**This book is to be returned on or before
the last date stamped below.**

-9. SEP. 1985   -8. FEB. 1995

-3 APR 1989   -1. MAR. 1996

22. DEC. 1989   31. OCT. 2005
-5. MAR. 1990

2 0 DEC. 1991

26. NOV. 1992

-9. FEB 1993

24. FEB. 1993

EUROPEAN COOKERY

EUROPEAN COOKERY

MASTER CHEF JEAN CONIL
Principal of the Academy of Gastronomy

Lida Hansley

PHOTOGRAPHY BY ROB MATHESON

CROOM HELM LONDON

1977 Jean Conil and Lida Hansley
Croom Helm Ltd, 2-10 St John's Road, London SW11

British Library Cataloguing in Publication Data

Conil, Jean,
    European cookery;
    1. Cookery, European
    I. Title II. Hansley, Lida
    641.5'94   TX723.5.A1

    ISBN 0-85664-505-2

Printed in Great Britain
by Redwood Burn Ltd, Trowbridge and Esher

Contents

Acknowledgements

I wish to thank all the persons concerned who have helped me to produce this gigantic gastronomic saga.

Firstly, my family: my wife Mary and my daughter Patricia for testing the recipes and sampling the food; my son Christopher for his expert suggestions on food presentation and general patisserie and confectionery recipes.

My own professional colleagues, too numerous to mention by name, but in particular the members of my catering staff: Michael Jones, Ernie White and Hannah Flynn for preparing many dishes and for assisting me in the cooking of dishes for the illustrations in this book. Also, the help of Janet Langford and Pat Forsythe.

I am much indebted to Embassy officials of the countries concerned for putting at my disposal a wealth of original information and data and for the collaboration of all the Foreign Trade representatives involved more directly in this project.

I am grateful for all the comments I have received from the Staff, Managers and Directors of Smiths Industries and for their constructive criticism.

I am also grateful to the team of hard working secretaries who have used their weekends and spare time to type the long manuscript: Misses Noelle and Caroline Dane, Jacqueline Berridge, Carol Mulkerin and Helen Hurley.

I am much indebted to Catherine Althaus of the British Tourist Authority for passing on much information about British Gastronomy.

To all the members of the Honorary Committee of the Jean Conil *Academy of Gastronomy*, my sincere thanks for their advice and technical assistance, particularly the Chairman, Charles Longman.

Lastly, I wish to thank our publisher, Christopher Helm, for his assistance and understanding, and Lida Hansley, my co-author, for her editorial help and for her contribution in writing my own biography.

Jean Conil

Introduction

Food has been a lifelong passion with me. From the cradle, I was brought up to enjoy it, to savour it and to appreciate its nutritive value. For the French child, training in gastronomy starts at an early age, and I was no exception.

My mother and my grandmother — and all the mothers of my family — knew their food instinctively and by sheer force of necessity. My grandmother was a market gardener who grew everything and turned her garden into paradise for little boys like me. Her apples were like melons, for she could graft a tree with the skill of a surgeon; her strawberries had the flavour of ambrosia and her jams were heaven. When all the flowers were in bloom and the gardens filled with the noise of birds, we hungry, lusty boys had to be fed every hour.

She never tired of tending to our whims. Her huge slices of wholemeal bread with lashings of butter which she made every week were daily fare to us. Her cheese had the freshness of the meadow; her cider and beer, her wines were nectar. She could distill and macerate fruits and turn their liquor into potions which could cure any of our complaints. Her lime trees and her herbs produced *tisanes* more flavoursome than tea and less harmful. Her honey was the natural sweetener for all her cakes, rum babas and country flans; and her *brioches* and *croissants* were so light that at the slightest provocation they would fly into our mouths.

Oh yes, grandmother Mathilda could cook, brew and process foods fit for the most fastidious gastronome. With a quick jerk of her wrist she could slaughter a rabbit or kill a pig, and turn its meat into sausages, pates, galantines, black puddings, spiced hams and pies.

We had fresh eggs every day and all the fruits we could imagine — figs, peaches, pomegranates, plums, nectarines and grapes from her vineyard, which, to us small boys, seemed to stretch for miles. But none gave us more pleasure than the apple trees in her orchard; we climbed for the sport and ate fruit from the trees until we were sick. We were never short of food, and yet in other ways we seemed so very poor, and often went tramping in the fields without shoes or sandals.

With my grandmother I started to learn about food technology and how to preserve most foods by pickling, canning and drying in the sun. Gradually I began to unveil through the years the mysteries of gastronomy.

My grandmother had no use for doctors or veterinary surgeons. She once saved my life when I was attacked by a swarm of angry bees by rubbing garlic juice on the stings; the swelling and pain disappeared instantly. On the occasions when I suffered from earache, she would take the seed of a poppy, mix it with olive oil and apply it to ease the pain. Little did I know then that it was morphia.

She was truly a miraculous woman. She sold the produce of her farm and bought very little in return, for she could make her own clothes, mend her own shoes and make people happy. She was a world of her own, a city, a tower of strength.

My concern for gastronomy started in my father's establishment. The hotel and restaurant which my family ran in Boulogne-sur-Mer was the centre of activities for the whole town. In contrast with what I was learning about raw materials at my grandmother's farm, in my father's kitchen I learned to process food for the table.

My father was the official town caterer in Boulogne, and very often we would be the centre of gastronomic feasts and culinary exhibitions. Boulogne is the largest fishing port in France, and our catering establishment was the Buffet de la Halle, where the fish was sold. There was every imaginable variety of fish: shark and turbot were landed as often as herring and whiting. So it was natural that my father would specialise in fish dishes, and many of his creations were incorporated in professional cookery books. The town often sponsored competitions for the best fish recipes and first my father, then I myself won a few prizes; but that was later.

On one hand I was learning the appetising preparation and presentation of food; on the other, my grandmother was teaching me about the very essence of life: nutrition. Mathilda was the first person to explain to me why Marie Antoinette should not have been derided for advising that the starving of France should eat *brioche*. *Brioche* is made with eggs and butter while bread is made with water. *Brioche* is more nutritious and has a higher protein content. Grandmere Mathilda never tires of telling me that for nourishment, no matter what the food, try always to add an egg to it. Whether it be mashed potato, bread, soup, sauce or vegetables, try always to add an egg and enrich your food with protein.

She grew beans for their protein content and sprouted mung beans in winter to make a salad rich in Vitamin C. 'Mange un bol de crudités' was her cure-all in winter; we did eat those delicious salads of raw vegetables and our cheeks were rosy and I can not remember having a bad cold.

This is why I began to associate food with its nutritive value from a very early age, and later, when I became a professional chef, I always assessed food on its nutritive and calorific values as well as on its culinary merit.

When I was ten, my mother thought it was high time I went to what she called a proper school, and sent me as a boarder to Chanlaire College, a very strict Catholic institution run by a highly disciplinary Jesuit order. Then on to Stanislas College in Paris where it was thought I would finish at the Military Academy of St Cyr and become eventually either a general or a President of the French republic. Instead I finished as a cook, the seventh generation of my family to do so, and I became president of an association of chefs.

My apprenticeship as a chef was spent in Paris. My father and grandfather were both restaurateurs and trained chefs, and as it was customary for Parisian restaurants to specialise in certain dishes, one had to work in these places to learn, progress and expand the culinary repertoire. One must remember that in those days chefs were very reluctant to pass on their recipes, and there were very few schools where one could improve one's professional knowledge to an advanced level. So my first establishment was a Drouant restaurant in the Gare de l'Est in Paris, where I learned all about fish cookery and oysters. It was the best fish restaurant in Paris, on a par with Prunier, and employed forty chefs and commis, catering for 300 to 400 *à la carte* meals every day. I learned what I could, and a year later moved to L'Ecu de France, which specialises in regional dishes like *saumon aux morilles* and *foie gras en croûte*. Butter was served in an enormous 28 lb mount on a dish, and nonchalantly the head waiter or head chef carver would give guests a small sliver of this Beurre des Charentes. Later the boss of this establishment opened a restaurant of the same name in London, which was bought by M Herbodeau, a disciple of Escoffier, and run successfully for many years by him.

For the next two years I moved every month to a variety of famous restaurants in Paris and on the Riviera where the owners were friends of my father, to learn a few specialities. Drouant on the Place Gayon taught me *faisan Souvaroff, cailles vigneronne* and *filet de sole vin blanc*; and the true *Bouillabaisse Marseillaise*. At the Escargot-Montorgueil I learned the correct way to stuff a dozen snails and cook frog legs. Chez Garnier, at the Gare St Lazare, I met the great Escoffier who was then retired and a regular visitor. He taught me that sometimes opposing flavours can bring out a dominant one, and how in producing a dish, he would always consider harmony of flavour and colour. His tip to me, at that time, was wild strawberries with a chocolate flavour. To the unitiated, this sounds rather unappetising, and yet the combination is as perfect as chocolate and mint.

Escoffier also taught me the secrets of a perfect consommé.

Then I moved on to one of the most celebrated and largest restaurants in Montparnasse, La Coupole, where I stayed a year. In those days the establishment had many specialities which I eagerly learned: *Canard Sauvage à la Presse, Truffles sous le Cendre, Moules Marinières* and *Tripes à la Mode de Caen*, truly delicious bathed in cider and applejack. Not long ago I visited La Coupole and was welcomed like a long lost son by the owner, who at eighty-five was still running the place with the same efficiency as forty-six years earlier when I was working there as a night commis.

By this time I was ready to be promoted to chef de partie. I had learned every possible style of cooking a sole or a chicken, I had a spell of pastry making and I knew how to prepare expertly a soufflé Grand Marnier or a lobster Americaine. I also knew how to scrub pots and pans, how to scrub a kitchen floor and a wooden table. I had beaten the record for opening a thousand oysters in six hours during a New Year's Eve night at La Coupole and I was capable of running a small kitchen brigade of six during the night.

I was just 18.

The Governor of the Transatlantic shipping line came in one day to La Coupole and liked my work. On his recommendation, I was engaged on the *Ile de France*, a liner famous for its cuisine in the first-class kitchen. I crossed the Atlantic several times and began to get acquainted with American tourists and their strange habits, such as freezing their tastebuds with iced water before tasting a delicate sauce, or drinking spirits throughout the meal at the risk of anaesthetising their palates.

At that time, the *Ile de France* was renowned for the excellence of its cuisine under head chef M Mangrin, probably the best French chef working at that time. The cold buffet was never complete without a display of huge water ice carved in the shape of an imperial eagle or a bear to hold the Russian caviar. It may look difficult, but for anyone with an eye for geometry and proportion it is not too complex, and I soon learned to do a swan, then an eagle, and then anything anyone wanted. The menu on the *Ile de France* was as large as a book. When a customer wanted a portion of duck, one cooked the whole duck and sent it with an elaborate garnish. The unwanted portions never came back. Baby lamb was roasted whole or as a baron, i.e. two legs plus the saddle, or sometimes just the saddle. The delicious petits fours from the patisserie were always served in a basket of spun sugar and adorned with pulled sugar flowers, an art I was to learn later in England. But for the time being I was a specialist in sauces and proud of it: was it not the great Brillat-Savarin who said that a good saucier is born but a roast cook may learn the trade? We often had to prepare as much as three gallons of the delicate Hollandaise sauce, as tricky to make as mayonnaise, except butter is used instead of oil, and it is served warm.

A speciality was *langouste au gratin*, a lobster without claws in a sauce. I had made a filling of mushrooms, shallots, fennel and chopped eggs, and flavoured the whole mixture with Pernod. Actually the chef wanted a glass of Pernod for himself and a glass of Port for the dish, but I had misunderstood the directions. When the compliments came from the Captain, who had enjoyed the unusual dish, the head chef still did not know what had happened. When asked for the name by the head steward, he said it was Langouste du Père Noël; the name stuck, and for many years they repeated the dish. But in my professional diary I entered the date of creation and called it Langouste Pernod. It was my first contribution to international gastronomy.

I was promoted to a job on the sister ship, the S.S. *Colombie* where I was able to travel for the first time to the tropics and South America. We featured the Caribbean and Latin American cuisine of the countries we visited, mostly based on Spanish and Creole cooking. We touched port every day from Martinique, Port de France, Guadeloupe, then Trinidad, Barbados, Jamaica, Cuba, Curacao, Colombia, Venezuela, Panama and back again. I soon learned the different specialities of each country and kept all the notes in my professional diary.

In Barbados we traded rum for wines, perfume and silk garments; in Martinique we bought the black rum to make Pomponette, a type of rum baba shaped like a rectangle with icing and whipped cream. We made ices from pineapple, reshaped with ice filling and served in a glassy wreath of spun sugar. Plantains, those huge bananas, were cooked like potatoes or used as a garnish for spicy stews. Many of the specialities I was to improve upon when I was appointed twenty years later to Frenchman's Cove in Port Antonio in Jamaica.

In 1938 I was conscripted to the French navy as a chef for the officers mess on the *Brestois*, a destroyer I boarded in Cherbourg. Not only did I have to cook, but I had to be my own labourer and fetch large bricks of coal from the very bowels of the ship to light my stove. The hatch to the store was vertical and the steps were steep and there was many a young sailor whom I bribed with money and wine to help me get those bricks. I learned a great deal about butchery when I had to cut the meat from large carcasses. And about bakery; all the bread was made fresh every day.

French officers eat well. Whether the meal was lunch or dinner, it would always begin with hors d'oeuvre or oysters, then a fish course: grilled sole, bream in wine sauce or even a *lobster à l'Americaine*. A meat course or two would follow, with vegetables, then desserts and a choice of half a dozen perfectly ripe cheeses, with wine to match.

In May 1940 the Germans invaded France. Our ship was in Lorient, and with the rest of the Northern French Fleet we received orders to go to England, to join the Royal Navy or the forces of General de Gaulle. The Navy was my choice, and I was drafted to a corvette, the *Aubrietia*, of the same flotilla as the one made famous by Montsarrat in *The Cruel Sea*; in fact it was our corvette which captured the German submarine mentioned in the book.

Life aboard was very uncomfortable. We were losing many ships on the Russian and American convoys, and morale was low; for months we were not allowed ashore. But I was learning English and Scottish cooking at its best. I traded my rum

ration for the skill of the ship's company cook and he taught me the lightest to treacle puddings; the secret was to blend the dough with lukewarm water, not to blend it too much, and to use freshly chopped beef suet from the kidney.

After a few months an infection meant I had to leave the corvette and go to convalesce in a stately home in Gourock, owned by the baronet Sir Hugh White. In this household taken over by the Royal Navy, the food was Scottish and unbelievably delicious. The cooking was done by a lady who had trained at a Royal Palace and had presided as head cook for many years. It was there that I learned that grouse must never be well done, but pinkish and cooked for 17 minutes at 400° F precisely. One minute more and they are ruined.

I made my acquaintance with haggis, but this oats and sheep's pluck concoction did not make the grade with me – I always find it too herby, and would prefer it if sage and oats were not so prominently used. But haddock in cream, buns and scones and venison roasts in port wine sauce were exquisite and I learned them all. The knowledge of English and Scots cooking earned me a promotion and I became a chief Petty Officers' cook in Skegness and finally I made it to London in 1943, as Head Chef to two Admirals, Sir Claude Barry and Sir George Creasey. At the Admiralty they entertained heads of state like the then Mr Churchill, Prince Bernhardt of the Netherlands and General de Gaulle. In spite of rationing and war-time restrictions, I was able to turn out some excellent dishes, some based on whale meat, best prepared as curries, goulash or in spicy sauces. I also made soups and stews with rooks and pigeons, and even seagulls met their fate in my pots.

During leave and on days off I was working in the Savoy as relief chef to learn the civilian aspect of cooking in Britain.

War-time affected the big hotels just like the rest of the country. No more three course meals permitted, and ice cream was prohibited. We managed to get around this by creating new dishes in the form of frozen custard cream puddings. The Savoy kitchens were staffed with old chefs, as the youngsters had been conscripted. One of my favourites was M Petit, with whom I collaborated on a book about Indian cooking and his experiences as chef at the Great Eastern Hotel in Calcutta.

Once the Second World War was over, I joined the staff at the Imperial College of Science and Technology and started the Academy of Chefs de Cuisine for full-time chefs to improve standards which had deteriorated during the war. André Simon was the first president and the academy had an advisory committee of the twenty-four best chefs in Britain. I also opened the Caprice restaurant in Arlington Street, in London, a famous eating place for the stars and personalities of the fifties. I featured Russian specialities and middle European food, as well as my own concoctions, often flambeed in brandy with a spectacular flourish; people were spending money like water after the hardships of the war, but rationing was still in force on a good many items.

The national Press became interested in the Academy, and my reputation was growing; Fortnum and Mason, that gastonomic temple of excellence, beckoned and I became their master chef. Here I was able to cater to the Royal Family, for the nobility and for the famous of the land, often creating new dishes in honour of my clients. I also published my first book, *Haute Cuisine*, which received a Gold Medal in Berne and is still a textbook in cookery schools.

At Fortnum and Mason I featured many of my creations: *Lobster Pernod, Selle d'Agneau St Jean, Sole Benedictine, Paillard de Veau Pompadour* and *Scampi Conil.* Unlike the chefs of my youth, I was happy to share the secrets of the kitchen with apprentices and housewives, and the *Sunday Times* in London published my recipes for seven years. I also started a new organisation, the Cercle Epicurien Mondial, and wrote a book, *For Epicures Only*, which was graciously accepted by the Queen.

Next I took over a restaurant in the Atheneum Court Hotel and made it a fashionable gathering place for the gastronomes of London. I appeared on the television show *Cafe Continental*, and developed new recipes and processes for Nestles and Cherry Valley Farms — whose *duck à l'orange* won for me the Gold Medal of the Comité de l'Excellence Européenne.

I have been a teacher, but I have also been a learner — all my life. From the three basics of being a competent master chef: patisserie, bakery and cooking, I wanted to develop a knowledge of food products and an understanding of the basic principles of appreciation. I learned how to evaluate every single component of each food in chemical terms as well as in physical effects. Organoleptic assessment on the basis of whether the food is chewy or soft or crunchy; green or white or brown; succulent or fibrous and flat; sour or sweet or salty or smoky — these are just some of the possibilities, the notes, if you like, from which a master chef orchestrates a harmonious whole.

Above all I tried to study the behaviour of the recipients of food and found a whole new science waiting to be explored: how people and animals react to certain foods, on the basis of associative elements built up from childhood and on the basis of cultural elements built up by our surroundings, religion and family customs. I called this the gastro-psychology of food, and defined it as a science concerned with the gastronomic behaviour of people with particular reference to their likes and dislikes. To be a true gastronome, I concluded, one must like the study of food, enjoy it, approach it with no prejudice and have a technical knowledge to help you analyse what you eat and why you should eat such food.

The development of a food consciousness is vital to our survival. Better nutrition makes better citizens; a well nourished individual is always more sociable, more cooperative, more gregarious and more peaceful. Food can build a better world, a stronger, more intelligent and more competent race.

Gastronomy accepts all factors of preference as long as they fulfil the criteria of nourishment and enjoyment. To achieve this aim, however, we must curb our food prejudice. We must be prepared to change our food habits. We must peep over the neighbour's garden fence and see for ourselves what he grows and how he lives. Our gastronomic journey is a necessary journey to a promised land — for who knows? We may find what is best for us. The appreciation of food should be common to us all, irrespective of class distinction. No God or Devil should interfere with our basic needs, and traditional conservatism in gastronomy may turn out to be nutritional suicide as the supply of our traditional foodstuffs diminishes.

To learn the cuisine of other nations is like studying maps in order to find the right road to one's destination — and get a nice view on the way. The culinary achievements of one country are merely pieces in the puzzle of the entire gastronomic picture which no man or woman with pretensions of education and intelligence can afford to ignore. The links between countries have been forged with sweat and bloodshed; now the fruits of these endeavours can be shared by an exchange of knowledge and practical experience. Eating or sampling someone else's brew is a small effort which may bring great dividends in broadening the mind. Further, improvement in our diet can be made much better and quicker if we try to appreciate someone else's fare.

This work is intended to dispel the mystique of gastronomy and the technique of haute cuisine; to present the subject not as a gratuitous sophistication but rather as it should be, as a science in survival and as an art in living wisely. A century ago a man's wealth could be seen to be proportionate to his girth. If he were rich, he could kill himself with the kindness of the table; if he were poor, he would the sooner know a narrow grave. Today the indications may be reversed, but now the rich man can usually afford to travel abroad and learn how the others live and profit by it.

So on this Grand Tour of Europe allow me to guide the gastronome to some of the best dinner tables in each country. Allow me to discuss with him the resources of the nation and explain the customs at table so that he may comport himself with dignity in every nation. Above all, allow me to wish him 'Bon Appetit' from every country and advise him how best his appetite may be stimulated.

The recipes selected are meant to reflect the main features of the national cuisine. In some cases we have employed professional tricks to enhance the national dishes, and in some cases I have even created new dishes to celebrate the excellence of local products which are perhaps not sufficiently appreciated in their own land.

Finding the original features of each national cuisine was in many cases like looking for a needle in a haystack. The delicious cake known as an apple strudel is a case in point: the Turks probably invented it, possibly drawing on the Persian cuisine; the Hungarians and Yugoslavs make it as a national dish and claim its invention, and the Austrians never cared from whence it came. They merely welcomed it and made it their own. So where does one put the strudel? We have made a diplomatic compromise and isolated several types, each with a different filling typical of the region. The rich tapestry of European history has meant that there are no bold dividing lines in the gastronomic map — there are gentle transitions and subtle influences at work in the kitchens of Europe. And yet in themselves these pressures brought about by treaties, diplomatic marriages, wars and invasions trace the ebb and flow of powerful nations and strong uprisings.

The history of the world may be written in its food. The cooking pots of Europe reveal who occupied whom and who was influenced by it. Sometimes the invaders were themselves influenced by a better style of cooking, sometimes they swept all before them and all but extinguished the flame of nationhood.

Not only the theory of food in Europe is fascinating. The practicalities of cooking it can be an inspiration to a creative cook. The subtle seasonings of a herring in Scandinavia may be applicable to a Cornish pilchard; the marinade for a sumptuous roast of venison may make an inexpensive mid-week roast of lamb a food fit for a feast. The middle European cook may have a way with yeast to inspire a cook who never used this lively stuff. The suet puddings of England may suit the capabilities of a cook in Germany or the purse of a Scandinavian. That is why the recipes have been chosen for the simplicity of their ingredients. Here and there, an exotic touch may creep in when one discusses an exquisite dish destined for a feast — but on the whole, the recipes are practical, inexpensive and delicious.

I have been particularly keen to bridge the gap from what is best of the old world in culinary matters and to introduce the new. Since Escoffier wrote his book in 1912 and Brillat-Savarin some forty years earlier, much progress has been made in food preservation and industrialisation. The introduction of preservatives and improving substances into our food has revolutionised the culinary industry. Standards of dishes have been more easily established and criteria of assessment more precise. As a result it is now possible to treat gastronomy as a practical science which can be taught to anyone with an interest in food. On the lowest level, the delivery of ready-cut chips, battered frozen fish and bulk oil has meant that even the standard of this basic but potentially good meal has become easier to assess. Steaming hot fish without grease and crisp chips of uniform gold mean that the chef knows his stuff — and he will be loved.

Yet there is something deeply satisfying in taking basic produce in season and starting to make a meal in the idiom of every land. There is a lesson to be learned from every country: the Spanish omelette is a fine example of a simple dish rich in protein. The coulibrac from Russia teaches the value of a pastry case and succulent filling in making the most of salmon, a potentially dry fish. Dumplings from middle Europe are an inexpensive filler when meat is scarce, and the Scandinavian cold buffet is a lesson for every hostess in enjoying her own party, with all the work done before the guests knock on the door.

Learn, enjoy and profit from your neighbour's table.

Oh, by the way — bon appetit!

Austria

For hundreds of years, Austria stood at the geographic and political centre of Europe. Its Golden Age was the time of Baroque, from around 1600 until the end of the nineteenth century; but for nearly 600 years, from 1282 until 1918, Austria, Hungary and Czechoslovakia formed the core of a Central European Empire, under the ruling house of the Habsburgs.

At one time, through a series of carefully arranged marriages, the Habsburgs ruled central Europe from the borders of Russia to the Adriatic sea, with more than a dozen nationalities making up the old Empire. The Turks tried to conquer it but failed, leaving behind a taste for coffee, exotic spices and delicate vanilla pastries made in the shape of the crescent on the Turkish flag, created in honour of the victory.

A taste for dumplings was brought to Vienna by the cooks from Bohemia and Moravia, employed by almost every bourgeois household. The Hungarians influenced the Austrians with their hot paprika and their roux made of lard, onions and flour, while noodles and nockerln are tastes from Italy, part of which was also included in the Empire.

Contacts with other countries, whether friend or enemy, may have influenced the gastronomy of Austria, but to all the imports, the Austrians have brought a light-hearted charm, an airy gaiety and a levity which transforms the classic recipes into something uniquely Austrian.

The Austrians have always regarded food as very important. Whoever travels to Vienna is going to a good kitchen, runs an old proverb, and never was this more true than at the Congress of Vienna, held in 1815 to try to bring peace to a shattered Europe after the fall of Napoleon. Politically it must have been a success, since it gave ninety-nine years of peace to Europe; but while the politicians were negotiating, the court was having a good time, and the great congress is often regarded as a time of wine, women and song in the Old World tradition.

France's delegate, Prince Talleyrand, recognised the relative importance of food in diplomacy, and told his sovereign, Louis XVIII, that he really needed more casseroles than written policies. The King took the point, and Talleyrand was allowed to take with him his own talented young chef, Antoine Careme, later to become one of the great masters of haute cuisine.

When the Empire collapsed in 1918 the republic of Austria stood on her own alongside the newly-formed republics of her former provinces. But Hitler annexed her, and after the Second World War, Austria decided to withdraw as much as she could from the hotbed of international politics. Austria is now a neutral country similar to Switzerland.

The real gastronomic impact of Austria has been in the area of pastries and confectionery goods. Chocolate is a popular flavouring, and the world-famous Sacher Torte typifies this: a chocolate sponge is covered first with sieved apricot jam, then with the unique Viennese bitter-sweet chocolate. It was created for Prince Metternich by his chef, Franz Sacher, because the famous diplomat found the traditional Viennese pastries too sweet.

Linzer Torte is a crisp tart filled with thick

raspberry jam and crisscrossed with a lattice of pastry; apricot dumplings are a substantial sweet while Salzburger nockerln are really a light soufflé. The Viennese pastrycook's art is world famous, and to sit in the most famous pastry shop of all, Demel's, and have a slice of one of their incredible tortes with coffee and Schlag (whipped cream) is still a gastronomic experience.

Each region of Austria has its own specialities, but if Vienna has a favourite dish, then it must surely be boiled beef. There are about twenty-four different cuts of beef available in Vienna, and they are all graded according to whether they are delicate or tasty and according to the texture of the fibres. The Tafelspitz, similar to a sirloin, is the most popular and celebrated, since it was the favourite cut of the Emperor Franz Josef.

Wiener Schnitzel is the most famous dish of Viennese cuisine, and traditionally should be so big that one cannot see the decoration around the edge of the plate. Its colour is important to connoisseurs, and the rich brown crust must not fall off the meat. Some cooks fry it in clarified butter or in oil, but more often it is fried in lard then finished with a little butter poured over it — foaming hot.

The third glory of Viennese cooking is backhendl, a piece of chicken floured, dipped in beaten egg and breadcrumbs and fried in exactly the same way as a Wiener Schnitzel. One also encounters the boiled smoked pork loin with sauerkraut and dumplings known as Gekochtes Geselchtes; red cabbage braised with sharp apples; Schinkenfleckerln — small square noodles boiled and then baked with a mixture of chopped ham, butter and eggs; germknodel, a yeast dumpling served with poppy-seed; strudels of all kinds, filled not only with apples but with paprika beef or a cabbage mixture. Kalbsbeuschel mit nockerln is a stew made of veal lungs, heart and melts, served with dumplings, and topfenpalatschinken are pancakes made with curd cheese. During Fasching, the weeks which precede the Lenten fast, Faschingskrapfen are a delicacy: a light dough-nut is filled with apricot jam and fried in deep hot fat or oil.

In Lower Austria there is game in season; wild boar, pheasant and venison flavoured with kirsch.

A peasant omelette is made with speck — bacon lovingly and slowly smoked in some farmer's own smokehouse, over vines or beech logs which give the speck its characteristic aroma. This is also the great vine-growing area.

Burgenland, 'castle country', has thick bean soup with bacon; roast goose, especially good in November and called the 'Martinigans' because it is eaten for St Martin's Day, served with hot spiced red cabbage; and stuffed paprika. This area also has the most full-bodied red wines in Austria.

Vorarlberg is proud of its 'Diegenes' — roast smoked pork with sauerkraut; and Burahockerle, a light pastry made with lard.

The great speciality of Styria is the poultry. Capons and poulards, plain roasted in butter with a crisp salad on the side, and new potatoes, are delicious. They also have heavy ragouts, made with pork or mutton, and one of the more unusual soups is a favourite here: sour milk, sour cream, potatoes and caraway seeds are the main ingredients.

The Carinthians are fond of noodles, especially small squares of noodle dough folded around a variety of fillings, sweet or savoury, and boiled in water. Fillings include meat, ham, mushrooms, cottage cheese, dried fruit and poppy seeds.

Salzburg has given the world not only its world-famous nockerln but also Wolfgang Amadeus Mozart as well as some of most spectacular Baroque architecture outside Vienna.

The great speciality of the Tyrol is the speck-knodel, a dumpling made with fat bacon smoked by the mountain farmers during the long winter. Onions are popular and fried onion rings are almost a trademark of Tyrolean cookery. Another great dish is the bauernschmaus, a dish of sauerkraut with smoked pork, fresh pork and pork sausages, again served with dumplings.

Austrian cookery is characterised by dishes garnished with dumplings or light escalopes fried plain or in breadcrumbs. Sauces are not reduced in the French style, but thickened with cream. Lard is used for frying, and caraway seeds, dill, capers, horseradish and paprika are popular flavourings. The profusion of sweets, cakes, ices, pastries and tortes make Austria a paradise for those with a sweet tooth.

Austria produces quality wines which are

highly regarded in the world. The white wines, made mainly from the Riesling grape, are the most famous and are drunk young and chilled. Some of the small vineyards around Vienna produce undistinguished but exceedingly pleasant white wines which are drunk in the same year as they are grown; going to the 'Heuriger' (This Year's) is a popular Viennese pastime. When the farmer considers his wine ready for drinking, he hangs out a branch of a fir tree. Guests come to drink the wine, sitting in his garden and drinking from plain water glasses. The menu is simple, too: dark peasant bread, cheese, smoked bacon and sausages, perhaps with a cucumber salad and a few home-grown radishes. Most of the 'heuriger' establishments are well within Vienna's limits, and recently the menu has become slightly greater because the tourists are discovering the charm of such an unforced evening. The farmer might even get out his old zither or piano accordion, and his guests join in a few choruses about how nice it is to be a Viennese — in three-four time, of course.

BILL OF FARE

Soup

LEBERNOCKERLSUPPE
Soup with liver dumplings

Meat Dishes

WIENER VIERLI
Strips of pork sauted Viennese style

FORSTER GOULASH
Venison goulash

KRAUTFLEISCH
Pork casserole with cabbage

WIENER SCHNITZEL
Veal escalop Viennese style

SADDLE OF VEAL METTERNICH with ROTKRAUT
Saddle of veal with red cabbage

Vegetables

WIENER ROTKRAUT
Red cabbage Viennese style

RICE PILAFF METTERNICH

Sweets

ZWETSCHEKNODEL
Prune or plum dumplings

MARILLENKNODEL
Apricot dumplings

AUSTRIAN STRUDEL
Rolly-pastry sweet with various fillings

WIENER GUGELHUPF
Yeast fruit cake Viennese style

FLORENTINER
Fruit and nut toffee round

METTERNICH SCHNITTEN
Apricot yeast cake Metternich

SALZBURGER NOCKERLN
Light sponge souffle

LINZERTORTE
Almond raspberry jam tart

WIENER BISCUIT
Piped shortcrust biscuit

KAISERSCHMARRN
Viennese torn raisin pancake

SACHER TORTE
Chocolate-coated gateau

SOUP

LEBERNOCKERLSUPPE
Soup with liver dumplings

Ingredients:

Beef bouillon 3 pints (1,800 mls)

Dumplings:

Ox or pig's liver 5 oz (150 g)
Chopped onion 2 oz (60 g)
White breadcrumbs 3 oz (90 g)
1 Egg
Butter 2 oz (60 g)
3 small dinner rolls 3 oz (90 g)
Pinch marjoram
Garlic $\frac{1}{8}$ oz (1 clove)
Salt and pepper
Milk 5 fl oz (150 mls)

Method: Soak rolls in milk until soft, then crumble
mixture and squeeze out surplus moisture.
Mince liver and onions and blend with bread and
egg. Fry crumbs in butter and add to mixture.
Season and add herbs. Shape dumplings into
1 oz (30 g) balls. Place on a greased tray barely
covered with stock and poach for 10 minutes
until they float. Serve in a rich beef or chicken
broth or in any clear vegetable soup.

MEAT DISHES

WIENER VIERLI
Strips of pork sauted Viennese style

Ingredients:

Lean pork meat cut in thin strips 2½ in x ¼ in
    8 oz (240 g)
Garlic or other cooked sausages 8 oz (240 g)
Green pepper cut in strips 4 oz (120 g)
Carrots cut in thin julienne 4 oz (120 g)
Onions thinly sliced 4 oz (120 g)
Button mushrooms thinly sliced 4 oz (120 g)
Lard 4 oz (120 g)
Water 1 pint (600 mls)

Vinegar 1 fl oz (30 mls)
1 clove chopped garlic
Salt and pepper
1 pinch of cumin
Tomato puree 2 oz (60 g)
4 fresh tomatoes, skinned, seeded and chopped
Sour cream 8 fl oz (240 mls)
Cornflour 1 oz (30 g)

Method: Heat lard in saute pan and brown all
meats first. Toss and stir for few minutes and
when brown add all the vegetables. Cover with a
lid and sweat to evaporate vegetable moisture for
5 minutes. Then add salt, spice and tomato puree
and fresh tomatoes. Add vinegar and water and
simmer, covered with a lid, for 45 minutes until
all ingredients are cooked. Disperse cornflour and
cream in a bowl. Add to the stew to thicken it
in order to cohere the mixture into a compact
mass. Check seasoning.

FORSTER GOULASH
Venison goulash

Ingredients:

Venison meat cut in ½ in cubes 2 lbs (960 g)
Wine vinegar 3 fl oz (90 mls)
Water 1½ pints (900 mls)
Sliced onions 2 oz (60 g)
Sliced carrots 2 oz (60 g)
Juniper berries 1 oz (30 g)
Salt and pepper, pinch of mace or nutmeg and
    a clove
1 bouquet garni
1 clove of crushed garlic
Tomato puree 2 oz (60 g)
Sugar 1 oz (30 g)
Sour cream 5 fl oz (150 mls)
Cornflour 1 oz (30 g)
Lard 3 oz (90 g)

Garnish:

Stewed plums ½ lb (240 g)

Method: Place meat in a bowl with all ingredients
except cream, flour and lard. Soak overnight.
Drain meat and vegetables, reserving liquid. Saute

meat in hot fat till brown, then add vegetables and cook 10 minutes with lid on pan. Add marinade liquor and as much water. Season and add bouquet garni and boil gently for 1½ hours until the meat is tender. Then thicken by stirring a slurry of cornflour and cream into boiling gravy. Mix well, cook 5 minutes. Remove bouquet garni and serve with redcurrant jelly separately — or plum compote.

KRAUTFLEISCH
Pork casserole with cabbage

Ingredients:

Lean pork cut in ½ in cubes 2 lbs (960 g)
Seasoned flour 2 oz (60 g)
Caraway seeds ½ oz (15 g)
Lard 3 oz (90 g)
Paprika 1 oz (30 g)
Sliced or chopped onions 3 oz (90 g)
Shredded cabbage or sauerkraut 6 oz (180 g)
Tomato puree 2 oz (60 g)
Vinegar 1 fl oz (30 mls)
Water 1½ pint (900 mls)
Sour cream 4 fl oz (120 mls) or plain yoghurt

Method: Toss the meat cubes in seasoned flour and caraway seeds. Heat lard and saute the meat with a lid on pan. Shake from time to time and cook until brown for 10 minutes. Then add ground paprika and sliced onions. Toss few minutes, add tomato puree and white cabbage or sauerkraut vinegar and cold water. Season with a little salt. Simmer gently for 1½ hours until the meat is tender. Add sour cream or plain yoghurt at the last minute.

WIENER SCHNITZEL
Veal escalope Viennese style

Ingredients:

Topside or cushion of veal 1 lb (480 g)
Seasoned flour 2 oz (60 g)
Beaten eggs 2
Fresh breadcrumbs 4 oz (120 g)

Lard or oil 3 oz (90 g) (clarified butter — melted and strained clear — or half clarified butter and oil or lard may be used)

Garnish:

4 thin slices of lemon
4 anchovy fillets
4 stuffed large olives
Sieved yolks of hard boiled eggs 2 oz (60 g)
Sieved or chopped white of hard boiled eggs 2 oz (60 g)
1 tbs of chopped parsley
4 tbs of capers
Salt and pepper
Fresh butter 3 oz (90 g)

Method: Cut against the grain four 4 oz (120 g) escalops). Wet each one. Place between wet piece of greaseproof paper or cloth. With bat or rolling pin, tap gently to stretch the escalope to a 6 inch area. Pass in seasoned flour then in beaten eggs and finally in crumbs. Heat a pan with lard or oil. Fry till brown on either side, cook gently for about 6-8 minutes. Place on a flat dish. Arrange a slice of lemon dipped in chopped parsley over or on the side with an anchovy fillet wrapped round a stuffed large olive, and on the side place a row of capers, egg yolks and egg whites arranged alternately.

In a pan add a lump of butter and when it is foaming pour over the escalopes. Serve immediately. No sauce or gravy is ever served with the Viennese Schnitzel, but a cold green salad and a garnish of saute potatoes cooked in oil and butter.

It is butter which gives the Schnitzel its characteristic final flavour. This is why some butter is used lastly — whether the escalopes were cooked in lard or oil. Basically veal is always used, but pork or chicken or even turkey meat can be cooked like Schnitzels too.

SADDLE OF VEAL METTERNICH with ROTKRAUT
Saddle of veal with red cabbage

This is one of three or four recipes dedicated to

Metternich, which were created in Vienna by various chefs. It is quite possible that Careme is one of them as he visited Vienna during the congress after Napoleon's downfall.

This recipe is classic and recorded in all the best professional reference books.

Ingredients:

(Recipe for 12 portions)
1 small saddle of veal 4 lb (1,920 g)
1 pint Bechamel sauce (600 mls)
Ground paprika 1 oz (3o g)
12 thin slices of truffles *or*
12 cooked button mushrooms
Parmesan cheese 2 oz (60 g)
1 pint gravy (600 mls)

Gravy:

Onions 2 oz (60 g)
Carrots 2 oz (60 g)
Bacon 2 oz (60 g)
Fat 2 oz (60 g)
Celery 2 oz (60 g)
Tomato puree 2 oz (60 g)
Water 1 pint (600 mls)

Thickening:

Cornflour ½ oz (15 g)
Water 5 fl oz (150 mls)
Salt and pepper

Garnish:

Rice pilaff 2 lbs (960 g)
Wiener Rotkraut 2 lbs (960 g)

Method: Place the trimmed veal saddle on a baking dish on a bed of thick chunks of bacon, carrots and onions and celery. Add a bouquet garni and a clove of garlic. Spread cooking lard and butter over the meat. Season and roast for 1½ hours at 400°F, basting from time to time. Remove joint. Flood meat tray with 1 pint (600 mls) water, add tomato puree and boil for 15 minutes. Remove and strain gravy. Thicken it with cornflour and water slurry so that it is not too thick but slightly cohered. Season. Prepare a Bechamel sauce. Add a pinch of paprika. Presentation of this dish: with the point of the

knife insert along the two middle parts of each loin to separate them. Remove the loins. Cut them in thick slices slantwise. Sandwich with sliced mushrooms and meat, rearrange the slices to constitute the saddle to its original shape. Coat the whole saddle with Bechamel sauce. Sprinkle grated parmesan cheese over. Brown under the grill and serve with the plain gravy with a garnish of red cabbage and rice pilaff.

WIENER ROTKRAUT
Red cabbage Viennese style

Ingredients:

Bacon or lard 2 oz (60 g)
Chopped onions 4 oz (120 g)
Sliced peeled apples 8 oz (240 g)
Shredded red cabbage 2 lbs (960 g)
White vinegar 5 fl oz (150 mls)
Sugar 3 oz (90 g)
Water 1 pint (600 mls)
Caraway seeds ½ oz (15 g) optional *or*
   pinch of cumin
1 bouquet garni and salt and pepper

Method: Heat lard and sweat chopped onions till tender but not brown. Add sliced apples and cabbage with vinegar. Season to taste. Flood with water, add seeds or bouquet garni and sugar. Boil 10 minutes then braise in oven covered with a lid for 45 minutes at 360°F. Remove bouquet garni. Serve as garnish with Saddle of Veal.

RICE PILAFF METTERNICH

Ingredients:

Long grain rice 1 lb (480 g)
Butter 2 oz (60 g)
Lard 1 oz (30 g)
Ground paprika ½ oz (15 g)
Water or stock 2 pints (1,200 mls)
Salt and pepper and 1 clove of garlic

Method: Melt butter and lard in saucepan. Add rice and stir to impregnate fat into rice without browning it. Cook 2 minutes then add paprika

and hot stock or water. Boil 5 minutes.
Transfer to a shallow dish. Season and add a
clove of garlic. Cover with a lid and bake for
20 minutes at 400°F. Each grain should
separate well.

SWEETS

ZWETSCHEKNODEL
Prune or plum dumplings

Ingredients:

Yeast ½ oz (15 g)
Lukewarm milk 3 fl oz (90 mls)
Water 5 fl oz
1 egg
Strong flour 1 lb (480 g)
Lard or margerine or butter 1 oz (30 g)
Sugar 1 oz (30 g)
Salt one pinch (3 g)

Fillings:

Fresh stoned plums or prunes
Butter 3 oz (90 g)
Cake crumbs 2 oz (60 g)
Icing sugar 3 oz (90 g)
Cinnamon

Method: The basic principle of this type of sweet
is the making of a yeast bun dough. Flour, water
and all ingredients should be at the same level
temperature of 76°F to ensure good fermentation
of yeast. Warm flour for 1 minute in medium
oven. Add salt and sugar. Blend milk and water
at 80°F with yeast crumbled into it. Add beaten
egg, and with the flour make a soft dough. Knead
well and gather into a ball. Cover with a basin
or cloth. Allow to ferment for 30 minutes. Blend
the soft fat and knead again until the dough is a
solid mass. Gather into a ball again and let ferment
for 10 minutes. Dust the pastry board with flour
and roll out the pastry ⅛ inch thick. Cut rounds
2½ inch diameter and carry on cutting the pastry
until you have made 20 rounds. Each round is
about 1 oz each (30 g).

On each round place one stoneless plum —
dust with cinnamon. Wet the edges with water
and top up with another round of pastry
(exactly as you would prepare a mince tartlet).
Brush the top with milk or water to prevent
pastry from skinning (as this would crack the
dough). Allow to ferment 15 minutes.

Heat a shallow tray with salted water and
poach the dumplings for 10 minutes. As soon as
they float they are ready. Remove and drain.
Place on a shallow dish. Add a piece of butter in
a pan and heat it until it foams. Add crumbs,
fry till brown, then pour over the dumplings.
Sprinkle with icing sugar and serve with sour
cream.

MARILLENKNODEL
Apricot dumplings

Method: Same preparation as prune dumpling.
Flavour apricots with Kirsch or a pinch of ground
cinnamon.

The drained cooked dumplings are fried in
clarified butter with a little sugar, simmering
like butterscotch, served in this syrup; or the
crumbs are fried in butter then the dumplings
are coated with the soft pourable fried crumbs
to enrobe them completely. Finally the
dumplings are dusted with icing sugar.

AUSTRIAN STRUDEL
Rolly-pastry sweet with various fillings

Ingredients:

Dough:

Strong flour 1 lb (480 g)
1 egg
Warm water 4 fl oz (120 mls)
Salt ¼ oz (7 g)
Melted butter 2 fl oz (60 mls)
Oil for brushing 2 oz (60 g)

Apple filling:

Peeled and sliced apples 4 oz (120 g)
Cake crumbs 2 oz (60 g)

Sugar 2 oz (60 g)
Pinch cinammon
Seedless raisins (sultanas or currants)
    2 oz (60 g)

Cherry filling:

Stoneless black or red cherries 4 oz (120 g)
Cake crumbs 2 oz (60 g)
Brown sugar 2 oz (60 g)
Pinch cinammon
Poppy seeds 1 oz (30 g)

Cottage Cheese filling:

Cottage or cream cheese 4 oz (120 g)
Castor sugar 2 oz (60 g)
1 egg
Grated lemon peel and juice of 1 lemon
Sultanas 2 oz (60 g)

Method: Beat egg and mix with water. Blend with
flour to obtain a firm dough. Rest 30 minutes,
then brush dough with oil. Roll it out as thinly
as possible. Spread a tablecloth on the table.
Dust it with flour then place the paste on the
cloth. With your two hands, stretch it into an
oblong shape as thinly as possible without
breaking. Sprinkle the surface with melted butter
and distribute the filling of your choice. Start
rolling then lift the cloth by the two corners of
one side to help the rolling motion so that the
strudel rolls itself. Transfer it into a greased tin
and bake at 400°F for 25 to 30 minutes. Cool and
when cold, dust with icing sugar.
Note: The thickness of the dough should be
about $\frac{1}{60}$th of an inch of ½ a millimeter
approximately.

WIENER GUGELHUPF
Yeast fruit cake Viennese style

Ingredients:

Yeast ½ oz (15 g)
Lukewarm milk 5 fl oz (150 mls)
1 egg
Sugar ½ oz (15 g)
Pinch of salt (4 g)
Strong flour 9 oz (270 g)

Butter 1 oz (30 g)
Seedless raisins 2 oz (60 g)
Juice and rind of 1 lemon
Icing sugar for dusting 2 oz (60 g)

Method: Crumble yeast in lukewarm milk. Add
sugar, salt, lemon juice and grated rind and
1 beaten egg. Blend flour to form a very soft
dough. Allow it to rise — covering it with a cloth
for 30 minutes. Add soft butter. Beat dough
again to blend the butter uniformly. Rest 15
minutes. Soak raisins in warm water for 10
minutes. Drain and dry. Blend to dough and place
dough in a greased Gugelhupf fluted mould
(with a hole in the centre). Dust the inside of the
greased mould with a little flour then half fill
the mould with mixture. Let it double in size for
30 minutes. Bake at 420°F for 30 minutes. Cool
on a rack and dust with icing sugar when cold.

FLORENTINER
Fruit and nut toffee round

This confectionery has a toffee-like texture
— snappy like a brandy snap, but with nuts and
fruit. It has a diameter of 2 inches and is coated
on one side with milk chocolate.

Ingredients:

Margarine or butter 4 oz (120 g)
Granulated sugar 4 oz (120 g)
Chopped nuts (nibs) 5 oz (150 g)
Cherries, Angelica 1 oz (30 g)
Peels 1 oz (30 g)
Double cream 1 fl oz (30 mls)

Coating:

1 milk chocolate bar 4 oz (120 g)
4 sheets of rice paper

Method: For accurate measurement of heat you
need a sugar thermometer which can be inserted
in the caramel mixture to record the exact
temperature corresponding to what is known as
the 'crack'. This is when sugar can be spun to a
thread.
    Place all ingredients except the chocolate in a

copper pan and boiler to a temperature of 280°F. Then remove from heat. Dip saucepan in basin of cold water and cool 10 minutes. Pour a spoonful of the mixture on a tray lined with rice paper and continue to produce about 18 Florentiners. Bake for 5 minutes only at 400°F. Remove from heat and cool. When cold brush the bottom side with melted chocolate. Make a design by waving the prong of a fork on the soft chocolate. On cooling it will harden. Then place each Florentiner on 2 inch paper cups.

To melt chocolate, place it in a bowl in a tray half filled with boiling water. Do not let water or moisture inside the chocolate as it would spoil it.

METTERNICH SCHNITTEN
Apricot yeast cake Metternich

This is another of the very few recipes dedicated to the famous Chancellor which was given to me by Mrs Balwin of the Austrian Institute in London and extracted from a classic Austrian reference book. Other recipes featuring meat, soup, etc., are also recorded in *Lexicon der Kuche* by Von Richard Herring (one of the most reliable international German reference books of culinary recipes).

Ingredients:

Baker's yeast ½ oz (15 g)
Lukewarm milk 2 fl oz (60 mls)
3 egg yolks
Sour cream 2 fl oz (60 mls)
Flour 12 oz (360 g)
Lemon juice 1 fl oz (30 mls)
Grated rind of lemon
Soft butter 6 oz (180 g)
Castor sugar 3 oz (90 g)
Pinch of salt (4 g)

Garnish for cake topping:

Apricot marmalade 3 oz (90 g)
3 egg whites
Chopped nuts 2 oz (60 g)
Castor sugar 3 oz (90 g)
Chopped glacé peels 1 oz (30 g)
Chopped glacé cherries 1 oz (30 g)
Chopped seedless raisins 1 oz (30 g)

Method: Crumble yeast in lukewarm milk, add yolks and warm sour cream — temperature at 78°F. Blend flour to form a stiff dough. Knead like a bun dough for few minutes until the mixture no longer sticks to the board and forms a solid mass. Gather into a ball and cover with a basin. Allow to prove for 35 minutes. Knead again and blend sugar, salt, lemon juice, soft butter and lemon rind. Knead for 5 minutes. Gather the mixture into a ball and again let it rest for 15 minutes to swell. Grease with lard an oblong tin 4 inch by 5 inch. Shape the dough into an oblong and place on tin. Brush top with milk. Allow to rest for 15 minutes, to recover and swell once more. This is an operation which is the key note of the success of all yeast cakes — to allow yeast fermentation and full dough expansion by gas pressure. When the cake has doubled in size, bake at 420°F for 25-30 minutes. Cool then brush with apricot jam.

Next prepare topping. Beat egg whites to a stiff meringue, add sugar gradually and beat between each addition. When the meringue peaks, add the nuts and fruits lightly. Spread the meringue thickly on the cake. Dust over a little castor sugar and bake 6 minutes at 380°F to set the meringue. Cool then cut cake in thin slices or finger shapes.

SALZBURGER NOCKERLN
Light sponge souffle

Ingredients:

5 egg yolks
Castor sugar 1 oz (30 g)
Soft flour 1 oz (30 g)
5 egg whites and 1 pinch salt
Castor sugar 2 oz (60 g)
Vanilla essence (few drops)
Butter 2 oz (60 g)
Icing sugar 1 oz (30 g)

Method: Beat egg yolks and 1 oz (30 g) sugar to a foam then blend flour. Beat egg whites and salt to a meringue. Add rest of sugar gradually.

Beat again until mixture peaks then fold gently into yolk mixture. Place butter in an oval shallow dish 2 inch deep. Add few drops of vanilla. Heat the dish in oven to melt the butter and when butter is foaming but not brown, pour mixture evenly. Spread it over the dish. Bake 10/12 minutes at 380°F. Serve immediately with the top dusted with icing sugar. Make sure oven has been preheated 15 minutes before use. This is a kind of souffle. It should be well puffed up and golden brown on top.

LINZERTORTE
Almond raspberry jam tart

Ingredients:

Butter 4 oz (120 g)
Lard 2 oz (60 g)
Icing sugar 4 oz (120 g)
Ground almonds 4 oz (120 g)
3 egg yolks 2 oz (60 g)
Juice and grated rind of 1 lemon
Flour 8 oz (240 g)
Cinammon ¼ oz (8 g)

Filling:

Raspberry jelly 4 oz (120 g)
1 egg
Flaked almonds 2 oz (60 g)
Icing sugar for dusting 1 oz (30 g)

Method: Grease a baking tray with a little lard. In a bowl cream butter and lard with sugar till fluffy then add ground almonds and yolks. Beat few more minutes, add lemon juice and stir well. Blend flour and cinnamon to produce a stiff dough. Add grated lemon and roll to a ball. Rest in refrigerator for 30 minutes.

Dust a board with flour and roll out the paste to ⅛ inch thick. Cut two 8 inch rounds. Place one round on tray. Spread raspberry jam and wet edges. Cover with second round of pastry. Brush top with beaten egg and sprinkle flaked almonds. Crimp edges round with fork handle. Bake at 400°F for 15-20 minutes. Cool and dust with icing sugar.

WIENER BISCUIT
Piped shortcrust biscuit

Ingredients:

Butter 4 oz (120 g)
Margarine 4 oz (120 g)
Icing sugar 5 oz (150 g)
Lard 2 oz (60 g) (for greasing tray)
2 egg yolks
Flour 8 oz (240 g)
Vanilla, lemon, almond essences (few drops)

Decoration:

Few glacé cherries or glacé ginger preserve
Icing sugar for dusting

Method: Grease a tray with a little of the lard. Cream soft margarine and butter with icing sugar and yolks. Add essences and half of the flour and beat well. Add rest of flour. Place mixture in a piping bag fitted with a large star tube. Pipe a small dollop or rosette on tray at regular intervals. Decorate centre with half a glacé cherry or ginger. Bake at 380°F for 15 minutes. Cool and dust with icing sugar.
Note: If mixture is hard to pipe, warm it a little and do not fill the bag too much so as to have a better leverage.

KAISERSCHMARRN
Viennese torn raisin pancake

Ingredients:

Milk 12 fl oz (360 mls)
4 egg yolks
Flour 6 oz (180 g)
Pinch salt and 4 egg whites
Seedless raisins 2 oz (60 g)
Vanilla essence (few drops)
Lard 1 oz (30 g)
Butter 3 oz (90 g)
Icing sugar for dusting 1 oz (30 g)
Castor sugar 2 oz (60 g)

Utensil:

One 10 inch frying pan

Method: Blend milk and egg yolks and with flour beat to a batter consistency. Beat egg whites with a pinch of salt to a meringue, gradually adding 3 teaspoonfuls of sugar only. Blend to batter mixture — lightly but thoroughly. Add raisins.

Heat a pan with lard. Tip off surplus. When hot pour enough of the batter to cover the pan thinly. Cook on both sides like an ordinary pancake. Then cut in pieces by tearing the pancake apart with two forks. Add a piece of fresh butter and toss the pancake bits until golden brown. Sprinkle icing sugar and castor sugar and serve on a dish with a compote of fruits of your choice, or with lemon wedges. Repeat the operation until the batter is all used up.

SACHER TORTE
Chocolate-coated gâteau

The basis of this gateau is a chocolate Genoese sponge type of mixture which, when baked, is sandwiched with apricot jam and iced with a chocolate dark icing.

It is best to bake the sponge first then store it overnight in a refrigerator as it will cut better. Sandwich it with apricot jam and complete as indicated.

Ingredients:

Butter 3 oz (90 g)
Margarine 2 oz (60 g)
Castor sugar 3 oz (90 g)
8 egg yolks
Melted chocolate 5 oz (150 g)
Flour 5 oz (150 g)
8 egg whites
Granulated sugar 3 oz (90 g)
Vanilla essence (few drops)

Filling:

Apricot pulp jam 5 oz (150 g)

Icing:

Chocolate couverture 5 oz (150 g)
Icing sugar 5 oz (150 g) ⎫
Water 3 oz (90 mls) ⎭ or butter

Method: Cream butter and margarine with castor sugar till fluffy then add melted chocolate. Stir well and beat in the yolks and vanilla essence. Fold in the flour gently. Beat the whites to a meringue then add the sugar gradually — beating between each addition of sugar. When the meringue is forming a peak fold into the cake mixture gently but thoroughly. Place in a torte tin 2 inch deep and 9 inch diameter. The tin should be lined with grease-proof paper — bottom and side — or greased with lard and dusted with flour. Level the mixture and bake at 380°F for 25 minutes. Cool on a rack and cover with foil. Store in refrigerator overnight. Split in two and spread with apricot jam. This can also be done in 3 layers.

Icing: Mix icing sugar with hot water then add melted chocolate. Flavour with a few drops of vanilla or instant coffee diluted to give the chocolate a darker and more pronounced flavour. Brush the top of the sponge with boiling hot apricot jam, then coat evenly with chocolate icing; top and sides. Spread level with palette knife. Place a small amount of mixture in piping bag and write the word 'Sacher' across the cake.

Hungary

Hungarian cuisine is a blend of basic recipes, tracing their origins back to antiquity, overlaid with a veneer of influences from successive invasions, friendly or otherwise. The gypsies, the Turks, the Austrians and their French chefs all brought a gloss to the basic cuisine.

Gastronomy began in Hungary more than a thousand years ago when the Magyars advanced from Asia to Central Europe during the period of human migration. They settled into a nation and their eating habits started to change as their way of life had changed, from nomadic wandering, fishing and hunting to agriculture and animal husbandry. In the Great Hungarian Plain, the Magyar tribes realised their good fortune in having found a land which could provide them with all the food they needed without having to rove endlessly. The blessed black humus and rich vegetation soon earned their country the name of 'Europe's Granary'. As late as the period between the two World Wars, Hungarian wheat produced the finest flour out of which, it was internationally acknowledged, the best bread was made.

Modern Hungary is a republic landlocked in central Europe between the Alps and the Carpathian Mountains. The climate is transitional between oceanic and continental, and the struggle for supremacy between the western, eastern and Mediterranean climates results in a most diversified agriculture. The high summer temperatures are excellent for wheat and maize, but can be dangerous when rainfall is below average. The tempestuous summer wind can wreak havoc with crops held by weak roots in a dry soil. The gentle, long autumns are valuable in ripening delicate crops like the fruit of the vine and cherries, apricots and the other exquisite fruits grown everywhere. The main part of Hungary, Transdanubia, falls into three main regions: the Kisalfold, producing wheat, rye, fodder plants and rearing cattle; the central highlands where forestry, fishing and tourist traffic supplement agriculture; and the third region, with similar activities to the second area but with more advanced mining and agriculture. The largest stretches of cereal land and cattle pasture are found on the true steppes east of the Tisa.

Hungarian cooking still bears traces of the most ancient periods of its history. *Tarhonya* is a classic example. It is a type of pasta, made of flour and eggs, with the dough shaped into small pellets as big as peas or grains of barley, originally dried in the sun, but now artificially dehydrated by the manufacturers. It is used in stews as the starchy complement. *Tarhonya* is sauted in butter or lard with chopped onions and paprika and then allowed to simmer until tender in stock. Another dish, fashionable today, is the planked steak which we associate more with Canada than with Hungary; however that is its place of origin as far as we can tell, and in ancient days it was cooked and served on a round piece of wood sawn from the trunk of a tree. Other names tinged with the romance of bygone days in Hungary are *Zsivanpecsenye* (bandit's roast), *Rablohus* (robber's meat) and *Ciganypecsenye* (gypsies' roast).

The Turkish conquest brought the all-important paprika to Hungary, and thus forever changed Hungarian gastronomy. It was added to the basic dishes to change their character totally, and now no one can even imagine a goulash without the rosy spice.

In the nineteenth century, the custom of employing leading French chefs at the Court of Austria and Hungary added to the national cookery its professional hallmark of distinction. Since that time, Hungarian cook books have adopted French cookery technology with the same terminology.

The most characteristic features of Hungarian cuisine are lard, onions, paprika and sour cream. The use of paprika as a condiment in Europe became widespread when the Napoleonic blockade in the early part of the nineteenth century prevented the importation of the ordinary pepper. Many varieties of paprika are grown in Hungary, ranging from the aromatic, very pungent *Bogyiszlo* type to much sweeter, milder types popular elsewhere. *Czeresznye* (cherry) paprika is the hottest of all. It is a thin-walled, cherry-sized variety, dark green when raw and turning into a ruby red when dry. Cherry paprika is an indispensable condiment in fish soup. For its pleasant flavour, fresh green paprika pods are added to practically every Hungarian dish prepared with a sauce. It is also eaten in omelets similar to the Spanish tortillas, with scrambled eggs, or stuffed with a variety of mixtures. It is high in Vitmin C and appears everywhere.

The foundation of most Hungarian recipes, the process which produces a typically Hungarian taste distinct from any other, is the basic frying of onions and paprika in pork fat. This is the beginning of any Hungarian recipe for stew or ragout. Hungarian onions — the reddish kind — are chopped finely, then carefully fried in fat until they become transparent and soft. The cook should stir them constantly to prevent burning at the high temperature. Only then should the paprika be added, lest it should burn, losing its red colour and turning bitter.

Pork fat is rendered at a high temperature in Hungarian cuisine; the crackling so obtained lends a characteristic taste to the fat. It is more of a dripping than lard, which is seldom used by good Hungarian cooks — they prefer to render their own pork fat.

Another favourite Hungarian ingredient is sour cream. No nation uses sour cream in so many ways and in such large quantities as the Hungarians. Except for certain beef dishes — *goulash*, a clear soup or stew traditionally garnished with dumplings; and *porkolt*, cubed meat stewed in a sauce thickened with roux — the Hungarians invariably add sour cream to any dish made with paprika and onion. They often serve a jug of cream on the side just in case there is not enough in the dish itself.

Freshwater fish is another favourite food in this landlocked country, and carp, sterlet, pike and bream are used extensively. But the 'King' of European freshwater fish is *Balaton Fogash*, a type of perch pike caught only in Lake Balaton. Its flesh is tender and white, and traditionally it is bent into a curled shape while cooking.

Hungary took with her independence the very best of the confectioner's skill and artistry, and Hungarian sweets, pastries and sugar confectionery have the same high quality as those found in Vienna. They claim that the strudel was actually invented in Hungary, where it is called *retes*; certainly a strudel made of Hungarian flour and filled with apple, morello cherries, cottage cheese with dill, poppy seed walnuts or even cabbage sauted with ground pepper and caramelised sugar is peerless.

The ecclesiastic year is celebrated not only in church, but at table in Hungary. Carnival doughnuts are served on Shrove Tuesday, sour eggs, sour cabbage and herrings are on the menu on Ash Wednesday, and on Good Friday there is wine soup, stuffed eggs and fish. However a layer of superstition combines with the ritual fasting and feasting, and on New Year's Day, sucking pigs are on the menu; with their snouts they are said to dig up good luck for the rest of the year.

Hungarian cuisine has attained a high standard. It has absorbed and modified many foreign influences yet developed a style distinctly its own, with a high enough standard to be ranked among the great gastronomic achievements of our time. It is now a cuisine which includes freshwater crayfish, frogs' legs, salmon trout and tasty pike and perch dishes among its delicacies.

Grape-vines grow extensively in the mild

climate of Hungary, and the country produces quality as well as quantity. When the Office of International Viniculture organised the first World Wine Competition in 1972 Hungary entered 66 wines, of which 54 were awarded the First Class Honorary Diploma, with 16 Grand Gold, 20 Gold and 18 Silver medals — proof indeed of the quality of Hungarian wines.

Wines from Tokaj and the Balaton regions have always had international acclaim. Tokay, which comes from a village in the Carpathian Mountains, can be sweet or dry. A measure of its sweetness is the number of baskets of grapes which go to make a certain quantity of wine — so the greater the number of *puttonyos* on the label, the sweeter the wine will be. The Tokay called *Esczencia* is not pressed at all mechanically. The sheer weight of the grapes themselves press out a little juice, which ferments when exposed to the open air. Although *Esczencia* contains little alcohol, it is a heavy, sweet wine more like a liqueur. It is also credited with marvellous rejuvenating powers for old men who wish to regain the vigour of former years.

A wide range of spirits is distilled from the wonderful fruit grown everywhere, and apricot, cherry and plum brandy from Hungary still taste of the fresh fruit which gave them birth. Even a type of champagne is made in Hungary, worthy of competing with the very best sparkling wines from France and Germany. The most exported wine is *Egri Bikaver*, or Bull's Blood, a wine as strong and powerful as its name.

BILL OF FARE

Soup

GULYAS
Beef paprika soup

UJHAZI
Vegetable soup

ORJA SOUP
Pork chine soup

PALOC SOUP
Mutton soup

SZEGED SOUP
Fish soup

Fish Dishes

CARP A LA RAC
Baked carp with vegetables

STERLET CARPATHIAN
Braised sterlet

HALASTLE
Fish stew

Light Entree Dishes

STUFFED PANCAKES HORTOBAGY
Pancakes stuffed with veal

STUFFED MUSHROOM EGER SAUCE
Mushrooms with a tomato and wine sauce

POACHED EGGS PANNOMIA
Grilled fish with poached egg

GOOSE LIVER CASSEROLE
Liver sauted with green and red peppers

Meat Dishes

PORK SZEKELY
Paprika-flavoured roast pork with sauerkraut

PAPRIKA CSIRKE
Chicken Hungarian style

ESTERHAZY ACHEM
Veal strips sauted in cream sauce

PAPRIKA CHICKEN
Sauted chicken with paprika and wine

STUFFED PULLET GODOLFO
Chicken with bread stuffing

SADDLE OF HARE
Roast saddle of hare with chestnuts and mushrooms

VEAL CUTLETS A LA MAGYAROVAR
Veal Cutlets topped with mushrooms, ham and cheese

STUFFED VEAL CUTLET
Veal cutlet stuffed with scrambled eggs

TRANSYLVANIAN HUNGARIAN MIXED GRILL
A mixture of grilled meats

BRIGAND'S ROAST
Cubes of meat grilled on a skewer

STUFFED PEPPERS

STUFFED CABBAGE KOLOZSVAR
Cabbage leaves stuffed with meat and braised in tomato sauce

SEVEN LEADERS' TOKANY
A casserole of various meats

SOUP

Regarding goulash or Gulyas if they are served as soups, more liquid and less paprika is used, otherwise basically the same ingredients are applicable but in different proportions, according to the type of goulash. Outside Hungary it has been the practice to list a dish as a goulash, entree or as a stew and not a soup. Most professional reference books do not list goulash as soup hence the difference of interpretation.

Here is an example of goulash as a soup:

GULYAS
Beef paprika soup

Ingredients:

Shin of beef ½ lb (240 g)
Onion 5 oz (150 g)
Lard 2 oz (60 g)
Ground paprika 1 oz (30 g)
Tomato puree 2 oz (60 g)
1 bouquet garni
Potatoes ½ lb (240 g)
Water 3 pints (1,800 mls)
Salt and pepper

Garnish: Tarhonya pasta
Flour 4 oz (120 g)
1 egg

Method: Cut meat in small ¼ inch cubes and chop the onion finely. Saute the meat and onion with lard in a saucepan until golden brown. Add the paprika. Stir well for few minutes, add tomato puree and cook few more minutes. Add water and bouquet garni and simmer 1½ hours till meat is tender. Add potatoes cut in ¼ inch cubes and cook 10 more minutes till tender but not mushy. Remove bouquet garni. Season with salt and pepper. Add cooked pasta to soup and serve.
Pasta: Blend egg and flour to a dough. Rest for few minutes then roll thinly. Either cut pasta in thin shreds or in small strips or squares. Boil 10 minutes in salted water. Drain and add to soup 10 minutes before serving to allow pasta to soften up.

UJHAZI SOUP
Vegetable soup

This is the Hungarian version of a rich Italian minestrone but with a flavouring of caraway seeds. It includes nine vegetables: carrots, onions, peas, beans, kohlrabi, green peppers, cabbage, carrots with tomato and vermicelli.

ORJA SOUP
Pork chine soup

It is made by boiling pig's head and trotters to obtain a stock. The broth is then clarified and garnished with diced meat and vegetables.

PALOC SOUP
Mutton soup

The Hungarian novelist, Kalman Mikszath, was a native of the region of the Paloc people to whom this soup is one of the regular features. It is made with diced mutton, paprika, beans and potatoes with soured cream added at the end before serving.

SZEGED SOUP
Fish soup

It is made with four kinds of fish: bream, carp, sterlet, trout with onions and paprika. It is similar to the classical matelote of French cuisine but with the paprika as its main characteristic.

FISH DISHES

CARP A LA RAC
Baked carp with vegetables

Ingredients:

Carp or similar fish 1 lb (480 g)
Sliced potatoes 1 lb (480 g)
Butter 3 oz (90 g)

Green peppers 4 oz (120 g)
Sliced onions 4 oz (120 g)
Skinned and seeded tomatoes 4 oz (120 g)
Diced bacon rashers without rind 4 oz (120 g)
Lard or other fat 2 oz (60 g)
Salt and pepper, paprika
Water 1 pint (600 mls) *or*
  half water and half white wine
Sour cream 8 fl oz (240 mls)
Cornflour 1 oz (30 g)
Chopped parsley 1 tbs

Method: Heat lard and butter and saute the sliced
onions and diced bacon. After 5 minutes add the
sliced green peppers and tomatoes. Place the
sliced potatoes on a shallow dish. Dot a few bits
of butter and add seasoning then cover with
pieces or fillets of carp. Spread cooked vegetable
mixture on top of fish. Season again, add seeds
and 16 fl oz (600 mls) of water or white wine. Cover
dish with greaseproof paper and bake 30 minutes
to 45 minutes in moderate oven (380°F). When
cooked strain fish liquor into a small saucepan,
boil it for 5 minutes and thicken it with a slurry
of cream and cornflour. Check seasoning and
pour over the fish. Sprinkle chopped parsley.

STERLET CARPATHIAN
Braised sterlet

Braise the sterlet till tender in a shallow dish half
filled with white wine. Add chopped onions.
Sprinkle a little paprika and salt and a lump of
butter. Cook for 20 minutes then add chopped
dill and sour cream. Garnish the sterlet with
boiled crayfish tail. Serve with potatoes in parsley
butter.

HALASTLE
Fish stew

Ingredients:

River fish (perch) 2 lb (960 g)
Onion 2 oz (60 g)
Water ½ pint (300 mls)
White wine ½ pint (300 mls)

Bay leaf, clove, thyme
Cream ½ pint (300 mls)
2 egg yolks
Cornflour 1 oz (30 g)
Salt and pepper
Paprika ½ oz (15 g)

Method: Cut skinned and boned fish in slices.
Place in a casserole dish with thinly sliced onions.
Add wine and water. Season and add herbs.
Bake with lid on for 35 minutes. Pour liquor in
saucepan, add blended cream, cornflour and yolks
gradually to thicken it like a custard. Pour this
sauce over the fish and check seasoning. Sprinkle
paprika and serve.

LIGHT ENTREE DISHES

STUFFED PANCAKES HORTOBAGY
Pancakes stuffed with veal

Stuff the pancakes with cooked, minced veal
meat, like a cannelloni. The sauce should be
creamy made from the veal stew liquor.

STUFFED MUSHROOM EGER SAUCE
Mushrooms with a tomato and wine sauce

Peel large mushroom caps. Wash and stuff them
with goose liver pâté. Pass each cap in seasoned
flour flavoured with paprika and in beaten eggs
and crumbs. Fry in pork fat till golden and
serve with a tomato paprika sauce made with
Eger wine.

POACHED EGGS PANNOMIA
Grilled fish with poached egg

Grill fillet of perch or sterlet and serve them with
a poached egg on top. Coat the fish with a
creamy sauce made with sour cream and paprika.

GOOSE LIVER CASSEROLE
Liver sauted with green and red peppers

Saute an equal quantity of green and red peppers
and onions in 1½ oz (50 g) lard, allowing 5 oz
(150 g) for each ingredient. When tender, add the
liver sauted separately in fat. Cook till tender
for 10 minutes. Then sprinkle paprika and
seasoning. Place the liver on top of the vegetable
mixture and serve as a hot hors d'oeuvre or light
entree.

MEAT DISHES

PORK SZEKELY
Paprika-flavoured roast pork with sauerkraut

Ingredients:

Rindless loin of pork 2½ lb (1,200 g)
Fat 2 oz (60 g)
Chopped onions 5 oz (150 g)
Sauerkraut 1 lb (480 g)
Salt, pepper and paprika ½ oz (15 g)
Caraway seeds (3 g)
1 clove garlic
Sour cream 8 fl oz (240 mls)
Cornflour 1 oz (30 g)
Water 1 pint (600 mls)

Method: Partly roast the meat at 400°F for 35
minutes. Remove some of the fat and fry the
chopped onions without browning. Blend to
sauerkraut and place in a shallow dish. Arrange
joint on top. Sprinkle paprika. Add few caraway
seeds on the side and all the seasoning. Cook
gently for another hour, basting with hot water
or stock. When cooked strain the liquor into a
saucepan. Boil the gravy and thicken it with
a slurry of cream and cornflour added to the
boiling liquid. Season. Slice the meat, pour sauce
over it and place it on the dish of cooked
sauerkraut. Sprinkle or dust a little paprika over.

PAPRIKA CSIRKE
Chicken Hungarian style

Ingredients:

1 by 2½ lb roasting chicken (1,200 g)
Onion 5 oz (150 g)
Lard 2 oz (60 g)
Ground paprika ½ oz (15 g)
Pinch pepper and clove, cumin and salt
Seasoned flour 2 oz (60 g)
White wine or water ½ pint (300 mls) with 1 tbs
    vinegar
Cream ½ pint (300 mls)
Lemon juice 1 fl oz (30 mls)

Method: Cut chicken in four pieces. Pass in
seasoned flour mixed with paprika and the other
spices.

Heat a saute pan with lard and saute chicken
for 15 minutes till well brown. Place a lid on
and cook gently during this operation. Remove
chicken pieces and in same fat fry onions till
soft but not brown. Drain fat and replace chicken
in pan. Add water or wine and lemon juice.
Boil gently for 20 minutes or cook in oven in a
casserole dish. Strain sauce into a pan and add
cream. Boil 5 minutes, check seasoning and pour
over chicken.

ESTERHAZY ACHEM
Veal strips sauted in cream sauce

Ingredients:

Veal cut in strips 2½ inch long and ¼ inch thick —
    1 lb (480 g) (from leg or loin)
Onion cut in thin slices or shreds 5 oz (150 g)
Red and green pepper 5 oz (150 g) (cut in strips)
Lard 2 oz (60 g)
Water 5 fl oz (150 mls)
Salt and pepper and a pinch of cumin
Paprika ½ oz (15 g)
Double cream 5 fl oz (150 mls)

Garnish:

Maize semolina 2½ oz (75 g)
Butter 1 oz (30 g)
Water ½ pint (300 mls)
Grated cheese 1 oz (30 g)
1 clove garlic

Pinch of nutmeg
Salt and pepper
4 lemon slices

Method: Heat lard in a saute pan and cook the meat gently along with the onion until brown. Add the pepper strips, toss, add water and condiments and cook gently for 20 minutes. Add cream and boil for 5 minutes. Check seasoning and serve with a dish of Polenta.
Polenta: Rub butter and maize semolina, season then cook with garlic in boiling water for 20 minutes. Pour into a greased tray to cool. When cold cut rounds 3 inch diameter with a pastry cutter. Pan fry the rounds. Sprinkle grated cheese flavoured with nutmeg. Garnish the meat around the dish with this maize gnocchi, and over the meat place the 4 lemon slices. Sprinkle a little chopped parsley or paprika over the lemon.

PAPRIKA CHICKEN
Sauted chicken with paprika and wine

Joint the raw chicken into 8 pieces and pass in seasoned flour flavoured with paprika. Saute in pan with pork fat until golden. Add chopped onion, red and green pepper and a cup of white wine. Bake in oven with a lid on for 20 minutes. Add a cup of sour cream and cook a few more minutes. Season. Serve with egg dumplings or noodles.

STUFFED PULLET GODOLFO
Chicken with bread stuffing

Soak 5 oz (150 g) of bread in milk then press moisture out. Blend one egg and chopped parsley and onion to form a forcemeat of firm consistency. Blend sauted chicken livers to this mixture and stuff the chicken at the neck end. Roast chicken till tender, basting with pork fat blended with paprika.

SADDLE OF HARE
Roast saddle of hare with chestnuts and mushrooms

Remove skin from saddle and lard it with strips of bacon. Roast 30 minutes and serve with a gravy flavoured with a rich red wine. Serve chestnuts and sprouts tossed in butter or just a puree of chestnut and button mushrooms and onions, flavoured with Tokay wine.

VEAL CUTLETS A LA MAGYAROVAR
Veal cutlets topped with mushrooms, ham and cheese

Ingredients:

4 veal cutlets
4 slices of cooked ham
4 slices of Gouda type cheese
Sliced mushrooms 5 oz (150 g)
Lard 1½ oz (50 g)
Salt and pepper and a pinch of paprika
Butter 1½ oz (50 g)

Method: Saute the sliced mushrooms in butter with a pinch of paprika for 5 minutes. Remove. Flatten the veal cutlets, pass in seasoned flour flavoured with paprika and toss in pan on both sides to brown — not to cook. Remove. Place a spoonful of the cooked mushrooms on top of each cutlet and cover with a slice of ham, finally topping each with a slice of cheese. Place the cutlets in a shallow dish and bake until the cheese is melted and golden brown.

STUFFED VEAL CUTLET HUNGARIAN
Veal cutlet stuffed with scambled eggs

Cut into a thick veal steak a slit on the side to make a pocket. Stuff this cavity with scrambled egg mixture. Seal the side with string sewn through. Pass the veal steak in seasoned flour with paprika and cook in the pan till tender. Serve with a garnish of cooked sliced mushrooms on a bed of rice. Prepare a sour cream gravy to serve separately.

TRANSYLVANIAN HUNGARIAN MIXED GRILL
A mixture of grilled meats

This is made up of pork chops, veal cutlets and fillet steaks cut smaller than usual and grilled together. Serve on a wooden platter with rashers of bacon, grilled tomatoes and grilled green peppers and french fried thin potatoes. The platter is also garnished with small containers of various vegetable chutneys and pickles.

BRIGAND'S ROAST
Cubes of meat grilled on a skewer

Cubes of fillet of pork, veal and beef with rashers of bacon impaled on skewers and charcoal grilled. Serve with fried potatoes on ornamental silver skewers. Mushroom caps can also be mixed with the meat. It is in fact a sort of Hungarian Kebab. For colour, a slice of red and green pepper is placed between each cube of meat.

STUFFED PEPPERS

Peppers filled from the stem part after removing seeds. The stuffing can be raw minced meat or cooked meats of any kind or just rice. Braise the peppers in tomato sauce till tender. Usually the pepper should be parboiled 5 minutes before being filled if the stuffing is already cooked.

STUFFED CABBAGE KOLOZSVAR
Cabbage leaves stuffed with meat and braised in tomato sauce

Parboil cabbage leaves for 5 minutes then refresh in cold water and dry each leaf with a cloth. Make up a ball of raw minced beef and pork, seasoned with raw grated onions, salt, pepper and paprika. Wrap the ball with cabbage leaves. Bake in a shallow tray in tomato sauce for 45 minutes.

SEVEN LEADERS' TOKANY
A casserole of various meats

This is made with an equal quantity of beef, pork, veal and bacon cut in 2 cm cubes and cooked till tender in stock with diced red and green peppers. The liquor is blended with sour cream and seasoned with paprika. Add peeled tomato pulp. Serve potato pancakes separately. These are made from an ordinary batter with an equal amount of raw grated potato.

VEGETABLES

MUSHROOMS HUNGARIAN STYLE
Sauted mushrooms with caraway seeds

Ingredients:

Button mushrooms 1 lb (480 g) (remove stalks) (morels, boletuses or any other edible mushrooms)
Butter 2 oz (60 g)
Chopped onions 5 oz (150 g)
Paprika ½ oz (15 g)
Double cream 5 fl oz (150 mls)
Chopped parsley
Pinch caraway seeds
Lemon juice 1 fl oz (30 mls) (1 lemon)

Method: Wash, trim stalks but do not peel button mushrooms if very fresh and white. In a saucepan heat butter and add mushrooms and chopped onions and paprika, cover with a lid and simmer gently with lemon juice for 5 minutes. Toss from time to time. Then add cream. Boil 5 more minutes and season. Sprinkle chopped parsley and caraway seeds and serve on fried bread or toast.
Note: If mushrooms are large, cut in two. Trim stalks or remove altogether. Peel mushrooms if large and brown.

POTATO HUNGARIAN
Potato, onion and paprika casserole

Ingredients:

Potatoes 2 lbs (960 g)
Sliced onions 1 lb (480 g)
Lard 3 oz (90 g) or vegetable fat or oil
Ground paprika 1 oz (30 g)
Tomato puree 3 oz (90 g)
Salt and pepper and a pinch of caraway seeds
Water 2 pints (1,200 mls)
Red pepper (capsicum) 4 oz (120 g)
1 clove garlic

Method: Peel and cut potatoes in half or quarters but all must be of even size. In saute pans, saute onions with fat till golden brown. Add red peppers, paprika and tomato puree and water. Boil 5 minutes. Add potatoes and rest of ingredients. Cook for 20 minutes till potatoes are tender — not mushy. Keep the dish covered with a lid during cooking. Season to taste.

LESCO
Pepper and aubergine pickle

Ingredients:

Green peppers 1 lb (480 g)
Red peppers 1 lb (480 g)
Tomatoes 1 lb (480 g) — skinned
Tomato puree 2 oz (60 g)
Sliced onions 1 lb (480 g)
Chopped garlic 1 clove
Salt ½ oz (15 g)
Pinch of pepper
Water ½ pint (300 mls)
Vinegar 3 fl oz (90 mls)
Sugar 2 oz (60 g)
Paprika 1 oz (30 g)
Oil 3 fl oz (90 mls)

Method: Remove seeds from peppers and tomatoes. Skin tomatoes and cut peppers in strips. Slice onions and chop tomatoes. Crush garlic and saute all ingredients in oil for few minutes without browning. Add vinegar and boil 5 minutes, then add water, seasoning and tomato puree. Simmer gently for 30 minutes. Cool and serve cold as a pickle for cold meat or poultry.

SWEETS

PANCAKES A LA GUNDEL
Stuffed pancakes with walnuts

Ingredients:

Flour ½ lb (240 g)
Milk 10 oz (300 mls)
2 eggs
Salt

Stuffing:

Chopped walnuts 5 oz (150 g)
Seedless raisins 2 oz (60 g)
Orange peel 1 oz (30 g)
Rum 2 fl oz (60 mls)
Butter 4 oz (120 g)
Sugar 4 oz (120 g)
Chocolate sauce ½ pint (300 mls)

Method: Make a batter for the pancakes. Cook the pancakes in a 5 inch (12 cm) pan.
Filling: Mix nuts and raisins and peel with sugar and just enough milk to blend to a paste. Stuff each pancake with this mixture. Roll and place pancake in buttered shallow dish. Pour a nut of butter over each pancake and sugar and flavour with rum. Bake in oven for 8 minutes at 400°F.

HUNGARIAN APPLE TART
Tart with apples and walnuts

Ingredients:

Bun dough:

Flour 1 lb (480 g)
Yeast ½ oz (15 g)
Butter 2 oz (60 g)
Sugar 2 oz (60 g)
Milk 6 fl oz (180 mls)

2 eggs
Pinch of salt

Filling:

Peeled grated apples 2 lbs (960 g)
Ground almonds 2 oz (60 g)
Chopped walnuts 5 oz (150 g)
Sugar 5 oz (150 g)
Cake crumbs 5 oz (150 g)
Pinch of cinnamon

Method: Mix salt into flour. Disperse yeast into
tepid milk. Then add eggs and sugar. Blend mixture
with flour to a dough, knead well and rest in basin
for 40 minutes at room temperature to allow yeast
to leaven paste. Then blend butter and roll dough to
an oblong 9 inch (18 cm) long and 3 inch (6 cm)
wide. Make another strip similar for topping.
Blend all ingredients for the filling. Grate apple
and squeeze the juice through a cloth before
adding the rest of ingredients. Spread the filling
on the bottom pastry layer. Cover with the other
layer. Brush with egg wash and rest on tray 30
minutes before baking, then bake at 400°F for
25 minutes. Cut in portions and serve with cream
or custard or apricot sauce.

Czechoslovakia

Every country has something for which it is famous. Czechoslovakia, more particularly, Bohemia, has always been known for the excellence of its cooks. During the golden days of Austria's Empire, every well-to-do middle-class household in Vienna had a cook from the then province of Bohmen. These efficient kitchen dictators brought with them the recipes for good, plain basic cooking and a great talent for the warm pudding which even now is one of the glories of Eastern Europe. Apricot dumplings served with melted butter, cherry pudding made with a rich batter, strawberry dumplings with a mountain of sieved curd cheese and melted butter — the country dishes were taken by the Austrians and adopted with enthusiasm as their own. The French-trained chefs may have improved them, but the recipes started life in the tiny villages and golden wheat-fields of Bohemia.

Now the young Czech food industry is becoming equally well known around the world. Prague ham, pickled vegetables, jams, sauerkraut, beer, chocolates and bonbons are exported everywhere. A wealth of fruit is grown in Bohemia and Moravia, and liqueurs and spirits based on fruit distillations are gaining in popularity. Liqueurs based on strawberries, blueberries, cherries, apricots, peaches and blackberries; the most famous is *slivovice*, a double distillation of plums, which is to the Czechs what whisky is to the Scots and cognac to the French. The glass industry has helped the young liqueur industry by designing and producing some highly decorative bottles. Prague ham has always been famous, and is incontestably the most delicious smoked ham in the world. Other delicatessen products include smoked tongue, frankfurters, ham and blood sausages, and the very fine pork sausage called *klobasy*.

The excellence of Czechoslovakia's food is largely due to the quality of her foodstuffs. The climate — hot summers, gentle autumns, cold winters — and the geography combine to make this a fertile land. Sugar beet, corn and high grade barley for beer making are cultivated in the low-lying areas, and higher up potatoes, rye and oats predominate.

As Czechoslovakia has no sea coast, the breeding of fish in ponds is an industry dating back to the sixteenth century. As in other predominantly Roman Catholic countries, a great deal of fish is eaten, and the traditional Christmas Eve dish is carp. The large scales of the carp are saved, and there is a superstition that whoever carries a few of these scales in his purse or wallet will not be short of money in the coming year.

Generally, the cooking is simple, rustic and tasty. Pork roasted with caraway seed, with sweet-sour cabbage and dumplings, made with diced bread, is probably the favourite dish of Czechs. Goose is the festive bird, roasted with a filling of whole, sharp apples, which are then pureed to make a sauce.

The Czechs like to eat, and the three meals a day of other countries are quite simply not enough. So the Czechs have invented snack bars which are quite unique. One, for instance, specialises in tripe soup, made with marjoram and cayenne pepper. Others offer the smoked sausages which the English call Frankfurters, the Americans call Wieners, and the Czechs who really did invent them, call *parky* — which means pairs, since they are sold in twos and one is not enough even for a child. Czech sausages are always steamed or boiled, and connoisseurs like them with a mild mustard and a slice of the rich, dark peasant bread which tastes like no other. Others might order some sauerkraut, potato salad or pickles.

Another unique snack bar is that dedicated to the open sandwich. Goose liver mousse with horseradish in whipped cream, Prague ham with sweet-sour cucumbers, freshwater crayfish with mayonnaise and a wafer-thin slice of lemon are just three from the selection of over a hundred open sandwiches at one popular Prague establishment. People drop in for a glass of wine or a cup of coffee and a quick sandwich when the cares of the day prove debilitating. Hostesses pick up a box of assorted sandwiches if they are having guests for coffee, but if the hostess has time, she will make equally exotic creations of her own. Every woman in Prague seems to have a repertoire of these sandwiches, and jealously guards her own recipe for a liver mousse or a stuffing for a cornet of the famous ham.

With the beer comes *topinky*, bread fried in lard and liberally spread with crushed raw garlic. The garlic stimulates the thirst and the thirst makes one hungry for the bread — and an evening passes in quiet contemplation of the world, and the mess it is in.

The forests of Czechoslovakia have always provided good sport, and most fairy tales begin: 'One day, when the King was out hunting . . .'. Venison is highly prized meat, and there are many recipes for hunter's stews and venison steaks, usually flavoured with juniper. As in other Central European countries, marjoram and caraway seed are popular flavourings, and poppy seed is used in many sweet dishes, as it is in traditional Jewish cookery. Another flavour which brings tears to the eyes of any expatriate Czech is *povidlo*, a dark plum jam which is so thick that a knife should stand up in the jar. Lard is used for frying and butter is usually added for flavouring as a finishing touch. A popular topping for cauliflower, dumplings and anything else with a bland flavour and soft texture is breadcrumbs fried in butter — it adds a crunchiness to the soft texture.

The Czechs not only have false soups — when they like a flavour, they improvise if the money will not stretch to the real thing. So there is a potato goulash: the sauce is the same but there is no meat in it; and the much appreciated paprika sauce is used not only with veal and chicken, but also with French beans and dumplings.

But then such a tiny country, historically always under someone's thumb, has had to learn to improvise.

BILL OF FARE

Hors d'Oeuvre

NADIVANE KORNOUTKY Z PRAZSKE SUNKY
Cream-filled ham slices

Soup

CESKA POLEVKA
Gammon soup with sour cream

MASOVA POLEVKA PO CESKU
Chicken and leek soup

BOHMISHER PIVO POLEVKA
Beer soup

Fish Dishes

PSTRUH PO CESKU
Salmon trout in cream sauce

KAPR NA CERNO
Carp with fruit and gingerbread sauce

MARINOVANY KAPR PO CESKU
Soused carp with cream

Meat Dishes

SVICKOVA NA SMETANE
Boiled salted beef with sour cream sauce

TELECI NA KMINE
Veal escalop in sour cream with caraway seeds

NADIVANA HOVEZI PECENE S OMACKOU
Stuffed fillet of beef in cream sauce

Vegetables

FAZOLE PO CESKU
Baked beans in cream sauce

BRAMBOROVA KASE
Mashed potatoes with cream and caraway seeds

KNEDLIK
Czech dumplings

HALUSKY
Cheese and potato dumplings

Sweets and Desserts

PECIVO (MILOSTI)
Fried pastries

LIVANCE
Bohemian pancakes

OVOCNE KNEDLIKY
Plum dumplings

ZEMLICKY (DALKEN)
Yeast bun fritters

PRAZSKY ORECHOVY DORT
Nut layer cake

VANOCKA
Christmas braid (plaited yeast cake)

JAHODOVY DORT SE SLEHACKOU
    LUDMILA 'VIE DE BOHEME'
Trifle with strawberries

HORS D'OEUVRE

NADIVANE KORNOUTKY Z PRAZSKE SUNKY
Cream-filled ham slices

Ingredients:

4 by 3 oz (90 g each) thin slices of Prague ham
12 oz (360 g)

Filling:

Liver pâté 4 oz (120 g)
Butter 2 oz (60 g)
Whipped cream 2 fl oz (60 mls)
Grated horseradish ½ oz (15 g)

Method: Blend filling together and pipe a rosette
in each slice folded like a cornucopia. Decorate
with cucumber and tomato.

SOUP

CESKA POLEVKA
Gammon soup with sour cream

Ingredients:

Lean diced gammon ½ lb (240 g) in ¼ inch cubes
Chopped onions 4 oz (120 g)
Lard 2 oz (60 g)
Flour 2 oz (60 g)
Water 3 pints (1,800 mls)
Salt and pepper, paprika to taste
Sour cream ½ pint (300 mls)
Chopped chives ½ oz (15 g)

Method: Saute diced gammon and onions with
lard till golden brown. Sprinkle flour and cook
5 minutes. Add water and simmer for 1½ hours
gently. Season and add soured cream when meat
is tender. Add chives. If the gammon is already
cooked the soup will be ready in 15 minutes
only.

MASOVA POLEVKA PO CESKU
Chicken and leek soup

Ingredients;

Chicken winglets and giblets 1 lb (480 g)
Leek ½ lb (240 g)
3 egg yolks
Cornflour 1 oz (30 g)
Sour cream 5 fl oz (150 mls)
Grated cheese 4 oz (120 g)
Salt and pepper

Method: Boil the giblets and winglets in cold water
till tender. Remove scum as it rises. Add the cleaned
and chopped leek and boil for 15 minutes. Strain,
season and thicken with a mixture of egg yolks,
cornflour and cream added firstly, into a bowl,
then poured back into the rest of the soup and
boiled to just cohere the mixture like a liquid
custard. Serve in a bowl with grated cheese. Note
that the diced leek can be left in the soup or
liquidised to a puree and added to the broth.

BOHMISHER PIVO POLEVKA
Beer soup

Ingredients:

Light beer 1 pint (600 mls)
Dark beer or stout 1 pint (600 mls)
Fresh grated ginger ¼ oz (8 g)
Cornflour 2 oz (60 g)
Sugar 2 oz (60 g)
3 egg yolks
Cream 5 fl oz (150 mls)

Method: Bring beers to the boil. Blend cornflour,
egg yolks and cream. Add half of the beer while
stirring. Add the mixture to the other
half of beer. Bring to the boil and stir while
mixture thickens. Add grated fresh ginger and
sugar.

FISH DISHES

PSTRUH PO CESKU
Salmon trout in cream sauce

Ingredients:

1 salmon trout 2 lbs (960 g)
White wine ½ pint (300 mls)
Water ½ pint (300 mls)
1 bouquet garni
Caraway seeds ½ oz (15 g)
Sliced onions 5 oz (150 g)
Ground paprika ½ oz (15 g)
Salt and pepper
Cornflour 1 oz (30 g)
Sour cream 5 fl oz (150 mls)

Garnish:

4 sliced tomatoes
4 pineapple cubes
4 orange segments

Method: Clean and gut salmon trout. Remove
scales. Wash and dry. Place on shallow dish with
water and wine, sliced onions and caraway seeds
and 1 bouquet garni and add seasoning. Bring to
the boil and simmer 30 minutes without boiling,
simmering it gently.

Remove from dish and place in a serving dish.
Strain liquor and boil it in a saucepan to reduce
by half its quantity to ½ pint (300 mls). Thicken
with a slurry of sour cream and cornflour. Check
seasoning and pour over the trout. Garnish with
tomatoes, orange segments and pineapple.

KAPR NA CERNO
Carp with fruit and gingerbread sauce

Ingredients:

Carp — gutted, scales removed ready for cooking
    4 lb (1,920 g)
Wine vinegar ½ pint (300 mls)
Water 1 pint (600 mls)
1 bouquet garni
Onions 5 oz (150 g)
Carrot 5 oz (150 g)
Salt and pepper
1 clove, 1 pinch nutmeg

Garnish for sauce:

Prunes 8 oz (240 g)
Seedless raisins 4 oz (120 g)

Brown sugar 1 oz (30 g)
Pinch cayenne pepper
Gingerbread crumbs 4 oz (120 g)
Fish stock 1 pint (600 mls)
Butter 2 oz (60 g)
Chopped walnuts 3 oz (90 g)

Method: Soak prunes in water until swollen.
Then cook them with brown sugar until tender.
Cool, remove stones and chop pulp. Poach fish
in water and vinegar with seasoning, vegetables
and bouquet garni for 30 minutes, simmering
gently without boiling. Leave fish in its own
liquor until cold. Then remove and peel off
skin. Place in a large shallow dish.
Sauce: Simmer gingerbread crumbs in melted
butter, add prunes, cayenne pepper, rasins and nuts
then dilute ¾ pint (450 mls) of the fish stock into
this mixture to reach a coating consistency.
Season to taste. Pour sauce over fish or serve it
separately.

MARINOVANY KAPR PO CESKU
Soused carp

Ingredients:

Carp filleted into 4 fillets of 5 oz (150 g) each
4 peeled slices of lemon

Vegetable garnish:

Chopped gherkins 1 oz (30 g)
Chopped capers 1 oz (30 g)
Chopped onions 2 oz (60 g)
Thinly sliced carrots 2 oz (60 g)
Thinly sliced celery 1 oz (30 g)
Lard and butter 2 oz (60 g) total
1 bouquet garni
White wine 5 fl oz (150 mls)
Water 5 fl oz (150 mls)
Sliced mushrooms 5 oz (150 g)
Chopped parsley 1 tbs
Salt and pepper
Mayonnaise 5 oz (150 g)

Method: 1. Fold carp fillet with a slice of lemon
inside. Place each fillet on a shallow dish well
greased with butter and lard. Add wine and

water, 1 bouquet garni and seasoning. Poach covered, 20 minutes in oven at 360°F. Strain liquor. Boil vegetable ingredients in liquor till tender for 15 minutes. Strain liquor and pour it over the fish. Add cooked vegetables to mayonnaise sauce. Serve separately.

Method: 2. Place all the vegetables in a shallow dish well greased with lard and butter. Arrange folded fish on top. Cover with wine and water. Season and bake in oven for 25 minutes at 380°F. Serve in same dish with plain mayonnaise. Make sure carrots are cut thinly to cook within the same time. Otherwise, cook them separately and add as garnish. Fish must *not* be over-cooked.

MEAT DISHES

SVICKOVA NA SMETANE
Boiled salted beef with sour cream sauce

Ingredients:

Boned salted silverside 2 lb (960 g)
Carrots 5 oz (150 g)
Leek 5 oz (150 g)
1 large onion studded with 2 cloves 5 oz (150 g)
Turnips 5 oz (150 g)
Celery 5 oz (150 g)
1 bouquet garni
Vinegar 5 fl oz (150 mls)

Sour cream sauce:

Sour cream ½ pint (300 mls)
Cornflour 1 oz (30 g)
Beef stock or broth ½ pint (300 mls)
Salt and pepper
Grated horseradish ½ oz (15 g)

Method: It is best to purchase from the butcher a piece of uncooked pickled silverside. Place it in water to desalt for 2 hours. Then cook it in cold fresh water and vinegar for 1 hour, removing scum as it rises. Then and only then add bouquet garni and clean vegetable roots: carrots, turnips and celery (and its roots if any). Simmer for another 30 minutes. Lastly add leek and onion. The leek should

be split open and well washed prior to cooking as it tends to be full of sand. Simmer for another hour. Add seasoning. Remove meat into a dish and surround with vegetables.
Sauce: Boil ½ pint (300 mls) of stock and add cornflour and cream slurry to thicken it. Blend grated horseradish and add seasoning.

TELECI NA KMINE
Veal escalope in sour cream with caraway seeds

Ingredients:

4 veal escalopes from cushion or undercushion of
    veal – allow 3 oz (90 g) per escalope
Seasoned flour 2 oz (60 g)
Frying oil or lard 3 oz (90 g)
Chopped onions 2 oz (60 g)
Diced apples 3 oz (90 g)
Sour cream 6 fl oz (180 mls)
Caraway seeds ½ oz (15 g)
Salt and pepper
Pinch of ground paprika

Method: Pass escalopes in seasoned flour. Pan fry in lard or oil until done. Place in shallow dish and keep warm.

In same pan, fry chopped onions till tender but not brown. Add sliced or diced peeled apples. Cook for few minutes. Remove surplus fat if any, then add cream, salt, pepper and caraway seeds and boil 10 minutes. Pour over escalops and dust with paprika. Serve with noodles or boiled potatoes.

NADIVANA HOVEZI PECENE S OMACKOU
Stuffed fillet of beef in cream sauce

Ingredients:

4 by 4 oz fillet steaks (120 g each)

Filling:

Cooked sausage meat 3 oz (90 g)
Crumbs 2 oz (60 g)
Chopped onions 1 oz (30 g)
Lard 2 oz (60 g)

1 egg
Salt and pepper
Seasoned flour

Sauce:

Chopped onions 2 oz (60 g)
Lard and butter totalling 1 oz (30 g)
Sliced mushrooms 2 oz (60 g)
Sour cream 5 fl oz (150 mls)
Czech brandy 3 fl oz (90 mls)
Paprika (a pinch)
Caraway seeds (a pinch)
Salt and pepper
Chopped parsley 1 tbs

Method: Fry the chopped onions in lard for few minutes. Cool and blend with sausage meat, egg, crumbs and seasoning to form a stuffing. Flatten each steak thinly and place a small ball of stuffing inside. Roll the steak and tie it up with two cocktail sticks or with strings. Pass in seasoned flour and pan fry in lard for 12 minutes. Place in shallow dish and cover with the sauce.
Sauce: Pan fry – without colouring – the chopped onions in lard and butter. Strain fat and add mushrooms. Cook 5 minutes. Blend cream and seasoning. Add brandy and pour over meat, with paprika and caraway seeds. Cover dish with a lid and braise for 30 minutes. Sprinkle chopped parsley and serve.
Note: Another way for larger parties is to stuff the whole fillet of beef by making a slit lengthwise and inserting the mixture. The fillet is tied up in string and roasted, the sauce is made separately and when ready, the fillet is sliced and sauce poured over. The previous method is more practical and simpler.

VEGETABLES

FAZOLE PO CESKU
Baked beans in cream sauce

Ingredients:

Pea beans ½ lb (240 g)
Bacon bones or trimmings 4 oz (120 g)

Sauce:

1 whole onion
1 whole carrot
1 bouquet garni
Lard 2 oz (60 g)
Chopped onions 2 oz (60 g)
Salt and pepper; caraway seeds
Vinegar 3 oz (90 mls)
Sugar 1 oz (30 g)
Garlic 1 clove
Sour cream 8 fl oz (240 mls)
Chopped parsley 1 tbs

Method: Soak the beans in water overnight. (If water is hard, use distilled water.) Boil beans for 30 minutes, remove scum as it rises then add 1 whole onion and garlic, 1 carrot and 1 bouquet garni, caraway seeds and bacon bones or trimmings. Simmer gently for 1 hour till tender either on top of stove or in a casserole dish covered with a lid. Remove bouquet garni, carrot and onion and all the bacon trimmings.

Fry chopped onions in lard till soft but not brown. Strain fat off. Add vinegar and boil few minutes then pour in cream and season. Blend sauce to beans and serve sprinkled with chopped parsley.

BRAMBOROVA KASE
Mashed potatoes with cream and caraway seeds

Ingredients:

Potatoes 2 lbs (960 g)
Lard 3 oz (90 g)
Chopped onions 3 oz (90 g)
Sugar 1 oz (30 g)
Sour cream 6 fl oz (180 mls)
Salt and pepper, paprika
Pinch caraway seeds
1 tbs white vinegar
Chopped parsley 1 tbs

Method: Cut potatoes in quarter and boil in salted water for 20 minutes. Drain off water. Fry the chopped onions in lard for 20 minutes till soft without browning. Add vinegar and boil 1 minute then add cream, sugar, seasoning and seeds. Blend potatoes with this sauce and serve with chopped parsley sprinkled over.

KNEDLIK
Czech dumplings

Ingredients:

Wheatflour 1 lb (480 g)
Salt ¼ oz (7 g)
2 egg yolks
Milk 3 fl oz (90 mls)
Butter 5 oz (150 g)
Bread cut in ¼ inch cubes (180 g)
Lard or oil for frying 4 oz (120 g)

Method: Sift the flour and salt into a bowl. Whisk the egg yolks in the milk. Mix with the flour to form a moist dough. Work with a wooden spoon until its surface is shiny and blisters form and break. The dough is ready when it no longer sticks to the spoon. Dust the dough with flour, cover with a cloth and allow to rest. Fry bread and drain on absorbent paper. Blend the bread to the dough and disperse the cubes evenly. Roll the dough into a salami loaf. Cut about one oz (30 g) of the mixture and roll it into a plum shape. Grease a tray, and half fill it with boiling water. Drop the dumplings into the water and poach for 10 minutes until they bob up. Melt butter and pour over the dumplings.

HALUSKY
Cheese and potato dumplings

Ingredients:

Potatoes 3 lbs (1,440 g)
Flour 1 lb (480 g)
Diced streaky bacon 2 oz (60 g)
Sheep's cream cheese or cream cheese ½ lb (240 g)
Salt ⅕ oz (5 g)
Chopped onions 2 oz (60 g)

Method: Grate the peeled potatoes and mix the flour. Add salt and cream cheese. Mix to a dough. Shape in small dumplings and poach in salted water for 10 minutes until they bob up. Drain and place into a shallow dish.

Fry diced bacon in little fat and brown onions at the same time. Cover the dumplings with this mixture. Serve hot.

SWEETS AND DESSERTS

PECIVO
Fried pastries

Ingredients:

Butter 2 oz (60 g)
Lard 1 oz (30 g)
1 egg
2 egg yolks
Milk 3 fl oz (90 mls)
Flour 1 lb (480 g)
Castor sugar 4 oz (120 g)
Vanilla essence, few drops
Lemon essence, few drops
Mixed spices, a pinch
Icing sugar 4 oz (120 g)
Oil or fat for deep frying

Method: Cream together butter and lard. Add eggs, milk, flour, castor sugar, the essences and spices. Form a stiff dough, knead a little and gather into a ball and rest in refrigerator for 30 minutes. Then roll out dough on a floured board to ¼ inch thick and cut into 2 inch to 3 inch triangles. Make a cut in the centre. Heat fat and fry at 360°F for 5 minutes. Drain, dry and dust with icing sugar when cold.

LIVANCE
Bohemian pancakes

Ingredients:

Milk 1 pint (600 mls)
4 beaten eggs
Grated lemon peel ½ oz (15 g)
Flour 5 oz (150 g)
Gingerbread crumbs 5 oz (150 g)
Pinch salt

Vanilla essence
Castor sugar 5 oz (150 g)
Lard 4 oz (120 g)

Method: Blend milk and beaten eggs, add crumbs and flour to form a soft, runny batter. Add rest of flavourings. Rest 30 minutes. Heat an omelette pan with a little lard, when hot tilt some of the fat and pour 2 oz (60 g) of mixture to cover the pan area. Cook on both sides like a pancake. Serve with sugar and wedges of lemon or with jam, especially the Czechoslovakian red plum jam.

OVOCNE KNEDLIKY
Plum dumplings

The characteristic of this dumpling is that it is made with cream cheese to flavour the dough.

Ingredients:

Butter 1 oz (30 g)
Cream cheese 5 oz (150 g)
1 egg yolk
Milk 4 fl oz (120 mls)
Flour 12 oz (360 g)
Grated peels ½ oz (15 g)

Filling:

12 firm, ripe red plums
Pinch of cinnamon
Salted water for cooking
Melted butter 6 oz (180 g)
Castor sugar 6 oz (180 g)

Method: Cream butter and cheese with egg till fluffy. Add grated peels then blend flour to obtain a stiff dough. Add milk. Knead well. Gather into a ball and rest for 30 minutes. Then roll like a salami. Cut 16 slices weighing 1 oz (30 g) each. With the palm of the hand flatten them lightly. Place a plum in the centre – or a half of one if it is large. Gather, purse-like, the ends of the pastry on top and shape like a ball. Drop dumplings in salted water and poach 8 minutes until they float. Drain well and pour

melted butter over and sprinkle with castor sugar mixed with cinnamon.

Instead of boiling in water, the dumplings could equally be fried in deep fat. Fruits other than plums can also be used.

ZENLICKY
Yeast bun fritters

Ingredients:

Baker's yeast ½ oz (15 g)
Lukewarm milk 4 fl oz (120 mls)
2 eggs
Pinch of salt and sugar
Lard 1 oz (30 g)
Flour (strong or bread flour) 1 lb (480 g)
Castor sugar 4 oz (120 g)
Pinch of cinnamon
Czechoslovakian red plum jam 6 oz (180 g)

Method: This yeast bun is really a doughnut which has found its way round the world under many names.

Crumble yeast into lukewarm milk. Disperse and add egg, salt and sugar. Blend flour and lard to form a stiff dough. Knead and gather into a ball. Rest for 30 minutes – cover with a basin turned upside down. Divide dough into 12 balls. Shape them round well. Place on greased tray to rise again. Brush a little milk or water to prevent crusting. After 20 minutes, fry in deep fat for 6 minutes, turning them all round. Do not pack the frying kettle. Frying temperature should be at 360°F. Drain and dry. Place jam in a piping bag fitted with a small plain tube. Inject a shot of jam inside each doughnut. Roll the doughnut in granulated sugar flavoured with a pinch of cinnamon and serve hot with coffee or tea.

PRAZSKY ORECHOVY DORT
Nut layer cake

I have modified this cake so that it can be served as a dessert or sweet.

Ingredients:

Sponge:

Butter 4 oz (120 g)
Castor sugar 4 oz (120 g)
4 eggs
Ground almonds 4 oz (120 g)
Flour 1 oz (30 g)
Grated peels ½ oz (15 g)
Breadcrumbs 4 oz (120 g)
Almond essence, few drops

Buttercream filling:

Butter 3 oz (90 g)
Icing sugar 2 oz (60 g)
Toasted ground nuts 1 oz (30 g)
Melted chocolate 1 oz (30 g) or cocoa powder

Cream for decoration:

Whipped cream 5 fl oz (150 mls)
8 Czech glacé plums

Method: Cream butter and sugar until fluffy.
Add eggs gradually, then almonds, flour, peels
and crumbs, and almond essence. Line a cake
tin (9 inch in diameter) with greaseproof paper
and spread mixture evenly. Level with palette
knife. Bake 30 minutes at 380°F. Cool on rack
and store in refrigerator overnight. Then split
and fill with chocolate butter cream.

Cream butter and sugar, add nuts and
chocolate. Add flavour if required. Fill sponge
with some of this buttercream and coat top
and sides with some cream. Apply a few toasted
nuts on the side. Pipe whipped cream pattern
on top and decorate with candied or glacé plums
or other fruits.

VANOCKA
Christmas braid (plaited yeast cake)

Ingredients:

Lukewarm milk ½ pint (300 mls)
Baker's yeast ½ oz (15 g)
Sugar 1 oz (30 g)
1 beaten egg
Flour 1 lb (480 g)

Butter 2 oz (60 g)
Pinch salt
1 egg for glazing

Fruits:

Seedless raisins 2 oz (60 g)
Lemon peels 1 oz (30 g)
Pinch ground mace or nutmeg and cinnamon
Grated fresh lemon, a pinch
Flaked almonds 3 oz (90 g)

Glaze:

Sugar 5 oz (150 g)
Water 2 fl oz (60 mls)

Method: Crumble yeast and blend in lukewarm
milk, add sugar and salt. Blend in the flour and
beaten egg to obtain a stiff dough. Knead for 5
minutes then gather round into a ball. Cover with
a basin turned upside down or with a cloth. Let it
prove until twice its size. Knead again and blend
in soft butter. Let it prove again for 15 minutes
then add fruits — previously soaked, drained and
dried — and all peels, spices and nuts. Knead well.
Divide the mixture into three balls. Shape each
into a well rounded form. Cover with a cloth
or basin and prove for 20 minutes. Roll each ball
into an elongated oblong loaf pointed at each end.
Rest 10 minutes and plait the three loaves which
should be 9 inch long each. Place the plaited loaf
on a greased tray. Brush with eggwash. Allow to
rest another 15 minutes. Bake at 400°F for 30
minutes. Meanwhile boil water and sugar to
obtain a thick syrup (boil only 5 minutes). Brush
loaf when it is removed from the oven. This will
produce an attractive gloss. Cool on a rack.

JAHOSOVY DORT SE SLEHACKOU
LUDMILLA 'VIE DE BOHEME'
Trifle with strawberries

I dedicate this creation to the ladies of
Czechoslovakia bearing the name.

Ingredients:

Czech white or red wine ½ pint (300 mls)
Ground gelatine 2 oz (60 g)

Castor sugar 5 oz (150 g)
Czech plum brandy 3 fl oz (90 mls)
Strawberry essence, four drops
Red colour, four drops
Sponge cake ½ lb (240 g)
Fresh strawberries 1 lb (480 g)
Whipped cream ½ pint (300 mls)
Toasted almonds (flaked or nibbed)
Crystallised violets 2 oz (60 g)

Method: Heat wine without boiling. Mix ground
gelatin and sugar and add to hot wine to
dissolve it. Remove from heat. Add essences and
colour, and brandy. Place diced sponge in a
trifle glass dish. Soak with hot wine jelly mixture.
Set in a refrigerator. When jelly is firm, place
cleaned strawberries on top. Decorate with piped
cream in criss-cross patterns. Decorate with
toasted almonds and violets.

The British Isles

What is British gastronomy? Is it the food of Imperial Britannia, with all the trimmings of the Victorian past? Is it the food of the famous hotels and restaurants, where some of the best chefs in the world made their names? Is it the food eaten by the ordinary people in their homes and in the fish and chip shops? Or is it the traditional foods of the regions, still cooked by industrious housewives for appreciative menfolk?

It is a combination of all of these together with the best traditional foods served in gentlemen's clubs, the halls of universities and even in the little country pubs where the tenant still cares about the food he puts in front of his customers. Good food may be found anywhere in the British Isles. It is a pity it is not found everywhere.

Political influence may now only be exercised through membership of the European Community; yet Britain is still one of the biggest importers of food in the world, and as such a big customer she can dictate her own terms. The produce which is grown here and that which is imported is the best in the world. The catering industry has the highest standards and some of the world's greatest chefs have made their home and name in London: Careme, Sover, Escoffier, Gouffe, Dutrey, Boulestin have all contributed to the standard of British cookery.

Gastronomy is alive in Britain. Perhaps what is wrong is that curious quirk in the British character which prevents a Briton who has had a disappointing meal from complaining about bad food and service.

It is not done to run down the food of your host. Worse still, one does not reprimand a bad cook in public or abuse the waiter who brings you such bad food. On the contrary, the traditional custom is to praise the meal, thank the host and praise God for having provided the food. Commendable — except that is the way in which shoddy service and indifferent food will perpetuate themselves.

For those who seek it out, the British Isles offer a great variety of food and a very civilised style of eating. The great British institution, copied throughout the world and nutritionally sound is the great British cooked breakfast. Fresh fruit juice, hot porridge with salt or with sugar and cream, a selection of grilled fish or kippers, smoked haddock poached in milk, or simply a few soft roes on toast are a prelude to the more solid food. Then come the bacon or ham and eggs, devilled kidneys, sausages grilled or fried, with or without mushrooms, tomatoes or liver. You can even have a few lamb cutlets. Lastly, with copious cups of tea, one may have the finest toast, crisp and hot and golden, with creamy butter and honey or the tangy marmalade made from bitter-sweet Seville oranges.

A cup of tea and a biscuit for elevenses is a mere comma on the face of the day, but the meal following still divides the country into two classes. The middle class call it 'lunch' and have light grills, roasts or other plain fare; the others call it 'dinner' and have rich foods or sandwiches.

The middle class has 'tea' at four and 'dinner' at eight; the others have tea 'at six and later in the evening 'supper'. There is no other country in the world where class difference is shown by eating habits to such a degree. Yet the ingredients in the dish of the middle class and that of the working class may be similar. It is not so much a question of money, but of attitude.

Whatever the main meal of the day and whatever one calls it, soup is a popular beginning, followed by fish. Nowadays many skip the fish course to go on to the meat, often a roast of beef or lamb with a variety of vegetables. The British love their vegetables and it is usual for the main meal to have up to four: roasted and boiled potatoes, a green vegetable and one of the root vegetables. Roasted birds are usually accompanied by bread sauce, gravy, chips, watercress and some type of jelly or relish.

A book could be written on the puddings of the British Isles alone. Solid steamed puddings so beloved in boarding schools, baked puddings with or without fruit, light airy confections like syllabub or lemon meringue pie vie with the nourishing puddings like custards and creams.

The afternoon tea ceremony may not be as intricate as the Japanese version, but it is arguably as enjoyable, with its selection of cakes, scones, buns, biscuits, jellies, thin bread and butter and dainty sandwiches. Tea is served with milk or slices of lemon — and the tea comes from India, Ceylon or China. A well-presented tea is a meal in itself.

The cooking of the British Isles is still very regional in style. To the Welshman it means cawl and girdle cakes and laver bread; to the Yorkshireman it means parkin and cold tripe and Yorkshire pudding; to the man from the shires it may mean Melton Mowbray pies and to the Scotsman it means scones, bannocks, shortbread and haggis. The differences are becoming less amongst the clientele of restaurants, and one is just as likely to find an excellent meal of international classics in Edinburgh, Dublin or Cardiff as in London.

Unfortunately, to the foreigner British cooking still means lumpy gravies, over-cooked roasts and watery vegetables. That, however, may no longer be the truth. Now the ordinary food of the people is much more likely to mean frozen meals, take-away snacks, food from the micro-wave cooker and canteen meals. As so many women now work, breakfast can be a skimped affair, lunch a non-event and dinner a convenience meal. Cooking is done at the weekends and, in some cases, as a hobby.

That is why British gastronomy is in such a state of flux as the end of the twentieth century approaches. On one hand there are the superb traditional dishes of England, Scotland, Ireland and Wales; on the other hand there are those cooks who have no time, no money and no inclination to recreate the wonderful dishes of the past. The international cuisine served in most restaurants is no more British than the food in those restaurants with Chianti bottles for candlesticks is Italian. Yet there is a revival, small but promising, of the true taste of good British food. When well done, it is delicious, nourishing and, like all native food, entirely appropriate to the climate and the people. It would be a pity to allow the true taste of Britain to become extinct.

England

Foreign tourists may seek out the roast sirloin of Olde England, juicy, succulent and tempting, but too often they miss the true country flavour of the numerous regions of this beautiful country. Roast beef is truly a wonderful dish when done properly; but there is a wealth of simpler dishes to explore in the various regions.

Some of the great culinary triumphs of English cookery are born of necessity and poverty: Yorkshire pudding was created by the thrifty housewives of the north to catch every last drop of juice escaping from the expensive roast, and to fill starving families before they attacked the meat. Lancashire hot pot is an economical way of stretching lamb to whatever the exchequer will bear; kidneys or even oysters may be added but the potatoes and onions may equally be increased to dominate the meat. A ham and veal pie wraps the expensive, tasty filling in a thick cocoon of hot water crust pastry, delicious but inexpensive.

When I first visited England in 1938, with my fellow countrymen I was a guest of the town of Penzance — the French fleet was in and our red pompoms were at a premium. Little did I think that this lush, green land would one day become my second home and that I would live through thirty years of its gastronomic traditions, dish by dish and meal by meal, sampling dishes and concocting them, one day for the King, the next for an illustrious politician like Winston Churchill, and soon afterwards for the young Queen who brought in the new Elizabethan era.

I travelled the British Isles, preaching, demonstrating and lecturing as a champion of gastronomy. The British housewife was and is the love of my life as the most interested pupil a master chef could wish for.

The produce of England is the strength of its gastronomy. There are the delicate herrings of Yarmouth, the lamb from the South Downs and beef from Herefordshire. Wiltshire hams vie with those of York in excellence, and Aylesbury ducklings, Norfolk turkeys, East Anglian pheasant and Northumbrian venison are just a few of the gastronomic miracles of this land.

The English are traditional with their food. They like their dishes plain, rich but not heavy. The simple cooking is still the food you encounter at the very best dinner tables in the land — roasts, grills, pies and stews made of well-flavoured ingredients with little in the way of rich sauces. The sauce cookery of England tends to be on the side of condiments more than on the traditional French sauce cookery of haute cuisine. Yet there is something to be said for those sauces of Cumberland, Gloucester, Worcester, Mint, Horseradish and Albert: they are distinctive and their aroma imparts a quite unique taste to the meat or fish with which they are served.

An English pie is a culinary masterpiece. Whether hot or cold, a veal pie in a pub or a steak and kidney pie in an expensive restaurant, the habit of wrapping delicious morsels of meat in a skin of melting pastry is very English.

Puddings of England deserve a whole book to themselves. Steamed or baked, boiled or chilled, the English pudding stands alone in its starchy glory — aromatic with dried fruit and spices, tart with fresh fruit in season or creamy with buttery milk and nutmeg, the puddings of England are wildly fattening and totally irresistible.

London is the capital and the city for which most tourists aim when they come to England. The Thames was once the source of much of London's food, and popular specialities still reflect this dependence. Salmon used to be so plentiful that it was the food of the poor, and apprentice boys of London would have a special clause written into their indentures absolving them from eating salmon more than twice a week. Smoked trout, haddock and eel remain London favourites. Jellied eels are the delicacy of the working man of London, and stalls in the open-air markets still offer a fine selection of these along with cockles, mussels, winkles and the more costly and fashionable scampi and prawns. Food from every corner of the globe is available in the capital, but the traditional dishes of succulent beef, steak, kidney and oyster pie, roast crown of lamb, a juicy London grill with kidneys, steak, chops and sausages with mushrooms and tomatoes, or the jam roly-poly are best eaten in the clubs where gentlemen drink brandy behind The Times and ladies are seldom if ever admitted. More accessible treats include the Chelsea bun, a sticky yeasty pastry which goes well with a cup of Indian tea, and Richmond maids of honour, little cakes which go down well at any time at all.

Yorkshire is a region of hearty eaters and industrious women, which augurs well for the gastronome. There is a legend that in the cutting of the beams for York Minster, the oak sawdust produced the smoke to flavour the succulent hams of the region. A tea, eaten in the early afternoon, with ham and a little apple pie for afters, is a traditional Yorkshire meal. The apple pie is eaten with slices of the rich, crumbly Wensleydale cheese. Typical Yorkshire dishes are black pudding, a blood sausage flavoured with herbs and spices; tripe, and faggots, made with pig's liver and salt pork. A treacly, gingery cake is the parkin, and there are curd tarts, Fat Rascals (griddle scones) and Harrogate toffee. The fishing ports of the area yield superb fish, and it is no accident that the best fish and chip shops are in this region.

Kent is the lovely garden of England, with its spectacular blossom and its fragrant fruit. The specialities of this region are fruit tarts and puddings, with fruit wines and ciders, mead, cherry ale and cherry brandy. Chickens scratch beneath the trees of any orchard, and they meet their fate in puddings and pies of the south-east. Game is abundant and Ashdown Forest has given its name to a partridge pie. The New Forest venison is rich, succulent and meaty.

Sea food comes from the rich fishing grounds around the Kent coast. If there were no other product than Dover sole, the sea food of this region would still deserve a mention.

Cumbria is the region of grey and green mountains which separate the glacial valleys to make the food of the area truly local: travel has been so difficult that the dishes created by the industrious local housewives have remained quite unique. Many specialities bear the name of their own town, such as Lamplugh with its pudding, Kendal with a mint cake and Hawkshead with its Havverbread. Morecambe Bay is rich with exquisite shrimps, exported all over the world, and fluke, a delicate fish rather like plaice but less well known. Cumberland sausage is a delicious coil served with apple sauce. The local lamb finds its way into many a dish, the best being the tatie-pot, a traditional stew with vegetables. Rum, brown sugar and spices are all a relic of the past in Cumbria, with its trade with the new world, based on Whitehaven.

The North produces the famous and adaptable Lancashire hot-pot along with the Cheshire and Lancashire cheeses. Liverpool Lobscouse is another lamb dish with ship's biscuits added, and Hindle Wakes is a chicken stuffed with prunes and breadcrumbs. Cakes and pastries are delicious, with oatcakes in the front row for delicacy and tastiness. Toasted with jam or honey, or fried with bacon and eggs, they add their nuttiness to the filling. Simnel cake, a delicacy traditionally made for Mothering Sunday, comes from this area. The garland of almond paste is traditionally left undecorated.

Melton Mowbray in the shires produces the best and most famous raised pork pies, traditionally flavoured with a dash of anchovy. The Melton hunt cake is a rum-flavoured fruit cake which used to be reserved for the hunting gentry. The cheeses Leicester, Derby and Stilton originate in the shires, and are traditionally offered with the Bramley apples of the area.

Thames and the Chilterns produce some of the food traditionally associated with childhood memories. Brown Windsor soup, Banbury cakes, Aylesbury duck and the Poor Knights of Windsor are all dishes which conjure up dusty classrooms smelling of chalk and a silky sward on the cricket pitch.

The West Country gives us some of the most tasty treats in the English repertoire of cooking. A Cornish pasty is known as a Tiddy Oggy in its own surroundings, and its much maligned commercial cousin bears no relation to the succulent original. Devon combines its name with one of those teas when jam, butter, scones and cream mingle in a happy acquaintance. Cider is made and drunk in both Devon and Somerset, and Cheddar cheese is a product of the Cheddar gorges in Somerset. Wiltshire offers superlative hams, pies and bacon, and the Cornish coast has fish and shell-fish to titillate the palate of the most discerning gastronome.

The area known as the heart of England produces a great number of specialities besides Worcester sauce and Malvern water. Cider comes from the cool cellars of Hereford, and the beef cattle give juicy, tender beef for pies and steaks. Shrewsbury lamb is deliciously tender and elvers are caught in the Wye River to be fried and eaten whole like whitebait.

East Anglia is principally known for its wide selection of fish landed at the important harbour of Lowestoft. Herrings are made into bloaters and kippers, and the oysters reared at West Mersea are small but delicate. Fresh fish abound in the rivers and are smoked along with the salt water fish. Turkey and duck are tasty birds reared in Norfolk, and pheasant introduces a welcome tang of game. Soft fruit bruises easily and most is sold at the roadside to be made into summer pudding and preserves. Maldon produces crystalline sea salt which is rich in iodine and minerals.

Above all, the food of England is simple and tasty, with a distinct bias towards grills and roasts. And with the quality of the raw materials, who would want anything more?

BILL OF FARE

Soup

WINDSOR SOUP
Brown meat soup made with calf's head and
herbs

ANGLIA SOUP
Creamy soup with ham and peas

Hors d'Oeuvre

SMOKED MACKEREL PÂTÉ
Cream mackerel paste with sherry and brandy

PRAWN MOUSSE ELIZABETH
Mousse lined with smoked salmon

SCAMPI ROSSLARE
Fresh Dublin Bay prawns cooked in wine

SCAMPI MORECAMBE
Scampi cooked with sherry and whisky in pastry
cases

POTTED HAM & CHICKEN
Ham and chicken brawn

Fish Dishes

DOVER SOLE NELSON
Fried sole stuffed with potted shrimps and
mushrooms

DOVER SOLE PRINCE PHILIP
Sole baked with cider and tomatoes

SALMON ROYAL
Whole salmon cooked in dry cider and coated with
a cream sauce

LOBSTER ASCOT
Lobster boiled in court-bouillon and served in
coupe with a mint and apple flavoured
mayonnaise

LOBSTER CLARENCE
Hot lobster meat cooked in curry sauce cohered
with yoghurt and served with rice

Meat Dishes

ROYAL CROWN OF ENGLISH LAMB
ELIZABETH II

Lamb garnished with potato pie and cauliflower
au gratin Elizabeth II

STEAK & MUSHROOM PIE
Diced top or silverside beef stewed in port wine
sauce and served with a pastry topping

STEAK & KIDNEY & MUSHROOM PUDDING
Raw diced meats steamed with suet pastry

LANCASHIRE HOT POT
Chops, potatoes and white vegetables baked in
an earthenware pot

SURREY JUGGED HARE
Stewed hare with port wine

BRAISED OX HEART VICTORIA
Sliced ox heart sauted and braised in oven with
vegetables

YORK HAM PASTIES
Ham turnover with mushrooms

CUMBERLAND MUTTON PIE
Diced mutton cooked with vegetables in cider

LONDON CITY SIRLOIN
Roast beef with Buckingham apple pudding

FILLET OF BEEF WELLINGTON
Fillet of beef wrapped in puff pastry, baked and
served with a port wine sauce

Vegetables

LINCOLN CROQUETTE
Potato croquette in pear shapes flavoured with
onions

ASPARAGUS REGENCY
Hot asparagus with a cream sauce flavoured with
fresh mint

DEVONSHIRE STEW
Casserole of potatoes and vegetables in tomato
sauce

LEEK NORTHUMBRIA
Leeks coated with cheese sauce

BAKED MARROW CAMBRIDGESHIRE
Stuffed marrow coated with cheese sauce

STUFFED ONION EAST ANGLIA
Onions stuffed with egg, crumbs and pork sausage
    meat

STILTON CUCUMBER
Cucumber stuffed with a stilton cheese mixture
    with tomatoes and chopped onions blended
    into the sauce

Savouries

ANGELS ON HORSEBACK
Oysters wrapped in grilled bacon rashers served
    on toast

DEVILS ON HORSEBACK
Kidney wrapped in bacon, coated with cheese
    sauce and served on toast

KNAVES ON HORSEBACK
Mushrooms stuffed with chicken liver, wrapped
    with bacon rashers, coated with cheese sauce,
    browned under the grill and served on toast

Sweets

OXFORD PUDDING
Sponge treacle pudding

CASTLE PUDDING
Sponge cake pudding with jam

CHRISTMAS PUDDING
Rich fruit pudding with rum

ELIZABETH SILVER JUBILEE PUDDING
Baked custard with meringue and raspberry filling

COLCHESTER PUDDING
Custard with fruit topped with meringue

SYLLABUB FARMHOUSE
Cream and wine served in glasses like junket

LEMON & TANGERINE PIE
Lemon curd and tangerine topped with meringue

MINCE TART DICKENS
Rich fruit tartlet flavoured with rum

BROWN BREAD AND BUTTER PUDDING
Bread custard pudding flavoured with mixed
    fruit, honey and nuts

GOOSEBERRY FOOL
Puree of gooseberries blended with whipped
    double cream

CONIL'S SHORTBREAD
A sablé type of biscuit

Cakes

CHELSEA BUN
Yeast bun coated with icing

SAFFRON CAKE
Yeast bread cake flavoured with saffron

FLAPJACKS
Confectionery made with syrup, sugar, nuts and
    oats

PARKIN
Treacle cake with spices

CURD CHEESE CAKE
Custard cheese cake

BRANDY SNAPS
A caramel confectionery

SCONES
Baking powder small bread or cake

WINDSOR CASTLE CAKE
Rich fruit cake

SOUP

WINDSOR SOUP
Brown meat soup made with calf's head and
   herbs (8 portions)

The original version of this soup is often described
as mock turtle soup. It can be made in two forms
– clear and thick. The essential meat ingredient
must invariably be calf's head and the flavour of
the herbs used for fresh or canned turtle soup –
basil, marjoram, sage, rosemary, thyme, coriander,
bay leaf and fresh mint (often forgotten), plus
6 white peppercorns.

   Allow 5 g of each and pack in a small muslin
bag. These herbs are available in the trade in
sachets.

Ingredients:

Clear version:

Water 4 pint (2,400 mls)
Half a calf's head 4 lb (1,920 g)
Carrots 5 oz (150 g)
Leeks 5 oz (150 g)
Celery 5 oz (150 g)
1 split onion (slightly browned in a pan and
   studded with 4 cloves)
1 bouquet garni
1 lemon
1 herb sachet

Mirepoix

Carrots 3 oz (90 g)
Onions 5 oz (150 g)
Bacon rashers 5 oz (150 g)
Wine sherry 5 oz (150 g)
Garlic 5 g

Clarification:

Minced beef 8 oz (240 g)
Minced leek 5 oz (150 g)
White of egg 2 oz (60 g)
Arrowroot ½ oz (15 g)

Garnish:

12 quenelles of chicken or veal blended with
   10 per cent chopped hard-boiled eggs

Or make from:
Raw minced chicken 8 oz (240 g)
2 egg whites
Butter or cream 4 oz (120 g)
(All blended together and shaped with a spoon.)

Brunoise:

Carrots 2 oz (60 g)
Turnips 2 oz (60 g)
French beans 2 oz (60 g)
   all cut $\frac{1}{8}$ inch cubes

Method: Singe the calf's head. Scald and rinse.
Rub well with lemon. Bone and remove the
brain. Keep for future use. Place meat bones and
vegetables in pot, cover with cold water and add
mirepoix cut in thick slices, bouquet garni and
garlic and bring to the boil and simmer for 1½
hours until meat is tender. Strain soup and add
sherry. Cut meat in small cubes and keep in
sherry. Cool liquid and add clarification mixture.
Stir well and reheat to boiling point. Simmer for
1 hour and strain like consomme. To the clear
broth add the sachet and infuse 5 minutes or
more. Prepare a slurry with arrowroot and water
and add to the boiling soup to thicken it (use only
one litre for four portions). Lastly add the garnish
allowing 20 g per portion. These quenelles are
optional if the meat is served as a garnish. Cook
quenelles in salted stock for 10 minutes before
adding them to soup.
Thick version: To half a litre of clear Windsor
add half a litre of demi-glace sauce and use the
same garnish, or instead use 75 g cooked brunoise
of vegetables.

ANGLIA SOUP
Creamy soup with ham and peas (4 to 6 portions)

Ingredients:

Lard 2 oz (60 g)
Bacon 2 oz (60 g)
Chopped onions 2 oz (60 g)
Green peas 1 lb (480 g)
Fresh mint, few leaves
Water 1½ pint (900 mls)
Milk 1 pint (600 mls)

Salt and pepper
Pinch of mace
Butter 2 oz (60 g)

Method: Heat lard in a saucepan and saute diced
bacon and onion until soft and tender. Add peas,
seasoning, mace and mint. Cook for 5 minutes
and then flood with water. Boil till tender and
add milk. Simmer for a few minutes and then
pass mixture through a fine sieve. Reheat soup
and stir in a pan of butter. Serve with bread
sippets. Season to taste.

HORS D'OEUVRES

SMOKED MACKEREL PÂTÉ
Cream mackerel paste with sherry and brandy

Ingredients:

4 large smoked mackerel fillets 1 lb (480 g)
Butter 4 oz (120 g)
Shallots or onions 2 oz (60 g)
Sherry 2 fl oz (60 mls)
Brandy 2 fl oz (60 mls)
Salt and black pepper
Double cream 4 fl oz (120 mls)
1 lemon
Nutmeg, cayenne pepper

Method: Saute the skinned smoked mackerel
fillets and chopped shallots or onions in butter
for five minutes. Add brandy and sherry, stir well
and add salt and black pepper. Remove from the
heat and when cool pass through a mincer. Cream
the mixture to a very smooth paste adding a little
double cream and the juice and grated rind of
the lemon. Add a pinch of nutmeg and cayenne
pepper. Chill and serve with sippets of brown
bread.

PRAWN MOUSSE ELIZABETH
Mousse lined with smoked salmon (8 portions)

Ingredients:

Milk ½ pint (300 mls)

2 egg yolks
Ground gelatine 1 oz (30 g)
Flour 1 oz (30 g)
White port wine 2 fl oz (60 mls)
Chopped shallots or onions 1 oz (30 g)
Sliced mushrooms 1 oz (30 g)
Oil 1 oz (30 g)
Butter 1 oz (30 g)
Double cream 5 fl oz (150 mls)
Single cream 5 fl oz (150 mls)
Pinch of paprika
Juice and rind of 1 lemon
Salt and pepper
Smoked salmon 4 oz (120 g)
Large peeled prawns 4 oz (120 g)

Aspic jelly:

Gelatine 1 oz (30 g)
Water ½ pint (300 mls)
Pinch of salt
Juice of ½ lemon

Decoration:

Cucumber 4 oz (120 g)
Red pepper 1 oz (30 g)

Method: Boil milk. Mix in a bowl egg yolks,
flour, ground gelatine and port wine. Gradually
add hot milk. Stir well add butter and reboil until
it thickens. Remove from heat, add proper
seasoning and cool. Strain. Heat oil in pan and
saute chopped onions without browning. Add
sliced white mushrooms and cook for a further
few minutes. Add prawns and toss ingredients
well. Season with paprika. Blend to egg sauce
and add juice and rind of lemon. Cool.
Aspic jelly: Dissolve gelatine in water, add salt,
lemon juice and cool. When cold pour gelatine
into small 5 oz tumblers, rotating the tumbler
to allow gelatine aspic for form a coating on the
bottom and sides. Pour surplus away. To speed up
the operation, have handy a basin of ice cubes
and rest tumblers on ice. Whip double and single
cream until it forms peaks. Blend this mixture
lightly with prawn sauce. Check seasoning, add a
pinch of cayenne pepper to hot it up, if desired.
Cut smoked salmon into thin strips and line each
tumbler with smoked salmon, which should

adhere easily on the semi-set jelly. Fill the cavity with prawn mousse. Chill for 2 hours. To unmould, dip mould in warm water and turn out on to flat dish.

Decoration: Groove an unpeeled cucumber to obtain a design, slice thinly and arrange around the dish. Place a strip of red pimento on each cucumber slice in a criss-cross fashion.

SCAMPI ROSSLARE
Fresh Dublin Bay prawns cooked in wine

Ingredients:

Fresh live Dublin Bay prawns 2 lb (960 g)
Water 1 pint (600 mls)
Onions 5 oz (150 g)
Carrots 5 oz (150 g)
Celery 2 oz (60 g)
Garlic ⅓ oz (10 g)
Vinegar 2 fl oz (60 mls)
Chopped parsley 1 oz (30 g)
Cream 4 fl oz (120 mls)
Mint ¼ oz (10 g)
Pinch of thyme
Salt and pepper
Water and white wine ½ pint (300 mls)

Method: Cut the heads off the prawns and boil in the water with an onion for 15 minutes to produce a stock. Strain. In a pan saute chopped onions, garlic, sliced carrot and celery for a few minutes without colouring, add vinegar and 1 pint of stock. Boil for 10 minutes until the vegetables are soft. Add prawn tails and white wine. Cook for 6 minutes with lid on. Remove lid and sprinkle with chopped parsley, mint and a little thyme. Add cream, salt and pepper and serve in their shells with sauce in a soup tureen or soup plates.

SCAMPI MORECAMBE
Scampi cooked with sherry and whisky in pastry cases

Ingredients:
Puff pastry ½ lb (240 g)

Frozen or shelled raw scampi *or*
    Dublin Bay prawns 1 lb (480 g)
Butter 2 oz (60 g)
Sherry 2 fl oz (60 mls)
Whiskey 2 fl oz (60 mls)
Fresh mayonnaise 5 oz (150 g)
Chopped parsley and fresh mint
Lemon juice
Salt and pepper

Method: Bake 4 bouchees 3 inch diameter and scoop out the centre to form a cavity. Fill each one with the following mixture, prepared in this manner:

Toss 1 lb scampi in butter for 5 minutes, add sherry and whisky, boil for 2 minutes only, season and cool. To this, add a rich mayonnaise flavoured with a teaspoonful of freshly chopped parsley and mint and lemon juice to taste.

POTTED HAM AND CHICKEN
Ham and chicken brawn (12 portions)

Ingredients:

1 capon 5 lb (2,400 g)
Gammon bacon 10 oz (300 g)
Sausage meat 10 oz (300 g)
Pig's liver 5 oz (150 g)
Capon liver and heart 2 oz (60 g)
Pork fat 5 oz (150 g)
Onions 5 oz (150 g)
Garlic ¼ oz (10 g)
2 eggs
Parsley ¼ oz (7 g)
Gin and sherry 5 fl oz (150 mls) of each
Salt ¾ oz (20 g)
Honey ¾ oz (20 g)
Black pepper small pinch (2 g)
Mixed spices small pinch (2 g)
Water ½ pint (300 mls)
Gelatine 1 oz (30 g)
Vinegar 3 oz (90 g)
Bacon rashers 8 oz (240 g)

Method: Bone and skin capon. Cut meat into cubes. Cube a piece of gammon bacon the same size. Blend the sausagemeat with minced liver, chopped onions, garlic, parsley, gin and sherry and seasoning. Bind the mixture with an egg. Saute the capon and bacon together in pork fat until golden. Add water, vinegar, gelatine and onions and cook gently for 1 hour. Season to taste and add spices and melted honey. Line a large earthenware dish with rashers of bacon which have been parboiled and refreshed in cold water. Place the minced raw mixture in alternate layers. Complete the dish by adding the capon and bacon mixture with its liquor and top up with the rest of the minced mixture. Bake for 45 minutes to 1 hour at 380°F. Cool and add a heavy weight to the mixture to press it down while it is being chilled overnight. Serve cold with hors d'oeuvre. The liquor should form a tasty jelly and the minced mixture will have a liver pâté flavour.

FISH DISHES

SOLE

The sole is the most recherché fish in the whole fish kingdom. This is probably why many chefs have used their imagination to compose as many as 300 to 400 different garnishes to accommodate it. Such is the value of the sole that most gourmets would assert the merit of the sole as sufficient, to be worthy of consideration on its own and to be palatable by the simplest method of grilling and served with a pat of butter.

Soles are in season all the year round and the best are those caught in the Channel and rightly called 'Dover sole'. In the menu description the word 'Dover' must precede 'sole' to indicate the authenticity of the dish. Serving a Torbay sole instead would constitute a fraud unless it is clearly specified.

For a fish course use an 8-10 oz (250-300 g) sole; for an à la carte use 10-14 oz (300-400 g).

SOLE PREPARATION

Scrape the end of the tail with a knife to loosen it. Grab it with a cloth and pull off from tail to head. Remove the white skin in the same way. Gut, wash and dry the sole. Trim fins with scissors. Some chefs remove the head but it has now become more widespread to keep it on, as it should be for all fish which are cooked and presented whole. So just cut off the end bit of the snout. Remove the eyes.

Pass in seasoned flour, pass in eggwash and breadcrumbs and deep fry for 8-9 minutes. Drain on a cloth and serve on a dish lined with Doyley paper. Garnish with half a lemon and fried parsley.

Fried sole invites a rather acid sauce such as tomato or anchovy.

DOVER SOLE NELSON
Fried sole stuffed with potted shrimps and mushrooms [Conil's creation]

Method: Gut, wash and dry the fish, trim the fins and remove the head. Make a pocket on the thick side by filleting the upper side without detaching completely the two fillets which must remain connected to the fish. Curl the fillets outwardly as for opening a book. Break the bone in two places with a knife or scissors. Pass in seasoned flour, eggwash and breadcrumbs. Deep fry until golden between frying wires to keep fish flat during cooking. Drain and remove the broken bones. Dish up on a flat tray lined with Doyley paper. Garnish with filling:

Filling (per sole):
Potted shrimps 2 oz (60 g)
Cooked mushrooms 1 oz (30 g)
Cream sauce 2 oz (60 g)
Gin, a small teaspoon

Method: Blend all the ingredients in white sauce and flavour with a spoonful of gin. When the sole is cooked (fried and the inside bone removed) stuff it with two spoonfuls of the mixture. Sprinkle with chopped parsley and serve with a wedge of lemon.

DOVER SOLE PRINCE PHILIP
Sole baked with cider and tomatoes (4 portions)
   [Conil's creation]

Ingredients:

8 by 2½ oz (75 g each) Dover sole fillets
   (2 fillets per portion)
Butter 4 oz (120 g)
Chopped onions 2 oz (60 g)
Sliced button mushrooms 4 oz (120 g)
Sliced peeled cucumber 4 oz (120 g)
Diced celery 1 oz (30 g)
Dry cider 5 fl oz (150 mls)
Chopped, skinned and deseeded tomatoes
   4 oz (120 g)
Chopped parsley and fresh mint

Method: Beat fillets to break fibres lightly. Season
and fold in two. Butter a shallow dish and place
fillets side by side. Cover with the diced or sliced
vegetables. Pour over cider and chopped tomatoes
and cover with greaseproof paper. Bake for 20
minutes at 360-380°F. Sprinkle with chopped
herbs and seasoning. Serve in same dish.

SALMON: DECORATION OF WHOLE FISH

There are three basic forms of presentation of cold
salmon: the flat surface where the fish is presented
on one side; the 'S' motion, or swimming
position; the 'barge' (to imitate the boat with
broad side) where the salmon is boned and stuffed.
There is another presentation known as the
'torpedo' which is similar to the barge but the
stuffed fish is not shown in such a broad
presentation, as the two sides of the fish are
brought closer towards the centre.

SALMON ROYAL
Whole salmon cooked in dry cider and coated
   with a cream sauce (12 portions)

Ingredients:

1 small salmon 4 lb (1,920 g)

Court-bouillon stock:

Carrots 4 oz (120 g)

Onions 4 oz (120 g)
Celery 2 oz (60 g)
Bouquet garni and 6 peppercorns
White vinegar 5 fl oz (150 mls)
Water 5 pint (3,000 mls)
Salt 1½ oz (45 g)

Sauce:

Button mushrooms 8 oz (240 g)
Dry cider ½ pint (300 mls)
Double cream ½ pint (300 mls) blended with
   cornflour 1 oz (30 g)
Salt and pepper
Gin 4 fl oz (120 mls)
Duchesse potatoes 1 lb (480 g)

Method: Gut, scrape scales and wash salmon.
Place in a shallow tray with court-bouillon
ingredients. Vegetables must be sliced very thinly.
Bring to the boil and bake for 30 minutes. Cool
in its liquor. Remove and very gently skin the
salmon on both sides. Split salmon by lifting
top fillets without breaking them. Reconstitute
the salmon on an oval flat dish 18 inch long.
Pipe all round with Duchesse potatoes (mashed
potatoes and egg) a cordon of mixture for
decoration.
Sauce: Boil the button mushrooms in cider for 6
minutes. Add seasoning and gin, and thicken with
cream and cornflour. Boil for a further 4
minutes. Pour over the fish. Serve with new
potatoes and cucumber salad.

LOBSTER

Preparation:

1 lobster 1½ lb (720 g) (2 portions)

1. Dip live lobsters for 10 minutes in salted water.
2. Place lobster on a board and chop off the
   claws and legs. Crack claws.
3. Cut the tip of the head lengthwise to remove a
   small angle of the head, including the two eyes.
   This kills the lobster. Remove the gravel bag
   ('queen'). Turn the lobster over — ventral side up.
4. Starting at the head, insert a large knife between

ECLAIR AU CHOCOLAT (France), EMINCE DE VEAU ZURICHOISE WITH RICE (Switzerland)
SALADE AMERICAINE, WIENER SCHITZEL (Austria)

KIRSCHTORTEN (Germany), WINECAKE AND CHOU CROWN WITH CREAM (Czechoslovakia),
GUGELUPF (Austria)

SALMON ROYAL (England)

CANARD A L'ORANGE (France)

the body and tail segments and split lobster in two lengthwise but do not cut through back shell if the whole lobster is to be served as one portion (cut shell if half lobster is required).

5. Remove the stomach, or lady, and discard it with the intestinal vein along the tail end.
6. The coral found in the female hen lobster is often removed and used with the liver or tamale for other products such as sauces or lobster butters.

Broiled or grilled lobster:

1. Place lobster in grill rack, shell side up, under a salamander or over a charcoal grill. Large claws may be baked in the oven with a little water to retain moisture.
2. Broil for 3 to 5 minutes, or until shells are red.
3. Fill head cavity with stuffing: cooked savoury rice, Duxelle or crumb fish stuffing, chopped eggs and crumbs, or chopped tomato Portugaise.
4. Place lobster on a roasting tray. Finish cooking in the oven for a further 15-20 minutes. Brush with oil from time to time.
5. Remove shell from claws and place meat on top of stuffing, near the head. Dish up and garnish with lemon and parsley sprigs. Serve with melted butter or a spicy tomato sauce.

Note: Broiled or grilled lobsters were originally served with no stuffing. It is commonly accepted now that when facilities require placing lobsters in oven without pre-cooking in broiler, a weight of some kind must be placed across the bottom of the tails to prevent curling. For baked stuffed lobsters, meat may be removed from claws and placed in the body cavity, then covered with crumb stuffing. Seafood may also be added to the lobster stuffing or chopped shrimp, cod or any minced fish blended in a spicy fish sauce.

LOBSTER ASCOT
Lobster boiled in court-bouillon and served in coupe with a mint and apple flavoured mayonnaise (4 portions)

Ingredients:
Diced cooked lobster 1 lb (480 g)

Sauce:
Diced cucumber 2 oz (60 g)
Diced gherkins 1 oz (30 g)
Diced, skinned and seeded tomatoes
    2 oz (60 g)
Fresh mayonnaise ½ pint (300 mls)
Chopped mint (freshly chopped)
Chopped red lobster coral
Shredded lettuce and Belgian endive chicory
    4 oz (120 g)

Method: Place in 4 by 5 oz (150 g) glasses some shredded lettuce and chicory. Blend together the diced lobster meat with cucumber, gherkins and tomatoes. Stir the mayonnaise with the mint. Place mixture on a bed of lettuce and decorate with chopped mint and red coral. Serve separately with wedges of lemon.

LOBSTER CLARENCE
Hot lobster meat cooked in curry sauce, cohered with yoghurt and served with rice (4 portions)

Ingredients:
2 cooked lobsters 1½ lb each (720 g)

Sauce:
Bechamel ½ pint (300 mls)
Chopped onion 2 oz (60 g)
Fat 2 oz (60 g)
Curry powder (1 level teaspoonful *only*)
Salt and pepper
Plain yoghurt 5 fl oz (150 mls)

Method: Split lobsters in half. Remove intestinal cord and red coral. Remove meat from shell and place it with meat from claws into individual shallow dishes greased with butter. Reheat lobster in oven while preparing the sauce. Make a bechamel sauce. Fry chopped onions in fat without browning them. Add curry powder and chopped lobster shells and cook for a few minutes. Add white sauce and boil for 5 minutes. Then blend the yoghurt and seasoning. Strain sauce after boiling for 5 minutes. Pour over hot lobster and serve with plain rice or pilaff. Sprinkle top with the red coral.

MEAT DISHES

ROYAL CROWN OF ENGLISH LAMB ELIZABETH II

Lamb garnished with potato pie and cauliflower au gratin Elizabeth II (12 portions)

Ingredients:

4 best-ends of lamb (24 cutlets)
Soya sauce 3 fl oz (90 mls)
Worcester sauce 2 fl oz (60 mls)
Brown sugar 2 oz (60 g)
Malt vinegar 2 fl oz (60 mls)
1 pinch red colouring powder
1 clove crushed garlic

Method: Blend together the last six ingredients for marinade.

THE BEST-END OF LAMB

The best-end is situated between the loins and the côtes découvertes (uncovered cutlets, middle neck) comprising 3 to 3½ lb (1,680 g). A single best-end has the spinal cord split down the centre half on each best-end.

Preparation of best-end

1. *Skin:* Cut through the outer skin (bark) at the rib end (belly) ¾-1 inch (2 cm) from the end. Lift the skin carefully and peel back *from head to tail and rib end to centre of back*. The head end is thicker and should have a small piece of the shoulder blade gristle showing.
2. Remove fat from the spine bone. Saw ½ inch (1 cm) from the centre of the spine bone, through *all* the rib bones. Take care not to damage the meat underneath. Remove chine bone with a boning knife.
3. *Gristle:* Remove the blade gristle and spine gristle from along the back.
4. *Handles:* Measure the 'eye' of the meat along both ends and allow an equal amount of fat. Cut off excess. Cut down the bones from the inside, pull the fat through and cut off. This will ensure a good clean cut from the fat side. Scrape the bones and finish by wiping with a

dry cloth. Trim the bones to equal length.
5. For roasting whole, score the fat lightly to decorate before roasting with the back of the knife. For Crown Joints use 4 best-ends (24 cutlets).

How to prepare a Crown Lamb

1. Remove the chine bone from 4 best-ends of lamb, prepared as shown above.
2. Trim cutlet bones and curve round so as to have the fat part of the joint on the inside.
3. Make a small cut between each rib near the eye of the meat to help the two joints curving without stress.
4. Wrap tips of ribs with foil to prevent carbonisation of rib bones during roasting.
5. Fill inside with a savoury filling (usually made up of pork sausages, sage and onions) or make a ball with tin foil.
6. To colour the crown as for barbecue ribs blend all marinade ingredients and brush the outside of the cutlets. Baste the joint with this marinade of soya during roasting. Roast at 380°F to 400°F for the first 20 minutes and then reduce heat for 10 to 20 minutes to 360°F. In this particular creation I have planned this dish to consist of a base made up of a potato pie and to include a cauliflower au gratin with cheese and ham sauce. For these recipes see below.
7. The meat can be cooked medium done for 30 minutes or well done for 45 minutes.

GRAVY

Ingredients:

Diced lean bacon 2 oz (60 g)
Chopped lamb bones 1 lb (480 g)
Chopped onions 2 oz (60 g)
Bacon fat 1 oz (30 g)
Tomato puree 2 oz (60 g)
Fresh mint 1 oz (30 g)
Juice of meat
Water 1 pint (600 mls)
2 beef bouillon cubes or use stock instead of water
Sprig of celery

1 bay leaf
Salt and pepper
Worcester sauce 1 fl oz (30 mls)
Redcurrant jelly 1 fl oz (30 mls)

Method: Brown bones and bacon and onion in
fat for a few minutes till tender. Add tomato puree,
cook for 5 minutes, add rest of ingredients except
redcurrant jelly and Worcester sauce, and boil
for 45 minutes. Strain, season and thicken
with ½ oz (15 g) arrowroot and 3 fl oz (90 mls)
water. Dissolve redcurrant jelly and lastly, add
Worcester sauce. The gravy should be glossy,
smooth and well reduced to acquire a mature
flavour. It is essential to boil the ingredients for
at least 45 minutes while the meat is being cooked.
The juice of the meat can be added minus the fat
dripping.

Leave the joint for 15 minutes before serving.
Then place it on a potato pie base over a flat
round dish (14 inch diameter). In the inside of
the crown fit in a piece of fried bread 3 inch high
with the same diameter as the inside of the crown
(5 inch). On top of the bread place a cooked,
glazed cauliflower au gratin. On the tip of each
cutlet place a silver frill made from foil. Serve
gravy separately and in addition a sauceboat of
cranberry or redcurrant jelly and mint sauce.

POTATO PIE

Ingredients:

Pancakes:

2 eggs
Milk ½ pint (300 mls)
Flour 6 oz (180 g)
Pinch salt
Lard or oil for pan

Potato filling:

Bechamel sauce ½ pint (300 mls)
2 eggs
Diced, half boiled potatoes 2 lb (960 g)
Fresh chopped parsley, 1 tbs
Grated cheddar cheese 4 oz (120 g)

Chopped onions 1 oz (30 g)
Salt and pepper

Method: Blend the eggs and milk with seasoned
flour to obtain a smooth batter. Heat an 8 inch
pan and use the mixture to make about four to
five pancakes. Toss and cook – not too brown
– on both sides.

Grease a 9 inch diameter (3 inch deep) cake
tin with lard and margarine or butter. Line the
mould with cold pancakes as if it was pastry.

Blend eggs to bechamel sauce and add diced
cold potatoes, stir well, add seasoning, chopped
parsley, onions and grated cheese. Fill mould
with potato mixture. Fold back flap of the
pancakes. Brush the top with melted butter and
bake for 45 minutes with the joint. Cool for a few
minutes and turn onto a flat round dish (14 inch).
Decorate with peeled tomatoes and parsley.

CAULIFLOWER AU GRATIN ELIZABETH II

Ingredients:

1 large cauliflower 3½ lb (1,680 g)
Bechamel sauce ½ pint (300 mls)
2 eggs
Grated cheddar cheese
Chopped red pimentoes 2 oz (60 g)
Diced ham 2 oz (60 g)

Method: Groove a hole in the centre of the
cauliflower core. Trim off leaves except a few.
Boil in salted water with a drop of white vinegar.
Boil for 20 minutes. Drain. Place on a dish. Blend
beaten eggs to bechamel sauce. Add chopped,
cooked red peppers and half grated cheese. Pour
sauce over cauliflower. Sprinkle rest of grated
cheese and brown in the oven till golden. Place
cooked cauliflower inside the lamb crown as
indicated and decorate top with diced red and
green peppers.

STEAK & MUSHROOM PIE
Diced top or silverside beef stewed in port wine
sauce and served with a pastry topping
(4 portions)

Ingredients:

Short or puff pastry 8 oz (240 g)

Filling:

Topside of beef 8 oz (240 g)
Ox kidney 2 oz (60 g)
Button mushrooms 4 oz (120 g)
Diced carrots 1 oz (30 g)
Chopped onions 2 oz (60 g)
Fat 2 oz (60 g)
1 bouquet garni
Tomato puree 1 oz (30 g)
Flour 2 oz (60 g)
Water 1 pint (600 mls)
Port wine 5 fl oz (150 mls)
1 bay leaf
Pinch ground thyme

Method: Prepare puff or short pastry in the usual method. Dice meat into ½ inch (2 cm) cubes. Wash kidney in water with a little vinegar, remove fat and nerve and cut in thin slices. Rub meat in flour and saute in saucepan with fat for 10 minutes till brown. Add chopped onions, mushrooms, carrots and bouquet garni. Cover with lid and sweat for 5 minutes. Add water, port wine and tomato puree and stew gently for 1½ hours, preferably in the oven. Cool and strain gravy. Thicken it with a roux (1 oz flour and 1 oz fat) or add 1 oz cornflour to water and blend into the gravy. Season to taste.

Place meat in a pie dish and cover with the cold sauce. Cover with a layer of pastry. Brush with egg glaze. Arrange a little design of pastry on top (leaves, diamond, strips, etc.). Bake for 25 minutes at 380°F.

STEAK, KIDNEY & MUSHROOM PUDDING
Raw diced meats steamed with suet pastry
    (4 portions)

Ingredients:

Suet pastry:

Flour 8 oz (240 g)
Beef suet 4 oz (120 g)

Baking powder ½ oz (15 g)
Water 4 fl oz (120 mls)

Filling:

Raw diced topside of thick flank or chuck beef
    meat ½ inch (2 cm) cubes 8 oz (240 g)
Lean ox kidney diced 2 oz (60 g)
Chopped onions 2 oz (60 g)
Sliced mushrooms 2 oz (60 g)
Port wine 5 fl oz (150 mls)
Salt and pepper
Pinch ground mace or nutmeg

Gravy:

½ pint (300 mls) brown sauce made separately

Method: Rub suet into flour and add baking powder. Add 4 fl oz lukewarm water to make a stiff dough. Leave for a few minutes, then roll and line a 1½ pint pudding basin. Fill with the ingredients, meat, vegetables, seasoning and port wine. Top with round of pastry. Crimp edges and cover with paper, foil and cloth. Steam for 2½-3 hours. Serve with brown gravy thickened with a little port wine.

LANCASHIRE HOT POT
Chops, potatoes and white vegetables baked in
    an earthenware pot (6 portions)

Ingredients:

8 middle neck cutlets *or*
    diced lamb or mutton 3 lb (1,440 g)
4 lamb kidneys (skinned and sliced)
Sliced potatoes 1 lb (480 g)
Sliced onions 8 oz (240 g)
Sliced turnips 2 oz (60 g)
Sliced parsnips 2 oz (60 g)
Sliced celery 1 oz (30 g)
Sliced white part of leek 1 oz (30 g)
1 bouquet garni
Water ¾ pint (450 mls)
Salt and pepper

Method: Place all ingredients in layers in earthenware pot ending with a final layer of potatoes. Add water and seasoning. Cover with a lid and bake for 2 hours at 360°F. Sprinkle chopped parsley and serve in the same pot.

SURREY JUGGED HARE
Stewed hare with port wine (6 portions)

This very basic recipe is a foundation for the continental jugged hare with the exception that the blood is not used to thicken the sauce as done in France, Belgium and other countries.

Ingredients:

1 hare 3½ lb (1,680 g)

Marinade:

Wine vinegar 5 fl oz (150 mls)
Oil 5 fl oz (150 mls)
Water 1 pint (600 mls)
Sliced onions 5 oz (150 g)
Sliced carrots 5 oz (150 g)
1 bouquet garni
Clove of garlic $^1/_3$ oz (10 g)

Sauce:

Fat 2 oz (60 g)
Sliced onions of marinade
Flour 2 oz (60 g)
Tomato puree 2 oz (60 g)
Marinade liquor ½ pint (300 mls)
Chopped liver of hare
Button mushrooms 6 oz (180 g)

Method: Cut hare into eight pieces. Place pieces in an earthenware jug or pot. Add wine vinegar and water and oil, sliced carrots, onions, garlic and bouquet garni. Marinade overnight. Next day, drain and dry meat and vegetables, then brown in pan with fat. Sprinkle with flour and add tomato puree and marinade liquid. Stew gently for 1½ hours till tender. Sprinkle with chopped parsley. Saute the diced liver in the pan for a few minutes and add to the stew. Serve redcurrant jelly as an accompaniment.

Red wine, cider or even beer can be used instead of water. Either way will produce a palatable sauce. Button mushrooms and onions can be added to sauce 10 minutes before the stew is ready.

BRAISED OX HEART VICTORIA
Sliced ox heart sauted and braised in oven with vegetables (4 portions)

Ingredients:

Ox heart 1 lb (480 g)
Salt ½ oz (15 g)
Seasoned flour 2 oz (60 g)
Pinch mace
Sliced onions 2 oz (60 g)
Sliced carrots 2 oz (60 g)
Sliced celery 2 oz (60 g)
Sliced apples 4 oz (120 g)
Tomato puree 2 oz (60 g)
Sliced mushrooms 2 oz (60 g)
Water 1 pint (600 mls)
Dry cider ½ pint (300 mls)
Cornflour 2 oz (60 g)
Cream ½ pint (300 mls)
Chopped parsley

Method: Soak sliced heart in salt water for 10 minutes. Rinse. Dry and toss in seasoned flour. Brown in fat with apples and vegetables for 10 minutes. Transfer to a casserole dish. Cover with cider, water, and add tomato puree, mushrooms and cover with a lid. Braise for 1½ hours at 360°F. Test meat heart, if not tender cook a little longer. Strain gravy and reduce by boiling the liquor first. Then add a slurry of cream and cornflour, stirring all the time. Season and add to the meat. Sprinkle with chopped parsley.

This is a dish which will be more tenderised if left in its gravy overnight and reheated next day.

YORK HAM PASTIES
Ham turnover with mushrooms (4 portions)

Ingredients:

Short or puff pastry 8 oz (240 g)
Diced cooked ham 4 oz (120 g)
Diced cooked potatoes 2 oz (60 g)
Chopped onion 1 oz (30 g)
Chopped mushrooms 2 oz (60 g)
1 pinch chopped parsley
Chopped gherkin 1 oz (30 g)

White sauce 4 fl oz (120 mls)
1 diced hard-boiled egg

Method: Roll out the pastry $^1/_8$ inch thick. Cut
into 6 inch rounds. Blend other ingredients to a
compact mixture. Place two dessert spoonfuls on
each round. Wet edges of pastry and fold over
like a Cornish pasty. Crimp well to seal edges.
Brush with egg glaze. Bake at 400°F for 15
minutes. Serve hot or cold.

CUMBERLAND MUTTON PIE
Diced mutton cooked with vegetables in cider
(4 portions)

Ingredients:

Diced lean mutton 1 lb (480 g)
Fat 2 oz (60 g)
Seasoned flour 2 oz (60 g)
Tomato puree 2 oz (60 g)
Diced carrots 2 oz (60 g)
Diced celery 1 oz (30 g)
Diced turnips 1 oz (30 g)
Diced potates 2 oz (60 g)
Water 1 pint (600 mls)
Pinch mace
Salt and pepper
Chopped parsley 1 tbs
Mashed potato 1 lb (480 g)
Cornflour 1 oz (30 g)   ⎫
Water 5 fl oz (150 mls)   ⎬ (Cornflour paste)
                          ⎭

Method: Brown meat in pan for 10 minutes.
Sprinkle with flour and stir well. Add tomato
puree and all but last three ingredients. Simmer
for 1½ hours. Cool. Transfer to a pie dish.
Strain gravy and thicken with cornflour paste.
Check seasoning. Add half gravy to meat and
cover with mashed potatoes. Brown the pie in
the oven for 15 minutes. Serve remainder of
sauce separately.

LONDON CITY SIRLOIN
Roast beef with Buckingham apple pudding
(6 portions)

Ingredients:

Strip sirloin with fat and side sinews removed
    2 lb (960 g)
Fat 2 oz (60 g)
Salt and pepper
1 carrot
1 onion
1 sprig of celery
Broken bones for gravy
Water 1 pint (600 mls)

Pudding:

1 egg
Plain flour 3 oz (90 g)
Water 5 fl oz (150 mls)
Sliced apple 5 oz (150 g)
Beef dripping 2 oz (60 g)

Method: Season the joint and place the meat on
chopped bones to act as a trivet. Roast for 20
minutes and then add the whole onion, split carrot
and sprig of celery. Continue roasting, basting
from time to time.

When cooked place the tray on top of the
cooker. Add water and boil until the liquid is
reduced by half. Strain and season. Add juice
from meat to gravy.

The gourmet prefers to eat roast sirloin underdone. Roast meat at 400°F. allowing 10 minutes
per pound plus 20 minutes to heat the oven.
Therefore cook for 40 minutes if required underdone, 1¼ hours for medium, 1½ hours for well
done.

Method for pudding: Heat beef dripping in a meat
tray. When hot add sliced peeled apple and cook
for 1 minute. Blend the egg, flour and water to a
smooth batter. Rest the batter 30 minutes before
use. Pour the batter over the apples. Bake at
360°F for 25 minutes. Serve with the sliced
beef.

This pudding is based on the basic Yorkshire
pudding.

FILLET OF BEEF WELLINGTON
Fillet of beef wrapped in puff pastry, baked
    and served with a Port wine sauce
(6 portions)

Ingredients:

Puff pastry 8 oz (240 g)
Trimmed fillet of beef 2 lb (960 g)

Stuffing:

Liver pâté 6 oz (180 g)
Chopped mushrooms 4 oz (120 g)
Chopped onion 1 oz (30 g)
Fat 2 oz (60 g)
Chopped parsley 1 tbs
1 egg
Minced liver 5 oz (150 g) or liver pâté
Chopped ham 3 oz (90 g)
Salt and pepper
Fat for roasting 2 oz (60 g)
Port wine ½ pint (300 mls)

Method: Roast the fillet at 400°F for 20 minutes to sear the juices. Cool and spread the following mixture: saute chopped onions and sliced or chopped mushrooms in meat fat for 5 minutes until soft. Remove and blend with the liver puree, chopped ham, parsley and seasoning to obtain a spreadable mixture. Coat the fillet with this paste and wrap in puff pastry. Decorate with pastry leaves cut in diamond shapes. Brush with egg wash and bake for 20 minutes at 400°F to cook the pastry. Prepare an ordinary gravy with port wine added instead of water. Serve hot with a mixture of green and root vegetables.

VEGETABLES

LINCOLN CROQUETTE
Potato croquette in pear shapes flavoured with onions

Ingredients:

Mashed potatoes 1 lb (480 g)
Chopped ham 4 oz (120 g)
Chopped cooked onions 4 oz (120 g)
2 eggs
Salt and pepper
Breadcrumbs 4 oz
Seasoned flour
Parsley sprigs or stems

Method: Boil potatoes and drain well. Dry then mash and pass through a sieve. Blend one egg, add ham and onion. Divide into 16 small portions. Roll into pear shape and pass in flour, beaten egg and breadcrumbs. Fry in deep fat for a few minutes. It is best to use a frying wire basket. Add stem of parsley on each croquette.

ASPARAGUS REGENCY
Hot asparagus with a cream sauce flavoured with fresh mint

Ingredients:

Asparagus 1 lb (480 g)
Skinned and seeded tomatoes 8 oz (240 g)
Chopped chives 1 oz (30 g)
White sauce 4 fl oz (120 mls)
Juice and rind of 1 lemon
Chopped mint ½ oz (15 g)
Salt and pepper

Method: Scrape asparagus, trim end of stalks and tie up in four bundles. Boil in salted water for 10 minutes. Drain and place on a shallow dish and cover tips with this sauce:

Blend in hot white sauce the chopped tomatoes and chives, add seasoning, lemon juice, grated lemon rind and chopped mint.

DEVONSHIRE STEW
Casserole of potatoes and vegetables in tomato sauce

Ingredients:

Fat 4 oz (120 g)
Chopped onions 4 oz (120 g)
Potatoes 1 lb (480 g)
Tomato puree 2 oz (60 g)
Water 3 pint (1,800 mls)
Peas 2 oz (60 g)
Beans 2 oz (60 g)
Celery 2 oz (60 g)
Carrots 2 oz (60 g)
Cauliflower 2 oz (60 g)
Turnips 2 oz (60 g)

Shredded cabbage 2 oz (60 g)
Salt and pepper

Method: Sweat chopped onions in fat without colouring in a large saucepan. Add potatoes and tomato puree. Stir well, add water and remainder of diced vegetables. Cook for 30 minutes. Serve with the juice. Season to taste.

LEEK NORTHUMBRIA
Leeks coated with cheese sauce

Ingredients:

Medium-size leeks 2 lb (960 g)
White sauce ½ pint (300 mls)
English grated cheese 4 oz (120 g)
Salt and pepper

Method: Trim leeks. Split in four by piercing the centre and cutting towards the green parts, wash well and boil in salted water for 10 minutes. Arrange on a shallow dish and cover with white sauce. Sprinkle with grated cheese and brown under the salamander. The alternative is to place the cooked leeks in a pastry casing and proceed the same, or in a pie dish as indicated and cover the tip with mashed potatoes.

BAKED MARROW CAMBRIDGESHIRE
Stuffed marrow coated with cheese sauce

Ingredients:

1 marrow 2 lb (960 g)

Stuffing:

4 beef sausages, cooked and sliced
Diced ham 2 oz (60 g)
White sauce ½ pint (300 mls)
Grated cheddar cheese 4 oz (120 g)
Salt and pepper

Method: Peel marrow and cut in half lengthwise. Scoop out seeds. Blanch in salted water for 3 minutes. Drain and place in a shallow dish. Blend sliced cooked cold sausage with white sauce. Add ham and half of grated cheese. Season to taste and

fill the marrow with this mixture. Sprinkle remainder of cheese over the marrow and brown in a hot oven or under the grill for 10 minutes.

STUFFED ONION EAST ANGLIA
Onions stuffed with egg, crumbs and pork sausage meat

Ingredients:

4 large onions 8 oz each (240 g)
Raw minced beef 2 oz (60 g)
Raw pork sausage meat 2 oz (60 g)
1 egg
Salt and pepper
Chopped parsley
Garlic salt
Grated cheese 8 oz (240 g)
1 cup of cream

Method: Peel and boil onions for 15 minutes. Remove centre to leave a two layer casing. Chop centre of onion and blend with the mince, sausage meat and egg. Season and refill onions with this mixture. Place on a greases shallow pie dish and add a cup of cream. Sprinkle with grated cheese and bake in the oven at 360°F for 30 minutes.

STILTON CUCUMBER
Cucumber stuffed with a Stilton cheese mixture with tomatoes and chopped onions blended into the sauce

Ingredients:

1 cucumber
Stilton cheese 4 oz (120 g)
1 egg
Breadcrumbs 4 oz (120 g)
Salt and pepper
Cream ½ pint (300 mls)
Butter 2 oz (60 g)
Cooked chopped celery 2 oz (60 g)

Method: Peel cucumber and cut in four. Remove seeds. Prepare filling by creaming the butter and cheese, add breadcrumbs, egg and seasoning. Stuff the cucumber pieces with cheese mixture. Place on greased shallow tray and add a little cream and celery. Bake at 380°F for 25 minutes. Serve in dish.

SAVOURIES

English savouries are a feature of English gastronomy. They are served at the end of an evening meal instead of sweets, traditionally served with a glass of vintage port. There are literally hundreds of savouries. I have selected two well-known ones and added two of my own.

ANGELS ON HORSEBACK
Oysters wrapped in grilled bacon rashers served on toast

Ingredients:

8 oysters
4 bacon rashers
4 oblong toasts
Butter 2 oz (60 g)
Pinch cayenne pepper
Grated cheese (optional)

Method: Blanch bacon rashers in boiling water for 3 minutes. Rinse and dry. Wrap each oyster in a slice of blanched bacon. Season with a pinch of cayenne pepper and sprinkle with a little grated cheese (optional) and grill for 5 minutes. Serve on buttered toast allowing 2 per person.

DEVILS ON HORSEBACK
Stuffed prunes with liver and bacon on toast

Ingredients:

8 stoneless cooked prunes
Liver pâté 2 oz (60 g)
8 small bacon rashers
4 oblong toasts
Butter 2 oz (60 g)

Method: Blanch bacon in boiling water for 3 minutes. Drain and dry. Stuff prunes with liver pâté. Wrap each prune with bacon rasher and grill for 5 minutes and serve on buttered toast. Instead of pâté, cooked chicken liver can be used.

KNIGHTS ON HORSEBACK
Kidney wrapped in bacon, coated with cheese sauce and served on toast

Ingredients:

4 sheep's kidney
3 bacon rashers
Grated cheese 4 oz (120 g)
Chutney 2 oz (60 g)
4 toasts
Butter 2 oz (60 g)

Method: Skin and split the kidney. Blanch the bacon rashers in salted water for 3 minutes. Grill or saute the kidney for a few minutes. Wrap the cooked kidney in bacon. Spread a spoonful of chutney on buttered toast. Grill the kidney for a few minutes and place on toast. Then sprinkle cheese on top and grill until melted.

KNAVES ON HORSEBACK
Mushrooms stuffed with chicken liver, wrapped in bacon rashers, coated with cheese sauce and browned under the grill and served on toast

Ingredients:

4 large peeled mushrooms
4 chicken livers
4 large stuffed olives
Grated cheese 4 oz (120 g)
Chutney 1 oz (30 g)
4 buttered toasts
Salt and pepper

Method: Chop chicken liver, season and place raw mixture inside the uncooked mushrooms. Place an olive in the centre and sprinkle with grated cheese. Bake in tray with fat for 10 minutes. Serve on buttered toasts with a little chutney on top.

SWEETS

OXFORD PUDDING
Sponge treacle pudding (4 portions)

Ingredients:

Margarine 4 oz (120 g)
Butter 1 oz (30 g)
Brown sugar 3 oz (90 g)
2 eggs
White crumbs 2 oz (60 g)
Self-raising flour 6 oz (180 g)
Pinch of mixed spice
Few drops vanilla and rum essence
Milk 2 oz (60 mls)
Treacle 6 oz (180 g)

Method: Cream fats and sugar together until
fluffy, add beaten eggs and stir well. Blend crumbs
and flour, add spices and essence to milk and stir
into the mixture. Put mixture in a 2 pint pudding
basin which has been well greased with margarine.
Cover with paper or foil and steam for 2 hours and
serve with hot treacle.

CASTLE PUDDING
Sponge cake pudding with jam

Ingredients:

Margarine 4 oz (120 g)
Castor sugar 4 oz (120 g)
2 eggs
Flour 5 oz (150 g)
Vanilla essence
Red or apricot jam 4 oz (120 g)

Method: Cream margarine and castor sugar until
fluffy, add beaten eggs and essence, stir well until
light, then fold in flour. Place a spoonful of jam
on greased individual moulds or a 1 pint mould or
basin and fill with mixture. Cover with paper,
foil and cloth. Steam the large pudding for 1½
hours or the small puddings for 1 hour. Serve
with custard.

CHRISTMAS PUDDING
Rich fruit pudding with rum

Ingredients:

Beef suet 6 oz (180 g)
Brown sugar 4 oz (120 g)
2 eggs
Breadcrumbs 2 oz (60 g)
Flour 6 oz (180 g)
Diced glacé cherries 1 oz (30 g)
Mixed peel 1 oz (30 g)
Sultanas 1 oz (30 g)
Seedless raisins 1 oz (30 g) } Soaked in hot water
Currants 1 oz (30 g) and drained
Grated carrots 1 oz (30 g)
Juice and grated rind of 1 lemon
1 small teaspoon of mixed spices
Rum 2 tbs (30 mls)
Dark treacle 2 oz (60 g)
Gravy browning or black jack—1 small teaspoonful

Method: Rub beef suet, sugar, flour and crumbs
together. Blend beaten eggs, rum and essences and
spices. Add fruits. Place in a 2 pint pudding
basin. Cover with paper, foil and a cloth and
steam for 3 hours. Serve with rum or brandy or a
sweet white sauce.

ELIZABETH SILVER JUBILEE PUDDING
Baked custard with meringue and raspberry
filling (6–8 portions)

Ingredients:

Seedless raspberry jam 8 oz (240 g)
Fresh breadcrumbs 2 oz (60 g)
8 egg yolks
Castor sugar 3 oz (90 g)
Milk 1½ pint (900 mls)
Rum 2 fl oz (60 mls)
Fresh crumbs 2 oz (60 g)
8 egg whites
Pinch of salt
Granulated sugar 6 oz (180 g)
Fresh or frozen raspberries 1 lb (480 g)
Flaked almonds
Gin 1 fl oz (30 mls)
Angelica 1 oz (30 g)
Crystallised violets 1 oz (30 g)
Double cream 5 fl oz (150 mls)

Utensil:

An oblong heatproof casserole dish 3 inch deep
 and 9 inch by 4½ inch

Method: Spread jam in bottom of dish and sprinkle
with crumbs. Heat dish to melt jam and absorb
crumbs. Blend beaten egg yolks and milk with
castor sugar in a bowl. Add rum flavour or vanilla
if preferred and place dish in a tray half filled with
hot water and bake at 360°F for 40 minutes.
Remove from the oven and spread raspberries
evenly over the top. Separate egg whites and place
in a clean bowl with salt. Beat until stiff, then add
sugar. Cover with meringue 2 inch thick. With
remainder of meringue pipe the inititals E.R. and
decorate with flaked almonds. Bake for 8 minutes
at 380°F to set the meringue without browning it.
Finally decorate with a few crystallised violets
and green angelica as leaves. Serve with fresh cream
flavoured with gin and sugar: 5 oz (150 g) cream,
1 oz (30 g) sugar and 1 fl oz (30 mls) gin.

COLCHESTER PUDDING
Tapioca custard with fruit, topped with meringue

Ingredients:

Milk 1 pint (600 mls)
Tapioca 1½ oz (45 g)
Pinch of salt
Castor sugar 2 oz (60 g)
Juice and grated rind of 1 lemon
Vanilla essence
Stewed pears and apples 8 oz (240 g)
3 egg yolks
3 egg whites
Castor sugar 3 oz (90 g)
Double cream 4 fl oz (120 mls)

Method: Heat milk and sprinkle in tapioca, salt
and sugar. Cook for 10 minutes while stirring.
Remove from the heat and cool. When cold blend
in 3 beaten egg yolks and essences. Place stewed
fruits into a shallow dish and cover with tapioca
mixture. Beat egg whites to a meringue, add sugar
in three intervals beating each time until mixture
peaks. Fold over the pudding evenly. Make a
pattern with criss-cross lines and sprinkle with a

little castor sugar. Bake for 8 minutes. Serve with
cream.

SYLLABUB FARMHOUSE
Cream and wine served in glasses like junket

Ingredients:

Castor sugar 3 oz (90 g) ⎫
Gelatine 1 oz (30 g)   ⎬ blend together
Pinch of nutmeg   ⎭
Dry cider 3 fl oz (90 mls)
Light beer 3 fl oz (90 mls)
Double cream 12 fl oz (360 mls)
Fresh currants ½ oz (15 g)
Sweet sherry 2 fl oz (60 mls)
Juice of ½ lemon

Method: Heat cider and beer to boiling point.
Dissolve sugar and gelatine. Cool and blend with
whipped cream, sherry and lemon juice and fill
the syllabub in individual fluted glasses as for
junket. Sprinkle the currants on top for decoration.

LEMON AND TANGERINE PIE
Lemon curd and tangerine topped with meringue

Ingredients:

1 x 8 inch diameter flan pastry case baked blind

Curd:

Cornflour 2 oz (60 g)
Milk 5 oz (150 g) ⎫
5 egg yolks   ⎬ mixed in bowl
Water 1 pint (600 mls)
Juice and rind of 2 lemons
Castor sugar 5 oz (150 g)
4 egg whites
Canned or fresh tangerines 5 oz (150 g)

Method: Boil water and thicken it with a slurry of
cornflour blended with milk and egg yolks. Add
grated lemon rind and juice last. Cool and pour
into the pastry case to a thickness of ½ inch. Beat
egg whites to a meringue. Add 3 oz of sugar
gradually while beating until mixture peaks. Spread
½ inch coating evenly over the lemon curd.

Decorate by piping meringue on top. Bake at 380°F for 8 minutes to set. Decorate top with tangerine segments.

MINCE TART DICKENS
Rich fruit tartlet flavoured with rum

Ingredients:

Sweet short pastry 12 oz (360 g)

Mincemeat:

Grated peels 1 oz (30 g)
Sultanas 1 oz (30 g)
Seedless raisins 1 oz (30 g)
Diced apples 1 oz (30 g)
Currants 1 oz (30 g)
Glacé cherries 1 oz (30 g)
Beef suet 3 oz (90 g)
Rum or brandy 3 fl oz (90 mls)
Crumbs 1 oz (30 g)
Pinch of mixed spices

Method: Blend all mincemeat ingredients together. Fill tartlets lined with short pastry and cover with another layer of pastry. Bake for 15 minutes at 400°F. Dust with icing sugar.

BROWN BREAD AND BUTTER PUDDING
Bread custard pudding flavoured with mixed fruit, honey and nuts

Ingredients:

4 slices of toasted brown bread cut in triangular shapes 4 oz (120 g)
Butter 2 oz (60 g)
Milk 1 pint (600 mls)
3 eggs
Pinch of mixed spices
Castor sugar 3 oz (90 g)
Few drops of rum and vanilla essence
Sultanas 2 oz (60 g)
Grated peels and glacé cherries 2 oz (60 g)
Chopped walnuts 2 oz (60 g)

Method: Butter the toast and cut into small triangular shapes. Line a pie dish with alternate layers of bread, chopped fruits, mixed spices, nuts and sugar. Beat eggs, add honey to milk and pour over the bread ingredients. Soak for 30 minutes and sprinkle with sugar. Bake at 360°F for 40 minutes in a tray half filled with hot water.

GOOSEBERRY FOOL
Puree of gooseberries blended with whipped double cream

Ingredients:

Creme de Menthe liqueur 1 fl oz (30 mls)
Fresh gooseberries 1 lb (480 g)
Castor sugar 4 oz (120 g)
Water ½ pint (300 mls)
Gelatine 1 oz (30 g) ⎫ blend together
Castor sugar 2 oz (60 g) ⎭
Double cream 4 oz (120 mls)
Single cream 2 oz (60 mls)
Pinch grated nutmeg

Method: Trim gooseberries and cook in water with sugar. Dissolve gelatine in gooseberries when pulpy. Pass mixture through a sieve and cool. When cool fold in whipped cream. Add a little grated nutmeg and the Creme de Menthe liqueur. Place in fluted glasses and serve with English shortbread biscuits.

CONIL'S SHORTBREAD
A sablé type of biscuit

Ingredients:

Butter 6 oz (180 g)
Icing sugar 3 oz (90 g)
1 egg yolk and 1 egg white for glazing
Sifted flour 9 oz (270 g)
Lemon and orange essence 4 drops
Castor sugar 1 oz (30 g)

Method: Cream butter and icing sugar until fluffy and light. Add beaten egg yolk and essences, blend flour. Mix well. Gather into a ball and rest in cold place 30 minutes. Roll on floured board to a ¼ inch thick. Cut into 6 inch diameter rounds. Place on greased tray and without making a complete separation, mark each round with a division of four. With the prong of a fork crimp edges. Brush top with thinned down egg white, sprinkle with castor sugar and bake at 400°F for 10 minutes. Cool.

CAKES

CHELSEA BUN
Yeast bun coated with icing

Ingredients:

Baker's yeast 1 oz (30 g)
Lukewarm milk ½ pint (300 mls)
1 egg
Strong flour 1 lb (480 g)
Butter or lard 2 oz (60 g)
Sugar 2 oz (60 g)

Filling:

Brown sugar 2 oz (60 g)
Granulated sugar 2 oz (60 g)
Mixed dried fruit 12 oz (360 g)
   3 oz each of the following:
   Currants
   Sultanas
   Seedless raisins
   Grated or glace peel
   Pinch mixed spice

Icing:

Icing sugar 6 oz (180 g)
Hot water 2 fl oz (60 mls)
A few drops almond essence
Flaked almonds 4 oz (120 g)

Method: Crumble yeast in lukewarm milk. Add beaten egg and blend to flour to form a firm dough. Knead well and leave for 40 minutes covered with an upturned basin. Blend in lard and knead dough again. Shape into a ball and leave for 15 minutes — again covered with the basin.
   Dust a board with flour. Roll pastry into an oblong ⅛ inch thick. Brush surface with beaten egg. Mix brown and granulated sugar with spices and scatter the mixed fruit all over. Roll up like a Swiss roll. Cut into slices ½ inch thick. Place each slice flat on a greased tray 1 inch apart. Allow 10 minutes to settle. Bake at 400°F for 20 minutes. Prepare icing by adding hot water, flavoured with almond essence, to the sifted icing sugar. Brush each bun with soft icing and sprinkle a few toasted almonds on each Chelsea bun.

SAFFRON CAKE
Yeast bread cake flavoured with saffron

Ingredients:

Baker's yeast 1 oz (30 g)
Lukewarm milk 5 fl oz (150 mls)
Warm water 5 fl oz (150 mls)
1 egg
Pinch salt
Pinch saffron
Strong bread flour 20 oz (600 g)
Sugar 1 oz (30 g)
Lard 2 oz (60 g)
Currants 4 oz (120 g)
Chopped peel 1 oz (30 g)
Pinch mace or nutmeg

Method: Crumble yeast in milk. Soak saffron in boiling water and let it brew for 8 minutes. Strain. Add saffron water to milk and beat in the egg. Blend to the flour, salt and sugar to form a stiff dough. Knead for a few minutes. Shape into a ball and leave for 45 minutes covered by an upturned basin. Knead again and blend in lard and fruit. Leave for 15 minutes in ball shape covered by the basin. Grease an oblong mould or bread tin with lard. Roll the dough like a salami. Flatten it lightly. Bring the two ends together and roll tightly to a loaf. Place the loaf in the tin. Brush with milk to prevent skinning. Leave for 30 minutes and then bake at 400°F for 30 minutes. Brush the top with syrup (4 oz sugar and 1 oz water boiled together).

FLAPJACKS
Confectionery made with syrup, sugar, nuts and
   oats

Ingredients:

Margarine 4 oz (120 g)
Brown sugar 2 oz (60 g)
Golden syrup 4 fl oz (120 mls)
Honey 1 oz (30 g)
Oats 6 oz (180 g)
Flour 8 oz (240 g)
Baking powder 1 oz (30 g)
3 eggs
Milk 1 pint (600 mls)
Oats for rolling cakes

Method: Grease an oblong tin with lard. Heat
margarine, brown sugar, honey and syrup
until liquid. Add oats. Sift flour and baking
powder and blend to mixture to obtain a
dough of dropping consistency, obtained by
adding the milk and the beaten eggs. Pour
this mixture into the greased tray. Level with
wet hands or palette knife. Sprinkle with a few
uncooked oats and bake at 380°F for 35–40
minutes. Cut in fingers or squares. Dust with icing
sugar.

PARKIN
Treacle cake with spices

Ingredients:

Butter 8 oz (240 g)
Flour 8 oz (240 g)
Castor sugar 8 oz (240 g)
Ground ginger 1 oz (30 g)
Good pinch mixed spice
Baking soda ½ teaspoon (5 g)
Oatmeal very finely ground 2 lb (960 g)
Golden syrup 2 lb (960 g)
Milk 3 fl oz (90 mls)

Method: Grease an oblong tin (2 inch deep) with
lard and line with greaseproof paper. Rub butter
with flour. Add sugar, spices and oatmeal. Heat
golden syrup and blend with mixture to obtain a
soft, almost runny, dough. Dissolve soda in cold

milk and add to mixture at the last moment. This
will produce the aeration during baking. Pour
mixture into the tin. Level with wet hands or
palette knife. Bake for 45 minutes at 360°F. Fig
parkins are made by adding 4 oz chopped figs to
the mixture.

CURD CHEESE CAKE
Custard cheese cake

Ingredients:

Shortcrust pastry 12 oz (360 g)

Filling:

Curd cheese 12 oz (360 g)
Butter 6 oz (180 g)
Castor sugar 4 oz (120 g)
Ground almonds 2 oz (60 g)
Almond essence 2 drops
Currants 4 oz (120 g)
Double cream 3 fl oz (90 mls)
Grated nutmeg 1 pinch
4 eggs
White port or sweet Madeira wine 5 fl oz (150 mls)

Method: Roll the pastry ⅛ inch thick. Cut into
3 inch rounds. Place in greased tartlet moulds.
Press pastry evenly and prick bottom. Rub curd
through a sieve or use cream cheese. Beat cheese,
butter and sugar. Add beaten eggs, ground
almonds and flavouring. Blend in cream and
Madeira or port and currants. Fill the tartlets
two-thirds full with the mixture. Bake for 20
minutes at 360°F.

BRANDY SNAPS
A caramel confectionery

These traditional biscuits are known as Mothering
Sunday Wafers in Hampshire where they are made
with orange water (not juice) instead of brandy.
In Devonshire they are served with cream and
jelly and known as Fairings and in Lancashire they
are known as Ormshirt Gingerbread.

Ingredients:

Butter 4 oz (120 g)
Treacle 4 oz (120 g)
Brown sugar 4 oz (120 g)
Flour 4 oz (120 g)
Pinch ground ginger
Brandy 1-2 tsp (5-10 mls)
Grated lemon

Method: Melt butter, sugar and treacle in a saucepan. Add flour and cook for a few minutes. Add spices. Pour spoonfuls of the mixture onto a greased tray. Leave 6 inch apart as they will spread on baking to a 4 inch diameter. Bake for 8 minutes at 350°F. Remove and immediately curl on an oiled stick or wooden handle. Cool and fill with whipped cream.

SCONES
Baking-powder small bread or cake

Ingredients:

Self-raising flour 1 lb (480 g) or flour and baking
    powder 1 oz (30 g) well sifted
Margarine 4 oz (120 g)
Sugar 2 oz (60 g)
3 eggs
Milk 3 fl oz (90 mls)
Beaten egg or milk for glazing

Method: Rub margarine and flour. Add sugar and blend in beaten eggs and milk. Form a firm but pliable dough. Roll the dough ¾ inch thick. With a pastry cutter make 2½ inch rounds. Place each round on a greased tray. Leave for 10 minutes and then brush with glaze. Bake for 10 minutes at 400–425°F.

The success of a perfect scone is to roll the dough evenly. If all the scones have the same thickness before baking they should rise level during baking. To serve, split and coat with butter or cream and jam.

WINDSOR CASTLE CAKE
Rich fruit cake

Ingredients:

Margarine 3 oz (90 g)
Butter 2 oz (60 g)
Lard 1 oz (30 g)
Castor sugar 6 oz (180 g)
3 eggs
Flour 8 oz (240 g)
2 oz (60 g) of each of the following fruit:
    glacé pineapple
    cherries
    peel
    ginger in syrup
Rum 2 fl oz (60 mls)
Few drops of vanilla essence
Walnuts 8 oz (240 g)

Method: Cream fats and sugar till fluffy. Add beaten eggs and beat mixture to a light creamy consistency. Add sifted flour and mixed, diced fruit, rum and essence. Line a greased 3 inch x 10 inch tin with greaseproof paper. Fill tin two-thirds full with the mixture. Level it. Arrange a few walnuts on top in a circular pattern. Bake for 1½ hours at 360°F.

LE PINTADEAU SANS RIVAL (France)

LANGOUSTE AU GRATIN GRANDE CHARTREUSE (France)

APPLE TURNOVER, TUTTI FRUITI TART, APPLE FLAN, PINEAPPLE FILLED WITH
SAUERKRAUT, FRANKFURTERS AND KNUCKLE OF BACON (Germany)

Scotland

The climate of Scotland is colder than that of England and the beef is more succulent. Scotland has always been a food-producing country and there are many districts which are more fertile than any in the British Isles. The moors and forests abound with game and cattle with flesh of the most marvellous tenderness roam the hills. To these are being added reindeer, to produce venison on the intensive farming principle. Rivers, lochs and the surrounding sea teem with fish. Scottish salmon, smoked or fresh, is a wonderful contribution to gastronomy, and kippers and haddock are smoked to juicy perfection.

Oats and barley have always been the staple grains, and porridge is a traditional breakfast dish. Barley bannocks and oatcakes have been popular for centuries, and barley is used in broths, stews and haggis, that highly individual way of using the liver and lights of a sheep. To foreign gourmets, haggis may be an abomination, but to the Scots it is a large and delicious minced meat sausage. The recipe differs with the chef and many a modern gastronome has had a hand in trying to improve it. But it is not to be despised, and even I have served it to unsuspecting clients as a pâté—without complaints.

As oatmeal and barley are the staple grains, so kale has been the staple vegetable, particularly in the lowlands. The highlanders prefer nettles in their broth. Turnips (or neeps as they are called) are used extensively in Scotland and always accompany haggis.

Salmon used to be so plentiful in the Scottish lochs and rivers and Dutch fishermen took advantage until it dawned on the Scots that they were being robbed of their benefits. Since then the good name of Scotch salmon is a fiercely preserved identity and is exported to all parts of the world.

There is a distinct French influence on Scottish cookery. It started with the early Stuarts and the 'auld alliance' which preceded the 'Entente Cordiale' between France and Britain by many centuries. King James I kept a French cook and this remained a habit for many centuries afterwards. Dessert was probably introduced at this time.

During the Reformation with the decline of the privileged classes the gastronomy of Scotland declined and haggis and porridge to a large extent sustained the whole population as well as the ordinary people.

Barley broth, Hotch Potch and Powsowdie (sheep's head broth with nettle) are the traditional soups of Scotland, with cock-a-leekie, a leek soup based on chicken stock, the most popular. Seafood includes the tasty crappit heids, fish stuffed with oatmeal and beef suet together with eggs and even lobster meat. Cropadeu is made from haddock liver, oatmeal and water, and partan pie is a tasty dish of stuffed crab.

Limpet stovies is a plebeian dish of limpets with potatoes, and roasted deer is a great dish for festive occasions. The Scotch Grouse which makes a much trumpeted entrance on August 12 is, in my opinion, the greatest delicacy in the world after partridge.

Collops of Scotland may be minced steaks or escalopes and Inky-Pinky is a sauted mixture of left-over beef and vegetables. Boiled leg of mutton with caper sauce is a rare delicacy in these days when sheep are killed so young, and so is mutton ham, cured and smoked in the traditional way.

Orange marmalade is one of the greatest products of Scotland and worthy to stand by the side of the butter-rich shortbread. The Scottish high tea is an institution not to be missed. There is a spread of bannocks, cakes, scones, breads and tea-cakes, which accompanies ham and eggs and is rounded off by wonderful fruit pies.

The women of Scotland know how to cook and particularly how to bake—and the men know how to appreciate the food. Good cooks and an appreciative audience—that makes for good gastronomy.

BILL OF FARE

Soup

PARTAN BREE
Scotch crab milky soup

COCK-A-LEEKIE
Leek and potato soup in chicken broth with
  prunes

SCOTCH BROTH
Mutton broth with pearl barley

Hors d'Oeuvre

COD'S ROE PASTE
Smoked cod's roe paste made with butter and
  cream

SMOKED SALMON TARTLET
Baked custard with a garnish of smoked salmon

Fish

ARBROATH SMOKIE PIE
Smoked haddock and potatoe pie

HADDOCK STRACHUR
Finnan haddock poached in stock and served in
  fresh cream

ST ANDREW'S PLATTER
A splendid assortment of Scottish sea-food with
  hard boiled eggs and a potato salad in a rich
  mayonnaise flavoured with apple sauce

Meat Dishes

CULLODEN COLLOPS
Minced beef pie flavoured with whisky and
  blended with oatmeal

HAGGIS
Sheep's innard pudding

STEAK BALMORAL
Sauted fillet steaks with a sauce made with cream
  and whisky

SPICED BEEF PRINCE CHARLIE
Braised beef highly flavoured with honey and
  spices

ROYAL SCOTCH GROUSE
Braised grouse in Port wine

Vegetables

KALE
A hardy winter vegetable with crisp curly leaves

KALE BROSE
Kale cooked with oats and onions

ONION CAKE
Onion and potato pie

BANFFSHIRE POTATOES
Stuffed potato filled with herbs

PUNCHNEP
Creamy potato and turnip pie

Sweets

MARMALADE BATTER PUDDING
Baked pudding with a marmalade topping

PERTHSHIRE BRAMBLE PUDDING
Blackberries flavoured with Drambuie

DRAMBUIE CREAM
Custard flavoured with Drambuie

SCOTS FLUMMERY
Custard with sherry and currants

WHIM-WHAM
Creamy sweet with white wine and sponge fingers

KIRRIE LOAF ANGUS
Spicy cake with sultanas soaked in tea

DUNDEE CAKE
Rich fruit cake

BALMORAL CHEESE CAKE
Mixed fruit tart with egg custard filling

ATHOL BROSE
A whisky-flavoured cream pudding made with
  oats

SOUP

PARTAN BREE
Scotch crab milky soup (4 to 6 portions)

Ingredients:

1 medium-size crab 2 lb (960 g) or frozen crab
meat 8 oz (240 g)

Broth:

Leek 4 oz (120 g)
Carrot 2 oz (60 g)
Butter 2 oz (60 g)
Lard 2 oz (60 g)
Oats 3 oz (90 g)
Water 2½ pint (1,500 mls)
1 bouquet garni
Salt and pepper
Sprig of celery
Cream 5 fl oz (150 mls)
Anchovy essence 1 teaspoon
Pinch cayenne
Juice of 1 lemon

Method: In a saucepan, heat butter and lard. Saute
the sliced vegetables for a few minutes without
browning. Add the water and boil them with
bouquet garni, till tender, then strain the broth.
Use vegetables elsewhere. Remove white and
brown meat of boiled crab or use frozen crab
meat. Add to soup with oats and boil for 10
minutes. Lastly add cream, reheat and serve.
In Scotland some cooks use rice instead of oats. It
is optional. Anchovy essence and lemon juice are
added at the last moment while checking seasoning.
Addition of cayenne is purely optional.

COCK-A-LEEKIE
Leek and potato soup in chicken broth with
prunes (4 to 6 portions)

Ingredients:

Chicken giblets 8 oz (240 g): winglets, necks,
gizzards or a fowl
1 bouquet garni
Water 2½ pint (1,500 mls)
Sliced potatoes 4 oz (120 g)
Sliced leeks 12 oz (360 g)
8 prunes soaked overnight
Salt and pepper

Method: Scald the giblets and winglets for 10
minutes, rinse and drain. Place in a soup pot with
2½ pint fresh water, bouquet garni, leeks and
potatoes and boil for 1 hour. Add prunes and
cook for a further 10 minutes. Season. Serve with
one winglet of chicken and 2 prunes on each
plate. The stock of a boiled fowl can be used in
the same manner and a little of the chicken meat
can be served with the soup.

SCOTCH BROTH
Mutton broth with pearl barley (4 to 6 portions)

Ingredients:

Diced shin of beef 8 oz (240 g)
Water 2½ pint (1,500 mls)
Onion 2 oz (60 g)
Leek 2 oz (60 g)
Carrot 2 oz (60 g)
Celery 2 oz (60 g)
Cabbage 2 oz (60 g)
Turnip 2 oz (60 g)
Potato 2 oz (60 g)
Parsnip 2 oz (60 g)
Peas 2 oz (60 g)
Barley 3 oz (90 g) (soak for 2 hours before
required)
Chopped parsley
Salt and pepper

Method: Scald the diced beef in water for 10
minutes, rinse and drain. Place in a soup pot with
2½ pint fresh water. Cook for 1½ hours. Add
vegetables and barley and simmer gently for ½
hour until the barley is cooked. Season with salt
and pepper. Serve sprinkled with chopped parsley.

HORS D'OEUVRE

COD'S ROE PASTE
Smoked cod's roe paste made with butter and
cream

Ingredients:

Smoked cod's roe 8 oz (240 g)
Fresh bread crumbs 2 oz (60 g)
Cream 4 fl oz (120 mls)
Juice of 1 lemon
White pepper
Chopped spring onion or chive ½ oz (15 g)
Oil 5 fl oz (150 mls)

Method: Place roe in a bowl. Blend in crumbs and cream. Add lemon juice, onion and pepper. Beat mixture while adding oil to obtain a smooth paste well emulsified. Place in individual pots. Chill and serve with hot toast.

SMOKED SALMON TARTLET
Baked custard with a garnish of smoked salmon
  (portions: 8 tartlets or 1 large flan 8 inch)

Ingredients:

Smoked salmon 4 oz (120 g)
Short pastry 8 oz (240 g)

Filling:

2 eggs
Cream ½ pint (300 mls)
Juice of ½ lemon
Pinch paprika
Salt and pepper

Method: Roll out pastry and cut 3 inch rounds with pastry cutter. Line greased tartlets, press pastry to prevent puffing up. Prick bottom, arrange a small slice of salmon on each tartlet. Beat eggs and add to cream and lemon juice. Season and fill each mould. Bake for 30 minutes at 360°F.

ARBROATH SMOKIE PIE
Smoked haddock and potato pie

Ingredients:

Smoked haddock 2 lb (960 g)
Water 1 pint (600 mls)
Milk ½ pint (300 mls)
Margarine 1 oz (30 g)

Flour 1 oz (30 g)
4 hard-boiled eggs
Chopped spring onions 1 oz (30 g)
1 tsp made mustard (5 mls)
Grated cheese 2 oz (60 g)
Salt and pepper
Juice and grated rind 1 lemon

Method: Place haddock fillets in water. Poach for 15 minutes. Drain. Discard bone and skin. Place fish in a shallow dish. Arrange sliced hard boiled eggs on top. Make a roux and dilute with boiling milk. Season. Add lemon juice, made mustard, grated rind and sprinkle with chopped green onion. Pour over fish. Sprinkle grated cheddar cheese. Brown under the grill or a salamander.

HADDOCK STRACHUR
Finnan haddock poached in stock and served
  in fresh cream

Ingredients:

4 fillets 8 oz (240 g) each
Water 1 pint (600 mls)
Onion 2 oz (60 g)
Celery sprig 1 oz (30 g)
1 bouquet garni
White vinegar 1 oz (30 mls)
Salt and pepper
Single cream 5 fl oz (150 mls)
Cornflour ¼ oz (8 g)
Juice of 1 lemon
Pinch of cayenne and paprika

Method: First, make a stock. Boil fish bones in water and vinegar with onion and celery for 20 minutes. Strain and add fillets of fish. Season and poach for 10 minutes. Drain, mix the cream and cornflour and boil for 5 minutes to thicken. Add lemon juice. Place fish on a shallow dish and pour sauce over. Sprinkle paprika and cayenne.

ST ANDREW'S PLATTER
A splendid assortment of Scottish seafood with
  a potato salad in a rich mayonnaise flavoured
  with apple sauce

Ingredients:

Sliced smoked salmon 8 oz (240 g)
Filleted smoked trout or mackerel 1 lb (480 g)
Skinned and filleted smoked eel 8 oz (240 g)
Cooked mussels 8 oz (240 g)
Potato salad 1 lb (480 g)
Rich mayonnaise 10 oz (300 g)
Apple puree 3 oz (90 g)
Horseradish sauce 5 fl oz (150 mls)
Chopped chive 1 oz (30 g)
Few leaves of lettuce, sliced cucumber and tomatoes
    tomatoes
Wedges of lemon
Boiled red pimento cut in thin strips

Method: Present the fish on a large platter on a bed of lettuce leaves, surrounded with sliced cucumber and tomatoes. Blend apple puree and mayonnaise and mix with diced cooked potatoes— sprinkle with chopped chive. Serve separately horseradish sauce and pickled mussels on sticks. *Note:* To decorate, place strips of red pepper in a cross to imitate Saint Andrew's cross.

MEAT DISHES

CULLODEN COLLOPS
Minced beef pie flavoured with whisky and
    blended with oatmeal

Ingredients:

Best quality lean minced beef 1 lb (480 g)
Fat 2 oz (60 g)
Chopped onions 4 oz (120 g)
Chopped mushrooms 4 oz (120 g)
Tomato puree 2 oz (60 g)
Salt and pepper
Pinch of mace
Oatmeal 2 oz (60 g)
Scotch stout 5 fl oz (150 mls)
Whisky 5 fl oz (150 mls)

Method: Heat fat in a pan and brown the meat, add chopped onions and mushrooms. Cover and simmer for 10 minutes, stir from time to time. Add tomato puree, stout beer and seasoning and cook gently

for 30 minutes. Add oats. Stir well. Transfer to a greased earthenware dish. Cover with a lid and cook for 60 minutes at 360°F. Add whisky and serve.

HAGGIS
Sheep's innard pudding

Gervase Markham described haggis as 'that pudding of whose goodness it is vain to boast because there is hardly to be found a man that doth not affect them'.

Ingredients:

1 sheep's bag or use greaseproof paper and a
    cloth as for boiled pudding
Sheep's heart 5 oz (150 g)
Sheep's liver 8 oz (240 g)
Sheep's lung 5 oz (150 g)
Suet or lard 12 oz (360 g)
Oatmeal 2 oz (60 g)
Chopped onion 8 oz (240 g)
Juice and rind of 1 lemon
1 pinch of clove, ginger, black pepper, mace,
    cinnamon (15 g)
Salt ½ oz (15 g)
Sugar ¼ oz (8 g)
And for good luck: 5 fl oz whisky (150 mls)

Method: Mince all ingredients and blend them thoroughly. Fill a well-washed sheep's stomach or skin or place in a pudding bowl. Wrap a piece of greaseproof paper around it, then a cloth and tie it up like a Christmas pudding. Steam for 2 hours. A teaspoonful of salpêtre can be used with the salt to improve the colour and act as a preservative.

STEAK BALMORAL
Sauted fillet steaks with a sauce made with
    whisky

Scotch beef is the finest in the world. The climate is ideal for breeding the finest specimen of beef cattle. The greatest treat a visitor can be offered is to be served with a delicious and tender fillet steak topped with a pat of Scotch butter.

Ingredients:

4 x 8 oz Scotch fillets of beef (240 g each)
  (1 inch thick)
Oil 2 oz (60 g)
White sliced mushrooms 4 oz (120 g)
Chopped onion 1 oz (30 g)
Tomato puree 1 oz (30 g)
Mushroom ketchup 1 oz (30 g)
Salt and pepper
Whisky 5 fl oz (150 mls)
Butter 2 oz (60 g)
Stout beer 5 fl oz (150 mls)

Seasoning:

pinch mace
salt and black pepper

Garnish:

Fresh boiled asparagus tips 1 lb (480 g)
Baked potatoes flavoured with butter and chopped
  chives

Method: Trim fillets of fat and skin. Season and
sprinkle a few drops of mushroom ketchup. Heat
oil in a pan and saute the fillets with lid on. Cook
according to requirement, e.g. rare, medium or
well done—10, 12 or 15 minutes if the steaks are
1 inch thick (2½ cm). When done, remove steaks
and keep warm. In the same pan, toss chopped
onions for 2 minutes, then add sliced mushrooms
and cook for 5 minutes. Add beer and tomato.
Boil for 5 minutes. Season sauce with a pinch of
salt, mace and black pepper to taste, add whisky
and pour gravy over the steaks. Surround with
cooked asparagus tips. On each steak place a pat
of parsley butter.

SPICED BEEF PRINCE CHARLIE
Braised beef highly flavoured with honey and
  spices (10 portions)

Ingredients:

Rib of beef 5 lb (2,400 g)
Butter 2 oz (60 g)
Lard 2 oz (60 g)
2 carrots

Pinch of mace, cinnamon, clove,
  paprika, ginger
Chopped garlic 5 g
1 teaspoonful mustard powder   } mix together
Brown sugar 3 oz (90 g)
Malt vinegar 3 fl oz (90 mls)
Honey 2 oz (60 g)

Method: Bone and roll rib of beef and tie with
string. Rub over with soft butter and lard, season
with salt and black pepper, roast in a tray set
with a few bones and two uncut carrots. Set the
oven at 400°F for the first 30 minutes to seal the
juices. Then reduce the heat to 370°F and cook for
another 30 minutes if required, underdone or 45
minutes if medium or 1 hour if well done.
Amateurs and gourmets prefer the meat very
underdone. When done, remove joint and place in
a shallow dish and leave for 20 minutes. Remove
the surplus fat, add 1 pint of water and boil 10
minutes with trimmings of meat and bones. Strain
and thicken with a little cornflour or arrowroot
diluted in water. Season and serve with the meat.

Now for the flavouring specific to this
particular beef dish: blend all spices with sugar,
vinegar and honey and *spread* all over the joint.
Set the oven high at 400°F and brown the joint
quickly for 5 minutes. Place on a dish and flavour
the joint also with a good glass of whisky poured
over the meat at the last minute.

Serve with baked potatoes, braised parsnips
and green sprouts. Pass round a sauceboat of
horseradish sauce and 2 or 3 kinds of mustard.

ROYAL SCOTCH GROUSE
Braised grouse in Port wine

Young grouse should be trussed, larded with
strips of fatty rashers placed on the breast and
roasted for 17–20 minutes at 400°F. They are
served on fried bread coated with a liver paste
with a garnish of gravy, bread sauce and crisps
and a bunch of watercress. The best other
accompaniment is a green salad or, when in season,
sea kale boiled in salted water and served with
melted butter.

In this particular recipe I have made use of

old grouse which require longer cooking, my recipe is in fact a sort of salmis.

Ingredients:

4 grouse (1 per person)

Marinade:

Vinegar 3 fl oz (90 mls)
Water 1 pint (600 mls)
1 sliced onion
1 sliced carrot
1 stick celery
Few peppercorns
1 bouquet garni
Tomato puree 3 oz (90 g)
1 clove garlic

Sauce:

Red port 5 fl oz (150 mls)
Double cream 5 fl oz (150 mls)
Cornflour 1 oz (30 g)
Water 5 fl oz (150 mls)
Salt and pepper
Lard or oil 3 oz (90 g)
Diced bacon 2 oz (60 g)

Method: Clean the grouse. Wash it well and split in two. Remove the rib bones. Soak in marinade overnight. Drain and wipe with a cloth. Dry all the vegetables of the marinade too. Pass the grouse in seasoned flour, then pan fry in oil or lard until brown on both sides. Place pieces into a shallow tray. Fry the bacon and vegetables and add to the meat. Boil the marinade liquor for 10 minutes. Add red port wine. Season. Braise in oven for 1 hour covered with a lid to avoid evaporation. Strain gravy and thicken it with a slurry of cornflour and cream. Boil it for 5 minutes. Pour over the grouse. Serve with fried croutons cut in heart shapes.

VEGETABLES

KALE BROSE
Kale cooked with oats and onions

Tartan Purry is another name for Kale Brose and is a corruption of the French *Tarte en Purée*.

Ingredients:

Kale 1 lb (480 g)
Oatmeal 1 oz (30 g)
Water 2 pint (1,200 mls)
Onion 2 oz (60 g)
Salt and pepper
Few meat bones

Method: Trim the kale and wash well. Boil for 8 minutes in salted water or stock. Drain, and in the liquor cook the oats to thicken the stock. Saute the chopped onions without browning and add to the liquid. Season to taste. Reheat the kale in this thickened broth and serve. Otherwise plain boiled kale can be served hot or cold with melted butter or vinaigrette dressing.

ONION CAKE
Onion and potato pie

Ingredients:

Sliced potatoes 1 lb (480 g)
Chopped onions 4 oz (120 g)
Oil and butter 4 oz (120 g)
Salt and pepper

Method: Grease a 6 inch diameter cake tin with butter and lard. It is best to use either a silicone dish or a tin which has been well conditioned to avoid potato sticking. Place a layer of sliced, washed and well dried potatoes and a good sprinkling of chopped onions, season and add another layer of potatoes. Dab the top with plenty of butter and bake at 380°F for 45 minutes. Press down the mixture and rest for a few minutes. Turn out into a dish.

BANFFSHIRE POTATOES
Stuffed potato filled with herbs

Ingredients:

4 large potatoes (8 oz each) (240 g)
Butter 2 oz (60 g)

Fresh chopped rosemary and chives
Salt and pepper
Fresh breadcrumbs 2 oz (60 g)
1 beaten egg
Milk 3 fl oz (90 mls)
Butter 4 oz (120 g)

Method: Bake washed potatoes for 1 hour. Cut potatoes across. Scoop out the pulp and sieve in a bowl. Blend with beaten egg, milk, butter and herbs. Pipe mixture or replace it into the skin casing. Sprinkle with crumbs and add melted butter. Bake for 15 minutes to brown the crumbs.

PUNCHNEP
Creamy potato and turnip pie

This is a Welsh dish which has found its way to Scotland.

Ingredients:

Mashed potatoes 8 oz (240 g)
Mashed white turnips or swede 8 oz (240 g)
Butter 2 oz (60 g)
Cream 3 fl oz (90 mls)
Salt and pepper

Method: Blend all ingredients. Serve on a shallow dish and sprinkle with chopped parsley.

SWEETS

MARMALADE BATTER PUDDING
Baked pudding with a marmalade topping
(8 portions)

Ingredients:

Flour 12 oz (360 g)
Pinch of salt
Castor sugar 4 oz (120 g)
Pinch of ground ginger
Grated rind and juice of 1 lemon and 1 orange
8 egg yolks
8 egg whites

Milk 2 pint (1,200 mls)
Coarse orange marmalade 6 oz (180 g)

Method: Sift flour and salt with sugar and ground ginger, and add grated rinds. Mix egg yolks, fruit juices and milk together and add to dry ingredients. Mix to a batter. Beat the egg whites until stiff and fold into the batter. Grease a shallow pie dish (3 inch deep) and pour in batter mixture. Bake for 20 minutes at 400°F. Turn out onto a plate and coat with hot melted marmalade.

PERTHSHIRE BRAMBLE PUDDING
Blackberries flavoured with Drambuie (4 portions)

Ingredients:

Blackberries 1 lb (480 g)
Drambuie 5 fl oz (150 mls)
Double cream 5 fl oz (150 mls)
Brown sugar 2 oz (60 g)

Method: Wash and drain berries. Flavour with liqueur and put them into glasses. Whip cream and pipe on top. Sugar added according to taste.

DRAMBUIE CREAM
Custard flavoured with Drambuie

Ingredients:

5 egg yolks
Drambuie 5 fl oz (150 mls)
Double cream 5 fl oz (150 mls)
Milk ½ pint (300 mls)
Cornflour 1 oz (30 g)
Single cream 4 fl oz (120 mls)
Castor sugar 3 oz (90 g)

Method: Mix egg yolks, cornflour and Drambuie with double and single cream in a bowl. Pour in hot milk, stirring it well into the mixture. Reboil until it thickens, like a custard, for a few minutes. Thoroughly stir in the sugar. Pour into fluted glasses and leave to cool. When set decorate the top with a few strawberries or other suitable fruit.

SCOTS FLUMMERY
Custard with sherry and currants (4 portions)

Ingredients:

Currants 1 oz (30 g)
Dry sherry 3 fl oz (90 mls)
Milk 6 fl oz (180 mls)
Double cream 5 fl oz (150 mls)
4 egg yolks
Castor sugar 2 oz (60 g)
Rose water 1 fl oz (30 mls)
Pinch of grated nutmeg

Method: Soak currants in sherry for 1 hour. Heat milk and cream, pour this mixture over the egg yolks in a bowl. While stirring add sugar, mix and strain. Add the rose water and nutmeg and reheat in a double saucepan, like a custard, until it thickens enough to coat a spoon. Stir all the time. Add currants and sherry. Serve in fluted glasses and let the flummery mixture set in a refrigerator. This mixture can also be flavoured with a spoonful of Drambuie or whisky.

WHIM-WHAM
A creamy sweet with white wine and sponge fingers (4 portions)

Ingredients

Double cream 12 fl oz (360 mls)
Dry white wine 6 fl oz (180 mls)
Castor sugar 2 oz (60 g)
Ground gelatine ½ oz (15 g)
Grated rind and juice of lemon
8 sponge fingers
Redcurrant jelly 4 oz (120 g)

Decoration:

Lemon jelly or segments of tangerines
Whipped cream 8 oz (240 g)

Method: Place the cream, wine, lemon juice and rind, sugar and gelatine in a bowl. Whisk mixture till frothy. Heat the mixture to 180°F. Place a layer of sponge fingers, cream mixture and

redcurrant jelly on individual dishes. Decorate dishes with tangerine and a rosette of whipped cream.

KIRRIE LOAF ANGUS
Spicy cake with sultanas soaked in tea

Ingredients:

1 tea bag ¼ oz (8 g)   } to brew tea
Boiling water ½ pint (300 mls) }
Sultanas 1 lb (480 g0
Castor sugar 8 oz (240 g)
3 eggs
Butter 4 oz (120 g)
Golden syrup 4 oz (120 g)
Plain flour 1 lb (480 g)
Baking powder 1 oz (30 g)
½ teaspoon of ground ginger and mixed spice
Pinch of salt

Method: Brew a tea bag for 5 minutes. Soak sultanas and sugar in hot tea. Melt butter and syrup in a saucepan and stir into the beaten eggs while stirring mixture. Add sifted flour, salt, baking powder and all the spices. Stir thoroughly and blend the currants and syrup of tea. Grease a round or oblong loaf tin and fill it two thirds full with the mixture. Bake for 1½ hours at 350°F.

DUNDEE CAKE
Rich fruit cake

Ingredients:

Butter 8 oz (240 g)
Castor sugar 8 oz (240 g)
5 eggs
Flour 9 oz (270 g)
Currants 3 oz (90 g)   } wash, soak and dry
Seedless raisins 3 oz (90 g) } before use
Sultanas 3 oz (90 g)   }
Grated or mixed peel 2 oz (60 g)
Grated orange rind and juice
Blanched split almonds 2 oz (60 g)

Method: Wash and soak fruit in hot water. Drain and dry. Cream soft butter with sugar until fluffy.

Then gradually add beaten eggs and flour. Then add the fruit, rind and juice and peel. Line an 8 inch tin with greaseproof paper. Fill the tin with cake mixture until two thirds full and level it with a palette knife. On the top arrange the split almonds in rows all round to completely cover the cake. Bake for 1½ hours at 360°F, or until cooked through. On removal brush with a little egg white to glaze the top. Cool on rack and store overnight in a tin.

BALMORAL CHEESE CAKE
Mixed fruit tart with egg custard filling

Ingredients:

Short pastry:

Butter 3 oz (90 g)
Lard 2 oz (60 g)
Flour 9 oz (270 g)
1 egg

Filling:

Butter 4 oz (120 g)
2 eggs
Castor sugar 8 oz (240 g)
Cake crumbs 1 oz (30 g)
Flour ½ oz (15 g)
Chopped glace cherries and angelica 2 oz (60 g)
Brandy 2 fl oz (60 mls)
2 egg whites
Granulated sugar 1 oz (30 g)

Method: Prepare pastry by creaming fat until fluffy. Then add beaten egg and lastly flour. Shape pastry into a ball and leave for 20 minutes. Roll into a thickness of $^1/_8$ inch and cut with a 3 inch diameter cutter, to fit tartlet moulds. Grease the moulds and line each one. Press fingers in the centre to even out. For the filling melt butter and blend beaten eggs in a bowl. Add the rest of the ingredients and lastly fold in the beaten whites which should be as stiff as a meringue. Spoon fill each tartlet and bake at 380°F for 15—20 minutes.

ATHOL BROSE
Whisky cream pudding made with oats

Ingredients:

Water ½ pint (300 mls)
Milk 1 pint (600 mls)
Oats 3 oz (90 g)
Pinch salt
Gelatine 1 oz (30 g)
Castor sugar 4 oz (120 g)
Whisky 5 fl oz (150 mls)
Juice and rind of half an orange and lemon
Whipped cream ½ pint (300 mls)
Glace cherries 1 oz (30 g)
Tangerine 2 oz (60 g)

Method: Blend water and fine oats (as used for porridge). Boil milk and add oat mixture. Season with a pinch of salt and half sugar, lemon and orange juice and grated rind. Boil 10 minutes until thick. Mix gelatine and castor sugar. Dissolve in the hot mixture. Stir well and cool, add whisky. Whip cream and fold into cool oat mixture. Place in long fluted glasses. Decorate with whipped cream, glacé cherries and tangerine.

Wales

Born of an eloquent poverty, the food of Wales is made up of centuries of thrifty recipes devised to economise on ingredients and to provide good fare at the cheapest cost. Yet the food is good, the flavours balanced and there is a proper regard for the freshness and intrinsic taste of the ingredients. It is a food of the people, savoury and hearty to feed the farmers, the shepherds and above all the miners of the country. The sheep is the most important animal in this hilly area, and Welsh ham is a leg not of pork but of the tender sheep.

Welsh rarebit is a renowned delicacy which is a great favourite with those gastronomes who still prefer a savoury end to their meal rather than a pudding. Originally it was simply a slice of Gloucester cheese on buttered toast, spread with mustard. Now it has been embellished to include beer in the spread, and Welch Rabbit of the nineteenth century has become the sophisticated Welsh Rarebit of the twentieth.

Welsh beef is the traditional way of preparing beef to retain and enhance its full flavour. It is flavoured with Jamaican pepper, stuffed with herbs and baked with a covering of pastry which was discarded once it had fulfilled its purpose.

Ffest y Cybydd may be translated as the miser's feast, and is a dish of boiled bacon, potatoes and onions. The miser managed to make two meals from the one bit of cooked bacon.

Leek porridge is a traditional meal with supposed qualities of improving male virility—not surprising, since many ancient cultures regarded the leek as a phallic symbol.

Bara Brith is the speckled bread made with raisins and citrus peel; cockle cakes are cockles in oatmeal fried in batter, and *crempog* is a batter which can be cooked in a pan or on a griddle. Pembrokeshire pie is filled with stewed lamb together with sugar and currants, rather like original mince pies of Christmas which also combined meat and fruit.

The five million sheep produced by Wales every year finish on the market as prime lamb. The value of Wales as a contributor of the finest lamb in Europe has been underrated too long: a saddle of Welsh lamb, roasted and served with redcurrant jelly and mint sauce is one of the finest dishes ever produced.

Bara crai is an unleavened bread, probably as old as the bible, but modified somewhere along the way to include bicarbonate of soda, a leavening agent. Laver bread is typical Welsh fare: a type of seaweed is mixed with oatmeal to make small cakes relished by the Welsh. Nutritionally excellent, the laver bread is definitely an acquired taste. *Bara ceirch* are biscuits made of oatmeal, hot water, and bacon fat, baked on a *maen* bakestone (the Welsh griddle) and kept in boxes like biscuits.

The excellence of Welsh food is undisputed, but it is not the regular daily fare of the people, and has not been since the Second World War. I found this out to my cost when I visited there with my wife Mary and baby daughter Patricia after they were evacuated during the war. The friendly Welsh people offered us hospitality on our arrival, and it was obvious that they knew I was a chef with the Navy and had prepared something special. The meal I got was simple, spartan and swiftly prepared, to say the least.

I, who prided myself on my sophistication and on my palate, had only one meal in Wales.

It was a chip butty.

BILL OF FARE

Soup

GOWER OYSTER SOUP
Oysters poached in broth and used as garnish to a
thick mutton broth

Fish Dishes

KIPPER FISH CAKES
Flaked kipper mixture with mashed potato shaped
into cakes

HERRING CASSEROLE
Baked herring fillets with potatoes and apples
flavoured with onions and mustard

COCKLE PIE
Cockles cooked in cream sauce with pastry topping

MACKEREL IN FENNEL SAUCE
Mackerel baked or grilled with butter

Meat Dishes

WELSH LAMB PIE
A pie of lamb and carrots baked with herbs and
served with a gravy made from the bones

TATWS A CIG YN Y POPTY
Boned breast of lamb roasted as a joint with
sliced potatoes

WELSH MUTTON VENISON STYLE
Leg of mutton marinaded in vinegar and port
wine and pot-roasted

Vegetables

LEEK PORRIDGE
Boiled sliced leeks served with cream

BARA LAWR
Laver bread. Boiled edible seaweed

LAVER SALAD

WYAU YNYS MON
Anglesey eggs with leek

TEISEN NLONOD
Onion cake

CAWS POBI
Welsh rarebit

Sweet/Cakes

WELSH BORDER TART
A tart filled with raisins and sultanas with a
meringue topping

TEISEN PLANC AFALAN
Welsh apple tart

PWDIN REIS MAMGU
Rice pudding blended with eggs

SOUP

GOWER OYSTER SOUP
Oysters poached in broth and used as garnish to a
  thick mutton broth

Ingredients:

8 oysters
Mutton neck 2 lb (960 g)
Water 2½ pint (1,500 mls)
1 onion 5 oz (150 g)
1 carrot
1 bouquet garni
1 sprig of mint

Roux:

Margarine 2 oz (60 g)
Flour 2 oz (60 g)

Method: Place mutton in boiling water to blanch
it for 10 minutes. Refresh in cold water. In a
saucepan add fresh water and blanched mutton.
Boil with onion, carrot, mint and bouquet garni
for 1½ hours. Strain the liquid and remove the fat.
Cook roux and thicken the stock with the roux.
Strain and season. Poach the oysters and their water
in a little stock for 5 minutes only without allowing
stock to boil. Serve soup with bread sippets and 2
oysters for each plate.

FISH

KIPPER FISH CAKES
Flaked kipper mixture with mashed potato shaped
  into cakes

Ingredients:

Kipper fillets 1 lb (480 g)
Mashed potatoes ½ lb (240 g)
1 egg
1 hard-boiled egg
Butter 1 oz (30 g)
Pinch pepper
Juice of 1 lemon or 1 tbs of white vinegar
Oil or lard for frying

Method: Flake fillets in pieces and blend with
beaten egg into mashed potatoes. Chop hard-boiled
egg and blend to mixture with melted butter and
pepper. Divide mixture into 2 oz (60 g) cakes.
Shape each cake like a scone. Pass in seasoned flour
and pan fry until golden on each side.
    This is an excellent breakfast or snack dish.

HERRING CASSEROLE
Baked herring fillets with potatoes and apples
  flavoured with onions and mustard

Ingredients:

Fresh herrings filleted 2 lb (960 g)
English made mustard 1 tbs
Salt and pepper
Sliced potatoes 2 lb (960 g)
Sliced apples 1½ lb (720 g)
Sliced onions ¾ lb (360 g)
Water 1 pint (600 mls)
Pinch fresh sage
Vinegar 2 fl oz (60 mls)
Butter 2 oz (60 g)

Method: Spread each fillet with made mustard.
Season. Arrange sliced potatoes in a buttered pie
dish with a layer of apples and onions. Place
herring fillets folded in two or rolled over the
mixture. Sprinkle fresh chopped sage, salt and
pepper. Cover with water and vinegar. Place lid
on dish and bake for 1 hour at 380°F.

COCKLE PIE
Cockles cooked in cream sauce with pastry
  topping

Ingredients:

Cockles 3 lb (1,440 g)
Water for soaking 5 pint (3,000 mls)
Vinegar 4 fl oz (120 mls)
1 bouquet garni
1 chopped onion 4 oz (120 g)

Roux:

Flour 1 oz (30 g)
Margarine 1 oz (30 g)
Milk ½ pint (300 mls)

Cockle stock 1 pint (600 mls)
Chopped parsley
Puff pastry ½ lb (240 g)

Method: Soak the cockles in water and vinegar for 2 hours. Strain and rinse again in cold water to eliminate sand deposit. Place cockles in water with vinegar, bouquet garni and onion, boil 5 minutes. Strain liquor. Remove cockles and discard shells. Cook roux and thicken with milk and cockle stock. Strain. Season, add chopped parsley and blend cockles. Place the mixture into a pie dish, cover with a thick layer of puff pastry and glaze with eggwash. Leave for 20 minutes then bake at 400°F for 20 minutes. Alternatively, use mixture as filling for pre-baked puff pastry cases or make small pastry turnover style, serving sauce separately.

Cockles are probably more delicious than mussels; the only inconvenience is the removing of the sand.

MACKEREL IN FENNEL SAUCE
Mackerel baked or grilled with butter

Ingredients:

4 large mackerel fillets 2 lb (960 g)
1 fennel ½ lb (240 g)
Butter 4 oz (120 g)
1 bouquet garni
Water ½ pint (300 mls)
Salt and pepper
Seasoned flour

Method: Place fillets of mackerel in salted water with 2 spoonfuls of vinegar to eliminate blood stain. Soak for 15 minutes and rinse. Drain and dry. Pass the fillets in seasoned flour and dip in melted butter. Wash and slice the fennel, place in a casserole dish with water and bouquet garni. Place fish on top. Season to taste. Cover dish and bake for 30 minutes at 380°F. Serve in the same liquor, hot or cold.

MEAT DISHES

WELSH LAMB PIE

A pie of lamb and carrots baked with herbs and served with gravy made from its bones

Ingredients:

Lamb meat from shoulder, neck, or middle neck
   1 lb (480 g)
Sliced carrots 1 lb (480 g)
Salt and pepper
Water 1 pint (600 mls)
1 tbs chopped parsley
Few chopped mint leaves
Pinch sugar

Short pastry:

Margarine 4 oz (120 g)
Lard 1 oz (30 g)
Flour 10 oz (300 g)
Water 3 fl oz (90 mls)

Method: Cut meat into ½ inch cubes. Season. Place in a pie dish with carrots and water, sprinkle with seasoning, herbs and sugar. Cover with short pastry. Bake at 350°F for 2 hours.

Boil bones with same amount weight for weight of water with 1 onion to obtain 1 pint (600 mls) of broth out of which you produce a gravy, slightly thickened with arrowroot and seasoned to taste. *Pastry:* Rub fat and flour, add water and mix to a dough. Roll to $\frac{1}{8}$ inch thick. Cover pie evenly. Make a design of pastry leaves.

TATWS A CIG YN Y POPTY
Boned breast of lamb roasted as a joint with sliced potatoes

Ingredients:

Boned and rolled breast of lamb 3 lb (1,440 g)
Sliced potatoes 2 lb (960 g)
Salt and pepper
Flour 1 oz (30 g)
Sliced onions ½ lb (240 g)

Method: Bone the breast. Remove as much fat as possible. Season and roll up like a roly-poly. Tie up with string. Partly roast at 400°F for 30 minutes. Remove joint from tray and discard fat to about 1 tablespoonful. Add potatoes, season and mix in flour. Place the onions on top and add 1 pint (600 mls) of water. Arrange the joint over the mixture. Cover with lid or another tray and bake gently at 375°F for 1 hour until the meat is cooked and the potatoes tender.

WELSH MUTTON VENISON STYLE
Leg of mutton marinaded in vinegar
  and pot-roast

Ingredients:

1 leg of mutton without pelvis bone 4 lb (1,920 g)

Marinade:
Malt vinegar 8 fl oz (240 mls)
1 sliced onion 5 oz (150 g)
3 cloves
1 bouquet garni
6 juniper berries
Salt 2 oz (60 g)
Saltpetre ¼ oz (8 g)
Crushed peppercorns, 1 pinch

Sauce:
Port wine 8 fl oz (240 mls)
Marinade stock 1 pint (600 mls)

Roux:
Flour 1 oz (30 g)
Fat 1 oz (30 g)

Method: Soak the leg of mutton for 48 hours in marinade ingredients. Keep in a refrigerator in an earthenware container. Turn meat from time to time. Drain and dry. Rub with fat and roast for 1½ hours at 380°F.

Fry sliced onion in fat until golden. Gradually add marinade and boil for 15 minutes. Make a roux and dilute it into stock. Reboil and strain. Add Port wine. Season to taste. Serve with mutton.

VEGETABLES

LEEK PORRIDGE
Boiled sliced leeks served with cream

Ingredients:
Leeks 2 lb (960 g)
Salt and water

Method: Clean and pierce leeks through the middle with knife to split open to release dirt. Wash thoroughly and cut in slices. Boil 10 minutes in salted water. Save liquid for soup. Serve in porridge bowl with some of the liquid and some cream.

BARA LAWR
Laver bread. Boiled edible seaweed

Laver bread and grilled bacon is a popular dish in Wales for breakfast. It can also be served with grilled meat or fish.

Ingredients:
Fresh laver 1 lb (480 g)
Oatmeal 1 lb (480 g)
Water 5 pint (3,000 mls)
Salt and pepper
Bacon fat 3 oz (90 g)

Method: Soak the laver for 3 hours in running water if possible to wash away the sand. Place in water and simmer for 3 hours until tender. When ready cut it coarsely or make a puree. Blend with oats and cook like porridge for a few minutes. Season to taste. To increase speed of cooking the laver, it can be chopped first then boiled in salted water until tender. Cook puree and when cold shape into little cakes. Pass in flour and beaten eggs and then in oats. Fry in hot fat like a fritter. Serve with rashers of bacon.

LAVER SALAD

Ingredients:
Cooked laver 1 lb (480 g)
Oil 2 fl oz (60 mls)
Cider vinegar 2 fl oz (60 mls)
Salt and pepper

Method: Blend all ingredients as for a salad, season with salt and pepper and sprinkle chopped onions for extra flavour.

WYAU YNYS MON
Anglesey eggs with leek

Ingredients:

6 small size leeks
Butter 2 oz (60 g)
Grated Welsh cheese 4 oz (120 g)
8 hard-boiled eggs
Mashed potatoes 1 lb (480 g)
Flour 1 oz (30 g)
Milk ½ pint (300 mls)
Salt and pepper

Method: Pierce leeks in the middle with the point
of knife and cut towards the green part to split the
leek in four from centre outward. Clean in plenty
of cold water. Tie up in a bundle and boil in salted
water for 10 minutes. Drain. Trim green part.
Mince the leek and mashed potatoes. Place on a
dish the hard-boiled eggs cut in halves. Prepare a
cheese sauce. Cook butter and flour, add milk and
grated cheese, season. Pour sauce over eggs.
Surround with mashed potato. Sprinkle grated
cheese and brown under the grill.

TEISEN NLONOD
Onion Cake

Onion and potato pie. Although it has a Welsh
name this dish is well known in Scotland.

Ingredients:

Sliced potatoes 1 lb (480 g)
Chopped onions 4 oz (120 g)
Butter 4 oz (120 g)
Salt and pepper

Method: Grease a 6 inch diameter cake tin with
butter and lard. It is best to use either a silicone
dish or a tin which has been well conditioned to
avoid potato sticking. Place a layer of sliced,
washed and well-dried potatoes and a good
sprinkling of chopped onions, season and add
another layer of potatoes. Dab the top with plenty
of butter and bake at 380°F for 45 minutes. Press
down the mixture and rest for a few minutes.
Turn out into a dish.

CAWS POBI
Welsh rarebit

This cheese savoury was credited to the Welsh as
far back as the fourteenth century and later
immortalised by Boorde in his 'Tales of Toasted
Cheese and St Peter'.

The flavour of the Welsh Rarebit will depend
on the type of cheese used; the strongest Cheddar
type cheese is recommended. The cheese should be
drier than usual as it is easier to grate.

WELSH RAREBIT (4 portions)

METHOD 1

Ingredients:

Cheddar cheese ½ lb (240 g)
Butter 1 oz (30 g)
Flat beer 2 fl oz (60 mls) or 3 tbs
1 tsp of made mustard
Salt and pepper
A pinch of cayenne
Few drops of Worcester sauce
4 slices of bread with crust removed

Method: Grate cheese and cream it with butter and
flat beer, add seasoning and mustard. Toast the
bread, butter each slice and coat with the mixture
evenly and thickly. Brown under the grill.

Alternatively the cheese mixture can be cooked
in a saucepan, then poured over the buttered toast.
Brown under the grill.

METHOD 2

Ingredients:

Cheddar cheese ½ lb (240 g)
Butter 1 oz (30 g)
2 tsp made mustard
1 egg
1 tbs strong beer
Salt and pepper
4 sliced buttered toast

Method: Cream all ingredients together and spread
on buttered toasts. Brown under the grill.

METHOD 3

Ingredients:

Cheddar cheese ½ lb (240 g)
Margarine 2 oz (60 g)
Flour 2 oz (60 g)
Milk ½ pint (300 mls)
2 teaspoons of made mustard
Few drops Worcester sauce
Salt and pepper
2 eggs
4 slices buttered toast
Butter 3 oz (90 g)

Method: Grate cheese. Melt margarine in a saucepan and add flour to produce a white roux. Cook until grainy for 4 minutes on a low heat, gradually add cold milk while stirring with a wooden spoon. Then when the paste is smooth add grated cheese and seasoning. Remove from heat, add beaten eggs and cool. When cold spread this cheese paste thickly on buttered toasts and brown under the grill.

SWEETS

WELSH BORDER TART
A tart filled with raisins and sultanas with a meringue topping

Ingredients:

Butter 1 oz (30 g)
Castor sugar 4 oz (120 g)
Seedless raisins 4 oz (120 g)
Sultanas 4 oz (120 g)
Few drops lemon juice and lemon rind
3 egg yolks
3 egg whites

Short pastry:

Margarine 3 oz (90 g)
Lard 2 oz (60 g)
Sugar 1 oz (30 g)
1 egg
Flour 9 oz (270 g)

Method: Prepare filling. Melt butter and mix with egg yolks. Blend juice and grated rind of lemon, add fruits previously scalded and dried to plum them up.
Pastry: Cream fat together until fluffy, add beaten egg and sugar and blend in flour to obtain a smooth dough. Rest for 20 minutes in refrigerator. Roll out ¼ inch thick to an 8 inch diameter. Line a greased flan tin with the pastry, fill with mixture and bake at 380°F for 20 minutes. Beat egg whites to a stiff meringue in a clean bowl. Gradually add sugar beating at each addition until it is stiff again. Fold meringue over the cooked tartlet, reserving some to pipe a small design or make a criss-cross pattern with a palette knife. Return to oven and bake at 360°F for 8 to 10 minutes until meringue has set.

TEISEN PLANC AFALAN
Welsh apple tart

Ingredients:

Short pastry:

Margarine 2 oz (60 g)
Lard 2 oz (60 g)
1 egg
Flour 8 oz (240 g)

Filling:

Sliced apples 8 oz (240 g)
Castor sugar 3 oz (90 g)
Butter 1 oz (30 g)
Pinch each cinnamon and nutmeg

Method: Cream fat until fluffy, add beaten egg and stir well, blend in the flour to obtain a firm dough. Rest 10 minutes. Roll our and cut 2 rounds ¼ inch thick and 9 inch in diameter. Place 1 round on a greased tray. Arrange sliced apples over pastry and sprinkle with sugar and spices and knobs of butter. Wet edges with water and cover with second pastry round. Crimp edges (seal with rounded design) and bake at 380°F for 30 minutes. Dust over with castor sugar and icing sugar blended together. Serve with Welsh cream.

PWDIN REIS MAMGU
Rice pudding blended with eggs

Ingredients:

Cream 1 pint (600 mls)
Water 1 pint (600 mls)
Pinch of salt and grated nutmeg
1 bay leaf
Pudding rice 4 oz (120 g)
Castor sugar 3 oz (90 g)
4 egg yolks
4 egg whites
Granulated sugar 2 oz (60 g)

Method: Boil or bake rice in water and cream with
salt and bay leaf for 30 minutes. Remove bay leaf.
In a bowl mix cooked rice with egg yolks and
castor sugar. Beat egg whites to a meringue adding
granulated sugar at intervals until the mixture
peaks. Fold meringue into rice mixture and
transfer into a buttered pie dish. Bake for 25
minutes at 360°F. Serve pudding with fruit, honey
or cream.

Ireland

Irish gastronomy is based on natural products from a very prosperous agricultural industry which exports to all major Common Market countries. Butter, cheeses, first-class beef and lamb and a wealth of seafood are sufficient to ensure the gastronomic future of Ireland for thousands of years to come.

But has Irish cuisine made any fundamental progress? The recipes of the kitchens of Ireland are based on a sad time of famine and despair. Irish stew is made with lamb and potato, but on analysis the recipe reads: 'take a few scrags of lamb, a few onions and potatoes and let the whole thing boil to pieces.' Yet a stew based on meaty lean lamb chops, with delicate new potatoes and thinly sliced onions could be a feast for any gourmet.

A recent influx of tourists to Ireland has promoted a revival of the tourist and catering industries. Majestic hotels have grown, good little restaurants are springing up everywhere. The chefs of Ireland are going abroad to pick up new tips and they are winning prizes along the way. The excellent produce is there — it is up to the new breed of chefs to use it.

The Irish are a charming and gracious people: indeed my wife, born Mary Groake, comes from Ireland. The imagination is there in the race — now it should be translated on to the tables of the country. There is great scope for new, exciting recipes based on the wholesome, fresh ingredients so abundantly available in this fertile island.

BILL OF FARE

Soup

ANRAITH OINNIUN GEALACH
A beefy onion soup flavoured with whiskey

ANRAITH MEIDREACH CIARRAT
Potato and mixed vegetable soup

ANRAITH AINT CHLAIR
Aunt Clare vegetable soup

ANRAITH PRATH TIR EOGAIN
Tyrone potage; milk soup with potatoes and
turnips

ANRAITH TIOBRAID ARANN
Tipperary soup: vegetable mixture

Fish Dishes

AOIBNEAS AN BRADAN SHANAGARRY
Fillet of salmon with Irish whiskey

AIGRAN GEALACH TRINSIUR CILL MANTAIN
Mixture of sea-food: scampi, haddock, scollops,
mussels and vegetables

Main Entrees

SCALTAN NAOMH PADRAIG
Chicken in cider and whiskey

STEIG GAMBUN CHRUITE LEIS UACHTAR
Gammon bacon flavoured with whiskey and
mushrooms

STEIG GAILLIMH
Steak braised in black stout

STOBACH GEALACH
Irish stew with lamb, onion and potatoes

BAGUN AGUS CABAISTE BHRUITE
Boiled bacon and cabbage

STEIG GEALACH
Sauted steak, flavoured with Irish Mist and
cohered with cream

EININ BALLYSADARA
Duckling braised in stout with apple fritters

Vegetables

ARAN BOXTY
Mashed potato cakes

PANTOG
Potato pancakes

CAL CEANNANN
Colcannon: cabbage and potato cake fried in
bacon fat

Sweets

PUTOG GEALACH
Cream Charlotte flavoured with Irish Mist liqueur

ARAN AGUS IRA PUTOG
Cream pudding flavoured with Irish Mist liqueur

SOUP

ANRAITH OINNIUN GEALACH
A beefy onion soup flavoured with whiskey
(6 portions)

Ingredients:

Pork fat 2 oz (60 g)
Butter 2 oz (60 g)
Onions 1 lb (480 g)
Beef brisket 4 oz (120 g)
Water 2½ pint (1,500 mls)
2 beef bouillon cubes or beef extract
Potatoes 8 oz (240 g)
Salt and pepper
Pinch of cayenne
Whiskey 4 fl oz (120 mls)
Grated cheese 4 oz (120 g)

Method: Heat pork fat in butter in saucepan and
fry sliced onions until golden brown. Add thin
slices of beef brisket cut in julienne and simmer
together. Complete the soup with water, adding
2 beef bouillon cubes or beef extract, and sliced
potatoes. Season. Boil until tender and pass
through sieve of liquidiser. Lastly, add one tot
of Irish whiskey and sprinkle Irish grated cheese
over.

ANRAITH MEIDREACH CIARRAT
Potato and mixed vegetable soup

Ingredients:

Potatoes 3½ oz (100 g)
Turnip 3½ oz (100 g)
Onion 3 oz (90 g)
Oil 3 oz (90 mls)
Sorrel 3 oz (90 g)
Lettuce 3 oz (90 g)
White stock 1½ pint (900 mls)
Milk 1 pint (600 mls)
Butter 3 oz (90 g)
Chervil sprigs
Salt ½ oz (15 g), pepper 1 tsp

Method: Peel, clean and cut potatoes, turnips
and onions in paysanne (thin slices). Sweat them

in oil, covered, for 5 minutes. Add shredded
sorrel and lettuce. Stir well and moisten with
white stock. Bring to the boil and cook for 18
minutes. Add milk and stir in butter. Whisk it
and serve with sprigs of chervil. Season to taste.

ANRAITH AINT CHLAIR
Aunt Clare vegetable soup

Ingredients:

White of leek 3 oz (90 g)
Cabbage 3 oz (90 g)
Turnip 3 oz (90 g)
Celery 2 oz (60 g)
Potatoes 3 oz (90 g)
Onion 3 oz (90 g)
Clarified butter 3 oz (90 g)
Water 2 pint (1,200 mls)
Salt ½ oz (15 g)
Sorrel 3 oz (90 g)
Spinach 3 oz (90 g)
Lettuce 3 oz (90 g)
Milk ½ pint (300 mls)
White pepper 2 g
Fancy soup pasta 3 oz (90 g)

Method: Chop coarsely all the vegetables, except
lettuce, spinach and sorrel, which should be finely
shredded. Sweat the *chopped* vegetables in butter
with lid on for 5 minutes then add water and
salt. Cook till tender then add the shredded
leaves. Cook 5 more minutes and add milk. Season.
Garnish with pasta cooked separately.

ANRAITH PRATH TIR EOGAIN
Tyrone potage: milk soup with potatoes and
turnips

Ingredients:

Turnips 2 oz (60 g)
Potatoes 4 oz (120 g)
Leeks 4 oz (120 g)
Clarified butter 3 oz (90 g)
White stock or consomme 1 pint (600 mls)
Milk 1 pint (600 mls) optional
Green peas 2 oz (60 g)

Beans 2 oz (60 g)
Shredded sorrel 1 oz (30 g)
Watercress leaves 1 oz (30 g)
Salt ½ oz (15 g), white pepper 2 g
Fresh butter 3 oz (90 g)

Method: Clean and wash root vegetables and cut them in paysanne. Sweat them in butter with lid on for 5 minutes. Add stock or water and cook 20 minutes. Add peas, beans, shredded sorrel and watercress leaves. Season and cook for 8 more minutes. Just before serving, add fresh butter.

ANRAITH TIOBRAID ARANN
Tipperary soup: vegetable mixture

Ingredients:

White of leeks 4 oz (120 g)
Potatoes 10 oz (300 g)
Clarified butter 5 oz (150 g)
Chicken stock 2 pint (1,200 mls)
Cream or milk 6 fl oz (90 mls)
White mushrooms 4 oz (120 g)
Salt $1/3$ oz (10 g), pepper, a pinch

Garnish:

Sliced mushrooms 3 oz (90 g)
Diced boiled new potatoes 3 oz (90 g)

Method: Boil new potatoes in jackets. Cool, skin and cut in small cubes for garnish. Peel old potatoes and cut in thin slices. Cut clean leeks in slices. Sweat in clarified butter. Add potatoes and moisten with stock. Cook 20 minutes till tender, sieve and add cream. Wash mushrooms, but do not peel. Chop finely and sweat in clarified butter, add cream and pass the mixture through a liquidiser to obtain a fine puree. Blend this to the potato mixture. Season. Wash and peel fresh mushrooms, cut in thin slices and add to soup. Saute the diced boiled new potatoes and add to the soup as a garnish.

FISH DISHES

Next to Scottish salmon the Irish produce the finest salmon in the British Isles. Apart from the usual smoked varieties and the many presentations of cold salmon with salads and mayonnaise sauce, there are exquisite dishes which can be concocted with various highly flavoured sauces. Salmon is an oily fish which demands an acid sauce or condiment. The following are ideas which could well be exploited:

AOIBNEAS AN BRADAN SHANAGARRY
Fillet of salmon with Irish whiskey

Ingredients:

4 large fillets of salmon 6 oz (180 g) each
Dry vermouth 4 fl oz (120 mls)
Irish whiskey 4 fl oz (120 mls)
Pork fat and butter 2 oz (60 g) of each
Shallots 2 oz (60 g)
Sliced mushrooms 4 oz (120 g)
Double cream 4 fl oz (120 mls)
Salt, pepper and cayenne
Pinch of tarragon, mint and parsley
Juice of 2 lemons

Method: Skin the fillets and soak them in vermouth and whiskey for ½ hour. Sweat in butter and pork fat the chopped shallots and mushrooms. Add the fish and liquor. Cover with a lid and poach gently in oven for 20 minutes. Strain and add cream. Boil sauce 5 minutes, season and add fresh chopped herbs and juice of lemons. Transfer salmon to dish and decorate with piped potatoes round the edges. Coat the fish with sauce and serve.

AIGRAN GEALACH TRINSUIR CILL MANTAIN
Mixture of sea-food: scampi, haddock, scollops,
    mussels and vegetables

Ingredients:

4 fillets of haddock
4 scampi
4 scollops
12 raw shelled mussels
White wine ½ pint (300 mls)
Butter 2 oz (60 g)
Chopped onions 2 oz (60 g)
Butter and flour 2 oz (60 g) of each

Milk 1 pint (600 mls)
Cauliflower 1 lb (480 g)
Runner beans ½ lb (240 g)
Carrots ½ lb (240 g)
Potatoes 1½ lb (720 g)
Cayenne pepper ½ g
Grated cheese 4 oz (120 g)
Butter 2 oz (60 g)
Chopped parsley
1 lemon

Method: In a large, well-buttered, shallow dish, place fillets of haddock, a few shelled raw scampi, scollops and raw shelled mussels. Add dry white wine, a few knobs of butter and chopped onions. Season with salt and pepper and add herbs. Cover with greaseproof paper. Bake 20 minutes in a moderate oven. Meanwhile prepare 1 pint (600 mls) of thick bechamel (butter 2 oz (60 g), flour 2 oz (60 g) and 1 pint (600 mls) of milk). Boil the vegetables for 10 minutes. Arrange on a large platter the cooked fish and surround with the vegetables in separate amounts — in contrasting colours. Add the fish liquor to the bechamel and season, with a pinch of cayenne. Coat the fish partly with the sauce, pouring the rest of the sauce over the cauliflower only. Leave rest of vegetables as they are. Sprinkle grated cheese over the fish and cauliflower and brown under the grill. Brush melted butter over the potato and sprinkle with chopped parsley.

MEAT DISHES

SCALTAN NAOMH PADRAIG
Chicken in cider and whiskey

Ingredients:

1 by 3 lb (1,440 g) roasting chicken
Oil 2 oz (60 mls)
Butter 2 oz (60 g)
Seasoned flour

Sauce:

Celery 2 oz (60 g)
Chopped onions 2 oz (60 g)

Diced bacon 2 oz (60 g)
Flour 1 oz (30 g)
Tomato puree 2 oz (60 g)
Cider ½ pint (300 mls)
Meat extract $^1/_3$ oz (10 g)
Salt, pepper and a pinch of cinnamon
Garlic $^1/_3$ oz (10 g)
Redcurrant jelly or bramble jam 2 oz (60 g)
Whiskey 5 fl oz (150 mls)
Button onions 2 oz (60 g)
Button mushrooms 2 oz (60 g)
Diced green peppers 2 oz (60 g)
4 sliced heart-shaped pieces of bread fried in oil
Chopped parsley

Method: Cut chicken into 4 pieces. Pass each piece in seasoned flour and saute in oil and butter, cooking gently for 20 minutes covered with a lid. Meanwhile prepare the sauce. In a saucepan fry diced celery, chopped onions and diced raw bacon in 2 oz of oil (60 mls). Add flour and cook till light brown. Then add tomato puree and dry cider. Bring to the boil, add meat extract, herbs and garlic. Then add the redcurrant or bramble jam. Simmer sauce and strain it. Season and add whiskey. Prepare the garnish by boiling button onions and mushrooms for 10 minutes, separately. Drain and saute in butter for 2 minutes. Saute diced green peppers and add to strained sauce. Place the cooked chicken in casserole dish. Cover with sauce, and seal with a lid. Braise in oven for 30 minutes. Serve surrounded with French croutons with tip dipped in sauce and chopped parsley.

STEIG GAMBUN CHRUITE LEIS UACHTAR
Gammon bacon flavoured with whiskey and
    mushrooms

Ingredients:

4 by 4 oz (120 g) slices of boiled gammon or ham

Sauce:

Butter 1 oz (30 g)
Oil 1 oz (30 mls)
Chopped shallots 2 oz (60 g)

Dry cider 5 fl oz (150 mls)
Cream 5 fl oz (150 mls)
Mustard (made up) 1 dessertspoon (10 mls)
Salt and pepper
Whiskey 5 fl oz (150 mls)
Chopped parsley

Method: Place the sliced ham in a metal or shallow dish. Keep it hot with stock or water. Drain surplus liquid when hot. Saute chopped shallots in butter and oil till tender. Add cider. Boil for 5 minutes then gradually add cream and lastly mustard and seasoning. Do not boil the sauce; simmer it while stirring it to a smooth consistency. Heat whiskey and set alight over the ham. Cover immediately with sauce. Sprinkle chopped parsley and serve with *pommes au gratin* (sliced potatoes in cheese sauce).

STEIG GAILLIMH
Steak braised in black stout

Ingredients:

8 by 6 oz (180 g) thin topside steaks
   (2 per portion)
Guinness 1 pint (600 mls)
Whiskey 4 fl oz (120 mls)
Seasoned flour
Pork fat or other fat 1 oz (30 g)
Onions 1 lb (480 g)
Tomato puree 3 oz (90 g)
Salt and black pepper
Chopped parsley

Method: Marinade the topside steaks in Guinness and whiskey with a little oil overnight. Drain and dry the steaks. Pass in seasoned flour and pan fry quickly to brown them on both sides. In the same pan, fry sliced onions till tender and brown. Place the steaks in a dish covered with a layer of onions. Boil the liquor and add tomato puree and salt and pepper. Pour over the steak and sprinkle with chopped parsley. Braise in an oven at 380°F for 1½ hours. Serve with baked jacket potatoes and Irish butter.

STOBACH GEALACH
Irish stew with lamb, onion and potatoes

Traditional Irish Stew was always prepared with mutton or lamb, potatoes and onions. No other vegetable or meat was used. A good Irish Stew is no longer made with scrags, but with good meaty cutlets. Pickled red cabbage is still always served as an important accompaniment with the Irish Stew. Today it is served as in the following recipe.

Ingredients:

[Either cut large chops from shoulder or best end
   of lamb]
Middle neck and best end of lamb cutlets
   3 lb (1,440 g)
Potatoes 1 lb (480 g)
Onions 1 lb (480 g)
White of leeks 2 oz (60 g)
1 bouquet garni (bay leaf, thyme, celery tops —
   2 oz (60 g))
Water 6 pint (3,600 mls)
Salt ½ oz (15 g)
Pepper — black (a pinch)
Chopped parsley
White cabbage leaves 2 oz (60 g)

Method: Scald the meat for 10 minutes and refresh in cold water to wash away the scum — an operation called blanching. In an earthenware pot place alternate layers of meat, sliced potatoes and onions and a little white of leek and cabbage for flavour. Add a bouquet garni and fill the pot completely with water. Season with salt and pepper. Bring the liquid to the boil and gently simmer for 2 hours. Serve with a generous sprinkling of chopped parsley.

This dish is very delicious providing the meat selected is plentiful and the right amount of cuts has been selected. The addition of a few white cabbage leaves can improve this dish by giving it a sweetened taste. Some Irish people add carrots as well, but this becomes another Irish Hot Pot which should be given a name, as it is actually a variation to the traditional Irish Stew.

BAGUN AGUS CABAISTE BHRUITE
Boiled bacon and cabbage (6 portions)

Ingredients:

Piece of gammon 2 lb 2 oz (1,020 g)
   (soaked overnight)
1 cabbage 2 lb (960 g)
Water 6 pint (3,600 mls)
Vinegar 2 oz (60 g)
Black pepper
1 bouquet garni

Method: Place the piece of bacon or gammon in
a pot of water and gently bring it to the boil with
bouquet garni and black pepper. Simmer 25
minutes per pound of meat. In the last 30 minutes,
add the cabbage and cook till tender so that the
bacon and cabbage are finished cooking at the
same time. Be careful not to overcook. Add
vinegar to take away the smell of cabbage. Remove
bouquet garni and bacon rind and sprinkle brown
crumbs if intending to use it cold. Slice the bacon
and serve with the cabbage and boiled potatoes.
Hot parsley or caper sauce may be served with
this dish.

STEIG GEALACH
Sauted steak, flavoured with Irish Mist liqueur
   and cohered with cream

Ingredients:

4 by 6 oz fillet or sirloin steak (180 g) each
Lard or butter 2 oz (60 g)
White vinegar 1 oz (30 mls)
Cream 4 fl oz (120 mls)
Irish Mist 4 fl oz (120 mls)

Method: Season the steaks and pan fry them for
5 minutes. Remove and in same pan add one
spoonful of white vinegar and boil up the juice.
Add cream and boil 5 more minutes, then add
Irish Mist liqueur. Season and pour over the steaks.
Note: The same procedure can be done with
veal escalopes or lamb cutlets with bones
removed before cooking

EININ BALLYSADARA
Duckling braised in stout with apple fritters

Ingredients:

1 by 5 lb duckling (2,400 g)
Guinness 1 pint (600 mls)
Water 5 oz (150 mls)
Malt vinegar 3 fl oz (90 mls)
Carrots, celery, onions 4 oz each (120 g)
Cornflour 2 oz (60 g)
Salt and pepper
Peeled apples, cut in rings or slices 1 lb (480 g)
Flour 2 oz (60 g)
Egg batter ½ pint (300 mls)

Method: Roast the duck for 1½ hours. Carve the
breast and legs and keep warm in a dish while
preparing the sauce.
   Make stock by boiling carcass, bones and
giblets with Guinness, vinegar and water for 30
minutes. Strain.
   Make the gravy by frying the chopped onions,
celery and carrots till brown. Add stock and boil
for 10 minutes, then thicken with cornflour and
season to taste. Pour sauce over the duck and
braise in oven for 40 minutes. Garnish with
apple fritters.
   Make garnish by passing sliced apples in flour,
then batter. Fry for 5 minutes in hot fat and
serve with the duck.

VEGETABLES

ARAN BOXTY
Mashed potato cakes

Ingredients;

Peeled potatoes ½ lb (240 g)
Mashed potatoes ½ lb (240 g)
Strong flour ½ lb (240 g)
Baking powder ½ oz (15 g)
Salt ¼ oz (7 g)
Pinch white pepper
Butter 2 oz (60 g)

Method: Spread a cloth on the table and grate
raw potatoes on it. Squeeze surplus moisture
into a bowl. Blend mashed potatoes and flour
and add grated potatoes. Collect starch deposit

from the liquid of the grated potatoes and add to mixture with salt and pepper. Add melted butter. Dust board with flour and roll out dough like a salami. Cut into small 2 oz (60 g) cakes — 2 inch in diameter and ½ inch thick; or divide mixture into 2 flat round cakes. Mark each one into quarters without dividing. Set on a greased tray with palette knife and make a marking design. Brush top with eggwash or milk and bake at 360°F for 40 minutes for the large cakes and 25 minutes for the small cakes.

PANTOG
Potato pancakes

Ingredients:

Boxty bread mixture (above) 1½ lb (1,440 g)
3 beaten eggs
Milk or buttermilk ½ pint (300 mls)
Lard for frying ½ lb (240 g)

Method: Dilute boxty bread with beaten eggs and add milk to make a thick batter. Heat a little lard in a frying pan and pour in about 2 oz (60 g) of batter. Cook like a pancake on both sides, using all the batter. Brush each one with freshly melted butter.

CAL CEANNANN
Colcannon: cabbage and potato cake fried in bacon fat

Ingredients:

Chopped onions 2 oz (60 g)
Cooked sliced potatoes ½ lb (240 g)
Cooked green or white cabbage ½ lb (240 g)
Salt and pepper
Milk 3 fl oz (90 mls)
Lard or bacon fat 2 oz (60 g)
Butter 2 oz (60 g)

Method: Cook chopped onions in fat till tender but not coloured. Add to mixture of coarsely cut cooked potatoes and cabbage. Season to taste and blend with a little milk to obtain a sort of compact mass. Divide into 2 oz (60 g) cakes.

Heat lard in a pan and fry each cake on both sides until golden brown. On serving, pour over hot melted butter.

SWEETS

PUTOG GEALACH
Cream Charlotte flavoured with Irish Mist liqueur

Ingredients:

Lard 3 oz (90 g)
Butter 4 oz (120 g)
Brown sugar 5 oz (150 g)
2 eggs

Dried fruits:

Seedless raisins
Sultanas
Diced apricots
Diced apples
Grated carrots
Grated lemon rind
Grated orange rind
Stoneless prunes
(2 oz of each of the above)

Ingredients:

Flour 4 oz (120 g)   ⎫
Breadcrumbs 4 oz (120 g)   ⎬ Sifted
Baking powder 1 oz (30 g)   ⎭
Cream 4 fl oz (120 mls)
Irish Mist liqueur 2 fl oz (60 mls)
Irish whiskey 2 fl oz (60 mls)

Method: Cream fat and sugar, add eggs and beat till fluffy. Add Irish Mist, dried fruits, sift baking powder, flour and crumbs and add to mixture with cream. Grease a pudding basin and fill it two-thirds full. Steam for 1½ hours and serve with a custard, flavoured with Irish Mist and Irish whiskey.
Note: Soak all fruits in Irish Mist.

ARAN AGUS IRA PUTOG
Cream pudding flavoured with Irish Mist liqueur

Ingredients:

Soft butter 2 oz (60 g)
Bread slices, cut in triangular pieces 5 oz (150 g)
Irish Mist 5 fl oz (150 mls)
Irish whiskey 5 fl oz (150 mls)
Scalded sultanas 3 oz (90 g)
Diced peeled raw apples 2 oz (60 g)
Brown sugar 3 oz (90 g)
Grated nutmeg
3 eggs
Vanilla essence
Castor sugar 3 oz (90 g)
Single cream 1 pint (600 mls)

Method: Butter sliced bread. Disperse the fruits
in the bottom of a well-greased shallow dish.
Spread the bread slices on top. Sprinkle with
brown sugar and nutmeg. Beat eggs and flavour
with vanilla essence and Irish Mist liqueur and
whiskey. Blend cream. Pour this mixture into
the pie. Bake in a tray half-filled with hot water
at 360°F for 45 minutes.
Note: The liqueurs can be added last, when the
pudding is cooked.

Belgium Luxembourg

Next to France, Belgium has the highest gastronomic standards in Europe. The quality and variety of available products is excellent, but more important, the Belgians are natural cooks and their chefs are the finest craftsmen. The majority of Belgian chefs are trained by the outstanding hotel schools in Brussels, Liege, Namur and Ostend.

One of the reasons why the chefs are so good is that their audience is amongst the most appreciative in the world. The Belgian is a natural-born gastronome who sets no store by any sort of hurried snack. He prefers to eat a good and carefully chosen meal, with plenty of hot, rich food and plenty of time to enjoy it – a major factor in gastronomic appreciation.

One of the most touching moments in my life was in Belgium, when I was in charge of catering on the French destroyer *Brestois* in 1939. We were on an official visit and the crew was invited to disperse so that we could all visit various parts of the country as guests. With three men, I was despatched to Liege, and we expected a boring 'official' day. But when we came from the station with our escort of Belgian officers, we saw the entire regiment standing to attention while the band played the 'Marseillaise' – and I, a humble non-commissioned officer, was invited to review the troops as if I were a high-ranking general. The banquet which followed was an example of the very best of Belgian food.

There was *Jambon des Ardennes* and the *pâté*, flavoured with a cognac of distinction, which is a pearl of international gastronomy. Thin slivers of breast of goose followed, delicately flavoured with a rich, unctuous demi-glace sauce which clung to every delicious morsel. Belgian endives, fried in butter, proved that their slight bitterness is a perfect foil to the richness of the goose. Finally a *Tarte Liegeoise* appeared and a formidable portion was cut for each of us. Coffee, cognac and speeches followed; not knowing how to thank them, I made up a rhymed sonnet extolling the cult of Bacchus, Ceres and all the patron saints of the arts. To this day I think of Belgians as not only good cooks and gourmets, but wonderfully hospitable people.

A year later Belgium was occupied by the Germans, and the barracks where we were treated so royally were the billets of the invaders.

Belgian gourmets will tell you they think French food is divine but Belgian food is better. They cook with wine and beer and lard and butter, and have a fine understanding of the importance of contrasting flavours and textures. Vegetable soups or clear meat and chicken broths are usually the beginning of the two main meals of the day. The glorious ham of Ardennes, smoked over sweet-smelling gorse branches and juniper berries, could be offered as a starter – or the delicious cold fish dishes, shell fish dressed in a pristine cloak of mayonnaise or the famous Ostend oysters. *Anguille au vert* is a justly celebrated dish of eels stewed in butter with a mixture of fresh herbs such as parsley, chervil, sorrel, sage, onions and chives. The fish stock is made into a rich sauce by the addition of egg yolks and cream.

Konijn met pruinen is a delicious rabbit stew simmered in a rich gravy with a garnish of large prunes. The *carbonnade flamande* is known the world over as tender morsels of steak braised in a gravy made rich with subtly bitter undertones of beer. Game is delicious and used a great deal, and special vegetables are hop shoots eaten in March with a creamy sauce, and the Brussels chicory (*witlof*) pleasant but slightly bitter. Fruit is used in large open tarts served in appetising wedges, often with dried fruit like prunes in winter, and a marvellous, refreshing version with rhubarb in spring and early summer.

Religion plays an important part in the lives of the ten million inhabitants of this small country. They never miss an opportunity of expressing their faith with feasts and processions, and christenings, weddings and first communions are all celebrated with much delicious food, The Belgians also like a snack in the morning and in the afternoon, between regular meals, and oysters, mussels and other fish specialities are offered in every cafe. Mussels with chips is probably the most popular combination, although you can buy a packet of the chips alone — *pommes frites* — or thick waffles dusted with icing sugar on every street corner. The *charcuterie* is every bit as good as that of France, and a chunk of bread with a huge slice of liver pâté, washed down with a bottle of wine or a pint of the local beer, is a gastronomic treat.

In Ardennes, try the fragrant Ardennes ham, carefully smoked. This is a region of walnut groves, fresh hot bread, cold beer and generously proportioned wenches happy to flirt with you.

Liège is one of the gayest cities in Belgium, as well as a centre of gastronomes. The Liègois were the first to join the French Revolution and the first to demand independence. The *Clou Doré*, the *Vieux Liège* and *Gourmet sans Chique* are the three best restaurants in this city of excellent food — although others are not too far behind.

The Belgian associations of gourmets maintain a standard every bit as high as their French counterparts, and such organisations as the *Club des 33, Club des Gastronomes and La Ligue des Amis du Vin* bestow their diplomas sparingly.

Beer is the national drink and there are many to choose from. *Faro* is reputed to have been brewed by the same methods for just over a thousand years. In the Brussels area, the beers are particularly strong. The light ale of Malines is delicious and refreshing, the dark ale of Charleroi is potent, and the white of Louvain has a deceptively innocent look. There are heavy, dark ales of the Trappist monks and beers from Antwerp, Oudenarde, Diest and Ghent.

It was in Mesopotamia that the first recipe for beer was found. There, on a crumbling clay tablet, the earliest details of the brewing process were unearthed, portraying the two men stirring the fermenting contents of an ancient brewer's vat, above a legend which explained the process. Beer, the relished refresher and health-giving drink, was consumed from the year 4232 B.C., and has remained a firm favourite for quenching the thirst ever since, nowhere more so than in Belgium. It is used in cooking, particularly in making the succulent *carbonnade* beer sauce, and most steaks and joints are particularly improved by being marinaded in a mixture of flat beer and malt vinegar. Any kind of beer may be used, as long as all the gas has been eliminated by exposure to the air for one hour.

All good chefs know that it is in the little pots that you can make the best sauces, and the tiny Grand Duchy of Luxemburg lives up to this statement. It may appear to come straight out of a Franz Lehar musical play, but it is an independent country with a third of a million inhabitants. Gastronomically they share the taste of the Belgian, German and French cuisine with a flavour of their own. The standard of cuisine is very high and competes favourably with its neighbours.

A meal often begins with paper-thin slices of the delicious Ardennes ham, followed by a trout or crayfish cooked in local wine. In winter, a dish of black pudding, *treipen*, with mashed potato, is hearty and savoury, and a tender roast of smoked pork with bread beans is so popular that it is almost the national dish. In the summer buffet, a cold jellied sucking piglet is displayed in all its pink lustiness with well decorated and seasoned salads.

Gras-Double in the Luxemburg manner is a nourishing dish of tripe cooked in wine instead of the French cider, and *Quenelles* of calves' liver with dumplings compete for lightness in a sea of delicate gravy.

The local rivers Sure and Moselle provide fine pike and perch, usually cooked in the acid Moselle wines. Jugged hare is prepared the German way, with cream. To round off the meal, a good choice is a huge slice of *Quetsch* or *Mirabelle* tart from an 18-inch diameter monster pastry tray.

Luxemburg produces quite a lot of light, dry and refreshing wine from the vineyards bordering the Moselle, but it is the liqueurs made from the sun-ripened fruit which are truly superb drinking. Kirsch, Mirabelle, Prunelle and Quetsch are all made locally, and the fiery liquid with its taste of fresh fruit is a welcome drop at any time. A fantastic blackcurrant wine is made at the Château de Beaufort.

BILL OF FARE

Soup

HOCHEPOT À LA GANTOISE
A rich soup made with boiled beef and assorted
vegetables

LUXEMBURG LEEK SOUP
A creamy potato and leek soup cohered with
cream and egg yolks

Hors d'Oeuvre

PÂTÉ DE CAMPAGNE DES ARDENNES
Pork and pig's liver pâté

PÂTÉ LUXEMBOURGEOIS
Boiled pig's head in aspic

Fish Dishes

ANGUILLES AU VERT À LA FLAMANDE
Stewed eels in herb sauce

MOULES OSTENDAISE
Mussels in cream sauce

TRUITE LUXEMBOURGEOISE
Salmon trout in sour sauce

Meat Dishes

PÂTÉ D'OIE NAMUROISE
Gosling pie

PÂTÉ DE LAPIN NAMUROISE
Rabbit pie

BOUDIN ENTRE-CIEL-ET-TERRE
Black pudding with apple and potato puree

CHOESELS AU MADÈRE
Rich mixed meat casserole in Madeira wine

FRICADELLES OR BALLEKJES
Belgian meat balls in savoury sauce

BOEUF BRAISE TABLE DU ROI LEOPOLD
Braised beef Belgian style

L'OIE DE VISÉ
Braised goose Belgian style

HUES MAT RAM
Roast saddle of hare with cream sauce
Luxemburg style

CARBONNADE FLAMANDE
Braised beef steak and onions with beer

FAISAN À LA BRABANÇONNE
Pot roast pheasant Belgian style

CANETON AUX CERISES BRABANÇONNE
Duck with cherries

**LES OISEAUX SANS TÊTE ET SANS
ÉSPRIT**
Stuffed and rolled veal or beef escalope on a bed
of Belgian endives

WATERZOI DE VOLAILLE PRINCE ALBERT
Chicken fricassee

Vegetables

ENDIVES BRAISÉES DE BRUXELLES
Belgian endives or chicory

ENDIVES MEUNIÈRE
Boiled endives pan fried in butter

CHOUX DE BRUXELLES
Sprouts tossed in butter with chestnuts

CHOUX ROUGE LUXEMBOURGEOIS
Red cabbage with chestnuts and apples

LES JETS DE HOUBLONS
Hop sprouts in butter and lemon

SALADE FLAMANDE
Raw chicory salad with vinaigrette dressing,
beetroot, celery and potatoes

Sweets

GÂTEAU AU FROMAGE LUXEMBOURGEOIS
Cheese cake Luxemburg style

APPEL KUCH LUXEMBOURG
Custard apple tart

FLAN LORRAIN
Ground almond flan

GAUFRES FLAMANDE
Thick Belgian waffles made with yeast

CRAQUELINS PRALINÉS
Belgian buns with jam

GÂTEAU DE VERVIERS OR
  CRAQUELINE
A yeast bun like a brioche with rum

CHAUSSON MATHILDA OR GOZETTES
Apple and apricot puff pastry turnover

CHAUSSON CHARLEROI
Almond cream turnover

FLAMICHOU AUX POMMES ISABELLA
Baked pudding with apple (Conil's creation)

PUDDING FLAMAND OR PUDDING SAXON
Light souffle pudding with apricot sauce

BEIGNETS SOUFFLES FLAMANDE
Light fritters made of chou pastry

PAIN À LA GRACHT
Almond sponge cake flavoured with kirsch

ROMBOSSES OR RABOTTES DE POMMES
Baked apple in sweet short pastry

PISTOLETS
Milk stick bread roll with a cut in the centre

SOUP

HOCHEPOT A LA GANTOISE

A rich soup made with boiled beef and assorted
  vegetables (8 to 12 portions)

Ingredients:

Silverside of beef 8 oz (240 g)
Oxtail 8 oz (240 g)
Breast of lamb 8 oz (240 g)
Pig's ears 8 oz (240 g)
1 knuckle of bacon 8 oz (240 g)
4 pig's trotters 1 lb (480 g)
Water 6 pint (3,600 mls)
Carrots 8 oz (240 g)
Turnips 8 oz (240 g)
1 head of celery
1 onion stuffed with 4 cloves
1 bouquet garni
1 small cabbage
8 small leeks

Garnish:

8 small beef chipolatas
Potatoes 2 lb (960 g)
Salt and pepper
1 fresh small sprig of mint leaves

Method: Bone, de-fat and tie each piece of meat
with string. Place in a large stock pot. Cover with
cold water. Bring to the boil gently and remove
scum as it rises. Simmer gently for 1½ hours.
Meanwhile clean, wash and prepare the vegetables
as follows: cut carrots and turnips in two. Clean
the head of celery, stem by stem. Wash each leek.
Make an incision right through the middle of the
leeks and cut away towards the green part to allow
dirt to be removed easily. Wash and tie up the
leeks in a bundle. Place all these vegetables in the
stock pot and cook for 30 minutes with the meat
so that all the ingredients are cooked correctly
and are ready at the same time. Add bouquet
garni and the fresh mint leaves to the vegetables.
Season. When the meat and vegetables are cooked
remove the meat and carve. Remove the vegetables
and arrange around the dish. Serve the broth with
sippets of bread as soup. Serve with boiled
potatoes and grilled beef chipolata sausages.

It is important to maintain the level of liquid
during the whole simmering process by adding
cold water. Avoid boiling too violently. Simmering
means cooking at 180°F, just under boiling
temperature.

The reader will, by now, realise that the *Hochepot* is a main meal consisting of the broth with
meat and vegetables cooked at the same time but
in different order of cooking. The cabbage is cut
in four with the core removed and added to the
soup 20 minutes before the dish is ready to be
served.

Meat 1½ hours, vegetables ½ hour — total
cooking 2 hours. This means the meat takes 2
hours to cook and within the time period the
vegetables are cooked for only ½ hour.

The usual garnishes are pickled gherkins or
cucumber, chutney, horseradish sauce and some
of the broth.

LUXEMBOURG LEEK SOUP

A creamy potato and leek soup cohered with
  cream and egg yolks (8 portions)

Ingredients:

Sliced potatoes 8 oz (240 g)
Sliced leeks 8 oz (240 g)
Lard 1 oz (30 g)
Butter 1 oz (30 g)
Water 3 pint (1,800 mls)
Salt and pepper

Thickening:

2 egg yolks
Cream 5 fl oz (150 mls)
Cornflour ½ oz (15 g)

Method: Saute, without browning, the cleaned
sliced potatoes and leeks. After 10 minutes add
the water. Boil for 20 minutes and then pass
through a sieve. Season. Mix the egg yolks, cream
and cornflour in a bowl. Add a cup of the soup.
Stir and pour this mixture into the soup while
whisking gently over heat to thicken. Boil for a
few minutes and serve.

HORS D'OEUVRE

PÂTÉ DE CAMPAGNE DES ARDENNES
Pork and pig's liver pâté

Ingredients:

Skinned pig's liver 8 oz (240 g)
Saltpetre ½ tsp
Water 5 fl oz (150 mls)
Sausage meat 8 oz (240 g)
Back pig's fat 8 oz (240 g)
Chopped onion 2 oz (60 g)
2 eggs
Milk 5 fl oz (150 mls)
Flour 2 oz (60 g)
Pinch mace, clove and ground cinnamon
Salt ½ oz (15 g)
Aspic gravy stock 5 fl oz (150 mls) *or*
    5 fl oz water, 1 oz gelatine and 1 beef bouillon
    cube
2 bay leaves
1 good pinch black pepper
6 blanched rashers of bacon with rind removed

Method: Dice the liver and put in a little water
with saltpetre for 30 minutes. Place these
ingredients with sausage meat and solid pork fat
and mince twice. Blend the rest of the ingredients,
except the aspic. Stir the mixture thoroughly.
Line an earthenware dish with the blanched
rashers of bacon (scalded for 5 minutes). Fill with
the liver mixture. Add a few bay leaves and place
dish in a tray half filled with water. Bake for
1½ hours at 360°F. Turn out on a rack over a
tray to collect the juice. Clean casserole dish.

   Make the aspic by dissolving gelatine and
bouillon cube. Replace the pâté and pour the
aspic. Cool and chill to set. Chill the juice and
remove the hardened fat. Melt it and pour over
the pâté to insulate the top from air. Store in
refrigerator.

PIG'S HEAD PÂTÉ LUXEMBOURG
Boiled pig's head in aspic

Ingredients:

Half pig's head
1 carrot
1 raw, peeled, sliced beetroot
1 onion studded with 2 cloves
1 bouquet garni
2 peppercorns
Salt and ground mace
Water 5 pint (3,000 mls)
1 tsp meat extract *or* black treacle to colour
    the broth

Garnish:

Diced pickled gherkins

Method: Boil the pig's head with all the
ingredients except garnish for 2 hours. Remove
head. Discard bone. Cut meat in small cubes.
Place in a bowl or earthenware oblong mould.
Boil the stock to reduce it by half. Strain and
add the same quantity, weight for weight, of
stock and meat. Blend the diced gherkin and
cool. Chill the mixture until it sets hard.

FISH DISHES

Next to mussels, eels are the most popular fish.
The eel is the only species of its genus and is a
great delicacy which is appreciated all over the
world. In the East End of London, the English
cockney will buy it in its own jelly and eat it at
his local pub with much gusto. Large eels are
skinned before cooking; small eels are not, but
the slime is rubbed off thoroughly with coarse
salt and a cloth. Eels are classified into two groups:
silver eels which are found in rivers and sea eels.

ANGUILLES AU VERT À LA FLAMANDE
Stewed eels in herb sauce

Ingredients:

Live eels 2 lb (960 g)
Chopped onion 4 oz (120 g)
Celery 1 oz (30 g)
Lard 2 oz (60 g)
Water 5 fl oz (150 mls)
White wine 5 fl oz (150 mls)
White vinegar 2 fl oz (60 mls)

Salt and pepper
2 egg yolks
Cream 5 fl oz (150 mls)
Fresh chopped herbs 2 oz (60 g):
   chopped parsley, spinach, sorrel, mint, chervil,
   sage, summer savory

Method: Cut the eels in small (2 inch long) pieces.
The operation is made easier if you can hold one
end of the eel with a cloth. Pin it down to a
chopping board with an ice pick inserted into its
head. Make an incision round the head and loose
the skin which can easily be pulled off from head
to tail or you may leave the skin. Have a basin
of water and vinegar ready and plunge the pieces
to wash away the slimy part on the skin. Rinse
and dry with a cloth.

   Heat lard in a pan, sweat the diced or sliced
vegetables for a few minutes. Add the eel and cover
with a lid. Shake the pan. Stir and add vinegar,
water and wine with the seasoning. Poach for 8
minutes. Add the chopped herbs. Thicken with a
roux — 1 oz (30 g) each margarine and flour,
add some of the liquid and stir back into the
stew. Mix two egg yolks and 5 fl oz cream in a
bowl, gradually add half the sauce. Stir this
mixture back to the eel and rest of sauce. Stir
well and serve in a soup tureen.

MOULES OSTENDAISE
Mussels in cream sauce

Ingredients:

Mussels 8 pint (4,800 mls)
Chopped shallots or onions 4 oz (120 g)
Butter 2 oz (60 g)
1 bouquet garni
Malt vinegar 4 fl oz (120 mls)
Belgian beer 1 pint (600 mls)
Salt and ground pepper

Cream finish:

2 egg yolks + cornflour 1 oz (30 g)
Cream ½ pint (300 mls)
Juice and rind of 1 lemon
Chopped parsley 1 tbs

Method: Clean, scrub and wash mussels. In a large
saucepan sweat, without browning, the chopped
onions for 2 minutes. Add vinegar and beer and
boil for 5 minutes. Add bouquet garni and
mussels. Cover with a lid and boil for 5 minutes
until the mussels open. Discard those which have
not opened. Pour all the liquid into a smaller pan.
Boil for 5 more minutes. Blend the eggs, cornflour and cream in a bowl. Add some of the
mussel liquor and stir well. Pour this mixture
into the rest of the fish liquor and gently reheat
it while stirring. Adjust seasoning. Do not boil.
Pour this sauce over the mussels, sprinkle with
fresh parsley and then add lemon rind and juice.
Cover with a lid, stir and shake mussels and serve.

   In Brussels, the mussels are served without the
egg and cream. Most cafes provide mussels with
chips at any hour of the day.

TRUITE LUXEMBOURG
Salmon trout in sour sauce

Ingredients:

4 by 10 oz salmon trout (300 g each)
Vinegar 5 fl oz (150 mls)
White wine ½ pint (300 mls)
Water 5 fl oz (150 mls)
Salt and pepper
1 pinch sugar
1 bouquet garni
Sliced onions 2 oz (60 g)
Sliced carrots 3 oz (90 g)
Sliced leeks 2 oz (60 g)
Sliced white mushrooms 2 oz (60 g)
Sliced peeled cucumber 2 oz (60 g)
Sour cream 5 fl oz (150 mls)

Roux:

Flour ½ oz (15 g)
Margarine ½ oz (15 g)

Method: Clean, gut and remove scale of trout.
Place the trout in a shallow dish with all the
ingredients except cream, flour and margarine.
Poach gently in moderate oven for 20 minutes.
Remove trout. Place in a clean shallow dish. Cool
and remove skin. Boil the stock to reduce it by half

and add cream. Cook roux for a few minutes.
Dilute it with sauce. Check seasoning. Pour sauce
over the trout with all the sliced vegetables
around.

Instead of individual trout a large fish can be
used allowing 10 oz fish per person.

MEAT DISHES

PÂTÉ D'OIE NAMUROISE
Gosling pie

Ingredients:

1 goose 8 lb (3,840 g)
Sausage meat 8 oz (240 g)
Pig's liver 8 oz (240 g)
Liver of the goose 3 oz (90 g)
1 egg
Chopped parsley 1 tbs
Chopped onions 2 oz (60 g)
Flour 2 oz (60 g)
1 clove of garlic
Brandy or rum 3 fl oz (90 mls)
Salt and pepper
Pinch mace and clove

Pastry:

Lukewarm water ½ pint (300 mls)
Yeast ½ oz (15 g)
Strong flour 1 lb (480 g)
Lard 2 oz (60 g)
1 egg
Salt 7 g

Jelly stock:

Water 2 pint (1,200 mls)
Gelatine 1 oz (30 g)
Meat extract ¼ oz (7 g)
1 onion
1 carrot
1 bouquet garni
Salt and pepper

Method: First prepare the dough. Crumble yeast
in lukewarm water and blend with flour and lard
to make a yeast dough. Add beaten egg and salt.

Knead well. Gather into a ball and leave for 45
minutes covered by a large upturned basin.

Prepare the forcemeat. Blend sausagemeat and
liver finely minced or chopped with all the
ingredients listed above. Clean and truss the
goose. Remove skin. Bone the meat and dice it.
Blend meat with forcemeat.

To prepare the stock, boil bones and skin with
1 onion and bouquet garni for 1½ hours. Strain
and season. For 1 pint stock add 1 oz gelatine
and 1 teaspoon meat extract.

Knock back the yeast dough which has swollen.
Knead again and roll into an oblong 9 inch by
4 inch. Place the forcemeat goose mixture along
the middle of the pastry layer. Fold the two sides
towards the centre. Seal with water and tuck in
both ends. Turn over this loaf on to a greased dish.
Brush top with egg glaze. Make a decoration with
pastry trimmings. Brush decoration too. Leave
for 30 minutes. Bake for 35 minutes at 400°F and
then for 30 minutes at 350°F. Cool and introduce
some of the jelly stock, which must be semi-set,
through a hole in the centre.

PÂTÉ DE LAPIN NAMUROIS
Rabbit pie

Ingredients:

1 rabbit 3 lb (1,440 g) – net meat 1½ lb (720 g)
Pork belly 8 oz (240 g)
Pig's liver 8 oz (240 g)
Chopped onions 2 oz (60 g)
1 clove garlic
Salt ½ oz (15 g)
Pepper 2 g
Pinch mace and ground clove
Dark beer ½ pint (300 mls)
2 bay leaves
Bread crumbs 3 oz (90 g)
2 eggs
Rum 3 fl oz (90 mls)
6 derinded and scalded rashers of bacon 1 lb (480
    1 lb (480 g)

Method: Bone the rabbit. Cut all the meat in
cubes. Remove gall from liver. Mince the heart,
the pig's liver and pork fat. Add eggs, crumbs,

beer, rum and seasoning. Blend the liver mixture and the diced rabbit. Grease an oblong earthenware dish with lard. Line it with the scalded rashers of bacon and bay leaves. Fill the dish with rabbit mixture. Place in a tray half filled with water and bake for 1½ hours at 360°F. Cool and chill. Pour melted lard over it to insulate it. This will assist in keeping pâté in good condition. Store in the refrigerator covered with foil.

BOUDIN ENTRE-CIEL-ET-TERRE
Black pudding with apple and potato puree

Ingredients:

Fresh black pudding 2 lb (960 g)
Mashed potatoes 1 lb (480 g)
Apple puree 4 oz (120 g)
Salt and pepper
Lard or oil for frying
4 slices of bread

Method: Slice the pudding and fry it in lard for few minutes. Blend the two purees, season. Place in a shallow dish and cover with pudding slices. Fry bread slices, cut in triangular shapes, and surround the dish with them.

CHOESELS AU MADÈRE
Rich mixed meat casserole in Madeira wine

Ingredients;

Ox tail 8 oz (240 g)
Stewing veal 8 oz (240 g)
Boned breast of lamb 8 oz (240 g)
Tripe 8 oz (240 g) — cut in 2 inch squares or
    thin strips
4 sheep trotters
1 ox kidney — cut in thin slices
Belgian beer 1 pint (600 mls)
Madeira wine ½ pint (300 mls)
Water 2 pint (1,200 mls)
1 bouquet garni
Sliced carrots 4 oz (120 g)
Sliced celery 2 oz (60 g)
Chopped onions 2 oz (60 g)

Lard for frying 4 oz (120 g)
1 clove garlic
4 calves brains
Tomato puree 2 oz (60 g)
Salt and pepper

Roux:

Flour 2 oz (60 g)
Lard 2 oz (60 g)

Meat balls:

Minced beef 4 oz (120 g)
Minced pork 4 oz (120 g)
1 egg
Chopped parsley 1 tbs

Method: Cut ox tail in segments. Remove the fat. Skin and remove sinews of kidneys. Cut the veal in cubes, the breast in squares and the tripe in smaller squares. Clean sheep trotters. Fry all the meat in fat for a few minutes. Transfer to a large earthenware casserole. In same frying pan brown vegetables. Add to meat with beer, wine, water and rest of ingredients. Cover with a lid and braise slowly for 2½ hours at 340°F. Remove bouquet garni. Strain liquor into a saucepan. Boil for 15 minutes. Thicken it with a cooked roux, diluted into sauce. Strain, season and add to meat.

Separately, blanch brains. Remove membrane. Fry brains in a mixture of butter and lard.

To make the meatballs, blend beef and pork with egg. Shape into 1 oz balls. Pass in flour and cook in a tray half filled with unthickened stock for 15 minutes. Add to stew. Lastly, sprinkle chopped parsley.

FRICADELLES OR BALLEKJES
Belgian meat balls in savoury sauce

Ingredients:

Minced beef 8 oz (240 g)
Minced pork 8 oz (240 g)
1 egg
Chopped parsley 1 tbs
1 clove garlic
Bread crumbs 2 oz (60 g)

Salt and pepper
Chopped onion 1 oz (30 g)
Pinch sugar and mace

Method: Blend all ingredients together. Shape into 2 oz balls. Pass in seasoned flour and fry for 8 minutes. Serve with a rich tomato gravy or baked in oven with beer like carbonnade of beef.

BOEUF BRAISÉ TABLE DU ROI LEOPOLD
Braised beef Belgian style

Ingredients:

1 cow's heel
Topside or silverside joint 3 lb (1,440 g)
Belgian beer 2 pint (1,200 mls)
Malt vinegar 5 fl oz (150 mls)
Brown sugar 1 oz (30 g)
Sliced onion 4 oz (120 g)
Sliced carrot 4 oz (120 g)
1 bouquet garni
1 clove of garlic
Sprig of celery
Tomato puree 2 oz (60 g)
Salt and pepper
Pinch mace and clove

Garnish:

Belgian endives 2 lb (960 g)
Button mushrooms 1 lb (480 g)

Roux:

Flour 2 oz (60 g)
Dripping 2 oz (60 g)

Method: Bone or split the cow's heel in two. It will provide the gelatinous element in the sauce. Place beef in a large earthenware bowl. Cover with beer, water and vinegar and marinade overnight. Drain, wipe dry and place in a roasting pan with a little fat. Roast for 30 minutes at 420°F to seal the juice in and brown the meat on the outside. Reduce heat to 360°F. Add beer and liquid of marinade with tomato puree, bouquet garni, cow's heel, onions and carrots, garlic, celery and sugar. Cover with a lid and braise for 1½ hours. Remove joint only. Transfer all ingredients in the tray into a large pot and boil the cow's heel for 30 minutes. Remove the meat and discard the bone. Strain the gravy. Thicken it with a diluted roux. Season and strain again. Carve the beef and dice the heel meat.

Separately, cook the garnish of braised endives as in recipe (see vegetable section). Toss the cleaned and washed mushrooms in a little fat and cook for only 4 minutes with a lid on. Add mushrooms to sauce. Check seasoning.

L'OIE DE VISÉ
Braised goose Belgian style

This dish can be prepared with large duck if goose is not available.

Ingredients:

Boiling goose 9 lb (4,320 g)
2 carrots
2 onions studded with cloves
2 small leeks
1 bouquet garni
Water 6 pint (3,600 mls)

Sauce:

Flour 2 oz (60 g) ⎫
Margarine 2 oz (60 g) ⎬ Roux
Stock 2½ pint (1,500 mls)
Cream 5 fl oz (150 mls)
2 egg yolks
Salt and pepper
Pinch nutmeg
Chopped parsley 1 tbs

Method: Place the trussed goose in a large pan with cold water. Bring to the boil. Remove scum as it rises and after 30 minutes add vegetables and bouquet garni. Simmer for 1¼ hours. Cool in the same liquor. Remove goose. Strain liquor and keep rest for soup, using only 2½ pint. Remove grease from stock by chilling it. This hardens it so it is easier to remove. Cook a roux and dilute in stock. Blend egg yolks and cream in a bowl with some of the sauce. Return egg mixture to rest of sauce. Bring to the boil. Strain. Season. Carve goose and pour sauce over. Sprinkle chopped parsley.

HUES MAT RAM
Roast saddle of hare with cream sauce Luxembourg style

Ingredients:

2 saddles of hare, 1 head and 2 front legs
Lard 2 oz (60 g)
1 pint water (600 mls)
1 bouquet garni
Red wine 5 fl oz (150 mls)

Sauce:

Chopped onions 2 oz (60 g)
Carrots 2 oz (60 g)
Tomato puree 1 oz (30 g)
Fat 1 oz (30 g)
Flour 1 oz (30 g) } Roux
Cream 5 oz (150 mls)
Salt and pepper
Pinch mace, nutmeg and cinnamon
Canned chestnut puree 8 oz (240 g)
Butter 2 oz (60 g)

Method: Remove skin from the saddle of hare. Brown legs and head with fat. Add 1 pint water and bouquet garni and red wine. Boil for 1 hour to produce a stock.

To prepare the sauce, brown vegetables in lard. Add tomato puree. Add to stock and boil for 30 minutes. Strain. Thicken with roux. Brown fat and flour and dilute into stock. Season.

Roast saddle for 30 minutes. Carve in thin slices. Place in a shallow dish. Add cream to sauce and boil for 5 minutes. Pour some of the sauce over the meat and serve rest separately. Heat chestnut puree with butter. Season. Serve as a vegetable.

CARBONNADE FLAMANDE
Braised beef steak and onions with beer

Ingredients:

8 x 4 oz steaks from top or silverside (120 g each)
    —total meat 2 lb (960 g)
Sliced onions 1 lb (480 g)
Brown beer 1 pint (600 mls)
Water ½ pint (300 mls)
Malt vinegar 3 fl oz (90 mls)
Brown sugar 1 oz (30 g)
Salt and pepper
Tomato puree 1 oz (30 g)

Roux:

Flour 1 oz (30 g)
Lard 1 oz (30 g)
1 bouquet garni
Pince ground mace, clove and cinnamon
Lard for frying 3 oz (90 g)

Method: Fry the steaks in lard for 5 minutes on both sides. Remove and place in a shallow earthenware dish. In the same pan fry sliced onions gently on a low heat without browning. Remove and cover steaks. In the same pan, add flour to fat. Cook like a roux. Gradually add beer and water. Boil this mixture for 10 minutes. Add tomato puree, sugar and seasoning. Strain over the meat and onions. Add bouquet garni. Cover dish with a lid and braise in oven for 1½ hours at 325°F, or until tender. Remove bouquet garni. Check seasoning.

FAISAN À LA BRABANCONNE
Pot roast pheasant Belgian style

Ingredients:

1 pheasant 2½ lb (1,200 g)
Lard 2 oz (60 g)
Butter 1 oz (30 g)
Diced carrot 2 oz (60 g)
Diced onion 2 oz (60 g)
Diced celery 2 oz (60 g)
Shredded endives 4 oz (120 g)
Tomato puree 1 oz (30 g)
Belgian beer 5 fl oz (150 mls)
Continental gin 2 fl oz (60 mls)
Pinch ground thyme
Sugar ½ oz (15 g)
Salt and pepper

Thickening:

Cream 5 fl oz (150 mls)
Cornflour 1 oz (30 g)

Method: Truss and clean pheasant. Season and rub with lard and butter. Pan roast quickly for 15 minutes at 400°F. Transfer into a casserole dish with all vegetables, tomato puree, beer, gin and a pinch of ground thyme. Cover with a lid. Braise in oven for 30 minutes. Strain the liquor into a saucepan. Blend cream and cornflour. Add to sauce and boil for 5 minutes. Pour over the pheasant. Season with salt, pepper and sugar.

CANETON AUX CERISES BRABANÇONNE
Duck with cherries

Ingredients:

1 x 5½ lb duckling (2,640 g)
Fat 2 oz (60 g)
Salt and pepper

Sauce:

Sliced onions 2 oz (60 g)
Sliced carrots 2 oz (60 g)
Tomato puree 1 oz (30 g)
Cinnamon 1 teaspoon
Beer 1 pint (600 mls)
Fresh mint few leaves
Pinch mace and nutmeg
1 bouquet garni

Thickening:

Cornflour 1 oz (30 g)
Water 5 fl oz (150 mls)

Garnish:

8 oz (240 g) stoneless red morello (very acid) cherries soaked in 2 fl oz (60 mls) gin

Method: Truss and clean duck. Season and rub with fat. Roast for 110–120 minutes–first 30 minutes at 400°F and rest of time at 360°F. Drain and carve. Place the carcass bone and giblets in a saucepan with 1 pint of water, beer and bouquet garni. Boil for 1 hour and strain. Brown sliced onions and carrots in fat. Add tomato puree and stock. Boil for 15 minutes and thicken with a slurry of cornflour. Strain. Add spices and seasoning. Place sauce over the duck and scatter the stoned cherries. Sprinkle a little Belgian gin over the duck and serve.

[I have modified this recipe to what I consider an improvement of the original. J.C.]

LES OISEAUX SANS TÊTE ET SANS ÉSPRIT
Stuffed and rolled veal or beef escalope on a bed of Belgian endives

Ingredients:

4 x 6 oz beef escalopes taken from topside, thick flank or silverside [or veal CUTS]
Lard 2 oz (60 g)
Seasoned flour 1 oz (30 g)

Stuffing:

Sausage meat 8 oz (240 g)
1 egg
Ham cut in 8 strips 2 inch x ¼ inch 4 oz (120 g)
4 gherkins

Sauce:

Lard 2 oz (60 g)
Sliced onions 2 oz (60 g)
Sliced carrots 2 oz (60 g)
Tomato puree 1 oz (30 g)
Beer ½ pint (300 mls)
Water ½ pint (300 mls)
Salt and pepper
Pinch mace and cinnamon

Thickening:

Cornflour ½ oz (15 g)
Water 5 fl oz (150 mls)

Method: Beat the escalopes with a rolling pin as thinly as possible. Season and pass in flour. Blend sausage meat with egg and season. Place a small ball of meat and 2 strips of ham and 1 gherkin on each escalope. Roll up and tie with string or cocktail sticks. Pass in seasoned flour. Brown the escalopes in lard. Place into a shallow dish. Cover with the sauce made as follows: Brown vegetables in fat for a few minutes. Add tomato puree, seasoning, spices, beer and water. Boil for 30 minutes. Add to meat. Cover with a lid and braise for 1 hour. Strain sauce into a saucepan and thicken it with a slurry of cornflour and water. Check seasoning.

A stuffed escalope in culinary parlance is called a 'paupiette'.

WATERZOI DE VOLAILLE PRINCE ALBERT
Chicken fricassee (6 to 8 portions)

Ingredients:

1 boiling fowl 5 lb (2,400 g)
Water 5 pint (3,000 mls)
2 leeks
1 carrot
1 onion studded with 4 cloves
1 sprig celery
1 bouquet garni

Meat balls:

Sausage meat 8 oz (240 g)
1 egg
Chopped parsley 1 tbs
1 clove of garlic
Salt and pepper
Flour 1 oz (30 g)

Sauce:

Flour 2 oz (60 g)   ⎫
Margarine 2 oz (60 g) ⎬ roux
Stock 2 pint (1,200 mls) ⎭
Cream 5 fl oz (150 mls)
2 egg yolks
Pinch nutmeg
Salt and pepper
Juice and rind (grated) of 1 lemon
Pinch cayenne pepper

Garnish:

Rice pilaff 8 oz (240 g)

Method: Place cleaned and trussed fowl in a
large pot covered with cold water. Bring to the
boil and remove scum as it rises. Simmer for 1
hour and then add the cleaned vegetables—leeks
tied up in a bundle, the carrot split in two, onion,
celery and bouquet garni. Cook for another 40
minutes. Cool in its liquor. Remove fowl, peel
off the skin and carve the meat. Remove
vegetables. Cut them attractively.

To make sauce take the stock and boil it. Add
roux and stir well, simmer for 15 minutes. Blend
egg yolks and cream and a cup of sauce in a bowl.
Add this mixture to sauce. Season. Add spices,
lemon juice and grated rind. Reheat for 5 minutes.

Pour sauce over meat and serve rest separately. Cook
rice as for pilaff (20 minutes only with chicken
stock). Season and serve as a garnish.

Blend sausage meat with egg and parsley, garlic
and seasoning. Divide into ½ oz balls. Place in a
tray, covered with stock and poach for 15 minutes.
Serve with meat.

VEGETABLES

ENDIVES BRAISÉES DE BRUXELLES
Belgian endives or chicory

Ingredients:

Belgian endives 2 lb (960 g)
Lemon juice 2 fl oz (60 mls)
White vinegar 1 fl oz (30 mls)
Butter 2 oz (60 g)
Bacon trimmings and bone 8 oz (240 g)
Salt and pepper

Method: Trim end of chicory. Wash and dry. Place
in a casserole dish with lemon juice, vinegar, butter
and bones. Cover with a lid. Braise for 45 minutes.
Discard bacon trimming and serve in the same
casserole. Season to taste.

ENDIVES MEUNIÈRE
Boiled endives pan-fried in butter

Ingredients:

Belgian endives 2 lb (960 g)
Water 2 pint (1,200 mls)
Lemon juice 2 fl oz (60 mls)
Salt and pepper
Pinch sugar
1 tbs white vinegar
Butter 4 oz (120 g)
Chopped parsley 1 tbs

Method: Trim endives near the stalks. Wash and
dry. Parboil in salted water with lemon juice, sugar
and vinegar for 20 minutes. Drain. Squeeze the
surplus moisture. Place in a shallow dish. Melt
butter in a pan. Add juice of lemon and when it

froths, pour over endives. Sprinkle chopped parsley.

CHOUX DE BRUXELLES
Sprouts tossed in butter with chestnuts

Ingredients:

Parboiled chestnuts 8 oz (240 g)
Parboiled sprouts 1 lb (480 g)
Butter 4 oz (120 g)
Lard 1 oz (30 g)
Salt and pepper

Method: Parboil the skinned chestnuts and sprouts till tender. Drain. Heat a pan with butter and lard. Add vegetables and toss for 5 minutes. Season.

RED CABBAGE LUXEMBOURGEOIS
Red cabbage with chestnuts and apples

Ingredients:

Shredded red cabbage 1 lb (480 g)
Sliced apples 8 oz (240 g)
Skinned parboiled chestnuts 8 oz (240 g)
Salt and pepper
Butter 4 oz (120 g)
Lard 1 oz (30 g)
Vinegar 5 fl oz (150 mls)
Sugar 2 oz (60 g)
Water ½ pint (300 mls)

Method: Blend all ingredients together. Place in a shallow dish and cover with a lid. Braise for 1 hour at 360°F.

LES JETS DE HOUBLONS
Hop shoots in butter and lemon

Ingredients:

Hop shoots 1 lb (480 g)
Salted water 2 pint (1,200 mls)
Juice and rind of 1 lemon
Vinegar 1 tbs
Salt and pepper
Butter 2 oz (60 g)

Method: Boil the hops in salted water with lemon juice and rind and vinegar for 8 minutes. Drain and serve with melted butter. Season to taste.

SALADE FLAMANDE
Raw chicory salad with vinaigrette dressing, beetroot, celery and potatoes

Ingredients:

Belgian endives cut in shreds 2 oz (60 g)
Cooked beetroot strips 4 oz (120 g)
Sliced celery 2 oz (60 g)
Cooked, diced new boiled potatoes 8 oz (240 g)
French mayonnaise ½ pint (300 mls)
Peeled, sliced acid apples 2 oz (60 g)
Chopped chives 1 tbs
Chopped red peppers 1 oz (30 g)
2 hard-boiled eggs

Method: Blend all ingredients and serve in a glass bowl. Decorate top with sliced hard-boiled eggs.

SWEETS

GÂTEAU AU FROMAGE LUXEMBOURGEOIS
Cheese cake Luxembourg style

Ingredients:

Sweet short biscuit pastry:

Margarine 6 oz (180 g)
Icing sugar 2 oz (60 g)
1 egg
Flour 10 oz (300 g)
Pinch cinnamon

Cheese filling:

Cream cheese 6 oz (180 g)
Castor sugar 2 oz (60 g)
4 egg whites
1 egg yolk
Grated lemon rind
Flour 1 oz (30 g)
Kirsch 2 fl oz (60 mls)

Topping:

Stoneless black cherries 8 oz (240 g)
Arrowroot ½ oz (15 g)
Red wine 5 fl oz (150 mls)
Sugar 2 oz (60 g)
Pinch cinnamon

Method, pastry: Cream margarine and sugar until fluffy. Add beaten egg, flour and cinnamon to form a stiff dough. Knead and gather into a ball to rest for 30 minutes. Roll ¼ inch thick. Line a well greased mould 8 inch x 2 inch. Fill it with dry beans. Bake blind for 20 minutes at 400°F.
Meringue cheese filling: Cream cheese, sugar and egg yolk. Add flour and Kirsch and lemon rind. Beat egg whites to a meringue in a separate bowl, and fold into mixture. Fill the pastry flan. Bake at 360°F for 20 minutes. Then remove. Go round with a knife to separate the filling near the pastry skin so that the filling will not rise like a mushroom. Return to heat and bake for a further 20 minutes.
Topping: Boil cherries in red wine with sugar and cinnamon. Thicken with arrowroot and a little water, added to the boiling mixture. Cook for a few minutes. Cool cherries. Cool the cheese tart and when cold place the cherries on top.

APPEL KUCH LUXEMBOURG
Custard apple tart

Ingredients:

Short pastry as for cheese cake 8 oz (240 g)

Filling:

Sliced apples 6 oz (180 g)
Castor sugar 2 oz (60 g)

Custard:

Pinch cinnamon, ground clove and netmeg
2 eggs
Cream ½ pint (300 mls)
Sugar 2 oz (60 g)
Vanilla essence

Method: Line a flan ring with short pastry. Place the sliced apples and sugar. Beat eggs. Add to cream with sugar, spices and vanilla essence. Pour half of the custard in. Bake for 20 minutes at 400°F and then add rest of custard. Reduce heat to 360°F for another 20 minutes.

FLAN LORRAIN
Ground almond flan

Ingredients:

Flour 10 oz (300 g)
Sugar 3 oz (90 g)
3 beaten eggs
Milk 2 pint (1,200 mls)
Ground almonds 2 oz (60 g)
Orange peel 1 oz (30 g)
Rum 2 fl oz (60 mls)
Butter 2 oz (60 g)
Lard 2 oz (60 g)
Icing sugar
Assorted compote 8 oz (240 g)

Method: Mix flour and sugar in a bowl. Blend eggs with milk, add to flour mixture. Add almonds, orange peel, rum and melted butter. Beat mixture well. Grease a 2 inch x 8 inch mould. Fill with mixture and bake at 360°F for 40 minutes. Cool and sprinkle with icing sugar. Serve with fruit compote and custard.

GAUFRES FLAMANDE
Thick Belgian waffles made with yeast

Ingredients:

Yeast ½ oz (15 g)
Lukewarm water or milk 1¼ pint (900 mls)
4 beaten eggs
Flour 1 lb (480 g)
Pinch salt
Pinch sugar
Vanilla essence

Method: Crumble yeast into lukewarm milk or water. Add beaten eggs. Blend in flour and rest of ingredients. Beat this batter for 5 minutes and let it rise covered with a cloth for 40 minutes. Heat a waffle machine, well greased with lard, and cook waffles. When ready to serve dust with icing sugar.

CRAQUELINS PRALINES
Belgian buns with jam

Ingredients:

Yeast ½ oz (15 g)
Lukewarm milk ½ pint (300 mls)
2 eggs
Strong flour 1 lb (480 g)
Castor sugar 2 oz (60 g)
Butter 2 oz (60 g)

Filling:

Apricot jam 5 oz (150 g)
Chopped almonds 3 oz (90 g)
Icing sugar 6 oz (180 g)
2 egg whites
Few drops of almond essence

Method: Crumble yeast in milk. Dissolve castor sugar in beaten eggs and blend with flour and soft butter to a soft dough. Knead and gather into a ball. Cover with an upturned basin. Leave for 45 minutes. Knead again. Flatten. Roll up into a small loaf to fit an oblong tin, well greased with lard. Place the loaf inside. Allow to recover for another 30 minutes. Brush top with milk and bake for 35 minutes at 400°F. Cool and when cold cut in thick slices. Spread apricot jam. Make a royal icing by blending egg whites and icing sugar. Add chopped nuts and spread this icing on the slices. Place the slices on a greased tray and bake for 8 minutes at 380°F. Cool.

This delicious pastry is an excellent way to use up stale fruit loaves.

GÂTEAU DE VERVIERS OR CRAQUELINE
A yeast bun like a brioche with rum

Ingredients:

Yeast ½ oz (15 g)
Lukewarm milk ½ pint (300 mls)
2 beaten eggs
Butter 2 oz (60 g)
Castor sugar 2 oz (60 g)
Pinch salt
Flour 1 lb (480 g)
Coarsely crushed cube sugar or coffee crystal
   candies 4 oz (120 g)
Rum 5 fl oz (150 mls)

Method: Crumble yeast in lukewarm milk. Dissolve castor sugar in beaten eggs and blend with melted butter and flour. Knead to a soft dough. Gather into a ball and leave on the board covered with an upturned basin for 40 minutes. Knead again and shape into 2 oz buns. Place on a greased tray. Brush with milk and make a cross on top or slit with a sharp knife, scissors or razor blade and sprinkle with crystal lumpy sugar flavoured with rum. Allow to rest for 15 minutes and bake at 400°F for 15 minutes on a round, greased tin 9 inch diameter. The buns will stick to each other and form a round cake which can easily be separated into small buns again.

CHAUSSON MATHILDA OR GOZETTES
Apple and apricot puff pastry turnover

Ingredients:

Puff pastry 8 oz (240 g)

Filling:

Sliced apples 4 oz (120 g)
Sliced apricots 4 oz (120 g)
Pinch cinnamon
Castor sugar 3 oz (90 g)
1 egg

Method: Roll pastry ⅛ inch thick. Cut into 6 inch rounds. Place apple and apricot in the centre of each round. Sprinkle sugar and cinnamon. Wet edges with water. Seal and crimp edges tightly. Brush top with egg glaze and leave for 15 minutes. Bake at 400°F for 20 minutes.

CHAUSSON CHARLEROI
Almond cream turnover

Ingredients:

Puff pastry 8 oz (240 g)

Filling:

Butter 2 oz (60 g)
Castor sugar 2 oz (60 g)
1 beaten egg
Ground almonds 2 oz (60 g)
Flour 1 oz (30 g)
1–2 drops almond essence
Apricot jam 4 oz (120 g)
1 egg glaze

Method: Roll pastry $\frac{1}{8}$ inch thick to a diameter of 10 inch or as big as it will roll. Cream butter and sugar until fluffy. Add 1 beaten egg and ground almonds plus the flavouring. Spread jam in the middle of the round. Top up with almond mixture. Brush edges with water. Fold over and place on a greased tray. Brush with egg glaze. Leave for 15 minutes. Prick pastry on top and bake for 20 minutes at 400°F.

FLAMICHOU AUX POMMES ISABELLA
Baked pudding with apple (Conil's creation)

Ingredients:

1 egg
Flour 3 oz (90 g)
Milk 5 fl oz (150 mls)
Rum 2 fl oz (60 mls)
Salt
Sliced apples 8 oz (240 g)
Butter 2 oz (60 g)
Lard 2 oz (60 g)
Pinch cinnamon
Seedless raisins 2 oz (60 g)

Method: Prepare batter by blending beaten egg, milk, rum, flour and salt. Leave for 20 minutes. Toss sliced apples quickly in a pan with butter and lard—not to cook them but to brown them slightly. Place apples and raisins in a hot shallow dish, well greased with lard and butter, sprinkle with cinnamon. Pour the batter into the hot mixture and bake for 40 minutes at 360°F. Sprinkle with castor sugar and serve.

PUDDING FLAMAND OR PUDDING SAXON
Light souffle pudding with apricot sauce

Ingredients:

Water 7 fl oz (210 mls)
Margarine or butter 2 oz (60 g)
Pinch salt
Flour 4 oz (120 g)
4 egg yolks
4 egg whites
Few drops vanilla essence
Granulated sugar 4 oz (120 g)
Margarine for greasing moulds 2 oz (60 g)
Castor sugar to sprinkle inside moulds 2 oz (60 g)

Sauce:

Apricot jam 4 oz (120 g)
Water 5 fl oz (150 mls)
Sugar 4 oz (120 g)
Cornflour $\frac{1}{2}$ oz (15 g)
Cold water 5 fl oz (150 mls)
Kirsch 2 tbs

Method: Grease 8 small 5 oz dariole moulds with soft margarine (not melted) and sprinkle inside with castor sugar. Shake off surplus. Boil water to melt margarine. Add flour as for a choux pastry. Dry it well and remove from heat. Cool and add egg yolks, salt and 1 oz sugar. Beat egg whites to a meringue. Add 2 oz sugar gradually and beat between each addition. Fold meringue into egg yolk mixture carefully, but throroughly. Add flavour. Fill moulds two-thirds full. Place them into a tray half filled with hot water and bake in oven at 360°F for 20 minutes. Turn over on a dish and coat with an apricot sauce made as follows: Boil apricot jam with water and sugar and thicken with a slurry of cornflour and cold water. Cook for 5 minutes and strain. Add 2 tablespoons of Kirsch.

BEIGNETS SOUFFLÉS FLAMANDE
Light fritters made of choux pastry

These are also popular in Holland and all Flemish regions.

Ingredients:

Water 5 fl oz (150 mls)
Margarine 2½ oz (75 g)

Flour 5 oz (150 g)
4 eggs
Salt
Grated cheese 1 oz (30 g)
Castor sugar for dusting
Oil for frying

Method: Make a choux pastry by boiling the water
and margarine until it is melted. Add flour and
stir with a wooden spoon to obtain a stiff paste
which will not stick to the pan after being dried
up for a few minutes. Remove from heat. Add
beaten egg a little at a time while beating mixture.
The mixture should have a dropping consistency.
Add grated cheese and a pinch of salt and sugar.

Heat a kettle of oil at 360°F and take a
spoonful of mixture at a time. Drop it into the
kettle until the kettle is almost full but not too
packed to allow for expansion of fritters on frying.
Let them cook for 8 minutes. Drain on absorbent
paper and sprinkle with sugar.

PAIN À LA GRACHT
Almond sponge cake flavoured with Kirsch

Ingredients:

Ground almonds 8 oz (240 g)
Castor sugar 5 oz (150 g)
Butter 3 oz (90 g)
Cornflour 1 oz (30 g)
3 eggs
Few drops vanilla, rum and almond essence or
    Kirsch liqueur

Method: Mix ground almonds and sugar with
cornflour. Beat eggs. Cream butter. Add eggs and
blend the dry ingredients. Flavour with essences or
Kirsch liqueur. Beat mixture for 5 minutes. Grease
a 3 inch x 8 inch tin or a cake tin lined with
greaseproof paper as for a cake. Fill two-thirds full
and bake for 30–40 minutes at 360°F. Cool on a
rack and keep wrapped in foil. Alternatively, the
mixture can be baked in small cake moulds for 15
minutes.

ROMBOSSES OR RABOTTES DE POMMES
Baked apple in sweet short pastry

Ingredients:

4 medium-sized (3 inch diameter) apples 3 oz each
    (90 g)
Short sweet pastry 8 oz (240 g)
Brown sugar 2 oz (60 g)
Butter 4 oz (120 g)
Mixed spice 1 teaspoon

Short sweet pastry:

Butter 2 oz (60 g)
Lard 2 oz (60 g)
Icing sugar 2 oz (60 g)
1 egg
Flour 8 oz (240 g)

Method: Cream fat and sugar until fluffy. Add
beaten egg and blend with flour to obtain a firm
dough. Roll into a ball. Leave for 30 minutes
before using.

Peel the apples and core the centre. Roll pastry
$^1/_8$ inch thick. Cut into 4 squares. Place
each apple on the centre of the square. Cream
butter, sugar and spices and fill the cavity of the
apples with this mixture. Brush the side with
water and wrap the pastry round by folding corners
over and under. Cut 4 small squares to form a hat
and cover its folds. Brush pastry with egg glaze
and place 1 square on each apple. Bake at 380°F
for 20–25 minutes. Serve with rum flavoured
custard.
Note: A Rombosse is baked apples without the
pastry.

PISTOLETS
Milk stick bread roll with a cut in the centre

Ingredients:

Baker's yeast ½ oz (15 g)
Water and milk ½ pint (300 mls)
2 eggs
Flour 20 oz (600 g)
Butter 2 oz (60 g)
Salt ¼ oz (8 g)
Sugar ¼ oz (8 g)

Method: Crumble yeast in water and lukewarm
milk. Add beaten eggs. Warm flour for a few

minutes at 80°F. Blend liquid with salt and sugar and add flour. Knead well for 5 minutes. Gather paste to a ball. Scatter the butter on top. Cover with a large basin upside down. Leave to ferment for 50 minutes. Knead again and mix butter in the dough. Divide it into 1½ oz (45 g) balls. Shape the balls to an even round. Roll into sticks 4 inch long. Place on a greased tray. Brush with warm milk or water. Leave to prove for 20 minutes. With a sharp knife or razor blade make a split on top from one end to the other. Bake at 400°F for 15 minutes. Cool on racks. If rolls are required crisp, rebake for 5 minutes at 420°F. The crispness will be obtained between a period of rest between the two bakings as the rolls must be cooled before being rebaked the second time to allow steam to escape a little.

France

In France, as in many continental countries, the appreciation of food is a major national characteristic. You do not have to be rich to appreciate fine wines and tasty foods — you merely have to have an educated palate. This education starts at the family table where the best, freshest food is lovingly cooked with skill and imagination until it is brought to its zenith at the tables of some of the most creative chefs in the world. The French gastronome stops learning only with his last meal and perhaps not even then — for a heaven without food and wine is inconceivable to the Gallic spirit.

Frenchmen, rich or poor, all enjoy more or less the same food and drink and use similar criteria in assessing what goes in their mouths. Because they have an educated palate, consumers are always right and to perfect their standards and knowledge, they turn to the professional chef or Cordon Bleu. This seeking of gastronomic perfection, on the part of the ordinary man in the street as well as the specialist student of gastronomy, has given rise to a very high standard of cookery where superlative quality is a basic rule.

Not all musicians become composers, not all composers are venerated artists — but the few whose talent, experience and culture raise them above the crowd are soon given the supreme accolade. So it is with French chefs who have as an audience one of the most dedicated nations of gastronomes. When large numbers of this highly critical audience grants one the accolade, then we know the applause is for a Master Chef.

Creativity in cooking is not the mere juggling of words on a menu card or a transposition of garnishes from one dish to another. It is the orchestration of flavour, texture, colour and taste into a pleasing harmony where no note jars on the nerves. This creative instinct is inbred in all French cooks. The Frenchman is an individualist by temperament, an intellectual by argumentative passion and a sensualist by nature. This is the tripod which supports his basic philosophy — to enjoy life and to get out of all natural things the pleasure and satisfaction that the mind can absorb and the body can digest.

Gastronomy has been defined as the art and science of good eating. It is more than an appreciative science; it is also the study of food and its analysis. Its purpose is to educate the mind and the palate of the consumer in nutritional and hedonistic techniques and in quality assessment and evaluation. The true gastronome, then, is that person who, by native wit, cultural and educational influence, is best able to analyse the aesthetic and nutritional value of food and to prescribe methods and processes which will elicit the maximum satisfaction.

The French, of course, like the Italians and Persians, are a sensuous race who expect the table to provide pleasure. This spirit was engendered in the Middle Ages by the jolly monks, thankfully lacking those puritan hang-ups which have made life across the channel rather less rich in aesthetic pleasures. These men were the first to provide refreshment for travellers and their monasteries soon developed the air of pubs, never calling time. Trained in the crafts of food production from farming the land to preparing food for the table, the monks were the inheritors of ancient Roman recipes for making preserves, wines and liqueurs.

They used the Roman methods of farm husbandry, gathering herbs to make medicine and using liqueurs and potions distilled from mead, cider and wine.

The simple, but nourishing fare offered by the good fathers was typical of French food of the time. Gastronomy began to be raised to an art at the time of Louis XIII of France, at whose court a succession of Spanish and Italian cooks began to influence the then somewhat barbarous style of cookery. This influence was brought to the attention of the public by the satirical observations on the mores of the aristocracy of the literary masters Moliere, Racine, Corneille and Boileau.

War brings people together more than peace. In time of war, food shortages encourage man to seek and develop his own supply of nourishment. The lowly potato and sugar beet was fostered by Napoleon when he battled his way to Moscow, and his cooks learned the cuisine of his victims. Rum baba was more popular in France during his adventure with Countess Waleska of Poland. Spaghetti and macaroni became the craze of Paris when Napoleon's son became, on his birth, the King of Rome. Everyone ate caviar when the Emperor of Russia came to Paris to befriend Napoleon.

French chefs were in great demand in many countries of the world and while improving their own style of cooking, they often learned the national cuisine of their employers. They would refine, improve and embellish the local dishes and often incorporate the new creation into the professional repertoire. Thus, French cuisine became more encyclopaedic and international as time went on. With a wealth of ingredients to draw on and a multitude of cultures to inspire him, no Master Chef could fail to adorn his canvas with at least one 'Chef d'Oeuvre'.

Basically simple, French cuisine attained its supremacy through the liberal use of wines, spirits, herbs and spices, orchestrated upon the theme of top quality basic foods. The search for perfect produce has always been one of the cornerstones of French cuisine; even now the top chef will go to the market and stand side by side with the ordinary housewife, united in a quest for fresh, tasty ingredients.

French gastronomy reached its peak, historically speaking, during the reign of Victoria of England. Her son, Edward, was probably the most famous patron of gastronomy and many dishes were named after him, both by Escoffier and by Victoria's chef, Francatelli. On the other side of the channel, Napoleon III, unlike his uncle, had become renowned as host to fabulous banquets.

August Escoffier was the first master chef of the modern era to organise cookery and to classify it into an acceptable professional repertoire. He abolished the use of superfluous garnishes and ornaments and instead provided each meat or fish course with an appropriate, edible vegetable garnish. In France, Prosper Montagne, author of the *Larousse Gastronomique*, continued this simplification by reducing both the intricacy of garnishes and the number of courses in a meal to a more manageable — and democratic — four or five.

For myself, I took a different course. I could see that although the ideal was always the best of the freshest ingredients, the way the world is going it will be an increasing challenge to feed people well with the available resources. So my own prevailing interest has been food technology, and I have worked in some of the best equipped food laboratories in Europe. The challenge to the chef of tomorrow will be to nourish the multitudes while still satisfying the gastronome; and the exotic world of flavours will be the magic to change basic foodstuffs — whether based on seaweed, strange fish from the uncharted depths of the sea, or textured vegetable protein — into delicious foods. So I have worked with world-famous scientists on developing flavours to enhance whatever tomorrow may hold.

Fortunately, the world as I write still has good food a-plenty and nowhere is this more true than in my own beautiful France. Wheat, for instance, is produced to within 15 per cent of the annual consumption to make the bread which is the Frenchman's chief staple. To eat anything without bread in France is regarded as bad table etiquette. Why? Does the average French workman mop his plate to enjoy the gravy or just to balance the diet? Certainly the sapid sauces of French cookery should not be wasted since they contain the quintessence of the good ingredients in the dish.

French soil produces practically the full home requirement for man and beast in other cereals, root crops, fruits and nuts. In milk, butter and cheese, France is self-sufficient and exports many cheeses to all parts of the world, particularly to England. French flocks and herds are well stocked with many varieties of breed, including an important section of the horsemeat trade for human consumption. Sentiments aside, the horse is a much under-rated animal whose flesh is far superior to beef.

The wine production of France is legendary and vast quantities are imported from Algeria, Spain, Greece and Tunisia to supplement the home product and to blend with it. Brandies, liqueurs, beer and cider are all produced from home-grown raw materials in sufficient amounts for national consumption as well as a considerable export trade.

Gastronomically, France can be divided into five parts; the north eastern, north western, south western, south eastern and the Parisian centre including Ile de France, Orleans and Touraine.

North Western Region

1. Flemish Gastronomy

The chilly north of France is dominated by the Flemish style of food, with warming heavy meals, and lots of hot soups. It is too cold for the wine, so beer rather than wine is the local drink. Some of the main specialities are: *Moules Marinières*; *Moules a la Boulannaise* (mussels); *Le Hochepot*; *Le Lapin Aux Pruneaux* (rabbit with prunes); and *La Flamique* (leek flan). Popular sweets are: *Flan de Pommes au Lait*; *La Rabote* (small honey cakes and rich waffles). A typical garnish of the more solid foods is fruit used with a meat dish — so prunes, raisins, apples could be served with sausage products and black pudding is traditionally served with raisins or apple puree.

2. Picardy Gastronomy

This rich agricultural region is famed for the exquisite delicatessen *pâtés* and salamis produced by its talented *charcutiers*. The duck pie from Amiens is justly famous, as is the black pudding

soubise and almond macaroons from this region. *Le pot-au-feu Amienois* is one of those long, slow-simmered soups which titillate the nostrils cruelly for hours before they are ready — meat and vegetables slowly murmur in an old stone pot until their broth has developed a rare unctuousness. Then the lid is lifted and the steaming, bubbling liquid is ladled on to large slices of brown farm bread in a soup tureen, together with the tender meat and melting vegetables — a meal in itself. The cheeses of this region include a Camembert as fine as the Normandy version and the locally grown vegetables are hurried along in greenhouses to give Paris its first taste of spring with out-of-season *primeurs*.

3. Gastronomy of Normandy

Some of the most delicious *pâtés*, sausages and *andouilles* are made in the delicatessen towns of Vire, Lisieux and Caen. But without a doubt, the most popular dish of the region is the *Tripes a la mode de Caen*, a dish of much complexity and requiring to be made in large quantities to be at its best. Nowadays, it is usually bought from one of the excellent butchers of the region and heated up at home or in a restaurant. It consists of tripe and ox feet simmered for about twelve hours in cider and calvados, with a flavouring of carrots, onions and herbs. The lack of enthusiasm for tripe in Britain is a constant puzzle to the French, who recognise it as highly nutritious as well as a succulent dish.

A great number of fish are used in the dishes of Normandy, often recognisable by the liberal use of cream, in *Sole Dieppoise, Marmite Dieppoise* and *Sole Normande*. Other specialities include *Canard Rouennais* (duck, underdone and with the sauce made of the blood and liver of the bird, with port wine, foi gras and cream); *Poulet Vallee d'Auge* (chicken laced with Calvados); the Normandy applejack; larks, quails and pigeons go into pâtés and pies; apples and cream go with almost everything. The local butter is so rich that it needs little persuasion to turn itself into a sauce and some of the most delicate cheeses come from this region. They include *Camembert*, a soft, cylindrical cheese with a floury crust, which when ripe should be soft but not runny, its flavour decided but never strong. It comes in a 4½-inch round, about 1½ inches thick. *Pont l'Eveque* is some 4 inches square, 1¼ inches thick, with an ivory colour, soft and with a stronger flavour than a Camembert. *Livarot* is the most ancient of the Normandy cheeses, a soft paste with a brownish crust and a strong flavour. It comes in rounds of 5 inches, 1½ inches thick.

Le Gâteau Benedictin is a type of sponge cake with apples, flavoured with Benedictine liqueur and *les Sables de Caen* and *les Galettes du Vexin* are some of the sweets worth mentioning.

4. Gastronomy of Brittany

The seafoods of Britanny are its most wonderful contribution to gastronomy. The beautiful sardines, sole, mackerel, lobsters, crab, oysters, skate, whiting and turbot are done in a variety of ways which enhance, without disguising, the quality of the fresh ingredients.

Dishes of this region include the *Maquereaux de Quimper* (poached mackerel served with a sauce based on egg yolks, with butter and herbs); *Limande Bretonne* (plaice garnished with shrimps) and *Cotriade de Poisson* (a mixture of fish cooked with onions and potatoes). In the field of meat dishes, the most celebrated is undoubtedly the *Gigot Bretonne* (roast leg of lamb served with haricot beans in a sauce of tomatoes and onions). *La Bardatte* is another local meat dish and of the sweet dishes, the best are *les Crepes de Sarrasin* (a rye pancake); *le Far Breton* (a flan) and *les Beignets de Mam-Goz* (fritters). Britanny produces excellent white wines of which Muscadet is the best known. Cider is produced locally and drunk in large quantities. *Elixir de Bretagne* and *Benedictine* are the two best known liqueurs of this region.

5. Gastronomy of Anjou

The Loire region is known for its wines and its castles, rather than for its food. But excellent delicatessen products are made here and every *charcuterie* window has its mountain of *rillettes*, a soft, melting kind of potted pork, and *rillons*, its close relative but with larger pieces of pork. *Les Gogues* is a black pudding with herbs and a popular dish is a chicken fricassee in cream sauce.

Shad, a much-maligned fish, is not nearly as bony as it is reputed to be and is served stuffed or with a sorrell sauce. The *Matelote Angevine* is a stew of eels in a rich, wine sauce.

The wines are simply superb. Among the well-known ones are Rosé d'Anjou, known as Cabernet-Franc, Sancerre, Saumur, Pineau de la Loire, Pouilly Fumé and the soft Vouvray.

6. Poitou and Vendée Gastronomy

In the Vendée region where I was born, there are some excellent specialities which are not well known abroad. The local oysters and seafood dishes are superb and there is a local *pate Vendeen* which is made with pork and rabbit. *Les Moujettes à la creme* is a dish of beans in cream sauce, and stuffed turkey and hake with mushrooms are other delights. The sweets of the region include the *Nougatines de Poitiers, Macarons de Lusigna* and *Le Tourteau Fromage*.

Wines produced here are Foye-Montjault, Mareuil, Thourcais, and many which are not exported and best drunk locally, such as the wines of Auzay, Rosnay, Gard and Sigournais. The best known wine of this region is the Pineau de la Loire, a rather sweet aperitif wine, and the Cabernet-Franc.

7. Gastronomy of the Charente

This is a rich wine region with the best brandies in the world. Here are produced the four internationally acclaimed brandies: Grande Fine Champagne and Fine Champagne; La Grande Champagne and La Petite Champagne all produce excellent brandy. To enjoy the taste of a good brandy to the full, the connoisseur first warms the glass in his hand, sniffing the fumes to savour the aroma, then sipping small mouthfuls allowing the liquid to linger on the tongue before swallowing it.

One of the best known products of the Charente is the truffle, a variety of parasitic mushroom which grows on the roots of oaks. The best variety is black, with a rough skin and a penetrating aroma — a small piece can flavour an entire pâté.

South-Western Region

8. Bordeaux Gastronomy

Bordeaux is the gastronomic centre of the south of France and it competes favourably with Burgundian cooking in claiming some of the finest dishes of the French repertoire. Obviously, they are cooked in the superb claret which comes from this region and include mussels, chicken and steak all done '*à la Bordelaise*'. For the sweet tooth, the *Gateau des Rois* of Bordeaux, a *brioche* type of cake is in great demand. But the real interest to the hedonist in this region is the amazing quality of the wine, with five 'Grands Premiers Crus' and one hundred and twenty 'Crus Classes'. The five top wines are Château Yquem (white and sweet) and Château Lafite, Château La Tour, Château Margaux and Château Haut-Brion, all red.

9. Gastronomy of La Gascogne

This region is rich in fish, game, light wines and dishes well flavoured with garlic. It also produces Armagnac, a spirit with a similar appeal to Cognac. The specialities are the black puddings, liver cooked with raisins, and river fish such as shad. The best dishes are *Poule au Pot Henri IV, Ortolan Landaise, Tourterelles Cante-Cante* (wild wood doves) and *Pain à la Gondrin* (ham pie made with bread dough). For desserts, the *Pastis Landais* (pastry flavoured with orange liqueur), and *Millas des Landes* (corn pudding) are worth trying.

10. Gastronomy of the Basque and Bearn

Garlic, tomatoes and red peppers reign in this part of France and loudly proclaim the Spanish influence. Goose fat and pieces of preserved goose are used in all manner of dishes and there are spiced little sausages, rather like the Spanish *chorizos*. The locally cured smoked ham is excellent, as are the pies, pâtés and salamis made in this region. Dishes worth trying in these parts include *Ttorro*, a kind of fish stew, *Paella*, very like the Spanish dish, *Salmis de Palombe*, a kind of game bird pate, and *Chipirones con su tinta,* baby octopus in its own ink. There is also *Morue a la Vizcaina* (salted cod fish), *Piperade* (a scrambled egg mixture with peppers, onions, smoked ham and tomatoes), *Poulet a la Basquaise* and a rich vegetable soup known as *garbure*. Beef is stewed in wine with garlic and onions in a closed pot in the

delicious dish known as *estoufat*.

The *Gâteau Basque* is a sweet delicacy.

11. Gastronomy of Roussillon and Comte de Foix

This is the region of delicious liver pâtés and *saucissons*. Among local specialities are *civet de langouste* (crawfish in red wine), *ouillade* (baked beans and vegetables), *Bouillinada du Barcares* (a fish soup or stew) and *Feuilleté de Collioure* (pastry filled with eggs and anchovies). A sweet wine known as *Banyuls* is drunk as an aperitif.

12. Languedoc Gastronomy

Two of the best dishes of French provincial cookery come from this area. The *cassoulet*, a rich savoury stew of haricot beans with preserved goose, pork, mutton, sausage, garlic and herbs, baked for many hours in a special pot. After the best part of a day in the oven, the cassoulet emerges with a light brown crust which parts to reveal an appetising mixture of beans which have taken on the savoury aroma of the meats. The other tasty Languedoc dish is the *brandade de morue*, a cream made of flaked salt cod with warm milk and a little olive oil and garlic, served with crisp triangles of fried bread.

The largest town in this area is Toulouse, the Paris of the South, which has always had an excellent standard of cuisine and has enriched the professional repertoire with many local specialities. Two of the most famous chefs also come from this region, Joseph Durand, who published his book *Le Cuisinier Durand* in 1830 and Prosper Montagne, compiler and editor of the *Larousse Gastronomique*.

Languedoc specialities include *saupiquets* (chopped liver with garlic and herbs) and *sanguete* (a black pudding pancake made from chicken blood). Garlic is widely used in the cuisine of the Languedoc and a bread crust rubbed with a clove of garlic is buried deep in the local salads to give an elusive aroma.

For dessert, there is the *Croustadine Languedocienne* (a type of almond tart).

The red wines of Corbieres are light and *Frontignan* is a sweet fortified wine drunk as an aperitif.

13. Perigord Gastronomy

This is the region which produced truffles, the 'Black Diamond of Haute Cuisine' along with Quercy and Rouergue; the most luxurious dishes of the region are therefore studded with this aromatic fungus. Specialities of the region are *la brioche de foie gras, la truffe sous la cendre, le mourtairol* (saffron soup), *fois gras a la Quercynoise* and *alicot* (a stew of duck with beans). The sauce known as *Perigueux* is a wine sauce flavoured with truffles and carp is stuffed with foie gras for a festive dish. The most interesting dish of the region is *poulet sauce rouilleuse* (very peppery) and *Lievre à la Royale* is a hare stuffed and cooked in wine. Even potatoes get the truffle treatment in that delicious dish, *pommes sarladaises*, in which they are thinly sliced and layered with truffles.

Rasimat, a type of jam made with grapes, is often served as dessert. The world-famous Roquefort cheese comes from this region.

A sweet aperitif wine, Monbazillac, is produced from over-ripe grapes which have dried to a state known as *pourriture noble*; although *pourriture* means rot or mould, the grapes are by no means rotten. They are merely sun-dried and have more sugar content and less moisture.

North-Eastern Regions

14. Champagne Gastronomy

This area produces 120 million bottles a year, on average, of that most luxurious and festive wine which bears its name. Invented by a monk, Dom Perignon, champagne is to drink what caviar is to food. Although most champagne drunk is white, it is produced from red grapes grown in a strictly delineated area around Reims and Epernay. It is roughly divided into four regions: la Montagne de Reims, la valée de la Marne, la Côte des Blancs and La Region de L'Aube. It comes as no surprise to find that many of the most famous local dishes are cooked · in champagne. Carp, eel, trout, veal, chicken and kidneys all come in for this royal treatment in the specialities of the region. Equally good are the delicatessen products such as chitterling sausages, *boudin blanc* (chicken sausage) and *jambonneau de Reims en croute* (ham in pastry),

as well as hare pie, snipe pâté and quails wrapped in pastry. The best of the local cheeses is probably *Brie* followed by *Coulomiers, Maroille* and creamed cheese with herbs.

Meringues, *nougat, gougères* (a type of choux pastry) and *pain d'epices* (gingerbread) are famous.

15. Gastronomy of Alsace and Lorraine

Politically speaking, these regions are provinces of France. But gastronomically, they are German, so it must be vexing for the French to have to admit that the standard of cuisine is one of the highest in France (and Germany) and of course both countries claim the credit for the excellent fare. The quality of the local dishes has a great deal to do with the high standard of fresh produce available. Alsace produces thirty-three varieties of apples, twenty-seven of pears, thirty-six of peaches, twenty-nine of apricots and one hundred and thirty crus of wine. From the river Rhine there is an abundance of fish and the surrounding forests yield game, such as hare, deer, pheasant, quail, partridge and wild duck.

Pate de foie gras (goose liver) is made in this area and was invented here by Chef Close in 1762, although historians claim that versions of this pâté have been known since the Romans. Besides the precious *foie gras*, the delicatessens of this area produce *salamis, pâtés, terrines, galantines* of all kinds. German types of soup made with beer, green wheat and hops are also popular. There are also soups made with frogs and a wonderful crayfish bisque.

The favourite dish of the region is the *choucroute garnie*, a dish of sauerkraut with ham, frankfurters, garlic salami, salted belly of pork and potatoes. Sauerkraut is also served as an accompaniment to other dishes, often flavoured with Kirsch. Alsace also produces two excellent cheeses: *Munster*, flavoured with caraway seed and *Romatour*.

The gastronomy of Lorraine is more French in style. It has been claimed that the *baba au rhum* and puff pastry were invented in Nancy, although the first was made in Poland two centuries before, and Greek baklava puff pastry was made several centuries before. It would probably be more correct to say that these two classic items were improved in Nancy. *Quiche Lorraine* is the best known dish of this region and its crispness contrasted with a creamy filling of bacon, eggs and cream must have graced countless dinner tables in Britain. Other specialities carrying the name of the region are a *potée* – a soup – a pancake and a pâté of veal and pork.

Stone fruits abound in this area and from them are made some exciting liqueurs and spirits. *Kirsch, Mirabelle, Framboise* and Apricot Brandy are justly famous. The wines of Alsace include Traminer and Gewurztraminer, Tokay, Riesling, Sylvaner and Edelzwicker, all white. The reds include Turkheim, Bergheim, Hunawihr, Roderer and Marlenheim.

16. *Gastronomy of Bresse and the France-Comté*

The birthplace of Brillat-Savarin lies in this area at Belley in the south-east corner of the Bugey district. His reputation has given the local food a sort of halo. Most famous is the fattened chicken of Bresse, acclaimed as the most tender and succulent in all France. High quality raw materials simply cooked are perhaps the keynote of this area and the local crayfish presented as *ecrevisses à la nage* or a *gratin d'écrevisses Nantua* are worth trying. Other famous Bresse dishes are the *poulet de Bugey, quenelles de brochet Nantua* (pike dumplings) and *Tarte au fromage* (cheese tart).

The wines of Bugey are high in alcohol (13 per cent); the most popular are rosés, which include Cerdon, Virieu, Montagnieu and Charveyron.

The Franche-Comté region has many dishes made with the local cheese, *gruyere*, such as a rich cheese soup. *Gaudes* is a bacon soup with corn – a tasty combination. *Poulet à la diable* (chicken with a very peppery sauce with mustard); *timbale de morilles et poulet* (a tasty mushroom dish with chicken) and *les grives à l'Arboisienne* (thrush cooked with grapes) are delicious local specialities.

The Jura and the Franche-Comté are the only regions in France which produce five distinct types of wine: white, yellow, rosé, red and straw-coloured. Best known are Château-Châlon, Pupillon, Ménétru, Lavigny and Arbois.

17. *Burgundy Gastronomy*

The brilliant wines and excellent food of this region make it every Frenchman's idea of paradise. The cuisine of Burgundy is recognised as the finest in all France and, in truth, it is the very essence of what is great in French cuisine. The ingredients are of the highest quality, cooked to perfection and served with those aromatic wine-dark sauces which have been gently reduced to make them unctuous, flavourful and intense. Most often there is a garnish of diced bacon, button mushrooms and tiny glazed onions with these dishes cooked in the Burgundian manner.

Where the local wines have not been used in the cooking, the dish is often made to complement them. Many of the local specialities use cheese as the perfect complement to wine and the *gougère* is a delicious example of this. It is a rich cheese pastry, made with choux paste studded with tiny cubes of gruyere, and goes well with the first glass of wine at dinner as well as with the last as a savoury. Other specialities include a *potée bourguignonne*, a salt beef, bacon and vegetable soup; the famous *coq au chambertin*; steak *Morvandiau*; *Râble de Lièvre Piron* and the delicious local version of potted ham in wine, *le jambon persillé de Bourgogne*. The little snails which crawl and feed on the vines are especially delicious prepared in rich garlic butter, although sadly now many snails served in French restaurants are in fact expatriates from Eastern Europe. Pigeon can be cooked *au Chambertin* in a similar way to the *coq au vin* and *poulet à l'estragon* is also popular.

The wines of Burgundy may be roughly divided into three regions: Bourgogne, Haute Bourgogne and Basse Bourgogne. In Bourgogne, the best wines include Mercurey, Givry, Macon, the white wines of Pouilly and Fuissé and the red Moulin-à-Vent. Basse-Bourgogne produces Chablis, Fley, Milly and Lignorel – all white – and Boivin, Vermenton, Migraine and Chainette are excellent reds. There is also a wonderful rosé, produced in Annay. Haute Bourgogne may be further divided into the three major areas: Côtes Dijonnaise, Côtes de Nuits and Côtes de Beaune. Among the best Cotes de Nuits wines are Chambertin, Clos de Bège, Clos de Tart, Bonnes-Mares, Clos de la roche, Musigny and Clos de Lambrays. White Musigny and Clos de Vougeot are also remarkable. Other famous wines of this region are the Romanée,

Romanée Saint-Vivant, La Tache and the Richebourg: Nuits Saint Georges, Nuits Vaucrains, Nuits-Cailles, Nuits-Porrets and Nuits Pruliers. Côtes de Beaune wines of distinction are Corton, Clos du Roi, Château de Grancey, Bressandes and the white Corton Charlemagne. There are also the red Pommard, Monthelie, Volnay, Chassagne and Montrachet. Meursault comes as a red and a white, although the white is better known.

South-Eastern Region

18. Provençal Gastronomy

Spicy, full-flavoured and brightly coloured, Provençal cuisine has a swinging southern charm. Olive oil, tomato, onion, garlic and all the herbs which grow on the sun-baked hillsides: basil, oregano, thyme and rosemary mingle happily to produce the most aromatic dishes in all France. The Mediterranean coastline yields no less than forty-five types of fish which land on the kitchen table to make the many seafood specialities. Of these, the *Bouillabaisse* is perhaps the most famous, in which many types of fish, mussels, crab and lobster are cooked at a rolling boil which amalgamates olive oil and water with the juices of the fish into a glutinous broth, flavoured with garlic, saffron, onions and tomatoes and served with slices of bread.

Boeuf Provençal, true to its name, is a rich stew in which onions, garlic and tomatoes add their special flavours. Sometimes the garlic of Provençal is over-done but it is a good therapeutic and a germ killer so nobody cares. The use of garlic in Provençal cuisine is brought to a zenith in *aioli*, also called 'the butter of Provence'. It is simply a mayonnaise, highly flavoured with garlic, served with as varied an assortment as possible of plainly boiled vegetables, white fish and cold meats. Nobody will speak to you for days, but it is worth it.

Other specialities of the region include a *daube* (stew) of mutton, *Caillettes de foies pugetoise, fassum* (stuffed cabbage), stuffed tomatoes and stuffed onions — stuffed vegetables of all kinds are everywhere. Rabbit is served Provençal style and there is a famous pâté made of larks. Garlic also comes into its own as *aigo* soup, based almost entirely on garlic and *bourride*, a fish soup potently flavoured with the aromatic bulb. There is a *moussaka Provençal*, a *pissaladiera*, like an Italian pizza but tastier and *anchoiade*, a paste of anchovies and garlic with olive oil served on a slice of toasted bread and finished in the oven. Delicious with a glass of wine.

A unique Mediterranean fish called *le Loup*, sometimes translated as sea-bass or sea-perch, is served grilled on a bed of fennel stalks to impart the special aroma. The best-travelled dish of this region is probably the *Salade Niçoise*, with anchovies and black olives, french beans and tomatoes.

Cheese of the region include those made of goat's milk and ewe's milk: *Tomme de Banon, Tomme de Brousses, Tomme d'Annot* and the *Banon Poivre d'Ane.*

For the sweet tooth, there are the many candied and *pralinées* flowers of Grasse, the candied fruits of Aix and many sweets made of almonds. Pastries include *fougassettes* and *echaudés*, as well as many types of *petits fours*.

The wines of Provence include some sweet rosés, notably Tavel. The Papal red wine, Chateau-Neuf du Pape, comes from this region and white wines of distinction are Cassis-sur-mer and Clairette de Lerins. La Ciotat is a sweet wine of the muscatel type. Near the coast, the Côteau de Vence is another type of rosé.

Corsica may be included in this gastronomic region for its Italian influence. Specialities on this island are *Pibronata* (tomato sauce with peppers), *misciscia* (goat fillet), *Lonzo* (smoked fillet of pork), *prizuttu* (smoked ham), *crawfish Corsicane* (with red peppers), *copa* (pork) and *Danizze* (corn and chestnut cakes or tarts).

The wines of Corsica are especially potent, notably red table wines such as Bocca-di-Valle, Figuri, Fiumorbo, Vico, Casinca and Coggia.

19. Dauphine Gastronomy

This is the region where cream, eggs and cheese mingle happily in a wide variety of gratin dishes. Stuffed pancakes, *cervelas* (a type of sausage) and pike are typical first courses of this area and *ris de veau Dauphinoise* is a wonderful way of preparing sweetbreads. Tripes are served in tomato sauce, chicken is served *en vessie* (cooked in skin) and there is a *caneton Dauphine* (duck dish) and *estouffade de sanglier* (boar stew).

For desserts, try the *pain brioche aux pommes* or the *potiron*. Montelimar produces a world-famous nougat.

20.   Gastronomy of Savoy

The Savoy is a region of hunting, so game is high on the list of local dishes. Chamois, partridge, hare and wild rabbit and many small birds such as ortolans, thrush, quail are often on the menu. A great variety of wild mushrooms are picked in the forests and fields and from the milk of the fat cattle and the herd of goats is produced some of France's finest cheeses of which *Roblochon* is the most appreciated for its strong but pleasant flavour.

Cream and eggs play an important part in the cooking of many dairy products. Heading the list is the *Fondue Savoyarde*, a melted cheese paste eaten with diced bread as a snack; *Gratin Savoyarde*, baked sliced potato with cream and cheese; *Potée Savoyarde*, a rich soup of bacon, smoked sausages and cabbage with cheese and sippets of bread. The main dishes are *Civet de porc*, a robust stew made with red wine and thickened with blood in the same style as French jugged hare.

Brillat-Savarin used to have an orgasm every time he ate *Foie de lotte*, the liver of lotte (a fish found in the lake Bourget). But other fish like *Truite au bleu* (trout cooked in stock) and other similar fish make up for the lack of seafood specialities.

In the sweet line, my favourite is *Farçon* (a sort of potato cake) and the *Brioche Saint Denis*, flavoured with pralines and local liqueur. The most celebrated cake is the Savoy sponge, delicately flavoured with vanilla pods.

Beer and cider are brewed locally and equally enjoyed with the wines of the region. The sparkling red wine of *Aise* is drunk on festive occasions. Vermouth Chambery is the daily aperitif and with the liqueur *la Lie*, a potent white spirit, is enjoyed with coffee. The wine of *Montmelian* is as pleasant as the Beaujolais but the best wines in Savoie are *Digny, les Roussettes, Frangy* and *Seyssel* — some dry, others sweet. *Crepy* is another sparkling wine

and *Altesses* is a wine with a violet aroma. The very best and rarest is *Malvoisie de Lasseraz*, whose vines were originally imported from Cyprus. The best red wines are *Princens* and *Arbin*, with a faint raspberry aroma and a high alcoholic content.

Although Savoy was annexed by France in 1792, it has kept its original gastronomic culture which, in many respects, is similar to Switzerland, its neighbouring country, sharing a lake full of delicious fish and a climate as healthy as the Himalayas.

21.   Gastronomy of Lyons

After Paris, Lyons is the principal gastronomic centre of France. Its food fairs attract tourists from all over the world. Every Frenchman daily samples the *Saucisson de Lyons* with its stick of bread, almost as a pagan ritual, symbolic of potency and *'joie de vivre'!* The list of Lyons specialities is qualified as *Lyonnaise*. The adjective agrees with the French feminine word *'mode'* (style of) and not with the food in question, thus *Tripes à la Lyonnaise* describes the style of cooking in red wine and not the gender of tripes. *Boeuf en daube au Beaujolais* is braised beef cooked in wine and the lightest dumplings in the whole culinary repertory. *Les Quenelles Lyonnaise*, a paste made from pike with fat, cream and whites of eggs and served with a delicious crayfish sauce, has been one of the greatest and most difficult dishes to prepare to perfection. *Les Grenouilles sautées*, frogs' legs in butter, are not everybody's cup of tea, but it has enthusiasts who would sell their soul for such a dish. Every restaurant in Lyons features the *Poularde demi-deuil*, chicken in mourning, because of the slices of black truffles inserted between the skin and flesh. This symbolic name need not depress people in spite of its funeral title; it is another glorious dish which has won acclaim.

Unusual vegetables such as *Cardons au jus*, a sort of stem from a thistle plant, like celery but tougher. Cooked salami in brioche pastry by the name of *Cervelas truffé en brioche*, is a popular hot hors d'oeuvre.

In the confectionery desserts, we note *Marrons glacés* (candied chestnuts) and candied fruit paste which are packed in attractive boxes and exported all over the world.

Interesting wines such as *Fleurie, Brouilly* and *Côte-Rôtie* were mentioned by the Romans, Pliny and Martial, centuries ago. The best white wines are from *Condrieu* but I particularly recommend Chateau-Grillet for its aggressive taste and its youngish freshness.

22. Auvergne Gastronomy

Two products stand out in the realm of cookery in this part of France: the excellent ham, as good as that of the Ardenne, and the local cheese known as *Cantal*. The cooking of the Auvergne is robust, hearty country cooking which one would expect from such hospitable people. Among local specialities are: *Mourtayrol* (hot pot soup with saffron), *Potée Auvergnate* (soup made of salted belly of pork with cabbage and sausages), *Cousinat* (chestnut soup), *Quenelle of pike*, frog's legs, *Gigot Brayaude* (ham with cabbage and beans), stuffed cabbage, potato cakes and a souffle of chard leaves. Besides the *Cantal*, notable cheeses are the *Bleu d'Auvergne* and the *St Nectaire*, a semi-soft cheese.

The sweet course might offer such delights as *bourriols bougnettes* (fritters), *pascades, a flaugnarde* (flan), *fouass* (brioche) and *milliard de cerises* (cherries cooked in batter).

The wines of Auvergne are not very well known abroad but are quite delightful just the same. Chanturgues, red or white, Dallet, Sauvagnat, Lavalle and Saint Flour. Best wines are Coteaux d'Entraygues, Ribeyron, Louchy, Saulcet and the dry white wine known as Saint Pourcain.

23. Ile de France – Paris – Gastronomy

This is Paris, the world capital of gastronomy, where each chef attempts to outdo his competitor in friendly but fierce competition. Every Master Chef knows that he will make his mark on gastronomy only if he can create several specialities of his own, and the sum of all these concoctions has produced a fantastic repertoire of dishes for all tastes.

My own father had a restaurant in Paris called 'Ducastaing' and when I started to help him he used to send me working for the competition to find out what they were up to. I ate my way around Paris – heaven for a growing boy – and developed a sure touch in analysing the herbs and spices which other restaurateurs were using in their creations. This analytical palate has stood me in good stead when I have developed new ways of creating classic sauces for the manufacturers of modern foods.

My father's restaurant was the haunt of some of the great names in the arts and in the theatre – uninhibited, bohemian people who were quite shocking by the standards of those days. After weeks spent helping in the kitchen, my father eventually decided that I was presentable and knowledgeable enough to make my first public appearance at a big dinner. I was to bring in the main set piece, a gigantic *Gateau St Honoré* on a cloud of spun sugar as the last course. In the meantime one of the most famous actresses in all Paris had imbibed too freely of the gift of Bacchus, and had been egged on by the assembled company to do an impromptu dance. When I entered the banquet, shy, young and terrified, I was met by the sight of Mimi, totally naked, dancing on the table directly in front of my innocent eyes. Quite overcome, I tripped and went sprawling with my magnificent cake, most of which landed upon the gyrating Mimi. After that first experience in the restaurant business, I figured that things could only improve – and so started my forty-five years in the vocation I love above all else.

Dishes garnished as elaborately as that memorable Gateau St Honoré are no longer fashionable, but the essence of good Parisian cuisine is simplicity and sauces which are neither too rich, nor watery nor heavily seasoned. The best sauces in the classic repertoire are *Bercy, Normande, Parisienne, Régence, Madère, Périgueux, Diane, Poivrade* and *Poulette*. The classic soups of Paris are the *Petite Marmite, soupe à l'Oignon* (onion), *soupe à l'oseille* (sorrel), *crème Saint Germain* (peas), *potage Parisien* (potatoes and leeks) and the *bisque de Homard* (lobster). Egg dishes are popular, and the *oeuf benedictine* (egg on pieces of fish with hollandaise sauce and truffle), *omelette aux morriles* (morel) and *oeuf en cocotte a la creme* are delicious and light.

Fish dishes include sole in all its forms such

as Dieppoise and Normande, *turbot soufflé de Boulogne* (stuffed turbot with very light fish paste in wine sauce); *Homard à l'Americaine* (lobster in tomato and wine sauce with brandy); *Civet de langouste au Chambertin* (crawfish stew); *gratin d'écrevisses Nantua* (crayfish in sauce); *filet de sole Bercy* (cooked in Bercy wine and herbs); *coquilles St Jacques Parisienne* (scollops in mushroom sauce); *mousseline de saumon* (light salmon (mixture); *sole au Vermouth*; *truite en chemise* (trout wrapped in pancake with butter sauce); *homard Thermidor* (split lobster with cheese and mustard sauce and herbs); and *langouste Parisienne* (crawfish salad with mayonnaise).

Poultry dishes of distinction are *Canard à l'Orange*; *pintade Royale* (guinea fowl); *poulet au Champagne*; and *coq au vin* (chicken in wine).

Classic entrees are *cervelle au beurre noire* (brains in black butter); *blanquette de veau* (veal stew); *steak au poivre* (pepper sauce); *filet de boeuf Lucullus* (beef fillet with rich brandy sauce); *tournedos rossini* (fillet of beef with goose liver); *ris de veau Princesse* (sweetbreads); and *rognons flambés au vin blanc et moutarde* (kidneys in white wine and mustard).

Favourite vegetables include *champignons sous cloche* (mushrooms in cream sauce with brandy), *artichauts Barigoule* (globe artichokes), *Epinards Viroflay* (spinach), *Salsifis beurre noisette* (oysterplant fried in butter), *gâteau de courge au fromage* (marrow pie with cheese), *courgettes à la creme* (baby marrows with cream sauce), *petits pois à la Française* (peas cooked with butter, onions and shredded lettuce); and *laitues braisées au jus* (braised lettuce).

Sweets which have become Parisian classics with an international reputation include the *Charlotte Parisienne* (scones with cream custard), *Souffle au Grand Marnier* (one of France's most celebrated custard sweets which is as light as a feather), *crèpes Suzette* (pancake flans in brandy and orange liqueurs), *Abricot Condé* (apricots and creamed rice), *Gâteau Moka* (buttercream spongecake), *Poire Hélène* (ice cream with pears and chocolate sauce) and *Pêche Melba* (fresh puree of raspberries, ice cream and peaches). And, of course, my personal favourite, *Gateau St Honoré* (custard gateau topped with little choux stuffed with cream).

24. *The Gastronomy or Orleans and Touraine*

Some French gastronomes describe the cooking of this region as honest and careful. *Tourangelle* cuisine produces light and delicate sauces with the ingredients carefully balanced — no harsh note shocks the tastebuds in this area. The *rillettes* (soft potted pork) and chitterling sausages are wonderful starters, to be followed by the excellent local fish from the Loire: bass and shad are most appreciated. The local *matelotes* (fish stews) are made with the soft Vouvray wine. Meat dishes include a *daube de beouf au vin de Chinon* (beef stew on the delicate Chinon wine), *epaule d'agneau farcie* (stuffed shoulder of lamb), *epigrammes d'agneau de Valencay* (breast and cutlets of lamb braised and grilled in breadcrumbs) and a *gigot de chèvre* (goat's leg). Vegetables are *cardons de Tours au gratin* (cardoon with ham) and stuffed artichokes. Poultry and game includes a delicious fricassée of chicken with white wine, a hare stew *au Bourgueil* and a *gibelote de lapin* (rabbit stew). There is a wide variety of delicious goat's milk cheeses, and there are local variations on the theme of almond cakes, called *Le Fromente*, and a *brioche gâteau*.

Wine is the life blood of French cookery. I learned this fundamental principle when I first trod the grapes in my uncle's vineyards. I acquired my knowledge of biochemistry in making wines by the barrel. Eventually I soon mastered the art of distillation and liquor blending, using herbs and spices in the same manner as the perfumer takes care in selecting his essences for that elusive scent which attracts the sophisticated customer. Without Grand Marnier the *soufflé* would be a mere custard and the *Crepe flambées* a soggy mess in a syrupy sauce. A *coq au vin* would lose its succulence and a *sole bonne-femme* its feminine appeal. As I demonstrated my art to live audiences while touring the country I modestly pointed out, while pouring wine lavishly into my sauce, 'one glass for the pot and two for the Chef, and the spirit never falters when the wine is worth drinking'.

BILL OF FARE

Soup

SOUPE À L'OIGNON AU MADÈRE
Onion soup with Madeira, wine and cheese

LA MOULARDE
Creamy mussel soup

LA CITROUILLETTE
Pumpkin and bacon soup

LA COTRIADE BOULONNAISE
Mixed fish soup

Hors d'Oeuvres

LE PÂTÉ MAITRE-JEAN
Liver pâté blended with chicken and pork in
    port wine

Hot Hors d'Oeuvre or Light Entrees

PETIT PÂTÉ EN CROUTE
Individual pâté in pastry

**LES ESCARGOTS DE BOURGOGNE AU
    PERNOD**
Snails in Pernod butter

LA QUICHE AUX FRUITS DE MER
Small flan filled with seafood mixture

**CHAUSSON DE CRABE COMTE DE
    BOULOGNE**
Crab and mushroom filling in a pastry turnover

Fish Entrées

**LANGOUSTE AU GRATIN GRANDE-
    CHARTREUSE**
Crawfish stuffed with vegetables and flavoured
    with Grand Chartreuse

SUPREME DE TURBOT BOULONNAISE
Baked turbot cooked in white wine with herbs
    and mushrooms

**TURBAN DE COLIN CASINO DE BOULOGNE
    À LA CONIL**
A crown-moulded hake dish with prawn, mussel
    and mushroom filling

Crustaceans

LE HOMARD AU PERNOD À LA CONIL
Lobster in cream sauce flavoured with Pernod

**LES FILLETS DE SOLE AUX FRUITS DE LA
    VIGNE**
Sole fillets cooked in wine sauce

**QUENELLES DE SAUMON DE LA LOIRE
    DUC D'ORLEANS**
Minced salmon dumplings in Loire wine sauce

Meat Dishes

MIGNONETTES D'AGNEAU POIVRADE
Loin steak of lamb with a peppercorn sauce

ROGNONS DE VEAU MONTPARNASSE
Calf's kidney in white wine

RIS DE VEAU LUCULLUS
Sweetbread in savoury sauce with olives and
    mushrooms

**ESCALOPE DE VEAU CYRANO DE
    BERGERAC**
Veal escalope and liver in cheese sauce

PAILLARD DE VEAU EN PAPILLOTTE
Veal steal with mushrooms and sweetcorn
    pancakes, baked in a paper casing

Poultry and Game

POULET SAUTÉ AU MÉDOC
Chicken in wine sauce with button onions, carrots,
    celery and buttered beans

**CANARD À L'ORANGE AU GRAND
    MARNIER**
Roast duck with a delicious demi-glace sauce
    flavoured with Grand Marnier

LE PINTADEAU SANS RIVAL
Pot roast guinea fowl served with shell pasta in a
    light creamy sauce flavoured with dry
    Madeira wine

PERDREAU BELLE-FLEUR
Partridge pot roasted on a bed of aromatic
    vegetables with a garnish of stuffed prunes

L'OISON AUX POIRES ET MARRONS
Goose pot roasted and served with a rich mushroom
 sauce with a garnish of cooking pears in red
 wine and chestnut stuffing

Vegetables

LES CHAMPIGNONS SOUS CLOCHE
Creamy mushrooms served in a bell dish

LES COURGETTES MATHILDA
A mixture of baby marrows and mushrooms in
 tomato sauce

LE GRATIN PARISIEN
Sliced potato cake baked in oven with ham and
 cream

SOUFFLÉ D'ÉPINARD JEANNE D'ARC
Spinach and egg and cheese souffle, baked in oven

LA SALADE DE GRAND-MÈRE MATHILDA
Dandelion, spinach, curly lettuce in Roquefort
 dressing

LA SALADE DU PÈRE CONIL
New potatoes, red peppers, celery, chives and
 watercress served hot with a french dressing

Desserts

LA GATEAU SAINT HONORÉ
A pastry flan with a border of choux in cream
 with a rum flavoured custard

BRITANNIA PRINCE CHARLES
Meringue gateau shaped like a boat flavoured with
 Benedictine and filled with apple compote
 cooked in butter and honey

LE GRAND SOUFFLÉ ELIZABETH II
Baked alaska filled with pistachio, vanilla and
 strawberry ice cream on a sponge with
 strawberry flavoured kirsch

CLAFOUTI AUX CERISES MORELLO
Cherry flan

SOUFFLÉ PRINCESSE ANNE
Vanilla and chocolate souffle with pears in
 chocolate sauce flavoured with rum

SOUFFLÉ GLACÉ MONTECHRISTO
Egg ice cream with whipped meringue and cream
 set on ice flavoured with ginger in syrup and
 pineapple

SOUP

Our classical repertoire of soups consists of many different types ranging from broths to creamy *veloutes*, from unstrained soups to the most sophisticated lobster *bisque*. Of all the soups possibly the hot pot soup known as 'Petite Marmite' which is a double beef broth with winglets of chicken, is the most appreciated and probably the best French soup. We call it the *Pot-au-Feu*. By boiling shin of beef with leek, carrots, turnip and onions a splendid flavour is obtained. If the soup is simmered gently it will not cloud, otherwise it has to be clarified with egg whites and minced beef. In this soup the chicken winglets are boiled in the first stock until tender. The soup is then garnished after clarification of the broth with carrots, celery and leeks, sliced beef and a few winglets and served in an earthenware Marmite pot. French bread and grated parmesan cheese are presented separately.

My selection is of necessity restricted and therefore based on my own idea of taste and these four soups could quickly become firm favourites.

SOUPE À L'OIGNON AU MADÉRE
Onion soup with madeira wine and cheese

Ingredients:

Sliced onion 10 oz (300 g)
Butter and lard 2 oz (60 g)
Beef bouillon 2 pint (1,200 mls)
Madeira wine ½ pint (300 mls)
Toasted french bread 4 slices
Grated Gruyere cheese 4 oz (120 g)
1 egg
Salt and pepper

Method: Saute the sliced onions in a mixture of lard and butter in a saucepan, cook gently without browning too much. Add the beef bouillon. Boil for 10 minutes, lastly add the wine and season. Cream grated cheese and beaten egg. Spread this mixture on toasted French bread and brown under the grill like Welsh Rarebit. Serve soup unstrained in individual soup pots with toasted cheese sippets.

LA MOULARDE
Creamy mussel soup

Ingredients:

Fresh mussels 4 pint (2,400 g)
Chopped onions 2 oz (60 g)
Butter and lard 2 oz (60 g)
White vinegar 2 fl oz (60 mls)
White wine ½ pint (300 mls)
Water ¼ pint (150 mls)
1 bay leaf
Ground pepper
Chopped parsley 1 tbs
Mint and sprig of thyme
Single cream ½ pint (300 mls)

Method: Saute the chopped onions in butter and lard until soft but not brown. Add the vinegar, boil for 1 minute then add cleansed mussels (well scrubbed and seaweed attachment removed). Place a lid on the pan and toss for 1 minute then add the white wine, 1 bay leaf, water, fresh sprig of thyme and two mint leaves and a pinch of coarsely ground black pepper. Cook for 5 minutes until mussel shells open then add chopped parsley. Strain the liquor into a saucepan, add cream and reheat for 5 minutes. Pour over mussels.

LA CITROUILLETTE
Pumpkin and bacon soup

Ingredients:

Pumpkin 10 oz (300 g)
Chopped onions 4 oz (120 g)
Butter and lard 2 oz (60 g) each
Bacon 4 oz (120 g)
Water 2½ pint (1,500 mls)
Salt and pepper
Cream ½ pint (300 mls)
Ground ginger

Method: Peel and dice the pumpkin. Saute in a pan with bacon, onions in butter and lard until almost tender — about 15 minutes. Add water and boil for 45 minutes. Mince or pass everything through a sieve or liquidiser. Season and add cream and a pinch of ginger.

My grandma used to prepare this soup every year when the pumpkins were in season.

LA CÔTRIADE BOULONNAISE
Mixed fish soup

Ingredients:

Oil 2 oz (60 g)
Leek 2 oz (60 g)
Onion 2 oz (60 g)   Cut in thin slices or
Carrot 2 oz (60 g)   strips or shredded
Garlic
Tomato pulp or concassee 4 oz (120 g)
4 by 5 oz (150 g) fish fillets
Toasted bread
Salt and pepper
Grated cheese
Chopped chervil
Saffron, 1 pinch
Boiling stock 5 oz (150 mls)

Method: Saute the leeks, carrots and onions in oil and then add tomato pulp and garlic and water and boil for 15 minutes. Cool. Place fillets of hake or cod or haddock in a saute pan. Cover with the soup. Sprinkle a pinch of salt and pepper and simmer for 15 minutes, gently so as not to break the fish. Toast French bread cut in thin slices, rub with a little garlic and place in soup tureen. Place the fish on the bread and cover with broth and vegetables. Serve with grated cheese and chopped chervil sprinkled on top. Steep saffron in a quarter of the broth brew for 5 minutes, strain and add to rest of soup.

HORS D'OEUVRE

LE PÂTÉ MAITRE-JEAN
Liver pâté blended with chicken and pork in wine

Ingredients:

Chicken liver ½ lb (240 g)
Pinch sodium nitrate or saltpetre (0.06 g)
Water 5 oz (150 mls)
Diced lean pork ½ lb (240 g)
Diced raw chicken ½ lb (240 g)
Diced green bacon 4 oz (120 g)
Diced raw lard of pork ½ lb (240 g)
Chopped onions 2 oz (60 g)
Lard 2 oz (60 g)
1 clove fresh garlic (5 g)
1 egg
Flour 2 oz (60 g)
Pinch mixed spices (half tsp — 5 g)
Salt ½ oz (15 g)
Black pepper (2 g)
Rum 3 fl oz (90 mls)

Aspic jelly stock:

Bacon and chicken bones 8 oz (240 g)
Chicken skin and pork rind 4 oz (120 g)
Gelatine 2 oz (60 g)
Water 1½ pint (900 mls)
Madeira wine 5 fl oz (150 mls)
Salt ⅙ oz (5 g)
1 bouquet garni
4 by 2 oz (60 g) slices streaky bacon
    (for lining casserole dish)
2 bay leaves

Method: In a bowl dissolve the nitrate or use saltpetre and soak the cleaned chicken livers for 30 minutes. Make sure to remove gall pocket without bursting it. Saute diced meats and chopped onions in a pan. Cover with lid and cook gently for 10 minutes until meats are a golden colour. Remove and mince. Mince liver, add to other meats and re-mince. Blend together meats, egg, flour and spices in a bowl, add rum and seasoning. Stir well and rest for 2 hours in refrigerator. Boil all aspic stock ingredients for 30 minutes. Remove bouquet garni and simmer for 1 hour. Strain and keep in reserve. Line a 4 inch deep earthenware casserole with a few strips of parboiled streaky bacon and 2 bay leaves. Cover with mixture, level with a palette knife. Place casserole on tray, bake for 1½ hours at 360°F. Place a pastry rack over a shallow tray. Turn out pâté on to tray and let the liquid and fat drain for 20 minutes. Clean the casserole dish, place half strained aspic (about 5 fl oz, 150 mls) in the dish and replace pâté brown side up. Leave pate to soak up aspic and if necessary pour remainder of aspic over pate. Chill and turn onto flat dish for serving. The pate should have a jelly like appearance and be firm enough to slice without crumbling.

HOT HORS D'OEUVRE OR LIGHT ENTRÉES

PETIT PÂTÉ EN CROUTE
Individual pâté in pastry

Ingredients:

Chicken or calves liver ½ lb (240 g)
Pork sausage meat ½ lb (240 g)
Chopped onions 2 oz (60 g)
Chopped mushrooms 2 oz (60 g)
2 eggs
Chopped parsley 1 oz (60 g)
Salt and pepper
Cognac or sherry 3 fl oz (90 mls)
Flour 1 oz (30 g)

Cooked ingredients:

Diced duck or chicken leg meat 3 oz (90 g)
Diced ham or ox tongue 1 oz (30 g)
Pistachio nuts 1 oz (30 g)

Puff pastry ½ lb (240 g) — 8 portions
Eggwash

Method: Blend minced liver and sausage meat with ingredients to a smooth soft mixture. Add diced cooked ingredients.

Roll out puff pastry to just under ½ inch (1 cm) thickness. Cut two pieces 9 inch by 3 inch. Wet edges with water. Place mixture in centre of pastry, cover with second piece, seal edges and crimp the border. Brush with eggwash and leave for 30 minutes. Bake at 420°F for 20 minutes. Cut 2 inch wide fingers and serve hot hors d'oeuvre.
Note: The cooked ingredients determine the type of pâté, i.e. chicken, duck, goose, partridge, ham, etc.

LES ESCARGOTS DE BOURGOGNE AU PERNOD
Snails in Pernod butter

Canned snails are available. Only the savoury butter needs to be prepared.

Ingredients:

Butter for 2 doz snails 6 oz (180 g)
Chopped shallots 1 oz (30 g)
Fresh chopped herbs (parsley and tarragon, only 1 tbs)
Salt and pepper
1 crushed clove garlic
Pernod 2 fl oz (60 mls)

Method: Cream butter, blend herbs, crushed garlic and Pernod. Blanch chopped onions in boiling water for 2 minutes. Strain and add to mixture. Stuff each snail with mixture and chill to harden. Place on a special snail plate (with cavity for shells) or use a shallow dish — 6 per portion. Bake in hot oven for 8 minutes until butter begins to froth. Serve piping hot with French bread to mop up sauce.

LA QUICHE AUX FRUITS DE MER
Small flan filled with seafood mixture

Ingredients:

Short pastry ½ lb (120 g)

Filling:

Cooked cod 4 oz (120 g)
Prawns 2 oz (60 g)
Sliced mushrooms 2 oz (60 g)
Chopped parsley 1 tbs
White wine 5 fl oz (150 mls)
Chopped onions 1 oz (30 g)
Salt and pepper
Pinch of ground thyme
   All cooked together
Chopped skinned and seeded tomatoes 2 oz (60 g)

Custard filling:

White sauce 5 fl oz (150 mls) ⎫
2 eggs ⎪ Blend
Fish liquor 3 fl oz (90 mls) ⎬ together
Seasoning, salt and pepper ⎭

Method: Poach fish and prawns with remaining ingredients for filling for 12 minutes. Strain fish liquor and add to white sauce with two beaten eggs. Blend fish and prawns and cool. Fill flan of small pastry shell with mixture and bake 45 minutes at 360°F for flan and 25 minutes for small tartlets until the sauce is firm and set like a custard.

CHAUSSON DE CRABE COMTE DE BOULOGNE
Crab and mushroom filling in a pastry turnover

This is to my mind one of the great hot hors d'oeuvre which can be served as the starter to a good meal.

Ingredients:

White crab meat ½ lb (240 g)
Sliced white mushrooms 4 oz (120 g)

Sauce:

Chopped onions 1 oz (30 g)
White wine or vermouth 5 fl oz (150 mls)
Pinch of ground thyme
White sauce ½ pint (300 mls)
2 egg yolks
Freshly chopped mint, 1 pinch
Salt and pepper
Puff pastry 1 lb (480 g)

Method: Either boil a large crab and extract the white meat from claws and legs or use frozen crab meat. Boil chopped onions and white wine in a saucepan for 5 minutes. Add crab meat and sliced mushrooms. Simmer 10 minutes. Add white sauce and boil for 5 minutes. Season. Remove from heat and blend two egg yolks and fresh herbs. Cool and use as filling for puff pastry turnovers. Roll pastry $\frac{1}{8}$ inch thick, 8 inch diameter rounds. Place 2 oz (60 g) of mixture on each round. Wet edges and fold over, seal and crimp edges. Place on greased tray, brush tops with eggwash and leave for 20 minutes before baking. Bake for 15 minutes at 400°F. Serve hot or cold.

FISH ENTREES

LANGOUSTE AU GRATIN GRANDE-CHARTREUSE
Crawfish stuffed with vegetables and flavoured with Grande-Chartreuse

Do not confuse this crustacean specimen with crayfish. A crawfish has no claws and is brownish-yellow to dark green when alive.

Ingredients:

2 crawfish 1½ lb (720 g) each

Stuffing:

Chopped onions 2 oz (60 g)
Chopped mushrooms 2 oz (60 g)
Fat 2 oz (60 g)
Chopped fennel and celery 2 oz (60 g)
White wine 5 fl oz (150 mls)
Bread crumbs 2 oz (60 g)
Chopped hard boiled eggs 2 oz (60 g)
Chopped parsley 1 tbs
White sauce ½ pint (300 mls)
 (the white sauce to be flavoured with 1 tsp
 made mustard)
Grande-Chartreuse liqueur 4 fl oz (120 mls)
Lemon juice 2 fl oz (60 mls)
Salt and pepper
Grated cheese 3 oz (90 g)

Method: The crawfish are usually sold frozen and cooked. Otherwise boil for 30 minutes in salted water. Split open, remove intestinal cord and gravel. Remove meat from shells and clean the inside of the shell. Cut meat into slices, prepare sauce and stuffing as follows.

Sweat the chopped onions and mushrooms in fat gently for 5 minutes. Add crumbs, chopped eggs, parsley and white sauce and liqueur. Boil for a further 5 minutes and reheat crawfish meat in this sauce. Place empty shells in shallow dish and fill from head to tail evenly with the mixture. Sprinkle lemon juice, seasoning and grated cheese, brown in hot oven for 12 minutes until golden brown on top.

SUPREME DE TURBOT BOULONNAISE

Baked turbot cooked in white wine with herbs
and mushrooms

Ingredients:

4 by 6 oz (180 g) fillets of turbot or brill

Stock:

Fish head and bones with skin 1 lb (480 g)
Sliced onions 4 oz (120 g)
1 bouquet garni
1 sprig of celery
1 pint water (600 mls)
White wine ½ pint (300 mls)

Sauce:

Sliced mushrooms 4 oz (120 g)
Sliced pickled gherkins 2 oz (60 g)
Chopped parsley
Juice 1 lemon
Salt and pepper
Butter 4 oz (120 g)
Cooked mussels 1 lb (480 g)

Method: Boil bones and skin together with stock
ingredients for 20 minutes, strain. Clean and season
fish fillets, place in shallow greased dish. Cover
with the stock. Add cleaned and sliced mushrooms,
sliced gherkins, juice of 1 lemon and seasoning.
Place a few pats of butter on top. Cover with lid
and bake in oven for 20 minutes, at 360°F. Check
seasoning and sprinkle chopped parsley on top.
Serve in the same dish surrounded by a dozen or
so cooked mussels.

TURBAN DE COLIN CASINO DE BOULOGNE À LA CONIL

Crown-moulded hake dish with prawn, mussel
and mushroom filling

Ingredients:

Hake fillets 1 lb (480 g)
Butter 2 oz (60 g)

Filling:

Skinned and filleted whiting 1 lb (480 g)
Chopped shallots 1 oz (30 g)

1 egg
Crumbs 1 oz (30 g)
Salt and pepper
Butter 2 oz (60 g)

Garnish:

Cooked mussels 2 oz (60 g)
Prawns 2 oz (60 g)
Button white mushrooms 2 oz (60 g)

Vermouth sauce:

Chopped shallots 1 oz (30 g)
1 sprig mint
Butter and oil 1 oz (30 g) each
Flour 1 oz (30 g)
Vermouth ½ pint (300 mls)
Fish stock ½ pint (300 mls)
   (water and bones boiled together for 20 mins)
Cream 4 fl oz (120 mls)
Salt and pepper

Method: Grease a savarin mould with butter.
Line the mould slantwise with thin slices of hake
fillets. Mince the fish filling ingredients to a paste
and place into the mould. Cover with more thin
slices of hake. Place mould in a tin half filled
with water and bake for 30 minutes at 380°F.
Leave for 10 minutes then turn out into a flat
round dish. Brush the top with hot water to
remove coagulated white fish albumin. Coat the
fish with Vermouth sauce and place in centre
the mixture of cooked mussels, prawns and
button mushrooms. Dust the top with ground
paprika. Serve the surplus sauce separately. Serve
with boiled new potatoes.

Vermouth sauce: Saute chopped shallots in butter
and oil until translucent. Add flour and cook like
a roux. Moisten with fish stock and Vermouth and
boil for 15 minutes. Strain and add cream and
seasoning.

Note: Reheat garnish in some of the sauce.

LES FILLETS DE SOLE AUX FRUITS DE LA VIGNE

Sole fillets cooked in wine sauce

Ingredients:

Stock:

Fish bones 1 lb (480 g)
Sliced onions 2 oz (60 g)
Margarine 1 oz (30 g)
Water 1 pint (600 mls)

8 by 2½ oz (45 g each) sole
Butter 3 oz (90 g)
Pernod 5 oz (150 mls)
Stock 5 fl oz (150 mls)
Salt and pepper
Juice of 1 lemon

Roux:

Flour 1 oz (30 g)
Margarine 1 oz (30 g)
Fish liquor 1 pint (600 mls)

Liaison:

2 egg yolks
Plain yoghurt 5 fl oz (150 mls)

Garnish:

Seeded white grapes 5 oz (150 g)
4 slices of lemon and orange serrated and cut in
   half moon shapes
Mashed potatoes ½ lb (240 g) blended with
   2 egg yolks to pipe round the dish

Method: To prepare fish stock lay fish bones,
sliced onions, a little margarine and water in a
saucepan and boil for 20 minutes. Strain. Place
the folded fillets of sole in a well buttered
shallow dish. Squeeze lemon juice over fish, add
Pernod and marinate for 15 minutes, then add
fish stock and white wine in equal quantities,
season and cover with greased proof paper and
bake for 15 minutes in moderate oven, 360°F.
Drain liquor into a bowl. Complete sauce
by cooking a roux, gradually add the fish
liquor to thicken to right consistency. Mix
egg yolks, yoghurt and some of the sauce
Reheat to boiling point, season and pour over the
fish. Pipe a cordon of mashed or duchesse
potatoes round the dish and glaze under the
grill. Decorate with thin slices of serrated orange
and lemon and seeded grapes.

CRUSTACEANS

In French gastronomy all the crustacean family
is popular. At the moment the French and
Germans are paying high prices for all shell fish.
   Plain salted, or sea water is ideal for boiling
shell fish. Acid or vinegar should never be used as
this bleaches the shell.

COOKING TIMES:

Shrimps	5 minutes	
Prawns	8 minutes	
Scampi	9 minutes	
Crayfish	10 minutes	
Lobster	20 minutes per 1 lb	
Crawfish	20 minutes per 1 lb	(480 g)
Crab	20 minutes per 1 lb	

QUALITY AND PURCHASING POINTS:

Lobsters should be purchased when alive. They
are bluish-black in colour turning red when cooked.
Good lobsters should have both claws attached.
Those without are called 'cripples' and should be
cheaper. Their weight must be related to their
volume. A male is tastier than a female, although
the female has more meat and a broader tail. Eggs
and coral are kept to flavour soups and sauces.

PREPARATION:

The parts of the lobster to discard are the stomach
(a little bag which lies behind the mouth at the tip
of the head). This is removed by cutting the part
slantwise with the two eyes. The intestinal cord
along the tail must also be removed in all crustaceans,
including the crayfish (Ecrevisse). The soft green
or creamy part is the liver and is used for sauce
and soup. This green matter turns red when cooked
and adds to the flavour and appearance of a
sauce. This can be accentuated by frying the shell
with carrots and onions as for *Lobster Americaine*
or *Soupe Bisque.*

COOKED LOBSTER:

If purchased cooked, the lobster should first be wiped with a damp cloth and rewashed in water. Break off claws and legs and remove the meat. Split open carcass and remove tail meat. Discard intestinal cord. To serve cold, place a little Russian mixed vegetable mixture in mayonnaise over the head cavity. Turn over the tail meat and replace in the tail shell. Glaze with aspic and serve with mayonnaise.

Lobsters are in season from April to October.

LE HOMARD AU PERNOD À LA CONIL
Lobster in cream sauce flavoured with Pernod

Ingredients:

Stock:

Water 2 pint (1,800 mls)
Onions 2 oz (60 g)
Carrots 2 oz (60 g)
Bouquet garni
Vinegar 2 oz (60 g)
Tomato puree 1 oz (30 g)

Roux:

Margarine 1 oz (30 g)
Flour 1 oz (30 g)
Lobster stock 1 pint (600 mls)
Cream 4 fl oz (120 mls)
Sliced button mushrooms 4 oz (120 g) (well washed)
Pernod 5 fl oz (150 mls)
Pinch fresh chopped parsley, tarragon, chervil and fresh mint
Cooked rice 10 oz (300 g)
2 lobsters 1½ lb (720 g) each

Method: To prepare stock heat oil in a saute pan and fry coarsely cut onions, carrots and chopped lobster shells. Add tomato puree, garlic and bouquet garni. Cover with water, simmer for 45 minutes and strain. Add vinegar. Make a roux. Cook margarine and flour gently to a sandy texture, gradually add 1 pint of the stock. Cook for 15 minutes. Add the cream, Pernod, chopped herbs and sliced button mushrooms. Boil for 5 minutes only for flavours to blend harmoniously. Saute the slices of cooked lobster in butter for 6 minutes, add sauce and bring to boil. Serve on a bed of rice pilaff.

QUENELLES DE SAUMON DE LA LOIRE DUC D'ORLÉANS
Minced salmon dumplings in Loire wine sauce

Ingredients:

Skinned salmon 1 lb (480 g)
2 egg whites
White breadcrumbs 1 oz (30 g)
Tomato puree ½ oz (15 g)
Double cream 4 fl oz (120 mls)
Salt and pepper
Juice of lemon
Butter 2 oz (60 g)

Sauce:

1 oz (30 g) each of butter and flour for roux
5 oz (150 mls) each of water and white wine
Juice of half a lemon
Chopped parsley and fresh mint
Salt and pepper to taste
2 egg yolks
Cream 4 fl oz (120 mls)
Peeled cucumber 4 oz (120 g) shaped like olives

Method: Mince the salmon flesh twice. Bind with egg whites, tomato puree, lemon juice and crumbs. Chill for 1 hour. Gradually add double cream to fish mixture beating all the time. Season. Chill again for 30 minutes. Shape the mixture like an egg with a spoon dipped in boiling water. Place the Quenelles in a greased shallow dish; cover with hot fish stock evenly. Poach until Quenelles bob up. Then drain and coat with Paloise sauce. Garnish with peeled cucumber cooked in yoghourt.
Sauce: Cook butter and flour gently without colouring. Add water or fish stock made with wine. Boil for 15 minutes. Strain. Add cream and egg yolks blended together. Season and add chopped herbs and freshly chopped mint.
Stock: Place fish bones in pan with 1 oz (30 g) margarine, 1 oz (30 g) onions and wine and water.

Boil for 20 minutes and strain. Use bones from white fish only. If not available use a couple of chicken bouillon cubes.

MEAT DISHES

The French make better use of animal offal. The British are not usually interested in tripe, sweetbread, spleen, heart, kidney, trotters, tail, tongue, brain and other parts of the animal. This is a pity as the protein content of any offal is the same as meat muscle which forms the best cuts. Furthermore, there is a food value in animal blood when used in a fresh state as in black puddings, a dish often praised by the most sophisticated French gourmets. The Belgians and Germans, indeed most continental people, accept it as part of their normal diet. Black pudding is also popular in Ireland, more so than in England.

Experience shows that several dishes have become more acceptable, ox tail being the most popular, followed by calves', lambs', pigs' and ox's livers for use in pies. Animal hearts are sadly neglected, yet braised sheep's or calves' hearts are truly delicious. Calves' Kidneys are more popular than sheep's kidneys and more tender than ox's kidneys.

In the offal series of dishes the animal heads have been included. A Calf's head boiled and served with a sharp sauce is probably one of the most popular dishes in Franch. Pig's head is used for brawn and because of its gelatinous texture, it is preferred as a sort of pâté. Tripe, the animal stomach, appears to be the least popular among the English, yet *Tripes a la Mode de Caen* is a famous Normandy dish. Tripe needs to be cooked for a long time in clear stock or water. The French recipes call for ten hours at least on a low heat. Once the tripe has been cooked it can be reheated and it is the second cooking process which produces the flavour and soft texture.

MIGNONETTES D'AGNEAU POIVRADE
Loin steak of lamb with a peppercorn sauce

Ingredients:

Each Mignonette finished weight 5 oz (150 g) — allow 2 per person or 4 lb (2 kg) approx on the bone
Oil 2 oz (60 g)
Butter 2 oz (60 g)
Shallots 2 oz (60 g)
Sliced mushrooms 2 oz (60 g)
Vermouth 5 fl oz (150 mls)
White vinegar 1 fl oz (30 mls)
Sour cream 4 fl oz (120 mls)
Peppercorns 1 g
Salt and cayenne
Scalded seedless raisins 5 oz (150 g)
4 courgettes 5 oz (150 g) each
Cooked rice 5 oz (150 g)

Method: Bone a loin of lamb. Remove thin skin, roll and tie as a joint with string placed every 2 inch. Cut between the string for small loin steaks. Pass in seasoned flour. Place in pan with oil, cover with lid and cook for 8 minutes. *Sauce:* Sweat chopped shallots and sliced mushrooms. Add sweet vermouth and vinegar, boil for 5 minutes then add *sour cream,* boil for 3 minutes. Season to taste, add a pinch of cayenne pepper. Add scalded seedless raisins. Place each Mignonette on a fried crouton cut to the same size, coat with a little sauce. Serve the remaining sauce separately. Garnish with stuffed courgettes with rice.

ROGNONS DE VEAU MONTPARNASSE
Calves' kidneys in white wine

Ingredients:

Calves' kidneys 1 lb (480 g)
Oil and butter 2 oz (60 g) each
Chopped shallots 3 oz (90 g)
Garlic
White wine 5 fl oz (150 mls)
Brown gravy 5 fl oz (150 mls)
Salt and pepper
Cream 5 fl oz (150 mls)
Made mustard 1 teaspoon
Chopped parsley 1 tbls
4 croutons of fried or toasted bread

Method: This dish can be cooked in 10 minutes. Saute the sliced kidney in a pan with oil and butter for 6 minutes. Remove and keep hot while making sauce. Using the same fat, saute the chopped shallots and a little garlic for 2 minutes. Add white wine and boil for 4 minutes, add gravy and reheat for 2 minutes. Add cream, boil for 5 minutes, season, add a teaspoonful of French mustard well diluted in the sauce. Stir well, pour over the kidneys. Serve on toast with a sprinkling of chopped parsley.

RIS DE VEAU LUCULLUS
Sweetbread in savoury sauce with olives and
   mushrooms

Ingredients:

4 sweetbreads 1½ lb each (720 g)
Water 1 pint (600 mls)
Vinegar 1 pint (600 mls)
Seasoned flour 2 oz (60 g)
Butter and lard or oil 2 oz (60 g) each

Sauce:

Oil and butter 2 oz (60 g)
Chopped shallots 1 oz (30 g)
Sliced mushrooms 4 oz (120 g)
Sliced stuffed olives 2 oz (60 g)
1 clove garlic
Tomato puree 1 oz (30 g)
Meat glaze 1 teaspoon or gravy 5 fl oz (150 mls)
Chopped parsley
Sweet Madeira wine 4 fl oz (120 mls)

Method: Trim some of the sweetbread cartilage. Place in a saucepan with cold water and vinegar and gently boil or poach for 10 minutes. Trim and remove unwanted skin and cartilage. Place sweetbread on a plate under a weighted board to press and keep air out. Pass the sweetbread, cut in thin escalopes, in seasoned flour. Place in a pan with oil and butter and fry for 5 minutes on both sides. Keep warm in a dish. Saute the chopped shallots and sliced mushrooms quickly in butter for 2 minutes only or until shallots are tender. Add sliced stuffed olives, a clove of garlic, a spoonful of tomato puree, ¼ of the

gravy and a glass of sweet Madeira wine. Boil 5 minutes. Cover sweetbread with sauce, simmer for 5 minutes and season. Sprinkle chopped parsley *Note:* A little drop of meat extract in the sauce will give more character if meat stock gravy is not available. For presentation pipe a cordon of mashed potatoes around the dish and place sweetbread inside the ring.

ESCALOPE DE VEAU CYRANO DE BERGERAC
Veal escalope and liver in cheese sauce

Ingredients:

4 x 6 oz (180 g) veal escalops
Calves liver 4 oz (120 g)
Chopped shallots
Salt and pepper
Crumbs 1 oz (30 g)
1 egg
Seasoned flour
Butter and oil 2 oz (60 g)
Cooked spinach 10 oz (300 g)
Cheese sauce 10 oz (300 g)
Grated cheese 2 oz (60 g)
Tomatoes 4 oz (120 g)
4 jacket potatoes

Method: Make a slit inside the veal escalope and pipe a small amount of calf's liver filling.* Pass escalopes in seasoned flour and fry in the pan for 8 minutes until cooked. Place the escalopes on a bed of cooked spinach flavoured with garlic butter. Coat them with a rich Mornay sauce. Sprinkle grated cheese and brown under the grill. Decorate the dish with sliced peeled tomato. Reheat for a few minutes and serve with baked jacket potatoes. *Filling:* Remove skin of liver. Mince, add cooked chopped shallots and crumbs, bind with an egg and season.

PAILLARD DE VEAU EN PAPILLOTE
Veal steak with mushrooms and sweetcorn
   pancakes, baked in paper casing

Ingredients:

4 large veal steaks cut from loin of veal 10 oz
   (300 g) each

Stuffing:

Chopped shallots 2 oz (60 g)
Chopped mushrooms 2 oz (60 g)
Sweetcorn 4 oz (120 g)
2 eggs
Milk 5 fl oz (150 mls)
Flour 5 oz (150 g)
Cooking oil 3 fl oz (90 mls)
Salt and pepper

Serve with a dish of baby marrow (Courgettes Mathilda).

Method: Season the veal steak. Fry with a little oil in a covered pan to keep moist. Turn twice during cooking to avoid over-colouration. Remove. Prepare batter in a bowl using beaten eggs, milk and flour. Add the mushrooms, sweetcorn and shallots. Season. Using a little oil heat the pan and fry small spoonfuls of batter like pancakes cooking on both sides. Place one pancake on top of each steak. Prepare the paper bag as follows: using a whole sheet of greaseproof parchment paper per steak cut a heart shape about 14 inch across at its widest point (7 inch wide when folded). Oil the outside of the paper and lay flat on the table oily side down. Place steak with pancake on top on one side of the paper, fold over and crimp and seal edges of the heart bag. When ready to serve place bags on a tray. Heat the tray on top of stove, this will create an air vacuum causing the bags to swell. As soon as this begins to happen transfer tray to hot oven 380°F, when the bags brown and puff out completely, serve immediately with rich gravy flavoured with Madeira wine and Courgette Mathilda.

POULTRY AND GAME

POULET SAUTÉ AU MÉDOC
Chicken in wine sauce with button onions, carrots, celery and buttered beans

Ingredients:

Chicken 3 lb (1,440 g)
Seasoned flour

Médoc wine ½ pint (300 mls)
Oil 2 fl oz (60 mls)
Lard 2 oz (60 g)
Flour 1 oz (30 g)
Chicken stock ½ pint (300 mls)
Salt and pepper
Cinnamon
Vinegar 3 fl oz (90 mls)
Button mushrooms 6 oz (180 g)
Onion 5 oz (150 g)
Celery 2 oz (60 g)
Carrots 2 oz (60 g)
1 bouquet garni
Garlic 5 g
Tomato puree 2 oz (60 g)
Tarragon

Method: The Médoc is more suitable for richer wine sauces. Similar wines, rich in tannin, give a better tang and more character to the sauce.

Cut chicken in 8 pieces; leg in 2, breast in 2 and 2 wings. Keep carcass and winglets for stock. Brown winglets and giblets in fat with 1 onion, carrots and bouquet garni. Then boil for 30 minutes and strain stock to obtain ½ pint of liquid. Pass chicken pieces in seasoned flour. Pan fry legs first for 5 minutes and then add breast and wings and cook for 12 minutes with lid on. Turn over for even browning. Remove from pan and keep in casserole dish. In same pan brown small onions, sliced carrots and celery and add to chicken. Use 2 oz (60 g) of the frying fat to make a roux with 1 oz (30 g) flour and cook till sandy brown. Then add tomato puree and crushed garlic and dilute the stock to a thickish consistency. Boil button mushroom caps and diced celery in red wine for 5 minutes only. Add a pinch of cinnamon and tarragon. Strain juice into thickened stock. Season and add to chicken pieces and braise in oven at 325-350°F for 40 minutes with a lid on. Remove half of the sauce. When cooked add the mushrooms and sprinkle with chopped parsley.

CANARD À L'ORANGE AU GRAND MARNIER
Roast duck with a delicious demi-glace sauce flavoured with Grand Marnier

Ingredients:

1 duck 5½ lb (2,640 g)

Special dye mixture:

Water 5 fl oz (150 mls)
Pinch of turmeric
Pinch of red powder
Gravy browning ⅛ oz (4 g)
Fat for roasting 2 oz (60 g)

Stock:

Cooked duck bones and giblets 1 lb (480 g)
Water 2 pint (1,200 mls)
Carrot 5 oz (150 g)
Onion 5 oz (150 g)
Mint leaves 5 g
1 bouquet garni
Tomato puree 3 oz (90 g)
White Port wine 5 fl oz (150 mls)
Good pinch of mixed spices
Cornflour 2 oz (60 g)
Water 5 fl oz (150 mls)
Salt and pepper

Caramel:

Cube sugar 4 oz (120 g)
White vinegar 1 fl oz (30 mls)
Water 1 fl oz (30 mls)
4 oranges ⎫
1 lemon ⎭ cut rind in thin strips 1 oz (30 g)
Morello cherries 4 oz (120 g)
Grand Marnier 5 fl oz (150 mls)

Method: Cut winglets and remove neck and truss ready for roasting. Mix ingredients for dye mixture and soak duck all over to produce an orange colour. Dry for 12 minutes, season and rub a little fat on the breast. Roast at 400°F for first ½ hour and then 360°F for 1 hour, basting from time to time to remove surplus fat. Cut duck in 4 portions and break up the body carcass bone in small pieces. Boil bones, neck and giblets in water with 1 onion, 1 carrot and bouquet garni for 1 hour. Strain. Add tomato puree, few leaves of fresh mint and Port wine to stock and boil for 5 minutes. Add spices and seasoning and thicken with a slurry of cornflour and water. Boil for a further 5 minutes and strain. Add caramel juice

made by boiling the 4 oz cube sugar and 1 tablespoon of water until it reaches the caramel stage. Add vinegar and orange juice to caramel and boil for 2 minutes. Add to sauce last with boiled strips of orange and lemon peel. Pour sauce over the duck and surround the dish with segments of oranges and scatter with a few stoneless morello cherries. Lastly, sprinkle the Grand Marnier all over the duck portions.

LE PINTADEAU SANS RIVAL
Pot roast guinea fowl in a creamy sauce flavoured with dry Madeira wine

Ingredients:

2 small guinea fowls 2 lb (960 g) each
Seasoned flour
Oil 5 oz (150 g)
Chopped onions 2 oz (60 g)
Garlic 5 g
Skinned, seedless chopped tomatoes 8 oz (240 g)
White port 5 fl oz (150 mls)
Tomato puree 2 oz (60 g)
Water 5 fl oz (150 mls)
Salt and pepper
Few black olives

Garnish:

Shell pasta 8 oz (240 g)
White sauce ½ pint (300 mls)
Cream 5 fl oz (150 mls)
2 egg yolks
Lemon juice 1 fl oz (30 mls)
White sliced mushrooms 5 oz (150 g)
Butter 3 oz (90 g)
Salt and pepper
Chopped parsley
Grated cheese 5 oz (150 g)

Method: Cut the guinea fowl in 2 and separate the legs. Pass in seasoned flour and pan fry with oil until golden on all sides. Then add chopped onions, garlic, tomato puree and tomato pulp, wine, water and seasoning. Cover with a lid and simmer gently for 40 minutes. Strain liquor into a pan and thicken with a slurry of cornflour and water. Add a few black olives and sprinkle with chopped parsley.

Garnish: Boil shell pasta for 15 minutes in salted water and drain. Blend white mushrooms fried in a little butter and oil for a few minutes only (half cooked) and add to the pasta. Season and place pasta in a buttered shallow dish. Blend cream, egg yolks and lemon juice to white sauce and mix with the pasta. Sprinkle with a little grated cheese. Place the guinea fowl portions on top with sauce and serve. Sprinkle with fresh chopped parsley and grated cheese.

PERDREAU BELLE-FLEUR
Partridge pot roasted on a bed of aromatic vegetables with a garnish of stuffed prunes

Ingredients:

4 partridges
Flour 2 oz (60 g)
Butter 5 oz (150 g)
Shallots 2 oz (60 g)
Lard 2 oz (60 g)
Port wine 5 fl oz (150 mls)
Gravy 5 fl oz (150 mls)
12 prunes
Liver pâté 5 oz (150 g)
1 egg
Flour
Breadcrumbs
Belgian endives
French dressing with blue cheese
Salt and pepper

Method: Each bird is split by introducing a knife through the back and cutting down the spinal bone. Open the partridge and remove breast ribs and giblets. Season and pass in flour. Dip in melted butter and roast quickly for 15 minutes at 400°F, basting from time to time.
Gravy: Sweat chopped shallots in lard until soft. Add 1 glass of red port wine and gravy and boil for 5 minutes.
Garnish: Serve cooked prunes stuffed with liver pate passed in flour, beaten eggs and crumbs and dipped fried.

Belgian endive salad with sliced hard-boiled egg and blue cheese dressing seems appropriate with this dish.

Note: This method can be applied to all small birds including young chickens.

L'OISON AUX POIRES ET MARRONS
Goose pot-roasted and served with a rich mushroom sauce with a garnish of cooking pears in red wine and chestnut stuffing

Ingredients:

1 goose 8 lb (3,840 g)

Stuffing:

Sausage meat 1 lb (480 g)
Cooked chestnuts 8 oz (240 g)
1 egg
1 glass rum
Chopped parsley 1 tbs
Chopped onions 2 oz (60 g)

Gravy:

1 onion 5 oz (150 g)
Celery tops 2 oz (60 g)
Carrot 5 oz (150 g)
Goose fat 2 oz (60 g)
Port wine 5 fl oz (150 mls)
Water 1 pint (600 mls)
Few sage leaves
Cornflour 1 oz (30 g)
Water 5 fl oz (150 mls)
Salt and pepper

Garnish:

Cooking pears (small types only) 1 lb (480 g)
Red wine ½ pint (300 mls)
Sugar 2 oz (60 g)
Cinnamon 1 pinch
Few red colour drops

Method: Clean, truss and singe goose. Blend all stuffing ingredients and fill goose through back cavity. Season and rub with lard. Roast for 1½ hours at 400°F, basting from time to time with stock made by boiling water and giblets for 1 hour. Collect the juice or gravy in a saucepan and add sliced carrot, onion, bouquet garni and sage. Season and boil for 30 minutes and strain. Thicken with a slurry of cornflour and water. Strain again and add Port wine. Peel and core pears and cook gently in oven in wine with sugar and spice for 35 minutes. Serve the carved goose with this compote of pears. Serve gravy separately.

VEGETABLES

In France the vegetables are usually served as a course. Most of the classic dishes are always garnished. The name of the dish indicates the type of garnish, i.e. Boulangere means sliced potatoes cooked with onion, Bretonne means haricot beans etc.

In the ordinary fare the French garnish all their dishes with potatoes or pasta. The range of potato dishes is enormous and covers 300 varieties from the humble boiled potatoes which can be flavoured with farm butter and chopped parsley to complex gratin potato dishes with cream, eggs and cheese, from the lean and dainty chips or pommes allumettes to the most difficult souffle potatoes.

The French cook in oil in all the Southern parts of France and in lard and dripping in the North. For frying a mixture of lard and beef dripping would produce delicious chips. It has been claimed, with justice, that frying in duck, goose or chicken fat makes the food even better.

We have devoted much space to potatoes in many sections and it is irrelevant to include the most simple and obvious potato recipes in the French section. Butter is used in cooking as a flavouring agent.

LES CHAMPIGNONS SOUS CLOCHE
Creamy mushrooms served in a bell dish

Ingredients:

Button mushroom caps 1 lb (480 g)
Shallots 2 oz (60 g)
Diced bacon 2 oz (60 g)
White port 5 fl oz (150 mls)
Cream 5 fl oz (150 mls)
Salt and pepper
Chopped parsley and chervil
4 large croutons or fried bread

Method: You will need a glass or heat resistant bell dish with platter and lid.

Saute well-washed mushroom caps with shallots and diced lean bacon for 2 minutes only in butter. Add white port wine, boil for 1 minute and then pour on cream, seasoning, chopped parsley and chervil. Transfer contents into bell dish lined with fried bread. Cover with the bell and bake for 5 minutes to obtain a vacuum of air which will keep the lid tightly closed. Serve in the same dish. This vacuum effect concentrates the flavour and improves the dish. Allow 1 dish per person.

LES COURGETTES MATHILDA
A mixture of baby marrows and mushrooms in tomato sauce

Ingredients:

Courgettes (marrows) 2 lb (960 g)
Chopped shallots or onions 3 oz (90 g)
Tomato puree 2 oz (60 g)
Sliced mushrooms 3 oz (90 g)
Tomato pulp 5 oz (150 g) (skinned and seeded tomatoes)
Chopped parsley and chervil
Grated cheese 2 oz (60 g)
Salt and pepper

Method: Scrub and trim the courgettes without peeling (young marrows need not be peeled). Cut in thick slices slantwise. Saute sliced mushrooms and onions in pan, add tomato puree and tomato pulp and cook for a few minutes. Then add courgettes, season and cook with lid on for 6 to 8 minutes. No water is required but make sure to keep lid on pan. Serve with a sprinkling of chopped parsley and grated cheese. Season.

LE GRATIN PARISIEN
Sliced potato cake baked in oven with cream

Ingredients:

New potatoes 2 lb (960 g)
Milk 1 pint (600 mls)
Cornflour 1 oz (30 g)
Water 6 fl oz (180 mls)

Salt and pepper
Crushed garlic
Butter 2 oz (60 g)
3 egg yolks
Cream ½ pint (300 mls)
Sliced ham 5 oz (150 g)

Method: Slice new potatoes thickly and scald for
5 minutes in boiling salted water and drain. Boil
milk and thicken with cornflour slurry. Add beaten
eggs and cream and season. Place the sliced
potatoes in a well greased shallow dish and cover
with egg mixture. Sprinkle with grated cheese and
bake in oven for 30 minutes at 380°F. A little
garlic sauce will give a pleasant flavour but it is
optional.
Note: Enrichment of this dish can be made by
adding sliced ham to the potatoes.

SOUFFLE D'EPINARD JEANNE D'ARC
Spinach, egg and cheese souffle baked in the oven

Ingredients:

Spinach leaves 2 lb (960 g)
Anchovies 3 oz (90 g)
Garlic 5 g
White sauce 5 oz (150 g)
2 egg yolks plus 1 whole egg
5 egg whites
Salt and pepper
Butter 2 oz (60 g)

Method: Pick over and remove stalks from spinach
leaves and boil in salted water for 5 minutes.
Drain and squeeze out surplus moisture completely
if possible. Chop leaves, add chopped anchovies
and garlic and blend a cup of thick white sauce
and two yolks and one whole egg. Season. Beat 5
egg whites to a meringue foam and fold gently
into spinach mixture. Fill a well buttered souffle
dish with the spinach mixture to the top. Make a
ring ¼ inch deep round with the thumb to prevent
mixture skinning and sticking to the edges. This
will assist the lifting of the mixture without forming a balloon or dome shape. Bake for 20 minutes
at 400°F in a tray half filled with hot water.

LA SALADE DE GRAND-MERE MATHILDA
Dandelion, spinach, curly lettuce in roquefort
  dressing

Ingredients:

Dandelion leaves 4 oz (120 g)
Spinach leaves 4 oz (120 g)
Curly chicory 4 oz (120 g)

Dressing:

Chopped celery 1 oz (30 g)
Blue cheese 2 oz (60 g)
Oil 2 fl oz (60 mls)
Vinegar 2 fl oz (60 mls)
Salt and pepper
Crushed garlic (optional)

Method: Clean and wash all leaves. Drain and dry.
Prepare French dressing with oil, vinegar and
seasoning and dilute with blue cheese. Toss salad
and sprinkle with chopped celery and garlic.

LA SALADE DU PERE CONIL
New potatoes, red peppers, celery, chives and
  watercress served hot with a French dressing

Ingredients:

New potatoes 1 lb (480 g)
Chopped chives 1 oz (30 g)
Diced red peppers 2 oz (60 g)
Watercress leaves 1 oz (30 g)

French dressing:

Oil 3 tbs
Wine vinegar 1 tbs
Salt and pepper
French yellow Dijon mustard 1 small tsp

Method: Prepare dressing. Boil new potatoes in
jackets, peel and cut in slices while still hot.
Place in a bowl. Parboil chopped red peppers for
3 minutes and add to the potatoes. Toss salad
in dressing, sprinkle with chopped chives and
arrange a few watercress leaves on top.

  The importance of eating a good green salad,
preferably with citrus fruit or tomatoes and
peppers for the intake of Vitamin C, cannot be

stressed enough. Salads are the best accompaniment for heavy meat grills or fish.

DESSERTS

LA GATEAU SAINT HONORÉ
A pastry flan with a border of choux in cream
  with a rum-flavoured custard

Ingredients;

Puff pastry 8 oz (240 g)
Choux pastry 8 oz (240 g)
Custard ½ pint (300 mls)
Caramel ¼ pint (150 mls) for dipping

Decoration:

Whipped cream ¼ pint (150 mls)
Glace cherries, angelica and few crystallised
  violets 3 oz (90 g)

In this recipe I shall give the choux and custard recipes only as puff pastry can be purchased ready made from shops.

Choux pastry:

Water ¼ pint (150 mls)
Margarine 2 oz (60 g)
Flour 4 oz (120 g)
Pinch of salt and sugar
4 eggs

Method: Boil water and margarine until the margarine has melted. Add flour and stir with a wooden spoon until mixture is a solid mass, not sticking to the pan. Reduce heat and dry a little for 5 minutes. Remove from heat and add the beaten eggs one by one. The mixture should have a dropping consistency (forming a thread). Add salt and sugar and mix well. Place mixture in a bag which has been fitted with a plain ¼ inch tube. Pipe 12 small buns as big as plums on a greased tray. Brush with egg wash and bake for 20 minutes at 400°F. Remove from oven and cool.

Roll out puff pastry into a round 8 inch diameter. Place on a greased tray and prick evenly with the prongs of a fork. Pipe the rest of the choux pastry round the puff pastry to form a border. Bake the pastry for 25 minutes at 400°F.

Custard:

2 egg yolks
Milk ½ pint (300 mls)
Cornflour 1 oz (30 g)
Vanilla essence
Rum 1 fl oz (30 mls)
Castor sugar 3 oz (90 g)
3 egg whites
Castor sugar 2 oz (60 g)

Method: Place egg yolks in a bowl with cornflour and half of the milk and stir well. Boil rest of milk and add to egg mixture, add essences and sugar and reboil to thicken for a few minutes. Keep warm. Beat egg whites to a meringue and add sugar gradually. Fold meringue into hot custard and mix well. Cool and pour into the centre of the pastry. Fill choux balls with the rest of the custard.

Caramel: Cook cubes of sugar with a few drops of water until it reaches caramel stage at 310°F. Remove from heat and place saucepan in a basin half filled with iced water to prevent further browning of the caramel. Dip each choux ball in the caramel making sure only the top is coated. Stick balls around the border of the gateau. Pipe a design of whipped cream and decorate with glacé cherries, angelica and crystallised violets.

BRITANNIA PRINCE CHARLES
Meringue gateau shaped like a boat flavoured
  with Benedictine and filled with apple
  compote cooked in butter and honey

Ingredients:

Sponge cake 7 oz (210 g)
Benedictine liqueur 5 fl oz (150 mls)
Quartered apples 8 oz (240 g) cooked in butter
  2 oz (60 g) and sugar 2 oz (60 g)

Meringue:

4 egg whites
Castor sugar 2 oz (60 g)

Custard:

4 egg yolks
Cornflour 1 oz (30 g)
Cream 1 pint (600 mls)
Benedictine liqueur
Sugar to taste
Vanilla essence

Decoration:

Few crystallised violets, angelica, glacé cherries
    and 2 oz (60 g) toasted flaked almonds

Method: Cut sponge in the shape of a boat 9 inch
long by 4 inch wide at the centre narrowing down
to each end. Soak with Benedictine liqueur, like a
tipsy cake. Hollow out the centre to form a
cavity for the filling. Fill with cooked apple
mixture and cover with custard and cool.

   Beat egg whites to a meringue and add sugar
gradually. Cover the sponge and apple completely
to imitate the white Britannia making sure the
top is level. Make a few portholes with glace
cherries on the sides at regular intervals and pipe
a border on top of the boat. Sprinkle with a few
flaked almonds and bake to brown the meringue
and set it like a marshmallow consistency for 8
minutes. Decorate with a few glacé cherries,
crystallised violets and almonds.

Custard: Boil cream and sugar. Add to
cornflour and yolks. Reboil to thicken mixture.
Flavour with vanilla and a little of the Benedictine
liqueur.

Cream sauce, to serve with this sweet: Boil cream
and sugar and kirsch. Cool and when cold serve
with the hot sweet.

LE GRAND SOUFFLE ELIZABETH II
Baked alaska filled with pistachio, vanilla and
    strawberry ice cream on a sponge with
    strawberry flavoured kirsch (8 portions)

I have had the honour to create this excellent
sweet in honour of the Queen's Silver Jubilee.
Once prepared it can be kept in a freezing cabinet
until required.

Ingredients:

Sponge cake 8 oz (240 g)
Fresh strawberries 1 lb (480 g)
Orange segment salad 8 oz (240 g)
Grand Marnier 5 fl oz (150 mls)
Orange Curacao 3 fl oz (90 mls)
Red currant or plum jam melted 5 oz (150 g)

Ice cream:

Pistachio ice 6 oz (180 g)
Vanilla ice 6 oz (180 g)
Strawberry ice 6 oz (180 g)

Meringue:

10 egg whites
Granulated sugar 10 oz (300 g)

Two piping bags needed:
    one with a plain star tube
    one with plain $1/8$ inch tube
Granulated sugar for last glazing

Method: Cut the sponge cake into a 9 inch by
4½ inch oblong and scoop out a little of the centre
to form a cavity 3 inch by ½ inch. In this cavity
place cleaned strawberries and cover with a little
melted jam. Sprinkle with some Grand Marnier an
and Curacao. Place the ice cream on top to form a
type of Neapolitan block of different ice flavours.
Smooth the ice to an oblong shape with a flat
surface. In a clean fat-free bowl place the egg
whites making sure to eliminate any specks of
yolk. Add a pinch of salt and beat to a meringue
until the mixture holds in the whisk. Gradually
add one third of the sugar and beat until the
mixture peaks again, repeat until all the sugar has
been used. Cover the ice and sponge with this
meringue allowing ½ inch all round which will
act as an insulator. Place some meringue in a bag
fitted with a star tube and pipe a cordon of shells
all around the base and top. Place the rest of the
meringue in the other bag which has been fitted
with a plain tube and pipe a swan design or the
initials E.R. on both the long sides of the baked
alaska. Sprinkle granulated sugar over the souffle
and bake at 380°F for 8 minutes to cook the
meringue to a setting consistency. Meanwhile
prepare the rest of the strawberry and orange salad

with a flavour of Curacao and Grand Marnier liqueuer. Place the strawberries on top and surround with orange segments to fill the cavity bordered by the piped meringue shells. Cover the top of the strawberries with melted red jam. Serve immediately.

See illustration.

CLAFOUTI AUX CERISES MORELLO
Cherry flan

Ingredients:

Fresh stoned Morello cherries 8 oz (240 g)
Fresh or canned stoned mirabelle plums 8 oz
  (240 g)

Batter mixture:

2 egg yolks
4 beaten eggs
Castor sugar 4 oz (120 g)
Flour 3 oz (90 g)
Milk 1 pint (600 mls)
Cream 6 fl oz (180 mls)
Kirsch 2 fl oz (60 mls)
Pinch of cinnamon
Icing sugar
Butter 2 oz (60 g)

Method: Grease a shallow dish 3 inch deep by 9 inch long or diameter with butter and place fruits in the bottom. In a bowl beat eggs with sugar and flour. Boil milk and cream and add to egg mixture gradually while beating. Add kirsch and pour this batter over the fruit. Bake for 45 minutes at 360°F until brown on top. Dust with icing sugar and ground cinnamon.

SOUFFLE PRINCESSE ANNE
Vanilla and chocolate souffle with pears in chocolate sauce flavoured with rum

Ingredients:

Cooked pears 8 halves

Chocolate sauce:

Dark chocolate 6 oz (180 g)

Butter 2 oz (60 g)
Double cream ½ pint (300 mls)
Icing sugar 2 oz (60 g)
Rum 3 fl oz (90 mls)

Souffle mixture:

Butter 3 oz (90 g) for greasing mould
Granulated sugar 2 oz (60 g) for sprinkling inside
  mould
Castor sugar 3 oz (90 g)
2 egg yolks
Flour ½ oz (15 g)
2 egg yolks
1 egg
Vanilla essence, few drops
Milk 5 fl oz (150 mls)
Sponge fingers 3 oz (90 g)
Rum 3 fl oz (90 mls)
4 egg whites
Icing sugar for dusting

Method: Grate chocolate and add butter. Melt in a tray half filled with water and when melted add icing sugar and double cream. Stir well, add rum and keep warm. Coat souffle mould 4 inch deep with a 7 inch diameter with soft butter (not melted) and sprinkle granulated sugar on the inside making sure that the bottom and sides are evenly coated, then cover with diced sponge fingers, soaked in rum.

Place egg yolks with flour and castor sugar in a bowl and cream. Add flavouring. Boil milk and add gradually to egg mixture. Reheat to thicken mixture, stirring all the time. Remove from heat when thickened like a custard. Add two more egg yolks and one beaten egg to the mixture and cool.

In a clean fat free bowl beat egg whites to a meringue until the mixture peaks. Add castor sugar in three stages beating each time to allow the meringue to peak again. Fold the meringue into the egg mixture gently but thoroughly. Place mixture in a souffle dish filling it right to the top. Make a criss-cross pattern with a fork on top to level up the mixture. The most important tip in making this souffle rise evenly without forming a mushroom dome is to go round with the thumb to form a small gullet or circle ¼ inch deep round the edge. This will prevent the mixture sticking and the souffle will rise straight up with a flat top. Place souffle dish in a tray and bake at 400° for 20/25 minutes. Dust with icing sugar when cooked and return to the oven for a further 3 minutes to allow the sugar to form a glossy glaze. Serve immediately with a compote of pears and a sauceboat of chocolate cream sauce.

SOUFFLE GLACÉ MONTECHRISTO
Egg ice cream with whipped meringue and cream
  set on ice flavoured with ginger in syrup and
  pineapple

Ingredients:

Cube sugar 6 oz (180 g)
Water 5 fl oz (150 mls)
Gelatine ½ oz (15 g)
Egg yolks 5
Crystallised pineapple 2 oz (60 g)
Crystallised ginger 2 oz (60 g)
Double cream 1 pint (600 mls)
8 egg whites
Granulated sugar 5 oz (150 g)
Cointreau 3 fl oz (90 mls)

Method: Boil sugar cubes with water and gelatine to obtain a syrup. Remove from heat. Place egg yolks in a basin and pour in the syrup while beating to thicken the mixture like a custard. Beat the mixture until it is cold. Dice the fruits and soak them in liquor. Add to the egg mixture. In another bowl whip the cream until it holds in the whisk and blend to the egg mixture. Beat egg whites to a meringue and add sugar gradually beating the mixture all the time to make it stiff again. Fold into the rest of the mixture. Use a mould dish 3 inch deep by 8 inch diameter. Surround the mould with a band of greaseproof paper 2 inch deep attaching the paper with string so that it will rise above the level of the mould by 2 inch. Fill this mould to the level of the paper, i.e. 2 inch above the mould. Chill in a freezer like ice cream and when set decorate the top with pineapple, ginger, angelica and glacé cherries and a few rosettes of cream. Remove the paper band showing the mixture above the mould thus giving the illusion of a souffle. Serve with sponge fingers or shortbread.

Switzerland

If one were to create a map of the food of Switzerland, it would correspond roughly to a map outlining the language divisions of the country. In the French-, German- and Italian-speaking sections, the cuisine reflects to a large degree the cultural origins of the population. However in all three sections of the country, the inventive Swiss have supplemented the usual list of specialities with innovations that can be found nowhere else; it is these local specialities which give infinite variety and add a unique charm to Swiss cuisine. Every region, indeed almost every town, has its special culinary delights.

Whatever the local dish, it is sure to be made from the best and freshest ingredients and served impeccably. Nothing is done in a slovenly manner in this tiny country with a population of six million people — half the size of Greater London. Life is very earnest, and hard work is the main virtue in life. For this reason the Swiss have one of the highest standards of living in the world. Their perfectionist standards carry over into the kitchens of the twenty-two cantons that go to make up this safety deposit box to the world. Women, who only recently expressed a wish to vote, have always played a contented part with homemaking and home economics as their chief interests. It is reflected in the spotless cleanliness of the home, with the smell of beeswax on the glossy furniture and serried ranks of home-made jams and pickles in the larder.

It is the same perfectionist standard which has made Switzerland the world centre of catering and hotel administration. The best hoteliers are those who pay infinite attention to details, and this is something that the Swiss are eminently suited to teach. But only 3 per cent of the population actually work in catering; modern Switzerland is a highly industrialised country, and 45 per cent of the national work force is in industry, and a further 17 per cent in agriculture.

In the French-speaking parts of Switzerland, the most characteristic dish is the melted cheese preparation known as *fondue*. Its preparation differs with the region, leaning heavily on the local cheeses fortified with suitable liqueurs. The cheese is melted, often with kirsch and white wine, in a pot set over a burner in the middle of the table. Any number of participants can enjoy this dish by spearing cubes of bread on a long fork and swirling it in the bubbling cheese to catch as much as possible. Greed is punished in a singularly pleasant way — he who drops in his cube of bread pays for the next bottle of wine.

As one follows the river Rhone further east, the *fondue* gives way to *raclette*, which in its simplest form is a block of *Gomser* or *Tilsit* cheese, held near an open fire until it melts, then scraped on to a heated plate to be eaten with hot boiled potatoes, gherkins and pickled onions.

In the Italian sections of Switzerland, the usual pasta dishes abound, but rice comes into its own with a delicious risotto, creamy yet with each grain of rice separate, flavoured with the wild mushrooms picked at dawn in the forests.

The basic character of Swiss cuisine leans much more heavily on the German culture than on the French or Italian. The abundance of potato dishes and the use of sauerkraut are just two of the marks of the Teutonic gastronomic tastes. Pork and veal are used more commonly than beef or lamb. The Genevans particularly are partial to *pieds de porc au madere* (pig's trotters with a madeira sauce) and the German influence is also seen in the wide variety of delicatessen products. The most delicious of these is the melting dried beef and pork of Valais, served as a snack as well as in hors d'oeuvre with pickles. Each canton seems to produce its own sausages: the Grisons boasts of its *Salsiz* (salami), *Tiges, Beinwurst, Engadinerwurst* and *Leberwurst,* very much like the German smoked sausages.

A gastronomic exploration of Switzerland could begin in Berne and the Swiss midlands, where the old traditional dishes are still popular. Amongst the most delicious is the *Berner Platte,* a mind-boggling serving of sauerkraut garnished with almost every type of pork product known to man: sausages, ham, smoked loin, various salamis and bacon simmered slowly in white wine and flavoured onions. In summer, the sauerkraut is replaced by beans. Other specialities are *Berner Ratsherrentopf, Rosti* potatoes, *Gnagi, Schnitz* and *Hardopfel* (stewed apples and potatoes). Notable sweets are apple charlotte, *Heitisturm* (stewed bilberries) and various types of meringue. The delicious nutty local biscuits are called *Berner Lackerli* and *Chneublatz.*

In the Canton Freiburg, *gruyere* and *vacherin* cheese are made, and the local speciality is of course *fondue.* Other delicacies include the *Freiburger Platte, pot-au-Feu, Beignets de Benichon,* known locally as *Chilbichuechli* or festival fritters, and *matafan* (gratinated bread slices). Then there is *fondue bourguignonne,* beef cubes on skewers dipped into boiling oil and served with a variety of sauces and condiments. This was originally a French dish; now it is one of Switzerland's national dishes. Other typical dishes of the region are the *tripes a la Neuchatel,* onion salad, cheese patties and the *seche au vin* (white wine tart).

Lake Geneva and the Jura district of the Canton Vaud owes a great deal to France gastronomically speaking, but particularly in Vaud, the dishes have been adapted to the tastes of the local countryside. Vaud offers a wide selection of smoked hams, sausages and pâtés, and

also the baked bread-and-cheese slices known as *gratin montagnard.* There are *Ramekins,* tripe cooked the local way and leeks.

In Geneva, they add eggs and butter to the fondue, offer frothy cheese souffle and *ombres chevalier,* wonderful fish found in Lake Geneva. Gratinated leeks are succulent and *sauce genevoise,* made with fish stock and wine, is a classic sauce.

The big features of Grisons' cuisine are imagination and richness. The air-dried meat known as *Bunderfleisch* needs no introduction to serious gourmets, and other specialities are Chur meat pie, game garnished with chestnuts or game goulash, Grisons bean soup, *polenta in flur* made with buckwheat, milk, cream and raisins, Chur meat fritters and *Maluns,* a potato dish. Engadine nut gateau is a delicacy that is sent all over the world.

To gourmets St Gall means *Bratwurst* (fried sausage) with onion sauce; Thugau means fish, particularly the excellent grilled *Gangfish* of Ebmatingen. There are also the delicate *Belchentaucherli* (birds from the Untersee region) and *Leberknopfli, Stupfete* (a potato dish) and potatoes cooked with pears.

In Appenzell they pride themselves on the *Mostmockli* and *Fenz* (a herdsman's dish made from cheese and milk) as well as *Biberfladen* and *Rahmfladen* (flat honey and cream confectionery) the recipes for which are passed down from one generation to the next.

Glarus offers not only *Chabzieger* cheese, made with herbs, but *Kalberwurste* (veal sausages), *Turkenriebel* (a dish made from maize, flour, milk and salt), cheese soup, *Glarus patties* (with plums) and *Brinbrot* (pastry filled with dried pears).

The people of Basle are gourmets with high standards, and support some of the finest pastry-cooks in the land. Salmon prepared the Basle way is excellent, flour and onion soups are specialities connected with the Basle carnival, and *Basleleckerli, Hypokras* and *Brunsli* are toothsome dainties.

The cuisine of Solothurn is refined but it has no special characteristics. Ragouts with brown or white sauce are served with tasty bread and onion puree and *Krausi* or *Fruggi* is a dish made from potatoes and sliced apple.

In Aargau — a vegetable and fruit growing district — there is a melting cabbage tart and a robust, moist carrot cake.

The Ticino is the gateway to Italian cookery, with *minestrone, busecca* (tripe soup), *spaghetti* and *ravioli, risotto con funghi* (with mushrooms), *osso bucco* (veal shanks), *gnocchi, uccelli scappate* (stuffed beef rolls), *pollo al diavolo* (chicken with rosemary), *castagnaccio* (chestnut souffle dessert) and *zabaione*, a sweet concoction of fresh egg yolks, sugar, wine and brandy. Unique Ticino specialities are *Gitzi* (young goat) and rabbit dishes.

In the Valais, the local *raclette* is made with *Gomser* cheese, which is also served with the maize mush known as *polenta*. The local *Kuchisuppe* includes potatoes, leeks and celery, and there are mouth-watering local versions of veal pasties. The vegetables grown in this area are succulent, and to finish a meal, the waffles are superb.

In central Switzerland around Lucerne, the cuisine is sturdy country fare alternating with refined classics. There is an unusual bacon and pear stew, with the fresh sweetness of the pears complementing the richness of the bacon. Sliced apples and potatoes are cooked together, and there are local pasties made of meat and mushrooms. *Felchen* is a delicious fish found in the lake, and pears make yet another appearance in the *Birnenwecken*, a pastry filled with the fruit. The spicy local gingerbread cakes are a typical Christmas treat but delicious at any time.

Zurich is the home of *Muesli,* that mixture of oats, nuts, dried fruit and wheatgerm which has staged a minor revolution on the breakfast tables of Europe. In Switzerland they eat it at any time, and call it *Birchermuesli* after Dr Bircher-Benner who founded a clinic here and first mixed the *Muesli* for his patients. On the whole, however, the people of Zurich are said to be fond of meat, and the local bill of fare underlines this preference: *Geschnetzeltes* (sliced veal) with *Rosti, Leberspiessli* (grilled liver on skewers) and *Cervelat*. Apple Charlotte is made well by the local chefs, and *Osterfladen* is an Easter flan made with rice or semolina and raisins.

The cooks of Schaffhausen have some interesting ways of preparing grayling and other fish caught in the Rhine. An outstanding dish of the area is an onion tart, known as *Bolledunne* and there are rich *schublingwecken* (sausage rolls) generally made for New Year's Eve.

Swiss patisserie is amongst the best in the world, and most bakers and confectioners learn at least part of their trade in Switzerland. The products are more subtle than the German and certainly better than the French. Highly commended are the *petits pains de rolee* (sugar buns), *cucheole* of Freiburg (large sweet bun loaves), *merveilles* (crisp wafers fried in oil), *gâteau au nillen* (a sort of lardy cake), *tresse* (plaited bread with milk and eggs) and the *panettone*, a plain fruit cake baked in a *gugelhupf* mould.

Food in Switzerland is not only a taste, it is an industry. For many years I worked in the major Swiss food company, Nestles, and while most people know that they produce sweet things, very few realise that they have helped underdeveloped nations to process their own milk into high quality cheeses. We worked on techniques in canning, freezing and food processing, and backed up the international team of scientists who were trying to produce food in areas of the world where people had for centuries been below the poverty line.

Serious as they are, the Swiss appreciate a good glass or three of wine. The local wines are excellent, but little known outside the country. There are two reasons for this: the wines are too delicate to travel well, and local production is barely big enough to satisfy the thirst of the Swiss. But the whites particularly are of a high standard, and much appreciated locally. Where the Englishman might have a beer and the American a rum and Coke, the Swiss will order two *decis* (decilitres) of white wine. The bouquet and savour of the wines of Switzerland is so different in each that it is impossible to generalise. But highly recommended are the whites named *Hermitage, Fendant, Johannisberg, la Cote, Dezaley* and *St Saphorin*. Names to remember in the reds are the *Dole* of the Valais and the white or rose of Neuchatel.

BILL OF FARE

Soup

CANTON SCHOYZ CHEESE SOUP
Cheese and bread soup

GSOD SUPPE
Bean and bacon soup with carrots and leeks

Fish Dishes

BALLEN FROM LAKE ZUG
Trout in court-bouillon

FISH FILLET MORNAY AU GRATIN
Fish fillets in cheese sauce

Cheese Dishes

CHEESE FRIBOURGEOISE
Toasted cheese savoury

CHEESE BALLS ST GALL
Cheese fritters

CHEESE VAUDOISE
Toasted cheese baked in white wine

SWISS PIZZA WITH CHEESE
Bread dough bun baked with cheese

SWISS FONDUE
Melted cheese in wine with Kirsch and garlic
   flavour

Meat Dishes

MEAT PIE VALAIS STYLE
Stew of veal and bacon with a pastry topping

TESSIN SPIESSLI
Kebab of veal, liver and bacon cooked on skewers

AARGAU SUASAGE FRITTERS
Potato fritters stuffed with sausages

MEAT DUMPLINGS
Meat balls wrapped in pastry with tomato sauce

EMINCÉ DE VEAU ZURICHOISE
Strips of veal in cream, mushrooms and red
   peppers

LEG OF MUTTON CHOPS
Braised leg mutton chops

ZURCHER LEBERSPIESSLI
Liver and bacon on skewers

GESCHNETZELTES WITH ROSTI
Small escalopines of veal with potato cakes

ROSCHTI
Fried potato cakes

Egg and Vegetable Dishes

BASEL SPINACH FROG
Spinach leaves stuffed with minced pork

EGG RAGOUT
Hard-boiled eggs in onions and cheese sauce

POLENTA GRISONS
Cornmeal porridge

Sweets and Desserts

GAUFRETTES SUISSES
Swiss waffles

ZURICH EASTER CAKE
Fruit semolina or groat flan

SCHENKELI
Fried doughnut Swiss style

OBWALDEN HONEY CAKE
Honey cake

BRICELETS OF VAUD
Waffle-type cakes

ZOUG TORTE
Kirsch flavoured torte

SOUP

CANTON SCHOYZ CHEESE SOUP
Cheese and bread soup (4 to 6 portions)

Ingredients:

Sliced bread 1 lb (480 g)
Grated cheese 1 lb (480 g)
Water 2½ pint (1,500 mls)
Salt and pepper
Dry white wine ½ pint (300 mls)

Method: Place bread and cheese in a saucepan
with boiling salted water. Boil 10 minutes. Crush
ingredients to a smooth paste. Whisk the mixture
while adding wine. Reheat and check seasoning.

GSOD SUPPE
Bean and bacon soup with carrots and leeks
    (4 to 6 portions)

Ingredients:

Water 2½ pint (1,500 mls)
Navy pea beans ½ lb (240 g)
1 onion studded with 2 cloves
Leeks cut in strips 2 oz (60 g)
Carrots thinly sliced 5 oz (150 g)
1 knuckle of green desalted bacon – diced
Celery – diced 2 oz (60 g)
1 bouquet garni
Salt and pepper
Butter 2 oz (60 g)

Method: Soak the beans overnight. Wash with
water and boil for 10 minutes. Remove scum then
add vegetables and bacon and simmer for 1½ hours
until tender. Serve in a soup tureen. The bacon is
served separately as a meat course. Season to taste
and whisk in a lump of butter.
Note: This soup can be strained and puree
collected with broth to form a thick soup, or
beans left in broth and eaten with diced cooked
gammon and cooked barley or even some pasta.
Some Swiss serve separately grated cheese.

FISH DISHES

BALLEN FROM LAKE ZUG
Trout in court-bouillon

Ingredients:

1 ballen or trout 2 lb (960 g) *or*
    4 by 8 oz (240 g) each
Salt and pepper
Fresh sage
Sliced onions 2 oz (60 g)
Sliced carrots 2 oz (60 g)
Vinegar 2 fl oz (60 mls)
White wine 10 fl oz (300 mls)
Water ½ pint (300 mls)

Method: Swiss trouts have a characteristic of their
own in appearance and flavour. Scrape, scale, gut
and clean fish. Prepare court-bouillon: boil
vegetables in water till tender, then add vinegar
and wine with the herbs. Arrange fish in a shallow
dish covered with court-bouillon and bake for 20
minutes at 360°F. Serve in the same dish with
hollandaise sauce.

FISH FILLET MORNAY AU GRATIN
Fish fillets in cheese sauce

Ingredients:

4 by 6 oz (180 g each) fish fillets – pike, carp,
    salmon, trout
White wine 5 fl oz (150 mls)
Chopped shallots 1 oz (30 g)
1 bouquet garni
Butter 2 oz (60 g)
White sauce ½ pint (300 mls)
Grated Swiss cheese 4 oz (120 g)
Salt and pepper

Method: Clean, wash and dry the fillets. Place
fish with bouquet garni in a shallow well
buttered dish. Cover with white wine and season.
Bake 20 minutes in a moderate oven. Remove the
bouquet garni and strain off the liquor into a
saucepan. Add chopped shallots and boil for 5
minutes. Blend white sauce to this liquor and add
half the grated cheese and brown under the grill.

CHEESE DISHES

CHEESE FRIBOURGEOISE
Toasted cheese savoury

Method: Fry bread in butter on both sides. Drain and place a slice of Emmental cheese on each fried slice. Brown under the grill until cheese melts and top the cheese with a slice of fried rasher of bacon.

CHEESE BALLS ST GALL
Cheese fritters

Ingredients:
Grated cheese ½ lb (240 g)
4 egg yolks
Tomato sauce ½ pint (300 mls)
Oil for frying
Flour – seasoned 1 oz (30 g)

Method: Blend egg yolks and cheese to a paste. Shape into small balls and pass in seasoned flour then fry in oil till golden. Serve with tomato sauce.

CHEESE VAUDOISE
Toasted cheese baked in white wine

Ingredients:
4 slices of bread
4 slices of Gruyere cheese 4 oz (120 g)
Butter 3 oz (90 g)
White wine 5 fl oz (150 mls)
Pinch paprika

Method: Toast bread and spread with butter. Cover with grated cheese as for Welsh rarebit. Place in a shallow dish. Add white wine and bake for 10 minutes at 380°F. Serve in same dish with a pinch of paprika sprinkled over.

SWISS PIZZA WITH CHEESE
Bread dough bun baked with cheese

Ingredients:

Bread dough:
Yeast ½ oz (15 g)
Lukewarm milk ½ pint (300 mls)
1 egg
Salt – a pinch
Flour 1 lb (480 g)
Butter 2 oz (60 g)

Filling:
Lard 2 oz (60 g)
Chopped fried onions 2 oz (60 g)
Mashed potatoes ½ lb (240 g)
Grated cheese ½ lb (240 g)
Cream cheese ½ lb (240 g)
Paprika – a pinch

Method: Crumble yeast into lukewarm milk, add beaten egg and a pinch of salt (8 g). Blend to flour to produce a firm dough. Knead well and gather into a ball. Let it rise, covered with a basin, for 30 minutes. Knock back by kneading again and blend in the soft butter. Divide dough into 12 buns. Shape them round and allow to expand for 15 minutes. Flatten each one or roll lightly like a small pizza. Prick with prongs of fork. Let it rest for 10 minutes.
Filling: Fry chopped onions in fat without browning. Add to mashed potato. Blend grated cheese and soft cream cheese and paprika. Spread this paste thickly on top of bun. Sprinkle a little grated cheese on top and bake for 20 minutes at 400°F.

SWISS FONDUE
Melted cheese in wine with Kirsch and garlic flavour

Ingredients:

1 clove of garlic
Grated cheese ½ lb (240 g)
Dry white wine 5 fl oz (150 mls)
Kirsch 3 fl oz (90 mls)
Potato flour or cornflour 1 oz (30 g)
Water 5 fl oz (150 mls)
Bread – cut into 1 inch cubes ½ lb (240 g)

Method: You need an earthenware dish or fire-proof glass casserole for this dish.

Smear the inside with crushed garlic. Add grated cheese, wine and kirsch and cook gently to obtain a smooth creamy cheese soft paste. Blend cornflour with water and stir into the hot cheese mixture to thicken it. Place the casserole on a hot plate in the dining room and the guests can help themselves by dipping cubes of bread into the cheese fondue. It is best to have individual casseroles. Potato flour is also better than cornflour as a thickener as it stands the acidity without breaking up the consistency.

MEAT DISHES

MEAT PIE VALAIS STYLE
Stew of veal and bacon with a pastry topping

Ingredients:

Puff pastry ½ lb (240 g)

Filling:

Stewing veal ½ lb (240 g)
Diced green gammon ½ lb (240 g)
White wine ½ pint (300 mls)
Water ½ pint (300 mls)
Chopped onions 2 oz (60 g)
1 bouquet garni
Fat 1 oz (30 g)
Flour 1 oz (30 g)
Pinch of ground spices
Salt and pepper
Sliced gherkins 2 oz (60 g)
Seeded grapes 4 oz (120 g)
1 tbs brandy or rum

Method: Cut meats in ½ inch cubes. Boil in wine and water with chopped onions and 1 bouquet garni for 1¼ hours till tender. Cook roux for a few minutes and add the meat liquor or stock (1 pint – 600 mls). Make up with water if there is not enough to make one full pint. Season and add sliced gherkins, grapes and brandy. Place meat in a pie dish covered with sauce. Roll pastry to ⅛ inch thickness. Place a layer of pastry on top of pie and brush with eggwash. Rest 15 minutes and bake at 400°F for 20-25 minutes.

TESSIN SPIESSLI
Kebab of liver, bacon and veal cooked on skewers

Ingredients:

Veal cubes ½ lb (240 g)
Calf's liver skinned and cubed ½ lb (240 g)
Diced cooked ham in cubes 4 oz (120 g)
4 mushrooms
4 button onions
4 bay leaves
Oil for basting
Salt and pepper
Few coriander seeds

Method: Impale the meats alternately with button mushrooms, onions and bay leaves. Brush with oil. Season and cook over charcoal fire or under the grill. Serve with a dish of pasta blended with Swiss cheese.

AARGAU SAUSAGE FRITTERS
Potato fritters stuffed with sausages

Ingredients:

Mashed potatoes ½ lb (240 g)
Flour 6 oz (180 g)
Butter 2 oz (60 g)
1 egg yolk
8 Vienna sausages

Method: Blend mashed potatoes with flour, butter and egg yolk to a fine paste. Dust board and roll like a salami. Cut thick slices and wrap each with a peeled cooked Vienna sausage. Pan fry in fat or place in a greased tray. Brush with eggwash and cook for 15 minutes at 400°F.

MEAT DUMPLINGS
Meat balls wrapped in pastry with tomato sauce

Ingredients:

Filling:

Minced veal 6 oz (180 g)
Minced pork 6 oz (180 g)
Minced beef 6 oz (180 g)
1 egg
1 tbs chopped parsley
1 chopped clove of garlic
Chopped onion 1 oz (30 g)
Salt and black pepper
Tomato sauce 1 pint (600 mls)
Grated cheese ½ lb (240 g)

Noodle paste:

2 eggs
Water 6 fl oz (180 mls)
Strong flour 1 lb (480 g)

Method: Blend all filling ingredients and mince
twice. Season. Divide into 1 oz (30 g) balls.
Blend beaten eggs and water and add flour to form
a firm dough. Rest it 20 minutes, then roll into
an oblong $\frac{1}{8}$ inch thick. With a 2 inch round
pastry cutter, cut as many rounds as you have
dough, reshaping the left-over pastry into a dough
– resting it and rolling it again until all is used:
like ravioli. On each round place a ball of meat.
Wet edges. Seal, crimp and place in a greased tray
half filled with hot water. Poach for 12 minutes.
Drain. Place the dumplings in a shallow dish with
tomato sauce. Braise 30 minutes in a moderate
oven. Allow ravioli to soak up in tomato sauce
overnight, then reheat. Sprinkle grated sheese
and brown under the grill.
Note: The overnight session enables a tenderising
process known as hydrolysis to take place, thus
rendering the ravioli more succulent and soft.
Fresh ravioli are always tougher.

ÉMINCE DE VEAU ZURICHOISE
Strips of veal in cream, mushrooms and red peppers

Ingredients:

Veal escalopes cut into 2½ inch strips 1½ lb (720 g)
Seasoned flour
Butter 3 oz (90 g)

Oil 1 fl oz (30 mls)
Chopped shallots or onions 1 oz (30 g)
Sliced mushrooms 2 oz (60 g)
Shredded red peppers 1 oz (30 g)
White wine 5 fl oz (150 mls)
Brandy 3 fl oz (90 mls)
Cream 5 fl oz (150 mls)
Salt and pepper
Chopped parsley

Method: Cut veal into 2½ inch strips with a ¼
inch thickness. Pass in seasoned flour. Heat a pan
with oil and butter and saute the meat with a lid
on. Add chopped shallots and sliced mushrooms
and red peppers after 5 minutes, then white wine.
Boil up for 10 minutes, then add brandy and
cream. Boil 4 more minutes and season and serve,
garnished with chopped parsley. Set in a crown
mould.

LEG OF MUTTON CHOPS
Braised leg of mutton chops

Ingredients:

4 leg chops 8 oz (240 g), cut across the grain on
    the bone
Seasoned flour 1 oz (30 g)
Lard 2 oz (60 g)
Salt and pepper
Sliced potatoes 8 oz (240 g)
Sliced onions 4 oz (120 g)
Sliced carrots 4 oz (120 g)
White wine ½ pint (300 mls)
Tomato puree 1 oz (30 g)
1 clove of garlic
1 bouquet garni

Method: Cut chops across the leg horizontally.
Pass in seasoned flour and pan fry for a few
minutes. Drain them and season. Place in a
casserole dish and fill with layers of potatoes,
carrots and onions in that order. Add in tomato
puree diluted with wine, the clove of garlic and
bouquet garni. Cover with a lid and bake 1½ hours
at 360°F.

ZURCHER LEBERSPIESSLI
Liver and bacon on skewers

Ingredients:

Calf's liver 1 lb (480 g)
Bacon rashers ½ lb (240 g)
Seasoned flour
Oil — for brushing
Salt and black pepper
Soya sauce or Worcester sauce
Chopped parsley

Method: Skin liver and cut into cubes. Blanch
the bacon without the rind. Wrap each cube in
bacon and impale on a skewer. Pass in seasoned
flour. Brush with oil and season. Charcoal grill
or grill under a salamander. Season with a few
drops of Worcester sauce and sprinkle chopped
parsley. Serve with Devil sauce.

GESCHNETZELTES with ROSTI
Small escalopines of veal with potato cakes

Ingredients:

Veal escalopes 1 lb (480 g)
Seasoned flour 2 oz (60 g)
Oil 2 fl oz (60 mls)
Salt and pepper
Chopped onions 2 oz (60 g)
White wine 5 fl oz (150 mls)
Stock or water 5 fl oz (150 mls)
Thyme — a pinch
Butter 1 oz (30 g)
Flour 1 oz (30 g)
Chopped parsley 1 tbs

Method: Cut veal into small 2 oz (60 g) escalops.
Pass in seasoned flour. Heat a pan with oil and
saute quickly for 5 minutes. Season and remove
from pan. Keep hot in a shallow dish. In same pan,
fry chopped onions, add wine and stock and boil
for 12 minutes to reduce and concentrate. Sprinkle
with a pinch of thyme. Thicken with a roux. Cook
butter and flour for a few minutes. Add to gravy.
Boil while stirring. Season. Strain over the escalops
and sprinkle chopped parsley. Serve with the
potato dish made as follows.

ROSTI
Fried potato cakes

Potatoes in jackets 1 lb (480 g)
Bacon dripping 2 oz (60 g)
Butter 2 oz (60 g)
Salt and pepper

Method: Half-boil jacket potatoes for 15
minutes only. Peel and cool. Slice and cut into thin
strips. Heat bacon fat and butter in a pan and saute
the seasoned potato strips so that they cook on
one side first. Toss like a pancake and brown on
the other side. The whole success of this dish
consists in frying in a small 6 inch omelette pan
so as to keep the potatoes compact. They should
look like thick potato pancakes.
Note: Half way through cooking, press the potato
before tossing.

EGG AND VEGETABLES

BASEL SPINACH FROG
Spinach leaves stuffed with minced pork

Ingredients:

Chard leaves or large spinach leaves 1 lb (480 g)
Minced pork ½ lb (240 g)
1 egg
Chopped onions ½ oz (15 g)
Salt and pepper
Cheese sauce ½ pint (300 mls)

Method: Blanch spinach leaves for 2 minutes
only. Drain. Spread on a cloth placed on a pastry
board. Blend meat with egg, chopped onions and
herbs. Season. Divide mixture into 1 oz (30 g)
balls. Place each ball on a spinach leaf and wrap
round in an oblong shape. Flatten and place the
spinach frogs into a greased shallow dish. Cover
with cheese sauce. Braise in oven, covered with a
lid, for 45 minutes at 360°F.

EGG RAGOUT
Hard-boiled eggs in onion and cheese sauce

Ingredients:

Chopped onions 2 oz (60 g)
White wine 5 fl oz (150 mls)
White sauce ½ pint (300 mls)
Salt and pepper
8 hard-boiled eggs
Grated Swiss cheese

Method: Boil chopped onions in wine for 5
minutes. Add to the white sauce and season.
Boil for 5 more minutes. Cut eggs in half and
place them in a buttered shallow dish. Cover with
sauce. Sprinkle grated cheese and brown under
the grill.

POLENTA GRISONS
Cornmeal porridge

Ingredients:

Milk 1 pint (600 mls)
Cornmeal 4 oz (120 g)
Butter 2 oz (60 g)
1 clove of garlic
1 egg – beaten
Salt and pepper
Seasoned flour
Mixture of 2 oz (60 g) butter and oil for frying
Tomato sauce
Grated cheese 3 oz (90 g)

Method: Grease a 2 inch deep flat tray with
butter. Boil milk and sprinkle cornmeal. Cool
10 minutes until it thickens like porridge. Remove
from heat, add butter, garlic, salt and pepper and
beaten egg. Pour mixture onto the tray. Cool
and when cold, cut mixture into 2 inch squares.
Pass each square in seasoned flour and fry on
both sides. Sprinkle with grated cheese and serve
with a tomato sauce.

SWEETS and DESSERTS

GAUFRETTES SUISSES
Swiss waffles

Ingredients:

Sour cream 4 fl oz (120 mls)
1 beaten egg
Milk 2 fl oz (60 mls)
Kirsch 2 tbs
Pinch of salt
Flour ½ lb (480 g)
Sugar 4 oz (120 g)
Juice and grated rind of lemon
Vanilla essence
Whipped cream ½ pint (300 mls)

Method: Mix sour cream, vanilla essence,
beaten egg and milk with kirsch, salt, flour, sugar,
lemon juice and rind. Beat well to obtain a thick
batter. Let it rest for 30 minutes. Heat a waffle
pan, well greased with lard, and cook a ladle-full
of mixture, or as much as the pan will take. Cook
and dust with sugar or shape while hot into a
cornet. Cool and fill with whipped cream.

ZURICH EASTER CAKE
Fruit semolina or groat flan

Ingredients:

Short pastry ½ lb (240 g)

Filling:

Milk 1 pint (600 mls)
Butter 2 oz (60 g)
Groats or semolina 3 oz (90 g)
Castor sugar 2 oz (60 g)
2 egg yolks
2 egg whites
Rum or Kirsch flavouring
Sultanas 2 oz (60 g)
Seedless raisins 2 oz (60 g)

Method: Roll out pastry to ¼ inch thickness and
line an 8 inch flan. Place paper inside, filled with
dried beans and bake blind for 15 minutes at
380°F. Remove from oven – discard beans.
Filling: Boil milk and butter, add groats or semolina and sugar and cook 12 minutes like porridge.
Remove and mix in egg yolks, flavouring and
sugar. Beat egg whites to a meringue and fold
into mixture. Blend in fruits (previously scalded

and drained). Fill the flan case and bake for 15 to 20 minutes at 360°F.

SCHENKELI
Fried doughnut Swiss style

Ingredients:

Butter 2 oz (60 g)
Castor sugar 4 oz (120 g)
2 eggs — beaten
Grated peels 1 tbs
Flour ½ lb (240 g)
Cooking fat
Granulated sugar

Method: Cream butter and sugar until fluffy. Add beaten eggs, grated peels and blend in flour. Form a mass and divide it into 1 oz (30 g) balls. Heat lard or oil and fry to a golden colour. Drain on absorbent paper and serve dusted with sugar or with jam.

OBWALDEN HONEY CAKE
Honey cake

Ingredients:

Honey 12 oz (360 g)
Milk 12 fl oz (360 mls) *or* sour cream
Sugar 6 oz (180 g)
Pinch cinnamon and ground clove
1 pinch nutmeg and crushed aniseed
Juice and grated rind of 1 lemon
Flour 1½ lb (720 g)
Bicarbonate of soda 1 level tsp
Cream 4 fl oz (120 mls)

Method: Boil honey and milk with sugar and add all spices and flavourings. Pour into a bowl. Add flour and stir well. Dissolve bicarbonate of soda with cream and add to mixture. Place mixture in cake tin, 9 inch by 5 inch, well greased and lined with greaseproof paper. Bake for 45 minutes at 360°F. Turn out on a rack to cool. When ready, brush cake with liquid honey or water icing.
Note: Water icing is made by using 3 oz (90 g) icing sugar and 2 tbs of water combined.

BRICELETS OF VAUD
Waffle-type cakes

Ingredients:

Butter ½ lb (240 g)
Castor sugar ½ lb (240 g)
1 egg and 1 egg yolk
Pinch of salt
Flour 1 lb (480 g)
Cream 5 fl oz (150 mls)
Water 2 fl oz (60 mls)

Method: Cream butter and sugar until fluffy. Add eggs and a pinch of salt. Blend flour, cream and water alternately to obtain a smooth but firm cake mixture. Shape into 1 oz (30 g) balls, flatten them a little and place them onto a greased baking tray or into a waffle pan. Cook for 4 minutes.

ZOUG TORTE
Kirsch flavoured flan

This torte is composed of 2 layers of Japanese nut paste and 1 layer of sponge, sandwiched together with a coating of buttercream. The sponge is soaked in syrup and kirsch.

Ingredients:

Japanese nut paste mixture:

10 whites of eggs
½ lb castor sugar (240 g)
Ground toasted hazelnuts 4 oz (120 g)
Ground toasted almonds 2 oz (60 g)
Cornflour 1 oz (30 g)
    (Mix the ground nuts with the cornflour)

Sponge mixture:

4 whole eggs
Castor sugar 4 oz (120 g)
Vanilla essence
Flour 4 oz (120 g)

Buttercream:

Butter 1 lb (480 g)
Icing sugar (blend with hot water) 12 oz (360 g)
Hot water 2 fl oz (60 mls)

Maraschino 1 fl oz (30 mls)
Kirsch 1 fl oz (30 mls)
2 egg yolks

Syrup

Sugar 3 oz (90 g)
Water 3 fl oz (90 mls)
Kirsch 3 fl oz (90 mls)
   (Sugar boiled with water — kirsch added when
   cold)

Method, Japanese mixture: Whisk the whites with
half of the sugar to a stiff meringue. (Do not mix
the sugar all at once). Fold in the remaining
sugar and almonds and hazelnuts mixture
gradually and lightly. Place the mixture in a
piping bag fitted with a large tube. Starting
from the centre — on a greased tray — pipe
in spirals 2 by 8 inch rounds. Bake for 20
minutes in a low oven (300°F). Cool.
Sponge mixture: Beat eggs and sugar in a bowl
over a saucepan of hot water for 5 minutes, until
mixture holds to the whisk and is light and foamy.
Add vanilla essence. Fold in the cake flour
carefully and place into an 8 inch sponge mould
lined with greased paper, for easy removal of
sponge. Bake near the top of the oven at 380°F
for 25 minutes.
Buttercream: Beat butter and icing sugar with a
little hot water. Add flavouring and kirsch. When
light and fluffy, add 2 egg yolks.
Torte assembling: Place 1 round of baked
Japanese mixture on a cake base, then evenly
spread a thin layer of buttercream. Place the
layer of sponge on top and sprinkle with syrup
and kirsch so that it is well soaked. Cover with
the second layer of Japanese mixture. Spread
the rest of the buttercream on top and round the
torte which, by now, should be at least 2 inch high.
Place a few toasted flaked almonds all round and
dust the top with sieved icing sugar.
Note: A decorative pattern can be produced by
using different buttercream flavours or colours.

Germany

Brass bands, beer and bratwurst are traditionally the essence of German gastronomy, and indeed Germany produces some 6,000 kinds of beer, 1,458 types of sausages, 200 kinds of bread and an atmosphere that is more oom-pa-pa than string quartet. But there is more to German cooking than that. Certainly there is an unmistakable taste in German cooking that's quite unique and unlike that of any other country. It is less spicy and less garlicky than many other continental countries, and appeals more to British tastes. It is a robust taste which depends on highly flavoured ingredients combined in original ways rather than on herbs and spices. Meat and vegetables are often served with fruit, and the humble potato is used in many interesting ways in German cooking, where it is combined with apples, pears, grated raw into pancakes and baked with caraway seed.

The German hausfrau is economically-minded even in the affluence of today, and not every meal has a meat course. The main meal is usually served in the middle of the day and is either a meat dish, prefaced with soup and followed by a pudding or fruit; or the main course could equally well be a high-protein dish such as cauliflower cheese or a casserole of lentils with a sweet-sour sauce. Breakfast could be porridge made with honey, ground nuts and dried fruit, or open sandwiches with cottage cheese, tomatoes, one of the hundreds of sausages or even the sharp, refreshing taste of radishes. Coffee is the usual beverage although hot chocolate and lemon tea are quite popular.

Supper is kept quite simple and often consists of a selection of cold meats and sausages, salads and a variety of bread and rolls. Raw fruit and vegetables are very popular, made into tasty salads. The German people are very health-conscious, and the old image of an overweight, huffing puffing businessman with a *Speckbauch* ('bacon' belly) is fast fading. The new generation of Germans tends to be much slimmer and healthier than their parents, with a vitality which has helped them to rise to their present affluence. They are hearty eaters, but they are also hard workers, and they have found that nutrition is a key factor to their productivity. While many traditional recipes lean heavily on lard, dumplings and potatoes, the modern German *Hausfrau* is well aware of calories, proteins, vitamins and minerals. The number of health-food shops and devotees of simple food is an eye-opener. On special occasions, however, the traditional meals are still cooked. One of the most beloved throughout the nation is *Sauerkraut,* cooked in white wine, cider, beer, champagne or flavoured with Kirsch, and served with frankfurters, pickled pork, garlic sausages and new potatoes. It is more than a meal—it is a feast which requires a hearty appetite and a relaxed atmosphere.

Religious occasions still have their traditional dishes, and banquets for the whole family are given on the occasions of a confirmation, engagement, wedding, funeral or christening. Christmas cooking alone could take up a whole recipe book, with every housewife baking up a store for weeks beforehand. Meat was forbidden during Advent by the Church, so the creative powers of the talented cook are turned towards baking the most sumptuous variety of cakes and biscuits. A selection of *stollen* (yeast breads) is baked, filled with nuts, dried fruit, poppy seed and curd cheese; tiny biscuits are baked weeks beforehand and allowed to mature. In many of them some of the flour is replaced by ground almonds to make them more delicate.

The Festive bird for all occasions tends to be a goose or a duck rather than chicken or turkey. This is real goose country, hence the *foie gras pâtés,* and roast goose with apple sauce. It is the stuffing of the bird which is the principal source of gastronomic delight. All kinds of fruit are used in these concoctions, usually leaning heavily towards prunes, apricots or raisins.

Pike and carp are the sumptuous fish of Germany, fancifully stuffed and served with rich sauces, redolent of raisins and spices. *Schnitzels* were originally a veal escalope, but now the term embraces everything from the breadcrumbed version known as *Wiener Schnitzel* to slices of fillet of pork, breast of chicken or even slices of thick wild mushrooms. Highly recommended are the veal escalopes coated in cream sauce or spread with filling like a *paupiette.* Some are covered with cheese sauce and grated cheese and browned in the oven. The height of *schnitzel* inventiveness is the *Holsteinschnitzel,* named after Baron Friedrich von Holstein. The *schnitzel* should be served framed with smoked salmon, caviar, mushrooms, truffles and crayfish tails, and the *Schnitzel* itself should be topped with a fried egg with a design of thin fillets of anchovies, a few capers and a sprig of parsley. Most chefs these days omit the trimmings and leave the escalope with only its egg and anchovies. *Kasseler Rippespeer,* a smoked loin of pork, can be served roast or boiled, often with an assortment of vegetables including chestnuts, mushrooms and potatoes. Minced meat is much used, notably in *Königsberger Klopse,* made from minced pork, veal or beef, poached and served with a piquant sauce, often made with anchovies.

Game is as German as beef is British—which is to say that it would be served more often if it were not so expensive, but it remains a national dream. It is marinated in red wine and vinegar, and served as roast, small entrees or in stews. Pheasant, partridge and woodcock are highly prized and served with lingonberries *(Preiselbeeren)* which taste rather like cranberries.

German shops now are filled with a large assortment of international foodstuffs; there are specialised pork and game butchers in every town. In Munich, the most spectacular food store is Dallmayr's. It is a veritable gastronome's paradise, with iced counters displaying Iranian caviar, and pools abundant with live fish. The cheese department alone has on sale over 180 varieties of cheese from every part of the globe, and customers may sample several hundreds of varieties of sausages.

In the *Koniterei*—the German pastry shops—one can sample hundreds of types of sweet specialities such as *torten, babbas, gateaux* and pastries stuffed with every imaginable fruit, served with dollops of whipped cream. The *Kaffeeklatsch*—coffee gossip time—is still a national institution. *Strudel* came to Germany by way of Hungary and derived from the Greek *baclava.* It is stuffed with cottage cheese, raisins, cherries and poppy seeds. The *Frankfurter Kranz* is the most extravagant cake in Germany.

But the most typically and uniquely German food product remains the sausage in all its forms, raised here from the humble status to the most esoteric heights of the charcutiers' art. Sausage making became a culinary art in the Middle Ages, but previously the Romans had perfected a way of preserving meat, and the word sausage is derived from the Latin salsus, meaning preserved in salt. The Romans were partial to sausages which included nuts and were flavoured with cumin seed, black peppercorns and aromatic herbs, as well as garlic. The Emperor Constantine prohibited sausage eating when he embraced Christianity, because sausages were a phallic symbol with obvious connotations of sexuality. The prohibition remained during the reign of several emperors but was eventually abolished because of popular protests and because of bootlegging.

Modern sausage factories employ extremely scientific techniques involving the latest theories of chemistry, biochemistry and bacteriology, which in this context are more important than the culinary art. The handling of sausage meat requires a great deal of hygienic care to avoid bacterial infestation. The sterile conditions are not enough; additives in the form of salpetre (sodium nitrate) must be used to prevent bacterial growth, as well as to give an appetising pink colouring to the hams, pâtés and salamis. Salt and sugar also play a part in curing pork and other meats prior to the cooking or curing process. Cured meat requires at least 3½ to 4 per cent salt intake to eliminate meat moisture.

Among notable German sausages and sausage products is the *Leberwurst,* made of liver, the *rindswurst,* made of beef, and *Fleischwurst* composed of a variety of meats. There is the *Bratwurst,* the ordinary sausage made of pork or beef, common the world over. *Weisswurst* is a white sausage made of veal, spleen and brains, and in Westphalia sausages are baked in pastry like a gigantic sausage roll. The *Bouillonwurst* of Hanover is served with lashings of mustard and a bowl of horseradish; *Milzwurst* is made of spleen and found all along the Danube; in Braunschweig you will find dishes of *Saiten* sausage served with lentils, and also the soft, spreadable sausages known as *Mettwurst.* *Knackwurst* is served heated in water below boiling point and resembles a very fat, short Frankfurter. *Zungenwurst* is made of tongue and *Blutwurst* is the dark, almost black sausage made of pork and blood, a close relative of black pudding.

The cooking of Germany remains strongly regional in character, as is to be expected in a large country which until recently was composed of dozens of independent states.

Baden

The former Grand Duchy of Baden is a gourmets' paradise, with mouth-watering specialities like larded pike, trout fried in butter and garnished with almonds, braised venison in wine sauce and chicken in Riesling. Game is casseroled with wild forest mushrooms, buttered noodles complement the rich meaty dishes, and for dessert there might be a rose-hip jam sponge or a honey cake. The classical sweet is the *Schwarzwalder Kirschtorte,* a chocolate sponge with two types of cream, cherries and Kirsch, delicately strewn with shavings of chocolate.

Baden-Baden is the main town in the Black Forest, and in the nineteenth century it was fashionable to take the waters there, as much as for the social ambience as for one's health. The local traditional recipes were embellished by the chefs brought by the eminent visitors and classical dishes were given a local touch to produce a gastronomic standard of international repute.

The German version of the French *Boeuf à la Mode* is the *Badisches Ochsenfleisch,* boiled beef served with horseradish sauce and a salad of melon, cherries, pickled cucumbers and plums. Another local speciality is the veal stuffed with hard-boiled eggs, and a veal stew with capers. *Petits fours* developed a whole new meaning in this international playground. *Kuchle* are pastries made with nuts and wild berries and served fried; *Rosenkuchle* are made with rose petals and the *Frauenschenkeli* are stuffed with fruits.

Among the most famous spirits from this region is the *Kirschwasser* made from the tasty, dark cherries, and *Himbeergeist,* which magically preserves the delicate, fresh flavour of the raspberries from which it is made.

Bavaria

This is the largest state in West Germany and of the most consequence in terms of gastronomy. It is a rich agricultural region, with Munich as its capital, newly international yet still with men wearing *Lederhosen* an ornate Loden jackets, and women in various types of *Dirndl,* that flattering combination of wide skirt, puffy blouse and dark waistcoat, with an embroidered Sunday best apron.

Weisswurst is the first local speciality encountered by visitors to the famous beer festival; it is a hot white sausage served with lashings of sweet Bavarian mustard on a split bread roll, and helps the beer along. Another seasonal dish in Munich is a whole ox roasted on a spit with white radishes cut into spirals served as a garnish: this is an extra-special dish for the Munich Beer Festival only, and aside from the last week in September and first week in October, you would ask for it in vain. But *Knödel*—dumplings—are staple Bavarian fare, whether savoury or sweet. One solid variation is made with little pieces of fried bacon dotting the dough, and others are filled with fruit to make a warm dessert.

A typical Bavarian meal is *Geselchtes;* pieces of mildly smoked ham or pork, black on the outside, eaten with rye bread and served with mugs of beer with *Schnapps* as a chaser. *Leberkas* is a soft glistening liver pâté spread on rye bread, and *brathendl* is chicken roasted on the spit. A traditional favourite is a huge shank of veal or pickled pork, known as *Kalbshaxe* or *Schweinshaxe* served with Bavarian potato dumplings.

Bavarian beers are truly world-famous, and notable brand names are *Dortmunder, Hansa, D.A.B., Beck, Holsten, Loewenbraeu, EKU, Hubertus Back, Herforder Pilsner* and *Dortmunder Union.* An interesting aperitif is *Enzian,* a spirit flavoured with the root of the gentian, reminiscent of the French *Suze* – and bitter as hell.

Franconia

This is the region of the castles where Minnesingers composed the verses which formed the beginnings of German lyric poetry. But the local food is rather more hearty; the local version of *sauerkraut* is served with tiny, succulent sausages seasoned with herbs, which go by the name of *rostbratwurste.* *Pressack* is a meaty jellied brawn, and the *Scalach-platte* is a lavish assortment of sausages and meat served with *Frankische Klosse,* a robust dumpling. *Meerfischli* are tiny crunchy fish fried like sprats.

Some excellent wines are produced in this region, notably *Wurzburger Stein, Neuberg, Randersackerer Teufelskeller* and *Rodelseer.* Franconia also has some good beers—the most unusual is the *Rauchbiere,* in which the distinctive smokey flavour is due to using smoked malt.

Württemberg

This is the region where *Spatzle* appear in all sorts of guises. They are thin bits of noodle dough, scraped from a pastry board directly into boiling water. There are also machines like a mouli to make the *Spatzle.* When cooked, the *Spatzle* may be served with melted butter and browned bread-crumbs, or drained and fried lightly in butter. There are larger versions, still torpedo-shaped, which are stuffed with various ingredients like mushrooms, meat or cheese.

The *Kalbsvogel* is a delicious veal escalope, flattened out with a mallet and rolled around a filling of egg, spinach and bacon. Some of the most succulent sauerkraut is made in the Württemberg area, and lentils with sausages is a Stuttgart speciality. *Maultasch'* is a meatier version of ravioli, and some lusty soups are on the menu – *Fladle,*

Riebele, Brisle and *Klossle.* Some excellent wines are produced in this region, but the local thirst is massive and none are exported. The *Unterturkheimer, Unbacher* or *Rotenberger* are well worth trying.

Hesse, Rhineland and the Palatinate

The main speciality of the area is *Rippchen mit Kraut,* bacon spareribs with sauerkraut, which can not be copied in any other party of the world—it is the local bacon which gives the dish its stout character and imparts to the sauerkraut its special smokey flavour. Equally hearty and delicious is the *erbsbrei mit sauerkraut,* pease pudding and sauerkraut garnished with slices of pig's head, and served with an unctuous sauce made with a variety of herbs—one of the best of German cuisine. The *Kartoffelpfannkuchen* are potato pancakes served with apple sauce, and generally speaking potato dumplings, potato soups and potato dishes of all kinds are popular in the lower Rhine region.

Himmel und Erde (heaven and earth) is a mixture of apple puree, mashed potatoes, slices of black pudding and onions, all fried together quickly in a pan. It is served with thickly buttered bread and washed down with beer or schnapps. The most popular dish is *sauerbraten,* marinated beef braised in a sweet-sour sauce and served with dumplings.

Some of the finest white wines are produced in this region and exported under the generic term hock. There is also a sparkling white wine made by the champagne method and known as *Sekt,* the life-blood of any festive occasion in Germany.

Westphalia

Broad beans, bacon and *Panhas Westfalischer Spielart*—a thick stew made with stock, fresh liver sausage, beef, pork and pumpernickel bread—are the typical Westphalian specialities. *Husumer Rolle* is a beef brawn, matured and fried in slices, usually served with a sharp sauce. The raw smoked ham of this area is renowned the world over and is served as a starter. It is to Westphalia what smoked salmon is to Scotland.

Schleswig-Holstein, Hanover, Mecklenburg

German caviar is made from the roe of a large fish similar to a sturgeon, caught in the North Sea. The smoked fish of Cuxhaven has a high reputation with gourmets, and praticularly appreciated are the *Raucheraal* (smoked eel), *Raucherherring* (smoked herring), smoked flounder and the tiny, crisp yet melting smoked sprats. The *Rollmopse* (pickled herring rolls) are the best in Europe. Roast *Heidschnucken* (lamb) served with beans is the most celebrated dish of this region. The lamb is a curly-horned variety peculiar to this area and has a similar reputation to the French lamb *des prés salés*–lamb which has grazed on the salt-marshes near the sea is always more succulent than its inland cousin.

There are myriad fish specialities, many smoked and most of them quite delicious. Memorable are the long curls of smoked fillets known as *Schillerlocken,* allegedly resembling the curls of that poet.

Lubeck is famous for its marzipan, that delicious mixture of ground almonds, egg whites and rose water which in Germany is made into thousands of shapes, usually fruit and vegetables, all realistically coloured. They are an indispensable part of the German Christmas and used as a tree decoration as well as a confection. A delicious dessert is produced here and popular throughout Germany: *rote grutze,* a puree of raspberries thickened with potato or cornflour.

Hamburg food has an international flavour due to its long history as an international meeting place of merchants. Best of the local dishes are the *Hummer-ragout Graf Luckner* (lobster stew), *Funkenwerder Fischsuppe* (fish soup) and *Snuten und Poten*, a hot pot of pickled pork and vegetables,

Saxony

This former kingdom is now entirely within East Germany, but the excellence of its specialities means that many of them are available all over Germany. The most renowned of these, and justly so, is the Christmas cake known as Dresdner Stollen, a rich concoction of yeast dough studded with almonds, raisins, currants, citron peel and candied fruits of all kinds, folded into a foot-long loaf two weeks or so before Christmas, to mature gently until its glorious appearance on Christmas Eve. Another Saxonian delicacy is the *Streuselkuchen,* made with a base of egg-rich yeast pastry topped with breadcrumbs made with butter, sugar and flour.

Dried fruit is an important part of Saxonian cooking, and often a compote of dried pears, apples, raisins, prunes, apricots and peaches is served instead of a vegetable.

Liver is a much-prized delicacy, and there is a variety of recipes for it. An interesting one is *leber im grünen bett*–liver in a green bed–in which the liver is sauteed, then simmered in wine with a great number of fresh herbs. An imaginative vegetable dish is *Leipziger Allerlei,* in which a variety of vegetables are cooked lightly in broth and then masked with a butter sauce thickened with cream and a little cornflour.

Berlin

Gastronomically speaking, Berlin is a typically cosmopolitan city where classical dishes in the French manner are available in the luxury hotels and restaurants. At home, the people eat rather differently; in the eastern part the food is simple but wholesome, with a preference for minced or scraped meat, as in the local versions of steak tartare: *Schabefleisch* (scraped beef served with onions and capers), and its close relative, *Hacke-peter,* made of lean minced pork and served raw. Meat loaves are excellent and imaginative–and help to stretch the expensive meat.

Cucumbers are a favourite vegetable in East and West, whether eaten as pickles flavoured with dill, or gently simmered in butter as a hot vegetable, or sliced paper-thin and sprinkled with sour cream and fresh dill as a salad.

Another speciality too wonderful to remain local is the *Berliner Pfannkuchen,* now known all over Germany as *Faschingskrapfen.* It is quite simply a doughnut, but the most delicate, melting, toothsome, appetising doughnut in the world. Never greasy, never heavy, it is filled with plum jam and fried in a deep bath of hot oil–traditionally lard, but cholesterol rules even the most traditional cooking in Germany now.

With their financial security, high standard of living and solid economy, who can blame them for wanting to stay healthy? They have so much to live for.

BILL OF FARE

Soup

GAME SOUP WITH ROSE-HIP
Game soup flavoured with port wine and garnished with German sausages

WESTPHALIAN BIERSUPPE
Cold beer custard soup flavoured with honey

GRUNER AAL HAMBURGER ART
Hamburg smoked eel soup or stew

Hors d'Oeuvre

HERRING IN SOUR CREAM
Herring and pickled cucumber salad in cream

GERMAN NOODLE SALAD
Noodles and German sausages with cheese in mayonnaise

KARTOFFELSALAT
Sausage and potato salad

GEFULLTE TOMATEN
Tomatoes stuffed with diced apple, cheese and frankfurter salad in mayonnaise

Fish Dishes

HEILBUTT UNTER DEM SCHNEEBERG
Poached halibut in cream sauce

FRIESISCHER PFANNFISCH
Baked fish with potatoes and flavoured with mustard and beer

FISCHE MIT APFEL KUMMELKRAUT
Fish fried with apples and caraway seeds

ROLLMOPS
Pickled herrings

KAISERHUMMER MIT HUHN
Chicken and lobster souffle William II

Meat Dishes

REBRUCKEN MIT ROTWEINSOSSE
Braised venison

KASSELER RIPPESPEER
Braised smoked loin of bacon with sauerkraut

SUSS-SAURE BRATWURST
Sausages in sweet and sour sauce

GANSEBRATEN MIT APFELN, ROSINEN UND NUSSEN
Roast goose with fruit mixture

SAUERBRATEN
Braised beef marinaded in vinegar

KONIGSBERGER KLOSSES
Meat dumplings in caper and lemon sauce

KLOSSE
Bread and bacon dumplings coated with butter sauce

KALBSROLLE
Braised stuffed breast of veal

GERMAN SAUCE
One of the leading sauces of international cookery

Vegetables

SPATZLE
German pasta

KURBISBREI MIT KASE
Pumpkin with chsse

GEFULLTER SELLERIE
Stuffed celeriac

KARTOFFELKLOSSE
Potato dishes

MOHREN
Carrots and apples with honey

SAUERKRAUT (German style)
Fermented cabbage cooked with bacon and juniper berries

BOHNEN MIT APFELN
Haricot beans with apples

ROTKOHL MIT APFELN
Red cabbage braised with apple

GRUNE BOHNEN MIT BIRNEN
Runner beans with sliced pears

Sweets and Desserts

STOLLEN
Yeast cake filled with almond paste

SCHWARZWALDER KIRSCHTORTE
A torte filled with cherries, cream and chocolate

APFELKUCHEN
German apple tart

KASEKUCHEN
Lemon cheese cake with morello cherries

FRUCHTSPEISE
Apple and blackberry pudding

GERMAN GUGELHUPF
A cake version of the Austrian yeast cake

BIREWECKA
A German mixed fruit bread loaf, also popular in
   Alsace

SOUP

GAME SOUP WITH ROSE-HIP
Game soup flavoured with port wine and garnished
with German sausages

Ingredients:

Canned German soup or sauce from jugged hare
2½ pint (1,500 mls) or any good brand game
soup

Garnish:

Diced carrots 2 oz (60 g)
Celery 2 oz (60 g)
Potato 2 oz (60 g)
Red port 5 fl oz (150 mls)
Pinch of mixed spices
2 frankfurters thinly sliced 4 oz (120 g)
Rose-hip jelly 4 oz (120 g)
Lard 2 oz (60 g)

Method: Brown all vegetables in fat for 10 minutes,
add game stock or soup and boil for a further 40
minutes. Season. Add frankfurter slices and jelly
and lastly port wine.

WESTPHALIAN BIERSUPPE
Cold beer custard soup flavoured with honey

Strange as it may seem, this soup is usually served
at the beginning of a meal in Germanic countries
but it can also be served as a sweet anywhere else.

Ingredients:

Pale ale beer 2½ pint (1,500 mls)
Sugar 2 oz (60 g)
Honey 3 oz (90 g)

Scalded fruits:

Seedless raisins 1 oz (30 g)
Dried apples 1 oz (30 g)
Dried apricots 1 oz (30 g)

Thickening:

4 egg yolks
Cornflour 2 oz (60 g)

Water ½ pint (300 mls)
Pinch of nutmeg and cinnamon

Method: Place fruits in beer until well soaked.
Cook gently for 20 minutes. Strain juice into a
saucepan and thicken with thickening ingredients
which have been well blended together. Stir while
adding egg mixture and add sugar, honey and
spices. Cool and chill.

GRUNER AAL HAMBURGER ART
Hamburg smoked eel soup or stew

A typical German soup with a sweet and sour
taste combining fish and stewed fruits. Generally,
when available, fresh eels are used for this soup
which is similar to the Belgian and Dutch soup.

Ingredients:

Smoked eel 2 lb (960 g)
White wine ½ pint (300 mls)
White vinegar 1 fl oz (30 mls)
1 teabag
Mixed soaked dried fruits (apricots, apples,
pears, prunes) 8 oz (240 g)
Water 1 pint (600 mls)

Vegetable stock:

Water 1½ pint (900 mls)
Leeks 2 oz (60 g)
Carrots 2 oz (60 g)
Shredded cabbage 2 oz (60 g)
1 bouquet garni

Thickening:

Cream 5 fl oz (150 mls)
2 egg yolks
Cornflour 1 oz (30 g)

Flavouring:

Chopped spinach, chervil, sorrel, parsley and fresh
mint 1 tablespoon

Seasoning:

Pinch of salt, pepper and nutmeg

Method: This kind of dish resembles the Flemish
Anguille au vert, the difference being that dried

fruit and smoked eel are used instead of the fresh eel.

Cut eel in 2 inch (5 cm) pieces. Remove skin and bone and place in a dish with wine and vinegar to soak for 5 minutes. Soak the dried fruit in tea for 30 minutes and cook in the same liquor. Slice vegetables and boil for 15 minutes to make a stock. Blend fish and liquid with the stock and reheat for 10 minutes. Drain and thicken liquor with a slurry of cornflour, egg yolk and cream and a little of the stock and then add to the remainder of the stock and boil for 5 minutes. Add the chopped herbs to the sauce and pour over the fish. Serve the compote of fruits separately as a garnish.

HORS D'OEUVRE

HERRING IN SOUR CREAM
Herring and pickled cucumber salad in cream

Ingredients:

Salted herring fillets 2 lb (960 g)

Marinade:

White vinegar ½ fl oz (15 mls)
Sugar ½ oz (15 g)
Water 1 fl oz (30 mls)
Sour cream ½ pint (300 mls)
Diced peeled pickled cucumber 4 oz (120 g)
Chopped or diced apple 4 oz (120 g)
Chopped spring onions 2 oz (60 g)
Pinch of chopped chives

Method: Desalt the herring in cold water for 2 hours. Drain and dry. Cut in small pieces and marinade in vinegar, sugar, water and cream for 2 hours. Then add chopped or diced cucumbers, apples, onions and chives.

GERMAN NOODLE SALAD
Noodles and German sausages with cheese in mayonnaise

Ingredients:

German egg noodle 8 oz (240 g)
Water 3 pint (1,800 mls)

Salt and pepper
German sausages 8 oz (240 g)
Tilsiter cheese cut in strips 6 oz (180 g)
Green pepper 2 oz (60 g)
Pickled gherkins 4 oz (120 g)
German mayonnaise 2 oz (60 g)
Plain yoghurt 5 oz (150 g)
German mustard 1 teaspoon
Pinch of paprika
Wine vinegar 2 tbs

Method: Boil the noodles in salted water for 15 minutes. Refresh in cold water for 10 minutes. Drain and dry. Cut frankfurters or other German cooked sausages in slices or strips, add cheese and shredded green peppers. Blend with rest of ingredients.

KARTOFFELSALAT
Sausage and potato salad

A mixture of egg, salami, apple and potatoes with salad dressing.

Ingredients:

German salami 10 oz (300 g)
Potato salad 10 oz (300 g)
Emmental cheese 3 oz (90 g)
Apples 5 oz (150 g)
Pickled cucumber 2 oz (60 g)
Chopped onions 2 oz (60 g)
3 hard-boiled eggs

Decoration:

Lettuce leaves, radishes and sliced cucumber

Dressing:

Mayonnaise ½ pint (300 mls)

Method: Dice or slice all ingredients and blend in mayonnaise. Decorate with lettuce leaves, radishes and sliced cucumber.

GEFULLTE TOMATEN
Tomatoes stuffed with diced apple, cheese and frankfurter salad in mayonnaise

Ingredients:

8 large tomatoes

Stuffing:

Diced Tilsiter cheese 2 oz (60 g)
Diced frankfurters 2 oz (60 g)
Diced pickled cucumber 2 oz (60 g)
Chopped onions 2 oz (60 g)
Mayonnaise 5 oz (150 g)

Method: Slice top of tomatoes, scoop out pulp and blend all other ingredients with mayonnaise. Refill tomatoes, topping with mayonnaise and sprinkle with chopped parsley. Replace top on each tomato.

FISH DISHES

HEILBUTT UNTER DEM SCHNEEBERG
Poached halibut in cream sauce

Ingredients:

Halibut fillets 1½ lb (720 g)

Fish stock:

Fish bones 1 lb (480 g)
Sliced onions 8 oz (240 g)
White wine 5 fl oz (150 mls)
Water 1 pint (600 mls)
Margarine 2 oz (60 g)
1 bouquet garni

Garnish:

Button onions 2 oz (60 g)
Diced pickled cucumber 2 oz (60 g)

Thickening:

Cream 5 fl oz (150 mls)
Cornflour 1 oz (30 g)

Seasoning:

Juice of ½ lemon
Pinch of paprika
Salt and pepper
Grated cheese 4 oz (120 g)

Method: Prepare fish stock by placing bones and margarine with sliced onions and bouquet garni in a saucepan and sweat for 10 minutes. Add water and wine and boil for a further 20 minutes. Strain.

Season the fish fillets and place in a shallow dish covered with stock. Braise in oven for 16 minutes at 360°F. Drain off the liquor and thicken with a slurry of cream and cornflour. Season to taste. Pour sauce over the fish, sprinkle with grated cheese and paprika and brown under the grill for 4 minutes. Serve additional sauce separately with a garnish of button onions (cooked apart) and diced pickled cucumber.

FRIESISCHER PFANNFISH
Baked fish with potatoes, flavoured with mustard and beer

Ingredients:

Sliced onions 5 oz (150 g)
Lard or oil 2 oz (60 g)
White fish (cod, haddock, whiting) 1½ lb (720 g)
    cut in fillets of 5 oz (150 g) each
German made mustard 2 oz (60 g)
Seasoned flour 2 oz (60 g)
Sliced raw potatoes 1 lb (480 g)
Salt and pepper
German beer 1 pint (600 mls)
1 bay leaf
1 sprig of thyme
Chopped parsley 1 tbs

Method: Pan fry sliced onion until soft but not brown. Coat the fish with made mustard and pass in seasoned flour. Place on a shallow dish and cover with the cooked onions and a layer of sliced potatoes. Season. Boil the beer and pour over the fish dish. Add herbs and bake in oven at 360°F for 20 minutes. Serve with a sprinkling of chopped parsley.

FISCHE MIT APPEL KUMMELKRAUT
Fish fried with apples and caraway seeds

Ingredients:

Fish fillets from cod, haddock, etc. 1½ lb (720 g)
Seasoned flour 2 oz (60 g)
Lard or oil 3 oz (90 g)
Sliced apples 3 oz (90 g)
Shredded white cabbage 8 oz (240 g)
Caraway seeds — a good pinch
Beer ½ pint (300 mls)
Salt and pepper
4 juniper berries
1 bay leaf
Juice of ½ lemon

Method: Pass the fish in seasoned flour. Pan fry in fat for 2 minutes on both sides. Grease a shallow dish and place shredded cabbage and sliced apples with beer in the bottom and cover with fried fish. Season and add herbs, berries and seeds. Bake with a lid on for 20 minutes at 360°F. Sprinkle with lemon juice on serving.

ROLLMOPS
Pickled herrings

Ingredients:

Fresh herrings 1½ lb (720 g)
Salt 1½ oz (45 g)
White vinegar 1 pint (600 mls)
6 peppercorns
2 chilli peppers
1 bay leaf
Few mustard seeds
Thinly sliced onion 5 oz (150 g)
3 juniper berries
Pinch of allspice
Pickled cucumber 4 oz (120 g)
Fresh water ¼ pint (150 mls)

Method: Scale, bone and fillet the herrings. Wash and dry. Place each fillet on the board and stuff with a strip of pickled cucumber and a thin slice of onion. Season with salt and pepper and roll up. Insert a cocktail stick and place in an earthenware dish. Boil water and vinegar with spices and 1½ oz (45 g) salt for 3 minutes. Cool and pour over the fish. Marinade for 48 hours. Store in a refrigerator.

KAISERHUMMER MIT HUHN
Chicken and lobster souffle William II

This recipe was created by Rudolf Boij, Chef to the late Emperor of Germany William II. It is interesting to note that Wilhelm II, who reigned from 1888 changed the language of the menus from French to German.

Ingredients:

Cooked lobster meat 8 oz (240 g)
Cooked chicken meat 8 oz (240 g)
Brandy 3 fl oz (90 mls)
Cream 5 fl oz (150 mls)
Butter 3 oz (90 g)
Flour 3 oz (90 g)
Chicken stock 1 pint (600 mls)
8 egg yolks
12 egg whites
Salt and pepper
Pinch of paprika
Tomato puree ½ oz (15 g)
Lobster coral ¼ oz (8 g)
Parmesan cheese, grated 2 oz (60 g)

Method: Cut the lobster meat in small cubes, add brandy, paprika and tomato puree and leave ingredients to macerate for 30 minutes. Dice the chicken, season and macerate with cream for the same period of time.

Meanwhile, prepare a thick sauce as follows. Melt butter in a saucepan and add flour. Cook without browning to obtain a pale roux. Gradually add the chicken stock (or milk), stir well and season. Remove from heat, add beaten yolks and reboil for 5 minutes stirring all the time. Remove from the heat. Beat egg whites with a pinch of salt in a clean bowl to a stiff meringue. When mixture sticks to the whisk it is ready.

Divide the egg custard in two parts. To one part add the diced lobsters with the brandy and to the other part add the chicken and cream. Mix each part well. Fold half of the meringue into the lobster mixture and the remainder into the chicken mixture.

Grease an 8 inch diameter by 3 inch deep souffle dish with soft butter. Sprinkle the inside with grated Parmesan cheese. Place alternate layers of lobster mixture and chicken mixture in dish and sprinkle with grated cheese. Form a circular gullet round the top of the mixture between the side of the dish and the mixture itself. This will prevent the mixture sticking to the sides of the dish and the souffle will rise upwardly without forming a mushroom dome. Place the souffle dish on a tray and bake at 380°F for 20/25 minutes. Serve immediately. The contrast of the two mixtures, one pink and one white, produces a pleasant effect and the flavour is harmonised without conflicting with each characteristic flavour.

MEAT DISHES

REBRUCKEN MIT ROTWEINSOSSE
Braised venison (10 to 12 portions)

Ingredients:

Saddle, leg or loin of venison
1 cow's heel 1 lb (480 g)

Marinade:

Water 3 pint (1,800 mls)
Red wine 1 pint (600 mls)
White vinegar 5 fl oz (150 mls)

Vegetables:

Sliced onions 10 oz (300 g)
Sliced carrots 10 oz (300 g)
1 bouquet garni
1 clove garlic
8 juniper berries
Tomato puree 2 oz (60 g)

Seasoning:

Salt and pepper
Pinch of mace and ground cloves

Thickening:

Cornflour 2 oz (60 g)
Cream 5 fl oz (150 g) (optional)
Water 5 fl oz (150 mls)

Fat for roasting and frying 2 oz (60 g)

Method: Boil marinade ingredients with vegetables for 5 minutes. Cool. Cut cow's heel in 4 pieces and boil in 2 pint water for 1 hour. Marinade venison for 48 hours, turning from time to time. Leave in a refrigerator for this period. Remove venison and wipe dry. Drain vegetables. Brown venison in a roasting tray with fat and roast at a high temperature to sear the juices for 20 minutes at 420°F. Reduce heat to 300°F and add vegetables, cow's heel, stock and marinade liquor. Cook for 2½ hours covered with a lid. Remove joint and place liquor in a saucepan with vegetables and meat from cow's heel. Boil for 30 minutes and strain. Use 3 pints of the liquor only. Mix cream, cornflour and water in a bowl. Add to the boiling venison liquor to thicken it to the right consistency. Check seasoning, carve the venison and pour some of the sauce over it. Serve remainder separately in a sauceboat with redcurrant jelly. Serve a compote of pears cooked in red wine as a garnish.

KASSELER RIPPESPEER
Braised smoked loin of bacon with sauerkraut
    (10 to 12 portions)

Ingredients:

Smoked short loin of bacon 4 lb (1,920 g)
Water 1 pint (600 mls)
Carrot 5 oz (150 g)
Onion 5 oz (150 g)
1 bouquet garni
Brown sugar 2 oz (60 g)
Ground mixed spices 1 tsp
Sauerkraut 1 lb (480 g)
Crushed pineapple 5 oz (150 g)
German gin 5 fl oz (150 mls)
4 juniper berries
Salt and pepper

Sauce:

Beer ½ pint (300 mls)
Meat stock ½ pint (300 mls)
Tomato puree 1 oz (30 g)

Thickening:

Cornflour 2 oz (30 g)
Water 5 fl oz (150 mls)

Method: Desalt the bacon overnight in cold water. Chine the joint by removing the spinal back bone. Place in cold water with 1 carrot and 1 onion studded with 4 cloves and 1 bouquet garni. Bring to the boil. Remove scum as it rises and simmer gently for 1 hour. Remove bacon from stock and place in a roasting tray. Remove rind and sprinkle with brown sugar and mixed spices. Brown in hot oven for 10 minutes at 380/400°F to obtain a nice glaze. Remove. Wash, drain and dry the sauerkraut. Boil with beer, tomato puree, juniper berries and some of the bacon stock for 30 minutes. Drain and collect the juice. Thicken it with a slurry of cornflour and water. Carve meat, sprinkle with gin, add some of the sauce and serve remainder in a gravy boat. Mix chopped pineapple with the cooked sauerkraut and serve with the meat.

SUSS-SAURE BRATWURST
Sausages in sweet and sour sauce

Ingredients;
Water 1 pint (600 mls)
Beef bouillon cubes ½ oz (15 g)

Thickening:
Cornflour 1 oz (30 g)
Water 5 fl oz (150 mls)

Salt and pepper
Made mustard 1 tsp
Pinch of mixed spices
Bratwurst 1 lb (480 g)
Sugar ½ oz (15 g)
Vinegar 1 fl oz (30 mls)
Seedless raisins 4 oz (120 g)

Method: Prepare a thin stock by dissolving bouillon cubes in boiling water. Season and thicken with slurry. Add sugar and vinegar and simmer Bratwurst in sauce for 20 minutes. Five minutes before end of cooking time, add seedless raisins and made mustard to the sauce.

GANSEBRATEN MIT APFELN, ROSINEN UND NUSSEN
Roast goose with fruit mixture (6 portions)

Ingredients:
Giblets (neck, gizzard, heart and winglets)
Water 2 pint (1,200 mls)
1 onion
1 carrot
1 bouquet garni
1 sprig of mint

Stuffing:
Goose liver 5 oz (150 g)
Sausagemeat 5 oz (150 g)
Breadcrumbs 3 oz (90 g)
Chopped parsley 1 tbs
Pinch of mixed sage and mint
2 eggs
Salt and pepper
Pinch of mace
Walnuts 2 oz (60 g)
Seedless raisins and sultanas 3 oz (90 g)
Diced apples and pears 4 oz (120 g)
Flour 1 oz (30 g)

1 goose 8 lb (3,840 g)
Butter 2 oz (60 g)
Lard 2 oz (60 g)

Thickening:
Cornflour 2 oz (60 g)
Water 5 fl oz (150 mls)

Seasoning:
Salt and pepper
Pinch of clove and nutmeg

Method: Prepare stock by boiling giblets in water with carrot, onion and herbs for 1 hour. Strain and thicken with a cornflour slurry. Blend minced liver and sausagemeat with crumbs, flour and beaten egg then add nuts and fruits with seasoning. Stuff goose in flap of neck and stuff remainder inside the bird. Rub the goose with butter and lard, season and roast for 100 minutes, first 30 minutes at 400°F and remainder at 360°F. Baste from time to time with gravy. Remove from tray. Add goose gravy to sauce, eliminate fat from gravy. Carve and serve with sauce.

SAUERBRATEN
Braised beef marinaded in vinegar
    (10 to 12 portions)

Ingredients:

Topside or thick flank beef 4 lb (1,920 g)
Same marinade and ingredients as for
    Rebrucken mit Rotweinsosse

Method: Follow same method as for Rebrucken mit Rotweinsosse.

KONIGSBERGER KLOSSES
Meat dumplings in caper and lemon sauce

Ingredients:

Chopped onions 5 oz (150 g)
Lard 3 oz (90 g)
Breadcrumbs 5 oz (150 g)
2 eggs
Cream 5 fl oz (150 mls)
Minced beef 8 oz (240 g)
Salt and pepper
Grated nutmeg
Chopped anchovy fillets 2 oz (60 g)
Chopped parsley 1 tbs
Seasoned flour

Sauce:

Margarine 2 oz (60 g)
Flour 2 oz (60 g)
Milk 1½ pint (900 mls)
Juice and rind of 1 lemon
2 egg yolks
Yoghurt 5 fl oz (150 mls)
Chopped parsley 1 tbs
Capers 2 oz (60 g)

Method: Fry chopped onions in lard without browning. Add to breadcrumbs and blend with remainder of ingredients, mixing them thoroughly in a bowl. Divide mixture into balls and pass in seasoned flour. Place in a greased

shallow tray and cover level with hot water and bake in oven for 30 minutes at 380°F. Drain off liquor and blend with milk. Make a roux: Cook margarine and flour together and add milk gradually. Season. Blend yoghurt and egg yolks and add to the sauce while stirring. Add capers and lemon. Pour sauce over dumplings and sprinkle with chopped parsley.

KLOSSES
Bread and bacon dumplings coated with butter
    sauce

Ingredients:

Fresh bread crumbs 1 lb (480 g)
Milk 5 fl oz (150 mls)
Diced cooked ham or bacon 8 oz (240 g)
Chopped onions 5 oz (150 g)
Lard 2 oz (60 g)
Chopped parsley 1 tbs
3 eggs
Flour 2 oz (60 g)
Salt and pepper
Grated nutmeg
Brown breadcrumbs 3 oz (90 g)
Butter 8 oz (240 g)

Method: Soak white breadcrumbs in milk. Squeeze out moisture so that the crumbs are as dry as possible. Melt lard in a pan and saute the chopped onions and bacon for 5 minutes. Place all ingredients in a bowl and mix well. Add beaten eggs, herbs and flour, and blend to a stiff dough. Divide the dough into small dumplings. Shape and roll on a floured board. Poach for 12 minutes in salted water until the dumplings bob up. Drain and place on a shallow dish. Fry brown breadcrumbs in butter so that mixture is fairly liquid and pour it over the Klosses.

KALBSROLLE
Braised stuffed breast of veal (10 to 12 portions)

Ingredients:

Breast of veal 4 lb (1,920 g)

Stuffing:

Minced pork 4 oz (120 g)
Breadcrumbs 1 oz (30 g)
1 egg
Chopped parsley 1 tbs
Salt and pepper
Chopped anchovy 1 oz (30 g)
Fat 2 oz (60 g)

Gravy:

Water 1 pint (600 mls)
1 onion 5 oz (150 g)
Pinch of sage

Thickening:

Cream 5 fl oz (150 g)
Cornflour 1 oz (30 g)
2 egg yolks
Pinch of nutmeg
Salt and pepper
Juice and rind of 1 lemon

Method: Bone the breast and make a slit between the skin and meat to form a pocket for the stuffing. Blend minced meat, crumbs, anchovy fillets and egg with herbs and seasoning and fill the pocket with this mixture. Season the joint and tie it up with string to prevent stuffing from escaping during cooking. Rub butter and lard all over and roast for 1½ hours. Baste with 1 pint water and after 1 hour add onion and sage to produce a gravy. Baste with this gravy for the remainder of cooking time and strain off into a saucepan. Mix cornflour, cream and water in a bowl, add lemon juice, grated rind and seasonings, and pour into the boiling gravy to thicken it. Carve the meat and serve with the sauce.

GERMAN SAUCE

This is one of the leading sauces of international cookery.

Ingredients:

White veal stock 1 pint (600 mls)
Sliced mushrooms 1 oz (30 g)

Thickening:

2 egg yolks
Cream 5 fl oz (150 mls)
Cornflour ½ oz (15 g)
Butter 1 oz (30 g)
Pinch of salt and grated nutmeg
Juice and rind of 1 lemon

Method: Mix yolks, cream and cornflour with one-third of the cold stock. Boil rest of stock with mushrooms and add thickening mixture, stirring all the time until it thickens like custard. Lastly add juice and rind of lemon and nutmeg and melted butter.

Or, instead, use a roux: 1 oz (30 g) flour, 1 oz (30 g) fat instead of cornflour. Strain.

VEGETABLES

SPATZLE
German pasta

Ingredients:

Flour 8 oz (240 g)
2 eggs
Water ½ pint (300 mls)
Pinch of salt

Method: Blend the mixture to a soft consistency but firm enough to handle and form into slivers. Prepare small slivers on a wooden platter. Boil salted water and drop slivers in the water as for pasta. Cook for 8 minutes, drain and dry.

Pan fry the Spatzle in fat until golden brown for 4 minutes and serve as a garnish or place Spatzle in a shallow dish with grated cheese or cheese sauce and serve like noodles.

The professional method of dropping the Spatzle in boiling water is to place the mixture in a piping bag fitted with a small plain tube and as the pasta comes out of the bag cut it by dipping a knife in hot water after each cut, as for Parisian gnocchi.

A simpler method is to place the Spatzle on a greased piece of wooden board and to immerse the board with the pasta balls in a tray of hot water. The Spatzle will detach themselves from the wooden board without losing their shape.

Spatzle can be purchased like any other pasta — ready for cooking.

KURBISBREI MIT KASE
Pumpkin with cheese

Ingredients:

Pumpkin 2 lb (960 g)
Salted water 1 pint (600 mls)
Pinch of ground ginger *or*
    fresh chopped ginger ½ oz (15 g)
Butter 3 oz (90 g)
Sliced apples 4 oz (120 g)
Grated cheese 4 oz (120 g)
Salt and pepper

Method: Cut pumpkin in segments and remove peeling and seeds. Boil in salted water with ginger and apples for 20 minutes until soft. Pass the pulp through a sieve and blend with butter. Season to taste. Place in a shallow dish, sprinkle with grated cheese and brown under grill.

GEFULLTER SELLERIE
Stuffed celeriac

Ingredients:

1 large celeriac 1 lb (480 g)
Minced cooked ham 4 oz (120 g)
2 hard-boiled eggs
Cheese sauce ½ pint (300 mls)
Grated cheese 2 oz (60 g)
Made mustard 1 tsp
1 lemon

Method: Trim and peel celeriac and rub the outside with lemon juice. Boil in salted water for 15 minutes. Scoop out centre from stem part and mince scooped out pulp with minced ham and chopped hard-boiled eggs. Add made mustard to flavour and fill the cooked celeriac with this mixture. Place celeriac in a shallow dish and cover with cheese sauce. Sprinkle with grated cheese and brown under the grill or salamander.

KARTOFFELKLOSSE
Potato dishes

Ingredients:

Bread slices cut in cubes ¼ inch 5 oz (150 g)
Butter and lard mixture 4 oz (120 g)
Sliced potatoes 2 lbs (960 g)
Semolina 2 oz (60 g)
Flour 2 oz (60 g)
Salt and pepper
Grated nutmeg
Melted butter

Method: Boil potatoes. Pass through a sieve and blend with flour and semolina to form a stiff dough. Fry bread cubes in butter and lard until golden. Cool mashed potato mixture and roll it on a floured board like a salami and cut into slices about 2 oz (60 g) each. Place a cube of bread in the middle and shape into a ball. Grease a tray with butter and lard and fill with boiling water. Separate the dumplings and drop into the boiling water. Bring to the boil again and poach dumplings for 8 minutes. Drain and dry and serve brushed with melted butter.

MOHREN
Carrots and apples with honey

Ingredients:

Young carrots 1½ lb (720 g)
Sliced apples 8 oz (240 g)
White vinegar 1 fl oz (30 mls)
Honey 1 oz (30 g)
Water ½ pint (300 mls)
Salt and pepper
Butter 2 oz (60 g)

Method: Peel carrots and apples. Toss in melted butter, add honey and vinegar and cook for 4 minutes. Add water and boil for 20 minutes. Allow liquid to evaporate as much as possible during cooking. Season to taste.

SAUERKRAUT (German style)
Fermented cabbage cooked with bacon and
  juniper berries

Ingredients:

1 can sauerkraut 1 lb (480 g)
German gin 2 fl oz (60 mls)
Bacon fat 2 oz (60 g)
Streaky bacon 4 oz (120 g)
Salt and pepper
6 juniper berries
German white wine 5 fl oz (150 mls)
Stock or water 5 fl oz (150 mls)

Method: Wash and drain sauerkraut. Reheat in a
saucepan with all the ingredients for 45 minutes.

BOHNEN MIT APFELN
Haricot beans with apples

Ingredients:

Haricot beans 8 oz (240 g)
Sliced apples 8 oz (240 g)
Sugar 1 oz (30 g)
Salt and pepper
Butter 4 oz (120 g)

Method: Soak the haricot beans for 2 hours.
Bring to the boil gently and cook until tender.
Remove scum. Drain and reheat the beans in a
saucepan with sliced apples and butter. Season
and cook gently for 10 minutes to allow apple
to soften and acidulate the beans.

ROTKOHL MIT APFELN
Red cabbage braised with apple

Ingredients:

Shredded red cabbage 2 lb (960 g)
Water 1 pint (600 mls)
Vinegar 4 fl oz (120 mls)
Red wine ½ pint (300 mls)
Brown sugar 1 oz (30 g)
6 juniper berries
1 bouquet garni

Sliced apples 8 oz (240 g)
1 bacon rasher 2 oz (60 g)
Salt and pepper
Pinch of ground clove and cinnamon

Method: Blend ingredients, place in an earthenware
casserole and bake for 1 hour at 360°F.

GRUNE BOHNEN MIT BIRNEN
Runner beans with sliced pears

Ingredients:

Runner beans 8 oz (240 g)
Sliced peeled pears 8 oz (240 g)
Butter 4 oz (120 g)
Salt and pepper
Sugar 1 oz (30 g)
Vinegar 2 fl oz (60 mls)

Method: Clean and trim runner beans and slice
thinly. Parboil in salted water for 12 minutes.
Drain and toss in butter with pears. Season to
taste and add sugar and vinegar. Stir well.

SWEETS and DESSERTS

STOLLEN
Yeast cake filled with almond paste

Ingredients:

Dough:

Yeast 1 oz (30 g)
Lukewarm water 4 fl oz (120 mls)
Lukewarm milk 4 fl oz (120 mls)
2 beaten eggs
Salt 7 g
Sugar 8 g
Strong flour 20 oz (600 g)
Lard 2 oz (60 g)

Dried fruits:

Seedless raisins 3 oz (90 g) ⎫ washed and
Sultanas 2 oz (60 g) ⎬ drained
Grated lemon or mixed peel

Chopped glacé cherries 1 oz (30 g)
Chopped angelica 1 oz (30 g)
Almond paste or marzipan 8 oz (240 g)
Apricot jam 4 oz (120 g)
Icing sugar 4 oz (120 g)
Water 1 fl oz (30 mls)
Flaked almonds 4 oz (120 g)

Method: Crumble yeast and stir in the lukewarm water and milk. Add beaten eggs and mix with flour to form a stiff dough. Knead and roll into a ball. Cover with an upside down basin and leave for 40 minutes. Blend with lard and knead again. Roll in a ball and rest for 15 minutes. Add the fruits. Knead and divide the dough in two balls. Flatten with rolling pin and place a piece of marzipan rolled like a sausage in the middle of each piece. Brush with water and fold the pastry over. Flatten the edge with rolling pin. Brush with milk or water and place the two stollen on a greased tray. Rest for 30 minutes and bake for 30 minutes at 400°F. Meanwhile melt apricot jam. Brush the baked loaves with apricot jam and coat with icing made from icing sugar and hot water or just dust the loaves with icing sugar without the apricot glazing.

SCHWARZWALDER KIRSCHTORTE
Torte filled with cherries, cream and chocolate

Ingredients:

Sponge:

4 eggs plus 1 egg yolk
Castor sugar 4 oz (120 g)
Cake flour 4 oz (120 g)
Cocoa powder ½ oz (15 g)
Melted butter 1 oz (30 g)

Custard:

2 egg yolks
Cornflour 1 oz (30 g)
Castor sugar 2 oz (60 g)
Ground gelatine ½ oz (15 g)
Milk ½ pint (300 mls)
Whipped cream 5 fl oz (150 mls)
Vanilla essence 4 drops

Topping:

Red or black morello cherry pie filling (canned)
   5 fl oz (150 g)
Cherry jam 2 oz (60 g)
Or fresh black cherries ½ lb (240 g)
Sugar 2 oz (60 g)
Water 5 fl oz (150 mls)
Starch or potato flour 1 oz (30 g)

Flavouring:

Kirsch 4 fl oz (120 mls)

Decoration:

Whipped cream 5 fl oz (150 mls)
Chocolate shavings 3 oz (90 g)
Toasted flaked almonds 3 oz (90 g)

Method: First grease an 8 inch sponge tin (2 inch high). In a bowl place the eggs and sugar, whisk until fluffy for 8 minutes. Sift flour and cocoa powder and add to mixture, lastly fold in the melted butter. Place in tin two-thirds full. Bake for 25 minutes at 380°F. Turn out on a pastry rack to cool. When cold store in refrigerator overnight. Split the sponge in three layers. Place one layer on a cake board. Sprinkle the kirsch and spread some melted cherry jam. Cover with another layer. Sprinkle kirsch again and spread with cold custard cream. Cover with last layer of sponge and arrange the cherry mixture in the centre, leaving the border clear for decoration. Spread some cream on the side with a palette knife. Coat some toasted nuts on the sides. Pipe a border of cream around the cherry topping and decorate the cream with shavings of dark chocolate.
Custard cream preparation: Place egg yolks, cornflour, sugar and gelatine in a bowl and half of the milk. Heat the remaining milk and add to mixture. Stir and reboil until it thickens. Cool, then add whipped cream flavoured with vanilla.
Topping: If fresh cherries are used, stone all cherries. Boil with sugar and water and thicken with a slurry of potato flour and water. Cook 5 minutes.
Chocolate shavings: Melt chocolate. Pour on to a clean oiled board. Cool and when cold roll shavings with a knife in a scraping action.
Whipped cream: Use half single and half double

cream. Whip until it holds in the whisk. Sweeten with 1 oz sugar per ¼ pint of cream.

See ilustration. This shows the use of red morello cherries.

APFELKUCHEN
German apple tart

Ingredients:

Short pastry:

Margarine 2 oz (60 g)
Lard 2 oz (60 g)
Icing sugar 1 oz (30 g)
Pinch of cinnamon
1 egg
Flour 8 oz (240 g)

Filling:

Sliced apples 8 oz (240 g)

Custard:

Cornflour 1 oz (30 g)
2 egg yolks
Milk ½ pint (300 mls)
Vanilla essence
Castor sugar 3 oz (90 g)
Butter 2 oz (60 g)

Method: Cream fat and sugar, add cinnamon and beaten egg and then flour to form a short pastry dough. Rest for 30 minutes. Roll to ¼ inch thick and line a greased 8 inch flan ring. Fill pastry with sliced apples and dust with sugar. Bake for 20 minutes at 400°F and cool. Cover apple with confectioner's custard and rebake for 8 minutes at 380°F to glaze.
Confectioner's custard: Blend cornflour, egg yolks, and sugar. Boil milk and add to egg mixture. Reboil for 4 minutes stirring all the time until the mixture thickens. Add vanilla essence and knob of butter to prevent skinning.

KASEKUCHEN
Lemon cheese cake with Morello cherries

Ingredients:

Sweet short pastry (as above) 8 oz (240 g)

Filling:

Cottage cheese 8 oz (240 g)
1 egg yolk
Cream 3 fl oz (90 mls)
Castor sugar 2 oz (60 g)
4 egg whites
Granulated sugar 2 oz (60 g)
Cornflour 1 tsp (8 g)
Grated rind and juice of 1 lemon
Cake crumbs 2 oz (60 g)
Morello cherry pie filling

Method: Line an 8 inch diameter by 2 inch deep flan ring with sweet short pastry. Fill bottom with morello cherry pie filling and sprinkle with cake crumbs. Add cream cheese mixture prepared as follows: Cream cheese, cream, egg yolk, cornflour and sugar together to a smooth mixture. Flavour with grated peels and lemon juice. Beat egg whites to a meringue, add granulated sugar and fold into the cheese mixture. Bake for first 10 minutes at 400°F and then reduce heat to 360°F for a further 40 minutes.

FRUCHTSPEISE
Apple and blackberry pudding

Ingredients:

Apple puree 8 oz (240 g)
Blackberries 2 oz (60 g)
Castor sugar 3 oz (90 g)
Ground gelatine 1 oz (30 g)
3 egg yolks
Cornflour 1 oz (30 g)
Whipped cream 5 fl oz (150 mls)
Granulated sugar 2 oz (60 g)

Method: Heat apple puree and blackberries. Blend sugar and ground gelatine and dissolve into puree. Pass mixture through a sieve. Mix cornflour and yolks, add to hot puree, stir well and reheat until mixture thickens. Cool and blend the whipped cream. Set in individual dishes. Serve with sponge fingers.

GERMAN GUGELHUPF
Cake version of the Austrian yeast cake

Ingredients:

Butter 5 oz (150 g)
Castor sugar 6 oz (180 g)
3 eggs
2 egg yolks
Flour (medium) 1 lb (480 g)
Baking powder ½ oz (15 g)
Milk ½ pint (300 mls)
Grated rind and juice of 1 lemon

Chocolate paste:

Melted chocolate 2 oz (60 g)
Butter 1 oz (30 g)
Cake crumbs 1 oz (30 g)
Vanilla essence or few drops of rum

Icing:

Water 2 fl oz (60 mls)
Icing sugar 6 oz (180 g)
Boiled apricot jam 6 oz (180 g)

Method: Cream soft butter with sugar until fluffy and add beaten eggs gradually. Sift flour and baking powder, add half to mixture with half of the milk. Add remainder of flour and milk and blend thoroughly without beating too much. Add juice and grated rind of lemon. Cream melted chocolate and butter with crumbs to obtain a paste. Add flavouring. Mix part of this paste into the cake dough and distribute it evenly without mixing completely so that it will leave streaks of chocolate paste throughout the whole cake mixture, to obtain a kind of marble effect. Grease a Gugelhupf tin with lard and sprinkle with a few flaked almonds on the bottom. Fill mixture two thirds full and bake at 380°F for 45 minutes. Turn cake out on a pastry rack to cool. When cold brush top and sides with hot apricot jam and coat with warm icing mixture. The icing is made by heating water, adding icing sugar and a few drops of vanilla essence or rum.

Readers should remember that the word Gugelhupf denotes the specific name of the mould with a hollow fluted centre. There are many variations of cakes baked in this mould. Some prepared with brioche mixture and others with cake batter as the one above. (See Austrian recipe for the yeast Gugelhupf.)

BIREWECKA
German mixed fruit bread loaf, also popular in
  Alsace

Ingredients:

Dough pastry:

Yeast ½ oz (15 g)
Water ½ pint (300 mls)
1 egg
Bread flour 1 lb (480 g)
Lard 2 oz (60 g)
Salt 7 g
Sugar 8 g
Milk for brushing 5 fl oz (150 mls)

Filling:

Dried mixed fruits (apples, pears, apricots,
  seedless raisins) 12 oz (360 g)
Water 2 pint (1,200 mls)
Tea leaves ½ oz (15 g)
Walnuts 4 oz (120 g)
1 tsp mixed spices
1 anis star or anisette liqueur 3 fl oz (90 mls)
Brown sugar 8 oz (240 g)
Honey 8 oz (240 g)

Method: Crumble yeast in lukewarm water, add beaten egg, sugar and salt and blend with flour. Mix and knead to a dough. Form into a ball and rest for 45 minutes covered with an upside down basin. Blend in lard and knead dough again. Shape into a ball and leave for 15 minutes — again covered with the basin. Add boiling water to tea to make a brew. Add honey and soak dried fruits in this brew for 1 hour. Add the nuts, spices and liqueur and cook for 30 minutes. Drain and keep syrup in reserve to make a sauce. Dust board with flour and roll pastry into an oblong. Place fruit and nuts in the middle and sprinkle with brown sugar. Wrap up pastry and shape like a long bread loaf. Place on a greased tray, brush with milk and let it rest at

room temperature for 30 minutes. Bake at 400°F
for 30 minutes.

Sauce:

Fruit syrup 1½ pint (900 mls)
Cornflour 1½ oz (45 g)
Cream 5 fl oz (150 mls)

Method: Boil syrup and add blended cornflour
and cream. Cook for 5 minutes until the mixture
is thick and smooth. Strain and serve with the
fruit loaf.

Greece

It is easy to dismiss Greek food as being Turkish in origin and based on inferior ingredients produced by a poor country. Yet there is something about the food of the Hellenes which has its roots at the dawn of civilisation. The primeval taste of the little black olives from the gnarled trees which were bearing fruit when Christ walked the earth have something of this ancient individuality. The aroma of lemons and aromatic herbs picked on an arid hillside, the pine scented aggressiveness of retsina are all typical of Greek food.

Many areas of Greece are barren, yet the Greeks love to eat. The Greek men are frankly gourmands rather than gourmets, and Greek women learn to cook the simple, fresh food at an early age. Where quality is not always dependable, quantity has a special appeal.

When I was Catering Manager and Executive Chef of Fortnum and Mason, I had the opportunity of catering to the rich and famous. On one occasion, I was asked to prepare a most elaborate party for the daughter of one of the Greek shipping tycoons. On the day, we descended on the house with a staff of twenty skilled chefs, six butlers and six vans of the most luxurious food one could gather in one meal. We laid it out on silver trays: the buffet was about sixty feet long. There was enough, by my calculations, to feed three times the 200 who were booked.

The splendid *Langouste en Belle Vue* vied for attention with the *Salmon Royale* in a sea of aspic; there were stylish *bouchees*, aspic salads, *faisan en volière* and even an entire peacock displaying all its feathers. The sweets were the entire French and Viennese repertoire of gâteaux, tortes, mousses and a *Croquembouche* which had taken three hours to make, set on a bed of spun sugar with a garland of pulled sugar flowers.

The musicians played Greek dances, the guests sipped champagne next door. At a signal from the hostess, the double doors opened and we prepared to serve, carve, dish out and gently help the guests to enjoy this Ritzy feast.

Helas! In ten minutes the buffet was in ruins. It was like a Battle of Waterloo with myself cast as Napoleon. They ate everything in any order. One fat lady was eating her way through my *croquembouche* although she had not yet started on the savoury food. They were like scavengers, like sea-gulls picking baby turtles off the beach. No pity. No leftovers, either, and the food was gone in one wild, frenzied hour.

We retreated to lick our wounded pride in the kitchens. Tea and sandwiches helped restore our composure, and we noticed a little old man in white with no cap on his head, making some stodgy macaroni puddings, ladling syrup over honeyed sweets and making a yellow sauce. Oh well, it is only for the staff, I thought, and was about to thank him for making so much food for my people when the hostess appeared again and asked for the next meal for her guests. Prepared to lose my temper I followed, only to be thoroughly disarmed when she said: 'Jean, come and taste real food now as my guests. Real Greek food!' So it was that I made my acquaintance with the intricacies and mysteries of Greek food at its best. The little old man was one of the great experts on Greek cookery, but he was so modest that I only know his first name was Alexis.

Here was Greek cooking at its best, with *Dolmas* in a lemon sauce; *Youvetsi*, macaroni baked with meat; *Souvlakia*, grilled lamb on sjewers, lemon-scented chicken soup, *kotosoupa avgholemeno; hilopittes me Kima,* noodles with minced beef; *dolmathakia avgholemeno,* stuffed vine leaves with egg and lemon sauce. The sweets were sticky, syrupy and delicious, with nuts, sesame seeds and honey as the dominant notes.

We also had on that memorable evening a lesson in the correct way of preparing what the Greeks call their own Turkish coffee. I am familiar with the Greek language, and the verses of Homer came flooding back. Archistratus, a poet, contemporary of Dionysius the Younger and tyrant of Syracuse wrote a book in 330 BC which collated the information he had gathered about gastronomical customs of the time. He called it *Hedypathia* — voluptuousness — and it earned him the title 'Hesiod of the Gourmets'. From the time of Alexander the Great and onwards, Greek cooking became a real art, and professional chefs made their appearance. Culinary schools were established where students worked for two years to pass the difficult examinations.

Sauce cookery became important and changed the character of basic ingredients. Eventually the chefs demanded so much money that clever employers gave them the most intelligent of their house-slaves to assist them as helpers, and these learned as much as they could about the chefs' techniques. Many slaves learned the art of cooking and replaced the high-priced chefs at no cost to their masters, and many were so good that they became politically knowledgeable. Cadmus, the founder of Thebes and inventor of the alphabet, was supposed to have worked as a cook.

Greek cooks were imported into Rome when the Roman Empire became great, and when the *nouveaux-riches* Romans wanted to titillate their barbaric palates. Masters of the culinary arts were brought to Rome until even Cato complained that the Greeks spoilt the primitive purity of the Romans. The Romans in turn influenced the Byzantine cuisine and so the Greek influence was felt for about 1,500 years from the Alps to Asia Minor; hardly a cuisine to be dismissed lightly.

The dishes of those days were elaborate, with rich sauces disguising the freshness — or otherwise — of the ingredients. Gradually they became simpler as the country became poor again, and the extravagance of the past was replaced by fresh ingredients, natural products and a reliance on aromatic herbs to accent the taste of fish and meat. There is an abundance of olives, and olive oil is the single most important ingredient of Greek cuisine. There are many different types and qualities, and enthusiastic Greek cooks keep several varieties each for a different purpose.

There are exotic vegetables ripening in every garden in sunny Greece, and they are stuffed with all types of meat and fish. Popular variations include *aginares yemistes* (stuffed artichokes); *melitzanes papoutsakie* (stuffed eggplants); *kolokithakia yemista* (stuffed zucchini); and *dolmathakia* (stuffed vine leaves). Other vegetables suitable for this treatment are the okras and sweet peppers, always eaten young and small.

Fruit is abundant in Greece: apricots, peaches, strawberries and the tangy lemons which add so much to the sauces used on meat, fish and vegetables.

Lemon, garlic, onions and tomatoes along with a flavour of coriander characterise Greek cookery. Fish is plentiful and cheap, although perhaps not as good as the fish of colder waters. The Greek fish stew, *caccavia*, called *bourtheto* on Corfu, is claimed as the ancestor of the bouillabaisse. It contains all kinds of fish in an emulsion of oil, pepper, paprika, tomatoes and seasonings, quickly boiled on a high heat in the same way as its famous offspring. Meat is still rare and expensive by comparison with fish, but in the north, where pastures are good, it is of high quality. It is most often roasted on a spit or grilled, but in the south it can be tough so it is usually minced and made into sausages, *moussaka* (rissoles) or combined with macaroni.

Lamb roasted on a spit is the traditional Easter dish, and roast sucking pig is for traditional feasts such as weddings and Christenings. *Souvlakia* is a delicately flavoured cubed lamb grilled on a skewer, marinaded in a mixture of herbs, wine and flavoured vinegar to give the quintessential Greek taste. Coriander, oregano, basil and fresh lemon rind are frequently used to scent the food to a perfect blend, harmonising without overpowering the other ingredients.

The immense plain of Thessaly is the granary of Greece, and white bread was already being enjoyed in Ancient Athens. Modern Greek bread is crusty with an open texture, sprinkled with sesame seeds on top. Pastries are sweet, often sticky with honey and based on the filo pastry, rather like single layers of puff pastry. They are usually bought by the kilo and only the most diligent or poor housewife would make her own.

The cakes and pastries are often eaten between meals with a spoonful of thick, sweet rose-petal or walnut preserve and a glass of cold water, the traditional offering of hospitality in villages and on the small islands. The *glyka koutaliou*, or spoon sweet, is eaten from the teaspoon, the water is drunk and the spoon returned to the empty glass. This charming ritual is usually followed by a small glass of liqueur and then by Turkish coffee.

Bread, the white, salty *feta* cheese, fruit and salad is the basic fare of the poor people. In more prosperous households, a meal is usually preceded by a long, cool sip of ouzo, the aniseed flavoured drink reminiscent of Pernod, and taken with little bites of *meze*, such as olives, nuts, cheese, small pieces of fish, tomatoes, pickle and slices of marinaded squid and stewed octopus. The main meal usually consists of meat or fish with vege-

tables, a rice sweet or *halva* made with semolina. Fruit and coffee are traditional endings to a meal.

Game is a much-prized meat in Greece, but there are quite a number of wild boar, hunted all year round in Macedonia, and there are deer, chamois, and roe on Mount Olympus. Feathered game such as pheasants, partridges, quail, wild ducks and wild hen are found in Macedonia.

Great care is taken in the preparation of each dish on a Greek menu; because of the lack of products, their value is enhanced in the eyes of the cook. Much is made of a small amount of ingredients by using stuffings and by making the delectable pies of flaky pastry which melt in the mouth and make more of the expensive filling.

The wines of Greece are good but have never achieved international recognition, although most of them are eminently drinkable. The famous retsina or resinated wine is an acquired taste it is all too easy to acquire, sitting in the dark red light on the slopes of Sunion, with the columns of the temple silhouetted against the sunset. One ponders on the ill-fated Theseus who came home with sails of the wrong colours and caused his father, Aegeus, to throw himself to his death here in the Aegean sea; one takes another bite of feta and nibbles an olive and sips the retsina — and suddenly it is blindingly clear why this brooding, arid land is the home of philosophy.

BILL OF FARE

Soup

TAHINOSOUPA
Peanut butter soup with lemon and onion

SPANAKOSOUPA
Spinach soup with yoghurt

MAYERITSA
Easter soup made with offal

Hors d'Oeuvre (Mezes)

GREEK PICKLED MIXTURE
Vegetables in lemon marinade

TARAMA KEFTEDES
Fish roe cakes

TYROPITES
Cream cheese tartlets

MIDIA YEMISTA
Fried mussels

TIGANITES KOLOKITHAKIA
Courgette fritters

SALINGARIA
Stewed snails

PANDZARIA
Beetroot pickle

SPETSOFAGI
Sausages with peppers and tomatoes

MELIDZANES
Aubergine pate (eggplant puree)

SALATA PSARI ME YAOURTI
Fish salad in yoghurt

FASSOLIA SALATA
Haricot beans in lemon dressing

Fish Dishes

PSARI MARINATO
Marinaded fish

PSARI GRATINI
Fish au gratin

PSARI ROULLO
Fish loaf

SKOUMBRI YAHNI
Casserole of mackerel

SOUPIES YAHNI
Cuttlefish in onion sauce

BAKALAIROS SKORDALIA
Puree of fish and potato emulsified with oil

Meat Dishes

ARNI STIHOS ME KOLOKITHAKIA
Breast of lamb with courgettes

ARNI GIOUVETSI
Fricassee lamb in lemon sauce

PODARAKIA ARNOU AVGOLEMONO
Sheeps' trotters in lemon sauce

KREATOPITTA KEFALONIAS
Lamb pie in lemon sauce

SOUVLAKIA
Lamb kebab

KEFTEDES TIS SKARAS
Lamb meatballs on a skewer

KYDONATO
Lamb stew with quinces

HIRONO AVGOLEMENO
Diced pork with lemon sauce

MOSCARAKI ROULLO
Veal escalope stuffed with ham and cheese in
    lemon sauce

APHELIA
Pork kebab

APHELIA AVGOLEMENO
Pork cubes marinaded in wine

HIRONO ME SELINORIZA AVGOLEMENO
Pork and celeriac casserole

SYKOTI TIGANITO
Fried liver in batter

MOUSSAKA
Minced beef with potatoes, aubergines and cheese
    sauce

Vegetables

KOLOKITHAKIA PLAKI
Fried courgettes

PIPERIES YEMISTES
Stuffed green peppers

KOUNOUPIDI ME AVGA
Cauliflower baked with eggs

SELINORIZA TIGANTI
Celeriac fritters

PILAFIA
Rice pilaff

SKORDALIA
Garlic sauce

Sweets and Desserts

HALVAS SIMIGDALENIO
Semolina dumplings with a syrup sauce

KARYDATA
Walnut sugar drops

MYZITHROPITA
Cheese cake

SKALTSOUNAKIA
Puff pastry filled with walnuts and honey

SOUP

TAHINOSOUPA
Peanut butter soup with lemon and onion

This soup is usually made from a paste made of sesame seeds (tahina).

Ingredients:

Water or chicken stock 2½ pint (1,500 mls)
Rice 4 oz (120 g)
Chopped onions 4 oz (120 g)
Juice and grated rind of 2 lemons
Sesame paste or peanut butter 4 oz (120 g)
Salt and pepper
1 chicken bouillon cube 10 g

Method: Boil rice for 30 minutes. Add peanut butter, chopped onions and bouillon cube. Simmer for 15 minutes. Season. Add grated lemon rind and juice.

SPANAKOSOUPA
Spinach soup with yoghurt (4 to 6 portions)

Ingredients:

Oil 2 fl oz (60 mls)
Butter 1 oz (30 g)
Chopped onions 2 oz (60 g)
Cleaned spinach leaves 2 lb (960 g)
Chicken stock 2½ pint (1,500 mls)
Yoghurt 5 fl oz (150 mls)
Salt and pepper
Pinch grated nutmeg

Method: Heat oil and butter in a saucepan and sweat chopped onions without browning for 5 minutes. Add cleaned, shredded spinach and simmer for 5 minutes. Blend in stock and boil for 15 minutes. Liquidise. Collect puree and juice. Season. Add yoghurt and stir well. Serve with fried sippets of bread.

MAYERITSA
Easter soup made with offal (6 to 8 portions)

Ingredients:

4 sheeps' trotters
Rumen and honeycomb tripe 1 lb (480 g), cut in thin strips
Sheeps' heart 8 oz (240 g), cut in thin slices
Sheeps' liver 8 oz (240 g), cut in small escalopes
Water 3 pint (1,800 mls)
White vinegar 5 fl oz (150 mls)
Oil 2 fl oz (60 mls)
Butter 2 oz (60 g)
Flour 2 oz (60 g)
Chopped onions 4 oz (120 g)
Yoghurt 5 fl oz (150 mls)
Cooked rice 4 oz (120 g)

Thickening:

3 egg yolks
Lemon juice 2 fl oz (60 mls)
Potato flour or arrowroot 1 oz (30 g)

Salt and pepper
Pinch grated nutmeg
1 tbs chopped parsley
1 tbs chopped dill

Method: Clean trotters and tripe. Place in cold water and bring to the boil for 1 hour, removing scum as it rises. Add vinegar. Sweat in oil without browning the chopped onions and diced heart. Sprinkle flour and add 1 pint of the soup stock. Simmer for 20 minutes and then blend all ingredients and cooked rice. Season to taste. Serve with a sprinkling of parsley and dill.

Mix the egg yolks, lemon juice and potato flour in a bowl. Add ½ pint of the prepared soup and pour the contents of this egg mixture into the main soup. Bring to the boil, without exceeding boiling point, stirring all the time. Remove trotters. Discard bones and cut meat in pieces. Fry thin slices of liver and add to soup or serve separately.

HORS D'OEUVRE (MEZES)

GREEK PICKLED MIXTURE
Vegetables in lemon marinade

Ingredients:

Marinade stock:

Oil 3 fl oz (90 mls)
Lemon juice 2 fl oz (60 mls)
White vinegar 1 fl oz (30 mls)
Sugar 1 oz (30 g)
6 peppercorns
6 coriander seeds
1 bouquet garni
Diced celery or fennel 2 oz (60 g)
Water ½ pint (300 mls)
1 clove of garlic
6 slices of lemon
White wine ½ pint (300 mls)
Salt 1 oz (30 g)
Pepper 3 g

Vegetables:

Button mushrooms 4 oz (120 g)
Button onions 8 oz (240 g)
Courgette slices 8 oz (240 g)
Celeriac 4 oz (120 g)
Diced carrots 4 oz (120 g)
Diced turnips 4 oz (120 g)
Swede 8 oz (240 g)

Method: Boil marinade for 5 minutes. Add cleaned vegetables and simmer for 15 minutes. Cool and serve in the same liquor.

TARAMA KEFTEDES
Fish roe cakes

Ingredients:

Skinned smoked cods' roe or fresh 8 oz (240 g)
White breadcrumbs 4 oz (120 g)
Cold mashed potatoes 8 oz (240 g)
Yoghurt 4 fl oz (120 mls)
White wine 2 fl oz (60 mls)
Juice and rind of 2 lemons
2 beaten eggs
2 cloves of garlic finely chopped
1 grated onion 3 oz (90.g)
Pinch chopped mint
Seasoned flour
Oil for frying

Method: Blend all but last two ingredients together to a firm paste. Divide into 2 oz (60 g) cakes. Toss in seasoned flour and then fry on both sides until golden. Serve with salad.

TYROPITES
Cream cheese tartlets

Ingredients:

Short pastry 8 oz (240 g)

Filling:

Cream cheese 6 oz (180 g)
Chopped garlic ⅓ oz (10 g)
1 egg
2 egg yolks
Salt and pepper
1 tbs chopped chives
Flour 1 oz (30 g)

Method: Roll and line greased tartlet moulds with pastry ⅛ inch thick. Prick bottom. Leave for 15 minutes. Cream all the filling ingredients to a smooth paste. Place a spoon of mixture into each tartlet. Bake at 360°F for 20 minutes. First 10 minutes at 400°F and then reduce heat.

MIDIA YEMISTA
Fried mussels

Ingredients:

Mussels 2 qt (2,400 mls)
Water 2 pint (1,200 mls)
Vinegar 4 fl oz (120 mls)

Filling:

Cooked rice 4 oz (120 g)
1 egg
Sultanas 2 oz (60 g)
Chopped walnuts 2 oz (60 g)
Chopped spring onions 2 oz (60 g)
Seasoned flour
2 beaten eggs
Brown breadcrumbs
Oil for frying

Method: Shell all the raw mussels and remove seaweed. Place in cold water with 10 per cent vinegar. Soak for 30 minutes. Drain. Blend egg and cooked rice with chopped walnuts, onions and sultanas to form a firm pasta. Divide into small 1 oz (30 g) dumplings. Insert one mussel in each ball. Pass in seasoned flour, then in beaten eggs and crumbs and fry for 6 minutes in deep fat until golden. Serve with tomato or lemon sauce.

TIGANITES KOLOKITHAKIA
Courgette fritters

Ingredients:

4 medium courgettes
Seasoned flour 2 oz (60 g)
Juice and grated rind of 1 lemon

Batter:

1 egg
Flour 4 oz (120 g)
Water ½ pint (300 mls)
Salt and pepper
1 clove of crushed garlic
Pinch of chopped chervil or fresh mint

Method: To make the batter, beat the egg and add to water and flour. Season. Add garlic and herbs and leave for 20 minutes.

Scrape but do not peel the courgettes. Cut in four lengthwise. Marinade in lemon juice and grated rind for 10 minutes. Pass in seasoned flour and then in batter. Deep fry for 5 minutes in oil. Drain and season with salt and pepper.

SALINGRIA
Stewed snails

Ingredients:

24 snails
Oil 2 fl oz (60 mls)
Chopped onions 2 oz (60 g)
1 clove of garlic
Chopped, skinned and seeded tomatoes 4 oz (120 g)

1 tbs chopped parsley
Salt and pepper

Method: Live snails must be left in a bucket with a heavy weight for 48 hours. Boil in water with 1 onion and carrot and bouquet garni for 2 hours at simmering point. Otherwise, canned snails can be used.

Saute the chopped onions in oil until tender but not brown. Add garlic and chopped tomatoes. Simmer for a few minutes. Reheat snails in this mixture for 10 minutes. Season and serve with chopped parsley.

PANDZARIA
Beetroot pickle

Ingredients:

Oil 2 fl oz (60 mls)
Boiled young beetroots 2 lb (960 g)
Chopped onions 2 oz (60 g)
Vinegar 5 fl oz (150 mls)
Sugar 1 oz (30 g)
6 coriander seeds
Water 1 pint (600 mls)
1 tbs chopped parsley

Thickening:

Cream or yoghurt 5 fl oz (150 mls)
Cornflour ½ oz (15 g)
Salt and pepper

Method: Saute the chopped onions in oil without browning. Add the peeled, quartered young beets with vinegar, sugar and coriander seeds. Simmer for 10 minutes. Add water. Bring to the boil and thicken with a slurry of yoghurt and cornflour added to the boiling mixture, while stirring. Season with salt and pepper. Cool and sprinkle with chopped parsley.

SPETSOFAGI
Sausages with peppers and tomatoes

Ingredients:

Lard or oil 2 oz (60 g)

Chipolatas 2 lb (960 g)
Chopped onions 2 oz (60 g)
1 clove of chopped garlic
Skinned and seeded tomatoes 8 oz (240 g)
Sliced green and red peppers 8 oz (240 g)
Water ½ pint (300 mls)
Vinegar 2 fl oz (60 mls)
Salt and pepper
6 coriander seeds
Tomato puree 1 oz (30 g)
Sugar ½ oz (15 g)

Method: Fry the chipolatas in oil for 5 minutes.
Drain fat and saute the chopped onions and
garlic until tender, but not brown. Add shredded
peppers and cook for 5 minutes. Add tomato
pulp, puree and water. Simmer for further 5
minutes. Season. Add chipolatas and cook for
4 minutes. Serve hot or cold. Lastly, add vinegar,
sugar and coriander seeds to the liquor.

MELIDZANES
Aubergine pâté (eggplant puree)

Ingredients:

4 large aubergines 2 lb (960 g)
Oil 4 fl oz (120 mls)
1 clove of garlic
Salt and pepper
White breadcrumbs 3 oz (90 g)
Chopped onions 2 oz (60 g)
Juice and grated rind of 1 lemon

Method: Bake aubergines until tender. Remove
peel and scoop out all the pulp. Place this pulp
in a bowl with finely chopped onions and garlic.
Gradually add oil while whisking to obtain a fine
emulsion. Season and blend with crumbs and add
lemon juice and rind. Chill and serve on croutons.

SALATA PSARI ME YAOURTI
Fish salad in yoghurt

Ingredients:

Flaked cooked cod 2 lb (960 g)

Sauce:

1 tsp made mustard
Vinegar or lemon juice 2 fl oz (60 mls)
Oil 3 fl oz (90 mls)
Salt and pepper
2 chopped hard-boiled eggs
Chopped onions 2 oz (60 g)
Capers 1 oz (30 g)
1 tbs chopped parsley
Sour cream 4 fl oz (120 mls)
Yoghurt 4 fl oz (120 mls)

Method: Place flaked cooked cod in a shallow
dish. Prepare the sauce by blending the mustard
with vinegar or lemon juice. Add oil and
remaining ingredients. Pour over the fish and
sprinkle with fresh chopped parsley.

FASSOLIA SALATA
Haricot beans in lemon dressing

Ingredients:

Soaked haricots 1 lb (480 g)
Water 3 pint (1,800 mls)
Salt ½ oz (15 g)

Vinaigrette sauce:

1 tsp made mustard
Lemon juice 3 fl oz (90 mls)
Oil 4 fl oz (120 mls)
Salt and pepper
Chopped spring onions 3 oz (90 g)
Chopped garlic ½ oz (15 g)
Chopped parsley 1 tbs

Method: Bake the beans with water in a casserole
dish until tender. Wash and strain. Season. Add the
vinaigrette. Serve hot or cold.

FISH DISHES

PSARI MARINATO
Marinaded fish

Ingredients:

White fish (haddock, cod, bream, sole, halibut,
    etc.) 2 lb (960 g)
Seasoned flour 2 oz (60 g)
Oil for frying 5 fl oz (150 mls)

Garnish:

Tomato pulp 4 oz (120 g)
Chopped onions 2 oz (60 g)
1 clove chopped garlic
Oil 2 fl oz (60 mls)
Tomato puree 1 oz (30 g)
Lemon juice 2 fl oz (60 mls)
Water 5 fl oz (150 mls)
White vinegar 2 fl oz (60 mls)
Salt and pepper
Pinch rosemary and few coriander seeds

Method: Clean, scale and gut the fish. Pass in
seasoned flour and fry in oil for 3 minutes on
each side. Transfer to a shallow dish.

    Saute the chopped onions in oil for 5 minutes
without browning. Add remaining ingredients.
Place on top of fish and cook for a further 5
minutes. Cover with a lid and bake for 20 minutes
in a moderate oven (380°F). Serve hot or cold.

PSARI GRATINI
Fish au gratin

Ingredients:

White fish (haddock, cod, bream, sole, halibut,
    etc.) 2 lb (960 g)

Vegetables:

Carrots 2 oz (60 g)
Celery 2 oz (60 g)
Leeks 2 oz (60 g)
1 clove of garlic
Water 1 pint (600 mls)
Vinegar 3 fl oz (90 mls)
Salt and pepper

Sauce:

White sauce ½ pint (300 mls)
Grated cheese 2 oz (60 g)
Juice and grated rind of 1 lemon

2 egg yolks
White breadcrumbs 2 oz (60 g)
Mashed potatoes 1 lb (480 g)
Salt and pepper
Butter 2 oz (60 g)

Method: Clean and fillet the fish. Place in a
shallow dish. Boil chopped carrots, celery, leeks
and garlic in water and vinegar for 5 minutes.
Season. Add this mixture to fish dish and bake
for 15 minutes at 370°F. Remove fish from liquor
and transfer to a pie dish. Cover with white sauce
— seasoned and with lemon juice and rind added —
and vegetables from the stock. Blend egg yolks to
mashed potatoes. Sprinkle with grated cheese
mixed with crumbs and dot with pieces of
butter. Brown in a hot oven for 8 minutes at
400°F.

PSARI ROULLO
Fish loaf

Ingredients:

Raw minced cod 1 lb (480 g)
White breadcrumbs 2 oz (60 g)
2 beaten eggs
Butter 2 oz (60 g)
Salt and pepper
Pinch sugar
Grated raw onions 2 oz (60 g)
Juice and grated rind of 1 lemon
1 tbs chopped parsley
Yoghurt 4 fl oz (120 mls)

Method: Blend all ingredients together. Place in a
shallow greased dish and bake at 360°F for 1 hour.
Cool and turn out onto a dish. Serve hot or cold
with appropriate sauce — lemon, Hollandaise,
tomato or vinaigrette.

SKOUMBRI YAHNI
Casserole of mackerel

Ingredients:

Filleted mackerel 2 lb (960 g)
Seasoned flour 2 oz (60 g)
Oil for frying 5 fl oz (150 mls)

Chopped onions 2 oz (60 g)
Chopped, skinned and seeded tomatoes 5 oz
    (150 g)
Tomato puree 1 oz (30 g)
Vinegar 3 fl oz (90 mls)
Pinch chopped dill
Pinch chopped parsley
White wine ¼ pint (150 mls)
Salt and pepper

Method: Clean, wash and dry fillets. Pass in
seasoned flour and then dip in oil. Fry or grill
for 8 minutes. Transfer to a shallow dish.

Fry chopped onions until tender. Add
remaining ingredients and cook for 8 minutes.
Place on top of fish and bake for 15 minutes at
380°F. Sprinkle with herbs.

SOUPIES YAHNI
Cuttlefish in onion sauce

Ingredients:

Cuttlefish 2 lb (960 g)
Sliced onions 4 oz (120 g)
Oil 5 fl oz (150 mls)
Seasoned flour 2 oz (60 g)
1 clove of garlic
White wine ½ pint (300 mls)
1 bouquet garni
Salt and pepper
Pinch saffron

Method: Cut cuttlefish in thin slices. Pass in
seasoned flour. Fry in oil for 8 minutes. Add
garlic and chopped onions and cook with a lid
on for 10 minutes on a slow heat. Drain off
surplus fat. Transfer to a dish. Add wine, bouquet
garni, saffron and simmer in a moderate oven for
1 hour; adjust seasoning. Sprinkle with chopped
parsley and serve.

BAKALAIROS SKORDALIA
Puree of fish and potato emulsified with oil

The Bakaliaros is a puree of cooked salted fish
with potato which is emulsified with cold oil to
a creamy consistency. It is served with sippets of
fried bread. When cold, the mixture can be fried
in fat like croquettes.

Ingredients:

Dry salt cod 2 lb (960 g)
Mashed potatoes 1 lb (480 g)
1 clove of garlic
Oil ½ pint (300 mls)
Juice and rind of 2 lemons
Ground almonds 2 oz (60 g)
White vinegar 2 fl oz (60 mls)
Salt and pepper

Method: Desalt the fish in cold water for 24
hours. Boil in fresh water until soft. Flake the
white pulp and pound or mince it to a paste.
Blend with mashed potatoes. Place this puree in
a large mixing bowl and add crushed garlic, lemon
juice and rind, ground almonds, vinegar and salt and
pepper to taste. Add oil gradually, while whisking
as for a mayonnaise. Serve in a shallow dish with
triangular sippets of fried bread.

MEAT DISHES

ARNI STITHOS ME KOLOKITHAKIA
Breast of lamb with courgettes

Ingredients:

Breast of lamb 2½ lb (1,200 g)
Water 2 pint (1,200 mls)
Salt and pepper
1 onion studded with 4 cloves
2 tbs vinegar
Oil for frying
Seasoned flour 2 oz (60 g)
2 beaten eggs
Breadcrumbs 4 oz (120 g)
Lemon sauce ½ pint (300 mls)
    — see recipe.

Method: Boil lamb with onion in salted water
and vinegar for 30 minutes. Remove from water
and use stock to make lemon sauce according to
recipe.

Discard the bones and cut meat into 2 inch squares. Press the breast pieces under a weight for 30 minutes and then pass in seasoned flour, beaten eggs and crumbs. Deep fry for 5 minutes and serve lemon sauce separately.

This is a similar dish to the French *epigramme*.

ARNI GIOUVETSI
Fricassee lamb in lemon sauce

Ingredients:

Diced lamb from shoulder or middle neck
    2½ lb (1,200 g)
Water 3 pint (1,800 mls)
Oil 3 fl oz (90 mls)
Diced onions 2 oz (60 g)
Diced carrots 2 oz (60 g)
Diced celery or fennel 2 oz (60 g)
1 clove of crushed garlic
1 tsp coriander leaves or seeds
Flour 2 oz (60 g)   }   for the roux
Margarine 2 oz (60 g) }

Cohering agent:

3 egg yolks
Juice and grated rind of 2 lemons

Salt and pepper
Pinch grated nutmeg or chopped lemon herb
    (citronelle)

Method: Heat oil in a large saucepan. Fry the meat until brown. Add vegetables and toss. Stir and cook for 5 minutes with a lid on. Cover level with water. Add herbs and simmer gently for 1½ hours. Strain liquor inro another pan. Mix egg yolks and lemon juice in a bowl with ½ pint of the stock. Cook a roux with margarine and flour. Gradually add the boiling remaining stock. Reheat this sauce until it thickens to the right consistency. Stir and strain over the meat and vegetables. Reheat the mixture for 15 minutes and, while stirring, add the egg mixture. Simmer for a further 5 minutes and season to taste. Serve with a sprinkling of lemon herbs or chopped parsley and grated lemon rind.

PODARAKIA ARNOU AVGOLEMONO
Sheeps' trotters in lemon sauce

Ingredients:

12 sheeps' trotters
Water 3 pint (1,800 mls)
Chopped shallots or onions 5 oz (150 g)
Carrots 2 oz (60 g)
4 cloves
1 bouquet garni
Vinegar 3 tbs
Lemon sauce ½ pint (300 mls)
1 tbs chopped parsley
1 tbs chopped shallots
2 tbs chopped hard-boiled eggs
Salt and pepper

Method: Clean, wash and boil the trotters in water with carrot, onion and vinegar, cloves, bouquet garni, salt and pepper for 1 hour until tender. Discard the bones. Cut meat in small pieces and serve in some of the stock with lemon sauce separate or reheat the meat in lemon sauce. Sprinkle with chopped parsley, diced or chopped hard-boiled eggs and chopped shallots.

KREATOPITTA KEFALONIAS
Lamb pie in lemon sauce

Ingredients:

Stewed lamb prepared as *Arni Giouvetsi* —
    same amount with sauce
Cooked rice 8 oz (240 g)
Short pastry 8 oz (240 g)

Method: Place the stew, when cold, in a shallow pie dish. Cover with cooked rice and arrange a thin layer of short pastry on top. Brush pastry with egg glaze and bake for 25 minutes at 400°F.

SOUVLAKIA
Lamb kebab

Ingredients:

Lean cubed lamb from leg or shoulder 2 lb (960 g)

Marinade liquor:

Olive oil 3 fl oz (90 mls)
Lemon juice 2 fl oz (60 mls)
Dry white wine 5 fl oz (150 mls)
Coriander seeds 1 tbs
Green pepper 5 oz (150 g)
Onion cut in wedges and separated in layers
     5 oz (150 g)
Button mushrooms 8 oz (240 g)
Square pieces of celery stalks 4 oz (120 g)
Green and red peppers without seeds and cut in
     1 inch squares 8 oz (240 g)
Salt and pepper
4 bay leaves
Seasoned flour 2 oz (60 g)

Method: Soak all ingredients, except flour, in marinade for 6 hours. Impale the meat and vegetables alternately on 9 inch skewers, e.g. meat, pepper, onion, mushroom and a bay leaf. Pass in seasoned flour and grill under the salamander or over a charcoal fire or just fry in a pan.

   Boil marinade liquor and strain. Baste the kebabs with this gravy or thicken it with egg yolks and a cornflour slurry to produce a lemon sauce. Serve the kebabs with rice pilaff.

KEFTEDES TIS SKARAS
Lamb meatballs on a skewer

This dish is the same as above but use raw meat-balls instead of diced meat. Lamb and beef can be mixed with or without pork to obtain a better texture and flavour.

KYDONATO
Lamb stew with quinces

Quinces impart a definite flavour to meat sauce and as a garnish have no rival.

Ingredients:

Diced beef, lamb or mutton in 1 inch cubes
     2 lb (960 g)
Peeled, diced quince 1 lb (480 g)

Diced onions 2 oz (60 g)
Diced carrots 2 oz (60 g)
Tomato puree 1 oz (30 g)
Red wine ½ pint (300 mls)
1 clove of garlic
1 bouquet garni
Rice 3 oz (90 g)
Water 1½ pint (900 mls)
Sugar 1 oz (30 g)
Salt and pepper

Roux:

Flour 2 oz (60 g)
Oil 2 fl oz (60 mls)

1 tbs coriander seeds
1 tbs chopped fresh mint leaves

Method: Scald the meat in boiling water for 10 minutes. Rinse and place meat in a clean pan with fresh cold water and remaining ingredients. Bring to the boil and simmer for 1½ hours until meat is tender. Strain liquir. Cook roux and gradually add to strained stock. Reboil and strain. Season and add to meat. Reheat and sprinkle with herbs and seeds.

HIRONO AVGOLEMENO
Diced pork with lemon sauce

This dish is the same as *Arni Giouvetsi*, but use pork instead of lamb.

MOSCARAKI ROULLO
Veal escalope stuffed with ham and cheese in
     lemon sauce

Ingredients:

4 veal escalopes 3 oz (90 g) each
4 thin ham slices 2 oz (60 g)
4 thin slices of hard cheese 2 oz (60 g)
Lemon sauce ½ pint (300 mls)
Seasoned flour 2 oz (60 g)
Oil for frying

Method: Beat escalopes with rolling pin or mallet to $\frac{1}{8}$ inch thickness. Season and on each escalope place a slice of ham and cheese. Roll them up and insert cocktail sticks to hold in position. Pass in seasoned flour and fry in oil until golden and cooked through. Drain and serve with lemon sauce and a garnish of rice pilaff.

APHELIA
Pork kebab

This dish is the same as *Souvlakia* but use pork cubes instead of lamb.

APHELIA AVGOLEMENO
Pork cubes marinaded in wine

Pork cubes marinaded in wine and stewed as *Arni Giouvetsi.*

HIRONO ME SELINORIZA AVGOLEMONO
Pork and celeriac casserole

This dish is the same as *Hirono Avgolemono*, but with the additon of diced celeriac as an extra vegetable.

SYKOTI TIGANITO
Fried liver in batter

Ingredients:
Lambs' liver cut in thin escalopes 2 lb (960 g)
Seasoned flour 2 oz (60 g)

Marinade:
Oil 2 fl oz (60 mls)
Juice and grated rind of 1 lemon
Salt and pepper
1 grated onion 2 oz (60 g)

Batter:
1 egg
Flour 3 oz (90 g)

Water 5 fl oz (150 g)
Salt and coriander leaves

Oil for frying 2 fl oz (60 mls)

Method: Marinade the lamb escalopes in lemon juice, onion, seasoning and oil for 1 hour. Drain and dry. Pass in seasoned flour. Dip in batter made by beating egg and water with salt, coriander and flour. Shallow fry for 5 minutes.

MOUSSAKA
Minced beef with potatoes, aubergines and cheese
   sauce

Ingredients:
Minced beef 8 oz (240 g)
Chopped onions 2 oz (60 g)
Fat 2 oz (60 g)
1 clove chopped garlic
Tomato puree 1 oz (30 g)
Flour 1 oz (30 g)
Water ½ pint (300 mls)
Salt and pepper
Aubergines 8 oz (240 g)
Seasoned flour 2 oz (60 g)
Salt ½ oz (15 g) – for aubergines
Sliced cooked potatoes 8 oz (240 g)
Lemon or cheese sauce ½ pint (300 mls)
Sliced tomatoes 8 oz (240 g)
Grated cheese 4 oz (120 g)

Method: Peel and slice aubergines and sprinkle with salt. Leave for 2 minutes. Rinse in cold water. Drain and dry. Pass in seasoned flour. Deep fry for 5 minutes. Drain on absorbent paper.

Brown meat with chopped onions in fat. Add garlic and tomato puree. Stir well and add flour and hot water. Stir. Simmer for 15 minutes. Season.

Place alternate layers of meat, fried aubergines and sliced raw tomatoes. Top with a layer or cooked sliced potatoes. Cover with cheese sauce and a generous sprinkling of grated cheese. Brown in a hot oven 400°F for 15 minutes.

VEGETABLES

KOLOKITHAKIA PLAKI
Fried courgettes

Ingredients:

Baby marrows 2 lb (960 g)
Skinned and seeded tomatoes 1 lb (480 g)
1 clove of chopped garlic
Salt and pepper
Seasoned flour 2 oz (60 g)
Juice and grated rind of 1 lemon
Olive oil for marinade
Grated cheese 4 oz (120 g)
Oil for frying

Method: Scrape the marrows. Cut in four
lengthwise. Marinade in oil and lemon juice and
rind for 10 minutes. Drain and dry. Pass in seasoned
flour and fry in a shallow pan until golden.
Place the marrows in a shallow dish and cover
with a layer of tomato pulp. Season. Sprinkle with
grated cheese and chopped garlic and place under
the grill until golden.

PIPERIES YEMISTES
Stuffed green peppers

Ingredients:

4 large green peppers 2 lb (960 g)
Minced raw beef or lamb 1 lb (480 g)
Chopped onions 2 oz (60 g)
Oil 2 fl oz (60 mls)
Salt and pepper
Tomato puree 1 oz (30 g)
1 clove chopped garlic
Stock or water ½ pint (300 mls)
Chopped mint and parsley 1 tbs
Cooked rice 4 oz (120 g)
Tomato or lemon sauce ½ pint (300 mls)

Method: Split the peppers lengthwise or cut off
the stem to obtain a cavity. Remove seeds. Scald
for 20 seconds. Fill with the following mixture.
Brown meat in oil with chopped onions and
garlic. After 5 minutes, add tomato puree,
seasoning and stock. Cook for 20 minutes. Blend
with the cooked rice and add the chopped herbs.
Place this mixture in the cavity of each pepper.
Place the peppers in a shallow dish and cover with
tomato or lemon sauce. Bake in a moderately hot
oven for 20 minutes (380°F).

KOUNOUPIDI ME AVGA
Cauliflower baked with eggs

Ingredients:

1 head of cauliflower 3 lb (1,440 g)
Water 3 pint (1,800 mls)
Lemon juice 2 fl oz (60 mls)

Egg custard:

Milk 1 pint (600 mls)
Cornflour 1 oz (30 g)
3 eggs
Salt and pepper
Pinch grated nutmeg
Grated cheese 4 oz (120 g)

Method: Clean and core the cauliflower. Remove
unwanted leaves. Rub the florets with lemon
juice. Boil for 20 minutes in salted water.
Separate the sprigs into florets and arrange in a
row on a shallow dish. Boil ¾ pint milk and with
the cold remainder, mix cornflour. Add this
mixture to the boiling milk to thicken it. Remove
from heat and blend 3 beaten eggs and half of
the cheese. Season the custard and pour over the
cauliflower. Sprinkle remaining grated cheese
and brown in oven for 15 minutes at 360°F.

SELINORIZA TIGANTI
Celeriac fritters

Ingredients:

Celeriac 2 lb (960 g)
Juice and rind of 1 lemon
Seasoned flour 2 oz (60 g)
Oil for frying

Batter:

1 egg

Flour 3 oz (90 g)
Water ½ pint (300 mls)

Method: Blend beaten egg and water with flour to obtain a smooth batter. Leave for 20 minutes. Peel and cut celeriac in sticks or thin slices. Marinade in grated rind and juice of lemon. Pass in seasoned flour and batter and fry in a shallow pan with oil until golden for 5 minutes. Drain and dry. If the celeriac are cut in sticks, they should be scalded for ½ minute, drained and dried. This process will soften the texture. This is not necessary if the celeriac is sliced thinly.

PILAFIA
Rice pilaff

Ingredients:

Long grain rice 8 oz (240 g)
Water 2 pint (1,200 mls)
Oil 2 fl oz (60 mls)
Cooked peas 2 oz (60 g)
Sultanas or seedless raisins 2 oz (60 g)
Chopped onions 2 oz (60 g)
1 clove of crushed garlic
Red peppers 2 oz (60 g)
Good pinch turmeric powder

Method: Boil rice in salted water for 20 minutes and dry. Fry chopped onion in oil until translucent. Add peas, garlic, red peppers and rice. Toss mixture until it is well reheated. Season and sprinkle turmeric to add colour. Lastly, add scalded raisins and sultanas.

SKORDALIA
Garlic sauce

This is a sauce well-known in all the Balkan countries.

Ingredients:

2 cloves of garlic
Chopped walnuts 5 oz (150 g)
Oil 5 fl oz (150 mls)
White vinegar 1 fl oz (30 mls)

Breadcrumbs 4 oz (120 g)
Water 2 oz (60 g)
Salt and pepper

Method: Pound garlic and walnut to a paste. Soak breadcrumbs in water. Squeeze out moisture and add to paste. Gradually pour the oil. Finally, add salt, pepper and vinegar or lemon juice.

SKORDALIA GARLIC SAUCE
    MAYONNAISE
    (known in France as *Aioli*)

Ingredients:

Crushed garlic 1 oz (30 g)
3 egg yolks
Oil ½ pint (300 mls)
Salt and pepper
Juice and grated rind of 1 lemon

Method: Pound garlic to a paste. Add egg yolks, salt and pepper. Gradually pour oil while whisking mixture to obtain a smooth emulsion. Add lemon juice.

SWEETS and DESSERTS

HALVAS SIMIGDALENIO
Semolina dumplings with a syrup sauce

Ingredients:

Butter 4 oz (120 g)
Semolina or couscous 6 oz (180 g)
Chopped walnuts 2 oz (60 g)
Sugar 2 oz (60 g)
Water 5 fl oz (150 mls)
Cream 5 fl oz (150 mls)

Syrup:

Water 5 fl oz (150 mls)
Sugar 10 oz (300 g)
Few drops rosewater essence

Method: Melt the butter in a pan and fry the couscous or semolina to impart a nutty taste.

Add nuts and cook for 5 minutes. Remove from pan. Place the mixture in a saucepan with cream, water and sugar. Cook for a further 5 minutes. Cool and pour into a well greased tray. When cold, cut in squares or rounds and place these 'gnocchi' in a dish. Cover with the syrup made by boiling water and sugar for a few minutes and flavour with rosewater essence or other flavouring.

The Italian Roman gnocchi is made similarly, but cheese and egg yolks are added to the mixture.

Note: I would suggest adding 2 egg yolks to the semolina after it has been cooked to enrich and give a better texture to the halvas.

KARYDATA
Walnut sugar drops

These are made exactly like Coconut Kisses.

Ingredients:

Chopped walnuts 4 oz (120 g)
Icing sugar 8 oz (240 g)
Few drops strawberry or kirsch flavouring
Granulated sugar 2 oz (60 g)
Few drops red colouring
Water 2 fl oz (60 mls)

Method: Melt icing sugar with hot water. Pound the walnuts with granulated sugar, add flavouring and colouring. Drop spoonfuls of the mixture on an oiled tray. Allow to set and place in paper cases.

MYZITHROPITA
Cheese cake

Ingredients:

Cream cheese 8 oz (240 g)
Butter or margarine 3 oz (90 g)
Grated cheese 1 oz (30 g)
Pinch grated lemon rind
Castor sugar 1 oz (30 g)
3 eggs
Self-raising flour 12 oz (360 g)

Scalded currants 3 oz (90 g)
A mixture of a few drops of lemon and vanilla essence

Method: Cream cheese and margarine with grated cheese and sugar. Add beaten eggs and beat until fluffy. Blend with flour and add dried, scalded currants and flavouring last. Leave the mixture in a refrigerator for 30 minutes. Roll on a floured board like a huge salami (2 inch diameter). Cut slices ¼ inch thick. Place the slices on a greased tray. Bake for 15 minutes at 400°F. Cool and dust with vanilla flavoured icing sugar.

SKALTSOUNAKIA
Puff pastry filled with walnuts and honey

Ingredients:

Puff pastry ½ lb (240 g)

Filling:

Walnut ½ lb (240 g)
Cake crumbs 2 oz (60 g)
1 egg
Honey 2 oz (60 g)

Icing sugar 2 oz (60 g)

Method: Roll the pastry to ⅛ inch thick. Cut in 4 inch round. Blend all filling ingredients. Walnuts are to be coarsely chopped and mixed with egg, crumbs and honey to a paste. Place 1 oz of the mixture on each round. Brush side with water. Fold in two like a turnover. Press edges and crimp to seal tightly the two sides of pastry. Brush top with eggwash. Rest 20 minutes. Bake at 400°F for 20 minutes. Serve with melted honey poured on top of the pastry.

The Skaltsounakia can be done with the filo paste exactly as a Baklava. Style changes according to region. This is a modified version.

Cyprus

Kopiaste is the most exciting word in Cyprus. It simply means 'come and share my food'. When you begin to experience Cypriot gastronomy you must think of ancient Greece, Egypt, Rome and Persia all at once, and combine them with a pastoral scene where the wine flows, the food is abundant, wholesome and spicy, and the people are happy to share it with you.

Your first sip of the delicious and potent Cyprus wine will enslave your palate for evermore; but first you must learn to eat with your drink and to do it slowly. To help you, the Cypriots have invented the *Mezedes,* a type of tidbits or hors d'oeuvre, always served with drinks at any time of day.

Mezes means delicacy, and these little appetisers, also known as *mezades* or *mezedakia.* In a Cyrpus cafe or restaurant, you are served a rich collection of up to 20 appetisers and savouries or snacks. Amongst them you might find various morsels of cheese, *kaskavalli, halloumi or feta,* tomatoes, olives, celery, sliced artichokes or smoked ham, *houmous* (ground chick peas made into a paste with olive oil, garlic, and lemon), octopus, small calamares, squid, shrimps, fresh fish steamed or fried, such as the delicious *barbouni* (red mullet); succulent snippets of turkey and chicken, cucumbers, green peppers, *sheftalia* (home-made) sausage), *dolmades* (stuffed vine leaves with lemon sauce), *koupepia* (stuffed marrow) and *beccaficos,* the baby woodcock which have been a great delicacy since the time of the crusades.

The local bread made from homegrown wheat, sprinkled with sesame seed on the crusty outside, with a village salad with fresh coriander, green olives, olive oil and lemon juice, beside a plate of cool, salty feta cheese can make the mouth water. So can *taramosalata,* the delicious paste made from fish roe with the aromatic olive oil of the island; and as if these were not enough, there are the savoury main meal courses: *mousaka,* made from minced meats, herbs, potatoes, aubergines and marrows; *tavas*—veal, onion and herbs cooked in earthenware bowls and served straight from the oven; a macaroni cheese pie with a layer of rich tomato flavoured minced meat. *Souvlakia* is the familiar Greek marinated lamb with an aroma of lemon juice and white wine, flavoured with onions and coriander seeds, grilled on skewers over charcoal.

The excellence of Cypriot cookery lies mainly in its ingredients. The dishes are the same as those in Greece, sometimes with a little local colour added in the form of extra herbs or spices—but the basics are the same, made of the succulent produce which this sunny island produces in abundance.

Cyprus offers a cornucopia of excellent fresh fruit—oranges, grapefruit, grapes, tangerines, melons, lemons, figs, cherries, apricots, pomegranates and various types of nuts to name but a few. *Avgolemeno* is one of the delicious lemon-scented soups, and indeed lemons appear everywhere, with every meal and every meat. Potatoes are large and tasty, and Cyprus grows some of the finest varieties in the world.

Fish such as synagrida, fangri, red mullet, vlahos and trout are plentiful, and are much appreciated simply grilled or fried, perhaps with a touch of mint or coriander seeds.

The national dish is *fasolada karavishia,* a simple

dish of beans, and *afelia* (pork), soaked in wine and fried in pepper, lentils or laurel.

Game on the island includes partridge, hare, woodcock, snipe and pheasant, and the favourite method of preparation is to roast them plain with a bunch of herbs.

The sweet course in Cyprus includes not only all the fresh fruits but also all the middle eastern types of confectionery like *halva, baklava* and *locoum,* or Turkish delight. There are preserves and fruit pastes made from all types of fruit and rose petals—even one made from tiny aubergines. Cyprus honey is excellent and often used in pastries such as *kadeifi* or *galatopureko* which are rich honey cakes. *Soumada,* made of almonds, is a favourite hot drink.

The wines of Cyprus are legendary and Commandaria, the rich sweet dessert wine of the Crusaders, is reputed to be the oldest wine known in the world. During Roman times, the Byzantine province of Cyprus was famous for the excellence of its wines. But successive invasions destroyed the industry, and it was not until the island was bought by the British in 1878 from Turkey that the wine industry started to rediscover its old traditions and importance. The total production yield is now 155,000 tons, and the grapes are processed to make a whole range of wines: red, white, sweet, dry, sherries, vermouths and ports.

The latest addition is a fine sparkling wine made by the champagne method.

Ouzo is as popular as it is in Greece, drunk with a little iced water to turn it into an opaque white liquid. In the heart of the Paphos forest, in the ancient monastery of Kykko, another strong distillate is made: zivania, a pink, cinnamon flavoured liquid with a soft taste and hard after-effects. Cyprus brandy is quite good and is made in various grades dependent on the time the spirit has rested in the wood: the V O means 3 years, the Extra means 8 years, the VSOP and Five Kings can be anything from 12 to 20 years. The sherries of Cyprus are made by the same system as those of Spain.

Coffee is drunk, thick and usually sweet. But there are various types, and for a traditional sweet coffee you ask for *Glykis,* made with a heaped teaspoon of powdered coffee, freshly ground, and 2 teaspoons of sugar. The medium coffee is *metrios,* with only 1 teaspoon of sugar, and *skettos* is the bland drink made by using less coffee and no sugar at all.

The history of Cyprus may have been troubled and the poverty of the people far from being solved. But young and old, rich and poor, all eat similar food, appetising with the scent of lemons and herbs—and to a visitor, they will always say : kopiaste.

BILL OF FARE

Soup

SOUPA AVGOLEMENO
Egg and lemon soup

FAKI XIDHATI
Lentil soup

LOUVANA
Yellow pea soup

PATSHA
Brain soup

Hors d'Oeuvre (Mezes)

KLEFTEDHES
Meat and potato rissoles

TARAMOSALATA
Cod's roe paste

TALATTOURE
Cucumber in yoghurt

PRASSA
Leek Cypriot style

XYDATA KREMMIDIA
Sweet and sour onions

Fish Dishes

SAVORO
Garlic flavoured fried fish

BACALIARO KLEFTEDHES
Fish rissoles

KALAMARIA KATHISTA
Squid in wine

Meat Dishes

PSITO OF LAMB
Roast lamb Cypriot style

TAVA
Casserole of lamb

CYPRUS STUFFING
Rice filling for poultry and game

AFELIA OF PORK
Pork cubes cooked with wine

MAKARONIA TOU FOURNOU
Cypriot macaroni beef pie

DOLMADES YEMISTA
Stuffed vine leaves

Vegetables

BAMIES
Okra Cypriot style

LAHANOPITTA
Spinach and cheese pie

Sweets and Desserts

CYPRUS TART
Lemon curd tart

CYPRUS CAKE
Almond and semolina cake with syrup sauce

FIGS IN OUZO
Figs poached in syrup flavoured with aniseed
liqueur

FILFAR ORANGES
Orange in syrup with Filfar liqueur

IYRAN
Yoghurt drink

MYZITHOPITA
Cream cheese cake

BAKLAVA
Puff pastry filled with nuts and soaked in syrup

DHAKTYLA
Pumpkin fritters

SOUP

SOUPA AVGOLEMENO
Egg and lemon soup (6 to 8 portions)

Ingredients:

Chicken stock: 1 fowl or giblets 2 lb (960 g)
1 leek
2 carrots
1 onion studded with 4 cloves
1 turnip
1 sprig of celery
1 bouquet garni
1 or 2 chicken cubes for added flavour
1 tsp monosodium glutamate
Salt and pepper
Water 3 pint (1,800 mls)
Cooked rice 8 oz (240 g)

Lemon mixture:

6 egg yolks
Potato or maize flour or arrowroot 2 oz (60 g)
Juice and rind of 3 lemons

Method: Place fowl or giblets in water and bring
to the boil. Remove scum until the broth is clear.
Simmer for 1 hour, then add all the vegetables
and seasoning and cook for 35 minutes. Serve
fowl and vegetables with lemon sauce made as
follows: strain 2 pint of stock into a saucepan
and reheat. Mix 2 oz (60 g) potato flour with
½ pint of cold chicken stock. Add this mixture
to the boiling stock. Place the egg yolks with
lemon juice and grated rind in a bowl. Add ½
pint of the thickened stock. Stir well and pour
the contents of this mixture into the remaining
thickened stock. Reheat to boiling point. Season
and serve with chicken as a meal or a soup. Garnish
soup with cooked rice—2 oz (60 g) per person.

FAKI XIDHATI
Lentil soup (6 to 8 portions)

Ingredients:

1 knuckle of bacon or veal
Water 3 pint (1,800 mls)
Lentils 8 oz (240 g)

1 carrot
1 onion studded with 4 cloves
1 tbs coriander seeds
1 bouquet garni
Vinegar 2 fl oz (60 mls)

Method: Soak lentils in water for 2 hours. Boil veal
or bacon in water for 1½ hour. Remove scum as it
rises. Add lentils and remaining ingredients. Simmer
for 45 minutes, until lentils are tender. Strain stock
into a saucepan. Pass lentils through a sieve or
liquidize with some of the stock. Blend the puree
to the stock including carrot and onion. Season,
add vinegar. Serve the knuckle of veal or bacon as
meat course.

LOUVANA
Yellow pea soup (4 to 6 portions)

Ingredients:

Water 2½ pint (1,500 mls)
Yellow peas 8 oz (240 g)
Potatoes 8 oz (240 g)
1 onion 5 oz (150 g)
1 carrot 5 oz (150 g)
1 turnip or swede 5 oz (150 g)
1 sprig of celery
Rice 3 oz (90 g)
Salt and pepper
Juice of 1 lemon

Garnish:

Green olives 4 oz (120 g)
Black olives 4 oz (120 g)

Method: Boil all ingredients until tender. Pass
through a sieve and reheat puree and liquid.
Garnish with a few green and black olives on
each serving. This soup should be fairly thick.

PATSHA
Brain soup (6 to 8 portions)

Ingredients:

1 calf's or sheep's head
Water 3 pint (1,800 mls)

1 onion
1 sprig of celery
1 carrot
1 bouquet garni
Juice and rind of 2 lemons
6 egg yolks
Potato flour 4 oz (120 g)
Salt and pepper
3 chopped hard-boiled eggs
Sliced olives 3 oz (90 g)

Method: Split and bone the head. Remove the brains. Soak the brains in cold water with vinegar for 10 minutes. Remove blood membrane from brains. Place the brains in water with vinegar and poach for 8 minutes without boiling. Cool in liquor. Cut the meat of the head in small squares and boil in water with carrot, onion, celery and bouquet garni for 1½ hours. Strain 3 pint of liquor into a saucepan. Reboil it. Blend potato flour in a bowl with ½ pint of cooled stock. Add this mixture to the boiling, remaining stock while stirring until it thickens. Blend egg yolks and lemon juice in a bowl and add ½ pint of the thickened stock. Stir well and pour into the remaining thick stock. Whisk for 4 minutes to obtain smooth soup. Add meat to the soup and serve sliced brains separately with sliced eggs and olives as garnish.

HORS D'OEUVRE (MEZES)

KLEFTEDHES
Meat and potato rissoles

Ingredients:

Potatoes 8 oz (240 g)
Minced beef 1 lb (480 g)
1 egg
Chopped onions 2 oz (60 g)
1 clove chopped garlic
Salt and pepper
Pinch chopped mint
1 slice of bread 2 oz (60 g)
Milk 2 fl oz (60 mls)
Oil for frying

Seasoned flour 2 oz (60 g)
Lemon or tomato sauce ½ pint (300 mls)

Method: Peel and grate the potatoes and squeeze out the moisture. Blend with meat and egg, chopped onions, garlic and seasoning. Add bread soaked in milk and well squeezed. Knead to obtain a smooth mixture. Divide into 1 oz (30 g) dumplings. Pass in seasoned flour and fry in oil like rissoles. Serve with tomato or lemon sauce, either hot or cold.
Note: For 4 oz (120 g) seasoned flour, add ½ oz (15 g) salt and 1 pinch pepper.

TARAMOSALATA
Cod's roe paste

Ingredients:

Slice of white bread without crust 2 oz (60 g)
Milk 2 fl oz (60 mls)
Smoked cod's (or any other) roe 8 oz (240 g)
Juice of 2 lemons
Salt and pepper
Small pinch of paprika for pink colouring
2 cloves of finely chopped and crushed garlic
Olive or salad oil 5 fl oz (150 mls)

Garnish:

Sliced gherkins and olives 2 oz (60 g)

Method: Soak the bread in milk and squeeze out the moisture. Pound to a paste with smoked roe. Add chopped garlic and lemon juice. Stir mixture while adding oil in a small thread to obtain a smooth paste. Season. Place in a shallow dish and decorate with sliced olives and gherkins. Serve with sippets of bread or toast.
Note: Bread can be replaced by 3 oz (90 g) cold mashed potato.

TALATTOURE
Cucumber in yoghurt

Ingredients:

1 peeled cucumber 8 oz (240 g)
Plain yoghurt 5 fl oz (150 mls)

Juice and grated rind of half a lemon
Salt and pepper
Chopped parsley

Method: Slice cucumber. Sprinkle with salt and soak to exhude bitter juices for 10 minutes. Rinse off and dry. Blend with yoghurt, lemon juice, seasoning and rind. Sprinkle chopped parsley.

PRASSA
Leek Cypriot style

Ingredients:
8 small leeks 2 lb (960 g)

Marinade:
Juice and grated rind of 2 lemons
Olive oil 5 fl oz (150 mls)
White wine 5 fl oz (150 mls)
Water 5 fl oz (150 mls)
1 tbs coriander seeds
Chopped celery 2 oz (60 g)
Chopped onions 2 oz (60 g)
1 small tsp made mustard—added to marinade when
    it is cold after boiling
1 bay leaf
1 tbs chopped parsley
1 small tsp sugar
4 peppercorns

Method: Boil all the ingredients of the marinade for 5 minutes. Cool. Clean and trim the leeks. Tie in a bundle and boil in salted water for 10 minutes. Drain and place in marinade. Soak overnight. Sprinkle chopped parsley. Alternatively, the leeks can be cooked in the marinade.

Care must always be taken to make sure no dirt remains inside the leeks. It is necessary to pierce the centre of the leek with a pointed knife, cutting in 4 from centre to leaves, leaving the white part in 1 stem. Wash leeks several times in water and tie in bundles of 6.

XYDATA KREMMIDIA
Sweet and sour onions

Ingredients:
Button onions 2 lb (960 g)
Same marinade as for leeks

Method: Boil for 10 minutes in leek marinade and cool. Serve in the same liquor.

FISH DISHES

SAVORO
Garlic flavoured fried fish

Ingredients:
Mixture of bream, red mullets or other fish cut in
    small pieces on the bone or filleted 2 lb (960 g)
Oil 2 fl oz (60 mls)
Sliced onions 2 oz (60 g)
Seasoned flour 2 oz (60 g)
Vinegar 5 fl oz (150 mls)
Water 1 pint (600 mls)
Salt and pepper
Chopped rosemary
1 clove chopped garlic

Method: Clean fish and fillet in small pieces. Toss in seasoned flour. Fry in oil till cooked on both sides. Place in a shallow dish. Fry sliced onion rings in same oil till tender but not too brown. Add garlic. Cook 10 seconds only. Place on top of fish. Add a little flour to oil to make a roux and gradually add vinegar and water to obtain 1 pint of brown acid sauce. Boil for 5 minutes. Season and pour over the fish. Sprinkle with chopped rosemary or parsley and serve with lemon wedges.

BACALIARO KLEFTEDHES
Fish rissoles

Ingredients:
Salted cod fish 1 lb (480 g)
Water 3 pint (1,800 mls)
1 egg
Peeled prawns 5 oz (150 g)

Batter:
½ clove chopped garlic
1 egg

Flour 4 oz (120 g)
Water 5 fl oz (150 mls)
Seasoned flour 2 oz (60 g)
Lemon sauce ½ pint (300 mls)

Method: Soak fish overnight. Boil in the same
water until tender. Flake the fish and blend it with
peeled prawns. Pound to a paste with 1 egg. Season
and shape into 1 oz (30 g) dumplings. Toss in
seasoned flour. Make batter by adding beaten egg,
water and garlic to flour. Dip the fish dumplings
in this batter and deep fry until golden for 5
minutes. Serve with lemon sauce.

KALAMARIA KATHISTA
Squid in wine

Ingredients:

Cleaned and prepared squid 1½ lb (720 g)
Oil 2 fl oz (60 mls)
Seasoned flour 2 oz (60 g)
Wine vinegar 2 fl oz (60 mls)
4 garlic cloves
1 bay leaf
Salt and pepper
Pinch grated mace or nutmeg
White wine 5 fl oz (150 mls)
Chopped onions 4 oz (120 g)
1 tbs chopped parsley

Method: Squid can be obtained already cleaned
and prepared in frozen packets. Cut the squid
in pieces and pass in seasoned flour. Fry in oil
for 5 minutes. Add chopped onions and garlic
and simmer in fat for further 5 minutes. Pour
wine and vinegar over the mixture and boil for
10 minutes; add bay leaf. Transfer to a casserole
dish. Cover with a lid and bake slowly in the oven
for 1 hour at 360°F. Season and sprinkle with
chopped parsley. Serve with rice pilaff.

MEAT DISHES

The Cypriot Sunday joint is often lamb or chicken
and the preparation is the same.

PSITO OF LAMB
Roast lamb Cypriot style (10 to 12 portions)

Ingredients:

1 leg of lamb 3½ lb (1,680 g)
6 garlic cloves
Salt and pepper
Seasoned flour
Oil 2 fl oz (60 mls)
White wine ½ pint (300 mls)
Tomato puree 2 oz (60 g)
1 tbs oregano or chopped mint
Peeled potatoes 3 lb (1,440 g)

Method: Make slits in the leg of lamb with a
pointed knife and insert halved cloves of garlic.
Remove pelvic bone for easier carving. Season and
rub with oil. Dust with seasoned flour.
Place leg in a shallow tray and roast at
420°F for 15 minutes. Then add wine and
tomato puree. Reduce heat to 380°F and cook for
another 30 minutes. Add potatoes and cook for
further 30 minutes (at 380°F), basting from time
to time. Strain the liquid into a saucepan to make
a plain gravy. Flavour it with oregano or mint.

TAVA
Casserole of lamb (6 to 8 portions)

Ingredients:

Stewing lamb from shoulder, neck or middle
    neck 2½ lb (1,200 g)
Sliced onions 8 oz (240 g)
Skinned and seeded tomatoes 1 lb (480 g)
Tomato puree 1 oz (30 g)
Finely chopped red peppers 2 oz (60 g)
Oil 2 fl oz (60 mls)
Flour 2 oz (60 g)
Salt and pepper
Pinch cumin and coriander seeds
Water 3 pint (1,800 mls)

Method: Place meat in a saucepan with water.
Bring to the boil and remove scum as it rises.
Cook for 1 hour and then add remaining
ingredients, except oil and flour. Simmer for 30
minutes and thicken with a roux made with

flour cooked in oil until sandy textured. Dilute roux in the liquor of the meat. Strain the sauce and then add to meat. Season to taste. Sprinkle with chopped parsley. Add spices and seeds. Serve with rice pilaff.

CYPRUS STUFFING
Rice filling for poultry and game

Ingredients:

Long grain rice 8 oz (240 g)
Water 1½ pint (900 mls)
Oil 2 fl oz (60 mls)
Chopped onions 2 oz (60 g)
Chopped liver 3 oz (90 g)
1 clove chopped garlic
Sultanas or currants 2 oz (60 g)
Flaked almonds 2 oz (60 g)
Juice and grated rind of 2 lemons
Pinch of sugar (5 g)
Salt and pepper to taste

Method: Fry in oil chopped onions until translucent. Add rice and stir for 5 minutes. Add water and cook for 15 minutes. Add liver, seasoning, fruits and nuts and simmer for 5 minutes. Season. Stir the lemon juice and grated rind into the rice and use for stuffing.

AFELIA OF PORK
Pork cubes cooked with wine

Ingredients:

Pork cubes 2 lb (960 g)
Oil 2 fl oz (60 mls)
Seasoned flour 2 oz (60 g)
Pinch coriander seeds
White wine ½ pint (300 mls)
Chopped onions 2 oz (60 g)
1 clove of garlic
Salt and pepper

Method: Toss the pork cubes in seasoned flour. Fry in oil for 10 minutes, until brown. Drain. Remove fat and add wine and seasoning. Cover with a lid and cook with onions until tender.

Season to taste and serve with rice pilaff.

The onion can be fried with the pork if desired, but cooked as described, the flavour is milder.

MAKARONIA TOU FOURNOU
Cypriot macaroni beef pie

Ingredients:

Macaroni (large tubes) 8 oz (240 g)
Water 3 pint (1,800 mls)
Salt ½ oz (15 g)

Meat mixture:

Minced beef 8 oz (240 g)
Oil 2 fl oz (60 mls)
Chopped onions 4 oz (120 g)
1 clove of garlic
Tomato puree 2 tbs (60 g)
Flour 2 oz (60 g)
Water ½ pint (300 mls)
Salt and pepper
Pinch chopped oregano or freshly chopped mint
    leaves

Cheese sauce 1 pint (600 mls)
2 egg yolks
Grated cheese 4 oz (120 g)

Method: Boil macaroni in salted water for 15 minutes. Refresh and drain. Blend in half of the cheese sauce. Add two egg yolks to remaining sauce.

Brown meat with chopped onions and garlic in oil. Add flour and tomato puree. Stir and add water. Cook for 25 minutes. Season. Add herbs. Place alternate layers of meat and macaroni into a shallow dish until full. Cover with egg cheese sauce. Sprinkle with grated cheese and brown in the oven at 380°F for 20 minutes.

DOLMADES YEMISTA
Stuffed vine leaves

Ingredients:

2 doz vine leaves (available in tins)
Minced beef 1 lb (480 g)

Chopped onions 2 oz (60 g)
Cooked rice 4 oz (120 g)
1 egg
Salt and pepper
Pinch grated nutmeg or mace
Stock 1 pint (600 mls)

Sauce:

Fat 1 oz (30 g)
Flour 1 oz (30 g)
Stock 1 pint (600 mls)
3 egg yolks
Juice and grated rind of 2 lemons

Method: If fresh leaves are used, blanch them in salted water for 5 minutes. Refresh and drain. Place on a board without stems.

Blend minced raw beef, onions and cooked rice with egg to form a smooth paste. Season. Divide into 1 oz (30 g) dumplings. Wrap with vine leaves until all the meat mixture is used. Place the Dolmades in a shallow tray. Cover with stock and braise in the oven at 360°F for 1 hour, basting from time to time.

Drain liquor and make up to 1 pint with more stock or water. Bring to the boil. Cook a roux with fat and flour until sandy textured. Gradually add the liquor, while stirring. Mix egg yolks and lemon juice with rind in a bowl. Pour half of the sauce into the egg mixture while stirring and reheat this mixture with remaining stock until smooth. Stir to avoid coagulation. Season and pour over the Dolmades. Serve hot or cold.

VEGETABLES

BAMIES
Okra Cypriot style

Ingredients:

Ladies fingers (okra) 1 lb (480 g)
Oil 2 fl oz (60 g)
Chopped onions 2 oz (60 g)
Skinned and seeded tomatoes 8 oz (240 g)
1 clove of garlic
1 tbs chopped parsley

Salt and pepper
Water 1 pint (600 mls)

Method: Remove the top of the ladies fingers' stems without cutting into the pod. Fry chopped onions until tender, but not brown. Add chopped garlic, tomatoes and okra. Cover level with water. Season and boil gently for 40 minutes. Serve with chopped parsley sprinkled on top.

LAHANOPITTA
Spinach and cheese pie

Lahana resembles spinach but has larger leaves and a celery flavour.

Ingredients:

Lahana or spinach 3 lb (1,440 g)
Cottage cheese 8 oz (240 g)
Salt and pepper
Grated nutmeg
2 beaten eggs
Filo pastry 6 oz (180 g) – can be purchased
  at Greek shops (see Baklava recipe)
Butter 2 oz (60 g)

Method: Wash, trim and drain lahana or spinach leaves if not available. Boil for 5 minutes in salted water. Drain and squeeze out the surplus water. Chop coarsely and blend with cottage cheese and beaten eggs. Season. Grease a shallow tin 12 inch x 8 inch and line with six layers of pastry. Brush each layer with melted butter before adding the next. Place spinach and cheese mixture on top and again place a layer of pastry. Brush with melted butter, adding another six layers of pastry, each one having been brushed with butter. Cover with greaseproof paper and bake at 380°F for 30 minutes. Remove paper and increase heat to 400°F and cook for a further 20 minutes, until the top is golden brown like puff pastry.

SWEETS AND DESSERTS

CYPRUS TART
Lemon curd tart

Ingredients:

Sweet short pastry:

Margarine 4 oz (120 g)
Icing sugar 1 oz (30 g)
1 egg
Flour 8 oz (240 g)

Filling:

3 eggs
Flour 1 oz (30 g)
Castor sugar 6 oz (180 g)
Juice and grated rind of 1 lemon
Butter 2 oz (60 g)

Method: Cream margarine, sugar and egg until
fluffy. Add flour. Roll pastry to a ball and leave
for 30 minutes. Line an 8 inch ring or flan mould
with pastry. Place a piece of greaseproof paper
inside the pastry and fill with dry beans. Bake
pastry case blind for 20 minutes at 400°F. Remove
beans and paper. Cool.

Whisk eggs, flour and sugar for 5 minutes
until frothy. Add melted butter, lemon juice
and grated rind. Fill pastry case with mixture and
bake for 20 minutes at 360°F to set the curd.
Cool and serve.

CYPRUS CAKE
Almond and semolina cake with syrup sauce

Ingredients:

Butter 6 oz (180 g)
Icing sugar 5 oz (150 g)
Baking powder 1 oz (30 g) ⎫ Mix the 3 dry
Fine semolina 10 oz (300 g) ⎬ ingredients
Ground almonds 4 oz (120 g) ⎭ thoroughly
4 beaten eggs
Few drops of mixed essences: vanilla, almond and
    lemon
Grated rind of 1 orange and 1 lemon
Syrup: juice of 1 orange and 1 lemon
Cyprus sherry 5 fl oz (150 mls)
Castor sugar 8 oz (240 g)
1 tea bag
Flavourings

Method: Blend all the dry ingredients in a bowl.
Cream butter and icing sugar until fluffy. Add
beaten eggs to creamed butter and the mixed dry
ingredients. Add essences and grated rinds.

Line a cake mould with greaseproof paper.
Fill with mixture until two-thirds full. Level
mixture with scraper or palette knife. Bake at 380°
380°F for 45 minutes. Cool and turn out onto a
pastry rack. Remove paper when cold and place
into a round shallow dish.

To make syrup sauce, boil wine and brew tea
bag for 5 minutes. Remove the bag. Add fruit
juice and sugar. Reheat to dissolve. Flavour
with essence—rum, brandy or liquor. Strain. Pour
this syrup over the cake. Serve cool with lemon
ice cream or fruit compote.

FIGS IN OUZO
Figs poached in syrup flavoured with aniseed
    liqueur

Ouzo is more Turkish than Cypriot or Greek, yet
it is to Greeks what Pernod is to the French — an
aniseed or anis star flavoured liqueur. Simply add,
to figs in syrup, a glass of Ouzo per kilo of figs or
5 per cent of the syrup used.

FILFAR ORANGES
Orange in syrup with Filfar liqueur

Ingredients:

4 oranges

Syrup:

Castor sugar 6 oz (180 g)
Water 4 fl oz (120 mls)
Orange juice or Filfar liqueur 4 fl oz (120 mls)—or
    orange curacao or Grand Marnier

Method: Peel the oranges with a potato peeler to
obtain a thin rind (zest). Cut the rind into very thin
strips (julienne—1½ inch long). Boil strips in water
for 10 minutes and refresh. Drain. Prepare syrup
by boiling water, sugar and blanched strips for 5
minutes. Cool and add orange liqueur.

Peel the white skin off the oranges. Cut oranges

FRIED AUBERGINES, COURGETTES IN LEMON SAUCE, STUFFED VINE LEAVES
LAMB KEBAB AND RICE PILAFF (Greece and Cyprus)

FARFALETTE SOPHIA LOREN, TAGLIATELLE VERDI ALLA MARINARA, PRESCIUTTO MELONE
(Italy)

SAVARIN POLISH STYLE (Poland)

CHEESE CAKE, RUSSIAN EASTER BREAD, BORTSCH (Russia)

into segments without pips. Place in the syrup and let them soak all night in a chilled cabinet. Serve with water or lemon sorbet ice.

IYRAN
Yoghurt drink

Ingredients:

Plain yoghurt ½ pint (300 mls)
Ice water ¼ pint (150 mls)
Pinch salt
Fresh chopped mint or peppermint liquor

Method: Blend together and serve as cold as possible.

MYZITHOPITA
Cream cheese cake

Ingredients:

Butter 2 oz (60 g)
Cream cheese 8 oz (240 g)
Castor sugar 5 oz (150 g)
4 egg yolks
4 egg whites
Few drops vanilla and lemon essence
Juice and rind of 1 lemon
Plain flour 5 oz (150 g)
Baking powder ¼ oz (8 g)
Seedless raisins 2 oz (60 g)

Method: Cream butter, cheese and sugar until fluffy. Add egg yolks, flavouring, lemon juice and grated rind. Blend the scalded and dried raisins to mixture. Sift flour and baking powder and blend to mixture lightly but thoroughly. Lastly, beat egg whites to a meringue and fold into mixture.
    Grease a flan ring 9 inch x 3 inch. Fill with mixture and bake for 25 minutes at 360°F.

BAKLAVA
Pastry filled with nuts and soaked in syrup

Ingredients:

Filo pastry:

Flour 1 lb (480 g)–strong or bread flour
Oil 1 fl oz (30 mls)
Water 5 fl oz (150 mls)
Salt 5 g
Or use 1 lb (480 g) prepared puff pastry

Method: Blend oil and water. Add to flour to obtain a smooth, but firm dough. Knead the dough well and form into 8 balls. Cover and leave in a refrigerator for 3 hours. Roll each ball as thinly as possible. (It should be almost transparent.)

Filling:

Walnuts 8 oz (240 g)
Chopped almonds 3 oz (90 g)
Ground almonds 2 oz (60 g)
Icing sugar 4 oz (120 g)
Mixed lemon peel and candied orange 2 oz (60 g)
Honey 2 oz (60 g)

Method: Blend all ingredients to a paste. Place each pastry layer on a greased tray. Brush each time with melted butter and form 4 layers on top of each other. Spread walnut mixture and cover with 4 more layers, brushing each layer with melted butter. This operation is important as it is the secret of the flakiness of the pastry. Brush the top layer as well and bake at 400°F for 25 minutes.

Syrup:

Sugar 6 oz (180 g)
Water 3 fl oz (90 mls)
Juice of half a lemon
Honey 1 oz (30 g)
Few drops of orange blossom essence

Method: Boil the ingredients for 5 minutes and pou pour over the pastry when cold.

DHAKTYLA
Pumpkin fritters

Ingredients:
Baklava pastry 8 oz (240 g) *or*
    puff pastry

Filling:

Diced pumpkin pulp 8 oz (240 g)
Sugar 4 oz (120 g)
Water 5 fl oz (150 mls)
Pinch cinnamon
Seedless raisins 2 oz (60 g)
Boiled rice 2 oz (60 g)

Method: Roll pastry as thinly as possible ($\frac{1}{8}$ inch thick). Cut into 3 inch squares. Place on a floured board.

To make the filling, cut pumpkin pulp into small cubes and cook with sugar, cinnamon and water for only 5 minutes until soft. Then add cooked rice and raisins. Drain and cool. Put a spoonful of mixture into each square of pastry. Brush edge and fold into triangles. Fry in hot fat for 5 minutes until golden. Drain on absorbent paper and serve with syrup as for Baklava.

Holland

God made the world, say the citizens of Holland, but the Dutch made the Netherlands. Nearly half of this democratic land's 15,450 square miles has been reclaimed from the sea, and the doughty inhabitants have been trying to keep it from slipping back ever since. Windmills and pumps work ceaselessly to keep the land dry, for more than half Holland lies below sea level and fighting the onslaught of the waves for centuries has always been an arduous task.

Much of the country was ruled by the Dukes of Burgundy in the fourteenth century and dominated by Spain in the sixteenth. Dutch independence was achieved under William the Silent, but there are still some traces of Spanish influence, gastronomically speaking.

Holland's most prosperous period was during the seventeenth century when she lived on the spoils of her East and West Indian colonies. With all the gold pouring into the national coffers, she could commission the best artists to paint and sculpt, and encourage the best chefs to cook to their heart's content.

Now Holland has thirteen million inhabitants to support and no colonies, but the hard-working Dutch are doing well and have a very high standard of living. They like to be *deftig*—decorous, dignified and respectable—and *gezellig*—cosy, merry and comfortable to be with—and have a high regard for family life, expressed through shared meals in the evening at the family table; meals, like lunch, taken outside the family circle tend to be snacks of open sandwiches rather than complete meals.

The cooking of the Netherlands is very individual; it is a dichotomy between the hearty, satisfying simple type of food evolved to combat the effects of the cold North Sea winters, and the exotic spiciness imported from the Dutch colonies in the east.

The Dutch begin the day with a hearty breakfast of meat, eggs, bread and coffee. Cheese and jam are popular toppings for the delicious freshly baked bread and rolls—like the French, the Dutch housewife buys her bread fresh before breakfast. After this substantial start to the day, lunch is a light affair consisting mainly of open sandwiches garnished with the superb cold meats and fish, often smoked. Coffee or chocolate with little cakes follow the selection of sandwiches. At four o'clock there is tea with biscuits and cakes, and a hearty evening meal of soup, rich dishes and large helpings.

Whatever the meal, the Dutch enjoy their food, and their appetites are titillated by the national institution of the *borreltje*—a little nip of the Schiedam gin, which has a more pronounced flavour of juniper than our English gin.

Basic ingredients for Dutch cooking are fresh and of high quality. Dairy produce of Holland is famous and excellent, and cream, milk and butter are ingredients of many typical dishes. The soil of Holland is fertile and rich, and the excellence of the vegetables grown in market gardens which dot the countryside is undisputed. These fresh and tender vegetables are picked young and often served as a dish on their own, sprinkled with parsley or nutmeg.

Meat dishes are not necessarily served every day. When it does make an appearance meat is often pot-roasted and this method is also used for poultry. Dutch veal is some of the best in the world and there are excellent fish and game.

The big Zeeland oysters and large mussels are simply superb. When I was with the French navy on an official visit to Holland before the Second World War in 1939, we were made royally welcome by the Dutch. The crew of my destroyer split up and we were all sent to various towns. With three colleagues, I was sent to Rotterdam. Official banquets followed by dancing with all the bright young things was the custom on all these official visits, and we were entertained in what was then Rotterdam's best cafe restaurant where a women's orchestra was playing all the latest pop songs. We joined in the chorus and after great draughts of Dutch beer and countless glasses of Genever (gin) with the oysters, I sang a score or more of Charles Trenet's best numbers in vogue at the time. It is amazing what gin and oysters can do to a man.

Steak and chips is a dish much appreciated by the Dutch and features on every restaurant menu. It is usually served rare as *biefstuk;* to have it served well-done one asks for a *doorbakken biefstuk* and a chopped steak is called a *duitse biefstuk.*

Large white asparagus is grown in Holland, and is excellent with the Dutch sauce—*Hollandaise*—which is the country's delicious contribution to international gastronomy. Dutch cheese is renowned for its excellence and 3 types are exported around the world: the red spherical *Edam,* the rounded, creamy *Gouda* and the *Leidse,* flavoured with cumin. But the Dutch make dessert cheese as well, notably the soft, creamy *Kernhem,* which does not travel well but is wonderful on its home ground.

Typical dishes of Holland are similar to German food—sauerkraut served with frankfurters, sausages, bacon and ham. More distinctively Dutch are the combinations of vegetables mashed together as in the substantial beef hot pot known as *hutspot met klapstuk* in which onions, leeks, carrots and cabbage are all mashed together with potatoes. Pea soup made the Dutch way is a meal in itself, with a knucklebone and pork, and so thick that the spoon should almost stand up in it. *Rode kool met rolpens* is a dish of red cabbage and spiced beef with apples and *Boerenkool met Rookworst* is a hearty combination of kale, smoked sausages and potato.

Pancakes are known as *pannekoeken* and *flensjes,* and eaten at any time and any place. They are large, about a foot in diameter, and served with sugar or a variety of sweet sauces.

Indonesian food is extremely popular in contrast to this traditional North European fare. One of the most spectacular dishes, which has become one of Holland's best-known exotic imports, is the *Rijsttafel,* a gargantuan meal of fluffy, dry boiled rice with thirty or more side dishes like *sate babi* (sweet and sour prawns), *kroepoek* (a fried prawn paste which crisps into a cracker rather like a game chip), *daging smoor* (a dark, rich meat sauce). *Loempia* is a spicy little pocket of dough stuffed with meat, and usually there are dozens of curried vegetables, fried bananas, fried coconut with peanuts and various oriental pickles. A well-prepared *Rijsttafel* is a feast for the eyes as well as the tastebuds, and takes hours to eat.

Dutch beer and gin are the best known of the alcoholic drinks. The gin produced at Schiedam is produced from a mash of cereals distilled three times in a pot still, juniper berries being added before the last distillation. There are also special *genevers,* such as lemon and blackberry gins, and a wide range of good liqueurs, and *advocaat,* the delicious egg brandy.

Dutch *curacao* is the best of its kind, and is the one to use when making orange sauce for duck, goose or spiced bacon. It is also ideal for puddings, *crepes suzette* and other flambe dishes as it imparts an aromatic orange flavour with a caramel undertone. It is made in Holland from bitter oranges—*citrus bigaradia*—which are also used for marmalade.

To savour Holland, have a glass of chilled *genever* with a salted Dutch herring, holding it by the tail and eating from the bottom up, next to the stall. Then look around at the flat fields of flowers grown from bulbs to export all over the world; at the dreamy little towns along the *IJsselmeer,* and at the solid gentlemen with briefcases who buy raw diamonds and have them cut by the unassuming artists with steady hands. Artistry and solid business sense go hand in hand—and that is why the sauerkraut lived so happily next to the Indonesian *Rijsttafel* in the shadow of the windmills.

BILL OF FARE

Starters and Hors d'Oeuvre

DUTCH OYSTERS EDAM
Oysters with cheese sauce

SMOKED HERRING JULIANA
Smoked herring fillets and potato salad

DUTCH ASPARAGUS
Large boiled asparagus with a Gouda cheese
sauce

Soup

KALFSPOELETSOEP
Veal and vegetable soup with egg and cream

ERWNTENSOEP
Pea and gammon soup

DUTCH CHICORY SOUP
Chicory and potato soup

Fish

WATERZOOISOEP
Fish and vegetable soup or stew

DUTCH SAUCE
The famous Hollandaise egg and butter sauce
which is one of our great professional sauces

CODLING WILHELMINA
Fish dumplings served with Dutch sauce

CODLING JULIANA
Cod poached with mushrooms and a flavour of
Dutch gin

Meat Dishes

HUTSPOT MET KLAPSTUK
Beef hot pot

RUNDERLAPPEN
Braised steak with cabbage and onion in Dutch
beer

GEHAKTNESTJES
Hard-boiled egg wrapped in minced beef and
fried coated with breadcrumbs

UITSMIJTER
Dutch cheese and ham rarebit

BITTERBALLEN or BALKENBRIJ
Pig's meat fritters (from the head)

VEAL VALKENBURG
Veal escalope stuffed with ham, Dutch cheese
and flavoured with Dutch gin

KESHY YENA UTRECHT
Tender loin beef fillets

PORK CHOP AMSTERDAM
Conil's creation in honour of the Dutch Royal
Family

Vegetables

HARICOTS ENKHUIZEN
Flageolet beans sauted with green beans in
Dutch butter

AARDAPPEL BROODJES
Dutch potato cakes

RODE KOOL
Braised red cabbage and apples flavoured with
vinegar

LOFSCHOTEL
Dutch chicory cooked and served with eggs

Sweets and Desserts

KAAPS WOLKEN
Meringue sweet

DUTCH PEACH QUEEN WILHELMINA
Peach and strawberry sweet

BESCHUITKOEK
Dutch bread fritter

FLENSJES REMBRANDT
Butterscotch pancakes

DRIE IN DE PAN
Small fruit pancakes

DUTCH MERINGUE PIE PRINCE WILLIAM
OF ORANGE
Apple and pear lemon meringue pie flavoured
with Dutch orange curacao

KERST KRANS
Dutch almond Christmas cake

DUTCH ADVOCAAT
Egg sabayon with brandy and orange liqueur

OLIEBOLLEN
Dutch doughnuts

SOUP

KALFSPOELETSOEP
Veal and vegetable soup with eggs and cream

Ingredients:

Veal breast or shin 1 lb (480 g)
Water 3 pint (1,800 mls)
Diced carrots 2 oz (60 g)
Diced onions 2 oz (60 g)
Diced celery 2 oz (60 g)
Diced leek 2 oz (60 g)
Green peas 2 oz (60 g)
Diced turnips 2 oz (60 g)
Fat 2 oz (60 g)
1 bouquet garni
Rice 3 oz (90 g)

Thickening:

Cream 4 fl oz (120 mls)
Egg yolks 2
Cornflour 2 oz (60 g)
Water 4 fl oz (120 mls)
Salt and pepper
Juice of 1 lemon

Method: Dice meat ¼ inch cubes. Partly boil for 10 minutes. Rinse meat in fresh water. Drain and place in large saucepan with water. Cook for 1 hour until meat is almost tender. Add diced vegetables, bouquet garni, rice and peas and boil for another 30 minutes. Strain off 1 pint of the stock into a saucepan.

Mix in a bowl the thickening ingredients. Stir well and gradually add the pint of stock. Pour this mixture into the soup while stirring, and reheat until it boils for 5 minutes to effect cohering and cooking of the starch. Season and add the lemon juice.

ERWNTENSOEP
Pea and gammon soup

Ingredients:

Green gammon 1 lb (480 g), use shin or knuckle
Dried green peas 1 lb (480 g), soaked for 3 hours
1 pig's trotter

Water 4 pint (2,400 mls)
Onion 5 oz (150 g)
Carrots 3 oz (90 g)
Celery 3 oz (90 g)
1 bouquet garni
Sliced potatoes 8 oz (240 g)
1 oz (30 g) of each of the following:
 Green herbs
 Spinach
 Chervil
 Chard
 Green cabbage
 Parsley
 Sorrel
Milk 1 pint (600 mls)
Unsalted butter 3 oz (90 g)
Frankfurters 8 oz (240 g)
Salt and pepper
Pinch monosodium glutamate

Method: Soak meat in cold water for 3 hours to desalt. Shave and singe the pig's trotter and scald it in boiling water for 8 minutes. Refresh and place the knuckle and trotter in a large saucepan with fresh cold water. Boil for 1½ hours before adding soaked peas, other vegetables, herbs and bouquet garni. Cook for another 40 minutes. Remove knuckle and trotter. Season soup with pepper. Add milk and a pinch of monosodium glutamate, which will improve the peas' flavour. Lastly, whisk in the butter. Reheat the frankfurter and slice into soup. Serve sliced meat separately. Season to taste.

This soup is a meal by itself.

DUTCH CHICORY SOUP
Chicory and potato soup

Ingredients:

Lard 3 oz (90 g)
Sliced or diced potatoes 8 oz (240 g)
Diced lean bacon 6 oz (180 g)
Sliced chicory 6 oz (180 g)
1 bouquet garni
Water 1 pint (600 mls)
Milk 1 pint (600 mls)

Salt and pepper
Juice of 1 lemon

Method: Place the vegetables and diced bacon with the lard. Sweat for few minutes while stirring over moderate heat, then add water and bouquet garni and boil until tender for 45 minutes. Remove bouquet garni. Season and pass the soup through a sieve or liquidiser. Reheat with milk and serve, adding lemon juice at the last moment.

STARTERS and HORS D'OEUVRE

DUTCH OYSTERS EDAM
Oysters with cheese sauce

Ingredients:

16 oysters (4 per portion)
Edam cheese 6 oz (180 g)
Dutch gin 2 fl oz (60 mls)
1 egg
1 lemon
Cream 2 fl oz (60 mls)
Pinch cayenne pepper

Method: Open all the oysters. Collect and strain the liquor in a bowl and mix it with gin, cream, grated cheese and beaten egg. Season and blend to a soft paste. Place two oysters per shell. Spread some of the cheese paste on top evenly. Brown under the grill. Serve with a wedge of lemon.

SMOKED HERRING JULIANA
Smoked herring fillets and potato salad

Ingredients:

Smoked herring fillets 8 oz (240 g)
Cooked diced or sliced new potatoes 8 oz (240 g)
Diced apples 4 oz (120 g)
Cream 4 fl oz (120 mls)
Chopped spring onions 2 oz (60 g)
Diced gherkins 2 oz (60 g)
Chopped parsley 1 tbs
Salad oil 4 tbs
White vinegar 4 tbs

Salt and pepper
Pinch sugar dissolved in vinegar

Method: Desalt the smoked herring in water for two hours. Drain, dry and cut into small squares. Blend with all ingredients.

DUTCH ASPARAGUS
Large boiled asparagus with a Gouda cheese sauce

In the markets of Great Britain this select vegetable is generally sold under the name 'Sparrow grass' — a term that has no other meaning, which usually refers to the thin tips of green appearance. Flavourwise, the green varieties are preferred, because they are more tender and the flavour is more delicate than the larger continental varieties. In Holland the asparagus is thicker and white in colour. They are served with vinaigrette sauce or Hollandaise, the national egg sauce.

Allowing four to six per portion, cut off the end of stems. Scrape the stalk without breaking it. Tie up the asparagus per bundle of six to eight and pack them up, tips upwards and boil in salted water without a lid. Cook for 15 minutes. Drain and serve on a folded napkin with the appropriate sauce.

Dutch sauce: Melted butter, vinaigrette, ravigotte and evenly grated cheese can be sprinkled over the tips and slightly gratinated.

Better still, coat the tip parts of the asparagus with a cheese sauce and sprinkle with grated Dutch cheese. Brown under the salamander and serve. Two thirds of the long Dutch asparagus can be eaten, the pulp being scraped on eating in a sucking motion, while the teeth squeeze the stalk to extract the pulp. As asparagus are eaten with the hands, finger-bowls should be served with a slice of lemon to wash the fingers after eating them.

Asparagus are also served as a course on their own, although like globe artichokes, they are best served as a starter — hot or cold.

The discarded stalks of the asparagus when cleaned can be used with the cooking water for making soups.

FISH

WATERZOOISOEP
Fish and vegetable soup or stew

Ingredients:

Lard and Dutch butter 4 oz (120 g)
Celery 3 oz (90 g)
Leek 4 oz (120 g)
Chopped onions 2 oz (60 g)
Water 3 pint (1,800 mls)
Assorted white fish 2 lb (960 g):
    Cod
    Haddock
    Whiting
    (Cut into 2 inch squares – no bones)
1 bouquet garni
3 fresh mint leaves
6 peppercorns
White vinegar 2 fl oz (60 mls)
Crumble short biscuits 4 oz (120 g)
Salt and pepper

Method: In a large pan, sweat the diced vegetables with lard and butter without browning. Add fish then water and rest of ingredients, except the crumbs. Simmer for 20 minutes, then add crumbs to thicken the liquor. Serve the soup in tureen as a soup or as a fish starter.

DUTCH SAUCE
The famous Hollandaise egg and butter sauce
    which is one of our great professional sauces

Ingredients:

5 egg yolks
2 tbs water
Juice of 1 lemon
Butter 1 lb (480 g)
Salt and pepper

Method: Place a tray of water on the stove to boil. In a saucepan put egg yolks, water and lemon juice. Whisk mixture over heat until it begins to thicken slightly. Add the soft butter bit by bit, until all is used up in the sauce, whisking all the time as for mayonnaise. The eggs coagulate during the cooking, producing a custard-like sauce. Season. Serve with poached fish.
Note: Use freshly ground white pepper – vinegar can also be used instead of lemon juice.

CODLING WILHELMINA
Fish dumplings served with Dutch sauce

Ingredients:

Cod fillets 1 lb (480 g)
Matzos 3 oz (90 g)
1 egg
Chopped onions 3 oz (90 g)
Salt and pepper
1 pinch sugar
Juice of 1 lemon
Butter 1 oz (30 g) or oil

Frying:

Oil ½ pint (300 mls)
Breadcrumbs 3 oz (90 g)
Flour 3 oz (90 g)
2 beaten eggs

Method: Mince the fish and blend rest of ingredients. Divide mixture into small 2 oz (60 g) balls. Pass them in flour and beaten eggs and crumbs. Fry in hot oil until golden for 5 minutes. Serve with chips and a spicy tomato chutney.

CODLING JULIANA
Cod poached with mushrooms and a flavour
    of Dutch gin (J.C.)

Ingredients:

Cod fillets 4 by 6 oz (180 g each)
Butter 2 oz (60 g)
Dutch lager 5 fl oz (150 mls)
Dutch gin 3 fl oz (90 mls)
Lemon juice ½ fl oz (15 mls)
Salt and pepper
White sliced mushrooms 5 oz (150 g)
Chopped shallots 1 oz (30 g)
1 bay leaf
2 fresh mint leaves
Grated Edam cheese 2 oz (60 g)

Cream 5 fl oz (150 mls)
Cornflour ½ oz (15 g)

Method: Place fish fillets in a well-buttered
shallow dish, and season well. Flood with beer, gin
and lemon juice. Sprinkle over sliced mushrooms,
chopped shallots, herbs, grated cheese and bay
leaf. Cover with a piece of paper or lid and bake
for 20 minutes at 360°F. Drain the juice into a
small saucepan. Blend cornflour and cream and
add to boiling fish liquor, stirring until thick.
Pour over the fish. Check seasoning and serve.

MEAT DISHES

HUTSPOT MET KLAPSTUK
Beef hot pot

This dish has given the famous French *Pot-au-Feu*
its style.

Ingredients:

Beef flat rib 1 lb (480 g)
Brisket 1 lb (480 g)
1 bouquet garni
Water 6 pints (3,600 mls)
2 large onions studded with 4 cloves
4 cleaned leeks tied up in one bundle
4 small turnips
4 medium carrots
1 small green cabbage
Salt and pepper
Celery leaves
1 lb mashed potato

Method: Boil the meat in 6 pints of water, removing scum as it rises. When the broth is clear after
40 minutes add bouquet garni, studded onions, leeks
few celery leaves, carrots and turnips left whole.
Season. Split cabbage in four and remove stem and
core: add to pot. Simmer the soup for 1½ hours.
Remove the meat and slice it. Mash all vegetables to
a puree with same quantity of mashed potato,
cooked separately. Garnish the dish with this puree.
Use the broth as either clear or vegetable soup.
Dilute puree into it or simply place broth over

sliced bread, as my grandmother used to prepare
it. Season soup to taste at the last minute.
Alternatively the vegetables can be served
whole or cut into slices.

RUNDERLAPPEN
Braised steak with cabbage and onion in
Dutch beer

Ingredients:

Braising steak from chuck or top side
4 by 6 oz (180 g each)
Sliced onions 8 oz (240 g)
Sliced of shredded cabbage 8 oz (240 g)
Dutch beer 1 pint (600 mls)
Water ½ pint (300 mls)
Dutch gin 3 fl oz (90 mls)
1 bay leaf
Malt vinegar 2 fl oz (60 mls)
Bacon fat 3 oz (90 g)
Seasoned flour 2 oz (60 g)
Salt and pepper

Method: Beat the steaks thinly. Season and pass
in flour. Saute in a pan with bacon fat, until
golden on both sides for 5 minutes only. In same
pan fry sliced onions till golden. Transfer steaks
and onions in a shallow earthenware dish. Add
shredded cabbage. Season, add beer, gin, bay
leaf, vinegar and water. Cover with a lid and
braise for 1½ hours. Serve in same dish.

GEHAKTNESTJES
Hard-boiled egg wrapped in minced beef and
fried coated with breadcrumbs

This is the original Scotch egg — created by
the Dutch.

Ingredients:

Hard-boiled eggs 8
Pork sausagemeat 1 lb (480 g)
Salt and pepper
Flour 3 oz (90 g)
Beaten eggs 3

Breadcrumbs 5 oz (150 g)
Frying oil

Method: Divide sausagemeat into 8 balls. Flatten each ball, dust with flour and wrap round each hard-boiled egg evenly. Pass in flour, beaten eggs and crumbs and fry until golden for 4 minutes. When cold, split in two and serve with a pint of Dutch beer.

UITSMIJTER
Dutch cheese and ham rarebit

Ingredients:

Buttered toasted bread 4 slices
4 slices Dutch ham
Sliced Edam or Gouda cheese 4 oz (120 g)
4 eggs
Bacon fat 3 oz (90 g)
Anchovy fillets 8
Chopped parsley and few capers

Method: Place the ham on top of buttered toasts. Top them with sliced cheese. Brown under the grill to melt the cheese. Then cover with an egg fried in bacon fat. Decorate with anchovy fillets criss-cross fashion and sprinkle chopped parsley and capers.

BITTERBALLEN or BALKENBRIJ
Pig's meat fritters (from the head)

Ingredients:

Half a pig's head
Water 4 pints (2,400 mls)
1 large onion studded with 4 cloves
1 bouquet garni
Salt
Black pepper ½ oz (15 g)
Sliced gherkins 4 oz (120 g)

Frying:

Oil
Flour 4 oz (120 g)
2 eggs
Breadcrumbs 5 oz (150 g)

Method: Boil the half pig's head in water with onion and bouquet garni for 1½ hours. Remove from liquid. Discard all bones. Dice the meat. Strain the liquor and add same weight of diced meat and seasoning. Reboil for 30 minutes. Cool. Add sliced gherkins. Place the mixture into a shallow oblong dish 3 inch deep. Chill until the brawn sets firmly enough to be sliced without crumbling. Slice the brawn ¾ inch thick. Pass in flour, then in beaten eggs and crumbs. Fry in pan on both sides like escalopes for a few minutes. Serve with a brown gravy made from stock.
Note: In setting the brawn, remember that the same amount of stock must be used with the same weight of cooked meat (i.e. ½ pint stock to 10 oz diced meat).

VEAL VALKENBURG
Veal escalope stuffed with ham, Dutch cheese
   and flavoured with Dutch gin

Ingredients:

Veal cutlets 4 by ½ lb (240 g each)

Filling:

Grated Edam cheese 2 oz (60 g)
Chopped ham 2 oz (60 g)
1 egg
Salt and pepper

Lard 2 oz (60 g)

Sauce:

Butter 2 oz (60 g)
Oil 1 fl oz (30 mls)
Sliced mushrooms 8 oz (240 g)
Chopped parsley 1 pinch
Dutch beer ½ pint (300 mls)
Tomato puree 1 oz (30 g)
Cream 4 fl oz (120 mls)
Salt and pepper

Method: On one side only, fry the veal cutlets in oil and butter for 6 minutes. Cool. On the fried side place a spoonful of the following mixture: Mix cheese, ham and egg to a paste and season. Divide into 4 and place one portion on top of the cooked side of veal cutlet. Place cutlets in a shallow dish. Disperse the sliced mushrooms over and add beer, diluted with tomato puree. Season and cover with a lid and bake for 20 minutes at 360°F. Stir cream to liquid and sprinkle chopped parsley at the last moment. Check seasoning.

KESHY YENA UTRECHT
Tender loin beef fillets

Ingredients:

Tail of fillet of beef 1 lb (480 g)
Seasoned flour 2 oz (60 g)
Bacon fat or lard or oil 2 oz (60 g)
Chopped onions 2 oz (60 g)
Sliced mushrooms 2 oz (60 g)
Sliced red peppers 2 oz (60 g)
Dutch beer ½ pint (300 mls)
Cream 4 fl oz (120 mls)
Dutch gin 2 fl oz (60 mls)
Sliced chicory 2 oz (60 g)
Juice of 1 lemon
Salt and pepper

Method: Cut the beef in 2½ inch by ¼ inch strips. Pass in seasoned flour. Heat a frying pan with lard or oil and saute for a few minutes. Add chopped onions, sliced red peppers, chicory and mushrooms. Season. Blend beer and boil for 5 minutes. Add the cream, and stir well and mix in the gin and lemon juice. Season. Serve with rice or baked jacket potatoes.

In many ways, this dish resembles the Russian Beef Stroganoff but with additional ingredients and with different flavouring.

PORK CHOP AMSTERDAM
Conil's creation in honour of the Dutch Royal Family

Ingredients:

Pork chops 4 by ½ lb (240 g each)
Lard or bacon fat 3 oz (90 g)
Chopped onions 2 oz (60 g)
Shredded white cabbage 8 oz (240 g)
Diced or sliced red peppers 2 oz (60 g)
Dutch gin 3 fl oz (90 mls)
Dutch beer ½ pint (300 mls)
Tomato puree 1 oz (30 g)
Salt and pepper

Method: Pan fry the chops on both sides for 5 minutes. Transfer into a shallow dish. Sweat in a saucepan with bacon fat, the chopped onions and cabbage for a few minutes. Add beer, gin, tomato puree and seasoning. Boil for 10 minutes. Transfer mixture onto the pork chops, season and cover with a lid. Braise for 20 minutes. Partly boil the diced red peppers for 4 minutes and sprinkle on top of the dish for decoration and flavour. Season.

VEGETABLES

HARICOTS ENKHUIZEN
Flageolet beans sauted with green beans in Dutch butter

Ingredients:

Haricot beans ½ lb (240 g)
Green beans ½ lb (240 g)
Pork sausages ½ lb (240 g)
Butter 3 oz (90 g)
Bacon rashers 4 oz (120 g)
Salt and pepper
Potatoes ½ lb (240 g)
Pinch of monosodium glutamate
Grated Dutch cheese
Chopped parsley 1 tbs

Method: Soak the dried beans in water for 3 hours and then boil till tender. Drain. In salted water, boil the green beans adding a pinch of monosodium glutamate for good flavouring. Drain and blend the two beans in a saucepan with butter. Season. Pan fry the sausages and bacon until cooked.

Boil the potatoes in their jackets, then peel and slice. In a shallow dish place a layer of potatoes and top with beans. Finally, arrange bacon and sausages over the top. Reheat in oven and serve with a sprinkling of grated Dutch cheese and parsley.

AARDAPPEL BROODJES
Dutch potato cakes

Ingredients:

Potatoes 2 lb (960 g)
2 egg yolks
Butter 2 oz (60 g)
Gouda cheese 2 oz (60 g)
Diced bacon 2 oz (60 g)
Fat 2 oz (60 g)
Salt and pepper
Seasoned flour

Method: Boil the potatoes until soft. Drain and evaporate over heat, then pass through a sieve to obtain a dried puree. Blend with yolks, cheese, butter and diced cooked bacon. Season to taste. Cool. When cold divide mixture into 2 oz cakes. Pass each cake in seasoned flour. Shape to an oval and pan fry in butter and oil until golden.

RODE KOOL
Braised red cabbage and apples flavoured with vinegar

Dutch gin is an optional addition.

Ingredients:

Red cabbage 2 lb (960 g)
Sliced apples ½ lb (240 g)
Bacon fat 2 oz (60 g)
Vinegar 3 fl oz (90 mls)
Stock ½ pint (300 mls)
Rice 4 oz (120 g)
Salt and pepper
Sugar 1 oz (30 g)
1 bouquet garni
Dutch gin 2 fl oz (60 mls) — optional

Method: Shred cabbage and mix with the sliced apples. Blend vinegar and gin. Toss in fat for few minutes and transfer ingredients with stock and rice, bouquet garni, sugar and seasoning into a

shallow dish. Cover with a lid and braise for 1 hour at 360°F.

LOFSCHOTEL
Dutch chicory cooked and served with eggs

Ingredients:

Dutch chicory 2 lbs (960 g)
Juice of 1 lemon
Butter 2 oz (60 g)
4 hard-boiled eggs
Grated cheese 2 oz (60 g)
1 tbs chopped parsley
Salt and pepper
8 thin slices of ham 2 oz (60 g) each

Method: Boil chicory with water and lemon juice, covered with a lid, after 20 minutes. Drain and place chicory in a shallow dish, making sure to squeeze off the surplus moisture first. Melt butter and pour over chicory. Decorate with sliced hard-boiled eggs and sprinkle with grated cheese and parsley. Season to taste.

Alternatively, wrap each boiled chicory in a slice of ham. Place in a shallow dish and sprinkle with grated Edam cheese. Brown under the grill.

SWEETS and DESSERTS

KAAPS WOLKEN
Meringue sweet

Ingredients:

Milk 2 pint (1,200 mls)
Castor sugar 6 oz (180 g)
8 egg yolks
Cornflour 1 oz (30 g)
Dutch orange curacao 5 fl oz (150 mls)
Crystallised violets
8 egg whites
Granulated sugar 4 oz (120 g)

Method: Boil the milk and place in a clean shallow tray. Beat egg whites to a meringue adding the castor sugar gradually. The mixture must peak when lifted. Drop a spoonful of this mixture into the hot milk and poach for 5 minutes. Turn over after a few minutes. Drain on a sieve. When all mixture has been used up strain milk.

Mix cornflour and egg yolks. Add 4 oz sugar and orange liqueur. Pour the milk while stirring, then reheat the mixture until it thickens like a custard (when it coats the spoon). Pour this custard into an earthenware and place the cooked meringue dollops on top. Decorate with crystallised violets. Serve cold.

DUTCH PEACH QUEEN WILHELMINA
Peach and strawberry sweet (created by Jean Conil for distinguished Dutch visitors)

Ingredients:

Strawberries 8 oz (240 g)
4 yellow peaches
Ice cream 8 oz (240 g)
Dutch gin 5 fl oz (150 mls)
Dutch curacao liqueur 5 fl oz (150 mls)
Sponge fingers 8 oz (240 g)
Apricot jam 3 tbs
Cream 5 fl oz (150 mls)

Method: Place pieces of sponge in individual glass bowls and soak in Dutch gin. On top of each, place a blob of vanilla ice cream. Flatten it smooth and level. Top up with half a peach and surround with strawberries. Melt apricot jam and flavour it with Curacao liqueur. Pour sauce over peach only. Pipe a dollop of cream round the peach or in the centre.

BESCHUITKOEK
Dutch bread fritter

Ingredients:

Milk 5 fl oz (150 mls)
Beaten eggs 4
Orange curacao 4 fl oz (120 mls)
4 slices Dutch bread
Oil 2 fl oz (60 mls)
Butter 2 oz (60 g)

Pinch cinnamon
Castor sugar 2 oz (60 g)

Method: Blend liquor and beaten eggs with milk. Soak the bread slices in egg mixture. Heat a pan with butter and oil. When hot fry each slice on both sides until golden. Sprinkle with sugar and cinnamon.

FLENSJES REMBRANDT
Butterscotch pancakes

Ingredients:

Batter:

2 eggs
Milk ½ pint (300 mls)
Flour 6 oz (180 g)

Lard 2 oz (60 g)
Sliced peaches 4 oz (120 g)
Orange curacao 5 fl oz (150 mls)
Castor sugar 2 oz (60 g)

Method: Beat eggs and blend milk with flour to form a batter. Rest for 1 hour. Heat pan with a little lard and cook the pancakes until the batter is all used (8 pancakes). Soak the peaches in orange curacao and stuff the pancakes with the soaked peaches. Pour the rest of liqueur over the pancakes. Sprinkle sugar and serve hot.

DRIE IN DE PAN
Small fruit pancakes

Ingredients:

2 beaten eggs
Milk ½ pint (300 mls)
Flour 6 oz (180 g)
Seedless raisins 3 oz (90 g)
Mixed peels 1 oz (30 g)
Diced apples 2 oz (60 g)
Vanilla essence
Oil or lard for frying 2 oz (60 g)

Method: Place a little oil in Yorkshire pan tins and heat them in oven for 5 minutes. Half fill each one with vanilla flavoured batter mixture and add a spoonful of mixed fruits. Bake at 380°F for 20 minutes. Dust with castor sugar.

Alternatively, mix fruits with batter and cook like pancakes. Roll up and dust with castor sugar.

DUTCH MERINGUE PIE PRINCE WILLIAM OF ORANGE
Apple and pear lemon meringue pie flavoured with Dutch orange curacao (J. Conil's creation)

Ingredients:

Short pastry ½ lb (240 g)

Filling:

Chopped pears 4 oz (120 g)
Chopped apples 4 oz (120 g)
Mixed peels 1 oz (30 g)
Butter 4 oz (120 g)
Castor sugar 3 oz (90 g)
Water 2 fl oz (60 mls)
Pinch cinnamon

Meringue topping:

4 egg whites
Castor sugar 3 oz (90 g)
Pinch salt
Segments of 1 orange
Dutch orange curacao liqueur 5 fl oz (150 mls)

Method: Line a pastry mould 2 inch deep and 8 inch diameter with short pastry. Prick sides and bottom. Toss the fruits in butter with sugar and cook for few minutes without browning. After 4 minutes, add 2 tbs of water. Boil up and cool. Spread this fruit mixture in the bottom of the pastry, sprinkle with cinnamon and curacao. Bake for 20 minutes at 380°F. Cool. Beat egg whites to a meringue with salt. Add sugar in three stages, beating between to get meringue stiff each time. Fold meringue over the tart. Level it up with a palette knife. Dust with granulated sugar and rebake for 8 minutes at 360°F.

KERST KHANS
Dutch almond Christmas cake

Ingredients:

Puff pastry ½ lb (240 g)
Apricot jam 2 oz (60 g)

Almond filling:

Butter 4 oz (120 g)
Castor sugar 3 oz (90 g)
Flour 1 oz (30 g)
2 eggs
Crumbs 1 oz (30 g)
Ground almonds 4 oz (120 g)
Orange liqueur 2 fl oz (60 mls) or Dutch anisette
Icing sugar 2 oz (60 g)

Method: Roll up the puff pastry into an oblong 12 inch long by 3 inch wide and ⅛ inch thick, making two strips of the same size — one for the bottom and one for the top. Spread some apricot jam in the middle of one strip of pastry, leaving a margin of ½ inch for sealing. Wet the edges.
Filling: Cream butter and sugar with beaten eggs and ground almonds, crumbs and flour into a paste. Add orange or anisette liqueur. Spread this mixture over the jam. Place another layer of pastry strip on top. Seal the edges along the strip. Crimp edges (pressured and rounded to make a design, or just apply the prongs of a fork on edges to seal tightly). Rest for 20 minutes. Make a few slits on top of pastry. Bake for 20 minutes at 380/400°F. Dust with icing sugar and reheat in hot oven at 400°F for 4 minutes, to glaze the icing sugar and obtain a fine gloss. Cool and cut into fingers 2 inch wide.

The shape may be varied if preferred, to a round mould 8 inch in diameter.

DUTCH ADVOCAAT
Egg sabayon with brandy and orange liqueur

Ingredients:

5 egg yolks
Castor sugar 3 oz (90 g)
Orange liqueur 3 fl oz (90 mls)
Dutch gin 3 fl oz (90 mls) or brandy

Lemon or orange juice 1 fl oz (30 mls)
3 egg whites
Granulated sugar 2 oz (60 g)
4 sponge fingers

Method: Place egg yolks, sugar, liqueur, gin and
juice in a bowl. Whisk over a tray half filled with
water, until the mixture thickens like a custard.
Remove. In a bowl beat egg whites to a meringue,
adding sugar when meringue peaks and beat
between each sugar addition. Fold the meringue
into the custard. Place mixture into fluted glasses
and chill. Serve with sponge fingers.

OLIEBOLLEN
Dutch doughnuts

Ingredients:

Bakers' yeast ½ oz (15 g)
Lukewarm water 5 fl oz (150 mls)
Strong flour 1 lb (480 g)
1 egg
Milk 4 fl oz (120 mls)
Lard 1 oz (30 g)
Pinch salt and sugar
Seedless raisins 2 oz (60 g)
Mixed peels 1 oz (30 g)
Glacé cherries 1 oz (30 g)
Oil for frying
Granulated sugar
Pinch cinnamon

Method: Crumble yeast in water. Beat egg and
mix sugar and salt, add lukewarm milk. Mix this
liquid to flour to form a stiff dough. Knead well
and form into a tight ball. Cover with a basin
upside down. Let it rise for 30 minutes. Knock
back and knead in the lard first. When well mixed
blend the fruits. Divide the dough into 16 balls.
Shape well and place on a board. Cover with a
clean cloth. Allow to rise for 30 minutes. Heat
oil in the frying pan to 360°F and fry each
doughnut for 5 minutes. Turn over to get an even
brownness. Drain on absorbent paper. Pass in
granulated sugar with a pinch of cinnamon and
serve hot.

SEAFOOD PLATTER (Scandinavian countries)

PAELLA VALENCIANA (Spain)

STUFFED GLOBE ARTICHOKE, PRAWN COCKTAIL, FRUIT SALAD IN WINE JELLY, LOBSTER PORTUGUESE, ASSORTED PORTUGUESE HORS D'OEUVRE (Portugal)

Italy

There is more to Italian gastronomy than gulping down plates of *tagliatelle* washed down with *Chianti* and saving the bottle for a lamp. Historically, Italy is the home of good cooking. Her chefs were summoned to the French court in the time of Louis XIII to work their skill on the barbarous style of cooking in France. Italian and Spanish cooks were at the court kitchens of half Europe before the French took over with their Haute Cuisine; so to dismiss Italian cooking as a plate of *spaghetti* is to do a disservice to the culinary arts — and to one's own tastebuds.

For centuries, Rome was the centre of gastronomy. Talented cooks were given their freedom, when they succeeded in creating new dishes good enough to satisfy the sophisticated palate of the conquering Roman generals. Virgil, Caesar and Cicero have described the Roman diets and the gluttonous orgies which contributed to the fall of the Empire.

The Renaissance period established Italy as the land of refinement and culture. The pasta and rice dishes were featured at the time after Marco Polo had introduced them from China, along with other dishes like the ice cream of which the Italian confectioners became the world's greatest experts.

Today the cooking of Italy may not include the brains of nightingales, but it is a varied and imaginative cuisine which makes excellent use of simple ingredients. Meat is expensive, but fresh vegetables abound and outside the cities many Italians grow their own, so vegetable dishes are popular. Meat is stretched by the use of the hundreds of types of pasta available, but even this is used in different ways according to area. In the North, they disdain *pasta asciutta* — pasta served with sauce — and use it mainly in *brode*, served in a clear broth. Their meat stretcher is *polenta*, a maize porridge, and rice. In the South, they make sauces out of everything from raw eggs to the most elaborate slow-simmered sauces of meat, garlic and onions or seafood for their spaghetti.

Common to all Italians is a love of veal, served in a myriad ways as escalopes, *scaloppine* and *involtini* — rolled around a stuffing. Poultry is used in interesting ways, and the *antipasta* — a plate of mixed hors d'oeuvre, with salami, olives and raw vegetables — is common to all. Italian cookery does not depend on desserts for its reputation, so fruit and one of the excellent local cheeses is the usual end to a meal.

Coffee is the most popular beverage, drunk strong and slightly bitter as an *espresso* or made with hot milk as a *capuccino*. But wine is the national drink of Italy, and besides the wonderful wines produced by the growers, a great number of Italians still make their own, even if they have to buy the grapes. Even modern flats are sold with a *cantina* attached — a small wine-cellar — and a visitor knows he has been accepted as a friend when his host offers him a glass, not of the great brand wines, but of his very own brew.

Valley of Aosta

Italian gastronomy is strongly regional in character, and the character of the cooking of the Valley of Aosta is as strong as the mountains that surround it. Food is spicy, with great roasts spiked with garlic and much use of herbs. But it is obvious that France is not very far away from the presence of stews of beef, veal fricassees, quenelles, majestic partridges and larded pheasants. Thrushes are roasted with a savoury filling and fallow deer is braised in light red wines. Haricot beans are baked with a flavouring of fresh rosemary and there is a cheese fondue, reminiscent of nearby Switzerland.

Local wines are superb and include Moscato d'Asti, Caluso, Inferno and the famous Vermouth di Torino. Barbera, Barberesco, Barolo and Grognolino are all delicious full-bodied reds.

Piedmont

In Piedmont the famous white truffles of Alba are used in dishes such as *risotto* or with thin turkey slivers garnished with cardoons, a celery-like artichoke with thick stems. *Ravioli*, little pockets of pasta filled with meat or mushrooms and cooked in a broth is the most popular form of pasta in this region. The finest, tastiest asparagus is served on its own, as are the baby globe artichokes edible with their chokes when young and tender. The young goats of Cuneo come to the table as roast kid, often cooked with a sprig of fresh rosemary to give its appetising aroma. Salami is made by local farmers as well as by food manufacturers; the most famous is that of Asti. *Rabiola* cheeses come from Roccaverane and the *grissini* of Turin adorn every Italian table the world over. *Gnocchi alla fontina* are a substantial start to a meal; little semolina cakes, flavoured with cheese and cooked in foaming butter until they are crisp and golden on the outside, with a melting core tangy with cheese.

Lombardy

Lombardy uses more rice than pasta, and a *risotto* may be made of any meat or vegetable available. The one with wild mushrooms which taste of the forest and the sun is perhaps the best. Sausages and salami are eaten at every opportunity, as a meal or by the slice with a glass of wine as a welcome snack with friends. *Busecca* is a tomato version of the French tripe, and *castellera alla Milanese* is a cutlet in breadcrumbs, served with spaghetti. *Osso buco* is so good that its fame has spread far beyond the shores of Italy, and you will find it on the most international of menus — it is a shank of veal cut into chunks across the bone,

slowly braised in a rich sauce of wine, garlic, tomatoes and pot herbs. Gradually the sauce metamorphoses into a glutinous rich liquid with a subtle aroma redolent of garlic. The meat becomes tender enough to cut with a spoon and the unctuous sauce clings to each mouthful.

Rice dishes in the north of Italy are often flavoured with saffron, and vegetables are fried in batter or served with grated cheese. The *stufato* is a slow cooked joint of beef flavoured with wine and herbs.

Barbagello is a red wine good with robust poultry dishes; Buttafuco is strong and good with anything roasted or grilled. Chiaretto del Garde is an almond-scented rose wine which complements sweet things, as does the strawberry-coloured Moscato di Casteggio. Sangue di Giuda is a wine rich as blood, with a subtle sparkle, suitable for drinking alone or with food. Villa is a superior table wine.

Trentino-Alto Adigea

The cooking of the Trentino-Alto Adigea area has its roots in Germany and Austria. Veal is roasted with rosemary, there are dumplings in soups and the strudel makes an appearance. Italian jugged hare, in local wine with fragrant herbs, competes favourably with the classical version, and the fish from the little mountain lakes are prepared simply to preserve their fresh taste. The Italian yeast bun flavoured with lemon and saffron would have made Queen Marie-Antoinette pale with envy. The wines of the area are light and dry. Casteller is sweet, and the Val D'Adige is a red, good after two years. Valle Isarce is best served as an aperitif.

Venice

The gastronomy of the Venetian area is memorable for the ways they have with liver, serving it lightly fried and pink inside, with a wine sauce, and the flavour of onions is used subtly. An unusual local vegetable makes its appearance here to confound and delight the tourist: it is the radicchio rosso, a fleshy purple wild chicory with a strong, but refreshing bitter taste, like Belgian endive. It is used with salads and stewed in butter. *Baccala alla viventina* is salted cod cooked in a garlic sauce, and *risi e bisi* is a classical mixture of rice, peas with ham or bacon. Game is often served with *polenta* to mop up the tasty juices, and young turkey might meet its fate sealed in a pot with pomegranate juice.

The wines of the area around Venice are good, and two of them, Valpantena and Valpollicella have achieved international fame. Valpantena is held by connoisseurs of Italian wine to be better after a few years. Recioto Amarone is a rare dry wine used with game and roasts, and Barbarano is a ruby red wine drunk with meals on any occasion. Breganze and Gambellara are dry whites of good quality and a light bite — excellent with fish. Moscato di Arque is a dessert wine.

Liguria

Liguria is scented by the smell of the sea which provides all the ingredients for the *Burrida* and *Ciupina*, a dish soup redolent of garlic and spices similar to the French *Bouillabaisse. Cappon Magro* is a mountain of fish and vegetables piled up in a colourful pyramid and needing an insatiable appetite — not for the weak or delicate this, but a true gastronomic masterpiece for those who can manage it.

Genoa

Genoese cooking is characterised by thick soups and all frying is done in oil. Chicken is used in imaginative ways as in *Fricassee di pollo*, in which a lemon-flavoured cream is used to give an extra sparkle to the excellent local birds. *Fritto allo stecco* is a mixture of veal, sweetbreads, brains and mushrooms, all fried separately in breadcrumbs. *Gnocchi* made with potatoes are light and delicious, served with *pesto delle Trenette*, a sauce made of ewe's milk cheese, garlic, walnuts and sweet basil. A vegetable delicacy, fresh and melting in the mouth, is a light puff pastry case, filled with baby artichokes and spinach leaves, set in a custard flavoured with anchovies and garlic. Tongue braised in Marsala is quite superb, and veal roasted with sage is amazingly good. *Foccacia* is cheese flavoured with sage, good as a snack with a glass of wine. For dessert, a slice of the *Pandolce Genovese* will revolutionise all your thoughts about fruit cake. This light concoction studded

with fruits and nuts soaked in Marsala is a dream. Cinqueterre and Coronata are fresh-tasting dry white wines which complement fish marvellously. Dolceaqua and Satricola are sweet wines to try with dessert.

Have you ever danced to the tune of a Tarantella, eaten a plateful of Tagliatelle from Bologna and drunk a pint of Lambrusco di Castelvetro? I have, and many times I have wished I could go back to those magic days when I could eat a ton of that delicious pasta and drink that sparkling, lively wine without feeling terrible the next day.

Emilia Romagna

Emilia Romagna is a school of gastronomy all its own. It is light, delightful and amusing, with tiny pastas stuffed with delicious morsels and combinations of flavours which stamp the cooks of this area as talented and creative in the best traditions. Try *cappeletti*, tiny little hats of pasta, stuffed with ricotta cheese and diced turkey. *Zampone* is a substantial sausage, made by boning a large pig's trotter and stuffing the skin with lean meat and herbs. It may be boiled and served hot, or allowed to cool and served in slices for a filling snack. It is delicious served with a barely cooked light vegetable to lift its heavy, nourishing texture — a bed of artichoke hearts is ideal.

Filetti di Tacchino are turkey fillets sandwiched with the smoked ham of Parma and cheese, sometimes with a thin slice of truffle, cooked in a fragrant wine sauce. A more simple dish is *risotto* made with duck meat and known as *Risotto con l'Anitra. Escalopes Bolognese* are thin veal cutlets fried in breadcrumbs and served with that sauce which has nothing to do with the reheated hash of yesterday favoured by some cafes, and which garnishes many a dish of sloppy spaghetti in the name of *Bolognese*.

In Romagna you can savour a dish of eels baked in a sauce flavoured with vinegar and have no other garnish than thin *lasagne al forno* with plenty of Parmesan cheese, or try the *tortellini* stuffed with pork, turkey, veal and herbs served in a clear beef broth. Parma of course produces the Parmesan cheese to impart its flavour to Italian cooking everywhere.

The wine known as Lambrusco is slightly sparkling on the tongue and is produced in a variety of forms, from sweet to dry and from dark red to palest white. Bianco di Scandiano is a sparkling sweet white wine which froths into the glass with vivacity. Sangiovese is a red wine of substance, which is ready for drinking after five years — and, with its violet perfume, is worth the waiting.

Tuscany

Tuscany, the region around Florence, is known for the simplicity of its cooking with great regard to the blending of flavours and contrasting textures. Spinach is a favourite vegetable here, much used with crisp dishes to give contrast in texture and in colour, so any dish styled *alla Florentina* is sure to have spinach in it. *Prochetta aretina* is roast suckling pig, cooked on a spit with an elaborate stuffing. The local version of a fish stew is a complicated dish of all types of seafood, strongly reminiscent of *Bouillabaisse*, which goes by the name of *Cacciucco*. It was probably the inspiration for the Marseillais version, although no Frenchman would admit it.

The Florentine version of *polenta* is made with chestnuts, and delicious it is, too. Game and fish are used with pasta, more than steak and veal, in this region, and small birds are shot with abandon for the table. Songbirds are particularly popular: thrushes and larks join the usual woodcock, quail, moorhen, wild ducks and geese on the groaning Tuscan tables. Freshwater fish and seafoods are used extensively, and octopus, eels and lobsters are used small, before they reach maturity.

Chianti is the wine grown in this area and needs no introduction in most parts of the world. It comes in red or white versions, and its wonderful taste and bouquet is due to the volcanic soil in which the grapes grow. Other notable wines of the area are the Vino Santo Toscano and Vino Nobile di Montepulciano. The Island of Elba, off the coast of Tuscany, has a notable 15° wine.

The Marches

The Marches is a region on the Adriatic coast where seafood wins the day. *Brodeto* is a thick soup made of rock fish and *Datteri Marinati* is a seafood cocktail. *Stoccafisco alla anconetana* is a pie made of salted cod richly flavoured with garlic. The *calcioni* is a miniature version of *ravioli*, and the *olivetti* are small escalopes of veal, beaten out into thin rounds and rolled around a stuffing to make them look like fat little olives. *Pan pepato* is literally 'pepper bread' and is a very hot pizza. *Porchetta* is the local version of roast suckling pig, and the *ravioli* in this region are often filled with ewe's milk cheese. *Tornedo alla Rossini* is usually a slice of fillet steak topped by foie gras and truffles, with a Madeira sauce — but beware: the version served in Pesaro is a fillet steak garnished with ham and mushrooms in a lemon sauce, delicious in its own way, but certainly not the classic Rossini.

A wonderful wine of the region is Verdicchio dei Castelli di Jesi, a slightly bitter, amber-coloured wine which goes with almost anything. Otherwise the Rosso Montesanto and the Piceno are the rosé wines of the district which go well with the local food.

Umbria

Umbria is perfumed by the smell of the black diamond of cookery — truffles — used in all the cooked meats, pates, galantines, and salamis of the region, along with pistachio nuts to give a distinctive black and green punctuation mark to the local specialities. Even spaghetti is served with truffles and garlic in a simple but distinguished dish. With truffles growing on the doorstep, why not?

Palombacce allo spiedo is not for the sentimental tourist — white doves are simmered in a sauce, tender and sweet. Why pigeons and wood pigeons are good eating but white doves escape on grounds of sentiment in other countries is not for us to explain. *Mezzafegato* is liver fried with coriander with a touch of garlic, and *Agnello all'arrabbiata* is a simple roast lamb. Cardoons, artichokes which resemble stalks of celery, are excellent in this area, often fried in batter to come out crisp and golden.

Orvieto is the equally crisp dry white wine of the region, and the Sacrantino is almost cherry red with a definite sparkle.

Latium

Latium, the region of Rome, has a substantial food tradition which goes back to the ancient Romans and their love of herbs. Tiny lamb chops in rosemary sauce, served with stuffed artichokes and known as *carciofi alla giuda* are tasty morsels. *Cipolline in agrodolce* are sweet and sour onions and *coda alla vaccinara* is an oxtail stewed in rich tomato sauce. *Coratella* is a dish of all the innards of lamb, served with a peppery onion sauce. *Lumache* is a stew of snails and *saltimbocca alla Romana* is 'jump in the mouth' tiny escalopes with a slice of ham on top, fried in butter and served with a sauce flavoured with Marsala. *Zuppa di Cozze* is a dish of mussels and *trippa alla Romana* is a flavoursome way with tripe. *Spaghetti* is served with every type of garnish imaginable: cheese, ham, raw eggs, fish, peas, mushrooms and all the herbs.

Colli Lanivivi is a marvellous dry white wine, smooth and tannic and good with fish; roses include the excellent Velletri and there is a wine worth trying, if only for the name, known as Est! Est! Est!

Abruzzi is the home of the dragee, a sugar-coated almond often claimed as a French invention. Alas, the Romans really did invent it, and the little perfumed morsels have been sold here for generation after generation to celebrate Christenings and weddings. *Maccheroni* is used here rather than *spaghetti*, and the local *salsicce* is a liver sausage made with pickled pigs' liver with a pâté texture. *Mortadella* made here is heavily flavoured with garlic, which also appears in *Polpo in Purgatorio*, a stew of octopus in its own ink. *Pincigrassi* is a fried pasta and *parozzo* is a delicious almond and chocolate cake. *Scapece* is fish, marinaded and delicately flavoured with saffron.

Local wines of distinction are the Cerasuolo D'Abruzzo, cherry red and pleasant, Montepulciano, garnet red and smelling of wild flowers, and the golden Trebiano, dry and fresh.

Campania

Campania is the region around Naples in the shadow of Vesuvius, and the dishes are hearty like the people. *Calzoni alla Napolitana* is pasta nestling in a thick, dark red tomato sauce flavoured with an abundance of garlic and anchovies. *Mozzarella in carozza* is a simple sandwich made with the cheese of that name, then dipped in beaten egg and fried in oil. *Pizza Napolitana* is a veritable meal, with its thick topping of tomatoes, anchovies and cheese. *Satru* is a timbale of rice with veal, mushrooms and mozzarella. Fish is eaten as a *fritto misto* or made into soups and stews. Vegetables are often stuffed with a meaty filling, and tomatoes are used in almost every dish — anything on a menu which is styled *alla Napolitana* is sure to have tomatoes and garlic as ingredients. Ices are excellent here, notably the lemon and orange flavours.

Apulia

Apulian cuisine offers strong tasty foods like *Capitone* (stuffed kid), and *Cozze Gratinate* (mussels flavoured with garlic in the shell). *Panzerotti* are little pockets of pasta stuffed with cheese and anchovies. *Maccheroni al forno* is a complete meal of macaroni, meat balls and *mozzarella* cheese. Fish is used for soups or thick stews. The local wine is strong and generous on the tongue; best are Barletta and Aleatice di Puglia, both strong reds good with pasta.

Lucania

The cooking of Lucania is full of surprises. Every dish seems to be dominated by the locally grown ginger. It is at its best in dishes like *Soppressata*, a piece of salted meat preserved in oil and served in a dressing flavoured with ginger. It also makes an appearance in *lepre alla cacciatora*, a dish flavoured with capers, olives and ginger. *Anguille del Lago Monticchio* are eels simply roasted on hot embers and the fresh mountain trout is served in garlic with or without almonds. The local wines are sweet and strong: Agrianico del Vulture is red and sparkling, Malvasia del Vulture is sweet and white, good with desserts, and the Moscato del Vulture is sweet, white and highly aromatic.

Calabria

In Calabria there is Greek influence on food and the *Lucanica* sausages could easily have come from any of the Greek islands. *Lasagne imbottite* is the familiar wide noodle with a ragout of meat topped with cheese. Aubergines come to the table with mushrooms as their companions and trout is roasted with a mayonnaise sauce. The wines of the region, when aged, are good, notably the Greco di Gerace, with an orange blossom bouquet. The Pellaro and Balbino d'Altromonte are sweet, delicate aperitif wines.

Sicily

Sicily and Sardinia are the two main islands under Italian jurisdiction; Corsica has been dealt with in the chapter on France.

Sicily has heady wines and hearty appetites. Pasta is served with strong sauces, garlic permeates almost everything and fish is served fried or in soups. The orange sauce which is served with duck in international restaurants probably originated in the orange groves of this fragrant island. Tuna fish is caught around Sicily and is processed there in a small but thriving industry. It also makes an excellent dish when served fresh, roasted with vegetables. Local dishes of distinction are *Arancine*, a moulded rice dish filled with meat and green peppers; fried *calamari*, those baby squid cut into rounds; *caponata*, a delicious mixture of aubergines, peppers, onions and tomatoes. *Farsumagru* is a joint of veal with an egg stuffing, and *cuscusu* is a fish soup with pasta. The fresh, sea-fragrant sardines are served with *maccheroni* and a pine-nut sauce. Sicilians are also very good pastry cooks. Their confectionery like *frutti di marturana* made with almond paste in various animal and fruit shapes, is very distinctive.

In the hot Sicilian summer, it is natural that the selection of ice cream should be large and imaginative. The *cassatas, granitas* and other moulded ices, with nuts and crystallised fruits, come in all the traditional flavours as well as those made with the crystallised fruits of the island. These same glacé fruits are eaten on their own as dessert. A highly recommended speciality is the *cannoli*, a pastry stuffed with candied fruit, nuts, ricotta cheese and chocolate.

The grapes of Sicily develop a great deal of sugar in the hot sun, so the wines are powerful in taste and effect. Excellent with meat is the Ambrato di Comiso, strong (16°) and red. Other red wines of a similar calibre are the Corvo Rosso, red Eloro, Etna, and Faro. Sweet white wines used as aperitifs and with desserts are Albanella di Siracusa, Malvasia di Liparo, Memerto and Moscato. Marsala is the most celebrated wine from this region, a strong, red-brown wine with a distinctive sweetness and aroma, used by all chefs in sauces to go with veal escalopes.

Sardinia

Sardinia has a wide repertoire of excellent fish dishes and a delicious way with game, but the most unusual dish in this island is the wonderful hard ham made of wild boar. It combines the flavour of game with the smokiness of the home-cured type of mountain ham. It is excellent in dishes but superb on its own as an antipasta or at any time. *Carne a Carragiu* is a typically Sardinian way of cooking meat on a bed of herbs in the open air. Sardinia also offers unleavened bread like a large *matzo*. *Cassola* is a delicious fish soup, *corda* is a dish of tripe in tomato sauce. *Porcedu* are sucking piglets spit roasted with myrtle leaves and the *favata* are beans, often cooked with bacon. Myrtle leaves are also used in cooking thrushes, and *sospiri* is a marvellously light almond flavoured fried pastry.

Sardinian wines are very alcoholic and often used as aperitifs or liqueur wines after a meal. Anghelu ruju, Cannonau, Malvasia, Moscata and Nasco are all delicious wines in this context, as is the Torbato Extra, which has a sparkle to it. Powerful red wines are Mandrolisai, Ogliastra and Oliena, and sharper red wines include Terralba and Perda Rubia.

Italian gastronomy stands at the cross-road where the Orient meets the Occident. All Mediterranean countries have a common link with Italian cookery. The accent is on vivid colours, warm and appetising food; lingering flavours permeating the whole atmosphere and a care-free interest in all foods without any inhibition. This is why food in Italy is always a memorable occasion; for every day brings joy in the families when it is time to eat.

BILL OF FARE

Soup (Zuppe)

MINESTRONE
Thick vegetable soup with bacon, garlic, grated
parmesan cheese and pasta

MINESTRA
Broth with pasta and vegetable strips

MILLEFANTI
Broth thickened with crumbs and egg yolks

ZUPPE PAVESE
Broth with fried bread, eggs and parmesan cheese

ZUPPE AL PESTO
Garlic flavoured vegetable soup served with
grated cheese

Hors d'Oeuvre (Antipasta)

CARCIOFI GIOVANOTTI
Young artichokes Italian style

FINOCCHIO NAPOLITANO
Fennel in sweet and sour sauce

CICORIA TORSOLO
Sliced cores of lettuce and chicory in salad
dressing with hard-boiled eggs

ZUCCHINE AGRODOLCE
Young marrow in sweet and sour sauce

SEDANO DOLCELATTE
Celery stalks stuffed with Dolcelatte cheese
paste

Pasta Dishes (Farinacei)

TAGLIATELLE VERDI ALLA MARINARA
Green noodles with sea-food in tomato and red
pepper sauce

**ROLLATINE IMBOTTITE ALLA
FIORENTINA**
Pancakes stuffed with minced beef, spinach and
coated with cheese sauce

CANNELONI ROMANA
Pasta filled with minced veal, beef and pork meats

RAVIOLI MARINARA
Pasta filled with cod and prawns

BILBAO FILLING TORTELINI
Pasta filled with cottage cheese and eggs

GNOCCHI ROMANA
Semolina dumplings with cheese

PIZZA
Round flat bread topped with savoury fillings

RISOTTO DEL BOSCAIOLO
Savoury rice with mushrooms and cheese

POLENTA SOLE MIO
Corn meal porridge with cheese

RAVIOLI TACCHINO DELIZIOSO
Ravioli stuffed with turkey, chestnuts and sprouts
with a rich tomato sauce

SPAGHETTI BOLOGNESE ALLA MASPRONE
Spaghetti with a meat sauce flavoured with celery

FARFALLETTE SOPHIA LOREN
Shell pasta with turkey in a rich tomato and
cheese sauce

Fish Dishes (Dalla Pesca)

FRITTO MISTO DI MARE
Mixture of fried fish with tomato sauce

SARDINE A BECCAFICO
Grilled fresh sardines with a Pernod butter

PESCE PERSICO IN UMIDO
Casserole of fish, scampi and vegetables

SCAMPI DORATI ALL'OLIO D'OLIVA
Sauted scampi with fresh herbs in oil

Meat Dishes (Piatti di Entrata)

SALSICCIA ALLA DIAVOLA
Grilled pork chipolatas in peppery sauce

CERVELLO DORATO AL BURRO
Fried calf's brains in batter with tomato sauce

TRIPPA ALLA EMILIANA
Calf's tripe Italian style

CASSERUOLA DI ANIMELLE AL MARSALA
Braised sweetbread in Marsala sauce

FEGATO DI VITELLO ALLA VENEZIANA
Calf's liver sauted with white wine

VITELLO ALLA MARENGO
Saute of veal with tomato garnished with fried
  eggs

BOLLITO MISTO VERDE
Mixed boiled meats Bologna

FARSUMAGRU
Stuffed breast of veal

SALTIMBOCCA ALLA ROMANA
Veal escalopes, liver and bacon on skewers

OSSO BUCO ALLA LOMBARDIA
Braised shin of veal in casserole

PETTI DI POLLO CAVOUR
Chicken breast with Italian cheese and ham

SCALOPINA DI TACCHINO ALLA
  TOSCANINI
Turkey escalope in Martini (J.C.)

VITELLO TONNATTO
Braised veal with tuna fish sauce

Vegetables

SPINACI ALLA PIEMONTESE
Leaf spinach flavoured with anchovy and garlic

ZUCCHINI ALLA VATICANO
Baby marrow stuffed with mushrooms

CAPONATA
Eggplant Sicilian style

Sweets (Dolce Vitae)

CASSATA ITALIANA
Flavoured ices with fruits

ZABAGLIONE ROMEO
Egg custard with wine and brandy

CREMA MAMA MIA
Lemon cheese pudding

PANETTO DI NAPOLI
Almond cakes

PANETTI ALLA CIOCCOLATA
Small choux buns filled with cream and coated
  with a rum flavoured chocolate sauce

SOUP (ZUPPE)

MINESTRONE
Thick vegetable soup with bacon, garlic, grated
  parmesan cheese and pasta

Ingredients:

Water 2½ pint (1,500 mls)
Streaky bacon 4 oz (120 g)
Crushed garlic 1 clove
Chopped parsley 1 tbs

Vegetables:

Leeks 2 oz (60 g)
Carrots 2 oz (60 g)
Turnips 2 oz (60 g)
Potatoes 2 oz (60 g)
Cabbage 3 oz (90 g)
Peas 2 oz (60 g)
French beans 2 oz (60 g)
Precooked Flageolet beans 2 oz (60 g)
Tomatoes 4 oz (120 g)
Tomato puree 1 oz (30 g)
Basil herbs, 1 pinch
Chopped chervil, 1 pinch

Garnish:

Grated parmesan 4 oz (120 g)
Vermicelli or thin spaghetti 3 oz (90 g)
Salt and pepper

Method: Fry the finely chopped, rindless bacon
for a few minutes in a large saucepan. Add garlic
and all vegetables except peas and beans. Cover
with cold water and boil for 20 minutes. Add peas
and beans. Cook for 15 minutes. Add chopped
herbs, tomato puree and seasoning. Add vermicelli,
cook for 8 minutes. Serve grated parmesan cheese
separately.

MINESTRA
Broth with pasta and vegetable strips

Ingredients:

Thin flank of beef 1 lb (480 g)
1 small shin of bacon 1 lb (480 g)
Water 4 pint (2,400 mls)

1 onion studded with 4 cloves 5 oz (150 g)
1 carrot 5 oz (150 g)
1 turnip 3 oz (150 g)
1 bouquet garni

Garnish:

Cut macaroni 5 oz (150 g)
Salt and pepper

Method: Place bacon and beef in cold water and
bring to the boil slowly. Remove scum as it rises.
Cook for 1½ hours. Add the remaining ingredients
and cook for further 30 minutes. Boil macaroni
in salted water for 14 minutes. Strain, refresh
and add to broth. Season to taste. The meat and
bacon can be utilised for stuffing canneloni
pasta. Fresh carrot, leek and turnip, cut in very
thin strips known as julienne can also be used in
the minestra. These vegetables are cooked in the
broth for 10 minutes. Allow 2 oz (60 g) for each
vegetable. Use extra broth for gravy or sauce.

MILLEFANTI
Broth thickened with crumbs and egg yolks

Ingredients:

Broth from Minestra 2½ pint (1,500 mls)
Fresh crumbs 5 oz (150 g)
Grated cheese 4 oz (120 g)
4 whole beaten eggs

Method: Bring the broth to the boil and whilst
boiling blend the crumbs and cheese with beaten
eggs and strain through a coarse sieve over the
saucepan of soup to form a coagulated (filament)
garnish.

ZUPPA PAVESE
Broth with fried bread, eggs and parmesan cheese

Ingredients:

Minestra broth 2½ pint (1,500 mls)
4 eggs
4 pieces of fried bread
Grated parmesan cheese 4 oz (120 g)
Salt and pepper

Method: Place the hot broth in a deep casserole dish. Arrange four pieces of fried bread in soup. Break an egg on each slice. Sprinkle with grated cheese and grill under the salamander enough to melt the cheese and coagulate the eggs.

ZUPPE AL PESTO
Garlic flavoured vegetable soup served with grated cheese

Ingredients:

Water 2½ pint (1,500 mls)
Sliced carrots 2 oz (60 g)
Sliced turnips 2 oz (60 g)
Sliced French beans 2 oz (60 g)
Sliced cabbage 2 oz (60 g)
Green peas 2 oz (60 g)
Sliced leeks 2 oz (60 g)
4 small marrows 1 lb (480 g)
Salt and pepper

Paste:

Fat bacon lard 2 oz (60 g)
Tomato puree 1 tbs
Crushed garlic 10 g
Pinch fresh basil herbs
Grated cheese 3 oz (90 g)
Cooked marrow
Skinned and seeded tomatoes 6 oz (180 g)
Vermicelli 3 oz (90 g)

Method: Boil the vegetables with the marrow (Zucchini, which must not be cut). Simmer for 40 minutes and check seasoning. Remove the marrows and prepare the garlic paste. Blend unrendered, minced lard with garlic, cheese, herbs and puree of marrow. Add tomato puree and chopped tomato pulp.

When the vegetables are cooked to the right consistency, dilute the above garlic paste into the soup. Stir and boil for 5 minutes.

Boil the vermicelli in salted water for 8 minutes. Strain and add to soup.

HORS D'OEUVRE (ANTIPASTA)

CARCIOFI GIOVANOTTI
Young artichokes Italian style

Ingredients:

16 young artichokes
Water 1 pint (600 mls)
Juice of 4 lemons
1 clove of garlic
1 bay leaf
6 peppercorns
6 coriander seeds
Button onions 8 oz (240 g)
Salt ¼ oz (8 g)
White vinegar 1 tbs
Italian mustard 1 tbs
Tomato puree 1 tbs
    diluted with 2 tbs vinegar
Oil 3 tbs
Water ½ pint (300 mls)   } to cook onions
White wine ½ pint (300 mls)

Method: Select very small artichokes which, of course, have no fern and can be eaten whole. Allow 4 per person. Remove the green leaves to expose the white or red leaves. Soak the artichokes in a bowl or saucepan of water with lemon juice and vinegar for 1 hour. Boil for 15 minutes, adding the seasoning, seeds and peppercorns. Cool. Add the oil and tomato puree diluted with vinegar. Boil the button onions in water and wine for 5 minutes. Add to the artichokes. Serve cold as a salad.

FINOCCHIO NAPOLITANO
Fennel in sweet and sour sauce

Ingredients:

2 fennel heads
Sliced onion 2 oz (60 g)
1 clove of garlic
Tomatoes 8 oz (240 g)
White wine ½ pint (300 mls)
Oil 5 fl oz (150 mls)
Salt ¼ oz (8 g)
6 peppercorns

6 coriander seeds
1 bay leaf
Water ½ pint (300 mls)

Method: Cut the fennels in four pieces. Wash and trim. Place in a saucepan with the ingredients. Skin tomatoes and cut in half. Boil gently for 15-20 minutes. Cool in the liquor and serve in an earthenware dish with the liquor. Alternatively, the fennel can be shredded, parboiled for 10 minutes and then cooked in the mixture above.

CICORIA TORSOLO
Sliced cores of lettuce and chicory in salad dressing with hard-boiled eggs

Ingredients:

Trimmed cores or stems of lettuce, chicory (particularly Cos lettuce) or cauliflower, cabbage, etc. 1 lb (480 g)
4 hard-boiled eggs
Chopped spring onions 1 oz (30 g)
Oil 3 tbs
Wine vinegar 1 tbs
Made mustard 1 tsp
Dolcelatte cheese 1 oz (30 g)
Water ½ pint (300 mls)
Salt and pepper

Method: Boil the sliced cores for 5 minutes in salted water. Drain. Dilute mustard and cheese in vinegar. Add the oil and chives or onions. Check seasoning. Place the cores into a dish, cover with dressing and surround with slices of hard-boiled eggs coated with sauce.

ZUCCHINE AGRODOLCE
Young marrow in sweet and sour sauce

Ingredients:

8 baby marrows 2 lb (960 g)
Chopped onions 2 oz (60 g)
1 clove of garlic
Oil 3 fl oz (90 mls)
Wine vinegar 3 fl oz (90 mls)
Brown sugar 2 oz (60 g)

Seedless raisins 4 oz (120 g)
Tomato puree 1 oz (30 g)
Honey 1 oz (30 g)
Chopped anchovies 1 oz (30 g)
Salt and pepper
Chopped parsley
Water ½ pint (300 mls)

Method: Scrape the marrows and slice thinly. Heat oil in a saucepan and saute the marrows and chopped onions for 5 minutes without browning. Add crushed garlic, tomato puree. Simmer for further 5 minutes and then add rest of ingredients. Boil for 10 minutes without a lid to allow as much evaporation as possible. Cool and serve on an earthenware dish. Sprinkle with chopped parsley.

SEDANO DOLCELATTE
Celery stalks stuffed with Dolcelatte cheese paste

Ingredients:

Celery stalks 2 lb (960 g)
1 lemon

Filling:

Dolcelatte cheese 4 oz (120 g)
Butter 4 oz (120 g)
Chopped hard-boiled eggs 4 oz (120 g)
Chopped anchovy fillets 1 oz (30 g)
Chopped onions 1 oz (30 g)
Sweet Martini or Marsala 2 fl oz (60 mls)

Decoration:

12 stuffed olives

Method: Shave the stems of celery to remove tough filaments. Cut in 3 inch sticks. Rub with lemon. Blend all ingredients of the filling mixture to a smooth paste. Pipe the mixture inside the hollow part of the stems. Decorate with slices of stuffed olives.

PASTA DISHES (FARINACEI)

The following list is well worth knowing and includes the Italian names for most industrially produced pasta.

Bucatini	very thin macaroni
Canneloni	rectangles of pasta
Capellini	thin vermicelli
Cavatelli	shaped like tiny caves
Ditali	larger macaroni
Farfallette	various sizes of butterfly bows
Fettucini	noodle types
Fideline	thin spaghetti
Fusili	twisted macaroni
Gnocchi	semilina dumplings
Lasagne	large noodles
Maccheroni	tubular sticks
Mafalde	crimped pasta ribbons
Manicotti	small canneloni
Margherite	flat fluted macaroni
Maruzze	shell pasta
Mezzani	grooved quill shape
Rigatoni	ribbed macaroni
Semini	seedlike pasta for soups
Spaghetti	stick like pasta
Spedini	horn shaped pasta
Stellette	stars used for soups
Tagliatelle	flat ribbons
Tortellini	rings shaped like doughnuts
Tubetti	small tubes
Yolanta	twisted noodles
Ziti	cut macaroni

TAGLIATELLE VERDI ALLA MARINARA
Green noodles with sea-food in tomato and red pepper sauce

Ingredients:

Green noodles 1 lb (480 g)
Scampi 8 oz (240 g)
White cod 8 oz (240 g)
Prawns 4 oz (120 g)
Button mushrooms 4 oz (120 g)
Chopped onions 2 oz (60 g)
1 clove garlic
Tomato puree 2 oz (60 g)
Skinned and seeded tomatoes 8 oz (240 g)
Red peppers 4 oz (120 g)
Lard 3 oz (90 g)
Butter 3 oz (90 g)
Grated cheese 4 oz (120 g)
Water for the noodles 3 pint (1,800 mls)
White wine ½ pint (300 mls)
Water ¼ pint (150 mls)

Thickening:

Cream 5 fl oz (150 mls)
Cornflour 2 oz (60 g)

1 pinch basil herb
1 pinch saffron
Salt and pepper
1 pinch mace

Method: Boil green noodles in salted water for 15 minutes. Drain and keep warm in a shallow dish with a pat of butter and seasoning well stirred into the pasta.

To prepare sauce, saute chopped onions with lard in a pan until soft but not brown. Add garlic, chopped pulp of tomato, shredded red peppers, mushrooms and tomato puree. Cook for 5 minutes. To this, add diced cod fillet, scampi and prawns. Cover level with water and wine. Add herbs and saffron. Simmer for 12 minutes. Blend cream and cornflour in a bowl and add to ingredients in pan, stirring well. Cook for further 5 minutes until it thickens. Pour over the noodles and sprinkle with grated cheese.

ROLLATINE IMBOTTITE ALLA FIORENTINA
Pancakes stuffed with minced beef, spinach and coated with cheese sauce

Ingredients:

4 small pancakes

Stuffing:

Cooked spinach leaves 4 oz (120 g)
Cooked minced beef 4 oz (120 g)
   (use boiled beef from Minestra)

PASTA NOMENCLATURE CHART

Type	Cooking Time	Uses
ABC or Stars	2 minutes	Soups
Rings	5 minutes	Soups and Entrees
Vermicelli	3 minutes	Soups, Milk Puddings
Spaghetti	10-14 minutes	Entrée, Garnish
Noodles	10-14 minutes	Entrée, Garnish
Noodles, fried	5 minutes	Entrée, Garnish, Chinese Dishes
Macaroni	14-18 minutes	Entrée, Milk Puddings
Shells	10 minutes	Entrée, Garnish
Ravioli	10-15 minutes	Entrée, Snacks
Canneloni	10-15 minutes	Entrée, Snacks

Tomato sauce 4 fl oz (120 mls)
Grated cheese 4 oz (120 g)
Cheese sauce 4 fl oz (120 mls)
2 anchovy fillets
1 clove garlic

Grated cheese for sprinkling 3 oz (90 g)

Method: Blend the cooked spinach and beef with tomato sauce and grated cheese. Add chopped garlic and anchovy fillets. Stuff the pancakes with mixture. Roll and place on a buttered dish. Cover with cheese sauce and sprinkling of grated cheese. Brown in oven for 15 minutes.

NOODLE PASTE FOR PASTA

The preparation of good pasta requires the use of strong flour from durum wheat. To ensure you have the right ingredient, it is best to use fine semolina to make paste for ravioli and canneloni.

Ingredients:

Basic paste with semolina:

Fine semolina 8 oz (240 g)
1 beaten egg 2 oz (60 g)
Warm water 2 fl oz (60 mls)
Pinch salt or 4 g
1 level tsp oil

Basic paste with flour (bread flour):

Flour 8 oz (240 g)
1 beaten egg 2 oz (60 g)
Warm water 2 fl oz (60 mls)
Pinch salt or 4 g
1 level tsp oil

Method: Blend all ingredients to a dough. Roll and gather to a ball. Rest 30 minutes before using.

SELECTION OF SUITABLE FILLINGS FOR RAVIOLI OR CANNELONI

1. Roman filling: minced beef, veal, pork and spinach in equal quantities.
2. Bilbao filling: cottage cheese with egg.
3. Marinara filling: minced white fish and prawns with mushrooms.

ROMAN FILLING

Ingredients:

Minced beef 4 oz (120 g)
Minced pork 4 oz (120 g)
Minced veal 4 oz (120 g)
Chopped onions 4 oz (120 g)
Salt and pepper
Chopped mint or oregano, 1 pinch
1 egg
Water ½ pint (300 mls)
Lard 3 oz (90 g)
Flour 1 oz (30 g)

Method: Fry chopped onions in lard and blend all
ingredients together to a fine paste, except the
egg, flour and water. Cook in a saucepan with
lard until brown. Add ½ pint (300 mls) water
and boil for 15 minutes. Cool. Add beaten egg
and flour.

BILBAO FILLING

Ingredients:

Cottage cheese 6 oz (180 g)
2 eggs
Sugar 2 oz (60 g) – optional *or*
    grated parmesan cheese 2 oz (60 g) if savoury
Juice and rind of 1 lemon
Flour or cake crumbs 2 oz (60 g)

Method: Blend all ingredients.

MARINARA FILLING

Ingredients:

Raw minced cod 6 oz (180 g)
Cooked prawns 4 oz (120 g)
1 egg
Salt and pepper
Butter 2 oz (60 g)
Flour 2 oz (60 g)
1 tbs lemon juice
Sugar ¼ oz (8 g)
Water 4 fl oz (120 mls)

1 pinch chopped parsley
1 pinch basil

Method: Blend all ingredients.

CANNELONI ROMANA
Pasta filled with minced veal, beef and pork
  meats

Ingredients:

Noodle paste 1 lb (480 g)
Romana filling 1 lb (480 g)
Skinned, seeded and chopped tomatoes 8 oz
  (240 g)
Chopped garlic $\frac{1}{3}$ oz (10 g)
Grated cheese 4 oz (120 g)

Method: Roll the paste $\frac{1}{8}$ inch thick. Cut into
oblong pieces 3 inch by 5 inch. Boil salted water
and blanch the pieces for 10 minutes. Drain and
dry with a cloth. Pipe some of the meat filling,
using a ¼ inch tube fitted to a bag. Roll each
piece round the filling. Place the canneloni into a
shallow dish well greased with butter. Cover with
the chopped tomatoes, garlic and grated cheese
(alternatively, coat the canneloni with cheese
sauce). Brown in the oven for 15 minutes.

RAVIOLI MARINARA
Pasta filled with cod and prawns

Ingredients:

Noodle paste 1 lb (480 g)
Marinara filling 1 lb (480 g)

Lemon fish sauce:

Fish bones 8 oz (240 g)
Water 1½ pint (900 mls)
Sliced onion 2 oz (60 g)
Bouquet garni
Juice of 1 lemon
Salt and pepper

Garnish:

Sliced mushrooms 2 oz (60 g)

Thickening:

Cream 5 fl oz (150 mls)
Cornflour 1 oz (30 g)
Grated cheese 4 oz (120 g)

Method: Roll paste to an oblong ¹/₈ inch thick.
Place fish into a bag fitted with a ¼ inch tube.
Pipe about 1 oz (30 g) of mixture at regular
intervals. Brush the paste with water between the
piped fillings. Cover with another layer of paste.
Mark the paste with a pastry cutter upside down
so as not to cut into the paste yet. Press two
layers firmly together with a knife or ravioli
roulette. Cut ravioli into squares using marks
made with a ruler as a guide. Sprinkle a tray with
uncooked semolina and lay the ravioli to dry for
1 hour. Make a stock by boiling fish or fish heads
with water, onions and bouquet garni. After 20
minutes, strain the stock into a deep tray. Bring
it to the boil again and cook the ravioli in it for 8
minutes. Let the ravioli cool in this liquor. When
cold, remove and put into a shallow dish. Add
seasoning, sliced mushrooms and lemon juice to
the boiled liquor. Thicken with cream and
cornflour and pour over the ravioli. Reheat in the
oven for 15 minutes at 380°F. Sprinkle grated
cheese and brown under the grill.

BILBAO FILLING TORTELLINI
Pasta filled with cottage cheese and eggs

Ingredients:

Bilbao filling 1 lb (480 g)
Noodle paste 1 lb (480 g)
Oil for frying
Castor sugar

Method: Roll the noodle paste to ¹/₈ inch thick
and with a 3 inch pastry cutter, make as many
rounds as possible – approximately 16. On 8
rounds, pipe 1 dessertspoonful of cheese filling.
Wet edges with water and cover with another
round. Seal edges and crimp round with the prongs
of a fork. Heat oil to 360°F and fry for 8
minutes. Drain and sprinkle with castor sugar.

GNOCCHI ROMANA
Semolina dumplings with cheese

Ingredients:

Ground semolina 3 oz (90 g)
Milk 1 pint (600 mls)
2 egg yolks
1 whole egg
Butter 1 oz (30 g)
Chopped garlic 10 g
Salt and pepper
Pinch nutmeg
Lard for greasing tray 2 oz (60 g)
Butter for buttering dish 2 oz (60 g)
Grated Gruyere or Parmesan cheese 2 oz (60 g)

Method: Grease an oblong tray (2 inch deep) with
lard. Bring milk to boil. Sprinkle semolina while
stirring vigorously. Cook for 10 minutes. Remove
from heat and add beaten eggs, butter, chopped
garlic and seasoning. Stir well and pour into the
tray. Level with a palette knife. Cool. When cold
cut into 2 inch rounds with a pastry cutter.

Place 4 gnocchi into individual gratin dishes.
Brush top with melted butter and sprinkle with
grated cheese. Brown under the grill or in a hot
oven.

PIZZA
Round flat bread topped with savoury filling

The dish known as pizza has a variety of
modifications according to the filling used. The
bread dough can be enriched with eggs and fat
and made as light as croissant or Danish pastry.
In my view, such a dish should be light and while,
traditionally, it is a bread dough flattened like a
tea cake and baked with its filling, in the realm
of Haute Cuisine an additional egg should be
added to the dough for nutritional enrichment.

Ingredients:

Basic bread dough:

Yeast ½ oz (15 g)
Water at 80°F ½ pint (300 mls)
Strong bread flour 1 lb (480 g)

Salt 6 g
Sugar 5 g
Lard ½ oz (15 g)

Basic egg dough:

Yeast ½ oz (15 g)
Water at 80°F 6 fl oz (180 g)
1 egg
Butter 2 oz (60 g)
Milk 2 fl oz (60 mls)
Sugar 6 g
Salt 6 g

Method: Crumble the yeast in lukewarm water, stirring well. Dissolve salt and sugar with it. Add to the flour and lard to form a stiff dough. Knead well. Shape into a ball. Cover with a basin upside down to allow for expansion for 40 minutes. Knead again and divide the dough into four pieces. Shape each one into a ball. Rest for 20 minutes. Flatten each ball into a flat cake with the knuckles of your hands. Brush top with oil and arrange topping. Rest again for 15 minutes on greased tray to allow the pizza to swell again. Bake at 420°F for 15-20 minutes. Sprinkle grated cheese. Return to hot oven to brown and melt the cheese for 4 minutes. Serve piping hot.

Topping for pizza:

4 anchovy fillets
4 tomato slices (skinned and seeded)
1 slice cheese or 4 oz grated cheese
8 stoneless olives

Meat filling is the same as above, but add 1 slice of ham for each pizza.

The same procedure applies to the egg dough except add the beaten egg and milk and water (same temperature − 80°F) to the yeast and then to the flour and butter.

RISOTTO DEL BOSCAIOLO
Savoury rice with mushrooms and cheese

Ingredients:

Piedmont rice plump grain 5 oz (150 g)
Oil 2 oz (60 mls)

Chopped onions 2 oz (60 g)
Water or chicken stock 15 fl oz (450 mls)
Sliced button mushrooms 6 oz (180 g)
1 bouquet garni
1 clove of garlic
Grated cheese 5 oz (150 g)
Pinch rosemary
Salt and pepper
Pinch nutmeg

Method: Heat oil in a saucepan. Add chopped onions and fry without browning. Add rice and stir well. Add sliced mushrooms, water and rest of ingredients. Simmer gently for 20 minutes. Remove bouquet garni. Season. Place in a shallow dish and sprinkle grated cheese.

POLENTA SOLE MIO
Cornmeal porridge with cheese

Ingredients:

Cornmeal 3 oz (90 g)
Milk 1 pint (600 mls)
1 clove garlic
Butter 1 oz (30 g)
Grated cheese 4 oz (120 g)
2 egg yolks
Salt and pepper
Pinch grated nutmeg

Method: Boil milk and add cornmeal. Cook for 10 minutes. Add butter and rest of ingredients away from heat. Pour into a dish and serve grated cheese separately.

RAVIOLI TACCHINO DELIZIOSO
Ravioli stuffed with turkey, chestnuts and sprouts
with a rich tomato sauce (4 to 6 portions)
created by Jean Conil

Ingredients;

Noodle paste 1 lb (480 g)

Filling:

Minced cooked turkey 4 oz (120 g)
Chopped cooked chestnuts 4 oz (120 g)

Chopped boiled sprouts 3 oz (90 g)
Butter 2 oz (60 g)
Lard 2 oz (60 g)
1 egg
Salt and pepper
Cream 3 fl oz (90 mls)

Tomato sauce ½ pint (300 mls)
Grated cheese 5 oz (150 g)
Semolina 2 oz (60 g)

Method: Roll the ravioli in two oblong pieces.
Blend ingredients for the filling together and
mince. Fill a piping bag with ¼ inch tube with the
mixture and pipe on the paste. Wet edges with
water. Cover with the other layer and seal. Mark
paste with cutter. Divide with a ruler. Sprinkle
uncooked semolina onto a dish and place the
ravioli to dry for 1 hour over heat. Boil salted
water and poach for 10 minutes. Remove and
cool in cold water. Drain. Place in a shallow dish
well greased with butter. Cover with tomato
sauce. Sprinkle grated cheese and brown in the
oven for 15 minutes.

(Sprinkling uncooked semolina on the tray
prevents the ravioli from sticking.)

SPAGHETTI BOLOGNESE ALLA MASPRONE
Spaghetti with a meat sauce flavoured with
  celery

During my career I have had the privilege to work
with leading Italian chefs and restaurateurs. When
I was a young commis working at the celebrated
Hermitage le Touquet in France, my chef was
M Brule and the restaurateur Sr Masprone, two
of the most eminent caterers in Europe at the
time. I owe this particular recipe to these two
men.

I have since served on various cookery com-
mittees with leading chefs like the two Trompetto
brothers — the younger of the two is at the Savoy
Hotel and Signor Calderoni, the most eminent
Italian chef in Europe who was, for a time, chef to
Princess Bonaparte. Since, I have been disappointed
to notice that the so-called Spaghetti Bolognese
has taken a turn for the worse in Britain with the

various concoctions served under that name.
I hope the present recipe will put the record right.

Ingredients (for 6 to 8 portions):
Spaghetti 1 lb (480 g)
Water 3½ pint (2,100 mls)

Sauce:
Chopped onions 2 oz (60 g)
Chopped celery 2 oz (60 g)
Chopped carrots 2 oz (60 g)
1 clove crushed garlic
Lard or oil 2 oz (60 g)
Best quality tender beef (chopped with a knife)
  8 oz (240 g)
Tomato puree 2 oz (60 g)
Calf's liver, skinned and finely diced 2 oz (60 g)
Water 5 fl oz (150 mls)
Marsala wine 5 fl oz (150 mls)
1 bouquet garni

Thickening:
Cornflour ½ oz (15 g)
Cream 5 fl oz (150 mls)
Salt and pepper
Pinch mace, ground clove and rosemary
Pinch fresh basil herbs or oregano
Butter 3 oz (90 g)
Grated cheese 4 oz (120 g)

Method: Heat lard in a saute pan and sweat the
vegetables slowly without browning. Add the
meat and liver and stir well. Cover with a lid and
cook for 5 minutes. Add tomato puree. Cook for
a further 5 minutes, then add water and wine and
seasoning. Cook for 15 minutes. Thicken with
cream and cornflour, added to the boiling mixture
at the last moment. Stir well and cook for a few
minutes to obtain a good cohering sauce — this is
not a pourable sauce but a soft meat puree. Boil
the spaghetti for 15 minutes 'al dente'. Refresh
under cold water. Plunge again in salted water for
4 minutes. Drain and reheat in a pan with butter.
Stir well. Add salt and pepper, grated cheese and
herbs. Place in a shallow dish and cover with the
Bolognese meat puree. Serve grated cheese
separately.

FARFALLETTE SOPHIA LOREN
Shell pasta with turkey in a tich tomato and
  cheese sauce (created by Jean Conil for the
  famous Italian film star)

Ingredients:

Pasta 1 lb (480 g)
Butter 3 oz (90 g)
Cream 5 fl oz (150 mls)
Salt and pepper
Grated Gruyere cheese 4 oz (120 g)
Cooked turkey breast 4 oz (120 g)
Sliced raw mushrooms 4 oz (120 g)
Shredded red and green peppers 4 oz (120 g)
Chopped onions 2 oz (60 g)
Lard 2 oz (60 g)
Butter 2 oz (60 g)
Skinned and seeded tomatoes 8 oz (240 g)
Salt and pepper
Pernod 3 fl oz (90 mls)
Grated cheese 4 oz (120 g)

Method: Cook the shell pasta for 10 minutes in
salted water. Drain and place in a shallow dish
blended with butter, cream, cheese and seasoning.
Toss the chopped onions, red and green peppers
for 5 minutes in a pan with butter and lard. Add
the turkey and mushrooms. Cook for a few more
minutes. Add the skinned and chopped tomatoes.
Season to taste and flavour with Pernod. Pour the
contents of this pan over the pasta and serve
grated cheese separately.

FISH DISHES (DALLA PESCA)

FRITTO MISTO DI MARE
Mixture of fried fish with tomato sauce

Ingredients:

Fresh cod fillet 8 oz (240 g)
Scampi 8 oz (240 g)
Fresh sprats 8 oz (240 g)
Button mushrooms 8 oz (240 g)
1 large onion cut in rings 5 oz (150 g)
Seasoned flour 3 oz (90 g)

Batter:

Yeast ½ oz (15 g)
1 egg
Water ½ pint (300 mls)
Flour 6 oz (180 g)
Pinch salt

1 lemon or ½ pint (300 mls) tomato sauce

Method: Crumble yeast into lukewarm water and
stir. Add beaten egg, salt and flour to produce a
thick batter. Cover with a cloth and let ferment
for 1 hour.

Clean fish. Mince cod to a paste and divide
mixture into 8 balls. Toss in seasoned flour, then
in batter and fry in deep fat for 5 minutes. Toss
scampi in seasoned flour, then in batter and fry
for 4 minutes. Apply the same treatment to each
ingredient — pass in flour, then batter and fry for
4-5 minutes. Cook onion rings at 360°F for 1
minute only.

Serve fish balls in pyramid, surrounded with
scampi and topped with onion rings and mushrooms. Serve spratts separately, with the tomato
sauce or lemon wedges.

SARDINE A BECCAFICO
Grilled fresh sardines with a Pernod butter

Ingredients:

Fresh gutted sardines 2 lb (960 g)
Seasoned flour 2 oz (60 g)
Oil 5 fl oz (150 mls)
Salt, pepper and cayenne

Pernod butter:

Butter 4 oz (120 g)
Pernod 2 fl oz (60 mls)
1 tbs chopped parsley

Method: Cream butter with Pernod and chopped
parsley. Roll in a sausage shape and wrap in
greaseproof paper. Freeze and when hard cut into
pats.

Scrape, clean, wash, dry and pass sardines in
seasoned flour. Dip in oil and grill for 8 minutes.
Serve with a pat of Pernod butter.

PESCE PERSICO IN UMIDO
Casserole of fish, scampi and vegetables

Ingredients:

Seasoned flour 2 oz (60 g)
Sole fillets 4 oz (120 g)
Canned artichoke hearts 4 oz (120 g)
Shelled cooked prawns 4 oz (120 g)
4 scollops
Cooked potatoes 4 oz (120 g)
Peeled cucumber 4 oz (120 g)
Chopped shallots 2 oz (60 g)
Sliced mushrooms 4 oz (120 g)
Lemon juice 1 fl oz (30 mls)
Butter 4 oz (120 g)
Oil 4 fl oz (120 mls)
Salt and pepper
1 tbs chopped parsley
Chopped garlic ½ oz (15 g)
Tomato puree 2 oz (60 g)

Method: Cut sole fillets in fine strips (2 inch)
and toss in seasoned flour. Cut artichoke hearts
in strips the same size. Toss shelled prawns in
seasoned flour. Blanch the scollops in salted water
with 1 tbs vinegar to ½ pint water. Cook for 5
minutes. Drain and pass in seasoned flour. Boil
potatoes in their jackets. Peel and cool, then cut
in chips. Peel cucumber, remove seeds and cut in
thin slices. Heat oil in a pan and saute the raw fish
for 6 minutes, then add the scollops and vegetables. Toss several times. Season, add tomato
puree and lemon juice. Simmer for 6 minutes.
Add butter, toss again and serve with a sprinkling
of chopped parsley.

SCAMPI DORATI ALL'OLIO D'OLIVA
Sauted scampi with fresh herbs in oil

Ingredients:

Seasoned flour
Scampi 1 lb (480 g)
Oil 4 fl oz (120 mls)
Chopped shallots 2 oz (60 g)
1 clove chopped garlic
Chopped tomato pulp 8 oz (240 g)
Sliced button mushrooms 4 oz (120 g)

Dry Martini ¼ pint (150 mls)
Cream 5 fl oz (120 mls)
Cornflour ½ oz (15 g)
Salt and pepper
Juice of 1 lemon
1 tbs chopped fresh parsley and mint

Method: Saute chopped shallots and garlic and
mushrooms in half the oil for 5 minutes, without
browning. Add Martini and tomato pulp. Boil for
5 minutes. Blend cream and cornflour. Add to
boiling mixture to thicken. Season.
    Pass the scampi in seasoned flour. Heat oil in a
pan and fry quickly for 5 minutes. Drain and add
scampi to sauce. Saute for 4 minutes in sauce and
serve sprinkled with chopped herbs and lemon
juice.

MEAT DISHES (PIATTI DI ENTRATA)

SALSICCIA ALLA DIAVOLA
Grilled pork chipolatas in peppery sauce

Ingredients:

Beef or pork chipolatas 1½ lb (720 g)
Lard or oil 2 fl oz (60 mls)
Chopped onions 2 oz (60 g)
1 clove of garlic
Sliced button or white mushrooms 4 oz (120 g)
Celery 2 oz (60 g)
Fennel 2 oz (60 g)
Tomato puree 1 oz (30 g)
Tomato pulp 4 oz (120 g)
1 pinch thyme and oregano or basil herb
Salt and pepper
White wine 5 fl oz (150 mls)

Thickening:

Cornflour 1 oz (30 g)
Water 5 fl oz (150 mls)

Method: Grill the chipolatas on a shallow tray.
Collect the fat and juice in the saucepan with
the lard and sweat the diced vegetables — onions,
celery and fennel for 5 minutes. Add rest of
ingredients and cook for 10 minutes. Thicken

mixture with slurry of cornflour and water. Boil for 5 minutes. Season and pour liquid over the chipolatas. Serve with green pasta.

CERVELLO DORATO AL BURRO
Fried calf's brains in batter with tomato sauce

Ingredients:

4 calf's brains
1 tbs vinegar
Fried onion rings

Batter:

1 egg
Flour 3 oz (90 g)
Water 5 fl oz (150 mls)
1 tsp oil

Seasoned flour 3 oz (90 g)
Tomato sauce ½ pint (300 mls) – prepare as for chipolatas above

Method: Remove membrane from brains. Soak in cold water with vinegar and 1 teaspoon salt, to eliminate the blood, for 10 minutes and rinse. Put 1 tablespoon vinegar in a saucepan with water and poach lightly for 8 minutes. Drain. Pass in seasoned flour. Prepare batter by blending beaten egg and water with flour. Leave for 20 minutes. Add oil to batter and stir. Pass pieces of brains in the seasoned flour and then in batter. Fry in oil at 360°F for 5 minutes. Drain and serve with a sauceboat of tomato sauce. Garnish with fried onion rings.

TRIPPA ALLA EMILIANA
Calf's tripe Italian style

Ingredients:

Calf's tripe 1½ lb (720 g)
4 calf's trotters
Sliced onions 4 oz (120 g)
Clove of garlic 10 g
Lard or oil 2 oz (60 g)
Flour 2 oz (60 g)
Tomato puree 2 oz (60 g)

Celery 1 oz (30 g)
1 bouquet garni
White wine ½ pint (300 mls)
Water 1 pint (600 mls)
Salt and pepper
Pinch mace, oregano, basil and chopped fresh mint as seasoning

Method: Cut the tripe (stomach lining) into very fine shreds. Clean and shave trotters. Blanch the tripe in cold water with 3 fl oz of vinegar to 3 pint of water. Boil for 30 minutes and refresh under the cold tap. Drain and dry. Place the trotters and the tripe pieces in a deep casserole dish. Cover with the following mixture. Fry the onions in oil for a few minutes without too much coloration. Add the finely crushed garlic and sprinkle the flour to form a roux. Cook for 5 minutes and add the wine, water, tomato puree, celery, bouquet garni, herbs and seasoning. Pour over the tripe. Place a lid on the dish. Braise in the oven at a low heat (300°F) for 2 hours. Remove and serve over tagliatelli verdi, spaghetti or plain noodles.

CASSERUOLA SI ANIMELLE AL MARSALA
Braised sweetbread in Marsala sauce

Ingredients:

Calf's or sheep's bread 1½ lb (720 g)
2 bay leaves
Seasoned flour
Vinegar

Sauce:

Chopped onions 2 oz (60 g)
Lard or oil 2 oz (60 g)
Chopped bacon 2 oz (60 g)
1 clove garlic
Tomato puree 1 oz (30 g)
Marsala wine ½ pint (300 mls)
Meat stock 5 fl oz (150 mls)
Pinch oregano or fresh mint
Pinch basil and mace
Salt and pepper
Pinch powdered thyme

Garnish:

Button mushrooms 4 oz (120 g)
Stoneless olives 2 oz (60 g)

Thickening:

Cornflour ½ oz (15 g)
Cream 5 fl oz (150 mls)

Method: Remove membrane of sweetbreads. Soak
in 3 pint cold water with 3 fl oz vinegar for 30
minutes and rinse. Place sweetbread in water with
vinegar and two bay leaves and season. Poach
gently for 8 minutes. Remove, drain and press
under a heavy weight to break up air cavities.
Leave under pressure for 30 minutes. Slice sweetbread and pass in seasoned flour. Fry quickly
for a few minutes. Place the slices in a shallow dish
and keep warm while making the sauce as follows.
Fry the chopped onions in fat till tender, but not
brown. Add diced lean bacon and garlic. Cook for
5 minutes. Add all ingredients including mushrooms and olives. Boil for 6 minutes and thicken
with cornflour slurry. Boil for 3 minutes and pour
over the slices. Cover the dish and braise for 15
minutes.

FEGATO DI VITELLO ALLA VENEZIANA
Calf's liver sauted with white wine

Ingredients:

Thin calf's liver escalopes 1½ lb (720 g)
Seasoned flour 2 oz (60 g)
Lard or oil 2 oz (60 g)
Chopped onions 2 oz (60 g)
Sliced mushrooms 2 oz (60 g)
1 clove of garlic
Tomato puree 1 oz (30 g)
Red pepper 2 oz (60 g)
Tomato pulp 4 oz (120 g)
Pinch mace, tarragon, chervil, mint, basil or
    oregano
White wine (preferably dry Martini) ¼ pint
    (150 mls)
Cream 5 fl oz (150 mls)
Cornflour ½ oz (15 g)
Salt and pepper
1 tbs chopped parsley

Method: Remove skin and sinews from liver. Cut
slantwise into 8 escalopes and toss in seasoned
flour. Fry in oil for a few minutes, keeping the
meat underdone. Place in a shallow dish. Meanwhile, prepare the sauce. Fry the chopped onions
in oil for a few minutes. Add sliced mushrooms,
garlic and red pepper and pulp. Toss a few times
and add rest of ingredients except cream and
cornflour. Boil for 8 minutes. Add cream and
cornflour slurry to thicken the sauce. Season
and pour over the liver. Sprinkle with fresh
chopped parsley.

VITELLO ALLA MARENGO
Saute of veal with tomato, garnished with fried
    eggs

Ingredients:

Veal from breast cut in 1 inch cubes
    1½ lb (720 g)
Seasoned flour 2 oz (60 g)
Oil 3 oz (90 g)
Chopped onions 5 oz (150 g)
1 clove garlic
Water 1 pint (600 mls)
White wine ½ pint (300 mls)
Tomato puree 2 oz (60 g)
1 tsp meat extract
Flour 2 oz
Skinned and seeded tomatoes 8 oz (240 g)
1 bouquet garni
Pinch basil, oregano, tarragon, chervil

Seasoning:

Salt and pepper
Pinch mace or nutmeg

Garnish:

4 heart-shaped croutons
4 eggs fried in oil
Button onions 4 oz (120 g)
Button mushrooms 4 oz (120 g)
1 tbs chopped parsley

Method: Toss the meat in seasoned flour and
brown in a large saute pan, covered with a lid,
for 10 minutes. Stir from time to time. Add

chopped onions and garlic. Toss for 5 minutes. Sprinkle with flour to absorb fat and form a roux. Stir well. Add tomato puree, pulp and meat extract. Add water, wine, herbs and bouquet garni. Cover with a lid and stew gently for 1½ hours, preferably in the oven. Saute the button mushrooms and onions in oil for 5 minutes. Cook for 10 minutes with a little water. Add to stew.

Fry bread in oil and top each crouton with an egg fried in deep oil so that the white completely surrounds the yolk as if it was a fritter. Sprinkle chopped parsley over the meat and serve with eggs and croutons on top of the dish.

BOLLITO MISTO VERDE
Mixed boiled meats Bologna

This is a simple dish of mixed boiled meats — thin flank, knuckle of gammon. Known as Zampone which is boned and stuffed to look like a Mortadella or large salami, it can be purchased from delicatessen stores. The meats are cooked with all the hot-pot vegetables — carrots, turnips, celery, fennel, cabbage, leeks, etc. It is served in its broth with the usual accompaniment of chutneys, pickles and the famous Salsa Verde.

SALSA VERDE
Green sauce

Ingredients:

Olive oil 5 fl oz (150 mls)
Pinch sugar
Wine vinegar 2 fl oz (60 mls)
½ tsp made mustard
Chopped chives, chervil, oregano, parsley, tarragon, capers and gherkins making a total of 1 oz (30 g) or 2 tbs
Salt and pepper

Method: Dilute mustard with vinegar. Stir in oil. Add seasoning of salt and pepper and a pinch of sugar, then all the herbs and condiments, finely chopped.

BOLLITO MEATS
Boiled meats (6 to 8 portions)

Ingredients:

Thin flank or brisket 1 lb (480 g)
1 zampino 1 lb (480 g)
Carrots 4 oz (120 g)
Leeks 8 oz (240 g)
Turnips 4 oz (120 g)
1 small cabbage quartered 1 lb (480 g)
Celery 4 oz (120 g)
Celeriac 8 oz (240 g)
1 bouquet garni
1 small stem fennel for flavour
Water 6 pint (3,600 mls)
Salt and pepper
1 large onion studded with 4 cloves

Method: Bone, defat, roll and tie the brisket or thin flank of beef. Place in water with the zampino and bring to the boil. Remove scum as it rises. Simmer for 1½ hours. Meanwhile, clean, peel and wash all vegetables. Tie the leeks in a bunch. Cut carrots, celeriac and turnips in quarters. Cut celery and fennel in small sticks. Place all vegetables in the stock after the meat has been simmered. Cook the whole mixture for 30 minutes — just enough to cook the vegetables. Add the cabbage 15 minutes after the root vegetables. In the last 10 minutes add seasoning and the bouquet garni. Strain the broth which can be used for soups or sauces. Cut the meat in thick slices and surround with vegetables neatly arranged around the meat. Serve a sauceboat of broth separately and one of green sauce with all the condiments mentioned above. All left-overs can be prepared for a second dish with pasta, by mincing thoroughly as stuffing for canneloni, ravioli and pancakes.

FARSUMAGRU
Stuffed breast of veal (12 portions)

Ingredients:

Breast of veal 3 lb (1,440 g)
Lard 3 oz (90 g)

Stuffing:

Sausagemeat 8 oz (240 g)
Chopped onions 2 oz (60 g)
Chopped calf's liver 5 oz (150 g)
1 tbs chopped parsley
1 egg
1 chopped clove of garlic
Salt and pepper
Breadcrumbs 2 oz (60 g)

Sauce:

Chopped onions 2 oz (60 g)
Celery 1 oz (30 g)
1 tsp meat extract
Water 1 pint (600 mls)
Salt and pepper

Method: Bone the breast of veal and flatten with
a rolling pin. Make a pocket between the skin and
flesh along the flap of the rib cavity. Blend all
stuffing ingredients to a compact mixture. Distribute the filling inside the pocket. Tie up to hold
the filling inside the breast. Season the meat and
rub with lard. Place in a roasting tray and bake for
1½ hours at 380°F, basting from time to time with
a ladle of hot water.

To make the gravy, remove the meat from the
tray, but keep juices. Fry the chopped onions and
diced celery in lard for 5 minutes. Add meat
extract and 1 pint of water. Season and boil for
15 minutes. Strain. Serve with plain noodles,
spaghetti in tomato sauce or green tagliatelle.
Serve left-over meat with salad.
Note: The same preparation can be made with
breast of mutton or lamb.

SALTIMBOCCA ALLA ROMANA
Veal escalopes, liver and bacon on skewers

Ingredients:

4 small calf's or sheep's liver escalopes 2 oz (60 g)
    each
4 lean back rashers of bacon 2 oz (60 g)
4 small veal escalopes 2 oz (60 g)
Seasoned flour 2 oz (60 g)
Chopped parsley 1 tbs

Sauce:

Lard or oil 1 oz (30 g)
Butter 1 oz (30 g)
Chopped shallots 1 oz (30 g)
Sliced mushrooms 2 oz (60 g)
Marsala wine 8 fl oz (240 mls)
Cream 5 fl oz (150 mls)
Salt and pepper
Juice of 1 lemon

Method: Toss the escalopes in seasoned flour and
fry quickly in a pan with the bacon rashers for 5
minutes. Remove and place neatly in rows on a
dish. In the same pan fry chopped shallots and
sliced mushrooms for 5 minutes, without colouring. Add Marsala wine. Boil for 6 minutes. Add
cream and stir well. Boil for 2 minutes. Season and
finally add lemon juice. Pour sauce over the liver
and veal escalopes. Leave the bacon rashers without
sauce. Sprinkle chopped parsley and serve with a
dish of Gnocchi Romaine or with shell pasta in
butter and cheese.

OSSO BUCO ALLA LOMBARDIA
Braised shin of veal in casserole

Ingredients:

4 by 6 oz (180 g) shin of veal cut across the bone
Seasoned flour 2 oz (60 g)

Sauce:

Lard or oil 2 oz (60 g)
Chopped onions 2 oz (60 g)
Diced carrots 2 oz (60 g)
Diced celery 2 oz (60 g)
Diced bacon 2 oz (60 g)
Tomato puree 3 oz (90 g)
White wine ½ pint (300 mls)
Water 2 pint (1,200 mls)
1 bouquet garni
1 clove garlic
Pinch oregano, fresh chopped mint and basil
Salt and pepper
1 tbs chopped parsley
Cornflour 1 oz (30 g)
Water 5 fl oz (150 mls)

Method: Pass the shin steaks in seasoned flour and fry until golden on both sides. Place in a casserole dish. Fry all the vegetables gently in same fat and add to meat with tomato puree, wine, water, herbs and seasoning. Cover with a lid and braise slowly at 330°F for 2½ hours. Sprinkle chopped parsley. Serve with pasta or potato gnocchi. Sauce can be thickened with a slurry of cornflour and water.

PETTI DI POLLO CAVOUR
Chicken breast with Italian cheese and ham

Ingredients:

4 chicken breasts
4 thin slices of ham
4 slices of Fontina or Gruyere cheese
4 small slices of truffles or mushrooms
Seasoned flour 2 oz (60 g)
3 beaten eggs
Breadcrumbs 4 oz (120 g)
Oil for frying
Salt and pepper

Method: Skin the breast of chicken and make a cavity in the side. Open the pocket and insert the slices of ham, cheese and truffles or mushrooms. Pass in seasoned flour, beaten egg and crumbs and fry in deep fat till golden for 6 minutes. Serve with a Green Sauce (see p.262).

SCALOPPINA DI TACCHINO ALLA TOSCANINI
Turkey escalope in Martini (J.C.)

Ingredients:

Breast of turkey 2 lb (960 g)
Foie gras (goose liver pâté) 2 oz (60 g)
Truffles 2 oz (60 g) tin
Seasoned flour 2 oz (60 g)
Butter 2 oz (60 g)
Oil 2 oz (60 g)

Garnish:

Thin asparagus 8 oz (240 g)
Gruyere cheese 4 oz (120 g)

1 tbs chopped parsley

Sauce:

Butter 1 oz (30 g)
Oil 1 fl oz (30 mls)
Lean bacon 2 oz (60 g)
Chopped onions 1 oz (30 g)
Sliced button mushrooms 2 oz (60 g)
Chopped pulp of tomatoes 2 oz (60 g)
Chopped red pepper 1 oz (30 g)
Chopped celery 2 oz (60 g)
Sweetcorn grain 2 oz (60 g)
Green peppers shredded 2 oz (60 g)
Dry Martini ½ pint (300 mls)
Cream 5 fl oz (150 mls)
Cornflour ½ oz (15 g)
Salt and pepper

Method: Cut the breast slantwise in four thick escalopes. In the thick side of each escalope make a slit pocket. Insert 1 oz of goose liver pate with truffle (a 2 oz can can be purchased from a delicatessen store). Pass the escalopes in seasoned flour and fry in butter and oil very gently till golden on both sides for 6 minutes. Place the cooked escalopes on a shallow dish. Keep warm.

Boil asparagus tips for 10 minutes in salted water. Drain and keep in reserve. Place the grated gruyere cheese over the escalopes and brown under the grill to melt the cheese.

To make the sauce fry the onions, bacon and mushrooms gently in butter and oil mixture for 5 minutes. Add peppers, celery, sweetcorn, tomatoes and wine. Boil for 5 minutes. Finally, thicken mixture with a slurry of cream and corn-flour. Cook for 3 minutes and pour over the cooked turkey escalopes. Top each one with four asparagus and sprinkle with chopped parsley. Serve with mushroom savoury rice.

This is a dish I have created in honour of the famous Italian conductor.

VITELLO TONNATTO
Braised veal with tuna fish sauce (10 portions)

Ingredients:

Thick cushion or under-cushion of veal (from the leg) 2 lb (960 g)

1 can tuna fish 8 oz (240 g)
Anchovy fillets 2 oz (60 g) (a small can will do)
Chopped onions 2 oz (60 g)
Lard 2 oz (60 g)
Seasoned flour 2 oz (60 g)
Juice and rind of 2 lemons
Dry Martini ½ pint (300 mls)
Water 1 pint (600 mls)
Mayonnaise 6 fl oz (180 g) —
    2 yolks and 5 fl oz oil
Juice of ½ lemon
Capers ½ oz (15 g)
Chopped gherkins ½ oz (15 g)
Chopped parsley 1 tbs
Salt and pepper
1 bouquet garni

Method: Season the joint and rub with lard and seasoned flour. Roast at a high temperature (420°F) for 20 minutes, turning the joint over after 10 minutes. Then transfer into a large casserole dish. Add the lemon juice and rind, chopped onions or button onions, water and dry Martini and 1 bouquet garni. Crumble the tuna fish and chop the anchovy. Add to the veal. Cover with a lid and cook slowly in the oven for 1½ hours at 300°F. When meat is done, remove from the casserole dish. Boil the contents of the sauce and pass through a coarse sieve. Make a mayonnaise with 2 egg yolks and ½ pint (300 mls) oil. Add juice of half a lemon and season. Blend this mayonnaise with the fish puree, stirring well to obtain perfect emulsification.

    Slice the veal thickly and coat with sauce. Sprinkle chopped parsley, chopped gherkins and capers.

    Dry white wine can be used instead of dry Martini but the flavour is less wholesome.

VEGETABLES

SPINACI ALLA PIEMONTESE
Leaf spinach flavoured with anchovy and garlic

Ingredients:

Leaf spinach 2 lb (960 g)

Anchovy fillets 2 oz can (60 g)
1 clove of garlic
Butter 2 oz (60 g)
Salt and pepper
Pinch nutmeg
Diced fried croutons 4 oz (120 g)

Method: Wash the spinach three times in plenty of cold water. Trim leaves and boil in salted water for 5 minutes. Drain and squeeze out all moisture thoroughly. Divide into four balls. Saute the spinach with chopped anchovy fillets in butter and chopped garlic with a pinch of nutmeg and serve with fried croutons.

ZUCCHINI ALLA VATICANO
Baby marrow stuffed with mushrooms

Ingredients:

Chopped onions 2 oz (60 g)
Chopped mushrooms 4 oz (120 g)
Breadcrumbs 2 oz (60 g)
4 chopped hard-boiled eggs
Tomato puree 1 oz (30 g)
Tomato pulp 8 oz (240 g)
Grated cheese 4 oz (120 g)
Oil 2 fl oz (60 mls)
Lemon juice ½ fl oz (15 mls)
1 tbs chopped fresh herbs — oregano, mint,
    parsley
Baby marrows (Zucchini) 2 lb (960 g)

Method: Fry the chopped onions and mushrooms in oil. Add crumbs and chopped eggs. Cook for 3 minutes and blend in tomato puree, pulp and grated cheese. Scrape the marrows without peeling. Split open and parboil for 4 minutes in salted water. Place in a shallow dish and cover each half with filling. Sprinkle with grated cheese and bake in a hot oven for 15 minutes. Lastly, sprinkle lemon juice and chopped herbs.

CAPONATA
Eggplant Sicilian style

Ingredients:

Aubergines 1 lb (480 g)

Seasoned flour 2 oz (60 g)
Sliced onions 1 lb (480 g)
Celery 8 oz (240 g)
Tomato puree 2 oz (60 g)
Oil 3 fl oz (90 mls)
Wine vinegar 2 fl oz (60 mls)
Sugar 1 oz (30 g)
Salt and pepper
Green stoneless olives 3 oz (90 g)
1 tbs chopped parsley and oregano

Method: If the aubergines are very fresh, slice without peeling. Sprinkle with salt and let moisture exude freely. Wash after 15 minutes and drain. Fry onions in oil till golden. Toss well. Blend tomato puree, vinegar, sugar, seasoning and olives and simmer for 10 minutes.

Toss the sliced aubergines in seasoned flour and fry in deep fat for 3 minutes. Drain and dry on absorbent paper. Place in a shallow dish and cover with sauce. Sprinkle with chopped parsley and cool.

SWEETS (DOLCE VITAE)

CASSATA ITALIANA
Flavoured ices with fruits

The basic ice is made with a mixture of syrup (at 32° Beaume density) to which egg yolks are added and cooked like a custard sauce. Flavour and colour are added according to requirement. The ice can be enriched with whipped cream or meringue to produce a different texture. The Italian pastry cooks have created over 400 different types of bombas and ice cream sundries, including such flavours as asparagus, pistachio, melon and other exotic fruits.

WATER ICE WITH EGG WHITES —
SORBET TYPES

Ingredients:

Water 1 pint (600 mls)
Sugar 6 oz (180 g)

2 egg whites
Juice of 2 lemons and lemon essence *or*
   the juice of any fruit

Method: Boil juice and water with sugar for 5 minutes. Cool. Add egg whites when cold and whip in the ice cream machine to freeze until small snowy crystals appear.

For liqueur ice cream add 2 fl oz (60 mls) of chosen liqueur to this basic ice. For creamy ice add 3 fl oz (90 mls) whipped cream.

EGG ICE BOMBA MIXTURE

Ingredients:

Water 1 pint (600 mls)
Sugar 6 oz (180 g)
16 egg yolks
Flavour and colour to taste

Method: Boil water and sugar to a syrup for 5 minutes. Pour over the egg yolks while whisking. Strain and reheat, whisking all the time until the mixture thickens like a custard. Do not boil. Add vanilla essence or rum or liqueurs.

For fruit ice, substitute water for the appropriate fruit and fruit puree, weight for weight.

CREAM ICE

Ingredients:

Milk 1 pint (600 mls)
6 egg yolks
Gelatine ¼ oz (7 g)
Ground sugar 8 oz (240 g)
Whipped cream 5 fl oz (150 g)

Method: Mix powdered gelatine with sugar. Add to boiling milk. Pour mixture over the egg yolks while stirring. Reheat without boiling to thicken mixture like custard. When it coats the spoon, the custard is ready. Cool and when cold place in an ice cream machine to freeze. Half way through the operation, add the whipped cream and whisk. Flavour and colour should be added before freezing. For chocolate add 2 oz (60 g) melted chocolate. For coffee add 1 tsp instant coffee diluted with 1 tbs hot water. For liqueur add 2 fl oz (60 mls) liqueur.

A cheaper way to make ice cream is to use starch to thicken milk and to use less egg yolks (half the quantity) – 1 oz (30 g) starch and 3 egg yolks instead of 6 egg yolks.

CASSATA TUTTI FRUTTI

Ingredients:

Diced glacé cherries 2 oz (60 g)
Diced glacé pineapple 2 oz (60 g)
Chopped orange peel ½ oz (15 g)
Chopped angelica ½ oz (15 g)
Maraschino 2 fl oz (60 mls)
Cream ice 1 lb (480 g)

Method: Mix all the fruits and soak in liqueur for 15 minutes and blend to ice cream. Place in a suitable bomb mould or pudding basin and freeze.

The mould can also be lined with a lemon or orange water ice, allowing ½ inch wall, with centre filled with the fruit ice cream as indicated above.

ZABAGLIONE ROMEO
Egg custard with wine and brandy

Ingredients:

Castor sugar 8 oz (240 g)
6 egg yolks 4 oz (120 g)
White wine 6 fl oz (180 mls) – brought to the
  boil
Lemon juice 1 fl oz (30 mls)
Brandy or liqueur 2 fl oz (60 mls)
Whipped cream 4 fl oz (120 mls)

Method: Place egg yolks and sugar in a metal basin over a tray half filled with the boiling water. Whisk mixture for 6 minutes until it begins to thicken. Add the hot wine, juice and liqueur and continue whisking until the mixture begins to thicken like a custard. Remove from

heat and beat for further 5 minutes. Cool and when cold whip the cream and fold into Zabaglione. Serve in fluted glasses.

If plain Zabaglione is required omit the cream.

If the Zabaglione is to be served cold, for better stabilisation add to the above 1 level teaspoon of gelatine dissolved in the hot wine. For easier setting, add 2 teaspoons of cornflour or potato flour to half a cup of cold wine blended to remainder of boiling hot wine. This will also produce a better stabilisation if the Zabaglione is to be served hot.

CREMA MAMA MIA
Lemon cheese pudding

Ingredients:

Cream cheese 8 oz (240 g)
Grated parmesan cheese ½ oz (15 g)
2 egg yolks
Rum 4 fl oz (120 mls)
Juice and grated rind of 1 orange and lemon
Cream 5 fl oz (150 g) – for decoration
Castor sugar 3 oz (90 g)
Powdered gelatine ½ oz (15 g)
Hot water 3 fl oz (90 g)
4 egg whites
Granulated sugar 1 oz (30 g)
Pinch salt

Method: Blend the cheeses and cream with egg yolks. Add rum (or other liqueur if preferred), lemon and orange juices and rinds. Mix gelatine and castor sugar and dissolve in hot water. Add the cheese mixture. Whip egg whites to a meringue with a pinch of salt, then add sugar and whip again until stiff. Fold into cream cheese mixture. Place in individual jelly dishes. Chill and serve with sponge fingers or wafers.

PANETTO DI NAPOLI
Almond cakes

Ingredients:

Butter 5 oz (150 g)
Castor sugar 5 oz (150 g)

2 eggs
Flour 8 oz (240 g)
Ground almonds 6 oz (180 g)
Few drops of lemon and almond essence
Apricot jam 8 oz (240 g)
Icing sugar 4 oz (120 g) — for dusting

Method: Cream butter and sugar till fluffy. Add beaten egg and essence and stir well. Blend flour and ground almonds to mixture to obtain a firm paste. Chill for 30 minutes in refrigerator. Roll on dusted board to a thickness of $^1/_8$ inch. Cut rounds 3 inch diameter and divide in equal numbers. Make a ring by cutting a centre of half of the rounds with a 1½ inch cutter. Place the plain rounds on a greased tray. Brush with water. Place the rings on top. Fill centre with soft apricot jam piped into the cavity. At this stage the Neapolitans look like vol-au-vent cases. Bake at 380°F for 12-15 minutes. Do not brown them. Cool and dust with icing sugar.

PANETTI ALLA CIOCCOLATA
Small choux buns filled with cream and coated
  with a rum flavoured chocolate sauce

Ingredients:

Choux pastry:

Water 5 fl oz (150 mls)
Margarine 2½ oz (75 g)
Flour 5 oz (150 g)
4 eggs
Pinch salt and sugar

Lard for greasing tray 1 oz (30 g)

Filling:

Double cream 5 fl oz (150 mls)
Sugar 2 oz (60 g)
Vanilla essence

Chocolate sauce:

Grated dark chocolate 6 oz (180 g)
Butter 3 oz (90 g)
Cream 3 oz (90 g)
Cornflour ½ oz (15 g)Rum 3 fl oz (90 g)

Method: To make the choux pastry, boil margarine in water until melted. Add flour and stir with a spoon to obtain a solid mass which will not stick to the pan after being dried for a few minutes. Remove from heat and one by one add the eggs, beating all the time, and a pinch of salt and pepper. The mixture should be of dropping consistency. Place in a piping bag fitted with a ¼ inch tube. Pipe little dollops (approximately 1 dessertspoon of choux mixture) on a greased tray. Brush with egg glaze and bake for 20 minutes at 400°F. Cool on rack.

Whip double cream. Add sugar and few drops of vanilla essence. Fill each bun with cream. Place in a shallow dish.

Melt chocolate and add butter, mix cream, cornflour and rum. Boil for 5 minutes and pour this sauce over the buns.

Yugoslavia

Until 1918, there was no Yugoslavia as we know it today; it was cobbled together from a hodge-podge of provinces, nations and cultures at the conclusion of World War I, so to understand the gastronomy of this complex land, one must understand something of its history, dominated by the Turks in the East, the Habsburg Empire in the West, and quite often both, in conflict, in the middle.

The Romans paid their soldiers with salt and their biggest source of supply was the Illyrian province. Since that time, many invaders have come, and for a thousand years parts of Yugoslavia have been under foreign domination. Even Napoleon tried to influence Slovenia by granting it independence, hoping to gain a grateful ally. The independence was short-lived, but ever since, the Slovenes have had a soft spot for the French.

Five basic nationalities make up this complex country: Serb, Croat, Slovene, Macedonian and Montenegrin; with three main languages: Macedonian, Serbo-Croat and Slovene. There are also four main religions: Muslim, Jewish, Orthodox Christians and Roman Catholics. So for the older generation, there is no such thing as being a Yugoslav. One is proud of the fact that one is a Serb, a Croat or a Macedonian, with a distinct language, a culture—and a distinct gastronomy. However the new generation is fast turning into a truly cosmopolitan nation while retaining their racial characteristics. The more sophisticated Slovenes can be mistaken for prosperous tourists. The Croats mind their own businesses well, and thrive. The Dalmatians talk with their hands in Mediterranean manner and enjoy their pasta just like exuberant Italians from Napoli. The Bosnians have remained puritanical, modest and abstemious in their land of honey, sunshine and green pastures. The Serbs are the gipsies of the republic; they like rude jokes, highly spiced pork stews and surrealist art. The Montenegrins are proud of their ancient traditions and are reputed to produce the most beautiful women in Europe.

Modern Yugoslavia, guided by its national idol, Tito, gives this variety of characters and nations room to develop side by side within their own framework of traditions.

Food is abundant and cheap, and the cuisine is interesting and varied. Pork is a favourite meat, except in Bosnia and Macedonia where the Moslem influence is strong. Fish, game and all types of domestic animals are used, with lard, butter, oil and cream. Soups are popular, based on fish, meat or poultry, or thick soups made of maize like *kacamak, polenta* or *mamaljuga.*

The country ranges from the southern sea coast, with jagged rocks and a soft Mediterranean climate, to the eastern mountains, with hard winters and warm summers. In the south, there are olives, tobacco, peppers, figs and vineyards; in the north, there are rye and wheat fields, apples, and root crops. Enemies, invaders and friends and neighbours have left their mark on the national cuisine: the Turkish influence is particularly strong in Bosnia, Herzegovina and Macedonia, while the Austrian chefs have left their mark on Slovenia. The neighbouring Hungarians have influenced the cooking pots of Croatia and parts of Serbia, and the Italians would approve of what the Montenegrins and Dalmations make of their specialities.

All Yugoslav cooking has one thing in common:

it is the sturdy, tasty cooking of the peasants, with lots of flavour, spices and aroma. Rich stews just made for the hard-working men on the farm are full of exotic flavours, in the shape of peppers, aubergines and tomatoes. The aroma of simple meat grilled on skewers is enriched by whole bay leaves strung between the pieces of meat.

A new tourist industry is now giving the basic peasant cuisine an international touch. The indigenous dishes are having to compete for the favours of the tourists, and in the process have become more subtle in texture and taste.

Slovenia

In the Slovene Alps, cattle and sheep graze in harmonious peace with wild deer, and the trees in the hillside orchards are heavy with wonderful fruit. Hilly and mountainous, this part of Yugoslavia has a large population of game to enrich the larder. Water fowl abound and make rich salmi and stews. Fallow deer and mouflon (wild sheep), goats and even bear and wild boar are still to be found on the wooded hillsides. Birds such as grouse, partridge, geese and ducks abound in the marshy deltas of the rivers, and hunting is a national sport as popular as fishing.

There are nearly 160 different species of freshwater fish to stretch the creative imagination of the dedicated cook. There is a soft-mouthed trout *mekousta* and the red trout, *zlatousta*. *Glavatica* and *mladica* are types of salmon-trout with a delicate flavour and texture. The *belvica* is almost a prehistoric fish found only in Europe; it is slightly bigger than a trout and belongs to the same family. Freshwater crayfish are a gourmet's delight and can be used in the same way as scampi; however they are at their best simply boiled in court-bouillon.

The most ancient Roman dish of which there is still a record is roasted dormouse and braised young wild boar. In rather more modern idiom, *ricet* is a dish made of smoked meat with boiled barley groats, and *pohana piska* is a chicken fried in crumbs with butter. The strudel pastries are of a very high standard, influenced by the Hungarian versions, and usually served with a fruit or cheese filling, known as *prieska gibanica.* Gorjanska crima is the popular red wine of Radgona, and this fertile fruitbowl also produces some excellent brandies and plum spirits.

Croatia

You ask for a glass of water and you get of jug of sljivovica, such is the extent of hospitality in Croatia. A meal usually begins with an acid soup, often flavoured with pork and cabbage. The Croatians have a saying that one should not touch liquor before the cabbage nor sing before the meat— so the cabbage and the meat tend to make an early entrance.

Sarma is the great speciality: cabbage stuffed with minced beef or pork, cooked in the oven until tender. In the southern part of France, near Lourdes, there is a similar dish called *Sou Fasum.*

The Croatians appreciate braised turkey with a rich tomato-flavoured pasta; partridge in red wine; a haunch of venison—and usually finish their meal with a piece of strong cheese, often made of sheep or goats' milk. The dishes with paprika are even more hot and spicy than the Hungarian versions, and the excellent wines Silvana and Moslavac, whites served chilled, help to cool the throat. The red Portugizac has the richness and body of a good port.

Serbia

The Serbs are great gourmets, so it is no surprise that they are also great cooks. Their cold buffets are as artistic and varied as the most elaborate Scandinavian table. Suckling pig and lamb; sturgeon and salmon; lobster and crawfish, venison and pâtés, all displayed against the fresh crispness of a dozen or so salads make up a sumptuous display. Serbia has the most distinctive regional dishes, with meat and vegetable casseroles, stews of mixed fish, grilled meats, pumpkin pie and strudels in variety. *Podvarku* is a roasted turkey hen and *djuvec* is a rich stew of meat and vegetables. Hospitality in Serbia takes the form of an offering of sljivovica, black coffee, and the Serbian speciality called *slatko;* it is a cross between preserved fruit and jam, with perfect, fresh ripe fruit slowly stewed in a thick syrup without touching it lest if fall apart. A good *slatko* has the fruit still whole and with its natural colour, embalmed in an unctuous syrup. It may be made from any type of fruit, and often of flowers like white violets and May roses. It is traditionally served with a glass of fresh water.

Cheese is popular in Serbia, served as a start to a meal, or a snack with some smoked meat. A hard pungent cheese called *kackavlj* is marvellous as a nibble with drinks. The local bread, *pogaca,* is served in long strips, and with some *kackavlj* and a bottle of Zumberak or Moslavina a simple repast turns into a gastronomic experience.

Dalmatia

The Adriatic coast is a fish paradise to the enthusiastic cook and gourmet; it is said that there are 365 varieties of fish in this warm sea, one for every day of the year. There are oysters of *Vrsar,* Adriatic prawns and the delicate mussels, cooked in wine with a shot of plum brandy: fantastic. In this sunny province there are also fresh figs, rich little melons, flavoured with plum brandy, and some of the best ham in the world, rubbed with salt, pepper and garlic and smoked for at least two months. There is a local cheese not unlike Gruyere and another cured in olive oil.

In all the resorts on the Adriatic, including those on the Italian coast, the preparation of mixed fish dishes is an art, and the coast near Dubrovnik is no exception. *Ribe przene na ulju* is perhaps the best, and consists of six or eight items all fried: scallops, prawns, mussels and assorted fillets—a scrumptious fry-up indeed.

Maraschino liqueur is made in Dalmatia and wines produced include Korcula, Vugava, Plavac, Teran and Vipava, and the smooth malvazija from the island of Susak.

Bosnia

The great speciality of Bosnia is a savoury, aromatic stew called *lonac,* from the deep earthenware pot in which it is made. It is unusual in that it uses at least four and sometimes more types of meat: pork, beef, lamb, calf's feet for richness, bacon for savour, lots of root vegetables and white wine, vinegar and garlic for aroma. It is baked for at least four hours, and at a low temperature it develops a richness and succulence while the flavours mingle in an unctuous sauce made of the natural juices.

There are still a number of Bosnians who obey the ancient Moslem laws of diet, drink no wine with meals and avoid pork. Certainly the Turkish influence makes lamb on the spit *musaka* and kebabs very popular. A well done lamb roasted on a spit is possibly one of the great miracles of simple cooking; I once did such a dish for a party of International motor racing drivers. A lamb of 28 lbs was enough for only fifteen portions, so popular was this crisp, succulent meat—and there was no way of getting even another sliver from the bones, so clean had they been picked. The taste was out of this world.

Montenegro

The Montenegrins are proud people, little influenced by friends or invaders. They never accepted Napoleon, Hitler or Stalin, yet they paid a tribute to Tito when they called one of their towns Titograd. In the same way their gastronomy has absorbed only what they wished to absorb from friend and foe. The Adriatic is a rich source of ingredients for their fish specialities: *zubatac,* the toothfish, or fried inkfish with garlic, or even salmon gently flavoured with mastika (a potent liqueur made with sesame seeds and tasting like Pernod).

In the hills and valleys of Montenegro the day starts with *lozovaca,* a potent brandy; the performance is repeated before each meal. White wine is often served before meals and red during the meal. Winter foods are all types of meat: pickled pork, beef, mutton and every kind of sausage imaginable; all these served with kale, cabbage or beans. Smoked ham from Njesus and dried, smoked mutton called Kastradine are local specialities.

Belgrade

Until 1876 when the Turks were finally driven out of Serbia, the border between Turkey and Austro-Hungaria was very close to Belgrade. The strife has ended, but a sort of dangerous excitement is there still, along with the international polish of a cosmopolitan city. Caviar of Belgrade is better than that of Russia, and just as expensive. But cheaper delicacies can be sampled—like *raznjici, culbastja* and *pljeskavica.* The Russian *coulibiac* is traditional but the Yugoslav is better and more elaborate: delicious layers of salmon and crayfish tails with mushrooms, piled on a bed of soft rice with fish roe, all wrapped in a huge pancake and a thin layer of puff pastry. When served it is a splendid dish which requires much wine by way of celebration.

Macedonia

Macedonian cuisine has borrowed heavily from the Turks and from the Greeks. The meal may begin with *meze* or with lemon soup, or a cold sliced cucumber soup with yoghurt known here as *tarator*. *Ohrid Trout, tetovski grah* (a bean dish), lamb roasted on the spit, and a great profusion of different meat stews served with spicy vegetables are amongst the classic dishes of this region.

The Turkish and Greek influence is strongest in the area of sweets. The Yugoslavs love sweets, and all over the country one of the favourite desserts is *strudel,* known here as *pita.* It is filled with a variety of fillings, influenced by the nearest country—so those provinces near Austria favour apples, those near Hungary savoury fillings, and the Macedonians like the version with nuts and honey, covered with sugar syrup. Another speciality is *kadaif,* nuts and almonds wrapped in thin noodles soaked in syrup. *Ratluk* is a hard jelly made with almonds and rose oil, and is eaten at any time of day.

Yugoslavia is living proof that an international gastronomy exists; the cuisine of this exuberant country is a vivid example of its development and success.

BILL OF FARE

Soup

KASAPSKI-DJUVEC
Mutton and vegetable soup

Fish

RAKPAPRIKAS
Scampi or crayfish or baby lobster in cream sauce

FOGAS ADRIATIC
Perch-like fillets in cream sauce

Meat Entrées

MUTTON DJUVEC
Mutton stew with vegetables

LEG OF MUTTON YUGOSLAVIAN STYLE
Boiled leg of mutton with rice and barley

VENISON STEAK TITO
Venison steaks sauted with mushrooms in wine
sauce

PORK DJUVEC
Braised pork chop with potatoes and peppers

CEVAPCICI WITH AJVARSALATA
Cigar shaped hamburgers served with a mixture of
peppers and aubergines

SARMA YUGOSLAVIAN STYLE
Minced beef pie with sauerkraut cooked in wine

Sweets

YUGOSLAVIAN SABAYON FRUIT CUP
Plum with sabayon

MONTENEGRO FLOATING ISLAND
Baked meringue pudding with a wine custard and
pears

SOUP

KASAPSKI-DJUVEC
Mutton and vegetable soup

Ingredients:

Diced lean mutton meat from shoulder cuts 1 lb
   (480 g)
Fat 2 oz (60 g) (oil or lard)
Diced onions 3 oz (90 g)
Seeded and finely shredded green peppers 5 oz
   (150 g)
Tomato puree 3 oz (90 g)
1 pinch of the following herbs: marjoram,
   coriander and mint
1 pinch of caraway seeds and paprika
Salt and pepper
Diced potatoes 8 oz (240 g)
Diced green beans 5 oz (150 g)
1 clove of garlic
Sour cream 6 fl oz (180 mls)
Water 3½ pint (2,100 mls)

Method: Remove fat from meat and cut in ¼ inch
cubes. Saute in fat for 10 minutes then add
chopped onions and green peppers. Cover with lid
and let mixture sweat for another 5 minutes. Stir
from time to time. Add rest of ingredients and
cover level with water. Simmer for 1½ hours until
meat is tender. Check seasoning. (Use
beans of the French varieties. Head and tail and
cut slantwise in thin slices). When soup is ready
add cream, stir and serve.

FISH

RAKPAPRIKAS
Scampi, crayfish or baby lobster in cream sauce

Ingredients:

Frozen scampi or crayfish tail 1 lb (480 g)

Seasoning:

Salt, pepper and paprika 1 good pinch

Flour 1 oz (30 g)
Oil 3 fl oz (90 mls)
Chopped onions 3 oz (90 g)
Chopped red and green peppers 3 oz (90 g)
Tomato puree 2 oz (60 g)
Yugoslavian white wine 5 fl oz (150 mls)
1 clove of garlic
Sour cream 5 fl oz (150 mls)
Cornflour 1 oz (30 g)
Chopped parsley 1 tbs

Method: Pass the scampi in seasoning and flour.
Shake surplus off. Heat a saute pan with oil and
toss the scampi, together with chopped onions,
garlic and green peppers. Cover with a lid. Shake
pan from time to time and saute for 5 minutes.
Add white wine and tomato puree. Boil 5 minutes.
Strain liquor into a small saucepan and boil it
10 minutes. Thicken it with a slurry of sour cream
and cornflour. Add rest of cooked ingredients.
Reheat. Check seasoning and serve with fresh
chopped parsley.

FOGAS ADRIATIC
Perch-like fillets in cream sauce

Ingredients:

4 x 10 oz fillets (300 g) Fogas
Seasoned flour 2 oz (60 g)
1 pinch of paprika and caraway seeds
Lard or oil 3 oz (90 g)
Thinly sliced onions 2 oz (60 g)
Sliced white mushrooms 2 oz (60 g)
Carrots thinly sliced in strips 1 oz (30 g)
Yugoslavian white wine 15 fl oz (450 mls)
Chopped parsley 1 tbs
Juice and rind of 1 lemon

Method: Pass fish in seasoned flour. Sprinkle
paprika and caraway seeds. Pan fry in heated oil
for few minutes on each side. Transfer fish into
a shallow dish. In same fat saute the vegetables
for few minutes. Drain fat and add wine to
vegetables. Boil 8 minutes. Pour contents over
fish. Cover with paper or a lid and bake in oven
at 380°F for 15 minutes, or until cooked.

Sprinkle grated rind of lemon and juice and chopped parsley.

MEAT ENTREES

MUTTON DJUVEC
Mutton stew with vegetables

Ingredients:

Diced lean meat of shoulder of mutton 1 lb (480 g)
Lard or oil 3 oz (90 g)
Chopped onions 5 oz (150 g)
3 oz (90 g) of each of the following vegetables:
   carrots thinly sliced; turnips, beans, cauliflower,
   green peppers, red peppers, potatoes, celery.
   (All vegetables cut in same size. Cauliflower
   divided into flowerets).
Tomato puree 3 oz (90 g)
1 clove garlic

Seasoning:

Salt and pepper, pinch of paprika and cumin
1 pinch caraway seeds
1 bouquet garni
Water 4 pint (2,400 mls)
Rice 5 oz (150 g)

Method: Brown the meat in hot fat for few minutes, add chopped onions and sweat covered with a lid for 5 minutes. Stir well then add rest of ingredients, except rice, add water. Check seasoning and add rice. Cook 20 minutes more and serve in soup tureen.

LEG OF MUTTON YUGOSLAVIAN STYLE
Boiled leg of mutton with vegetables

Ingredients:

3½ lb (1,680 g) leg of mutton
Medium-size onions 1 lb (480 g)
Pearl barley 5 oz (150 g)
Rice 5 oz (150 g)
Dried yellow peas 5 oz (150 g) (soaked 3 hours in
   warm water)
Leeks 8 oz (240 g)
Dried red and green peppers 8 oz (240 g)

Tomato puree 3 oz (90 g)
1 clove garlic
1 bouquet garni
Salt and pepper
1 pinch paprika

Method: Bone the leg. Season and tie up with string. Place in cold water in a large saucepan or soup stock pot. Bring to the boil and remove scum as it rises. After 45 minutes add peeled onions, leeks (cleaned and tied up in a bundle), sliced seedless peppers, garlic, bouquet garni, rice, barley and peas. Simmer for 1¼/1½ hours at boiling point. Add seasoning. Make sure the broth boils. Add tomato puree and a little more water to keep the stock level all the time. Remove vegetables when they are cooked. The joint is ready if no blood comes out of the meat when pierced with a needle. Arrange meat and vegetables neatly on a dish, and serve the broth separately with rice, barley and peas as soup. Check seasoning.

VENISON STEAK TITO
Venison steaks sauted with mushrooms in wine
   sauce

Ingredients:

4 x 6 oz (180 g) venison from loin
Seasoned flour 2 oz (60 g)
Lard 2 oz (60 g)
1 pinch paprika and caraway seeds
Red wine 5 fl oz (150 mls)
Chopped mushrooms 3 oz (90 g)
Chopped onions 2 oz (60 g)
6 juniper berries or 2 fl oz (30 mls) gin spirit
Sour cream 5 fl oz (150 mls)

Method: Pass steaks in seasoned flour blended with ground paprika and caraway seeds. Heat a saute pan and quickly fry the steaks 5 minutes. Remove from pan and keep warm in a shallow dish. In same fat saute mushrooms and onions for few minutes. Add red wine and boil 6 minutes rapidly to reduce it by half. Add cream, boil 2 minutes. Check seasoning and pour this creamy sauce over steaks. Add juniper berries or gin and cover with a lid. Cook in moderate oven for 15 minutes.

PORK DJUVEC
Braised pork chop with potatoes and peppers

Ingredients:

4 x 8 oz (180 g) pork chops
Lard or oil 2 oz (60 g)
Chopped onions 2 oz (60 g)
Chopped seeded green peppers 5 oz (150 g)
Potatoes cut in 1 inch cubes 1 lb (480 g)
Tomato puree 2 oz (60 g)
1 pinch caraway seeds
1 bouquet garni
Celery 2 oz (60 g)
1 garlic clove
Water 2 pint (1,200 mls)
Chopped parsley 1 tbs

Method: In frying pan, brown pork chops for few minutes only without cooking them through. Transfer into shallow dish or casserole.

In same pan fry chopped onions until tender, add green peppers and toss few minutes. Transfer into saucepan with water, add potatoes and rest of ingredients. Boil 15 minutes. Transfer contents into the casserole with chops. Cover with a lid, add bouquet garni and braise for 40 minutes. Remove bouquet garni and sprinkle chopped parsley. Check seasoning.

CEVAPCICI WITH AJVARSALATA
Cigar shaped hamburgers served with a mixture of peppers and aubergines

Ingredients:

Minced beef ½ lb (240 g)
Minced pork ½ lb (240 g)
Salt 5 g
Black pepper 2 g
Pinch chilli pepper
Seasoned flour
Sliced onions 1 lb (480 g)
Sliced seeded green peppers ½ lb (240 g)
Fat or oil 3 oz (90 g)
Tomato puree 2 oz (60 g)
Peeled aubergines 5 oz (150 g)
Salt and pepper

Method: Blend the minced meats. Add seasoning and divide into 16 balls. Elongate each ball. Flatten each lightly and quickly pass in seasoned flour and pan fry a few minutes only. Keep warm in dish while you prepare garnish.

In saute pan heat oil and saute sliced onions and green peppers and aubergines until soft. Add tomato puree, seasoning and 1 cup water. Boil 10 minutes. Place this garnish in shallow dish. Arrange Cevapcici on top. Cover with a lid and bake for 15 minutes at 380-400°F. Serve in same dish.

SARMA YUGOSLAVIAN STYLE
Minced beef pie with sauerkraut cooked in wine

Ingredients:

Minced beef 1 lb (480 g) lamb, mutton or any
    other meat may be used equally

Filling:

Chopped onions 8 oz (240 g)
1 clove garlic
Tomato puree 3 oz (90 g)
Cooked rice 4 oz (120 g)

Salt and pepper
Pinch of paprika
Blanched cabbage leaves or Sauerkraut 1 lb (480 g)
White wine ½ pint (300 mls)
Few juniper berries (6)
Lard or oil 2 oz (60 g)
Water ½ pint (300 mls)

Method: Prepare forcemeat as follows:
Fry chopped onions for few minutes. Add to meat and blend rice, garlic, tomato puree and season. Mix well. Grease a shallow dish with lard or other fat. Place a layer of sauerkraut and a layer of meat and repeat again. Cover with wine and water with few juniper berries. Cover with a lid and braise for 45 minutes at 380°F. Serve in same dish.

If fresh cabbage leaves are used they should be blanched in salted water for 5 minutes. Filling should be placed in each leaf, wrapped like a stuffed cabbage ball. Braise in wine and water as indicated. When the liquid is almost evaporated the Sarma is ready.

SWEETS

YUGOSLAVIAN SABAYON FRUIT CUP
Plum with sabayon

Ingredients:

Fresh sliced red plums 1 lb (480 g) (peaches or
    apricots can also be used)
Plum brandy 5 fl oz (150 mls)
Maraschino 2 fl oz (60 mls)
Castor sugar 1 oz (30 g)

Sabayon:

5 egg yolks
Castor sugar 3 oz (90 g)
White wine 5 fl oz (150 mls)
Grated lemon and juice ½ oz (15 g)

Method: Place sliced plums in a bowl and add
brandy, maraschino and sugar: macerate 1 hour.
Then transfer and divide into 4 glasses (8 fl oz
size).

    In a basin place yolks, sugar and wine with
lemon juice. Beat 5 minutes over a tray half
filled with boiling water. The sabayon is ready
when it is of pouring custard consistency but
frothy. Top up the glass with the thick sabayon
and do not heat it at a higher temperature than
180°F as it is at this stage it will begin to
coagulate. At higher temperature it would curdle.

MONTENEGRO FLOATING ISLAND
Baked meringue pudding with a wine custard and
    pears

Ingredients:

4 ripe pears, peeled and cut in halves
Sweet white wine 1 pint (600 mls)
1 pinch cinnamon
Castor sugar 2 oz (60 g)
Lemon essence few drops
Rose essence few drops
6 egg yolks
Potato starch 1 oz (30 g) or use arrowroot
6 egg whites
Castor sugar 6 oz (180 g)
Crystallised violets 1 oz (30 g) or glacé cherries

Method: Place pears in large glass bowl. Moisten
with 4 spoonfuls of wine. Boil rest of wine with a
pinch of cinnamon. In another bowl beat egg yolks
and sugar, add potato flour or arrowroot and
gradually pour in the boiling hot wine. Whisk and
return to heat until it thickens like an ordinary
custard. Add lemon and rose essences. As soon as
it boils remove custard. Cool and pour over the
pears, filling two-thirds of the bowl only. Keep
the rest for meringue pudding. Beat in a clean, fat
free mixing bowl the egg whites. Add a pinch of
salt and whisk until the mixture peaks. Add the
6 oz sugar in 3 stages, beating between each stage
and making sure the meringue peaks each time.

    Grease with soft butter 1 pint cake or
pudding mould. Dust the inside with castor sugar.
Fill it with meringue mixture. Pad it well to
avoid air pockets. Cover with a greaseproof paper.
Place mould in a shallow tray half filled with
water and bake at 360°F for 20 minutes. Remove
from the oven and cool. When cold apply
pressure with your hand on the top of the baked
meringue to ease it out of the mould and turn it
into a shallow round dish. It should look like a
white blancmange. Coat with wine custard
completely. Serve with the accompaniment of
custard and pears. Decorate with crystallised violets
or glacé fruits.

Romania

Soft ewes' cheese on fir bark, served in pottery dishes with carved wooden spoons, and a dish of *mamaliga* (maize porridge) with a huge bowl of vegetable salad were offered to me once by a local shepherd when I visited Romania. The offering was typical of the race: colourful, traditional and hearty. Romania is the Latin land of central Europe, and like Italy it has flamboyance, love of colour, love of food, of wine and song. Its capital, Bucharest, is known as the City of Parks and was designed by the French architect Le Corbusier. Outside this cosmopolitan city with wide, modern thoroughfares you can still see women on their knees washing their clothes in the river. The new and the old mix in picturesque ways in this exciting land. Flamingoes and pelicans in their thousands roam over the wide plains and boar and chamois wander free through the Carpathian mountains. It is a glorious country trying to leap into a modern way of life with a bagload of traditions and exciting folklore.

You can eat and drink well in Romania. The wines are exhilarating and the food is simply exquisite in the freshness of its ingredients and its quality. In the Carpathians you can enjoy snipe, quail or even a joint of wild boar or chamois, delicious in wine sauce.

The Danube Delta is a Mecca for fishermen, and a considerable commercial asset. After the Volga fisheries, those of the lower Danube are the most extensive and the richest in Europe. On the other hand, the sea fisheries on the Romanian coast are negligible. The lagoons near Giurgiu and Oltenitsa at Calarshi, Cernavoda and Harsova and near Ostrov are the most productive. Three million kilos of carp are caught annually, and 1½ million kilos of sturgeon with its caviar roe.

In wheat, rye and other grain Romania is one of the richest countries in south-east Europe, with a wheat production one-fifth that of Canada. The wheat is of the finest quality and produces the highest quality bread. The Romanian deposits of mineral oil and gasoline are enormous and have brought added prosperity to an already rich land.

Romania is a large plain, intersected by a succession of rivers, and surrounded by the USSR, Hungary, Yugoslavia and the Black Sea. Over forty species of freshwater mussels have been observed in the Romanian rivers, quite apart from the numerous fish which constitute the main element in Romanian gastronomy.

In my younger days in the twenties, Elvire Popesco was the star of the Parisian stage, and her tempestuous personality was everyone's idea of the national Romanian character. At the same time King Carol of Romania and his girlfriend Lupescu hit the headlines, as the most romantic pair in Europe. Suddenly the Romanians were fashionable, and it became evident that there was more money in mineral oil than in cooking oil.

The cuisine of Romania is rich and aromatic. East meets West in Romania, and the centuries of Turkish domination are evident in the style of seasoning and garnishing. The most favoured dishes are charcoal-grilled meats and roasts on the spit, and *mititei* is a highly spiced type of hamburger, grilled to order in any cafe and restaurant. The *patricieni* is another popular cheap snack, not unlike a frankfurter. Heavy soups with plenty of vegetables are very common. The Moldavian *borshch* is a Russian type of soup based on cabbage and much in favour; some, like *ciorba de prisoare* are garnished with fish or meat balls, others like *taraneasca* are made with meat and vegetables. Fish soup is popular, and the many garnishes including sour cream and eggs make the range as varied as the Hungarian repertoire.

Young and old have their daily quota of the national porridge, *mamaliga,* based on cornmeal or flour. It can be eaten with milk, cream or poached egg, and is served morning, noon and night. The next most popular dish is *Sarmale,* cabbage leaves stuffed with meat like the Greek *dolmades.* The *Sarmale* is braised in a stock which is then used as the base for a soup. *Sarmale* and *mamaliga* are often served together.

One of the best and most nutritious vegetarian dishes is made in Romania: *ghiveci,* with as many as twenty vegetables simmered in their own juices and a touch of oil, eaten hot or cold. It looks like a more varied version of the French *Ratatouille Niçoise.* A flat meat patty, known as *parjoale,* is served as a snack, and often taken to the fields by the workers.

In the realm of haute cuisine, the *scorcolea* is worthy of attention when served with crayfish or scampi as an accompaniment. It is made with tender walnuts, bread, milk, oil and seasonings, served as a paste and used as an accent, rather like a chutney.

Romania has a wide variety of fish dishes, one of the best being *carp umplut,* where the fish is stuffed with olives. The other dish worthy of international fame is Julienne stew, with five or six meats—ham, chicken, beef, veal, venison—with carrots, leeks, peppers, onions and mushrooms all tossed together in oil and cooked gently in their own moisture, with garlic, tomatoes and a little wine for flavour. The finishing touch is a uniquely Romanian one: a garnish of white seeded grapes which have been soaked in brandy.

In the Iliad we read: 'The Greek warriors went to Thrace in search of wine'—and one of the ancient kings, Burebista, ordered the vines of the region to be uprooted because too many barbarians were drawn to his country by the quality of the wine. In modern times, the dry wines of interest are Odobesti, Cotesti and Panciu: the yellow-green nectar wines like Feteasca and Galbena are worth trying: after a bottle of Feteasca Neacra I felt like a man with twin souls—and I felt even better after a glass of Furmint, a wine with a honey tobacco flower bouquet.

Pre-war Bucharest as I remember it was the gayest, wickedest capital in the Balkans. Today the excitement has been chanelled into opera, ballet, the theatre, concerts and good food, though Bucharest still provides romantic meals with gipsy orchestras.

BILL OF FARE

Soup

BUCHAREST HOT POT
Vegetable broth soup with smoked sausages

Fish

CARP UMPLUT MAMAIA
Stuffed carp wrapped in pancakes and baked

SCORCOLEA
Walnut paste

Vegetables and Cereals

MAMALIGA
Corn pudding

MAMALIGA GNOCCHI
A poached version with sauce

GHIVECIU CALUGARESCU
Fricassee of vegetables

Meat Dishes

MICI
A sort of sausage shaped hamburger

Sweet

KACHA RUMANIA
Semolina pudding with a fresh apricot sauce
    flavoured with plum brandy liqueur

SOUP

BUCHAREST HOT POT
Vegetable broth soup with smoked sausages

Ingredients:

Lard 3 oz (90 g)
3 oz (90 g) each of the following cut in fine
    julienne or strips: beef, celery, leeks, onions,
    cabbage, carrots, turnips
5 oz (150 g) each of the following cut in small
    cubes: potatoes, tomatoes, red peppers
Sliced frankfurters 5 oz (150 g)
Bay leaf
Rosemary
Salt and pepper
Yoghurt 5 fl oz (150 mls)
1 lemon cut in wedges
Water 3½ pint (2,100 mls)

Method: Cut beef and cooked frankfurters in thin
strips and pan fry in lard for few minutes, then
add thinly shredded cabbage, onions, peppers,
turnips, carrots, leeks and celery. Simmer 8 minutes
then add sliced potatoes, tomato pulp and herbs.
Cover with water and simmer gently for 1 hour
until meat is tender. Season and serve with yoghurt
and wedge of lemon separately.
Note: Strips of cooked beetroot can be used as
garnish too.

FISH

CARP UMPLUT MAMAIA
Stuffed carp wrapped in pancakes and baked

Ingredients:

1 carp 3½ lb (1,680 g)

Stuffing:

Crumbs 5 oz (150 g)
Fried onions 5 oz (150 g)
Chopped herbs (parsley, chives) 1 oz (30 g)
Sliced olives 2 oz (60 g)
2 eggs

Salt and pepper
White wine 6 fl oz (180 mls)
4 large cooked pancakes 8 inch diameter
Fish stock 1 pint (600 mls)

Method: Clean and scrape scales of fish. Split open
the fish from the back so that it will hold from the
belly flap. Remove bone and season. Spread the
stuffing and fold the fish to reconstitute it to its
original form. Wrap the fish in several cooked
pancakes, or a large one. Place on a greased shallow
dish and add enough fish stock and white wine to
baste the fish during cooking. Cover with a lid and
bake in a moderate oven for 40 minutes. Serve in
same liquor.

Filling: Mix chopped cooked onions and sliced
olives with crumbs and herbs and seasoning. Add
eggs to bind mixture.
Stock: Boil in 1 pint water fish bones and head
together with sliced onions for 20 minutes. Strain
and season.
    The fish liquor can be thickened lightly with
a roux or a slurry of cornflour and water. Serve
with Scorcolca (the walnut paste).

SCORCOLE A
Walnut paste

Ingredients:

Walnut meat 1 lb (480 g) same weight of white
    bread crumbs
Milk ½ pint (300 mls)
Oil 3½ fl oz (100 mls)
Juice of 2 lemons
Salt and pepper

Method: Soak bread crumbs in milk, add walnut
and pound mixture to a paste or use a liquidiser.
Gradually add oil and lemon juice. Season and
pass through a sieve if required of a finer texture.
Not necessary if you have used a liquidiser.

VEGETABLES AND CEREALS

MAMALIGA
Corn pudding

Ingredients:

Cornmeal ½ lb (240 g)
Butter or oil 2 oz (60 g)
Water ½ pint (300 mls)
Milk 6 fl oz (180 mls)
Salt

Method: Rub a little oil or melted butter in
cornmeal then add the water and milk and boil
for 15 minutes till cooked. Season with a pinch
of salt. Serve hot with cream or milk or with
grated cheese or poached eggs or as a garnish for
meat or fish.

MAMALIGA FRIED

Method: Simply pass the cold small cooked pieces
in flour then in beaten eggs and in crumbs and
fry like croquettes.

MAMALIGA GNOCCHI
Poached version with sauce

Ingredients:

Cooked mamaliga 1 lb (480 g)
2 eggs
Grated cheese 3 oz (90 g)
1 clove of garlic

Method: Prepare the same mixture as above but
when cooked add two beaten eggs, and pour
mixture on oiled or greased tray. Cool. When cold
cut in small oblong pieces. Place on another tray
well apart. Sprinkle grated cheese and brown
under grill. The mixture can be flavoured with a
little garlic.

GHIVECIU CALUGARESCU
Fricassee of vegetables

Ingredients:

Oil 4 oz (120 g)
4 oz (120 g) each of the following:
    Aubergines
    Peppers
    Onions
    Potatoes
    Carrots
    Celery
    Cabbage
    Lady fingers
    Cauliflower sprigs
Garlic (10 g)
Peeled tomatoes 5 oz (150 g)
Chopped parsley 1 tbs
Mixture of chopped fennel and chives 2 oz (60 g)
1 bouquet garni
Meat or chicken stock or water 2½ pint (1,500 mls)
Lentils, peas, leeks, green beans 4 oz (120 g) each

Method: Saute the diced vegetables in oil with a
lid on saucepan. Tossing from time to time. Add
a little stock after 10 minutes and cook gently for
15 minutes until vegetables are tender. Season to
taste. Vegetables can be baked in a casserole dish
instead but for 40 minutes with the lid on.
Note: All vegetables should be fresh and tender,
peeled and diced uniformly, except carrots, leeks
and onions which should be thinly sliced or cut
in shreds.

MEAT DISHES

MICI
Type of sausage-shaped hamburger

Ingredients:

Minced beef 1 lb (480 g) plus
   2 oz (60 g) breadcrumbs
Pork or beef fat 4 oz (120 g)
Pinch cumin
Chopped garlic ¼ oz (7 g)
8 blanched rashers or bacon

Method: Mince all ingredients, except bacon rashers. Season and shape into balls 2 oz (60 g) each. Roll each ball into a sausage shape and wrap each one with a rasher of bacon, previously scalded in boiling water. Chill for 2 hours and pan fry like a sausage, or grill.

SWEET

KACHA RUMANIA
Semolina pudding with a fresh apricot sauce
  flavoured with plum brandy liqueur

Ingredients:

Semolina 5 oz (150 g)
Water ½ pint (300 mls)
Milk 1¾ pint (1 litre)
Sugar ½ lb (240 g)
Vanilla
4 yolks
4 egg whites
Chopped glacé fruits 4 oz (120 g)

Fruits:

Cherries, angelica, peels, ginger. etc.
  1 oz (30 g) of each

Sauce:

Sugar 3 oz (90 g)
Apricot jam 3 oz (90 g)
Same amount of water
Cornflour ½ oz (15 g)
Water 5 oz (150 mls)
Plum brandy liqueur 3 fl oz (90 mls)

Method: Stir in a bowl 5 oz (150 g) of fine semolina into ½ pint (300 mls) water. Boil the milk with the sugar and add semolina mixture and cook for 10 minutes. Stir in the egg yolks. Cool mixture in a bowl. Add vanilla. Beat the egg whites to a meringue and fold into mixture with chopped glacé fruits. Place mixture in well buttered pudding mould (angel cake or savarin mould). Bake at 360°F in a tray of water for 40 minutes. Rest a few minutes then turn on to a dish and pour apricot sauce flavoured with a plum brandy or apricot liqueur.

Sauce: Boil water, sugar and apricot, then thicken with slurry of cornflour and water till clear. Strain and add liqueur.

Bulgaria

The Bulgars are a long-lived race, with at least a few centenerians in every village. The secret of their long life is supposed to be hard work and yoghurt, and indeed they have given their name to the culture which turns milk into yoghurt: *cremolis bulgaricus*. Whatever the claims for this form of curdled milk, it is certain that centenerians could not live to their ripe old age without good food, and one suspects that the true secret of the Bulgarians' vigorous longevity is the simple, basic good food which is the national cuisine of their country. Coupled with an agricultural way of life which is in tune with the seasons, the simple diet of natural foods sustains a nation where a man of 100 still had all his faculties, and where, allegedly, a man of 60 starts a family as a matter of course.

Present-day Bulgaria is essentially a modern state, having little relation either territorially or socially to the Bulgar Empire of the ninth and tenth centuries.

The word 'Bulgar' means a cultivator or a ploughing peasant. Bulgaria has fertile lands with lagoons rich in fish, especially carp and sturgeon. Maize, tomatoes and peppers are grown extensively and form a large part of the diet. The wheat grown is excellent, and much is exported.

The nation started when the Bulgars, a race akin to the Huns and Abars, came westward behind the Huns during the great wave of migration from Asia into Europe. They found a fertile land and settled, a proud and individual race; the invasions of Turks gave her new ideas of cooking without taking away the individuality. So the strong flavours of Turkish cooking found no favour among this race. Yet some techniques were adopted, so that thin leaves of pastry stuffed with cheese or vegetables are now almost a national dish; but while they may melt in the mouth, they could never be mistaken for the Turkish version.

No wonder then that one of the national emblems of this small, aloof and independent country is the rare *Balkanska Zvezda*, a form of edelweiss and a symbol of stubborn pride. From her neighbours, whether friend or foe, she has chosen according to her needs. For five hundred years Bulgaria withstood the pervading influence of Turkish cooking, yet openly adopted the essence of Greek gastronomy. From her Slavonic neighbours she has borrowed techniques and ingredients and distilled them into something which has a definite identity in spite of an inevitable overlap between gastronomic boundaries.

Bulgaria is a small country, but her landscape is very varied. Some say it is the original horn of plenty, and where there is abundance, there is joy and merrymaking. Every nook and cranny of the country is covered with luxuriant grasses and fragrant herbs. Her flocks are vast and well-tended, and as in the rest of the Balkan countries, the national dish is lamb and potatoes.

In the homes of the country people, the hearth takes pride of place in the house. From it hangs a chain to which a cauldron is attached; from it issue tantalising odours, for there is always something simmering. This is where the diligent Bulgarian housewife officiates. On her way to and from the fields, she gathers various aromatic herbs like wild garlic, thyme, bay leaves, chillies and peppers, and neatly ties them in bunches over the hearth. Herbs, fresh in summer, dried in winter, are used in most dishes; it is impossible to think of fresh dill and not think of the Bulgarian cold soup *tarator*. The herb savory is used for a rich, sustaining lentil soup; caraway seeds are used in bread and cakes; jams from the aromatic fruits are given an added dimension with geranium leaves. As in every agricultural country, the housewife is the creator of the national cuisine.

The characteristics are not based on strong flavourings, as is Turkish and Indian food, but on its wholesomeness. The ingredients are of the finest quality, utilised to preserve their succulence, colour, texture and flavour. Braising in fat or pot-roasting is used to combine the flavours of meat and vegetables. The food is extremely nutritive and rich in protein. Special dishes are prepared for particular holidays: baked carp with nuts for St Nicholas' Day; many types of pork dishes at Christmas; roast lamb for St George's Day; roast capon on St Peter's Day. Big dinner tables are set, the family assembles and the wine flows. Everyone welcomes everyone else with the pick of his kitchen pot. Festive tables are still set under the vines in fields and meadows during the hot summer. The tables are covered with embroidered or handwoven gaily coloured spreads. Traditional breads are prepared – *vechernik* for Christmas Eve, *ovcharnik* for the shepherds,

pogacha, a family ritual bread with meaningful patterns, figures and unique designs.

In the Rhodope Mountains are the ruins of Dionysius' sanctuary – a reminder that Bulgaria was once as dedicated to the god of wines as the Greeks. Bulgaria produces some wines still, mainly for home consumption. The bialo vino are white wines of the hock type, the best among them Tcherpan and Evsinograd; the red ones to choose are Tcherveno Trakia or Mavroud. All over Central Europe, plums are distilled into potent brandy – and the Bulgarian Slivova is a real killer. For an aperitif, Boza is potent and pleasant, and would remind you of Pernod if it were not made of fermented sesame seeds. You buy it by the jugful and drink it by the hour.

With the expansion of the booming tourist industry, the national cuisine of Bulgaria is changing into an international gastronomic experience. The Americans and the British join the privileged holidaymakers from the Eastern European bloc in the new playground stretching from Sozopol to Balchik, where the Black Sea looks anything but sombre. But for a taste of old Bulgaria, wander through the meadows where the dill grows wild, and climb the ancient hills to seek the Balkanska Zvezda – the star of the Balkans. Until the scientists find why the Bulgars regularly live to be a hundred, enjoy the years you have!

BILL OF FARE

Soup

TARATOR
Cold cucumber and yoghurt soup

KURBAN CHORBA
Bulgarian mutton hot-pot

Hors d'Oeuvre

KYOPOOLOU
An aubergine spread flavoured with onions,
  tomatoes and peppers

BUREK
Fried stuffed aubergine

Meat Dishes

KEBACHES
Square veal and pork hamburgers, Bulgarian style

STOMNA
Bulgarian lamb casserole

KEBAB BULGARIAN STYLE
Cubes of lean meat charcoal grilled

POEK KAVARMA
Pork casserole in wine

SURMI
Vine leaves stuffed with meat and rice

Cheese Dishes

CHEESE A LA SHOPPE
Baked egg and cheese Bulgarian style

CHEESE FLAN
Cheese and egg custard flan

BULGARIAN CHEESE PIE
Baked cheese in puff pastry

Sweets and Desserts

TIKVENIK
Pumpkin flan Bulgarian style

YEAST POGACHA
Bulgarian ritual bread

MLIN
Bulgarian buns

SOUP

TARATOR
Cold cucumber and yoghurt soup

Ingredients:

Cucumber ½ lb (240 g)
Yoghurt ½ pint (300 mls)
Water ¼ pint (120 mls)
Vegetable oil 1 oz (30 g)
Juice and grated rind of 1 lemon
1 garlic clove
Salt and pepper
Chopped parsley 1 tbs
Walnuts 3 oz (90 g)

Method: Peel and remove seeds from cucumber.
Cut in small cubes. Place in a bowl. Dilute
yoghurt and water, add seasoning and flavouring
and mix with cucumbers. Serve with chopped
walnuts and parsley on top.

KURBAN CHORBA
Bulgarian mutton hot-pot

Ingredients:

Diced lean lamb or mutton 6 oz (180 g)
Diced lamb or mutton lung or liver 6 oz (180 g)
Water 5 pint (3,000 mls)
1 bouquet garni
Vegetable oil 2 oz (60 g)
Chopped onions 3 oz (90 g)
Flour 2 oz (60 g)
Tomato puree 2 oz (60 g)
Salt and pepper
Pinch paprika and marjoram and chillies, mint
Rice 2 oz (60 g)
Chopped parsley 1 tbs
2 eggs

Method: Bring lamb to the boil. Remove scum and
boil for 1 hour. Add diced liver or lung with
bouquet garni. Simmer for another 30 minutes.
Strain the broth. Keep the meat in a shallow dish.

Fry in fat the chopped onions and peppers for
few minutes without browning. Then add flour
to absorb fat and produce a roux. Cook few
minutes. Gradually add 2 pint of the meat stock.
Bring to boil and simmer. Add seasoning.

Boil rice in 1 pint remaining stock for 20
minutes. When cooked add all ingredients: meat,
rice and thickened broth.

Peel and remove seeds from 4 tomatoes. Dice
the pulp and add to soup for colour. Check
seasoning.

In the soup tureen beat two eggs thoroughly,
add a cupful of soup while whisking mixture and
rest of soup just before serving. Sprinkle chopped
parsley and fresh mint or fresh marjoram. The
addition of powder or pod chillies is left to the
discretion of the guest as it is powerfully hot and
burning.

HORS D'OEUVRE

KYOPOOLOU
An aubergine spread flavoured with onions,
tomatoes and peppers

Ingredients:

Aubergines (eggplants) 1 lb (480 g)
Green peppers 4 oz (120 g)
Large tomatoes 8 oz (240 g)
Chopped spring onions 4 oz (120 g)
Vegetable oil 4 fl oz (120 mls)
Chopped garlic 5 g
Stoned green olives 2 oz (60 g)
Lemon juice 1 fl oz (30 g)
1 lemon
Salt and pepper
White vinegar 1 fl oz (30 g)
Sour cream 3 fl oz (90 mls)
Breadcrumbs 3 oz (90 g)

Method: Bake aubergine for 20 minutes till soft.
Cut in two and scoop the pulp. Place it in a bowl.
Split the peppers. Remove seeds and grill them
outwardly for few minutes, remove skin and cut
in small cubes or chop them finely. Add skinned
and seeded tomato, garlic and rest of ingredients.
Pound to a paste or liquidise the mixture to
obtain a well emulsified mixture. Check seasoning
and serve with sippets of toasted bread.

BUREK
Fried stuffed aubergines

Ingredients:

4 medium-sized aubergines
Seasoned flour 2 oz (60 g)
Frying oil

Stuffing:

Cream cheese 5 oz (150 g)
Chopped walnuts 5 oz (150 g)
Chopped garlic (10 g)
Salt and pepper
3 beaten eggs
Breadcrumbs 5 oz (150 g)

Sauce:

Yoghurt 8 fl oz (240 mls)
Chopped dill, a pinch

Method: Split the aubergines lengthwise. Make cut into the pulp with point of a knife. Season with salt and let moisture exhude for 20 minutes. Wash and wipe dry. Pass in seasoned flour then fry few minutes to soften the pulp. Drain. Scoop pulp into a bowl, add cream cheese and chopped walnuts and 1 beaten egg. Season with chopped garlic, salt and pepper. Place a spoonful of this mixture inside the aubergine skin. Shape the skin like a cigar. Pass in seasoned flour then in beaten eggs and breadcrumbs. Fry in deep fat for 5 minutes. Serve with yoghurt flavoured with chopped dill or garlic.

MEAT DISHES

KEBACHES
Square veal and pork hamburgers Bulgarian style

Ingredients:

Lean veal ½ lb (240 g)
Lean pork ½ lb (240 g)
Cumin seed, a pinch
Salt and pepper
Oil for grilling 5 fl oz (150 mls)

Garnish:

Large onions 1 lb (480 g)
Red and green peppers ½ lb (240 g)
1 cucumber
4 tomatoes
Oil and vinegar salad dressing 5 fl oz (150 mls)

Method: Mince veal and pork, flavour with cumin and a little salt (5 g only). Refrigerate for 1 hour. Shape into 4 oz balls approx. Flatten the ball lightly and square the edges to have burgers 2½ by 1 by 2½ inches. Brush with oil and charcoal grill till cooked (10 minutes).

Split peppers and grill them. Peel the skin and cut into shreds. Season with oil and vinegar as for a salad garnish.

Cut the onions horizontally in thin rings, pass in seasoned flour and fry in deep fat or saute in the pan till tender and brown. Serve also as a garnish, tomato and cucumber salad.

STOMNA
Bulgarian lamb casserole

Ingredients:

Diced lean lamb from shoulder 1 lb (480 g)
Oil 3 fl oz (90 g)
Flour 2 oz (60 g)
Onions cut into rings ½ lb (240 g)
Chopped parsley, mint and savory herb
  (Sarriette) 1 tbs
2 cloves of garlic
Tomato puree 2 oz (60 g)
Water 3 pint (1,800 mls)
Salt and pepper
Pinch cayenne or chillies (optional)

Method: Brown meat in hot oil for five minutes, add onions and cover with a lid. Stir well and after ten minutes transfer meat and onions without the oil into an earthenware casserole. In same oil make a roux with flour. Cook to a pale brown, add tomato puree and gradually stir in 3 pint of boiling water. Simmer the mixture 10 minutes, add seasoning and herbs and pour over the meat. Cover with a lid and braise in oven for 2 hours moderate heat 360°F. The surplus gravy can be used for soup or sauce.

LAMB KEBAB BULGARIAN STYLE
Cubes of lean meat charcoal grilled

Ingredients:

Lean lamb from loin or from thick part of leg,
  known as the topside or cushion cut
  1 lb (480 g) net weight

Marinade:

White wine ½ pint (300 mls)
White vinegar 2 oz (60 mls)
Oil 2 fl oz (60 mls)
Coriander seeds and leaves 1 oz (30 g)
Pinch cumin, black pepper, salt and sugar
Few fresh mint leaves

Onions cut in quarters and segmented into layers
  ½ lb (240 g)
2 crushed cloves of garlic

Oil for brushing
Skewers (9 inch long)

Method: Place 1 inch cubes of meat in a bowl and
cover with marinade liquid. Stir well and leave to
soak overnight. Dry and impale meat on skewers
with alternate layers of onion cut the same size.
Sprinkle seasoning. Brush oil and charcoal grill
10 minutes or until tender or pan fry or bake in a
hot oven according to the cooking apparatus
available. Use marinade to baste the kebab during
cooking. Boil the rest for 10 minutes and use it as
a gravy.

POEK KAVARMA
Pork casserole in wine

Ingredients:

Lean pork meat cut in 1 inch cubes 1 lb (480 g)
Lard or oil 3 oz (90 g)
Seasoned flour 2 oz (60 g)
Leeks 1 lb (480 g)
Tomato puree 2 oz (60 g)
White wine ½ pint (300 mls)
Water ½ pint (300 mls)
1 bouquet garni
1 clove of garlic

1 tbs chopped mint and parsley
Salt and pepper (black)
Pinch of chilli pepper

Method: Clean leeks. Pass the meat in seasoned
flour. Heat lard or oil in a pan and saute meat
till brown, covered with a lid for 10 minutes.
Stir well and transfer meat into a casserole dish.
Saute without browning the sliced leeks. Add
sauted leeks to meat, tomato puree, wine,
seasoning and bouquet garni. Add water, cover
with a lid and braise in moderate oven for 2 hours
at 360°F.

SURMI
Vine leaves stuffed with meat and rice

Ingredients:

Chopped onions 5 oz (150 g)
Long rice 5 oz (150 g)
Lard or oil 3 oz (90 g)
Paprika ¼ oz (7 g)
Turmeric one pinch
Tomato puree 2 oz (60 g)
Water 1 pint (600 mls)
Minced raw lamb, beef or veal 1 lb (480 g)
Fresh or tinned vine leaves (16 leaves)
Water or stock made with beef bouillon cubes
  1 pint (600 mls)
1 clove of garlic

Method: Heat oil or lard in a saucepan and saute
chopped onions without browning for few minutes,
add rice and stir well. Pour water and rest of
ingredients (except meat and vine leaves)
to flavour rice mixture. Boil 20 minutes
until rice is cooked and water evaporated.
Cool. Blend meat and rice. Check seasoning and
divide mixture into 16 balls. Boil fresh vine
leaves 5 minutes in salted water, refresh and dry
(or use canned vine leaves). Place a ball on each
leaf. Wrap it round neatly and arrange the 'Surmi'
on a shallow dish, each tightly packed against each
other. Cover with bouillon or broth or with garlic
or water. Season and braise in a moderate oven
for 45 minutes, covered with a lid. The Surmi
can be eaten hot or cold.

CHEESE DISHES

CHEESE A LA SHOPPE
Baked egg and cheese Bulgarian style

Ingredients:

Any hard cheese grated 1 lb (480 g)
Butter 4 oz (120 g)
Oil 4 fl oz (120 mls)
Tomatoes skinned and seeded ½ lb (240 g)
Pinch paprika
4 eggs

Method: Use individual egg dishes. On each dish place 1 oz butter and oil. Add 4 oz grated cheese per portion. Heat in oven and add chopped tomatoes on each dish when cheese is melted. Break 1 egg on top and bake in hot oven until cooked. Dust over with paprika.

CHEESE FLAN BULGARIAN STYLE
Cheese and egg custard flan

Ingredients:

Pastry:

Flour 8 oz (240 g)
Margarine 4 oz (120 g)
1 egg

Filling:

Butter 4 oz (120 g)
Chopped spring onions 2 oz (60 g)
Cream cheese 4 oz (120 g)
Yoghurt 4 fl oz (120 mls)
2 eggs
Salt and white pepper
Pinch of paprika

Method: Make a short pastry by rubbing flour and margarine and blend with one egg. Rest pastry 15 minutes. Roll to ¼ inch thick and line an 8 inch flan tin well greased with lard or margarine.

Cream butter and cheese, add beaten eggs and chopped spring onions. Season, blend yoghurt and fill flan with this mixture. Bake first 10 minutes at 400°F and at 380°F for 25 minutes. Serve with a jug of yoghurt.

BULGARIAN CHEESE PIE
Baked cheese in puff pastry

Ingredients:

Puff pastry 1 lb (480 g)

Filling:

Butter 4 oz (120 g)
Cream or grated cheese ½ lb (240 g)
Yoghurt 4 fl oz (120 mls)
2 eggs
Pinch paprika and pepper

Yoghurt custard mixture:

Yoghurt ½ pint (300 mls)
2 eggs
Soda water 5 fl oz (150 mls)

Method: Roll out the puff pastry thinly ⅛ inch. Cut two oblong pieces the size of an oblong tray 3 inch deep. Grease the tray and line with pastry. Prick the bottom — bake blind 15 minutes at 400°F. Cool.
Filling: Blend butter and cream with yoghurt and beaten eggs, season with paprika and pepper. Spread this cheese mixture on the pastry layer. Cover with the second layer. Prick the top with the prongs of a fork at several places. Bake the cheese pie at 400°F for 20 minutes. Reduce heat down to 360°F.

Blend the beaten eggs and yoghurt and soda. Pour this custard mixture over the raised pie and bake for another 20 minutes to set the custard at 360°F.

Make sure you have a tray 3 inch deep at least, as the pastry of the pie will rise to 1½ to 2 inches (4 cm).

SWEETS and DESSERTS

TIKVENIK
Pumpkin flan Bulgarian style

Ingredients:

Puff pastry ½ lb (240 g)

Filling:

Pumpkin pulp 1 lb (480 g)
Honey 6 oz (180 g)
Chopped fresh ginger ¼ oz (8 g)
Water ½ pint (300 mls)
Rind and juice of 1 lemon
Chopped walnuts 3 oz (90 g)
Pinch cinnamon
4 eggs

Method: Cook diced pumpkin pulp with honey
and water until tender for 15 minutes. Cool.
Blend chopped ginger, cinnamon, walnuts, lemon
juice and rind and stir in the beaten eggs. Place
mixture in a large oblong dish, 9 inch by 5 inch.

Roll out puff pastry ¼ inch thick. Use
to cover pumpkin mixture. Brush top with
beaten egg. Let it rest in kitchen temperature
for 30 minutes before baking. With the point of a
knife make a criss-cross pattern on top and crimp
edges. Bake at 400°F for 25 minutes.

The same pie can be done with short pastry if
required. Serve with yoghurt.

YEAST POGACHA
Ritual Bulgarian bread

Ingredients:

Strong flour 1 lb (480 g)
Yeast ½ oz (15 g)
Lukewarm milk ½ pint (300 mls)
Sugar ½ oz (15 g)
Butter ½ oz (15 g)
Salt ¼ oz (7 g)
Caraway seeds ¼ oz (7 g)
1 egg

Method: Crumble yeast into lukewarm milk and
stir to disperse it evenly. Add sugar and salt and
blend into flour and butter to obtain a smooth
dough. Knead and roll into a ball. Rest 35 minutes
covered with a basin upside down. Knead again.
Shape like a large ball as tight as you can roll it.
Allow to rest 15 minutes. Flatten the ball to 2
inch high (5 cm) and about ⅞ inch diameter.
Place it on a greased tray, with fingers, make
few holes on top. Brush with beaten eggs and

sprinkle caraway seeds all over. Rest 30 minutes
before baking to recover and swell. Bake at 400°F
for 30 minutes.

MLIN
Bulgarian buns

Ingredients:

Strong flour 1 lb (480 g)
Yeast ½ oz (15 g)
Lukewarm milk ½ pint (300 mls)
2 eggs
Butter 2 oz (60 g)
Sugar 2 oz (60 g)
Pinch salt
Scalded and drained seedless raisins 3 oz (90 g)

Glazing:

Icing sugar 5 oz (150 g)
Hot water 2 fl oz (60 mls)
Aniseed liquor or essence, few drops

Method: Crumble yeast in milk, add beaten eggs,
sugar, and salt to flour to form a stiff dough.
Knead well and form into a ball. Rest for 30
minutes covered with an upside down basin.
Knead again with soft butter and add raisins.
Distribute them evenly while kneading the dough
which should be softer to handle. Roll into a ball
again. Cover with a basin upside down and rest
for 15 minutes. Divide mixture into 2 oz (60 g)
buns. Shape each one to a ball. Place on a greased
tray at regular intervals and allow to recover for
another 20 minutes. Bake at 400°F for 20 minutes.

Meanwhile, melt icing sugar and water, add
aniseed liquor. Brush each bun with this mixture
while the buns are still hot. Cool and serve
with coffee.

Poland

Polish feasts have been famous since the reign of Poland's first crowned king, Boleslaw Chrobry (the brave). When he was host to Otto III, ruler of half Europe, Boleslaw made Otto a gift of all the precious gold, silver and tin platters which had been used to bring the feast to the table. But there was one item that Boleslaw would not share: the spices, more precious than gold, which were kept in heavy wooden chests in the custody of a specially appointed spice keeper. This royal office was started by King Casimir the Great in 1454 and existed until the end of the sixteenth century. Until the middle the of the sixteenth century, the dining was simple yet good; bouillon, *barscz* (beetroot soup), *zur* (a very acid broth), boiled meat, collops, tripe, sausages, *bigos hultajski* ('Rogues' bigos' — a sauerkraut and meat dish), *kolduny* (meat turnover), *pierogi* (dumplings) and *kluski* (noodles). At more sumptuous feasts, guests were served giant geese in cream, or roasted with a black gravy dyed with a wisp of burnt straw. Dessert dishes were sweetened with honey, as sugar was not yet known.

Polish gastronomy took a new turn in the middle of the sixteenth century when the second wife of King Sigismund, Bona Sforza d'Aragona, came to Poland from Spain and brought her own cooks. Now vegetables came into their own, and Jan Sobieski, who vanquished the Turks at the battle of Vienna, introduced potatoes. But roast bison and buffalo were still favourite meats, along with bears' paws, beaver tails, elk's nostrils, venison braised in acid wines with sauces flavoured with wild berries and strong herbs.

Later, the tables of the Polish nobles were famous for their refinement and elegance, with dishes from Italy, France, Russia, Turkey, Hungary and Austria, slightly adapted to the Polish tastes. These were accompanied by beers, mead and wegrzyn, a Hungarian wine of the Tokay family. Amongst the most popular dishes in the eighteenth century were the extravagant 'pieces montees' confectionery often on a cloud of spun sugar, six feet high and with ornaments and details like rococo or baroque buildings. But the Poles have always had a sweet tooth, and in more simple vein, one of the traditions in the country is a 'sweet supper' given by bridegrooms-to-be on the eve of the wedding.

Modern Poland has an intensive agricultural economy, producing rye, potatoes, milk and dairy products, and with extensive stock breeding. Pork and beef are used extensively, supplemented by game from the forests: deer, boar, grouse, wild duck and geese are festive fare. Also from the forests come wild mushrooms in great variety, used to garnish meat, as vegetables in their own right, and dried and pickled for winter. Cucumbers fermented in dill are a Polish speciality which is fast gaining international fame. The lactose of the cucumber changes into lactic acid, thus preserving the fresh crispness. It is an entirely different process from pickling in vinegar, although both processes are used in central Europe. Fresh cucumbers are also popular, as salad in yoghurt or sour cream (*mizeria*) traditionally served with chicken and Polish stuffing.

The last time I was in Poland, I landed in Gdynia on my way to Leningrad. I shall never forget the reception we had, nor the potent wines and cocktails which hit us like a firing squad. My host lectured me on Polish gastronomy and Karl Marx in roughly equal quantities, taught me that in Poland vodka is always served on ice with appetisers, and supported me on my homeward way when a Francophile barman destroyed me with a cherry brandy-vodka concoction which he named *Roza Warsaw*, in my honour. But I recovered rapidly and enjoyed the food of Poland: the *bigos*, the *pyzy* (potato dumplings), carp, *polewka kminkowa* (caraway soup) and *kissel* (berry fruits pulped and thickened with potato flour).

Of course I was not the first Frenchman to be in tune gastronomically with Poland: Napoleon met Countess Marie Walewska over an Easter feast in Warsaw in May 1809, and decided to live with her while fighting the Russians. A special meat croquette made of the flesh of partridge was offered to him on a bed of pease pudding. He left the puree but asked for more *crepinette de perdreau*; and to his last days in his lonely exile on St Helena, he always demanded his favourite Polish *crepinette*. And it is said that the wretched man suffered all his life from indigestion and lack of love!

In Poland there is a sharp separation between food served in restaurants and the food of the ordinary people, found in the farmhouses where the mistress cooks not only for her family but all the workers on the farm. I was brought up in such surroundings, and believe you me, when that big soup tureen comes around with chunks of home-made bread — that is real food to me! real gastronomy; it is folklore cuisine and you can still find it in Poland today. There are soups like *zalewajka* (acid onion soup), *zur* (sour soup) and thick vegetable soups enriched with buckwheat, with diced sausages and bacon so thick the spoon will stand up. That type of nourishing, slow-simmered, aromatic soup is a meal in itself.

On the Polish farmhouse table you might find a thick rasher of boiled back gammon with *kopytka*, the local potato dumplings, *kaszanka* (black pudding and gruel sausage), potato pancakes and *bida* (poverty sausage), *parzybroda* (chin scalder — cabbages cooked with potatoes) or a plateful of knuckle of pork with peas, baked veal

shank, or dumplings with rich gravy. The peasants need no sweet course after such a meal. They down a cup of vodka and can work around the clock to boost the production of the Polish Democratic Republic; while we in Britain eat less and less and have not the strength to work for more than a plate of baked beans.

The haute cuisine of Poland conforms closely to the classic international gastronomy, yet with national overtones in the shape of traditions and customs. This in no way detracts from the excellence of the food — on the contrary, it makes it more interesting.

The cold buffet is popular in Poland, and among the cold side dishes one might find several river and lake fish: pike-perch in aspic, stuffed pike, smoked carp, salmon, and eel, marinaded fish in sour cream dressing, herrings and rollmops. There would be all kinds of pâtés and terrines, made of game, pork and poultry; stuffed meat rolls, suckling pig, pigs' trotters, smoked deer tenderloin, Polish sausages like *kabanosy* (long, thin and highly spiced) and *mysliwska* (hunter's sausage with pork and game); there could be smoked bacon and ham, and chicken and duck in aspic stuffed with foie gras. Hot side dishes might include braised pike and perch with mushrooms, carp in a semi-sweet black sauce with raisins, pilaff of fish and rice, *bigos* (sauerkraut and meat) or meat balls with prunes, or crayfish poached with dill.

Soups are extremely popular in this climate, where winter temperatures are usually below zero and a bowl of hot soup can thaw out a man faster than even a vodka. Borsch in all its variations is popular, with beetroot being the only constant ingredient; sorrel is used for a summer soup with a garnish of hard-boiled egg, but a soup based on pig's blood, dark like a jugged hare, is warming winter fare. Wild mushrooms make a light soup in summer and a spicy one in winter: the flavour of dried mushrooms intensifies. Buckwheat groats and barley are often used to thicken stews, and prunes are used to give a rich sweetness to sauces and stuffings. The Poles use raisins and nuts in a slightly acid sauce to serve with rich, soft-textured meats like tongue and heart. Meat is often stuffed to stretch it and make it more interesting, whether in a small way as in beef olives or in a full-sized roast.

Beans and peas are basic ingredients in many of the winter dishes. Pulses have been cultivated in Poland for many years, and are of excellent quality. They add richness, diminish the grease of many inexpensive cuts of meat, and have a high nutritive value in the form of protein.

Rabbits are now a big export item for Poland, but the tradition of keeping them for food goes back much further than the present industry. They are usually stewed in a rich sauce, or larded prior to roasting, as their flesh can be dry without careful cooking. However, it has the property of absorbing flavours, and the Poles take advantage of this by making the sauces interesting with aromatic vegetables, spices and herbs. Typically Polish flavours are dill, marjoram, caraway seeds, dried mushrooms and pickled vegetables of all kinds.

Vodka in all its forms is a national drink — and it seems to have more forms in Poland than even in Russia. One which brings tears to the eyes of expatriates is Zubrowka, flavoured by infusing with bison-grass, and always with a blade of the grass in the bottle. Others are kminkowka, with caraway seed, tarniowka, with sloe plums, krupnik, with honey and spices, marvellous on a cold night, and wisniowka, with black cherries and smelling of summer.

Wine is drunk with meals, and there is an interesting range of meads, made of honey, with the addition of suitable fruit juices: apple, rose-hip, blackthorn, raspberry, cherry, strawberry and juniper. Many of these are now exported, and a few sips while listening to a Chopin nocturne gives one a new appreciation of the sweet things of life.

BILL OF FARE

Soup

CLEAR BEET BARSZCZ
Clear beetroot soup

RYE ZUR
Rye sour soup

USZKA POLISH DUMPLINGS
Dumplings for soups

ZALEWAJKA
Acid onion soup

Hors d'Oeuvre

POLISH CHEESE PASTE
Cheese salad flavoured with caraway seeds

HERRING PASTE
Herring paste used as a spread

CHOPPED LIVER
Polish pate

HERRING IN SOUR CREAM
Soured herrings cut up in salad with sour cream

Fish

POLISH/JEWISH PIKE IN ASPIC
Gefillte type of dish

Meat Dishes

BRAINS POLISH STYLE
Fried brains with capers and chopped eggs

MEAT LOAF POLISH STYLE
Baked meat loaf served with sour cream

PORK AND CABBAGE RISSOLES
Rissoles made from pig's knuckle

KNEDLIKI
Bread and bacon dumplings

PYZY WARSAW
Potato and meat fritter

GRENADIN OF PORK CHOPIN
Fried pork chops with sour cream sauce

CHICKEN POLISH STYLE
Chicken fried in crumbs with a butter and egg
     crumbing

RABBIT POLISH STYLE
Cooked as for stew with a cream finish

DUCK POLISH STYLE
Marinaded braised duck with a cream sauce

POLISH BURGER MARITZA
Potato and lamb burger fried in crumbs

HARE POLISH STYLE
Casserole of hare with a cream finish

BACON AND CAULIFLOWER POLISH STYLE
Gammon served with cauliflower in a cheese sauce

BIGOS
The Polish national dish — pork, bacon and
     sauerkraut with mushrooms, tomato flavoured

Vegetables

POLISH CAULIFLOWER
Boiled cauliflower coated with an egg and crumb
     butter mixture

BEETS IN SOUR CREAM

KOHLRABI IN SOUR CREAM

KOPYTIKA
Potato dumplings

DILL CUCUMBER
Pickled cucumber Polish style

Cakes and Sweets

POLISH BABA
Yeast cake soaked in syrup

POLISH RING FRITTER
Fritter made with choux pastry shaped in a ring

MAZUREK
Almond cake

SOUR FLAKY MAZUREK
Fruit and almond cake

KISIELS
Fruit puree thickened with potato flour

SERNIK
Cheese flan

POLISH GINGERBREAD
Carrot flavoured gingerbread

MARMALADE POLISH ROLL
Sponge roly-poly stuffed with orange
　　marmalade

PACZKI
Polish yeast doughnuts

POLISH ALMOND CAKE
Rum flavoured cream tart

PREZEKLADANIEC
Polish Easter cake roll

SOUP

CLEAR BEET BARSZCZ
Clear beetroot soup

Ingredients:

Vinegar 5 fl oz (150 mls)
Water 2 pint (1,200 mls)
Small beetroots 1 lb (480 g)
Shin of beef 1 lb (480 g)
Leeks 2 oz (60 g)
Carrots 2 oz (60 g)
Swedes 2 oz (60 g)
Celery 2 oz (60 g)
Field mushrooms 2 oz (60 g)
Onions 2 oz (60 g)
1 clove garlic
1 bouquet garni
Salt and pepper
Beetroot juice 1 pint (600 mls) – fermented

Fermented juice:

Sliced peeled red beetroot 1 lb (480 g)
Water 3 pint (1,800 mls)
2 slices of rye bread
Sugar 8 oz (240 g)
Yeast 1 oz (30 g)

Method: Wash and peel beets, cut in slices and
boil in water and vinegar for 30 minutes. Strain
juice and keep. Cut beetroot in strips and add to
juice. Boil shin in 5 pints water, remove scum as
it rises. After 1½ hours add the thinly sliced
vegetables and boil for a further 30 minutes with
bouquet garni. When cooked, remove shin and
cut meat in small pieces or slices. Add the first
juice and red beetroot to soup and lastly add
1 pint of fermented beetroot juice.
Garnish: Meat pasties made with the beef, sour
cream, croutons, stuffed ravioli, potatoes, the
garnishes are endless.
Fermented juice: Crumble up yeast and place in
water at 80°F, add sugar, rye bread and slices of
raw red beetroot and the juice of cooked beetroot
to make up to 3 pints of liquid. Cover with a
polythene cloth and allow to ferment at a
temperature of 78°F to 80°F for 10 days. Strain
or filter. Bottle and keep in a refrigerator. This
is in fact an alcoholic drink which can be made
stronger by adding more sugar to the ratio of 3 lb
per 8 pints of liquid maximum. Absolutely clean
utensils and sterile ingredients should be used. For
safe measure, use Camden tablets to rinse equipment.
 Ordinary wine can be used as a substitute in
soup recipe.

RYE ZUR
Rye sour soup

This is fermented soup which is used as a soup
strengthener.

Ingredients:

Water 2 pint (1,200 mls)
Oats and rye meal 6 oz (180 g)
Yeast 1 oz (30 g)
Sugar 5 oz (150 g)
1 clove garlic

Method: Boil water and cool to 80°F. Crumble in
yeast and add sugar and garlic. Sprinkle in meal
and cover with a polythene cloth. Let ferment for
3 days at 80°F. Strain and filter. Use this
fermented type of beer to dilute your soups.

ISZKA POLISH DUMPLINGS
Dumplings for soups

Ingredients:

2 beaten eggs
Water 5 fl oz (150 mls)
Flour 1 lb (480 g)

Stuffing:

Chopped mushrooms 5 oz (150 g)
Chopped onions 2 oz (60 g)
Raw minced beef 8 oz (240 g)
Salt and pepper

Method: Blend beaten eggs and water with flour
to make a ravioli paste. Knead well and rest for
30 minutes. Roll like a thick salami 3 inch diameter
and cut in 1 oz slices. Flatten each slice and place

a ½ oz meatball made from stuffing ingredients on top and wrap round evenly into a ball. When all the paste is used up place in a tray half filled with soup broth. Poach for 12 minutes until the dumplings bob up. Drain and add to soup tureen.
Stuffing: Blend all ingredients together to a smooth but firm paste.

ZALEWAJKA
Acid soup onion

Ingredients:

Water 2 pint (1,200 mls)
Chopped or sliced onions 3 oz (90 g)
Lard 2 oz (60 g)
Sliced potatoes 6 oz (180 g)
Diced bacon 2 oz (60 g)
Sour Rye Zur 1 pint (600 mls)
Salt and pepper

Method: Fry chopped onion in lard without browning and add diced bacon. After a few minutes blend in sliced potatoes and then add water. Boil for 40 minutes and strain. Season. Add fermented rye zur. Serve the sour cream separately or add it to the soup.

HORS D'OEUVRE

POLISH CHEESE PASTE
Cheese salad flavoured with caraway seeds

Ingredients:

Cottage cheese 10 oz (300 g)
Cream cheese 5 oz (150 g)
1 level tsp of caraway seeds
Few lettuce leaves

Method: Blend two cheese together and add caraway seeds. Spoon on to lettuce leaves.

HERRING PASTE
Herring paste used as a spread

Ingredients:

Chopped roll-mops 10 oz (300 g)
Chopped onions 2 oz (60 g)
Chopped cucumber or pickled gherkins 1 oz (30 g)
Pinch of pepper
Double cream 3 fl oz (90 mls)

Method: Chop finely or mince all ingredients to a paste. Serve on lettuce leaves.

CHOPPED LIVER
Polish pâté

Ingredients:

Cooked chicken liver 10 oz (300 g)
2 hard-boiled eggs
1 raw egg
1 tsp made mustard
1 grated onion 1 oz (30 g)
Butter or chicken fat 3 oz (90 g)
6 anchovy fillets
Chopped chives 1 tbs
Salt and pepper

Method: Saute chicken liver in butter or chicken fat for 5 minutes with pan covered. Cool. When cold, chop finely and blend with raw egg, chives, mustard and grated onion, and then season. Serve on toast or lettuce leaves, garnished with hard-boiled eggs and anchovy fillets.

HERRING IN SOUR CREAM
Soured herrings cut up in salad with sour cream

Ingredients:

Smoked herring fillets 10 oz (300 g)
Hard-boiled eggs 2
Sour cream 5 fl oz (150 mls)
Chopped onions 1 oz (30 g)
White vinegar 1 fl oz (30 mls)
Sugar ½ oz (15 g)

Method: Desalt the smoked herrings in cold water for 3 hours. Rinse and dry. Mince herrings and blend all ingredients together. Serve on lettuce leaves.

FISH

POLISH/JEWISH PIKE IN ASPIC
Gefillte type of dish

Ingredients:

Pike or white mullet or bass 4 lb (1,920 g)
Breadcrumbs or matzo crumbs 3 oz (90 g)
Sugar ½ oz (15 g)
Salt ½ oz (15 g)
Ground pepper
Chopped onions 2 oz (60 g)
Butter 2 oz (60 g)
2 eggs
Pinch of grated nutmeg

Stock:

Water 4 pint (2,400 mls)
Sliced carrots 3 oz (90 g)
Sliced celery 2 oz (60 g)
Sliced onions 2 oz (60 g)
1 bouquet garni
Fish bones and skin
White vinegar 4 fl oz (120 mls)

Method: Scrape fish, gut and fillet. Retain skin
as it will be used for wrapping up minced fish.
Mince fish with all ingredients and blend into a
paste. Wash skin. Divide fish into large balls and
wrap each one with a piece of skin. Keep in
refrigerator for 1 hour. Boil ingredients for stock
for 30 minutes. Cool. Place fish in shallow dish,
cover with stock completely, cover dish with lid
and bake in a moderate oven for 20 minutes.
Season and serve with chopped horseradish pickle
and decorate with sliced cooked carrots from
stock. Serve in same stock.

MEAT DISHES

BRAINS POLISH STYLE
Fried brains with capers and chopped eggs

Ingredients:

4 calf's brains
White vinegar 2 fl oz (60 mls)
Water ½ pint (300 mls)

Polish batter mixture:

Butter 6 oz (180 g)
Breadcrumbs 2 oz (60 g)
1 chopped hard-boiled egg
1 tbs chopped parsley
Juice of 1 lemon
Salt and pepper

Method: Remove membrane from brains. Soak
in salted water and vinegar for 1 hour. Poach in
water for 8 minutes. Place in a shallow dish. Melt
butter and cook crumbs, add chopped egg and
pour over the brains. Squeeze lemon juice over
brains and sprinkle with chopped parsley. Season
to taste.

MEAT LOAF POLISH STYLE
Baked meat loaf served with sour cream

Ingredients:

Minced pork 8 oz (240 g)
Minced beef 8 oz (240 g)
Chopped onions 2 oz (60 g)
2 eggs
Breadcrumbs 2 oz (60 g)
Chopped parsley 1 tbs
Chopped garlic 1 clove
Salt and pepper

Sauce:

Chopped onion 1 oz (30 g)
White vinegar 1 fl oz (30 mls)
Water ½ pint (300 mls)
Sugar ½ oz (15 g)
Salt and pepper
Sour cream ½ pint (300 mls)
Pinch paprika
Pinch caraway seeds

Method: Combine all meats and ingredients
listed in first part. Grease an oblong dish 3 inch
deep by 6 inch long by 4 inch wide. Line with
cooked pancakes or leave plain. Fill with
mixture and place in a tray half filled with water
and bake for 1¼ hours at 360°F. Turn out onto
a dish. Serve with sour cream sauce, made as
follows: Boil chopped onions in water and vinegar

for 15 minutes. Season, add sour cream, sugar, paprika and caraway seeds and boil for a further 10 minutes. Strain and serve separately.

PORK AND CABBAGE RISSOLES
Rissoles made from pig's knuckles

Ingredients:

1 cabbage
1 knuckle of gammon (soaked overnight)
2 carrots
2 eggs
Breadcrumbs 6 oz (180 g)
Salt and pepper
Seasoned flour 2 oz (60 g)
Bacon fat for frying

Method: Boil pig's knuckle, cabbage and carrots together for 2 hours until meat is tender. Drain when cool. Mince the meat (rindless), cabbage and carrots together and add the crumbs and eggs. Season to taste. Shape into 2 oz (60 g) balls, pass each ball in seasoned flour and pan fry in bacon fat until golden on both sides.

KNEDLIKI
Bread and bacon dumplings

Ingredients:

Diced bacon 8 oz (240 g)
Breadcrumbs 8 oz (240 g)
Lard 2 oz (60 g)
Self-raising flour 8 oz (240 g)
2 eggs
Salt and pepper
Stock ½ pint (300 mls)

Method: Fry diced bacon in lard for a few minutes. Add crumbs and cook until flavoured and then remove. Blend in self-raising flour to mixture, and add eggs to form a stiff dough. Season. Shape the mixture into 1 oz (30 g) dumplings and steam or poach

in stock for 12 minutes in a shallow tray placed in the oven at 400°F.

PYZY WARSAW
Potato and meat fritter

Ingredients:

Chopped onions 4 oz (120 g)
Bacon fat or lard 1 oz (30 g)
Minced beef and pork meat 8 oz (240 g)
Salt and pepper
Chopped parsley 1 tbs
Raw grated potatoes 10 oz (300 g)
Mashed potatoes 10 oz (300 g)
Flour 1 oz (30 g)
Stock

Method: Fry chopped onions in lard until soft and brown. Cool. Blend onions to raw meat and add salt, black pepper and a little chopped parsley. Grate raw potatoes and squeeze out surplus moisture. Blend grated potatoes with sieved mashed potatoes and flour. Season. Shape into 1 oz (30 g) balls. Make a cavity in each ball and fill with a small ball of raw meat mixture. Form oval cakes and place in shallow dish half filled with stock. Bake at 400°F for 20 minutes.

GRENADIN OF PORK CHOPIN
Fried pork chop with sour cream sauce

Ingredients:

4 boneless pork chops 8 oz (240 g)
Sour cream ½ pint (300 mls)
Chopped onions 1 oz (30 g)
Salt 10 g
Pepper 1 g
Oil 2 fl oz (60 mls)

Method: Heat oil, saute the chops in a pan with a lid till cooked. Add chopped onions and simmer for a few minutes. Then add the cream and boil for 5 minutes. Season and serve.

CHICKEN POLISH STYLE
Chicken fried in crumbs with a butter and egg
crumbing

Ingredients:

4 raw chicken portions (from breast)
Breadcrumbs 4 oz (120 g)
2 eggs
Flour 2 oz (60 g)
Paprika 5 g
Caraway seeds 5 g
Chopped parsley 5 g
Butter 4 oz (120 g)
Oil 4 fl oz (120 mls)
Pinch pepper (2 g)
Juice of 1 lemon

Method: Remove skin from chicken. Pass in
unseasoned flour, then beaten eggs and rub crumbs
all over. Fry till golden in hot oil for 8 to 10
minutes. Drain. Transfer pieces to a dish and add
fresh melted butter and seasonings. Squeeze
lemon juice over and cover. Bake in oven for
10 minutes. Sprinkle with chopped parsley before
serving. Alternatively, the chicken can be baked
with half butter and oil in the oven.

RABBIT POLISH STYLE
Cooked as for stew with a cream finish

Ingredients:

1 rabbit loin and hind legs
Fat 2 oz (60 g)
Flour 1 oz (30 g)
Soured cream ½ pint (300 mls)
Salt

Marinade:

Vinegar 4 fl oz (120 mls)
Onions 2 oz (60 g)
Pimentoes 8 oz (240 g)
2 bay leaves
4-6 juniper berries
Water 2 pint (1,200 mls)

Method: Boil water with sliced onion, pimentoes
and spices, set aside to cool and add vinegar. Place
meat in an earthenware dish, pour the cold
marinade over the meat and keep in a cool place
for 2-4 days, turning the meat every day. Remove
meat from marinade, rinse, remove membrane, lard
the loin and add salt. Heat the fat in a roasting pan,
sprinkle the meat with fat and water and place in
a hot oven. Roast for about 2 hours, until tender,
basting frequently. Add water to thicken sauce.
Remove meat and cut into pieces. Arrange on
an oblong heated platter. Add flour to sauce,
bring to the boil, add soured cream and colour
with caramel. Add salt to taste. Pour sauce over
the meat. Serve either with potatoes, macaroni,
beetroots, bilberry jam, horseradish or red
cabbage salad.

DUCK POLISH STYLE
Marinaded braised duck with a cream sauce

Ingredients:

Duck 5 lb (2,400 g)
Sour cream ½ pint (300 mls)
Oil 2 fl oz (60 mls)
Flour 1 oz (30 g)
Onions 2 oz (60 g)
Allspice, pepper, salt, ginger and nutmeg
Wine vinegar ½ pint (300 mls)
Water ½ pint (300 mls)
Sugar 1 oz (30 g)
Bouillon cube 10 g

Method: Marinade duck in water and vinegar
with all the spices, sugar and seasoning. Soak
overnight. Wipe duck and roast at 400°F for
100 minutes. Keep duck warm. Boil marinade,
juice of duck and the sliced onion until
reduced by half. Add a bouillon cube and
check seasoning. Boil 10 minutes. Strain
gravy, then add cream and reboil for a few
minutes. Sauce should be sharp. Carve duck in
four portions, pour sauce over and serve with
oodles of potato dumplings.

Same procedure for hare, venison or any other
game. Vinegar may be replaced by red or white
wine.

POLISH BURGER MARITZA
Potato and lamb burger fried in crumbs

Ingredients:

Minced raw lamb 8 oz (240 g)
Mashed potatoes 6 oz (180 g)
Chopped fried onions 1 oz (30 g)
1 egg
Salt and pepper
Chopped garlic clove
Seasoned flour 1 oz (30 g)
2 eggs
Crumbs 2 oz (60 g)

Method: Mince the raw lamb and blend with
crumbs and mashed potatoes. Add seasoning,
chopped garlic, egg and chopped fried onions.
Shape into 2 oz (60 g) cakes. Pass in seasoned
flour, then beaten eggs and then crumbs. Fry in
oil till golden. Serve with a garlic tomato sauce.

HARE POLISH STYLE
Casserole of hare with a cream finish

Ingredients:

1 hare 6 lb (2,880 g)
Fat 2 oz (60 g)
Flour 2 oz (60 g)
Strip of lard to lard back of hare
Sour cream 5 fl oz (150 mls)
Seasoning

Marinade:

Thickly sliced carrot 5 oz (150 g)
Thickly sliced onions 5 oz (150 g)
Garlic 5 g
1 bouquet garni
Red wine ½ pint (300 mls)
Wine vinegar 2 fl oz (60 mls)
6 juniper berries
Tomato puree 1 oz (30 g)

Method: Cut hare in three pieces; front legs, back
and hind legs. Marinade hare for 24 hours in a
suitable vessel. Leave in refrigerator. Dry hare,
pass in seasoned flour and then rub with melted
pork fat. Season. Roast for 45 minutes at 400°F.

Prepare sauce. Pan fry onions and carrots till
brown, add tomato puree and garlic and then
flood with marinade juice. Boil for 45 minutes and
strain. Thicken mixture with a roux: 1 oz fat and
1 oz flour cooked till grainy in texture and then
added to sauce. Add pinch of rosemary, black
pepper and salt to taste. Strain sauce, reheat and
add sour cream at last minute. Carve the back
piece of hare in thin slices and cut legs in two to
obtain 4 pieces.
Butchery method: Remove the skin of the back
and loin of the hare before cooking. With a larding
needle insert strips of lard along the back, one at a
time 2 inch long so that both ends are shown.
Otherwise after the skin has been removed from
the hare wrap the back with strips of bacon before
roasting.

BACON AND CAULIFLOWER POLISH STYLE
Gammon served with cauliflower in a cheese sauce

Ingredients:

4 gammon steaks 8 oz (240 g) each
1 large cauliflower 3 lb (1,440 g)

Sauce:

Cheese sauce 1 pint (600 mls)
Chopped parsley 1 tbs
Caraway seeds 1 tsp
Grated cheese 2 oz (60 g)

Method: Boil cauliflower in salted water for 20
minutes. Place in a shallow dish and coat with
cheese sauce. Sprinkle with grated cheese and
caraway seeds and brown under the grill.
Sprinkle with chopped parsley and serve with
grilled gammon.

BIGOS
The Polish national dish — pork, bacon and
 sauerkraut with mushrooms, tomato flavoured

Ingredients:

Canned sauerkraut 1 lb (480 g)
White cabbage 5 oz (150 g)
Diced pork from shoulder 1 lb (480 g)

4 pork sausages
Chopped onions 2 oz (60 g)
Pork fat 2 oz (60 g)
Clove of garlic
Sliced mushrooms 5 oz (150 g)
Tomato puree 2 oz (60 g)
Water 1 pint (600 mls)
Salt and pepper
1 bouquet garni
Flour ½ oz (15 g)

Roux:

Flour 1 oz (30 g)
Lard 1 oz (30 g)

Method: Wash sauerkraut and drain. Place in a
saucepan with water, add fresh shredded cabbage,
sliced mushrooms, garlic, chopped onions and
tomato puree. Cover and boil. Brown meat in fat,
sprinkle with flour and seasoning and add water to
cover it. Add bouquet garni. Simmer for 1 hour
and add to sauerkraut. Pan fry sausages and add
to the dish. When cooked, strain off the juice
and thicken it with a roux: fat and flour cooked
to a semi-brown and diluted with meat stock.
Strain and blend with mixture. There should
be very little sauce in the Bigos, just enough to
keep it moist. Season to taste.

VEGETABLES

POLISH CAULIFLOWER
Boiled cauliflower coated with an egg and crumb
    butter mixture

Ingredients:

Cauliflower 3 lb (1,440 g)
Water 3 pint (1,800 mls)
Vinegar 2 fl oz (60 mls)
Butter 8 oz (240 g)
Breadcrumbs 4 oz (120 g)
2 chopped hard-boiled eggs
Chopped parsley 1 tbs
Juice of 1 lemon

Method: Clean, remove unwanted leaves and
slightly hollow out core of cauliflower. Boil in
water and vinegar for 20 minutes. Drain and break
up into sprigs. Place on a dish and cover with
following mixture: Fry crumbs, chopped eggs,
parsley and lemon juice in butter for 1 minute
only. Pour this mixture over the cauliflower.

BEETS IN SOUR CREAM

Ingredients:

Young beetroots 1 lb (480 g)
Butter 2 oz (60 g)
Vinegar 5 fl oz (150 mls)
Sugar 1 oz (30 g)
Salt and pepper
Sour cream ½ pint (300 mls)
Cornflour ½ oz (15 g)

Method: Wash and boil beetroots. Peel and slice,
blend with vinegar, butter, sugar and 5 fl oz water.
Season. Thicken with cream and cornflour slurry
and boil for 5 minutes.

KOHLRABI IN SOUR CREAM

Ingredients:

Kohlrabi 1 lb (480 g)
Butter 2 oz (60 g)
Chopped onions 1 oz (30 g)
Water 1 pint (600 mls)
Sour cream ½ pint (300 mls)
Cornflour 1 oz (50 g)
Salt and pepper
Pinch of caraway seeds

Method: Peel kohlrabi, cut in slices or cubes and
toss in butter. Add water and cook with onions for
15 minutes. Thicken with a cream and cornflour
slurry and boil for 5 minutes. Season and add
caraway seeds.

KOPYTKA
Potato dumplings

Ingredients:

Mashed potatoes 1 lb (480 g)
Flour ½ lb (240 g)
1 egg
Salt and pepper
Butter 4 oz (120 g)

Method: Blend mashed potatoes and flour with beaten egg to form a stiff dough. Season to taste. Form into a ball and divide into small dumplings 1 oz (30 g) each. Flatten balls and make a well in the middle. Heat water in a tray and poach dumplings until they bob up afrer 8 minutes. Drain and serve with melted butter.

DILL CUCUMBER
Pickled cucumber Polish style

Ingredients:

Dill cucumber 2 lb (960 g)
Water 2 pint (1,200 mls)
Salt 4 oz (120 g)

Method: Blanch neat, oblong, healthy cucumbers of uniform size in an enamel earthenware pot with a weak solution of alum for a few minutes. Drain off water and place cucumbers on a clean, dry cloth. Pack into a glass jar when dry. Alternate dill, horseradish, morello cherry leaves and a few peppercorns at the bottom and arrange layers of cucumbers. Mix 4 oz (60 g) salt with 2 pints (1,200 mls) water and bring to the boil. Pour boiling liquid slowly into the heated jars packed with cucumbers. Seal jars tightly with ox-bladder or sterilised caps, not tightly packed. Place jars in a well aired place and within two days the liquid will start to cloud and fermentation will begin. The lactose of the cucumber will change gradually into lactic acid and the liquid will clear when fermentation has been completed. Do not use parchment paper to seal cucumbers but ox-bladder only. Fill jars up with cold salted water, previously boiled, after 1-2 weeks when the liquid diminishes.

CAKES and SWEETS

POLISH BABA
Yeast cake soaked in syrup

A rum flavoured cake imported by the Turks to Poland and made famous by Maria Leczinska, the Polish wife of French King Louis XV.

Ingredients:

Yeast 1 oz (30 g)
Milk 5 fl oz (150 mls)
4 eggs
Butter or margarine 8 oz (240 g)
Sugar ½ oz (15 g)
Flour 1 lb (480 g)
Currants 3 oz (90 g)

Syrup:

Water 1 pint (600 mls)
Sugar 1 lb (480 g)
Ceylon tea 1 oz (30 g)
Vanilla, lemon and orange essences, few drops
Spirit rum 5 fl oz (150 mls)
Whipped cream for decoration

Method: Crumble yeast in lukewarm milk at 80°F. Dissolve the sugar in eggs and blend with mixture. Incorporate the flour and soft butter to form a fairly soft dough. Allow to prove covered with a cloth for 45 minutes. Then add scalded currants which have been properly dried. Fill small 5 oz (150 g) size moulds which have been *well greased* with soft margarine. Allow room for expansion. Let the babas rise well over the brim of the mould in a dome shape. Bake in a very hot oven at 400°F for 15 minutes and turn out on to a rack to cool. When cold soak quickly in syrup to saturate with the liquid without breaking. Place in a shallow dish and coat with melted apricot jam. Sprinkle spirit rum over and when cold pipe a rosette of whipped cream on top.

SAVARIN CHANTILLY

A savarin is made from a baba paste without the currants. It is baked in an 8 inch crown mould for

20 minutes. It is then soaked in kirsch syrup and glazed with apricot jam. The inside of the crown is then filled with fruit salad and decorated with cream. (*See ilustration.*)

POLISH RING FRITTER
Fritter made with choux pastry shaped in a ring

Ingredients:

Water ½ pint (300 mls)
Lard or butter or mixed fat 4 oz (120 g)
Pinch of salt
2 pinches of sugar 8 g
Sieved flour 8 oz (240 g)
Eggs

Method: Boil water and fat until melted with salt and sugar. Add flour and stir with a wooden spoon to obtain a stiff paste which will not stick to the pan after a drying process lasting a few minutes. Remove pan from heat and when cold add beaten eggs, beating mixture between each addition until the mixture has a pouring consistency yet still holds thread when tested with whisk or spoon. Prepare 20 small pieces of paper 3 inch by 4 inch and grease well. Pipe a ring of mixture using a ½ inch tube on each piece of paper. Heat a pan of oil to 360°F and slip the fritters in one at a time. Fry on both sides and drain after 4 minutes. Sprinkle with granulated or castor sugar.

MAZUREK
Almond cake

Ingredients:

Flour 8 oz (240 g)
Ground almonds 8 oz (240 g)
Butter 6 oz (180 g)
Castor sugar 5 oz (150 g)
Vanilla essence, few drops
3 egg whites
Icing sugar 4 oz (120 g)
Water 1 fl oz (30 mls)
Red plum jam 2 oz (60 g)
Orange and almond essences, few drops

Method: Cream butter and sugar, add beaten egg whites loosely then flour and ground almonds. Flavour with vanilla essence. Spread mixture into a greased tray 2 inch deep and bake at 360°F for 40 minutes. When cool split and spread with red plum jam. Add hot water to icing sugar and a few drops of essence (orange and almond). Coat top of cake with this soft icing and cut into fingers.

SOUR FLAKY MAZUREK
Fruit and almond cake

Ingredients:

Flour 1 lb (480 g)
Butter or margarine 4 oz (120 g)
2 egg yolks
Double cream 5 fl oz (150 mls)
Icing sugar 1 oz (30 g)

Filling:

Seedless raisins 2 oz (60 g)
Currants 2 oz (60 g)
Granulated sugar 2 oz (60 g)

Topping:

Egg white
Flaked almonds
Granulated sugar 1 oz (30 g)
Icing sugar 2 oz (60 g)

Method: Rub flour and fat together. Dissolve sugar in egg yolks and cream and beat well. Blend to flour mixture to form a sort of dough. Place in a bowl, dust with flour and chill overnight. Roll dough into oblong piece about ¼ inch thick. Sprinkle with fruits and granulated sugar and roll up like a roly-poly. Brush top with egg white and sprinkle with flaked almonds and granulated sugar. Prick with a fork and bake at 380°F for 25 minutes. Cool and dust with icing sugar.

KISIELS
Fruit puree thickened with potato flour

Kisiel is a very popular dessert. It is tasty, inexpensive and easy to prepare. It is a type of blanc-mange made with potato flour as the thickening agent. Due to the principal ingredient, the kisiel may be divided into two groups — fruit and milk kisiel. The basis of a fruit kisiel is the juice and pulp, or the boiled syrup of sour and aromatic fruits. The other ingredients are sugar and potato starch. Fruit kiesel is served throughout the year with respect to the fruit in season. It is made of white, red or black currants, raspberries, morello cherries, lemons, strawberries, cranberries, apples and fruit pulp.

Milk kisiel is usually flavoured with coffee, caramel or chocolate. A small amount of butter (5 per cent) is added to a milk kisiel.

Ingredients:

Juice and pulp of 1 lb (480 g) fruit
Sugar 3 oz (90 g)
Potato flour 1 oz (30 g)
Cream 5 fl oz (150 mls)

Method: Heat the liquid to be thickened and remove from heat. Dilute the potato flour with three times the amount of cold water and pour into the boiling liquid. Add sugar. Stir for a few minutes and cook until thick and smooth, stirring all the time. Cool and serve with cream and sugar. (Same procedures as for English custard.)

SERNIK
Cheese flan

Ingredients:

Pastry:

Flour 8 oz (240 g)
Lard 2 oz (60 g)
Butter 2 oz (60 g)
1 egg
1 spoonful of water
Sugar 1 oz (30 g)

Cheese filling:

Cream or cottage cheese 5 oz (150 g)
Flour 1 oz (30 g)
Sugar 2 oz (60 g)

3 egg yolks
3 egg whites
Peels 1 oz (30 g)
Lemon juice 1 fl oz (30 mls)
Lemon essence few drops

Icing:

Icing sugar 3 oz (90 g)
1 tsp of rum
1 tsp of water

Method: This excellent cheese flan is made by prebaking a pastry case in a flan ring, filling it with cheese mixture and topping it with pastry. Bake as for a flan.

Prepare short pastry by creaming fat, sugar and egg together, add flour and water if necessary. Rest dough for 2 hours in a chill cabinet and then roll out into two rounds 9 inch diameter. Line a flan ring with first round and bake blind for 10 minutes at 400°F. Cream cottage cheese with egg yolks, flour, peels, juice and essence and sugar. Add beaten whites. Fill flan level and cover with second layer of uncooked pastry dough. Prick top and bake for 45 minutes at 380°F. After cooling spread with water icing, flavoured with rum.

POLISH GINGERBREAD
Gingerbread flavoured with carrots

Ingredients:

Lard 4 oz (120 g)
Butter 4 oz (120 g)
Brown sugar 4 oz (120 g)
Honey 4 oz (120 g)
Black treacle 4 oz (120 g)
Polish beer or stout 1 pint (600 mls)
Strong flour (well sifted) 1½ lb (720 g)
½ tsp of bicarbonate soda dissolved with
    3 fl oz (90 mls) milk and 2 tsp mixed spices
Sultanas 2 oz (60 g)
Seedless raisins 2 oz (60 g)
Mixed peels 1 oz (30 g)
Pinch of caraway seeds
Grated carrots 2 oz (60 g)
Walnuts 3 oz (90 g)

Method: Line and grease an oblong tin 2 inch deep by 8 inch long by 4 inch wide. Cream butter and lard with brown sugar until fluffy and light. Boil treacle and honey in the beer. Add dissolved bicarbonate of soda to mixture and mixed spices and seeds. Blend the flour into the creamy mixture alternately with the beer and treacle. Add fruits, carrot and nuts last. Pour into tin and bake for 2½ hours at 360°F.

MARMALADE POLISH ROLL
Sponge roly-poly stuffed with orange marmalade

Ingredients:

5 egg yolks
5 egg whites
Castor sugar 5 oz (150 g)
Cake flour 5 oz (150 g)
Soft orange marmalade 5 oz (150 g)
Icing sugar 2 oz (60 g)

Method: This is nothing more than an English swiss roll filled with marmalade.

Line an oblong tin with greaseproof paper 18 inch by 9 inch. Place a cloth on a board which has been dusted with granulated sugar. Beat yolks and castor sugar for 5 minutes until foamy. Add flour. In another bowl beat egg whites to a meringue and fold into the yolks lightly. Spread mixture on tray evenly starting from one corner to another going round then in the centre with a palette knife or cake spreader. The mixture must be level. Bake for 6-8 minutes at 380°F. Turn out on to the sugared cloth and cool. When cool remove paper. Spread marmalade (slightly whipped for easy spreading) and then roll the sponge by lifting the cloth. Wrap in the cloth for a while to keep its shape. Place roll in dish and dust with icing sugar.

PACZKI
Polish yeast doughnuts

Ingredients:

Strong flour 1 lb (480 g)
Peel 1 oz (30 g)
Yeast 1 oz (30 g)
Butter 2 oz (60 g)
Sugar 2 oz (60 g)
Milk 5 fl oz (150 mls)
Egg 3 oz (90 g)
Red jam 4 oz (120 g)
Castor sugar 5 oz (150 g)

Method: This consists of a bun dough mixture which has been cut with a pastry cutter into 3 inch rounds, the centre filled with cherry jam and fried when it has recovered.

All ingredients for yeast goods should be warmed at 80°F to allow yeast to produce carbon dioxide and expand dough. Place all ingredients (flour, eggs, sugar, fat and peel) in a bowl. Disperse the yeast in milk and water at 78°F and then blend and knead dough for 5 minutes. Form into a ball and allow to recover at room temperature for 40 minutes in a covered bowl. Knead dough, shape into a ball again and allow to recover for a further 20 minutes. Dust pastry board with flour and roll out dough to a thickness of ½ inch. Cut into rounds 3 inch diameter with a plain pastry cutter. Allow to recover on a tray which has been dusted with flour for 15 minutes. Brush the dougnut with warm milk to prevent skinning before the last recovery period. When twice the original size fry in deep fat at 360°F for 5 minutes turning on the other side to give an even colouring. Oil is the best medium for frying doughnuts. Drain on absorbing paper or cloth and pass in castor sugar. Pipe jam inside the doughnut.

POLISH ALMOND CAKE
Rum-flavoured cream tart

Ingredients:

Flour 8 oz (240 g)
Margarine or butter 4 oz (120 g)
1 egg
Icing sugar 2 oz (60 g)
Apricot jam 2 oz (60 g)
Diced apple 3 oz (90 g)

Almond cream:

Butter 3 oz (90 g)

Sugar 1 oz (30 g)
Ground almonds 4 oz (120 g)
Rum 2 fl oz (60 mls)
2 egg yolks
2 egg whites

Method: Prepare short pastry by creaming butter
and sugar, then egg and lastly adding flour. Rest
dough for a while. Roll out ¼ inch thick and line
a pastry flan 9 inch diameter. Prick bottom and
spread with a little apricot jam. Cover jam with
chopped apples. Prepare almond cream as follows:
Cream butter and sugar, add yolks, ground almonds
and rum. Separately beat whites to a meringue
and fold into yolk mixture lightly. Place almond
mixture inside flan case. Bake for 45 minutes at
380°F (first ten minutes at 400°F and then reduce
heat for rest of time).

PREZEKLADANIEC
Polish Easter cake roll

Ingredients:

Dough:

Strong flour 1½ lb (720 g)
Yeast 1½ oz (45 g)
Lukewarm water 8 fl oz (240 mls)
Milk 6 fl oz (180 mls)
Sugar 1 oz (30 g)
Salt ¼ oz (7 g)
4 egg yolks
Melted butter 4 oz (120 g)

Filling:

Red jam 5 oz (150 g)
Apricot jam 5 oz (150 g)
½ oz each of following:
   Diced figs
   Dates
   Raisins
   Sultanas
   Lemon peel

Almond filling:

4 egg whites
Butter 4 oz (120 g)

Castor sugar 4 oz (120 g)
Ground almonds 4 oz (120 g)
Flour 1 oz (30 g)
Almond essence
Walnuts and almonds 4 oz (120 g)

Method: This is like a roly-poly made with a
yeast dough. The dough is nothing more than an
English bun mixture. The professional style could
be improved by preparing a Danish of French
crescent pastry. We will, however, produce the
exact Polish recipe with a plain dough mixture.
This cake is in three layers with several fillings of
fruit, jam and almond paste.
Dough: Place flour on table and make a well in
middle. Place warm water, yeast, sugar, milk, egg
yolks and melted butter in cavity and blend to a
smooth dough. Knead well until it forms a ball.
Place a basin over the dough and let it prove to
twice its size for 40 minutes. Then knock it back
by kneading again and add butter. Knead and
gather round the dough into a firm ball again and
let it recover for a further 15 minutes. Divide the
dough into three balls.
Filling I almond: Cream butter, ground almonds,
flour and sugar together, add egg whites and
flavour with a few drops of almond essence or
rum. Add a few chopped walnuts.
Filling II rose jam or strawberry.
Filling III apricot jam.
Filling IV: Mix chopped dates and figs with seedless raisins and sultanas.

Method: Grease an oblong tray 4 inch by 9 inch.
Roll out the first ball of dough to a thickness of
¹/₈ inch. Spread with red jam and then almond
paste and a third spreading of chopped fruits. Roll
out the second ball of dough to the same thickness and place on top of mixture to form a second
layer. Repeat with jam, almond and fruits. Cover
with a third layer of dough. Brush the top layer
with beaten egg yolks and water. Allow the dough
to recover and expand for 30 minutes and then
bake for 25-30 minutes at 430°F. Cool and
brush with melted apricot jam and sprinkle with
chopped toasted nuts or brush with water icing
and sprinkle with toasted almonds.
Note: For brushing top of pastry use egg whites.

Russia and the Baltic States

For many years, Russian cooking, to me, was the fabulous cuisine of the court of Catherine the Great. My knowledge of Russian gastronomy was based on the tales of the emigres who flocked to France after the Revolution. Every restaurant and taxi rank in Paris must have had its Russian Prince or Count, ready to talk nostalgically of the old days, when caviar was served by the kilo, any fish other than salmon was not worth eating and even bread was served on gold plates.

During World War Two, I fled from France to Britain, and joined British Naval Intelligence. When I discovered that my ship was bound for a visit to Russia, I felt a rising excitement in the pit of my stomach; at last I would see for myself the exotic foods of this country where gastronomy was a way of life.

Our arrival was an anti-climax. The country was grey, bleak and dismal, and the people seemed to be the same. A woman commissar started an argument with us the minute we arrived, and when I tried to turn on the charm, she was ready to arrest me. That evening we stumbled into a local restaurant and there she was again, beautifully dressed and with a smile especially for me. Apparently she had a special face to go with the uniform.

She took us on a tour of the local restaurants, and my image of Russian food slowly faded. Instead of tables groaning beneath Beef Stroganoff, sour cream, mushrooms, caviar and blinis and salmon poached whole, there were fifteen variations of cabbage soup, stuffed cabbage rolls, black bread and very little else. The real food of the people was stodgy and greasy; but in the bitter winters, people who live in such cold have to lay on an extra layer of fat, like a fur overcoat beneath the skin. For the same reason, many Russians seemed to get a lot of their calories from alcohol.

My visions of Russian cooking slowly disappeared on that short visit to Russia. My knowledge of Russian gastronomy was in fact based on the dishes invented for the nobility by my French colleagues, who had been imported to Russia by the very rich. Even Careme had gone there for a time, on the understanding that he would be paid in diamonds. Chicken Kiev has its gastronomic roots in Maxim's, and Beef Stroganoff actually comes from nowhere more exotic than the French Riviera.

But from whichever part of the world his food comes, the Russian likes to eat good food and plenty of it. 'We Russians have learned how to starve—so we know how to eat', I was told by a survivor of the 900-day siege of Leningrad. Indeed the groaning table and the heaped dish of Russian hospitality are no ostentation; they are a defiant gesture of a warm-hearted people to the spectre of hunger which has lurked outside the door throughout Russian history.

In the early seventies I devised a Russian banquet for a trade delegation from Moscow, visiting a British electronics factory. The food was the great old food of Imperial Russia, and the chief Trade Minister wrote me a personal letter to thank me for a banquet the like of which he had never seen. Even to him, the best Russian food was the food of Imperial Russia.

Yet the Russian gastronomy is far more varied; after all, modern Russia is the largest of all nations. Its eight and a half million square miles cover one-sixth of the world's land mass, and its sixteen republics have over 230 million inhabitants with 170 nationalities, many with their own language, customs and cuisine. The distance from its most northern point to its southern border is 3,000 miles, and when the sun is setting over the Baltic, a new day is dawning over Siberia.

In international gastronomy, the most famous Russian food is the Slavic cuisine of the Ukraine, Byelorussia and Great Russia, the territory from Leningrad to the Urals. Then comes the cuisine of the three Baltic states, Lithuania, Latvia and Estonia, which have been influenced by German invaders and Scandinavian neighbours. In the Caucasian area, Armenia, Georgia and Azerbaidzhan each have their own gastronomy, as has Turkestan, the oriental land beyond the Caspian sea.

The Slavic cuisine has developed as two types side by side. There is the simple, nourishing and warming food eaten by the people, typified by *borscht,* (beetroot soup), *shchi* (cabbage soup) and *golubtsy* (cabbage leaves stuffed with meat). On the other hand the rich Russian upper class began to tour Europe and bring back a taste for foreign dishes, along with the chefs poached from some of the best restaurants in the world to create them. This influx of chefs, mainly French, caused a blending of Russian and French cuisines. The famous *Salade Russe,* for instances, is the creation of a French chef, M. Olivier, chef to Nicholas the second. In Russia, it is known as *Salat Olivier.* Similarly, all Russian cream and puree soups can be traced to the French.

The fame of Slavic cooking was further enhanced by the number of Russian emigres who came to Europe and America after the Revolution. A large number went into the catering and restaurant trade because good food was something they knew about. So the fashion for *zakuski, caviar,* vodka, *kulebiak* and *borscht* grew. Many of the most popular dishes like steak tartare and beef stroganoff are still favourites on classic menus in Western countries.

Russians believe that food should not only be plentiful but immediately visible. Dinner guests are immediately confronted by a vast array of *zakuski* (snacks) usually set out in a daunting buffet in the drawing room. They will range from little tidbits which would be in character at a cocktail party, through caviar to major hot dishes which require a plate, knife and fork. The custom of the laden *zakuski* table stems from the old days when a family might come a hundred kilometres or so in a horse-drawn sleigh to visit friends. They would be in need of warming foods, washed down with vodka, to help them to thaw out before they embarked on the dinner proper. The most important ingredient on the zakuski table is a bowl of caviar, its quality and amount giving an indication of the solvency of the host and the importance of the guest. The name caviar comes from the Turkish word for roe, *Khavyah.* The Russians know it as *Ikra* and serve it on *blinis* (buckwheat pancakes), or on small squares of bread. The roe comes from four types of sturgeon. The most rare is the golden roe of the Volga sterlet, traditionally reserved for royalty. The Baluga is the largest fish giving the largest roe. They range in colour from black to grey with a pearly sheen. The Ocietrova is a medium-sized egg and the sevruga is the smallest. The best quality caviar is generally held to be Baluga, slightly salted (malossol). Pressed caviar is cheaper but still delicious. Other types of 'caviar' on the market include salmon, herring and lumpfish roes, salted and treated the same way. Caviar should be kept at a temperature below 45°F (7C) but it must not be frozen, as the cellular structure is permanently destroyed below 32°F (0C).

Zakuski are usually followed by soup, invariably accompanied by a side dish. *Borscht* has an accompaniment of *pirozhky,* and *shchi* comes with *vatrushky* (Cottage cheese tarts). Fish and meat normally follows the soup course and some of the most ingenious ways of cooking poultry belong to Russian cuisine. *Chicken Kiev,* with a thin cutlet of breast of chicken enfolding a finger of chilled butter and wrapped in a delicate coating of breadcrumbs was created by a French chef for a Russian nobleman; minced chicken mixed with seasoning and reshaped to a cutlet form, breadcrumbed and fried in butter is a Sunday best dish in many homes.

Vegetables are not prominent in Slavic cuisine. The short summer does not allow any but the most hardy vegetables to ripen, so cabbage and beetroot along with potatoes are the staple vegetables of the northern regions. Cucumbers of a particularly hardy variety are the most popular pickled vegetable, and wild mushrooms in infinite variety are gathered and dried for use during the long, bitterly cold winter.

Desserts and puddings include an amazing variety of pastries, baked and deepfried, stuffed and plain. A summer favourite is a fruit puree thickened with potato flour known as *kissel*.

Tea is served at all times of day, usually with a little side dish of jam. Strong tea is brewed in the pot which stands on top of the samovar, and diluted to taste in the cup with water from the samovar—an urn heated by charcoal in a vertical tube in its centre.

The national drink, however, is vodka, drunk plain or flavoured with lemon, orange, cherry stones, blades of buffalo grass, black or white peppercorns, blackcurrant leaves, tea and anis seeds. In the days of intrigue and ruthless enemies, it was believed that a grinding of pepper would take any impurities, including poisons, to the bottom, and make the vodka pure and safe to drink. A number of vodka drinkers still perform this ceremony, insisting that the vodka tastes better.

Vilnius, the largest city in Lithuania has a strong Roman Catholic tradition and foodwise this is reflected in the numerous fish specialities featured in all the eating places. A friend of mine who went recently on tour was escorted by Miezlaiskis Juozas, a man with a weatherbeaten face who holds the title of Hero of Socialist Labour, while inspecting the Sesupe collective farm, near Kapsukas, of which he is the chairman. Juozas told my friend that all but 10 of the 137 families who live on their farm own their lodgings. The collective and its members have 1.5 million rubles (1 million pounds) in savings. Most families own their car too.

The gastronomy of the Baltic States combines Scandinavian, German and Slavic cooking into a unique combination peculiar to each of the three countries. Lithuanian cooking takes a great deal from the Ukraine and Byelorussia, for the old Lithuanian kingdom stretched from the Baltic to the Black Sea, centuries ago. The origin of the Lithuanians is shrouded in mystery, but their language is the closest living relative of Sanskrit. The Latvians are closely related to them, but influenced more by the Germans, while the Estonians are of Finno-Ugric origin, like the Finns.

The Baltic States are very fertile pasture land, and this, coupled with the ice-free ports and rich fishing grounds, has made the three small countries natural targets for invasion through the centuries. But whether the masters of the moment were the Danes, the Germans, the Swedes, the Poles or the Russians, the Baltic States have remained independent in spirit. . .and in gastronomy.

Lithuanian cuisine makes great use of rich natural ingredients such as cream, butter, eggs, milk, bacon, potatoes and cottage cheese. Pork, ham and bacon are popular meats, but lard is never used in Lithuania. All cooking is done in butter. Favourite salads are tomatoes, onions, radishes, spring onions and cucumbers, while carrots, cabbage and beetroot are the winter vegetables. Fried diced bacon is used as a topping for many foods, and poppy seeds are used in savoury and sweet dishes.

Latvia is an industrial country involved more in Russian activities. Riga is the second largest Baltic port, teeming with Western sailors and tourists and boasts of the finest restaurants for miles around. (A rarity in the USSR.) When I visited Riga in 1937, the central market in the heart of the town was cracking with radishes, green lettuce and carrots and mountains of eggs, butter and carcasses of fresh meat. My journalist friend told me it is exactly the same today — Riga is a gourmets' paradise.

The Latvians are the great fishermen, and marinated sprats are almost a national dish. Various types of meat are combined in many dishes, and pork with beef is a favourite. Caraway seeds are widely used because they are believed to aid digestion, and they are the usual flavouring for sauerkraut. Latvian pastries are mouth-watering, and the Aleksandr-Torte is one of the tests of a good Latvian cook.

As soon as you cross the Narva River from Russia into Estonia, you know you are in a different land. The fields, dotted with apple and cherry trees and bordered by colourful flowers, are trim. The houses are tidy. Estonia shows few symbols of State socialism. Lawns are mown (lawn mowers are rarities in Moscow). The suburban shopping centres around Tallin, the

Estonian capital, stock such rarely seen items as toasters and modern kitchen utensils. No delays, no long queues so prevalent in the USSR. Tallin's sales-clerks are courteous and helpful — another difference. Tallin is packed with Finnish tourists who come to relax in the city's new Finnish-built hotel and watch its lively floor shows, extremely daring by Soviet standards. Vana Thomas, a cellar bistro on the square in the old part of the capital, provides you with the finest pates, smoked fish delicacies and French crescents, while a jazz flutist wails out Western songs.

The Estonians and the Soviets seem to have struck a symbiotic balance. This smallest republic has the highest output per capita of any of the other sixteen republics in the USSR. Its exports of meat and dairy products must be the reason for this unusual tolerance. Says Gustav Tonspoeg, vice chairman of the council of ministers: 'We are raising the people to be socialists, but we are encouraging and deepening our Estonian traditions.' Estonian traditions are for meaningful living. Gastronomy is an art practised in every home, and is expanding into Latvia and Lithuania. The Estonians share with their Scandinavian neighbours a love of buffet with cold meats, fish of all types, and salads, very like the Smorgasbord. Veal is popular, and cold veal combined with herrings and vegetables makes the traditional salad *Rossolye*.

Before the Revolution, Tallin, the capital of Estonia, had some of the best pastry shops in the world. The chefs were either French or French-trained, and elaborate pastries were intricately fashioned to order. Massive cakes floating on clouds of spun sugar soared upwards, and thirty layers in a towering cake were not unusual.

Much of the fish caught in the Baltic is processed for Russia and the problem of finding more fish is getting more acute in spite of ocean fleet and fish factories being fitted for sea-processing in many parts of the world. Russia is gradually increasing its range of fishing expeditions, a fact causing alarm in many European fishing populations out of work at this present time. Fish farming naturally has become a major activity and an ambitious programme of development has already started not only for increasing the fish production for home use but also to repopulate the fish at sea.

It was on Soviet initiative that measures were taken to protect the fish stock of the Baltic Sea and North-east Atlantic, and to restrict herring fishing in parts of the Pacific. Experts say 90-100 million tons of fish a year can be caught in the sea without damage to nature, providing this fishing is done sensibly. Mankind already catches two-thirds of this amount, but the oceans produce thousands of millions of tons more seafood every year. The trouble is that they do so without considering man's wishes and the only way to alter that is to modify natural processes. This interference has already begun. The first correction is artificial reproduction of stocks of fish and other marine foods. The Soviet Union has over 140 fish-breeding farms and acclimatisation stations. These release some 12,000 fry of such valuable commercial fish as the sturgeon and the salmon into the sea every year. Many countries already have benefited — Japan, Norway and Holland. Their fishermen are finding types of fish never caught before in their own waters.

All over the world fish farming is becoming a major industry, rearing turtles, trout, salmon and bream. Lobster farms are already established in America and Canada, where measures to prevent lobsters killing each other have been successful. Oyster and mussel breeding has been controlled for many centuries too. Molluscs release their larvae in surface water which carries them long distances, so simple collectors — ceramic plates strung on ropes — are used to catch them, so that they do not drop to the sea-bed and get eaten by predators. Up to 6 lbs can grow in eighteen months.

The day after leaving Archangel, the Russian port where we had brought our war supply to the Soviets, I discovered that the entire meat consignment was unfit for human consumption and with annoyance that our Russian allies had somehow cheated us, I was instructed to ditch the whole rotten pork overboard. All we had apart from a few groceries and canned pickled cucumbers was flour kept for such emergencies. So each day I would bake bread and pastries. But a stroke of luck saved the day. We successfully repulsed a submarine attack in the North Sea and one of the depth charge stations I manned brought forth a shoal of fish of the like I have never seen since: black, brown, red, big, small, flat and rounded — every species was represented. We had a field day picking them up as they floated, killed by the explosion but intact and good to eat.

Never would I have dreamt that fish would ever be in short supply one day. We had the previous year been stationed for a while in Iceland, and there you only had to put your hand in the water and you could catch a fish. But chasing the *Bismarck* in all directions gave us no time for proper fishing and afterwards we were bound to America and Canada in regular convoys where the loss of cargoes on each trip was so distressingly alarming. But our war supplies to Russia helped enormously in winning the war against the Germans.

Caucasian cooking differs radically from the cooking of Northern and Western parts of Russia. There is a Greek and Turkish influence, with stuffed vine leaves, yoghurt soups, salads with walnuts and pomegranate juice dressings, and lamb is the main meat. Vegetables are more those of the Mediterranean countries, with zucchini, okra, green peppers and eggplants. Bread from this region is thin and white, and very little butter is used; lamb fat is used for cooking and olive oil in salads. Flavourings used in this part of the world are quite unique; dried mint, crushed barberry, dried apricots and cumin seeds, dried eggplant, parsley and dill. Goat and yoghurt cheeses are eaten throughout the day, and cheese and olives stay on the table throughout a meal, even during desserts.

Shashlik comes from this part of the world, and every village seems to have its own way of cooking it. Meat is usually served in pieces, and a whole joint is rare. Meat balls are popular throughout the region, and vary in size from the tiny meatballs of the Armenians to the giant Azerbaidzhan *keufta*, which has a whole chicken embedded in its centre.

Armenian cookery has a taste of the Near East about it, and many of the dishes bear Turkish names: *dolma, halva, bakhlava.* Salads are eaten at almost any hour of the day, from light snacks served to guests to a substantial version which constitutes a whole meal. Meat is usually com-

bined with vegetables in Armenia to produce stews known as *Misof*s. If the meat is not served alongside the vegetables, it is served inside them, and stuffed vegetables are a national dish. One form of *dolma* even consists of baby eggplants, peppers, tomatoes and apples, all stuffed and cooked together in a casserole.

Instead of *zakuski*, Armenians start their meals with *meze*, a type of hors d'oeuvre with perhaps stuffed mussels, flaky cheese pastries stuffed with vegetables and bread with chickpea paste used as a dip. Soup follows, with yoghurt the main ingredient, thickened with farina or barley, flavoured with dried mint. Then lamb or chicken in meatballs, stew or *shashlik*, and the meal ends with fruit and cheese. Nuts are used in sweets combined with honey in the Near East manner, or in sticky, delicious flaky pastries soaked in syrup, rather like those of Turkey and Greece. Raki is the national drink rather than vodka.

Azerbaidzhan has a gastronomy of its own in relation to the rest of Russia. Its dishes are very closely related to Central Asia, and the pilaff is the everyday dish, made with several varieties of meat and fish together. Pomegranate seeds and saffron are used as flavourings, and lemon juice is often served on its own, in a jug on the side of a dish, so that guests can add it to sauces. Cinnamon is a spice used throughout the range of dishes, with meat and soups as well as in sweet dishes.

Soups are so thick that they are more like stews, and the lamb stew known as *piti* is flavoured with an assortment of vegetables and the fat cut from beneath the tail of lamb especially bred for its fat. This fat, known in Azerbaidzhan as *kyurdyuk*, is used in most cooking and gives the dishes of the region their distinctive taste. Butter can be substituted in cooking Azerbaidzhan dishes, but the flavour is not the same. Fat from ordinary lamb, melted down, will not do, as the flavour is entirely different.

The traditional flavours of Azerbaidzhan are tart and sour, because of the hot summers and very mild winters, and even savoury dishes served instead of dessert are sharpened with vinegar or lemon juice to refresh the mouth.

Georgia, a tiny mountainous nation where all the men seem to have rich moustaches and gleaming teeth forever smiling, has a distinctive gastronomy. The best known all over the world is chicken in walnut sauce, with garlic, vinegar, hot red pepper and coriander pounded with the walnuts. Hot, peppery foods are traditional with the Georgians, but very few sweet dishes are eaten. Corn is a popular grain, and makes a type of *kasha* in Western Georgia. It is also used in the local bread, sometimes served with a cheese stuffing. Herbs of all types grow wild in this rich country, and are often served raw as a snack, or as a salad without dressing. Red and black radishes are used freely, and saffron, watercress, spring onions and basil are traditional flavourings.

Turkestan has a gastronomy of its own, affected by the physical features of the country. It is a huge plain, once an inland sea, with high mountains on its south eastern border, and consisting mainly of plateaus. There are great extremes of temperature in the northern steppes, and generally the climate is dry. But in the fertile southern valleys, the climate is temperate, and grapes, melons, cherries and plums grow in wild profusion. Because of the hot summer sun, fruit here has a high sugar content, and the local cooks take advantage of this by boiling down fruit juices until it is a thick syrup, used in place of sugar in local sweetmeats.

In the more rigorous climate of the north, the inhabitants are nomadic herdsmen, who eat horsemeat, lamb and mutton, and drink fermented mare's milk known as *kumiss*. *Pilaff* is traditional in this area, often cooked with fruit as well as meat and onions, and pumpkin and hot red pepper distinguishes much of central Asian food.

The history of Russian gastronomy is related to its economic agricultural development and its success in making the collective farms work more efficiently. In Stalin's time many peasants died for not co-operating and millions of people in many Soviet republics starved to death during the periods of famines, when the harvest was poor. The cold climate in most parts of Russia explains also the types of diets mostly composed of heavy soups.

In Moscow all kinds of delicacies can be purchased in the 'gastronoms' – shops only opened to tourists and the Russian elite. Elsewhere, the main meal is often a soup garnished with *Moskowskii Sociskii*, a type of frankfurter sausage and smoked belly of pork. The southern part of Russia near the Caspian Sea is privileged in food production: where the vine grows the food flows, they say. But in general the Russian appreciate good food or any food because it is not that plentiful.

However, to cover the entire field of the culinary repertoire of Russia would involve as much research and study as to cover all the other countries of Europe put together. The increased interest in touristic holidays in various parts of Soviet Russia may invite further enquiries helping to promote its gastronomic aspects. In general, Russian gastronomy includes Siberian, Ukrainian, Caucasian, Georgian, Armenian and Turkestan cookery styles. Northern peoples will sup soups and sip vodka in larger quantities than the lucky and happy going Caucasian with his abundance of wines to cheer him up. The food of Transcaucasia is closer to that of the Middle East, and its cuisine will be described in the second volume of this series.

Russian catering is very much industrialised. With women able to leave their children all day or night in nursery schools, they can enjoy the food in the canteens where they work, prepared by professional chefs whose standards are as good technically as their Western colleagues. Like the British and the Chinese, the Russians prefer their own cuisine to any style from abroad. The Great Elizabeth insisted that her French chef include all Russian specialities like *Koulibiaka* and *Gretchnevaya Kasha*, a buckwheat concoction as heavy as baked beans and mutton stew.

Russians are big eaters, as reported by the *Soviet News* in 1976. Six men in Azerbaidzhan feasted on two sheep, twelve capons and drank twenty bottles of vodka and brandy. The paper did not say whether they were made heroes of Soviet Russia or not.

Beverages

Georgia and the southern parts of Russia produce wines, spirits and liqueurs of high quality. Vodka is now made under licence in many countries of the world. Originally vodka was made entirely from rye, barley, malt to the extent of 15-20 per cent being used to effect saccharification, but at the present day potatoes and maize are the staple raw materials from which this spirit is manufactured, and as a rule, green rye is now used instead of barley. In 1917, the Soviets made an attempt to enforce general prohibition, but failed. As a result the Soviet press reports many cases of increased alcoholism among the younger population – a state which alarmed the Soviet authorities. Softer drinks like Coca-Cola are now produced with the help of American manufacturers and other soft drinks are getting more popular. A great deal of encouragement is given by dieticians for the return of hot beverages made from plants and herbs.

Tea was introduced in 1640 from the Mongol horde. It was praised then for its medicinal powers and ability to refresh and purify the blood. It was also noted that it would keep one awake during church service. The brewing of the tea in a samovar is very traditional. This vessel resembles a barrel with a cock at one end and a chimney pipe in the middle into which coal was stocked; this thermos had no bottom draft. The traditional, spherical, cylindrical and tapered samovar dates back to the eighteenth century and when introduced to Britain became the tea-kettle as we have it in most households today.

The word 'Chai' in Russian cooking is applied to a number of hot drinks other than tea. Chai brewed of linden blossoms, lime tree leaves, raspberries, bilberries and other plants are known for their medicinal properties. Allow 1 oz (30 g) of tea or herbs per pint of boiling water.

Sweetbriar vitamin tea: Rich in vitamin C, this tea is drunk twice daily as an insurance for good health. Crush the fruit slightly, add to one glass or cup of boiling water, boil 5 minutes and brew for several hours. Strain and filter then add when cold additional juice of the fruit. Blackcurrant juice is a classical example of a berry rich in vitamin C. Notice that by adding fresh fruit juice to a cold boiled juice made of the same fruit you preserve the vitamin C which is easily destroyed by heat.

Bilberry tea: One cup of bilberry leaves brewed in one pint of boiling water. This infusion has diuretic, astringent and antiseptic effects.

Diaphoretic tea: Use $^1/_3$ oz (10 g) per half pint (300 mls) of boiling water of raspberry, linden or lime tree leaves. Boil for five minutes.

Sbiten: Sbiten was very popular in the eighteenth and nineteenth centuries. It was peddled by street vendors or served at inns and taverns, at tea houses and hotels. The sbiten vendor was a figure so common in the street of nineteenth-century Russian towns that he became one of the characters frequently portrayed in folk drawings known as the lubok. The following are two recipes for sbiten:

1. *Ingredients:* To 1¾ pints (1 litre) boiling water add: 5 oz (150 g) sugar – same amount honey; 2 g bay leaves; 5 g cloves; 5 g cinnamon; 5 g ginger; 5 g cardomom.
2. *Ingredients:* to 1¾ pints (1 litre) boiling water add: 4 oz (120 g) honey and 1 oz (30 g) sugar; 0.2 g clove; 0.2 g fresh mint; 3 g hops.

Method: To the boiling water add the sugar and honey and dissolve. Add other ingredients (ground spices or herbs). Brew 10 minutes without boiling and strain into earthenware pots.

Flavoured liqueurs

Vodka can be used as the main source of alcohol. Dilute 50 per cent of the vodka to any fruit syrup. Then flavour each liqueur with a few drops of an essential oil which will give it its characteristic. Examples:

Creme de Menthe type: Use ½ pint (300 mls) syrup made with 8 fl oz (240 g) sugar and 4 fl oz (120 mls) water. Macerate freshly chopped mint (spearmint plant) in vodka for a week then add syrup. Strain, or add a few drops of peppermint essence instead of the fresh mint.

Orange Liqueur: Use ½ pint (300 mls) vodka. For the syrup use ½ lb (240 g) sugar; 4 fl oz (120 mls) water; few drops of orange essence; 1 oz (30 g) caramel sugar. Blend all ingredients adding the essence last and syrup when cold.

Fermented cordial drinks

Cranberry Mead: Use 17 oz (510 g) honey; 4 pints

(2,400 mls) cranberry juices; 5 g cinnamon; 2 oz (60 g) yeast. Boil water and honey and cool to 80°F then disperse yeast into mixture. Add cranberry juice and ferment for 10 days, cover with polythene cloth. Strain and bottle in a jar fitted with an air lock. Ferment for 3 months, until fermentation ceases, then bottle and cork.

Meads

Meads are what the ancient Greeks called the fermented drink popular among the Slavic tribes. Ancient European travellers to Russia are known to have described how they enjoyed the wines or cordials made from cherry, plum, juniper, raspberry, bird cherry and spiced meads drunk all over Russia.

In all cases of fermenting drinks we advise our readers to observe the strictest rules of sterilisation. All chemists sell the Camden tablets used in dilution to sterilise the equipment and vessels containing the fermenting drink. Lack of hygienic techniques would produce a bad brew infected with unwanted bacteria. All equipment for making home-made drinks can be obtained from specialised brewing firms who will also advise on the usual preparation methods.

Russian wines

Wines are produced in the Don, Black Sea, Kuban and Terek areas of the Caucasian region. The Don wines have a good reputation but the Kuban and Terek wines are drier. Champagne produced in this region is of the sweeter kind. From maize products brandy and vodka are made in large quantities too.

In the republic of the Crimea where the Russian Riviera stretches from Cape Sarych to Feodosiya the region is studded with summer sea-bathing resorts — Alupka, Yalta, Gursuv, Alushta, Sudak and Theodosia. A country rich in culture and resources. The vineyards produce very good wines and many liqueurs are made from fruit and plants. Brewing and distilling industries are more developed in Ukraine, one of the last republics to join the Soviet Union in 1920.

Krasnaya means both 'red' and beautiful in Russian. You can qualify the crenellated red brick walls of the Kremlin with the word or use to describe the best vintage wines of the Kuibishev Vineyard in Massandra near Yalta. This major wine-making centre has a collection of 45,000 bottles of the Soviet Union's finest wines, some dating from the eighteenth century. There are as many brands as we have in France and Italy, many of superior qualities and the same applies to brandies and liqueurs. The sunny Georgian and Armenian slopes produce the largest quota.

Tap water as a rule is not safe to drink but mineral waters from the exotic Caucasian towns of Sukhumi-Poti and Batumi surrounded by citrus fruit trees, olive plantations, bamboo groves. Much of the bottled mineral water sold in the Soviet Union comes from this area, under the ubiquitous brand known as 'Narzan'. The best beer in Russia is made in Leningrad (known before the Revolution as Saint Petersburg). Hot mulled wines are sold everywhere and frukovaya voda (bottled fruit juice) are sold in most cafes.

BILL OF FARE

Soup

SHCHI
Cabbage soup

BORSCHT
Beetroot soup

RASSOLNIK
Pickled cucumber and kidney soup

SOLYANKA
Fish soup

BATWINIJA
Cold herb soup

Hors d'Oeuvre

CUCUMBER IN SOUR CREAM

BLACK RADISH SALAD

FISH SATSIVI
Fish in walnut sauce

AUBERGINE CAVIAR
Aubergines with onions, garlic and tomatoes

HERRING POZHARSKI
Herring fish cakes

CRAB SALAD

BEETROOT AND EGG CAVIAR
Beetroot with horseradish and hard-boiled egg

MUSHROOM CAVIAR
Mushrooms in a sour cream or mayonnaise sauce

CAVIAR WITH BLINIS
Caviar with Russian pancakes

MOSKOWSKAYA KUSNIK
Small chicken pies

CHICKEN POZHARSKI
Chicken cutlets fried in egg and breadcrumbs
   with a mushroom sauce

BLINIS
Russian pancakes

KVASS
Fermented beer used with stews

Fish

STEAMED SPRAT PUDDING
Minced poached sprats with tomato sauce

ESTONIAN SMOKED SPRAT IN SOUR CREAM

BALUGA IN BRINE
Beluga fillets baked with cucumber and mushrooms in brine

STUFFED FISH RUSSIAN STYLE
Poached stuffed fish

TELNOYE
Russian fish loaf

SHASHLIK OF STURGEON LATVIA
Skewered fish cubes with bacon or ham and
   mushrooms

FISH SOLYANKA
Baked fish in tomato and garlic

SCAMPI TALLIN
Fried scampi in sour cream

CRAB PIE LITHUANIA
Crab meat mixed with mushrooms and
   topped with mashed potatoes

HALIBUT RED ARMY
Halibut baked in white wine and vodka

KOULIBIAC MOSCOVIANA
Poached salmon in a pastry case

Meat Dishes

SOLYANKA TOLSTOY
Meat stew with sauerkraut

CASSEROLE OF BEEF WITH KVASS
Stew of beef from shank, topside of flank
   with beer

VEAL ZRAZY
Stuffed veal escalopes

LIVER IN SOUR CREAM

CHICKEN KIEV
Chicken escalope stuffed with parsley butter

GOLUBTSY
Stuffed cabbage balls

CHANAKHI
Lamb stew Georgian style

BEEF STROGANOFF
Strips of fillet of beef in a sour cream sauce

SHASHLIK BREZHNEV
Skewered lamb and kidney cubes

PUSHKIN STEAK
Braised steak with walnuts

RUSSIAN PELMENI
Russian type of ravioli

KISSLIJA KAPUSKA
Sauerkraut with frankfurter sausages

TSYPLENOK-TABAKA
Fried chicken Georgia with Tkemali sauce

TSCHAKKUM-BILI
Caucasian chicken

GLUKARS SMIJETANA SAUSUM
Black grouse, Caucasian style

RUSSIAN HOT POT LJUBUSHCHKIN
Oxtail with sauerkraut, herbs and sour cream

Vegetables

POTATO OLADYI
Potato pancakes

POTATO KNISHI
Stuffed potato balls

SWEET-SOUR SPINACH
Spinach with vinegar and tomatoes

CASSEROLED BEETROOT WITH SOUR
CREAM

POTATO ZAPEKANKA
Mashed potato topped with fried onion

CUTLETS DOYTOSKI
Fried vegetable cakes

CAKES and SWEETS

VARENIKI
Sweet noodle paste filled with fruit

KASHA
Various types of cereals used as savoury or
    sweet dishes

GEORGIAN RICE PLOV
Rice pudding

ARMENIAN RICE ARRAT
Rice crown filled with fruit

KULICH
Yeast fruit cake

PICKLED PEARS
Pears marinaded in red wine

STRAWBERRY KREMLIN
Sponge with Kummel liqueur, fresh strawberries
    and cream

FRUIT SOUPS

KISSEL

KACHA GOURIEFF
Semolina pudding

GOZINAKH
Walnut sweetmeat

PASHKA
Cheese pudding

COTTAGE CHEESE PUDDING

CREAM CHEESE PANCAKES

UKRAINIAN GALUSHKI
Cheese dumplings

COULIBIAC
Straight ban dough mixture.

KUZAKH (BELYASH)
Minced beef pie

VATRUSHKA
Type of fried doughnut filled with cream cheese

LIDA AND PETER'S BALTIC TORTE
Red berry cheese cake

SOUP

At the time of Peter the Great, soups were served as a main course under the name of pokhlebka. Today in Soviet Russia soups are still as good and nourishing as a meal as they were in the sixteenth and seventeenth centuries.

The most distinctive soups are: *Shchi*, cabbage or sauerkraut; *Borscht*; red beets; *Rassolnik*, pickled cucumber; *Ukha*, fish soup; *Solyanka*, sauerkraut, with fish or meat.

Cream and puree soups are also popular and are prepared in the same way as in most countries of the world.

The following recipes in this section are based on the popular Russian cookery of today's fare in average households.

SHCHI
Cabbage soup

Ingredients:

1 knuckle of bacon
Water 3½ pint (2,100 mls)
5 oz (150 g) each of the following sliced vegetables:
    Carrots
    Onions
    Cabbage
    Potatoes
1 bouquet garni
Bacon fat 2 oz (60 g)
Salt and pepper

Method: Boil a knuckle of green bacon in water with a bouquet garni for 2 hours. Strain broth. Sweat thinly sliced vegetables in fat for few minutes. Season to taste. Carve meat and serve with soup. (Soak knuckle 2 hours if green, 6 hours if smoked before cooking in fresh water.)

SHCHI
Sauerkraut

Same as above but substitute sauerkraut for fresh cabbage and garnish soup with a few sliced frankfurters.

BORSCHT
Beetroot soup

Ingredients:

Shin of beef tied up in one piece and a few bones
    2 lb (960 g)
Potatoes ½ lb (240 g)
1 onion
3 carrots
1 sprig celery
Raw beetroot 1 lb (480 g)
Baked beetroot 8 oz (240 g)
Water 3½ pint (2,100 mls)
Bacon fat 2 oz (60 g)
Shredded cabbage 5 oz (150 g)
Tomato puree 1 oz (30 g)
Vinegar 2 fl oz (60 mls)
Sugar 2 oz (60 g)
Sausagemeat 3 oz (90 g)
Puff pastry 6 oz (180 g)
Salt and pepper
Sour cream as garnish 5 oz (150 g)
Flour 2 oz (60 g)

Method: Prepare a beef stock by boiling in water the beef and bones for 2 hours. Strain broth. Keep meat in reserve to be used as main dish. Sweat in bacon fat the vegetables cut in thin strips or slices except the cooked beetroot. Sprinkle the flour and stir, then add tomato puree and dilute the stock gradually. Cook this soup until vegetables are tender for 20 minutes. Grate the cooked beetroot then add vinegar and sugar. Blend this mixture to soup when ready. Season and serve separately the sour cream and small sausage rolls made with puff pastry and pork or beef sausagemeat.

SUMMER BORSCHT

Same as above but the soup is not thickened with flour but with egg yolks. Place the yolks in soup tureen. Add a cup of the soup first while stirring then pour rest of soup and serve sour cream and meat pies or sausage rolls (*piroghi*). Allow 4 egg yolks per pint of soup.

In modern Russia potatoes are used in Borscht as a thickener. Clear Borscht ingredients are flour, potatoes or egg yolks. In addition to beef, fowl or duck giblets can be used for improving the flavour of this typical Russian soup.

BORSCHT
Russian hot pot (12 portions)

This is the most conventional recipe.

Ingredients:

Onions 5 oz (150 g)
Celery 6 oz (180 g)
Carrots 3 oz (90 g)
Potatoes 10 oz (300 g)
Cabbage 6 oz (180 g)
Leeks 5 oz (150 g)
Streaky bacon 5 oz (150 g)
Bacon fat 2 oz (60 g)
Skinned and seeded tomatoes 6 oz (180 g)
Tomato puree 2 oz (60 g)
Raw peeled beets 6 oz (180 g)
Shin or shank or thick flank of beef 2 lb (960 g)
Beef and pork chipolatas 8
1 bouquet garni
1 red pepper
Salt and pepper
Water 8 pint (4,800 mls)

Garnish:

Cooked beetroot 6 oz (180 g)
Vinegar 3 fl oz (180 mls)
Sugar 1 oz (30 g)
Sour cream 6 fl oz (180 mls)
1 pinch caraway seeds (optional)
8 *piroghi* made with a filling of meat using puff or Danish pastry or plain pastry

Method: Peel and cut all root vegetables in small cubes. Finely shred cabbage and celery and pepper. Saute all the vegetables in bacon fat for a few minutes. Add water and the piece of beef and bacon (bacon could be a knuckle). Boil for 2 hours, with tomato puree. Blend the cooked grated beetroot of garnish not used in soup with vinegar and sugar. Serve separately with cream. Cut beef in

thin strips (julienne) and add to soup with the red juice of the garnish beet.

Piroghi are made like small turnovers stuffed with some of the minced beef and pork (see recipe). Pan fry the chipolatas and cool, then cut in slices and serve with soup.

Note: There are many versions of making Borshch as there as other ways of spelling the word. Other Borshch recipes in Polish and Jewish gastronomy will be found with certain modifications.

RASSOLNIK
Pickled cucumber and kidney soup

Ingredients:

Ox kidney cut in thin slices 1 lb (480 g)
Sliced carrots 2 oz (60 g)
Sliced onions 5 oz (150 g)
Celery 1 oz (30 g)
Potatoes ½ lb (240 g)
Butter or fat 2 oz (60 g)
Pickled cucumber in dill, canned with some of the brine 5 oz (150 g)
Sour cream 5 fl oz (150 mls)
Chopped parsley
Salt and pepper
Water 3½ pints (2,100 mls)

Method: Saute the sliced kidney in fat till brown for few minutes. Add diced cucumber, chopped onions and carrots. After few minutes add the water and pickled brine, the celery and bouquet garni, sliced potatoes and cook gently for 1½ hours till meat is tender. Season to taste. Serve separately sour cream. Sprinkle chopped parsley and dill in soup, just before serving.

Rassolnik can be made with other meat, chicken or giblets. The characteristic is the sour flavour of pickled cucumber.

SOLYANKA
Fish soup

Ingredients:

Fish bones 1 lb (480 g)
Fish fillets 8 oz (240 g)

Chopped onions 5 oz (150 g)
1 sprig of celery
Pickled cucumber 6 oz (180 g)
Tomato puree 2 oz (60 g)
6 olives
Chopped parsley
Salt and pepper to taste and a few caraway seeds
Butter 2 oz (60 g)
Flour 2 oz (60 g)
1 bouquet garni (bay leaf, thyme, celery)
Water 3½ pints (2,100 mls)

Method: Make a stock by boiling fish bones in water for 20 minutes. Strain and thicken with a roux. Saute the onions in butter till tender but not coloured, add diced raw fish and cook 5 minutes then add diced cucumber, bouquet garni, chopped celery, tomato puree and stock. Simmer 10 minutes and season. Add caraway seeds and chopped parsley. Serve with a wedge of lemon and garnish with olives. To thicken soup, cream butter and flour (1 oz (30 g) each) and add to hot broth. Stir well.

BATWINIJA
Cold herb soup (6 portions)

Ingredients:

Shredded spinach and chard beet or sorrel leaves
    5 oz (150 g) of each
Shredded cooked beetroot 5 oz (150 g)
Shredded leeks 2 oz (60 g)
Butter 3 oz (90 g)
Bacon fat 3 oz (90 g)
Sliced peeled potatoes 10 oz (300 g)
Vinegar 2 fl oz (60 mls)
Sugar 1 oz (30 g)
1 glass white wine
Coriander seeds 1 oz (30 g)
Chopped fennel or caraway seeds 1 oz (30 g)
Salt and pepper
Water 3½ pints (2,100 mls)

Method: Place strips of cooked beetroot in vinegar with sugar to marinade for 20 minutes. Saute the strips of leeks and shredded leaves (chard and spinach) in butter and bacon fat for few minutes and add the sliced potatoes. Cook with 3 pints (1,800 mls) water and the chopped fennels and caraway seeds until the potatoes are soft and mashy. Pass mixture through a sieve. Add the beetroot and its juice together with the wine. Boil mixture and season to taste. Cool and serve chilled.

Garnish: Canapes of smoked salmon, hard-boiled eggs and pickled cucumber in dill.

HORS D'OEUVRE (ZAKUSKI)

CUCUMBER IN SOUR CREAM

Ingredients:

Cucumber 10 oz (300 g)
Salt and pepper
Sour cream 5 fl oz (150 mls)
Wine vinegar or lemon juice
Chopped dill and parsley

Method: Peel and slice cucumber. Remove some of the seeds if the cucumber is too mature. Sprinkle salt. Let stand for 20 minutes. Wash and drain. Blend sour cream, and season with salt and pepper and add the juice of half lemon, or the equivalent in vinegar. Sprinkle chopped dill and parsley.

BLACK RADISH SALAD

Ingredients:

Black radishes 10 oz (300 g)
Oil 2 fl oz (60 mls)
Vinegar 1 oz (30 g)
Salt and pepper
1 hard-boiled egg
Made mustard 1 tbs

Method: This variety of radish is not very well known in Britain but can be obtained and grown. The black radish is a root of the same shape as a long turnip or carrot — each can weigh 8-10 oz (240-300 g). Wash and peel the radishes. Slice thinly and blend with a salad dressing made by adding a sieved hard-boiled egg to oil and vinegar, salt and pepper and a little made mustard.

FISH SATSIVI
Fish in walnut sauce

Ingredients:

Fish fillets 2 lb (960 g)
1 bouquet garni
Coriander seeds 1 tbs
Sliced onion 2 oz (60 g)
Water 2 pint (1,200 mls)
Wine vinegar 5 fl oz (150 mls)
Salt and pepper
Walnuts 8 oz (240 g)
3 cloves garlic
Pinch mixed spices

Method: Place the fish fillets in a shallow tray, covered with water and vinegar with a bouquet garni and coriander seeds, salt and pepper. Poach or bake in oven for 25 minutes. Remove herbs and strain fish liquor. Arrange fish in a serving dish. Complete sauce by adding to fish liquor the walnut and garlic pounded to a paste and add chopped onions. Boil this sauce for 10 minutes. Check seasoning and pour over the fish. Serve cold.

AUBERGINE CAVIAR
Aubergines with onions, garlic and tomatoes

Ingredients:

Eggplants 10 oz (300 g)
Tomato pulp 5 oz (150 g)
Chopped onions 5 oz (150 g)
Oil 3 fl oz (90 mls)
Vinegar 2 fl oz (60 mls)
Salt and pepper

Method: Bake the aubergines. Cut in half when soft. Scoop pulp and chop it finely. Fry chopped onions and garlic in oil. When soft add tomato pulp and cook for a few minutes. Blend in the aubergine pulp. Season to taste. Add vinegar and a little oil. Boil for a few more minutes. Serve cold.

HERRING POZHARSKI
Herring fish cakes

Ingredients:

Herring fillets 1½ lb (720 g)
Breadcrumbs 2 oz (60 g)
Sour cream 2 fl oz (60 mls)
1 egg
Salt and pepper
Seasoned flour 1 oz (60 g)
1 egg
Breadcrumbs 4 oz (120 g)
Oil for frying 5 fl oz (150 mls)

Method: Fillet, skin and mince the flesh of herring to a paste. Blend crumbs and sour cream and beaten egg. Season and shape into fish cake. Pass each cake in seasoned flour, beaten egg and breadcrumbs. Fry in oil or fat on both sides.

CRAB SALAD

Ingredients:

Frozen brown crab meat (liver) 8 oz (240 g)
White meat 8 oz (240 g)
Thick mayonnaise 5 fl oz (150 mls)
2 hard-boiled eggs
Breadcrumbs 2 oz (60 g)
Salt and pepper
Lettuce leaves

Method: Prepare the liver part of the crab by blending crumbs and chopped hard-boiled eggs with the same amount of thick mayonnaise. Blend the white meat with half amount of mayonnaise. Place a spoonful of each mixture on lettuce or blinis.

BEETROOT AND EGG CAVIAR
Beetroot with horseradish and hard-boiled egg

Ingredients:

Beetroot 8 oz (240 g)
Grated horseradish 1 tbs
Oil 2 fl oz (60 mls)
Vinegar 1 fl oz (30 mls)

1 hard-boiled egg
Salt and pepper
Lettuce leaves
Grated onions

Method: Bake beetroot for one hour. Cool and peel. Grate and blend with a little grated horse-radish, oil and vinegar and chopped hard-boiled egg. Serve on a bed of lettuce leaves with chopped or grated onions.

MUSHROOM CAVIAR
Mushrooms in the sour cream or mayonnaise sauce

Ingredients:

Mushrooms 12 oz (360 g)
Chopped onions 6 oz (180 g)
Breadcrumbs 2 oz (60 g)
Chopped parsley 1 oz (30 g)
2 hard-boiled eggs
Thick mayonnaise 4 fl oz (120 mls)
Salt and pepper
Blinis

Method: Chop mushrooms and onions. Saute in oil or butter for five minutes. Add crumbs and chopped parsley, then chopped hard-boiled eggs. Cool then blend mayonnaise or sour cream. Serve hot or cold with blinis.

CAVIAR WITH BLINIS
Caviar with Russian pancakes

Ingredients:

Caviar 1 oz (30 g) per person
Half an egg
Chopped shallots

Blinis:

2 eggs
Yeast 1 oz (30 g)
Flour 4 oz (120 g)
Warm water 4 fl oz (120 mls)
Pinch salt

Method: Caviar should be served fresh out of the tin or in a jar. Serve separately a dish of chopped hard-boiled eggs and chopped shallots and allow two blinis per person.
Blinis: Beat eggs and blend to flour with a little water to which yeast has been dispersed. Allow to ferment for 1 hour. Add salt and then make small 3 inch pancakes in pan.
Note: Salmon caviar or sturgeon roes can be served the same way.

MOSKOWSKAYA KUSNIK
Small chicken pies

Ingredients:

Diced chicken 8 oz (240 g)
Chopped onions 8 oz (240 g)
Butter 1 oz (30 g)
Chopped mushrooms 4 oz (120 g)
Chicken sauce 4 fl oz (120 mls)
Cream 2 fl oz (60 mls)
Chopped gherkins 1 oz (30 g)
Oil 1 fl oz (30 mls)
Salt and pepper
Short pastry 5 oz (150 g)
Puff pastry 5 oz (150 g)
1 egg for egg wash
1 egg for blending chicken mixture

Method: The Kusnik are small pies filled with chicken and pickled gherkin mixed with cream and chicken veloute sauce. Puff pastry is usually better for the topping and short pastry for the base.

Saute the chopped onions in butter till soft then add diced cooked chicken. Blend with thick chicken sauce and a little cream. Add diced pickled gherkins or cucumber. Season. Saute diced mushrooms for two minutes in oil then blend to mixture, and add beaten eggs. Stir well and cool. Line small deep individual moulds with short pastry. Prick bottom then fill with chicken mixture. Top up with small rounds of puff pastry (same technique as for mincepies). Brush top with eggwash. Rest 15 minutes then bake 20 minutes at 400°F. Serve hot or cold.

CHICKEN POZHARSKI
Chicken fried in egg and breadcrumbs with a
  mushroom sauce

Ingredients:

Chicken breasts 4
White breadcrumbs 2 oz (60 g)
Milk or cream 2 fl oz (60 mls)
Salt and pepper
2 eggs
Seasoned flour
Brown breadcrumbs 4 oz (120 g)
Oil for frying
Bechamel sauce ½ pint (300 mls)
Chopped mushrooms 2 oz (60 g)
Butter 1 oz (30 g)
½ lemon
Salt and pepper

Method: Mince the flesh of chicken without the
skin. Blend breadcrumbs and milk or cream.
Season. Divide mixture in 2 oz (60 g) cakes
shaped in triangular form like a cutlet. Pass in
seasoned flour then in beaten eggs and lastly in
breadcrumbs. Pan fry in clarified butter or in oil
for 4 minutes on each side. Serve separately a
mushroom sauce.
Mushroom sauce: Saute chopped mushrooms in
butter 2 minutes then add a cup of Bechamel
sauce, juice of ½ lemon and seasoning.

This dish was first served by Laguipiere,
Napoleon's chef during his wretched Russian
campaign. The recipe was created by a Russian
chef who worked for a Russian aristocrat called
Pozharsky. But according to modern Soviet
information, Pozharsky was an innkeeper in the
old Russian town of Torzhok. Alexander Pushkin
recommended to his friends 'the cutlets fried at
Pozharsky's'.

BLINIS
Russian pancakes

Ingredients:

Bread flour 1 lb (480 g)
Buckwheat or wholemeal flour 4 oz (120 g)
Milk 1 pint (600 mls) or half milk, half water

1 egg
Butter 2 oz (60 g)
Sugar 10 g
Salt ¼ oz (7 g)
Yeast 1 oz (30 g)

Method: Disperse yeast in lukewarm milk and
water. Add beaten egg and sugar and gradually
add flour to obtain a smooth batter. Add salt and
soft butter last. Let the batter ferment for 1 hour.
Then cook small pancakes 3 inch diameter — not
too thick or thin.

KVASS
Fermented beer used with stews

Ingredients:

Rye bread 1 lb (480 g)
Yeast 1 oz (30 g)
Sugar 1½ lb (720 g)
Raisins 2 oz (60 g)
12 pints water (6 litres approx.)
1 Camden tablet

Method: Boil water and sugar two minutes. Cool
to a temperature of 90°F then add raisins, bread
and yeast and one Camden tablet. Place
mixture in a bucket. Cover with a polythene
cloth and ferment at 80°F for ten days.
Strain and transfer into a gallon jar fitted with an
air lock. Make sure the jar has been sterilised
with a Camden tablet (metabisulphite). Allow to
ferment for another two months until clear and
fermentation has ceased. Store in bottles and
chill for three days before using it like a beer.

FISH DISHES

STEAMED SPRAT PUDDING
Minced poached sprats with tomato sauce

Ingredients:

Filleted sprats 1 lb (480 g)
Breadcrumbs 2 oz (60 g)
4 egg yolks

4 egg whites
Milk 2 fl oz (60 mls)
Sour cream 2 fl oz (60 mls)
Butter 4 oz (120 g)
Seasoning

Method: Mince the fish to a paste, add crumbs,
milk, sour cream and egg yolks, season. Beat whites
to a meringue and fold into mixture. Place into
shallow mould well greased with soft butter. Place
mould into tray half filled with hot water. Poach
in moderate oven for 30 minutes. Serve with
tomato sauce.

ESTONIAN SMOKED SPRAT IN SOUR CREAM

Ingredients:

Smoked sprat 1 lb (480 g)
Sour cream 8 fl oz (240 mls)
Chopped onion 3 oz (90 g)
Pinch of allspice
Salt and pepper

Method: Boil sour cream with chopped onions.
Add seasoning. Pour over skinned smoked sprats.
Reheat in shallow dish and serve with a sprinkling
of chopped parsley. Garnish the dish with
mashed potatoes.

BALUGA IN BRINE
Baluga fillets baked with cucumber and
   mushrooms in brine

Ingredients:

Baluga fillets 1 lb (480 g)
Pickled cucumber in dill 8 oz (240 g)
Sliced mushrooms 8 oz (240 g)
Pickled brine 2 fl oz (60 mls)
Butter 2 oz (60 g)
Salt and pepper
Water ½ pint (300 mls)
Flour 1 oz (30 g)

Method: Place the small fillets of fish in a shallow
dish with strips of pickled cucumber and sliced
mushrooms. Season and cover with some of the

cucumber brine (canned cucumbers in dill are
adequate) and the water. Cover fish with lid or
paper and bake 25 minutes in oven at 380°F.
Cream 1 oz (30 g) flour and 1 oz (30 g) butter
and dilute into the boiling liquid to thicken it.
If too thick add more brine or water.

STUFFED FISH RUSSIAN STYLE
Poached stuffed fish

Ingredients:

1 large pike or sander, carp or bream
Matzo 3 oz (90 g)
Chopped onions 6 oz (180 g)
Small red beets 6 oz (180 g)
Carrots 8 oz (240 g)
Sugar 1 oz (30 g)
2 eggs
Oil 1 fl oz (30 mls)
Salt and pepper
Vinegar 2 fl oz (60 mls)
Dill
Bouquet garni

Method: Bone and skin the fish taking care to
leave the skin intact. Mince the fish with onions.
Add crumbs or matzo, egg, salt, oil, pepper and
sugar. Arrange this paste on the skin (previously
well scraped). Reconstitute the fish to its original
shape. Place in a shallow tray covered with water
and vinegar. Add thinly sliced carrots, beets and
sliced onions, and 1 bouquet garni. Poach fish for
40 minutes in oven at 360°F. Make sure fish is
covered with lid or paper. To ensure that vegetables are cooked, boil them in water first then
cool liquor and use to cook fish as indicated.
Serve in the same liquor hot or cold with a sprig
of dill.

TELNOYE
Russian fish loaf

Telnoye in Russian is a fish loaf. Reference to this
type of dish can be found in sixteenth- and
seventeenth-century manuscripts.

Ingredients:

White fish 1 lb (480 g) — salmon may be used
    when available)
Breadcrumbs 3 oz (90 g)
2 eggs
Butter 2 oz (60 g)
2 cloves of garlic
Milk 5 fl oz (150 mls)
Salt and pepper

Method: Grease a shallow dish with soft butter.
Mince fish and garlic and add rest of ingredients
to obtain a smooth paste. Place mixture in dish
and bake in a tray half filled with hot water for
45 minutes at 380°F. Turn the Telnoye out
into a flat dish. Serve with hard-boiled eggs and
pickled cucumber and tartare sauce. Hot or cold.

SHASHLIK OF STURGEON LATVIA
Skewered fish cubes with bacon or ham and
    mushrooms

Ingredients:

Fillet of sturgeon cut in small cubes 1 lb (480 g)
Diced ham or bacon 5 oz (150 g)
Button mushrooms 5 oz (150 g)
Salt and pepper
Oil and vinegar
Dill or caraway seeds
Flour 2 oz (60 g)

Method: Pass the fish cubes in seasoned flour
then dip in oil. Insert the fish into skewer,
alternating with a piece of bacon or ham and
mushrooms. Sprinkle caraway seeds and charcoal
grill or fry. Season to taste and sprinkle with
few drops of vinegar. Serve with French chips.

FISH SOLYANKA
Baked fish in tomato and garlic sauce

Ingredients:

White fish fillet (cod, haddock, hake, etc.)
    1 lb (480 g)
Butter or bacon fat 2 oz (60 g)
Tomato puree 2 oz (60 g)

Breadcrumbs 2 oz (60 g)
Pickled cucumbers 2 oz (60 g)
Water ½ pint (300 mls)
Vinegar 2 fl oz (60 mls)
Sugar 1 oz (30 g)
Salt and pepper
Olives 2 oz (60 g)
Sliced or chopped onions 4 oz (120 g)
1 clove of garlic
Flour 2 oz (60 g)
Cornflour 1 oz (30 g) and water 3 fl oz (60 mls)

Garnish:

Sauerkraut 1 lb (480 g)
Chopped onions 1 oz (30 g)
Caraway seeds 1 oz (30 g)
Sour cream 5 fl oz (150 mls)
Lard or butter 2 oz (60 g)
Chopped parsley

Method: Saute chopped onions in butter or
bacon fat. When soft add tomato puree and
crushed garlic, crumbs, sugar and water. Boil few
minutes. Thicken mixture with cornflour dispersed in cold water (slurry). When the sauce is
thick, add vinegar. Place the fillet of fish into a
shallow dish and cover with mixture. Bake in oven
20 minutes at 380°F. Season to taste.
Garnish: Saute sauerkraut with chopped onions
in bacon fat or butter. Add sour cream, caraway
seeds and seasoning. When cooked serve with fish
placed on top of sauerkraut. Or dispose fish
mixture and sauerkraut in shallow dish in two
alternate layers like a fish pie. Top up with sliced
boiled potatoes dotted with melted butter and
sprinkled with chopped parsley, sliced cucumbers
and sliced olives.

SCAMPI TALLIN
Fried scampi in sour cream

Ingredients:

Frozen or fresh scampi 1 lb (480 g)
White wine 5 fl oz (150 mls)
Chopped onions 1 oz (30 g)
Pinch caraway seeds
Sour cream 5 fl oz (150 mls)

Salt and pepper
Butter 2 oz (60 g)
Seasoned flour 1 oz (30 g)
1 bay leaf and 1 sprig thyme

Method: Pass the shelled scampi in seasoned
flour. Saute the chopped onions in butter until
soft and translucent. Add the scampi and cook 5
minutes; add sour cream and seasoning together
with the wine. Boil 5 more minutes and reheat
scampi in sauce. Serve with sliced boiled potatoes.
Note: Crayfish can be prepared in the same way.

CRAB PIE LITHUANIA
Crab meat mixed with mushrooms and topped
with mashed potatoes

Ingredients:

White frozen crab meat 1 lb (480 g)
Flour 1 oz (30 g)
Butter 1 oz (30 g)
Sour cream ½ pint (300 mls)
Grated cheese 2 oz (60 g)
Caraway seeds
Chopped parsley
Sliced mushrooms 2 oz (60 g)
Made mustard 1 small tsp
1 small glass vodka
Mashed potatoes ½ lb (240 g)
1 egg yolk

Method: Thaw the crab and marinade with vodka
and caraway seeds. In pan make the sauce as
follows: cook butter and flour till sandy texture,
add sour cream and boil till thick. Add sliced
peeled white mushrooms and cook 2 minutes
only then add crab meat and reheat till very hot.
Season and blend made mustard. Place in small
shallow dish. Pipe round a cordon of mashed
potatoes, brush with egg yolk and sprinkle the
crab meat with grated cheese. Brown under the
grill and serve with vodka.

HALIBUT RED ARMY
Halibut baked in white wine and vodka

This is a dish I have the pleasure of creating for
special celebration buffet parties in relation to
the peace of the world and the friendship of all
nations.

Ingredients:

8 small boneless steaks of halibut 5 oz (150 g)
   each
Dry Russian white wine ½ pint (300 mls)
vodka 4 fl oz (120 mls)
1 pinch caraway seeds
Caviar 4 oz (120 g)
4 hard-boiled eggs
Sour cream 5 fl oz (150 mls)
Sliced onions 1 oz (30 g)
1 carrot
1 stick celery
1 bouquet garni
Fish bones 1 lb (480 g)
Margarine 4 oz (120 g)
Flour 1 oz (30 g)
Butter 1 oz (30 g)
2 egg yolks
Sliced mushrooms 4 oz (120 g)
Chopped parsley 1 tbs
Tomato puree 1 oz (30 g)
Salt and pepper

Method: Prepare a strong fish stock as follows:
Place fish bones in saucepan with sliced onion
and margarine and saute 5 minutes without
browning. Then add 1 pint (600 mls) water with
chopped celery, sliced carrot and the bouquet garni
Boil 20 minutes. Strain. Melt butter and cook flour
to produce a roux. Gradually add stock and when
thick, season. Add caraway seeds and sour cream.
Boil 10 minutes and strain.
Fish: Place fish in shallow tray greased with
butter. Spread a little tomato puree over the fish
and add the sliced mushrooms and parsley. Cover
with white wine and vodka. Arrange a piece of
paper on top and bake 20 minutes at 380°F.
Drain juice, add it to sauce. Add yolks, stir well.
Cool fish and place on clean flat silver or
earthenware dish. Coat the fish with cold sauce.

Decorate with cucumber, tomatoes and lettuce leaves. Top fish with a teaspoonful of caviar. Separately serve wedges of lemon, hard-boiled eggs cut in quarters and brown bread. Drink Russian champagne and vodka.

KOULIBIAC MOSCOVIANA
Poached salmon in a pastry case

This is a spectacular dish for a party, and a good way to make a 4 lb salmon serve 12 people. One of the ingredients is *vesiga*, the dried marrow from the bones of a sturgeon. It is available in some exclusive delicatessens, but if it is unobtainable, the finished dish will be almost as good.

Ingredients:

1 salmon 4 lb (1,920 g)
6 eggs
Cooked rice 1 lb (480 g) or couscous
Sliced mushrooms 1 lb (480 g)
Diced onions 8 oz (240 g)
Salt and pepper
Peeled and sliced pickled cucumber 1 lb (480 g)
Vesiga 8 oz (240 g) soaked 24 hours
Chopped parsley
Butter 8 oz (240 g)
Danish or puff pastry 3 lb (1,440 g)
Chopped prawns 4 oz (120 g)

Sauce:

Bechamel sauce 1 pint (600 mls)
Kummel liqueur 2 fl oz (60 mls)
Vodka 1 fl oz (30 mls)

Court-bouillon:

Water 3 pint (1,800 mls)
Vinegar 2 fl oz (60 mls)
Carrots 2 oz (60 g)
Onions 2 oz (60 g)
1 bouquet garni
Small pinch salt
Few peppercorns

Method: Poach salmon gently in court-bouillon for 30-45 minutes. Cool in its own liquor. Sweat chopped onions in 2 oz butter and oil until translucent but not brown. Boil the eggs for 10 minutes. Saute sliced mushrooms for 2 minutes in 6 oz butter and oil. Chop finely and boil vesiga 3 hours. Lift salmon off the bone in two fillets, skin. Roll out pastry into rectangle, 18 inch by 9 inch. On it, arrange layers of salmon, sliced egg, rice, mushrooms, pickled cucumber, and vesiga twice over in a fish shape. Fold pastry over the make a fish-shaped parcel, tucking the ends in. Use any pastry trimmings to make small triangles to resemble fish scales, and place them on the fish. Brush over with eggwash. Mark eyes of fish with pastry dots and bake in a hot oven (400°F) for 30 minutes until golden. Serve with bechamel, flavoured with kummel and vodka, or any other fish sauces.

MEAT DISHES

SOLYANKA TOLSTOY
Meat stew with sauerkraut

Ingredients:

Sauerkraut 12 oz (360 g)
Minced beef 4 oz (120 g)
Minced bacon 4 oz (120 g)
Chopped onions 4 oz (120 g)
Tomato puree 2 oz (60 g)
1 glass vodka
2 juniper berries
Sugar 2 oz (60 g)
Salt and pepper
1 bay leaf
Vinegar 1 fl oz (30 mls)
Capers 1 oz (30 g)
Bacon fat 2 oz (60 g)
Meat stock or water ½ pint (300 mls)
Flour 1 oz (30 g)
Breadcrumbs 4 oz (120 g)
Fat or butter 6 oz (180 g)

Method: Brown chopped onions (half of onions) in bacon fat till tender then add sauerkraut and tomato puree and stock. Boil gently for 20 minutes. Flavour with vodka and juniper berries. Saute the rest of onions in bacon fat and when tender add minced meat, seasoning and sugar and flour to absorb surplus fat. Cook 5 minutes at this stage. Place alternate layers of sauerkraut and minced meat in a shallow dish. Add a little more stock to keep mixture moist. Sprinkle few capers, 1 bay leaf, add vinegar. Cover dish with a lid and bake in oven for 40 minutes at 380°F. Brown crumbs in bacon fat or butter and sprinkle over the dish when the meat is cooked.

CASSEROLE OF BEEF WITH KVASS
Stew of beef (from shank, top side or flank) with beer

Ingredients:

Diced beef 1½ lb (720 g)
Fat 2 oz (60 g)
Diced carrots 5 oz (150 g)
Diced onions 5 oz (150 g)
Tomato puree 2 oz (60 g)
1 bouquet garni
Breadcrumbs 2 oz (60 g)
Salt and pepper
Kvass or beer 1 pint (600 mls)

Method: Saute meat in fat till brown then add diced carrots and onions. Stir well and cover with a lid. Sweat mixture till brown then add tomato puree and rest of ingredients. Simmer gently and keep the level of liquid the same by adding either beer or more stock. Cooking time 2 hours.

VEAL ZRAZY
Stuffed veal escalopes

Ingredients:

Seasoned flour 1 oz (30 g)
Stock ½ pint (300 mls)
Tomato puree 2 oz (60 g)
Diced bacon 1 oz (30 g)
Chopped onion and celery 1 oz (30 g)
Cornflour 1 oz (30 g)
Cold water 4 fl oz (120 mls)
8 thin veal escalopes 2 oz (60 g) each

Stuffing:

Breadcrumbs 4 oz (120 g)
Milk 8 fl oz (240 mls)
1 egg
Chopped onions 2 oz (60 g)
Salt and pepper
Fat or butter 3 oz (90 g)

Method: Prepare stuffing as follows. Sweat in fat chopped onions till tender but not brown. Add breadcrumbs and remove from heat. Add milk and egg to obtain a stiffish paste. Season.

Spread this mixture on thin battered veal escalopes. Roll each one and tie with cocktail sticks. Pass in seasoned flour then pan fry in bacon fat till brown all round. Transfer into shallow dish and cover with a stock made up of the bones as follows.

Gravy. Fry diced onions and bacon till brown. Drain fat away, add stock and tomato puree and bouquet garni. Boil 15 minutes and add to meat. Bake meat 40 minutes in shallow dish with a lid at 380°F. Strain liquor and thicken with a cornflour and water slurry. Reheat and boil. Season and strain and pour over meat. Serve with a bowl of rice pilaff or with a dish of sauerkraut.

LIVER IN SOUR CREAM

Ingredients:

8 by 2 oz (60 g) thin escalopes from calf's liver or lamb's liver
Sour cream 6 fl oz (180 mls)
Seasoned flour 1 oz (30 g)
Meat stock 6 fl oz (180 mls)
Chopped onions 2 oz (60 g)
Bacon fat or butter 2 oz (60 g)
Salt and pepper

Method: Pass the liver escalopes in seasoned flour. Pan fry in fat till done to requirement for few minutes (do not overcook). Transfer liver into shallow dish. In same pan saute chopped onions till tender but not coloured then add meat stock. Boil down till reduced by half then add sour cream and seasoning. Boil few more minutes, pour this sauce over the liver and serve.

CHICKEN KIEV

Chicken escalope stuffed with parsley butter

Ingredients:

4 chicken breasts
Breadcrumbs 6 oz (180 g)
Flour 2 oz (60 g)
Salt and pepper
2 eggs
Butter 4 oz (120 g)
Oil for frying

Butter filling:

Butter 8 oz (240 g)
Chopped parsley 1 oz (30 g)
Pinch pepper
1 or 2 chopped anchovy fillets
Juice of ½ lemon

Method: Cream butter and add chopped parsley, pepper, juice of half lemon and chopped anchovy fillets to obtain a smooth paste. Chill a little.

Remove skin and bone from breast of chicken. Lift away the under fillet and place chicken between wet papers. Beat slightly to thin it down like an escalope. Place about 1 oz (30 g) parsley butter and shape it like a small thin sausage. Place this butter in the middle of the breast and cover with a piece of the under-fillet. Roll the chicken round the butter to form a secure parcel. Tie with string or cotton. Pass in seasoned flour then in beaten eggs and breadcrumbs. Pan fry in oil or clarified butter till golden for 10 minutes. The whole secret of this dish is to prevent the butter inside the chicken from escaping or frying. If well wrapped as explained it will stay inside until the consumer carves it, when it will flow out of the chicken.

Note: The parsley butter can also be flavoured with garlic or chopped chives. It is a matter of taste and style.

GOLUBTSY

Stuffed cabbage balls

This dish is found in many countries with modified versions.

Ingredients:

8 large green cabbage leaves
Chopped onions 2 oz (60 g)
Fat 2 oz (60 g)
Minced beef 8 oz (240 g)
Minced pork 6 oz (180 g)
Chopped garlic 5 g
Chopped parsley 1 tbs
2 eggs
Flour 2 oz (60 g)
Tomato puree 4 oz (120 g)
Salt and pepper

Gravy:

Chopped onions 2 oz (60 g)
Diced bacon 2 oz (60 g)
Meat stock ½ pint (300 mls)
Salt and pepper
Cornflour 1 oz (30 g)
Water 4 fl oz (120 mls)
1 bay leaf
Sour cream 4 fl oz (120 mls)
Dill

Method: Blanch the leaves of cabbages minus the core and stem for 5 minutes. Refresh and drain. Place leaves on a board to be filled with the following mixture.

Mixture: Blend raw chopped meats and finely chopped onions, flour, tomato puree, garlic, salt and pepper. Then add eggs and chopped parsley. Divide into 2 oz (60 g) balls. Place each ball on cabbage leaf. Wrap round like a parcel. Place stuffed cabbage leaves into shallow dish. Cover with the following sauce.

Sauce: Fry chopped onions and bacon till brown, add meat stock and seasoning. Boil 10 minutes then add to cabbage balls.

Braise covered with a lid for 45 minutes. Strain gravy and thicken it in a saucepan with cornflour and cold water added to boiling liquid. Check seasoning, stir in cream and pour over the cabbage balls. Sprinkle chopped parsley or dill.

CHANAKHI

Lamb stew Georgian style

Ingredients:

Stewing lamb 1½ lb (720 g)
Diced onions 5 oz (150 g)
Fat 2 oz (60 g)
Tomato puree 2 oz (60 g)
Tomato pulp 4 oz (120 g)
Peeled and sliced aubergines 8 oz (240 g)
Diced French beans 4 oz (120 g)
Garlic 5 g
Pepper and salt
Coriander seeds
Water 2½ pint (1,500 mls)
Potatoes 1 lb (480 g)

Method: Saute the meat in fat till brown then add diced onions and rest of vegetables. Season and cover with water. Simmer for 2 hours till meat is tender. Sprinkle chopped parsley and serve.

BEEF STROGANOFF
Strips of fillet of beef in sour cream sauce

This dish was claimed by the French chef of Count Stroganoff.

Ingredients:

Fillet of beef tail end 1 lb (480 g)
Sour cream 6 fl oz (180 mls)
Chopped onion 2 oz (60 g)
Butter 2 oz (60 g)
Seasoned flour 1 oz (60 g)
Worcester sauce, few drops
Salt and pepper
Sliced mushrooms 2 oz (60 g)

Method: This dish has been modified to the fancy of the cook. It is usually prepared by the head-waiter. Some add mushrooms, others do not. Tomato ketchup or even mustard has been added. I reproduce here the dish as it was done originally in Russia.

Cut the fillet of beef in thin strips 2 inch long and ¼ inch thick. Pass in seasoned flour. Saute quickly in fat or clarified butter till tender and done (do not overcook). Transfer meat into a shallow dish and keep warm while completing the sauce. In same pan saute the chopped onions or shallots till tender but not brown, add the cream and boil 5 minutes. Season and add a few drops of Worcester sauce or ketchup, stir well and pour over the meat. Garnish with fried potatoes or rice pilaff. Sprinkle chopped parsley and serve.

SHASHLIK BREZHNEV
Skewered lamb and kidney cubes

Ingredients:

Loin of lamb 1 lb (480 g)
Lamb's kidneys 2
8 small button onions
Vinegar 2 fl oz (60 mls)
Juice of 1 lemon
Salt and pepper
Few coriander seeds
Few crushed black peppercorns
Chopped parsley
4 bay leaves
Tomato ketchup 2 tbs (60 mls)
Sugar 1 oz (30 g)
Seasoned flour 2 oz (60 g)

Method: Cut the lamb and kidney in cubes. Free of fat and skin. Marinade in a bowl with vinegar, sugar, lemon juice and onions for 6 hours. Pass the meat in seasoned flour then dip in oil and insert onto 9 inch long skewers, alternating meat, kidney pieces and button onions with a bay leaf until the skewer is full. Season and sprinkle crushed peppercorns and coriander seeds. Grill for 10 minutes. Sprinkle chopped parsley and serve with rice pilaff. Pass ketchup sauce as accompaniment.

PUSHKIN STEAK
Braised steak with walnuts

Ingredients:

4 by 6 oz (180 g) steaks from topside
Oil 2 fl oz (60 mls)
Salt and pepper
Seasoned flour 2 oz (60 g)
Chopped walnuts 8 oz (240 g)

Coriander seeds ½ oz (15 g)
Tomato puree 2 oz (60 g)
Vinegar 2 fl oz (60 mls)
1 chilli
Garlic ½ clove
Red wine 8 fl oz (240 mls)
Cornflour 1 oz (30 g)
Water 4 fl oz (120 mls)
Salt and pepper
Sour cream

Method: Flatten each steak as thinly as possible.
Pass in seasoned flour. Pan fry for few minutes
till brown on each side. Cool. Prepare sauce
mixture as follows: Chop walnuts to a paste with
chopped garlic. Blend tomato puree, chilli, salt
and pepper. Spread mixture over each steak.
Place steaks into a shallow dish and cover with
wine and vinegar and water and few coriander
seeds and 1 bay leaf. Place a lid over dish and
braise for 45 minutes to 1 hour till tender. To
sauce add 4 spoonfuls sour cream well diluted
and serve with chopped parsley sprinkled on top.

RUSSIAN PELMENI
Russian type of ravioli

These types of ravioli are preserved by freezing in
the natural temperature of Siberia, as soon as they
are prepared. On thawing out and being reheated
in sauce they acquire a very distinctive texture
which is soft and pleasant. The Pelmeni can be
filled with many kinds of mixtures: cabbage and
pork; mushrooms and rice; fish or chicken or game.

Ingredients:

Flour 11 oz (330 g)
1 egg
Water 4 fl oz (120 mls)
Salt ¼ oz (7 g)

Method: Beat egg, add to water and salt. Blend
flour to a dough with liquid. Rest 1 hour then roll
out like pastry to ⅛ inch thick. Cut into 3 inch
rounds (6 cm), put 1 oz (30 g) filling in the

centre, wet the sides with cold water and fold
over, half moon shape, the rounds, like a turnover. Press the edges firmly. Draw the two points
over making a purse-like shape. Allow to rest
for 1 hour.
Cooking: Place boiling salted water in a tray and
poach pelmeni in it till they rise to the surface
after 10 minutes. Drain and place in shallow dish
and cover with tomato sauce or just melted
butter or sour cream or au gratin with cheese.
Allow 8 portions per 2 lb (960 g) of pelmeni.
It is best to braise the pelmeni in sauce for 40
minutes.

Filling 1: Beef and pork:
    Minced beef 4 oz (120 g)
    Minced pork 4 oz (120 g)
    Chopped parsley 1 tbs
    Chopped onions ½ oz (15 g)
    Salt and pepper
Blend to a smooth paste.

Filling 2: Cabbage filling:
    Minced beef 4 oz (120 g)
    Chopped green cabbage 2 oz (60 g)
    Chopped onions 1 oz (30 g)
    Salt and pepper
Mince together.

Filling 3:
    Cooked rice 4 oz (120 g)
    Raw diced mushrooms 4 oz (120 g)
    Cooked chopped onion 1 oz (30 g)
    Salt and pepper
Mix together.

Filling 4: Fish filling:
    Minced raw white fish 4 oz (120 g)
    Raw minced onion 1 oz (30 g)
    Pinch chopped parsley
    Anchovy fillet 1 oz (30 g)
    Salt and pepper
    Pork fat 1 oz (30 g)
Blend together.

KISSLIJA KAPUSKA with MOSKOWSKII SOCISKII
Sauerkraut with frankfurter sausages

Ingredients:

Sauerkraut (canned) 17 oz (510 g)
Sliced mushrooms 4 oz (120 g)
Chopped onions 4 oz (120 g)
Caraway seeds 1 oz (30 g)
Bacon fat 3 oz (90 g)
Russian white wine 10 fl oz (300 mls)
Sour cream ½ pint (300 mls)
1 bouquet garni
Frankfurters 1 lb (480 g) — 8 in number
Salt and pepper

Method: Saute the chopped onions in bacon fat
till soft but not coloured. Add the strained sauerkraut and toss in fat. Blend the caraway seeds and
bouquet garni, add white wine and salt and
pepper. Cover with a lid and braise for 1 hour
adding mushrooms for last 10 minutes. Then
add sour cream. Garnish with reheated
frankfurter sausages or sliced cooked gammon
or ham.

TSYPLENOK-TABAKA
Fried chicken Georgia with Tkemali sauce

Ingredients:

1 roasting chicken 2½ lb (1,200 g)
Butter 2 oz (60 g)
Salt and pepper
Chopped garlic ½ oz (15 g)
Flour 2 oz (60 g)

Sauce:

Red plums ½ lb (240 g)
Plum juice ½ pint (300 mls)
Sugar 4 oz (120 g)
Pinch cinnamon
Cornflour 1 oz (30 g)
Pinch red cayenne pepper

Method: Cream the butter with chopped garlic.
Brush mixture over chicken split in two through
the back without cutting breast part — spatcock

fashion. This is done by introducing a knife into
the bird and cutting spine bone. Discard rib bones.
Dip in flour. Season to taste and roast in oven at
400°F for 25 minutes or charcoal grill. Baste with
butter from time to time.
Sauce: Poach plums with water, cinnamon and
sugar in oven. Strain juice and thicken it with
cornflour. Add cayenne pepper. Serve chicken
with this sauce to which the sieved pulp of plums
has been added.

TSCHAKKUM-BILI
Caucasian chicken

Ingredients:

1 chicken 3 lb (1,440 g)
2 oz (60 g) each of the following
  Carrots
  Onions
  Marrow
  Pickled cucumber
  Celery
  Fennel
  Oil
  Flour
Red wine 5 fl oz (150 mls)
Same amount of water or stock
Salt and pepper
Sour cream 8 fl oz (240 mls)
Pinch coriander seeds
2 cups cooked rice (*see* Pilaff, p. 000)

Method: In a biography of Stalin we learned that
his favourite meal was this chicken dish. Stalin
was very keen on cooking and often used to
prepare his own meals when on holiday.

Cut chicken in 8 pieces. Pass in seasoned flour
and pan fry with oil till tender for 20 minutes —
covering with a lid. Turn pieces from time to
time. Remove chicken and transfer in a shallow
dish. In same fat fry sliced onions, celery, sliced
carrots, marrow and pickled cucumbers for few
minutes then add to chicken. Season. Add
chopped fennel or aniseed or coriander seeds
and 1 bouquet garni. Cover level with a glass of
red wine and water. Place a lid on the dish and
roast for 40 minutes at 400°F. Strain gravy, add

a cup of sour cream and boil 5 minutes — pour over chicken. Serve with rice pilaff and pickled cucumber.

GLUKARS SMIJETANA SAUSUM
Black grouse Caucasian style

Ingredients:

4 black grouse (enough for 4 portions)
Butter and oil 1 oz (30 g) each

Sauce:

Chopped shallots 2 oz (60 g)
Sour cream 8 fl oz (240 mls)
Grated cheese 2 oz (60 g)
Salt and pepper

Method: Truss and season grouse. Roast for 20 minutes at 400°F. Carve breast and remove legs.
Sauce: Sweat in butter chopped shallots till soft then add sour cream. Boil for a few minutes. Cover the meat with sauce. Season and sprinkle with grated cheese. Brown under the grill.

RUSSIAN HOT POT LJUBUSHCHKIN
Oxtail with sauerkraut, herbs and sour cream

Nicholas Ljubushchkin was one of the most famous pre-war chefs in Russia. He worked at the hotel in Leningrad known as hotel d'Angleterre.

Ingredients:

Oxtail 4 lb (1,920 g)
Sauerkraut 1 lb (480 g)
Chopped onions 2 oz (60 g)
Stock 5 fl oz (150 mls)
Juniper berries 1 oz (30 g)
1 bouquet garni
Salt and pepper
Sour cream 8 fl oz (240 mls)
Grated horseradish 1 oz (30 g)
Sliced carrots 2 oz (60 g)

Method: Cut oxtail in sections. Remove surplus fat. Roast for 20 minutes to sear the meat at 400°F. Then place in shallow dish with layers of sauerkraut, sliced carrots, juniper berries, chopped onions and herbs. Moisten with stock, season and bake — covered with a lid — for 3 hours at 360°F. When cooked add sour cream and grated horseradish.
Note: Canned sauerkraut can be used as indicated.

VEGETABLES

POTATO OLADYI
Potato pancakes

Ingredients:

Potatoes 1 lb (480 g)
Flour 4 oz (120 g)
Yeast 1 oz (30 g)
Water 3 fl oz (90 mls)
1 egg
Salt ¼ oz (7 g)

Method: Peel and grate the potatoes. Disperse yeast in warm water at 80°F. Beat egg, add to mixture with salt and flour. Beat mixture to obtain a smooth thickish batter. Allow to ferment for one hour. Pan fry like pancakes in bacon fat or clarified butter, or mixture of both. Cook 1 spoonful at a time. Serve with sour cream or butter.

POTATO KNISHI
Stuffed potato balls

Ingredients:

Peeled potatoes 1 lb (480 g)
1 egg
Flour 4 oz (120 g)
Salt ¼ oz (7 g)
Butter 1 oz (30 g)

Method: Boil and mash potatoes and combine with beaten egg and flour and salt to form a stiff dough. Divide mixture into 8 balls. Flatten slightly like a little scone. Make a depression in the centre and fill with various mixtures. Brush with eggwash and place on greased tray. Bake 20 minutes at 380°F.

Filling 1: Cream cheese and chopped green onions or chives: Blend 4 oz (120 g) cheese with chopped chives ½ oz (15 g).

Filling 2: Blend chopped ham 4 oz (120 g) and chopped cooked mushrooms 3 oz (90 g). Bind with thick egg sauce 1 oz (30 g).

Filling 3: Blend minced beef 4 oz (120 g) and chopped cooked onions bound with 1 egg.

SWEET-SOUR SPINACH
Spinach with vinegar and tomatoes

Ingredients:

Spinach 1 lb (480 g) (frozen can be used)
Chopped onions 3 oz (90 g)
Bacon fat 1 oz (30 g)
Flour 1 oz (30 g)
Vinegar 1 fl oz (30 mls)
Sugar 2 oz (60 g)
Salt and pepper
Skinned and seeded chopped tomatoes 4 oz (120 g)

Method: Boil spinach 5 minutes. Drain and squeeze moisture out. Saute the chopped onions in fat till soft and not brown. Add flour, then dilute with vinegar. Mix in sugar and chopped tomatoes. Blend in the blanched or pre-cooked spinach and stir well. Season to taste with salt and pepper or a little crushed garlic.

CASSEROLE BEETROOT WITH SOUR CREAM

Ingredients:

Small beetroot 1 lb (480 g)
1 celeriac root
1 large carrot
Vinegar 1 fl oz (30 mls)
Sugar 1 oz (30 g)
Sour cream 5 fl oz (150 mls)
Cornflour 1 oz (30 g)

Salt and pepper
Bay leaf or pinch of carway seeds

Method: Peel celeriac and beetroot and carrot and cut in julienne (strips). Mix together in a bowl with vinegar and sugar and seasoning. Add ½ pint (300 mls) water or stock and cook gently till tender for 20 minutes. Blend cornflour and sour cream and add to mixture while boiling to thicken it at the last moment. Add a bay leaf or caraway seeds and simmer for another 10 minutes.

POTATO ZAPEKANKA
Mashed potato topped with fried onion

Ingredients:

Potatoes 1 lb (480 g)
1 egg
1 onion — 5 oz (150 g)
Milk 4 fl oz (120 mls)
Butter 1 oz (30 g)
Salt and pepper

Method: Boil and mash potatoes. Add salt and pepper, egg and milk. Place mixture in greased shallow pie dish. Saute sliced onion and spread on top. Bake in hot oven till brown then serve with sour cream or mushroom sauce.
Note: The sliced fried onions can also be mixed into the mashed potato puree instead of being spread, and grated cheese sprinkled on top and browned under the grill.

CUTLETS DOYTOSKI
Fried vegetable cakes

Ingredients:

5 oz (150 g) each of the following vegetables:
    Carrots
    Turnips
    Marrow
    Pumpkin
    Cabbage
Semolina 4 oz (120 g)
Milk 1 pint (600 mls)
3 eggs

Breadcrumbs 4 oz (120 g)
Sugar 1 oz (30 g)
Butter 2 oz (60 g)
Salt and pepper

Method: Peel and slice all vegetables and boil in
1½ pints (900 mls) water till tender, then drain.
Boil semolina in hot milk for 10 minutes. Cool and
blend all cooked ingredients together. Add egg
yolks and seasoning. When cold shape into cakes.
Pass each cake in seasoned flour and in beaten
whites of egg and breadcrumbs. Fry in butter or
oil till brown on both sides.

SWEET DISHES

VARENIKI
Sweet noodle paste filled with fruit

This is the larger version of the Pelmeni. It is made
with a sweet noodle paste and filled with fruit
like an apple turnover. It can be fried or poached
in syrup.

Ingredients:
Flour 10 oz (300 g)
Milk 3 fl oz (90 mls)
1 egg
Sugar ½ oz (15 g)
Butter ½ oz (15 g·)
Pinch salt

Method: Make a dough as directed for pelmeni
(see p. 334). Roll to ⅛ inch thickness. Cut round
5 to 6 inch diameter. Place a fruit mixture in the
centre. Wet edges and fold over half-moonshape.
Place on a tray half filled with syrup and poach
gently for 15 minutes. Allow to cool in the same
syrup overnight.

FRIED VARENIKI

Fry the vareniki in deep frying oil heated to
360°F and cook for 8 minutes till golden brown.
Sprinkle sugar and cinnamon.

FRUIT FILLINGS FOR VARENIKI

Apricot and apple: 5 oz (150 g) each peeled and
diced apples and apricots blended together
with 2 oz (60 g) apricot jam. Flavour with
a pinch of cinnamon.

Apple and blackberry: Diced peeled apples 8 oz
(240 g) and blackberries 2 oz (60 g), bound
with a little plum jam, flavoured with
cinnamon.

Cheese and raisin: Cream cheese 5 oz (150 g) (or
cottage cheese); 1 egg; 2 oz (60 g) sugar;
flour 1 oz (30 g); juice of ½ lemon; seedless
raisins 2 oz (60 g); vanilla essence.
Method: Cream cheese and sugar and flour,
add egg and lemon juice to obtain a smooth
paste then blend the seedless raisins.

Sour morello cherries: Stoned morello cherries
5 oz (150 g); cake crumbs 2 oz (60 g);
brown sugar 1 oz (30 g); pinch of cinnamon.
Blend together.

KASHA
Cereals

Kasha in Russia are various types of cereals used
as savoury or sweet dishes; including porridge
made from rye, oats and other plants, like buckwheat groats.
    The millet Kasha or semolina can be obtained
in London as 'couscous'. This fine semolina is
very nourishing and easy to prepare.

MILLET PUDDING BALLERINA

Ingredients:
Semolina 8 oz (240 g)
Milk 1½ pint (900 mls)
Sugar 2 oz (60 g)
Diced peeled pumpkin 8 oz (240 g)
Pinch salt
Pinch ground ginger

Method: Boil the milk and cook the diced pumpkin till tender (10 minutes). Stir in the semolina and sugar and salt and ginger. Cook for another 15 minutes. Transfer the mixture into a buttered pie dish. Bake in moderate oven for 10 more minutes.

BUCKWHEAT PORRIDGE WITH CHEESE

Ingredients:

Buckwheat groats 8 oz (240 g)
Cottage cheese 6 oz (180 g)
2 eggs
Milk 1 pint (600 mls)
Pinch salt
Butter 2 oz (60 g)
Sugar 3 oz (90 g)
Sour cream 4 fl oz (120 mls)
Breadcrumbs 2 oz (60 g)
Vanilla essence

Method: Bring the milk to the boil and cook the groats for 16 minutes as for porridge. Add cottage cheese and liquidise mixture. In a bowl blend the mixture with beaten eggs, sugar and sour cream, salt and add vanilla essence or any other flavour. Grease a shallow dish with plenty of soft butter and dust the inside with crumbs and sugar. Place mixture into the dish and bake for 40 minutes like a custard at 360°F. Serve with melted butter or sour cream.
Note: Same pudding can be made with semolina or oats. Zapekanka is made of thick porridge or with potato.

GEORGIAN RICE PLOV
Rice pudding

Ingredients:

Rice (patna style) 4 oz (120 g)
Butter 2 oz (60 g)
Sugar 3 oz (90 g)
Seedless raisins 4 oz (120 g)
Water 1 pint (600 mls)
Sweet wine 4 fl oz (120 mls)
Sour cream 4 fl oz (120 mls)
Juice of ½ lemon

Method: Melt butter and add rice. Cook 2 minutes to allow the butter to soak the rice, add hot water. Bring to the boil and cook 5 minutes, transfer to a pie dish. Bake 20 minutes at 400°F until rice is cooked and fluffy and separates into grains. Mix in the sugar and raisins, previously soaked in sweet wine. Serve separately the sour cream to which lemon juice has been added.
Note: Flaked almonds or walnuts or other glacé fruits can be used equally to modify this interesting drier form of rice dish.

ARMENIAN RICE ARARAT
Rice crown filled with fruit

Ingredients:

Rice (pilaff rice) 4 oz (120 g)
Butter 2 oz (60 g)
Water 1 pint (600 mls)
Salt
Sugar 2 oz (60 g)
Diced apple 2 oz (60 g)
Diced dried soaked apricots 2 oz (60 g)
Quince jelly 3 oz (90 g)
Diced pineapple 2 oz (60 g)
Segment of 1 orange
Strawberries 4 oz (120 g)
1 glass of brandy
1 glass of orange liqueur
Flaked almonds 2 oz (60 g)
Glacé cherries 1 oz (30 g)

Method: Soak the diced fruit and liqueur and brandy and quince jelly. Cook the rice as Georgian Plov. When cooked place in a crown buttered dish (savarin mould). Press rice down to form a shape. Turn over into a flat dish. Place fruit in the centre. Heat a little brandy and pour over on serving. Sprinkle also the toasted flaked almonds.
Note: Blending the fruits with quince jelly will add the characteristic flavour. It must be remembered that the rice must be well grained and cooked like a savoury pilaff – well separated. Hence its characteristic. No milk is used as a binder as in Western puddings.

KULICH
Yeast fruit cake

Ingredients:

Yeast 1 oz (30 g)
Milk 5 fl oz (150 mls)
Warm water 3 fl oz (90 mls)
2 eggs
Strong flour 1 lb (480 g)
Butter 3 oz (90 g)
Seedless raisins 3 oz (90 g)
Pinch saffron
Sugar 2 oz (60 g)
1 pinch cardamom

Method: Disperse yeast in lukewarm water. Add milk at same temperature. Beat eggs and blend all liquid together to flour. Beat mixture to a firm dough. Cover with a lid or cloth and ferment for 1 hour. Knead dough again and blend butter. Mix all fruits, sugar and essence and a little saffron and cardamom brewed in 2 oz (60 mls) hot water. Place in a well-buttered savarin or other mould. Fill two-thirds of the mould only. Let mixture swell to the top of the mould. Then bake at 420°F for 30 minutes. Cool then turn over and dust with icing sugar.

PICKLED PEARS
Pears marinaded in red wine

Ingredients:

Pears 2 lb (960 g)

Marinade:

Water or red wine 1 pint (600 mls)
Honey 2 oz (60 g)
Sugar 6 oz (180 g)
White vinegar 5 fl oz (150 mls)
Pinch mixed spice or cinnamon
1 dry chilli
Salt 1 tbs

Method: Peel and core pears and cut in quarters. Boil marinade ingredients and pour over the pears. Soak overnight and pack in jars.
Note: Do not overcook the pears. The marinade will tenderise and pickle the pears to the right texture which must be chewy and not soft.

STRAWBERRY KREMLIN
Sponge with kummel liqueur, fresh strawberries and cream

Ingredients:

1 sponge 8 oz (240 g)
Strawberries 1 lb (480 g)
Raspberry jam 4 oz (120 g)
Kummel liqueur 2 fl oz (60 mls)
Whipped cream 6 fl oz (180 mls)
Egg custard ½ pint (300 mls)
Crystallised violets 2 oz (60 g)
Orange segments 8 oz (240 g)

Method: Place a round of sponge into a bowl. Sprinkle Kummel liqueur. Cover with fresh strawberries. Coat with melted raspberry jam. Cover with thick egg custard. Leave to set. Flavour the whipped cream with Kummel and cover the custard with a layer of cream. Pipe the rest and decorate with crystallised flowers and orange segments. Serve chilled.

FRUIT AND BERRY SOUPS

APPLE AND CRANBERRY SOUPS

Ingredients:

Cranberries 10 oz (300 g)
Apples 1 lb (480 g)
Sugar 8 oz (240 g)
Potato flour 2 oz (60 g)
Water 1 pint (600 mls)

Method: Peel and core apples and boil with sugar, add berries and water. Pass puree through a nylon sieve. Thicken it with potato flour and cold water added to the boiling puree. Serve separately sour cream.

APRICOT AND APPLE SOUP

Ingredients:

Apricots 10 oz (300 g)
Apples 1 lb (480 g)
Sugar 8 oz (250 g)
Potato flour 2 oz (60 g)
Water 1 pint (600 mls)

Method: Use fruit in the same way with the same method of preparation.

RASPBERRY AND APPLE SOUP

Method: Follow similar methods as above.

MIXED DRIED FRUIT SOUP

Ingredients:

Mixed dried fruit ½ lb (240 g)
Potato flour 2 oz (60 g)
Sago 3 oz (90 g)
Sour cream 5 fl oz (150 mls)
Pinch of cinnamon

Method: Soak the dried fruit for 2 hours in hot water. Cook in 1½ pint (900 mls) water with sugar and cinnamon till tender. Cook the sago in 1 pint (600 mls) milk and sweeten with 3 oz (90 g) sugar. Thicken the juice with potato flour dispersed with a little cold water. Serve separately the sago pudding and sour cream.

DRIED FRUIT SOUP WITH MACARONI

Method: Follow a similar method to the one above, but cook the macaroni in water till tender, for 15 minutes. Drain and reheat with ½ pint (300 mls) sour cream and sugar to taste. Dish up the cooked macaroni with some of the fruits on top.

KISSEL

This essentially Russian dessert was made with soured cereal water known as 'keesel'. Potato flour began to be used as the jellying agent in the nineteenth century. Kissel may be made of any fresh berries or stone fruit pulp and juice. Allowing 2 oz (60 g) of potato flour per 1 pint (600 mls) of fruit juice and pulp mixture, depending on the pulp texture.

Kissel is usually served cold like a blanc-mange with a jug of sour cream.

Modification of this sweet is made by adding gelatine and transforming it into a jelly dessert known as Muscovite.

APPLE AND BLACKCURRANT KISSEL

Ingredients:

Peeled apples 4 oz (120 g)
Blackcurrants 4 oz (120 g)
Water 5 fl oz (150 mls)
Sugar 4 oz (120 g)
Potato flour 2 oz (60 g)
Cold water 4 fl oz (120 mls)

Method: Boil apples and blackcurrants with water and sugar. Pass the pulp and juice through a nylon sieve. Collect the mixture to obtain 1 pint (600 mls), if not enough, make up with water and reboil. Blend potato flour and cold water and add to boiling fruit mixture. Cook 5 minutes until thick. Cool and serve in individual jelly bowls or porridge pudding basins. Serve with sour cream or decorate with whipped cream.

STRAWBERRY OR RASPBERRY MUSCOVITE

Ingredients:

Water 1 pint (600 mls)
Sugar 6 oz (180 g)
Few drops of kirsch liqueur
Red colouring if needed 1 oz (30 g), or few drops
Puree of fresh or canned strawberries or raspberries 1 lb (480 g)
Gelatine 2 oz (60 g)

Method: Boil water and sugar to obtain a syrup. Add puree of fruit passed through a sieve. Dissolve gelatine and place mixture in a jelly mould. Chill and set. When firm turn over on a flat dish and decorate with whipped cream. *Note:* If powdered gelatine is used, blend it with all the sugar first, then dissolve in boiling water. Add kirsch liqueur at the last minute.

The two desserts above illustrate the method and quantities. Other fruits can be used either on their own or with half apple puree to provide pulp texture. Rhubarb, plums, apricots, peaches, and every kind of berry can be combined with apple puree.

If potato flour is not available, use half corn-flour and half gelatine. Potato granules can be used instead of the flour when it is not available.

KACHA GOURIEFF
Semolina pudding

Ingredients:

Milk 1½ pint (900 mls)
Water ½ pint (300 mls)
Semolina 6 oz (180 g)
Castor sugar ½ lb (240 g)
Mixed chopped peels, cherries, pineapple, angelica 8 oz (240 g) all together
Grated chocolate 2 oz (60 g)
Apricot sauce 4 oz (120 g)
4 egg yolks
4 egg whites
liqueur 2 fl oz (60 mls)

Method: Soak semolina in cold water. Boil milk and sugar then add soaked semolina. Cook 15 minutes like porridge. Cool and blend yolks and flavour with kummel liqueur or orange liqueur or vanilla essence. Mix in diced glacé cherries, angelica, peels and pineapple and grated chocolate. Beat whites like meringue. Fold into mixture lightly. Place in greased mould and bake in tray half filled with hot water. Poach for 45 minutes in oven at 330°F. Unmould into flat dish. Cover with melted apricot sauce flavoured with kirsch or other liqueur.

GOZINAKH
Walnut sweetmeat

Ingredients:

Walnuts 8 oz (240 g)
Thick honey 8 oz (240 g)
Icing sugar 4 oz (120 g)
Oil 2 oz (60 g)

Method: Chop walnuts and toast them for few minutes in oven. Boil honey and icing sugar. Add to nuts and cook 15 minutes. Oil a dish and place mixture in it. Cool. When cold, cut in squares. Mixture can also be cooled on oiled marble board within a framework of wood. Cut like toffee.

PASKHA
Cheese pudding

Ingredients:

Cream cheese 1½ lb (720 g)
Whipped cream 8 fl oz (240 mls)
Castor sugar 8 oz (240 g)
Glacé cherries 4 oz (120 g)
Peels 4 oz (120 g)
Glacé pineapple and same amount seedless raisins or sultanas 4 oz (120 g)
Orange liqueur
Vanilla essence
4 egg yolks
Piping jelly for decoration

Method: Cream the cheese with yolks and add cream and sugar. Mix the peels and chopped nuts and glace cherries and sultanas. Add vanilla essence or rosewater or kirsch. Place in a pyramid mould or pudding basin to set. Chill. When cold turn over like a blanc-mange. Decorate with whipped cream and glacé cherries. With piping jelly write 'X.B.' or 'J.C.' and interpret this sign as you wish. This sweet is served at Easter. Serve this cream cheese with brioche or koulitch cake.

COTTAGE CHEESE PUDDING

Ingredients:

Cottage or cream cheese 1 lb (480 g)
1 egg
Sour cream 3 fl oz (90 mls)
Vanilla essence and grated lemon
Fine uncooked semolina 2 oz (60 g)
Seedless raisins 3 oz (90 g)
Honey 6 oz (180 g)
Butter 2 oz (60 g)
Pinch salt

Method: Mix all ingredients except butter and honey. Place in a pie dish. Brush top with butter and bake 20 minutes at 360°F. Serve with fruit compote, melted honey and sour cream separately.

CREAM CHEESE PANCAKES

Ingredients:

Pancakes:

Flour 4 oz (120 g)
1 egg
Milk ½ pint (300 mls)
Pinch salt
Oil

Filling:

Cream cheese 4 oz (120 g)
1 egg
Sugar 2 oz (60 g)
1 lemon (juice and grated rind)

Method: Make batter and rest for 1 hour. Cook pancakes as thinly as possible. Cream the cheese mixture ingredients. Fill each pancake and roll up. Dust with icing sugar and serve hot.

UKRAINIAN GALUSHKI
Cheese dumplings

Ingredients:

Cream cheese 1 lb (480 g)

2 eggs
Sugar 3 oz (90 g)
Butter 2 oz (60 g)
Flour 8 oz (240 g)
Breadcrumbs 4 oz (120 g)
Salt
Sour cream 4 fl oz (120 mls)

Method: Blend cream cheese, sugar and salt with beaten eggs and flour. Place mixture on a floured pastry board. Roll the mixture sausage-like about 1 inch diameter. Cut in small piece 2½ inch long. Shape with hand to make sure each 'galushki' is of a regular shape. Place in a tray filled with hot salted water and poach until they rise to the top. Remove and drain. Pass in melted butter and crumbs and pan fry lightly till golden. Serve the galushki with sour cream or with fruit compote.

RUSSIAN PIES AND PASTRIES

In common with British people, the Russians are very fond of pastries, pies and dumplings. There are three categories of pastries which must not be confused. Pirozhki (Russian spelling) are small closed pies, patties or turnovers of various shapes made from a yeast dough or bun dough to be exact. Pirogi are the same but bigger, made of the same bun dough, and Kulebyaki are large pies of six to eight portions.

COULIBIAC
Straight bun dough mixture

Ingredients:

Strong bread flour 1 lb (480 g)
Yeast 1 oz (30 g)
Butter 1 oz (30 g)
Lukewarm milk 8 fl oz (240 mls)
1 egg
Pinch salt
Same amount of sugar

Method: Disperse yeast in lukewarm milk with sugar. Allow 15 minutes of fermentation and blend to flour with salt to form a smooth dough adding beaten egg and soft butter. Knead well and gather into a ball as you would do with bread. Cover with a large basin and let ferment to double in size for 45 minutes. Then knead again and start using like ordinary pastry, rolling and cutting to the required size.

KAZAKH (BELYASH)
Minced beef pie

Ingredients:

Yeast dough 1 lb (480 g)

Filling:

Cooked minced beef ½ lb (250 g)
Onions 2 oz (60 g) bound with 1 egg, salt and
    pepper

Method: Roll out yeast pastry and cut into 5 inch rounds. Place a ball of beef mixture in the centre. Wet edges and fold over and let the turnovers stand for 15 minutes. Fry in deep fat till golden. Use coarsely crushed black pepper in seasoning the beef.

Same procedure for Pirozhki using any kind of meat or filling but shaped in rectangles (like sausage rolls).

VATRUSHKA
Doughnut filled with sour cream

Ingredients:

Yeast dough 1 lb (480 g)

Filling:

Cream cheese 4 oz (120 g)
Flour 1 oz (30 g)
Sugar 1 oz (30 g)
1 egg beaten until smooth

Method: Divide fermented bread or bun dough into small 1½ oz (45 g) balls. Place each ball on a tray and let them ferment like bread rolls, brushed with eggwash to prevent skinning. After 20 minutes, fill them with cream cheese mixture —

like doughnuts. Allow to swell again for 10 minutes and fry them in oil till golden. Dust with castor sugar.

LIDA AND PETER'S BALTIC TORTE
Red berry cheese cake

Ingredients:

Sweet short spice biscuit pastry:

Flour 6 oz (180 g)
Butter 4 oz (120 g)
Lard 1 oz (30 g)
Icing sugar 1 oz (30 g)
1 egg
Pinch of cinnamon

Cheese filling:

Cream cheese 6 oz (180 g)
Grated cheese 1 oz (30 g)
Sugar 2 oz (60 g)
Flour 1 oz (30 g)
2 egg yolks
3 egg whites
Orange essence
Grated peels
Vanilla essence

Topping:

Cranberry pie filling 5 oz (150 g)
Cornflour 1 oz (30 g)
Sugar 3 oz (90 g)
Red port wine 5 fl oz (150 mls)
Gelatine 1 oz (30 g)

Method: Prepare a sweet short pastry: Cream fat and sugar with ground cinnamon till fluffy. Add beaten egg then flour. Knead well. Rest 30 minutes. Roll out to ¼ inch thick, 9 inch diameter and line a 2 inch deep torte flan mould or ring.
Filling: Cream cheeses, flour and sugar. Add yolks. Fold whites beaten to a meringue and blend peels and add flavour. Place mixture inside pastry case. Bake at 400°F for the first 15 minutes. Reduce heat to 380°F and bake for another 30 minutes.

Cool and when cold place fruit topping thickened
with cornflour.

Topping: Boil cranberry with port wine and sugar.
Blend cornflour, gelatine and water and add to
boiling mixture. Cook 4 minutes until it clears.
Cool. Pour over the cold torte while still warm
and soft. Chill.

Scandinavia

There are two certainties in the life of every man: that he was born, and that he must die. To this, the Scandinavians add one other: that winter must come. Winter comes early, stays late and banishes the sun from the sky for its duration. So in the short season when everything grows, the Scandinavians traditionally preserve, pickle, smoke and dry the food to last them through another winter. As a result, the national cuisine uses fresh ingredients some of the time, but many specialities include foods traditionally preserved. The Vikings started this frenzy of preserving meat and fish, and implements to cut up the dried cod which was their staple diet have been found on a funeral boat excavated in Norway. The preserving processes may have improved since their day, but dried cod, smoked meat, even dried bread folded like a table napkin for storage to be used in the dreary, barren winter are still to be found throughout the Scandinavian countries.

Rugged coastlines mean good fishing in the five principal Scandinavian countries, and because they are so plentiful and easy to preserve, cod and herring have become the most important fish on Scandinavian tables. Cod may be dried and salted to preserve its nutritional values almost indefinitely, and it can be reconstituted to make a wide variety of dishes. Herring is even more versatile. Each country in Scandinavia has its own special way of dealing with this silvery fish, each of which furnishes about half the protein a full-grown active man needs in a day. One of the most usual ways of eating herring in all Scandinavian countries is in the cold buffet which is a feature of all Scandinavian cuisine (the Swedes call it *smorgasbord*, the Danes *smorrebrod*). The Norwegians often have it for breakfast, the Icelanders include dried fish which has been hammered rather than cooked, and the Finns, independent to the last, call it *voileipapoyta*.

The bases of preparing and eating it are similar in all of those countries. At first it may look like a giant sampler of all the food available that day, but there is a pattern and a reason to it. Abroad, the *smorgasbord* may be a selection of open sandwiches — each laden with meat, fish or cheese, and garnished with vegetables, sauces and flavours of all kinds, often with elaborate trimmings such as radish roses or pictures made of strips of truffles. But this is only one type of *smorrebrod*: the Danish open sandwich.

The Swedes, Icelanders, Finns and Norwegians do it rather differently: they arrange, simply and without any elaborate frills, large varieties of food, each in its own dish, and with bread served separately for those who want it. The gigantic *smorgasbord*s in the best hotels in these countries look like a random arrangement, but there is a very definite order in which the dishes are laid out. First come the cold dishes based on herring, which are the traditional first course. Next come other fish dishes like smoked salmon and eel, jellied salmon, cod roe or lumpfish caviar. Next are the cold cuts of meat and various salads, and the last step is the selection of hot dishes at the opposite ends of the buffet to the herring end. The hot dishes might include such delicacies as meat balls, always served without sauce in Sweden, deep-fried fish, an omelette or some pork chops. The final course is a sweet, served from a separate table, often a fruit salad or a fresh, unfermented cheese, such as the Icelandic *skyr*. The entire meal is helped down by schnapps or akvavit.

The Scandinavian countries produce excellent lager beers but the star of any gastronomic display is undoubtedly the schnapps or akvavit, served ice-cold in small glasses.

The feeling still clings to my mind of those days during my visit to Stockholm in 1937 — when I sipped schnapps after schnapps at the Grand Hotel — and missed my boat.

Sweden

Sweden is the largest of the Nordic countries and the most affluent. About 15,000 years ago, Sweden was entirely covered by a thick blanket of ice. As the ice gradually withdrew northwards, it left behind a landscape of incredible beauty: forests, lakes, mountains, plains — Sweden is blessed with the lot. The Gulf Stream warms the shores of Norway, giving a more temperate climate than Alaska at the same latitude to the entire peninsula.

The Swedes are extremely modern in outlook and there are skyscrapers everywhere in the larger cities; yet they cling to some of the old ways from the time when Sweden was a nation of peasant farmers. They are worldly and their restaurants offer some of the most elaborate and delicious creations in the style of haute cuisine, for they have a long tradition of royal patronage for grand dishes. Yet side by side with this sophisticated cuisine is the plain, basic cooking of the people, with pea soup made from dried yellow split peas and a slice of fat bacon; salt herrings with sour cream; baked brown beans; fruit soups; beer-flavoured stews and potato dumplings stuffed with minced pork.

All the usual European vegetables grow in Sweden, but the most popular in Swedish cookery are cabbage, carrots, beets and the potato. A typically Swedish flavouring is dill, used on all sorts of food from potatoes to crayfish.

A relatively new industry in this highly industrialised country is the production of reindeer meat, available frozen in supermarkets in Sweden, Norway and Finland, and now finding export markets.

In a country as far north as Sweden, the basic rhythms of the year are determined by the sun and its absence. Winter means hot soups thick as porridge, fat meat, salt herrings and dried fish. Vegetables which taste best are those that can be stored in the long night of winter, and cabbages, onions and beets were the only ones available before modern technology gave every housewife a freezer.

Summer food is distinctively light and fresh. Fish, crayfish, pork and veal come into their own. Berries grow in the forests and are eaten with pancakes and on their own with sugar. Lightness is all, and people stay up late to enjoy the long, long days.

The crayfish season starts on 7th August, and the tiny crustaceans are caught in wire traps set in the lakes. They are very close relatives of the lobster, and have a delicate taste which is intensified by the dill in their boiling water. The secret of getting the right flavour is to leave them in the dill-flavoured water until it has cooled. They are eaten with the fingers between long sips of akvavit. For two months or so, the sound of crayfish parties punctuates the late summer evenings.

The long winter can become immensely depressing, so the welcome feast of Christmas is celebrated in Scandinavia with a gusto unequalled anywhere. Christmas Eve is the most important day of the festival, and traditional foods are eaten. Lightly salted ham is boiled or roasted as part of a gigantic *smorgasbord*, along with roast spare ribs and sausages in memory of the slaughtering of pigs to provide fresh meat for the Yuletide table. Dark bread is dipped into the water in which the ham was boiled in traditional remembrance of the days when even that little bit of nourishment could not be wasted in winter. *Lutfisk* is another traditional Christmas dish: dried ling fish is soaked, boiled and served in a white sauce, and an indispensable part of Christmas is rice porridge, a humble peasant dish which even the most sophisticated Swede would not miss on Christmas Eve.

A unique dish for which the expatriate Swede yearns is the *surstromming*, Baltic herring which has been immersed in brine, cleaned and then stacked in barrels to ferment in the sun for a day. Space is left at the top of the barrel so that any gases formed will not cause an explosion. The barrel of fermenting herrings is then put into a cool room to slow down the fermenting. Their aroma gets progressively stronger until they are just ripe enough for their enthusiastic public; they are then canned. The fish is eaten, unless the tin has exploded, with thick bread and boiled potatoes. Even some Swedes say that the most difficult part is to get it past your nose.

BILL OF FARE

Soup

KALSOPPA MED FRIKADELLAR
Beef and cabbage soup

ARTER MED FLASK
Split pea soup with pork

NASSELKAL
Nettle soup

Hors d'Oeuvre

FAGELBO
Anchovy salad with potatoes, beets and spring
   onions

TIVOLI SALLAD
Herrings, beef, potato and apple salad

HONS I PEPPARROTSMAJONNAS
Swedish chicken salad in mayonnaise

JANSSON'S FRESTELSE
Hot anchovy and potato pie

LAX MED PEPPARROTSGRADE
Cornucopia of smoked salmon with whipped
   cream and horseradish on rye bread

ROKT LAXLADA
Smoked salmon custard tartlets

MEDALJONGER AV RAKOR
Shrimp or prawn cake

Fish Dishes

FYLLDA PANNKATKOR MED RAKSUVNING
Pancakes stuffed with scampi, prawns or
   crayfish and diced cooked potatoes baked
   like a pudding in a mould

TORSKROMPASTEJ
Cod's roe cake

KORT LUTFISK
Salted cod or ling boiled with potatoes

Meat Dishes

SMA KOTTBULLAR
Swedish meat dumplings

KOKT GRILJERAD SKINDA
Ham Swedish style

SJOMANSBIFF
Sailor's beef stew with potatoes and onions

Vegetables

VITKALSOPPA
Braised white cabbage

BONOR OCH SVAMP
Green beans with mushrooms in cream

Sweets and Breads

RAAMUNKAR or RARAKOR
Potato griddle cakes

SEMLOR
Shrove Tuesday buns

SMORBAKELSER
Swedish puff pastry

JULSTJARNOR
Christmas star

KONVOLUT
Pastry envelopes

PEPPARKAKOR
Christmas ginger snaps

SPRITSKRANSAR
S-shaped almond biscuits

MANDELFORMAR
Almond tartlets

RAGKAKOR
Rye cookies

JULGLOGG
Christmas wine cup

SOUP

KALSOPPA MED FRIKADELLER
Beef and cabbage soup   (4 to 6 portions)

Ingredients:

White cabbage 2 lb (960 g)
Butter 2 oz (60 g)
Lard 2 oz (60 g)
Golden syrup 1 oz (30 g)
Water 2½ pint (1,500 mls)
Salt and pepper

Frikadeller:

Minced beef 4 oz (120 g)
Minced pork 4 oz (120 g)
Minced ham 2 oz (60 g)
Breadcrumbs 2 oz (60 g)
Chopped onions 2 oz (60 g)
1 egg
Salt and pepper
Flour 1 oz (30 g)

Method: Trim cabbage and remove core, ribs and coarse leaves. Cut in shreds and wash well. Heat lard and butter in a large saucepan and add shredded cabbage, syrup and water. Season and boil for half an hour. Garnish with cooked frikadeller made as follows.
Frikadeller: Blend all the meats and other ingredients to a compact mixture. Divide into small dumplings 1 oz (30 g) each and roll in flour. Place in a tray with the cabbage stock and cook in the oven for 20 minutes at 380°F.

ARTER MED FLASK
Split pea soup with pork

Ingredients:

Yellow split peas 8 oz (240 g)
Water 2½ pint (1,500 mls)
Salted belly of pork or streaky bacon 8 oz (240 g)
Leeks 2 oz (60 g)
Onion 2 oz (60 g)
Pinch of mace, nutmeg and cloves
Cream 5 fl oz (150 mls)

Method: Soak peas overnight and cook in cold water. Stir the peas and bring to the boil gently. Remove coagulated albumen and when clear add chopped onion, leek and bacon. Simmer gently for 1 hour and remove bacon. Pass through a strainer and season. Complete the soup either with a little milk or cream. The bacon can be eaten cold with mustard and pickles or served as a garnish for the soup.

NASSELKAL
Nettle soup (4 to 6 portions)

Ingredients:

Nettle tops 2 lb (960 g)
Water 2½ pint (1,500 mls)
Giblets or a piece of streaky bacon 8 oz (240 g)
Leek or onion 2 oz (60 g)
Lard 2 oz (60 g)
Salt and pepper
Potatoes 8 oz (240 g)
Cream 5 fl oz (150 mls)

Method: Wash and drain nettle tops. Saute chopped onions or leeks in a large saucepan, add the nettle tops and simmer for 5 minutes. Cover with water, add giblets or streaky unsmoked bacon. Add sliced potatoes and cook for a further 15 minutes. Pass through a sieve or liquidiser and season to taste. Add cream or milk and serve with giblets or streaky bacon separately or as a garnish.

HORS D'OEUVRE

FAGELBO
Anchovy salad with potatoes, beets and spring onions

Ingredients:

Diced cooked potato 8 oz (240 g)
Diced cooked beets 4 oz (120 g)
Chopped spring onions 2 oz (60 g)
Oil 3 tbs (45 mls)
Vinegar 1½ tbs (22 mls)

Salt and pepper
Anchovy fillets

Method: Blend all ingredients together with dressing and decorate with anchovy fillets in a criss-cross pattern.

TIVOLI SALAD
Herrings, beef, potato and apple salad

Ingredients:

Cooked diced silverside beef 4 oz (120 g)
Diced herring rollmops 4 oz (120 g)
Diced boiled new potatoes 8 oz (240 g)
Diced apples 4 oz (120 g)
Diced pickled cucumber 4 oz (120 g)
Chopped celery 2 oz (60 g)
Chopped onions 2 oz (60 g)

Swedish sauce:

Chopped hard-boiled eggs 4 oz (120 g)
Chopped parsley 1 tbs
Capers 2 oz (60 g)
Oil 4 tbs (60 mls)
Vinegar 2 tbs (30 mls)
Salt and pepper
Made mustard 1 tsp

4 large lettuce leaves
16 oysters

Method: Mix all the diced ingredients and celery and onions. Prepare a dressing by diluting the mustard with vinegar, add oil, then chopped eggs, capers, parsley and seasoning. Blend dressing to the main mixture and garnish with lettuce leaves. Open oysters and serve on the shell around the salad with brown bread and butter.

HONS I PEPPARROTSMAJONNAS
Swedish chicken with salad in mayonnaise

Ingredients:

Diced cooked white chicken meat 8 oz (240 g)
Shredded celeriac 4 oz (120 g)

Diced apples 4 oz (120 g)
Rich mayonnaise 4 oz (120 g)
Whipped cream 3 fl oz (90 mls)
Grated horseradish sauce 2 oz (60 g)
Chopped celery 2 oz (60 g)
Anchovy fillets 4 oz (120 g) for decoration
2 chopped hard-boiled eggs
8 lettuce leaves

Method: Blend all but last three ingredients together. Smooth the top and decorate with criss-cross lines of anchovy fillets. Sprinkle with hard-boiled eggs and serve on lettuce leaves.

JANSSON'S FRESTELSE
Hot anchovy and potato pie

Ingredients:

Diced boiled new potatoes 1 lb (480 g)
Cream ½ pint (300 mls)
Chopped onions 2 oz (60 g)
Butter 2 oz (60 g)
Lard 2 oz (60 g)
Salt and pepper
Anchovy fillets 4 oz (120 g)
Grated cheese 2 oz (60 g)

Method: Sweat chopped onions without browning in lard and butter for 5 minutes. Add the cream and boil for a further 4 minutes, season. Place the diced cooked potatoes in a shallow dish and cover with the cream sauce. Sprinkle with grated cheese and bake at 380°F for 15 minutes. Cool and when cold decorate with anchovy fillets in a criss-cross pattern. Serve cold.

LAX MED PEPPARROTSGRADE
Cornucopia of smoked salmon with whipped cream and horseradish on rye bread

Ingredients:

Horseradish cream in jar 1 oz (30 g)
Whipped cream 4 fl oz (120 mls)
Prawns 4 oz (120 g)
Smoked salmon cut in slices thin 6 oz (180 g)

8 small slices of buttered rye bread
Pinch of paprika
Ground gelatine ½ oz (15 g)
Hot fish stock or water 2 fl oz (60 mls)
Pinch of salt
Pinch of sugar
Maggi aspic jelly crystals ½ oz (15 g)
   with water 2 fl oz (60 mls)

Method: Blend salt and sugar with ground gelatine
and add boiling water or stock to melt. Heat the
mixture a little and add horseradish cream or
grated horseradish, prawns and paprika. Cool and
blend lightly to the whipped cream when
completely cold but not jellified. (The gelatine
will set the cream like a mousse mixture.) Make
cornets with the smoked salmon slices by
wrapping the slices inside metal horns. Brush with
aspic jelly and set in the refrigerator. Remove the
salmon cornets from the metal horns and fill them
with the prawn and cream mixture. Place one
cornet per slice of bread.

ROKT LAXLADA
Smoked salmon custard tartlets

Ingredients:

Short pastry 8 oz (240 g)
Smoked salmon trimmings 4 oz (120 g)
2 eggs
Milk ½ pint (300 mls)
Salt, pepper and paprika

Method: Line greased tartlet moulds with short
pastry as for minced tarts. Put salmon trimmings
in bottom of each. Beat eggs and blend with
milk. Strain and season. Half fill tartlets with
egg custard mixture and bake for 10 minutes
at 420°F. Remove and fill tartlets to the top with
rest of custard. Bake at 380°F for 15 minutes.
Serve hot or cold with wedges of lemon.
   Use tartlet mould 1½ inch deep by 3½ inch
diameter.

MEDALJONGER AV RAKOR
Shrimp or prawn cake

Ingredients:

Cream cheese 8 oz (240 g)
Shelled shrimps or prawns 6 oz (180 g)
1 egg
White breadcrumbs 2 oz (60 g)
Salt and pepper
1 garlic clove or chopped chives 1 tbs
   $^1/_5$ oz (5 g) *only*
Seasoned flour
1 beaten egg
Breadcrumbs and seasoned flour
Frying oil

Method: Blend beaten egg with cream cheese and
breadcrumbs and add seasoning, crushed garlic and
shrimps. Shape like scones and pass in seasoned
flour, beaten egg and crumbs, and fry in deep fat
for 4 minutes until golden. Serve hot or cold.

FISH DISHES

FYLLDA PANNKATKOR MED RAKSUVNING
Pancakes stuffed with scampi, prawns or
   crayfish and diced cooked potatoes baked
   like a pudding in a mould

Ingredients:

Pancake batter:

1 egg
Milk ½ pint (300 mls)
Flour 5 oz (150 g)
Yeast ¼ oz (7 g)
Lard 2 oz (60 g)

Filling:

White sauce 6 fl oz (180 mls)
Boiled scampi, prawns or crayfish tails 8 oz (240 g)
Chopped or sliced mushrooms 4 oz (120 g)
Butter 2 oz (60 g)
Diced cooked potatoes 4 oz (120 g)
Oil 2 fl oz (60 mls)
Chopped onions 1 oz (30 g)

Vinegar 1 fl oz (30 mls)
1 beaten egg
Salt and pepper
Butter and lard for greasing 2 oz (60 g)

Method: Mix beaten egg and lukewarm milk together and add crumbled yeast. Blend flour and stir mixture to obtain a thickish batter. Let mixture ferment for 1 hour at kitchen temperature. Heat a pancake pan with a little lard and cook pancakes. Spread pancakes on a clean board to cool. Prepare prawn mixture as follows. Sweat onions in oil and butter until tender. Add mushrooms and cook for 4 minutes only. Add vinegar, boil for 2 minutes and blend white sauce, seasoning, potatoes and prawns. Reheat until mixture boils and cool. When cold add 1 beaten egg. Grease a shallow dish with butter and lard and line with cold pancakes to cover the bottom and sides and overlapping slightly. Fill the inside with prawn mixture and cover with more pancakes. Brush with melted butter and bake at 360°F for 25 minutes. Serve cold.
Note: I have modified this dish as a contribution to Swedish gastronomy.

TORSKROMPASTEJ
Cod's roe cake

Ingredients:

Smoked cod's roe 8 oz (240 g)
White sauce ¼ pint (150 mls)
Diced cooked potatoes 4 oz (120 g)
Chopped raw onions 2 oz (60 g)
Salt and pepper
Juice and grated rind of 1 lemon
1 beaten egg
Seasoned flour and breadcrumbs
Oil for frying

Method: Skin cod's roe and blend with finely diced cooked potatoes and chopped onions. Mix with the cold white sauce, season to taste and add lemon rind and juice. Divide the mixture into 8 cakes and pass in seasoned flour, then beaten egg and breadcrumbs. Fry in a shallow pan on both sides for 5 minutes. Serve hot or cold with wedges of lemon and brown bread and butter.

KOKT LUTFISK
Salted cod or ling boiled with potatoes

Ingredients:

Soaked salted cod 1 lb (480 g)
Water 2 pint (1,200 mls)
White sauce ½ pint (300 mls)
Butter 4 oz (120 g)
Boiled potatoes 2 lb (960 g)
Salt and pepper
Black pepper
Green peas 6 oz (180 g)
1 bouquet garni
Onion studded with 2 cloves

Method: Soak fish overnight. Boil in water gently for 20 minutes with 1 onion and 1 bouquet garni. Remove skin, season and serve on a dish coated with white sauce, with potatoes, peas and melted butter.

MEAT DISHES

SMA KOTTBULLAR
Swedish meat dumplings

Ingredients:

Minced beef 8 oz (240 g)
Minced pork 8 oz (240 g)
Chopped onions 2 oz (60 g)
1 egg
Breadcrumbs 2 oz (60 g)
Salt and pepper
Pinch of mace and cloves
Stock ½ pint (300 mls)

Method: Blend all ingredients except stock together and re-mince again. Divide the mixture into 2 oz (60 g) dumplings. Place in a greased tray and cover with stock and bake for 20 minutes at 380°F. Serve hot or cold with tomato sauce.

KOKT GRILJERAD SKINDA
Ham Swedish style (10-12 portions)

Ingredients:

Small green gammon 4 lb (1,920 g)
Water 5 pint (3,000 mls)
1 bouquet garni
1 onion studded with 4 cloves
Vinegar 5 fl oz (150 mls)

Glaze:

2 egg whites
Mustard powder ¼ oz (7 g)
Castor sugar 2 oz (60 g)
Mixed spices 1 level tsp (5 g)
Brown breadcrumbs 6 oz (180 g)

Method: Place gammon in a large pot and cover level with cold water and vinegar. Bring to the boil slowly and remove scum as it rises. When the stock is clear add bouquet garni and studded onion. Simmer gently for 2 hours and cool in its own liquor. Remove the rind, trim fat a little and place the gammon in a roasting tray. Blend glaze mixture by adding sugar and spices to mustard and egg white. Coat the ham with this paste and bake at 400°F for 8 minutes to add colour and caramelise. Remove, cool and roll in brown breadcrumbs. Serve cold with salads and pickles.

SJOMANSBIFF
Sailor's beef stew with potatoes and onions

Ingredients:

4 thick slices of topside beef 8 oz (240 g) each
Sliced onions 8 oz (240 g)
Sliced potatoes 1 lb (480 g)
Lard 3 oz (90 g)
Salt and pepper
Pinch of mace or black pepper
Water 1 pint (600 mls)
Beer ½ pint (300 mls)
1 bouquet garni
Chopped parsley 1 tbs
Vinegar 2 tbs (30 mls)
Sugar 1 oz (30 g)

Method: Pan fry the steaks in lard for 5 minutes to sear the juices. Place in a shallow dish and add bouquet garni. In same fat fry onions till golden brown and add to steak. Season and cover dish neatly with sliced potatoes. Boil water and beer with vinegar and sugar and add to mixture. Bake in a moderate oven for 1 hour. Serve with a sprinkling of chopped parsley.

VEGETABLES

VITKALSOPPA
Braised white cabbage

Ingredients:

Cabbage 3 lb (1,440 g)
Chopped onions 8 oz (240 g)
Brown sugar 2 oz (60 g)
Malt vinegar 2 fl oz (60 mls)
Water 2 pint (1,200 mls)
Bacon trimmings
1 bouquet garni

Method: Clean, core and shred cabbage. Place in a saucepan with chopped onions and remaining ingredients and braise gently for 40 minutes. Remove bacon trimmings and bouquet garni and serve with frankfurters.

BONOR OCH SVAMP
Green beans with mushrooms in cream

Ingredients:

Green beans 1 lb (480 g)
Sliced white mushrooms 8 oz (240 g)
Butter 4 oz (120 g)
Salt and black pepper
Cream 4 fl oz (120 mls)
Sugar ½ oz (15 g)

Method: Head and tail beans and cut in slices slantwise. Boil in salted water for 8 minutes, refresh and drain. Wash mushrooms and slice. In a saucepan melt butter and add mushrooms. Toss for 2 minutes, add beans and stir in cream. Season and add sugar.

SWEETS and BREADS

RAAMUNKAR or RARAKOR
Potato griddle cakes

Ingredients:

Potatoes 1 lb (480 g)
Lard for frying 4 oz (120 g)

Batter mixture:

1 egg + 1 egg yolk
Flour 5 oz (150 g)
Milk ½ pint (300 mls)
Pinch of salt and sugar

Method: Blend beaten eggs with milk and flour to obtain a smooth batter. Add seasoning and rest for 20 minutes. Grate potatoes and squeeze the moisture through a cloth. Add to batter and stir well. Heat a pan with lard and fry a spoonful of this mixture at a time. Turn over like a fritter and cook for a few minutes. Serve with rashers of bacon or fried sausages or with sugar or jam.

SEMLOR
Shrove Tuesday buns

Ingredients:

Saffron 1 sachet (5 g)
Water 5 fl oz (150 mls)
Baker's yeast 1 oz (30 g)
Salt ¼ oz (7 g)
Sugar 2 oz (60 g)
1 egg
Butter 2 oz (60 g)
Milk 6 fl oz (180 mls)
Strong flour 1 lb (480 g)
Pinch of mixed spices

Syrup:

Water 2 fl oz (60 mls)
Sugar 6 oz (180 g)
    (Boil together for 4 minutes)

Method: Brew saffron leaves in boiling water away from heat. When cold strain. Add sugar, salt and spices. Crumble yeast in lukewarm milk, add beaten egg and melted butter and blend to flour. Mix with the saffron water. Knead the dough well and roll into a ball. Cover with an upside down basin and ferment for 40 minutes. Knock back by kneading again and blend raisins. Roll into a ball again and rest for a further 20 minutes. Divide mixture into 1½ oz (45 g) buns, shape round with fingers on a board and place on a greased tray. Brush with milk and rest for 30 minutes in a warm kitchen to prove to the right size. Bake at 420°F for 15 minutes. Remove and brush with syrup.

SMORBAKELSER
Swedish puff pastry

Ingredients:

Butter 10 oz (300 g)
Strong flour 1 lb (480 g)
Lard 2 oz (60 g)
Iced water 9 fl oz (270 mls)
Lemon juice ½ fl oz (15 mls)
Pinch salt

Method: Cut butter in ¼ inch cubes. Rub lard into flour and add cubed butter. Add lemon juice and water with a pinch of salt and blend to a dough without crushing the butter cubes. Place on board and roll into an oblong 9 inch by 3 inch. Fold in three and turn sideways so that the three layers are facing you. Roll again into an oblong the same size. Rest for 20 minutes in a refrigerator and repeat twice again with two turns each time. Rest between turns in the refrigerator. The pastry is then ready for use.

JULSTJARNOR
Christmas star

Method: Roll pastry $\frac{1}{8}$ inch thick. Cut into four 1 inch squares and place 1 tablespoon of jam in the centre of each. Press together and slit each corner 1½ inch towards centre. Fold alternate points into the centre and press together. Brush with beaten egg and bake in a hot oven at 425°F for 8 to 10 minutes.

KONVOLUT
Pastry envelope

Method: Cut pastry into 4 by 1 inch squares and place a tablespoon of jam in centre of each. Fold two opposite corners and then fold to almost join the centre. Brush with beaten egg and bake as above.

PEPPARKAKOR
Christmas ginger snaps

Ingredients:

Lard or fat shortening 2 oz (60 g)
Brown sugar 2 oz (60 g)
Black or golden treacle 1 oz (30 g)
Water 1 fl oz (30 mls)
Grated lemon peel ¼ oz (7 g)
Flour 8 oz (240 g)
Baking soda 1 level tsp (5 g precisely)
Pinch of cinnamon, ground cloves and cardamon

Method: Cream fat and sugar with treacle and add water and lemon rind. Sift flour with baking soda and spices and add to creamed mixture. Blend well to a stiff dough and rest in the refrigerator for two hours. Roll on a floured board and with a pastry cutter make various biscuit designs. Place on a greased tray and bake at 360°F for 10 minutes. Cool and brush with water icing.

SPRITSKRANSAR
S-shaped almond biscuits

Ingredients:

Butter 4 oz (120 g)
Castor sugar 2 oz (60 g)
1 egg yolk
Ground almonds 2 oz (60 g)
Flour 6 oz (180 g)
Almond essence, few drops

Method: Cream butter and sugar until fluffy, add egg yolk and almond essence and blend the ground almonds and flour to form a stiff dough. Rest for 2 hours in a refrigerator. Roll to ¼ inch thick and

cut fancy shaped biscuits. Place on a greased tray and bake at 380°F for 10 minutes until golden. Biscuits are usually shaped into 'S'. Just cut into sticks and wave in snake like fashions to make the 'S' design.

MANDELFORMAR
Almond tartlets

Ingredients:

Butter 3 oz (90 g)
Castor sugar 3 oz (90 g)
Ground almonds 3 oz (90 g)
1 egg + 1 egg yolk
Flour 8 oz (240 g)
Almond essence, few drops

Filling:

Jam 4 oz (120 g)
Whipped cream 4 fl oz (120 mls)

Method: Cream butter and sugar until fluffy. Add beaten eggs, ground almonds and essence. Blend flour to form a stiff dough and chill well for 2 hours. Roll to ⅛ inch thick and line greased tarlets with this almond pastry. Prick bottom and place a spoonful of jam in each one. Bake for 12 to 15 minutes at 380°F and cool. Pipe whipped cream into each tartlet when cold.

RAGKAKOR
Rye cookies

Ingredients:

Butter 4 oz (120 g)
Icing sugar 2 oz (60 g)
1 egg yolk
Rye flour 4 oz (120 g)
Sifted all purpose flour 4 oz (120 g)

Method: Cream butter and sugar and add the egg yolk. Blend the two flours first and add to cream mixture. Mix to a stiff dough and rest in a refrigerator for 20 minutes. Roll to ⅛ inch and cut in small rounds 2 inch diameter. Place on a greased tray and bake for 10 minutes at 360°F.

JULGLOGG
Christmas wine cup

Ingredients:

1 bottle Swedish Acquavit or gin
2 bottles Burgundy
Seedless raisins 3 oz (90 g)
Castor sugar 3 oz (90 g)
Cardamom seeds ½ oz (15 g)
1 stick of cinnamon
1 sliced lemon
1 sliced orange
Few sprigs of mint (fresh)

Method: Place all ingredients except the Aquavit
in a saucepan and bring to the boil, do not exceed
boiling point. Remove from the heat and add
Aquavit. Set alight and serve in jugs with fruits.

Norway

Norwegian food is always plentiful and made from the delicious fresh raw materials which abound in this beautiful, open country. The visual sense is highly developed in the Norwegians, and food appeals to the eyes as well as to the palate. Large hotels and restaurants make a feature of these culinary displays, but in smaller establishments you are more likely to find the ancient simple foods of the people.

Breakfast comes as a surprise to visitors. The Norwegians are quite sports-mad, and start the day bright and early so that they can finish in time to ski, sail or simply walk through the countryside. For their physical activity, they need food, lots of it, and they need it at the beginning of the day. So the traditional Norwegian breakfast is the *Koldtbord*, which literally means cold table. It looks like an informal *smorgasbord*, and herrings are prominent. There is usually porridge, salted and pickled fish, salads, cold and cured hams, cold meats, salads, pastries, cheeses and eggs cooked in various ways. Fruit juice, milk, buttermilk, tea and coffee are the usual breakfast drinks.

The people of Norway do not stop work for lunch — that would keep them in their place of work for an extra hour, and that is better spent on sport. So the workers break off in relays to have tea or coffee with open sandwiches brought from home. Fillings could be raw meat with egg yolk (tartar), shrimp and lobster, egg and anchovies, roast beef, meat salad tongue or liver pâté, each with an appropriate garnish to make the food look delicious.

Dinner is usually the cold table again in restaurants and hotels, but this time fortified with hot dishes. The Norwegian cod with melted butter, halibut or sole may not sound distinctively Norwegian, but one will not find better anywhere. Fish from the cold northern waters has a much better taste and delicate texture, and the Norwegians use more fresh fish than their neighbours. Mutton and lamb figure much more on the menu than anywhere else in Scandinavia and there are various one-pot stews which are nutritious but easy to prepare — the national wish to be out and about and not wasting time in the kitchen extends to the Norwegian housewives.

Rake trout is almost a national dish, and is a half-fermented trout served cold in fillets with crispbread and butter. Spring nettles, caraway shoots and delicate spinach are used fresh and in soups.

In Norwegian homes, often a single nourishing dish will constitute a meal. So a thick soup with lots of vegetables, based on a rich stock and made even more nourishing with slices of hard-boiled eggs or slivers of meat may be followed by a few berry pancakes to count as a complete meal. The desire to be in the fresh air has made the way of eating free from international customs.

Mutton and cabbage is another one-pot dish easy to make, and cabbage rissoles, meat cakes fried with onions and *lapskaus*, a stew, are all traditional dishes. Sweets and desserts contain less pastry and more fruit and berries than in most other countries, and cloud-berries make a heavenly dessert with whipped cream.

The quality of Norwegian beer is excellent, both the pils, in the style of a lager, and the somewhat stronger export. Bayer beer is stronger and darker than the others.

BILL OF FARE

Soup

BLABAERSUPPE
Blueberry soup

OLMSUPPE
Beer soup

SONG OF GRIEG
Veal soup with caraway sprouts

Hors d'Oeuvre

SMORGAS PLATTER
Selection of ideas for items suitable for this
    food presentation

GRAVLAX or RAKORRET
Cured salmon Scandinavian style

SILDSALAT
Herring salad with eggs and beetroot

LOFOTEN CAVIAR
Caviar made with cod or herring's roe

NORWEGIAN PRAWN PÂTÉ
Prawn and egg mixture bound with cream and
    sherry wine

Fish Dishes

NORWEGIAN QUICHE
Custard flan with prawns

LAKSPUDDING
Salmon pie Norwegian style

FEVIG MACKEREL
Baked mackerel with potatoes and sour cream

FISKBOLLER
Haddock minced balls with sour cream

Meat Dishes

FAAR I KAAL
Mutton and cabbage

FENALAAR
Cured or pickled mutton

STEKTE HJORTEKOTELETTERS
Venison steak burgers

ARFUGI I FLOTESAUS
Pot roast ptarmigan flavoured with juniper
    berries

Sweets

TILSLORTE BONDENIKER
Apple crumble

OLLEBROD
Beer custard

BERTINES MANDELBUNN
Almond merginue shells with baked apple and
    egg custard

SOUP

BLABAERSUPPE
Blueberry soup

Ingredients:

Water 2½ pint (1,500 mls)
Brown sugar 8 oz (240 g)
4 lemon slices
Blueberries 1½ lb (720 g)

Thickening:

Potato flour or arrowroot 1 oz (30 g)
Cold water 5 fl oz (150 mls)
Pinch of salt

Method: Boil all ingredients for 10 minutes and thicken with a slurry of arrowroot or potato flour. Boil for a further 5 minutes and serve hot or cold.

This soup can be sieved through a nylon strainer if desired and served with cream. It is traditional to eat this soup as a first course in the Scandinavian countries although it is also a perfect dessert item at the end of a meal.

OLMSUPPE
Beer soup

Ingredients:

Ground rice 2 oz (60 g)
Milk 1 pint (600 mls)
Mild beer 1½ pint (900 mls)
Grated lemon
Pinch of cinnamon
Castor sugar 2 oz (60 g)

Method: Mix ground rice and milk. Boil beer and add to rice mixture. Cook until smooth for 12 minutes and season.

SONG OF GRIEG
Veal soup with caraway sprouts

Ingredients:

Caraway sprouts (*not* the seeds) 5 oz (150 g)

Veal stock 2½ pint (1,500 mls)
Butter and oil 2 oz (60 g)

Thickening:

Cream 5 fl oz (150 mls)
2 egg yolks
Cornflour 1½ oz (45 g)
Salt and pepper

Method: Saute the caraway sprouts in oil and butter for 5 minutes. Add veal stock and boil for 15 minutes. Mix cream, egg yolks and cornflour in a bowl. Add a cup of the soup and stir well. Pour this mixture into the remainder of the soup and reheat until it begins to boil. Remove from heat and season to taste.

HORS D'OEUVRE

SMORGAS PLATTER
Selection of ideas for items suitable for this food presentation

Norway is famous for her open sandwiches, and, like Denmark, she competes for the best selection. Smorbrod is the name for open sandwiches and smorgas for the platters or hors d'oeuvre. The famous goat cheese Gjetost is prominently featured in many presentations. Spiced caraway cheese called Nokklelost and smoked cheese are served with *flatbrod* and *Knekkebrod* and butter.

PLATTER I

Use a wooden platter 18 inch by 12 inch. Place a plain tray d'oyley on the platter. Arrange the food in rows but in an attractive pattern. Buttered on rye bread, ryvita and cream crackers with two or three different cheeses and butter pats.

(i)   Dish of hard-boiled eggs stuffed with anchovy fillets.
(ii) Peeled tomatoes, cucumber and green peppers seasoned with vinaigrette.

(iii) Slices of pâté, salami, smoked ham and brawn with gherkins and pickled cucumber.

(iv) Cold roast veal, beef, ham and ox tongue thinly sliced with small saucers of sweet pickles.

(v) Celery stalks, lettuce leaves and Belgian endives.

(vi) Potato salad with cream dressing and chopped chives.

PLATTER II

(i) Prawns on lettuce leaves with sprigs of dill.

(ii) Cornets of smoked salmon stuffed with cream horseradish dressing.

(iii) Sardines in oil with hard-boiled eggs.

(iv) Smoked herring salad with gherkins and apples.

(v) Roll-mops with onions and cream cheese.

(vi) Scampi or lobster cocktail in glasses with shredded lettuce leaves.

PLATTER III

(i) Cream cheese on celery sticks.

(ii) Selection of hard cheeses with sweet chutney and pickles.

(iii) Cheeses garnished with apples, grapes or pears.

(iv) Cubes of Cheddar or Emmentaler cheeses on cocktail sticks with pineapple.

(v) Blue cheese on canape or croutons with prunes.

(vi) Toasted cheese decorated with red peppers.

GRAVLAX or RAKORRET
Cured salmon Scandinavian style

This speciality of pickled salmon is the main attraction of Scandinavian gastronomy.

Ingredients:

Fresh salmon 2 lb (960 g)

Curing mixture:

Salt 3 oz (90 g)
Saltpetre ¼ oz (7 g)
Sugar 3 oz (90 g)
8 sprigs of dill
Coarsely ground black pepper 2 g

Method: Fillet salmon and remove skin. Wash and dry. Mix salt, sugar and saltpetre together and rub fish with this mixture. Place in an earthenware dish a layer of fish, then dill and so on until the dish is full. Sprinkle with coarsely ground black pepper and lay the fillets thick side to thin side. Place a weight on top and marinade in a refrigerator for 48 hours. Serve cut in thin slices with dill. This fish can also be cured for as long as 2 months.

MUSTARD SAUCE
(For serving with gravlax)

Ingredients:

4 egg yolks
Oil 6 fl oz (180 mls)
Chopped dill 5 g
Made mustard ¼ oz (7 g)
Salt and pepper
Malt vinegar 2 tbs (30 mls)

Method: Blend all ingredients together by whisking to a smooth emulsion. Gravlax can also be served on bread or crispbread covered with dill.

SILDSALAT
Herring salad with eggs and beetroot

Ingredients:

Diced cooked potatoes 8 oz (240 g)
Diced cooked beetroot 4 oz (120 g)
Diced pickled cucumber 4 oz (120 g)
Smoked herring cut in ½ inch squares 8 oz (240 g)
Onion rings 4 oz (120 g)

Salad dressing:

Oil 3 tbs
Vinegar 1 tbs

Salt and pepper
Made mustard 1 tsp

Chopped parsley
1 finely chopped hard-boiled egg

Method: Blend herring, potatoes, beetroot, onion
rings and cucumber together. Dilute mustard with
vinegar, add salt and pepper and stir in oil. Mix
dressing with salad and decorate with a few onion
rings. Sprinkle with chopped parsley and egg.

LOFOTEN CAVIAR
Caviar made with cod or herring's roe

Ingredients:

Fresh cod's roe 1 lb (480 g)
Water 4 fl oz (120 mls)
Salt ¼ oz (7 g)
White pepper 1 g
Sugar ½ oz (15 g)
Saltpetre 2 g
Sugar ¼ oz (7 g)
Oil 6 fl oz (180 mls)
Juice of ½ lemon

Method: Soak skinned roes in salt, water, sugar,
saltpetre and pepper for 1 hour. Boil for 15
minutes. Then cream mixture, adding oil as for a
mayonnaise while whisking, to obtain a good
emulsion. Add lemon juice and store in jars under
refrigeration conditions.

NORWEGIAN PRAWN PÂTÉ
Prawn and egg mixture bound with cream and
  sherry wine

Ingredients:

Pinch of dill
Oil 1 fl oz (30 mls)
Chopped onions 1 oz (30 g)
Peeled prawns 8 oz (240 g)
Sweet sherry 3 fl oz (90 mls)
Cooked cod fillets 4 oz (120 g)
2 hard-boiled eggs
Butter 4 oz (120 g)

Salt, pepper, paprika and cayenne
White breadcrumbs 2 oz (60 g)
Juice and grated rind of 1 lemon
Double cream 4 fl oz (120 mls)

Method: Soak dill in oil in a jar with the lid on
overnight. Saute chopped onions in same oil for 5
minutes until translucent, add prawns, cod, sherry
and chopped eggs, breadcrumbs and season. Pass
mixture through a liquidiser or mincer. Blend butter
and cream, add lemon juice and place in a basin or
pot. Chill and serve with prawns.

Fish Dishes

NORWEGIAN QUICHE
Custard flan with prawns

Ingredients:

Short pastry 8 oz (240 g)

Filling:

Prawns 8 oz (240 g)

Sauce:

Sherry 4 fl oz (120 mls)
White sauce ½ pint (300 mls)
2 eggs
Sliced mushrooms 2 oz (60 g)
Salt, pepper and paprika

Method: Line an 8 inch flan ring with short pastry
¼ inch thick. Fill with dry beans and bake blind
for 15 minutes at 400°F. Remove beans and bake
in oven for a further 5 minutes. Soak peeled
prawns and mushrooms in sherry wine for 1 hour.
Blend beaten eggs and white sauce, and add
seasoning and prawn mixture. Fill flan case with
mixture and bake for 25 minutes at 380°F.
Serve hot or cold with lemon wedges and salad.

LAKSPUDDING
Salmon pie Norwegian style

Ingredients:

Boiled spinach 8 oz (240 g)
Butter 2 oz (60 g)
Salt, pepper and nutmeg
Smoked salmon 8 oz (240 g)
Sour cream 5 fl oz (150 mls)
4 slices of lemon
6 beaten eggs
Milk 3 tbs   } Beat together
Salt and pepper
Butter 2 oz (60 g)

Method: Remove moisture from spinach and reheat in butter, add seasoning. Place in a shallow pie dish and cover with thin slices of smoked salmon. Beat eggs with milk and scramble lightly. Place on top of smoked salmon. Boil cream and pour over the eggs. Serve piping hot with croutons of fried bread.

FEVIG MACKEREL
Baked mackerel with potatoes and sour cream

Ingredients:

Peeled sliced potatoes 1 lb (480 g)
Sliced onions 2 oz (60 g)
1 bouquet garni
Sprig of dill
Butter 2 oz (60 g)
Mackerel fillets 8 oz (240 g)
Sour cream ½ pint (300 mls)
Chopped chives or dill 1 tbs
Salt and pepper

Method: Place alternate layers of potatoes and onions in a well greased shallow dish. Dot with knobs of butter, cover with mackerel fillets and add sour cream. Season and add bouquet garni and sprig of dill. Bake for 40 minutes at 380°F until potatoes are cooked. Sprinkle chopped chives or dill on serving. This dish can be made with any type of fish.

FISKBOLLER
Haddock minced balls with sour cream

Ingredients:

Raw skinned and minced fresh haddock 1½ lb (720 g)
Sour cream ½ pint (300 mls)
2 beaten eggs
Ryvita crumbs 8 oz (240 g)
Salt and pepper
Pinch of nutmeg
Sugar ½ oz (15 g)
Juice and rind of 1 lemon

Method: Blend all ingredients together. Divide mixture into small dumplings 1 oz (30 g) each. Place in a greased tray and cover with hot water and 1 sliced onion. Poach lightly for 10 minutes in the oven at 380°F, or fry in deep fat. Serve with prawn sauce.

PRAWN SAUCE
(For Fiskboller)

Ingredients:

White sauce ½ pint (300 mls)
Diced peeled prawns 4 oz (120 g)
Sweet sherry 3 fl oz (90 mls)
Salt, pepper and paprika

Method: Heat these ingredients together, adjust seasoning to taste.

MEAT DISHES

FAAR I KAAL
Mutton and cabbage

Ingredients:

Diced lean mutton 2 lb (960 g)
Shredded cabbage 1 lb (480 g)
Pinch of caraway seeds
Salt and pepper
Water 3 pint (1,800 mls)
Chopped parsley

Method: Place meat in water and bring to the boil. Remove the scum as it rises and when clear add remainder of ingredients. Cook gently for 1½ hours. Sprinkle with chopped parsley and serve.

FENALAAR
Cured or pickled mutton (8 portions)

Ingredients:

1 leg of lamb or mutton 3½ lb (1,680 g)
Brandy or schnapps 4 fl oz (120 mls)
Salt 4 oz (120 g)
Sugar 2 oz (60 g)
Saltpetre ½ oz (15 g)
Treacle 5 oz (150 g)
Water ½ pt (300 mls)

Second brining:

Water 9 pint (5,400 mls)
Salt 2 lb (960 g)
Saltpetre ½ oz (15 g)
Sugar 8 oz (240 g)

Method: Remove pelvis bone from leg, season with all ingredients for first brining and marinade for 1 day. Chill for 1 night. Prepare second brine by boiling salt and water. Add saltpetre and sugar and cool. When cold soak the leg and marinade for 6 days, completely immersed. Dry and smoke and let leg hang to dry in an airy place for about 3 months.

STEKTE HJORTEKOTELETTERS
Venison steak burgers

Ingredients:

Venison meat finely minced 1 lb (480 g)
Lard 2 oz (60 g)

Sauce:

Chopped onions 1 oz (30 g)
Sliced mushrooms 2 oz (60 g)
Brown beer ½ pint (300 mls)
Cream ¼ pint (150 mls)
Salt and pepper

Pinch of mace
4 juniper berries

Method: Shape the minced venison in 3 oz (90 g) steak burgers. Pan fry in lard for 8 minutes. Keep warm in a shallow dish while making sauce. In same pan fry chopped onions and mushrooms for 5 minutes and add beer and berries. Boil for 15 minutes, then add cream and boil for a further 5 minutes. Season and pour over the burgers. Serve with chestnuts and sprouts.

ARFUGI I FLOTESAUS
Pot roast ptarmigan flavoured with juniper berries

Ingredients:

4 small birds
4 rashers of bacon
Lard 2 oz (60 g)
Butter 2 oz (60 g)
Diced carrots 2 oz (60 g)
1 onion cut in quarters
1 bouquet garni
Beer ½ pint (300 mls)
Schnapps 4 fl oz (120 mls)

Thickening:

Cornflour ½ oz (15 g)
Cream 5 fl oz (150 mls)
Salt, pepper and paprika
Pinch of caraway seeds

Method: Clean, truss and season the birds. Cover with bacon rashers and cook in oven for 15 minutes. Remove birds and place in a casserole dish, add vegetables, herbs and liquid and cover with a lid. Cook for another 20 minutes and remove birds. Pour contents of casserole into a saucepan and boil for 10 minutes. Thicken with a slurry of cream and cornflour. Strain sauce and season. Place each bird on fried croutons. Serve sauce separately. Garnish dish and serve with a green salad and chip potatoes.

SWEETS

TILSLORTE BONDENIKER
Apple crumble

Ingredients:

Sliced apples 2 lb (960 g)
Butter 4 oz (120 g)
Sugar 8 oz (240 g)
Pinch of cinnamon
Cake crumbs 4 oz (120 g)
Butter and lard 8 oz (240 g)
Double cream ½ pint (300 mls)
Chocolate shavings 3 oz (90 g)

Method: Place apples, sugar, cinnamon, and butter in a saucepan and cook gently for 10 minutes. Remove and cool. Place in a shallow dish. Fry cake crumbs in butter and lard and pour over the apples. Cool and decorate top with whipped cream and sprinkle with shavings of chocolate.

OLLEBROD
Beer custard

Ingredients:

Lager beer 1 pint (600 mls)
Sugar 5 oz (150 g)
Pinch of cinnamon

Thickening:

6 egg yolks
Cream 5 fl oz (150 mls)
Cornflour 1 oz (30 g)
Water 5 fl oz (150 mls)

Lime cordial

Method: Boil beer and sugar with cinnamon. Blend cream, egg yolks and cornflour with water and add hot beer. Stir well and reheat mixture while stirring until it has the consistency of a custard. Add lime cordial and serve in glasses with shortbread biscuits. For adults only — add 5 fl oz (150 mls) Schnapps, Aquavit, rum or brandy.

BERTINES MANDELBUNN
Almond meringue shells with baked apple and egg custard

Ingredients:

Dry meringue mixture:

6 egg whites
Pinch of salt
Castor sugar 3 oz (90 g) — add 2 drops of almond essence
Granulated sugar 3 oz (90 g)

Filling:

Sliced apples 1 lb (480 g)
Sugar 4 oz (120 g)   Cook in saucepan
Cinnamon 1 pinch   until soft
Butter 2 oz (60 g)

Custard:

2 egg yolks
Castor sugar 2 oz (60 g)
Arrowroot ½ oz (15 g)
Beer ½ pint (300 mls)
Cream 5 fl oz (150 mls)

Method: Place egg whites in clean and fat free bowl. Add a pinch of salt and whisk until mixture peaks and will hold in the whisk. Continue adding sugar and beating until mixture peaks again. Place the mixture in a piping bag fitted with a ¼ inch plain tube. Pipe on a tray lined with greaseproof paper in the form of wells or nests as cases. This is done by piping round starting from the centre and piping a border 1 inch high. Place meringues in hot plate at 200°F for 5 hours to dry. When dry fill with cooked apple compote or puree. Serve a beer custard separately, made as follows.
Custard: Blend yolks, cream, sugar and arrowroot in a bowl. Boil beer, add to cream mixture, re-heat, stirring until it reaches custard consistency.

Denmark

There is a Scandinavian saying that the Norwegians eat to live, the Danes live to eat, and the Swedes eat to drink. Certainly the Danes are enthusiastic eaters and manage to cram five meal-times into a day. Some of this may be due to their inborn sense of friendship and hospitality — and where better to show love than at table?

But when the Danes eat, it is not just a hurried ingestion of available calories, they do it in style, with flowers and candles on the dinner tables of even the poorer families. They like to set a beautiful table and then draw the curtains against the bitter night outside to enjoy their families, their friends — and their food.

The Danes are great party goers. They celebrate birthdays and anniversaries with tremendous enthusiasm, and just the gathering of a few friends will produce the right atmosphere for food, drink and an instant party. *Smorrebrod* is the usual food at these gatherings, the fabulous Danish open sandwiches which are a meal on a slice of bread. A cold table is for more formal gatherings, with a delection of hot and cold dishes in spite of its name. Dinner parties give the hostess an opportunity to shine and display that uniquely Danish talent of creating *hygge* — sense of cosiness and comfort, physical and mental, in her guests.

For everyday eating as well as for parties, the favourite meal is pork, roasted plain or stuffed or minced for a *frikadeller*, a tasty fried meat patty. Potatoes and winter vegetables, mainly the roots, which keep, are the most popular and important.

The produce of Denmark needs no introduction to most of the kitchens of the world. Butter and cream, a variety of cheeses, bacon, ham, smoked pork products, eggs, chickens, beer and salami flow from this lush land as from a gigantic cornucopia.

There are two basic types of cooking in Denmark — the French-influenced court cookery which started in the seventeenth century with the coming of the French professional chefs, and the simple cookery of the people, with a primitive, rustic style. This is still maintained with a kind of nostalgia, and there are Danes who still love beer soup made with crusts of bread, grain porridge of various kinds, dried cod and salt herrings. But in the Danish kitchen, these days there are much better things bubbling than grain porridge.

The most delicious product of the Danish kitchens is probably the Danish pastry in all its infinite varieties. It is appreciated all around the world, but nowhere more than in Denmark, where people are not above having some for breakfast, a few after the open sandwich lunch, and of course everyone has some with coffee in the middle of the afternoon, and it tastes just right for a snack before bed. The flavours of the fillings of Danish pastry are never agreessive but are mainly delicate tastes: almonds, citrus peel, cinnamon, cardamoms and curd cheese. The pastry itself is buttery, flaky and light thanks to the quantity of butter used. Danish women still make their own in many cases, although working wives buy them from the excellent bakers on their way home. The pastries are time-consuming but not difficult to make. With a cup of coffee, sugared and liberally laced with thick cream, they are a real taste of Denmark — and produce instant *hygge*.

BILL OF FARE

Soup

GROENAERTE-SUPPA MED GAASE
Goose and pea soup

Hors d'Oeuvre

SMORREBROD
Open sandwiches

AAL I GELE
Jellied eels Danish style

Fish Dishes

PLUKFISK
Cubed cod fillets with potatoes

ROSPAETTE FILLET MED CITRON
SMORSOVS MED TETER
Plaice with prawns and lemon sauce

Meat Dishes

KRVORET MORBRAD MED
CHAMIGNONSOVS
Pork tenderloin with mushroom sauce

STEGT SVINEHAM MED AEPLER OG
SVESKER
Roast loin of pork Danish style

Vegetables

SUKKERBRUNEDE KARTOFLER
Caramel potatoes

Sweets

DANISH PASTRY
Four different types

AEBLEKAGE
Danish apple cake

DANSK LAGKAGE
Danish layer cake

SOUP

GROENAERTE-SUPPE MED GAASE
Goose and pea soup (6 to 8 portions)

Ingredients:

1 old goose 8 lb (3,840 g) *or* use goose giblets
   (neck, gizzards, winglets and bones)
   2 lb (960 g)
Water 4 pint (2,400 mls)
1 bouquet garni
1 onion studded with 4 cloves 5 oz (150 g)
1 carrot 5 oz (150 g)
1 sprig of celery 2 oz (60 g)
Frozen or fresh peas 1 lb (480 g) *or*
   dried peas 5 oz (150 g)
Salt and pepper

Method: Roast goose for 40 minutes at 400°F,
drain, place in a large saucepan and cover level
with water. Bring to the boil and remove scum
and fat as it rises. When the stock is clear add
bouquet garni and vegetables and simmer for a
further 1½ hours. Remove the goose. Cool and
carve meat in small slices. Return all bones to
the soup and boil for another hour. Strain and
add peas. Cook for 15 minutes if fresh or frozen
peas are used, otherwise 40 minutes. Liquidise
or pass through a sieve to obtain a smooth
puree soup. Season to taste and garnish with
slices of meat. The best part of the goose can be
used for another meal. Remove surplus fat from
soup as it floats.

   Use surplus stock to make gravy or others
soups or sauces.

HORS D'OEUVRE

SMORREBROD
Open sandwiches

Ingredients:

1. Slices of hard-boiled eggs topped with herring caviar on rounds of rye bread.
2. Scrambled eggs on buttered rye bread topped with anchovy fillets.
3. Creamed cheese on rounds of rye bread topped with a piece of roll-mop.
4. Rounds of buttered white bread with a slice of ham and pineapple.
5. An oblong of buttered rye bread with a piece of liver pâté topped with a pickled cucumber.
6. An oblong of buttered rye bread with a slice of smoked salmon filled with whipped cream flavoured with creamed horseradish dressing.
7. An oblong of buttered rye bread with a piece of fresh cooked salmon decorated with fresh peeled cucumber.
8. A piece of cured salmon with a sprig of dill (see recipe in Swedish section).
9. An oblong piece of toasted bread with smoked deer's tongue decorated with sour beet.
10. An oblong piece of white bread with turkey, cheese and cranberry.
11. A square piece of bread with ham, cheese and pineapple.
12. An oblong piece of buttered rye bread with prawns and dill.
13. An asparagus tip wrapped up in a piece of ham, chicken or turkey and topped with strips of red pepper.
14. A round piece of bread topped with a chunk of cucumber filled with cream cheese.
15. Strips of smoked salmon, red and green peppers, anchovy fillets and hard cheese blended in dressing and placed on small tartlets.
16. A tartare steak on a piece of bread with chopped onions, gherkins, capers and anchovy fillets served with vinaigrette sauce. The raw minced steak is hollow and a raw egg yolk placed in the cavity.

The possibilities are endless and hundreds more
could be devised similarly.

AAL I GELE
Jellied eels Danish style

Ingredients:

Eels 2 lb (960 g)
White wine ¼ pint (150 mls)
Vinegar 2 fl oz (60 mls)
Water 5 fl oz (150 mls)
Sliced onions 2 oz (60 g)
1 bouquet garni
Sliced carrots 2 oz (60 g)
Pinch of chopped dill
Salt and pepper
Salt ¼ oz (7 g)
Pepper 2 g
Gelatine 1 oz (30 g)   ⎫
Sugar 1 oz (30 g)   ⎭   Mix together

Method: Pin eel on a board with an ice pick.
Grab eel with a cloth and make an incision round
the neck. Cut the skin round it to loosen. Grab a
portion of the loose skin and peel off from head
to tail. Gut and clean. Cut in 3 inch long pieces
and place in vinegar to soak for 15 minutes.
Boil rest of ingredients for 15 minutes and place
eel pieces in the marinade and poach gently
for 20 minutes. Dissolve gelatine in stock and cool.
Serve in the same liquor with vegetables. Remove
bouquet garni and check seasoning.

FISH DISHES

PLUKFISH
Cubed cod fillets with potatoes

Ingredients:

Cod fillets cut in 1 inch cubes 2 lb (960 g)
Potatoes cut in 1 inch cubes 2 lb (960 g)
Seasoned flour 2 oz (60 g)
Water ½ pint (300 mls)
Chopped onions 2 oz (60 g)
Chopped parsley 1 tbs
White sauce ½ pint (300 mls)
Juice and grated rind of 1 lemon
Salt and pepper

Method: Pass fish cubes in seasoned flour and mix
with potato in buttered shallow dish. Sprinkle
with chopped onions and add juice and grated
rind of lemon. Season to taste. Cover level with
water and bake for 30 minutes at 380°F. Pour
white sauce over the fish and sprinkle with
chopped parsley.

ROSPAETTE FILLET MED CITRON
SMORSOVS MED TETER
Plaice with prawns and lemon sauce

Ingredients:

4 place fillets 8 oz (240 g) each
Prawns 8 oz (240 g)
Danish beer ½ pint (300 mls)
Salt and pepper
4 lemon slices
Salt and pepper
Ground mace or nutmeg
Chopped parsley 1 tbs
Butter 4 oz (120 g)
Chopped onions 3 oz (90 g)

Method: Skin, wash and season the fish fillets.
Place fish and prawns into buttered shallow dish,
sprinkle the chopped onions and cover with lager
beer. Season. Bake for 15 minutes at 380°F.
Serve with lemon. Sprinkle chopped parsley.
Serve with mashed potatoes.

MEAT DISHES

KRVORET MORBRAD MED
CHAMPIGNONSOVS
Pork tenderloin with mushroom sauce

Ingredients:

4 boneless pork loin steaks 6 oz (180 g) each cut
    ½ inch thick
Lard 2 oz (60 g)
Seasoned flour 2 oz (60 g)
Chopped onions 1 oz (30 g)
Sliced mushrooms 4 oz (120 g)
Danish beer ½ pint (300 mls)

Sauce:

Water 5 fl oz (150 mls)
Double cream 5 fl oz (150 mls)
Cornflour 1 oz (30 g)
Salt and pepper
Pinch of paprika and garlic salt or powder

Garnish:

4 skinned tomatoes
4 bacon rashers

Method: Pass pork loin steaks in seasoned flour
and fry in lard on both sides for 5 minutes.
Transfer the steaks to a shallow dish. In the same
fat fry chopped onions without colouring, add
mushrooms and toss for 5 minutes. Drain off
surplus fat, add beer and boil for 5 minutes.
Thicken mixture with a slurry of cream, water, and
cornflour and boil for 4 minutes. Season with
paprika, garlic salt or powder and pepper. Pour
sauce over the meat and surround with peeled
tomatoes and fried rashers of bacon. Cover with a
lid and bake for 20 minutes at 400°F. The bacon
rashers can be added on serving the dish. Serve
with baked potatoes or rice.

STEGT SVINEHAM MED AEPLER OG SVESKER
Roast loin of pork Danish style (8 to 10 portions)

Ingredients:

Sliced onions 2 oz (60 g)
Lard 2 oz (60 g)
Sliced apples 4 oz (120 g)
Red cabbage finely shredded 8 oz (240 g)
Sugar 1 oz (30 g)
Vinegar 2 fl oz (60 mls)
Loin of pork with rind and bone removed
    3 lb (1,440 g)
Water 1 pint (600 mls)
Salt and pepper
Soaked prunes in brewed tea 8 oz (240 g)
    with juice ½ pint (300 mls)

Method: Pan fry onions in lard until golden
brown. Add sliced apples and red cabbage. Toss
well and add vinegar, sugar and water. Bring to the
boil and transfer into a shallow dish. Season.
Place joint of pork on top, season again and bake
for 1½ hours at 360°F. Brew half pint of tea and
soak prunes until soft and tender. Simmer gently
for 10 minutes before the joint is ready. Add half
of juice to other ingredients. Make a thin gravy
with the remaining juice and serve the prunes as a
garnish.

VEGETABLES

SUKKEBRUNEDE KARTOFLER
Caramel potatoes

Ingredients:

New potatoes in jackets 2 lb (960 g)
Butter 2 oz (60 g)
Castor sugar 2 oz (60 g)
1 level tsp vinegar
Salt and pepper

Method: Scrub potatoes and boil in their skins.
Drain and peel. Heat sugar and vinegar until
syrupy and add butter. Pass potatoes in caramel
mixture making sure they are completely coated.
Season and serve.

SWEETS

DANISH PASTRY

Ingredients:

Baker's yeast 1 oz (30 g)
Cold milk 6 fl oz (180 mls)
Pinch of salt
Sugar 1 level tsp
1 egg
1 egg yolk
Flour 1 lb (480 g) – strong bread flour must be
    used
Butter 10 oz (300 g)
Flour 2 oz (60 g)

Method: Crumble yeast in milk, add beaten eggs and dissolve salt and sugar in this liquid. Add flour to make a stiff dough and knead well for 5 minutes. Form into a ball and cover with an upside down basin to allow to ferment. Rest for 30 minutes. Work butter and 2 oz (60 g) flour to a paste and roll out to $\frac{1}{8}$ inch thick, dust board with flour to make it easier or cut with a knife in thin slices. Roll pastry into an oblong 12 inch long by 4 inch wide and place slices of butter mixture over two-thirds of the surface leaving one-third plain. Fold pastry up making three layers as for puff pastry. Rest in a refrigerator for 20 minutes and repeat the operation twice. The dough is then ready for use.

WINDMILL

Ingredients:

Apricot jam 2 oz (60 g)
Danish pastry dough (as above)

Filling Confectioner's custard:

2 egg yolks
Castor sugar 3 oz (90 g)
Cornflour 1 oz (30 g)
Butter 1 oz (30 g)
Milk ½ pint (300 mls)
Vanilla essence, few drops

Syrup for glazing:

Sugar 6 oz (180 g)
Water 2 fl oz (60 mls)

Decoration:

Glacé cherries or pineapple 2 oz (60 g)

Method: Place cornflour, egg yolks and sugar in a bowl and stir well. Add three spoons of cold milk. Boil remainder of milk and add to the mixture. Reheat and continue stirring until it thickens. Blend in butter and vanilla essence and cool. Roll out Danish pastry to $\frac{1}{8}$ inch thickness and cut into 3½ inch squares. Using a sharp knife make 4 incisions in each square by cutting the pastry from the corners to within ½ inch from the centre. Brush over with a damp brush and fold corners to

the centre. Fasten the 4 corners by placing a small disc of Danish pastry in the centre of each square. Place on a greased tray, brush with eggwash and rest for 30 minutes to allow for fermentation and further rising. Bake at 420°F for 12 minutes. Brush with syrup made from sugar and water. Cool and pipe a blob of custard cream in the centre of each and decorate with half a cherry.

DANISH TURNOVERS

Roll out Danish pastry to $\frac{1}{8}$ inch thick and cut out circles with a 3 inch plain pastry cutter. Damp edges with water and fold. Brush with eggwash and rest for 30 minutes on a greased tray. Bake for 15 minutes at 400°F/420°F. Cool and split with a knife. Fill with apricot jam and custard cream.

DANISH TWISTS

Ingredients:

Danish pastry dough (as above)
Melted apricot jam 2 oz (60 g)
Toasted flaked almonds 2 oz (60 g)

Almond filling:

Cream together as a paste the following:
    ground almonds 4 oz (120 g)
    castor sugar 2 oz (60 g)
    1 egg white
    Almond essence, few drops

Method: Roll pastry 18 inch long by 4 inch wide by $\frac{1}{8}$ inch thick. Spread almond filling over two-thirds of the pastry and fold to the centre. Fold again in order to have three layers on top of each other. Cut in thin strips ¼ inch thick with a sharp knife and twist the stick over a board using two hands for the operation. Form an 'S' by rolling half of the stick one way and the other half in the opposite direction. Place all sticks on a greased tray and allow 30 minutes proving. Bake at 400°F for 12 minutes. Brush with boiling apricot jam and sprinkle with flaked amonds.

AEBLEKAGE
Danish apple cake

Ingredients:

Sliced apples 1½ lb (720 g)
Butter 3 oz (90 g)
Oil 1 fl oz (30 mls)
Castor sugar 3 oz (90 g)
Grated rind and juice of 1 lemon
Water 2 fl oz (60 mls)
White breadcrumbs 4 oz (120 g)
Double cream ¼ pint (150 mls)
Chocolate – grated or shavings 1 oz (30 g)
Glacé cherries and angelica 1 oz (30 g)

Method: Peel and core apples and slice thinly.
Cook in half of butter with half of sugar, water,
grated rind and lemon juice. Cool and place in a
shallow dish. Heat oil with remaining butter and
fry crumbs until golden. Add remainder of
sugar and stir well. Cool and sprinkle crumbs over
top of apples. Decorate top with whipped cream
and sprinkle with chocolate shavings. Garnish
with glacé cherries and angelica in an attractive
pattern.

DANSK LAGKAGE
Danish layer cake

Ingredients:

Butter 5 oz (150 g)
Castor sugar 5 oz (150 g)
2 eggs
Flour 5 oz (150 g)
Apricot jam 5 oz (150 g)
Whipped cream 5 fl oz (150 mls)
Nuts 3 oz (90 g)
Glacé cherries 2 oz (60 g)
Grated chocolate 3 oz (90 g)

Method: Cream soft butter and castor sugar
together until fluffy, add beaten eggs gradually
and fold in sifted flour lightly but thoroughly.
Line two 8 inch flan rings with greaseproof paper
making sure it fits exactly to the sides. Fill flan
rings with mixture and bake for 30 minutes at
360°F. Cool and store in a refrigerator overnight.

This makes the cake easier to split without
crumbling. Split the cakes and spread with jam,
fill with cream and top by brushing with very hot
melted apricot jam. Spread cream on sides and
coat with toasted flaked almonds. Make sure
almonds are cold before applying to the cream.
Decorate the gateau with whipped cream, glacé
cherry designs and chocolate shavings.

Finland

Finland is a country of a thousand lakes entirely surrounded by forests in the south and ice in the north. Even Helsinki gives the impression that it is carved from the forest which surrounds it, and there are little plantations of pine trees in the parks to remind the citizens that the forest starts just outside city limits.

The forests, the lakes and the sea all affect the cookery of the Finns. The forest is there in the scent of wild mushrooms and in the juiciness of the unusual berries: *lakkabeeren*, called the orange of the north and rich in vitamin C; the cranberries, whortleberries, cloudberries and lingonberries. These are made into jams and preserves, but perhaps the best way of using them is the *kiisseli*, a fruit syrup thickened with potato flour and eaten with cream, not unlike the Russian *kissel*.

Finnish cuisine appreciates the fish of the lakes and the sea. Fish dishes are garnished with potatoes and salmon often goes into a type of pie called a *lohipiiras*, rather like the Russian *koulibiac*. The Russian influence on the cooking of Finland is stronger than the Finns care to admit, but the mixture of Swedish and Russian cuisines has produced a distinctive gastronomy in this fertile land.

The Finns have a great appetite for game, and hare, elk and even bear are hunted and eaten. *Karhunkapala* is a gelatinously tasty paw of bear grilled on a bed of charcoal; a *karhunkinkku* is the hindquarter of the bear smoked in the traditional way like a ham. They like game so much that they even hang chicken, after rubbing it with juniper berries, for a few days until it gets a gamey taste.

Reindeer is a speciality and the flesh is smoked, grilled, braised or made into a consomme. Particularly delicious is the marrow of the bones, and smoked reindeer tongue, served with pumpkin chutney, scrambled eggs and cranberry sauce is a delicacy which deserves to be better known.

The bread of Finland is sour rye dough fermented with malt, and a similar dough is stuffed with vegetables, eggs or cheese. Cardamom, juniper, dill and allspice are the basic flavourings of Finnish cookery, and the preference is for strong but natural tastes. Sour cucumbers, sour milk, soups based on the innards of an animal are all typically Finnish tastes. Porridge and gruel made of various types of grain are much appreciated, and the traditional Easter dish is *mammi*, a pudding made with rye flour, malt, molasses and bitter oranges.

Karelian hot pot is a succulent stew made of various meats such as pork, beef, mutton and lamb, rather like a pot au feu and eaten in every house. There are hearty baked casseroles of meat with beans and root vegetables, high in caloric content to keep the body warm in these arctic regions.

From the region of Karelia also comes a selection of pies and pasties, with the filling lightly held by a thin rye crust. One of the best is *piirakka*, filled with rice.

A wonderful Finnish institution is the *ryyppy*, a short of icy vodka, which is the national drink rather than snaps or akvavit. Beer is popular and drunk in vast quantities: the Finns are a thirsty nation.

But with wolves and bears in the forests, ice and snow for half the year and a night that is six months long, who would not be?

BILL OF FARE

Soup

KALAKEITTO
Fish chowder with potatoes

KESAKEITTO
Scampi and vegetable soup

Hors d'Oeuvre

JATKAN LOHIPOTTI
Salmon fillets pickled with dill and served with
sour cream

Fish Dishes

PATAKUKKO
Fish and onion pie topped with pastry

Meat Dishes

KARJALANPAISTI
Mixture of game and butcher's meats cooked as
a stew

MAKASALAATIKO
Liver dumpling served with potatoes

DILLILAMMAS
Mutton hot pot with dill

KALALAATIKO
Pork and herring pie

Sweets

PUOLUKKALIEMI
Finnish apples and berries

SOLSKENSKAKA
Pineapple pudding with apricot sauce

FINNISH RYE BREAD

SOUP

KALAKEITTO
Fish chowder with potatoes

Ingredients:

Chopped or sliced onions 2 oz (60 g)
Lard and butter 2 oz (60 g) each
Sliced potatoes 8 oz (240 g)
Water 2½ pints (1,500 mls)
Cod fillets cut in small pieces 8 oz (240 g)
Salt and pepper
Chopped parsley 1 tbs
Chopped dill 1 tbs
Sour cream ½ pint (300 mls)

Method: Fry the chopped onions in lard without browning and add sliced potatoes. Stir well and cover with water. Bring to the boil and cook for 15 minutes. Add fish and dill and season. Simmer gently for 12 minutes. Add cream and boil for a further 5 minutes. Serve sprinkled with chopped parsley.

KESAKEITTO
Scampi and vegetable soup

Ingredients:

Vegetables 2 oz (60 g) of each:
    Cauliflower
    Peas
    Beans
    Potatoes
    Carrots
    Celery
    Turnips cut into ¼ inch cubes
Water 2½ pint (1,500 mls)
Shredded spinach 4 oz (120 g)
Frozen scampi 8 oz (240 g)

Thickening:

3 egg yolks
Cream ½ pint (300 mls)
Cornflour 3 oz (90 g)

Juice and grated rind of 1 lemon
Salt and pepper
Pinch of caraway seeds

Method: Boil the vegetables in water for 30 minutes. Add shredded spinach, caraway seeds and scampi and simmer for a further 8 minutes.

Place egg yolks, cream and cornflour in a bowl and mix well with ½ pint of the soup stock. Add this mixture to the remaining soup mixture and reheat while stirring to obtain a smooth thickish liquid. Season and finally add lemon juice and grated rind.

HORS D'OEUVRE

JATKAN LOHIPOTTI
Salmon fillets pickled with dill and served with
  sour cream

Ingredients:

Salmon fillets 1½ lb (720 g)
Sugar 1 oz (30 g)
Salt ½ oz (15 g)
Saltpetre ¼ oz (8 g)
Dill leaves 1 oz (30 g)
Juice of 6 lemons
Sour cream 5 fl oz (150 mls)

Method: Place the salmon fillets in alternate layers with the dill leaves, sugar, saltpetre and salt in an earthenware dish. Cover with lemon juice and refrigerate for 2 days. Drain and serve with sour cream.

FISH DISHES

PATAKUKKO
Fish and onion pie topped with pastry

Ingredients:

Pastry:

Rye flour 4 oz (120 g)
Wheat flour 4 oz (120 g)
Lard 2 oz (60 g)
Margarine 2 oz (60 g)
1 egg

Liquid:

Fish fillets 8 oz (240 g)
White sauce ½ pint (300 mls) + vinegar 1 tbs
Sliced mushrooms 4 oz (120 g)
Chopped anchovy fillets 2 oz (60 g)
Chopped dill, one pinch
Salt and pepper

Method: Mix the two flours and rub in fats until crumbly. Blend beaten egg to form a stiff dough and rest for 30 minutes, rolled in a ball.

In a shallow dish place the fillets seasoned with salt and pepper and sprinkled with chopped dill and anchovy fillets. Cover with white sauce. Roll the pastry $^1/_8$ inch thick and place a layer over the fish. Make a design with the pastry trimming and brush the top with milk or eggwash. Bake at 380°F for 25 minutes.

MEAT DISHES

KARJALANPAISTI
Mixture of game and butcher's meats cooked as a stew (6 to 8 portions)

Ingredients:

3 oz (90 g) each of the following meats:
  Bacon
  Pork
  Venison
  Beef
  Mutton
  Veal
Lard 4 oz (120 g)
Diced onions 3 oz (90 g)
Diced carrots 3 oz (90 g)
Diced celery 3 oz (90 g)
Diced swedes or turnips 3 oz (90 g)
Shredded cabbage 6 oz (180 g)
1 bouquet garni
6 juniper berries
1 clove of garlic
Water 4 pint (2,400 mls)
Salt and pepper

Method: In a large saucepan saute the chopped onions and carrots in lard until soft but not brown for 5 minutes. Add the meat and brown for a further 12 minutes covered with a lid. Stir from time to time. Add rest of ingredients and simmer for 1½ hours. Season to taste and serve with boiled potatoes.

MAKASALAATIKO
Liver dumpling served with potatoes (8 portions)

Ingredients:

Patna rice 8 oz (240 g)
Water 3 pint (1,800 mls)
Calf's liver 1 lb (480 g)
Raw sausagemeat 1 lb (480 g)
2 eggs
Salt and pepper
Chopped onions 5 oz (150 g)
Chopped dill and parsley 1 tbs
Breadcrumbs 2 oz (60 g)
Chopped anchovy fillets 2 oz (60 g)

Garnish:

Boiled potatoes 1 lb (480 g)
Compote of mixed dried fruits (pears, apricots and apples) 1 lb (480 g)

Method: Boil rice for 30 minutes, drain and cool. Mince liver and sausagemeat with onions and blend with rice. Blend egg, crumbs, chopped herbs, anchovies and seasoning. Grease a pudding basin with lard and fill with mixture. Place in a tray half filled with hot water and bake for 1 hour at 380°F. Turn out on a hot dish and serve with brown gravy, potatoes and a garnish of fruit compote.

DILLILAMMAS
Mutton hot pot with dill (8 portions)

Ingredients:

Diced mutton from shoulder 2 lb (960 g)
Water 3 pint (1,800 mls)
Sliced onions 8 oz (240 g)
Sliced potatoes 8 oz (240 g)

Sliced spinach 6 oz (180 g)
Chopped dill 1 tbs
Salt and pepper
Sugar 1 oz (30 g)
Cream 5 fl oz (150 mls)

Method: Place the mutton in a saucepan with water and bring to the boil. Remove scum as it rises. Boil for 1 hour, then add potatoes and cook for a further 20 minutes. Add rest of ingredients and cook for 10 minutes. Serve in a soup tureen.

KALALAATIKO
Pork and herring pie

Ingredients:

Herring fillets 4 by 4 oz (120 g) each
Thin pork steaks 4 by 4 oz (120 g) each
Sliced onions 4 oz (120 g)
Chopped dill 1 tbs
Beer ½ pint (300 mls)
Malt vinegar 3 fl oz (90 mls)
Water 5 fl oz (150 mls)
Salt and pepper
Breadcrumbs 3 oz (90 g)
Grated cheese 6 oz (180 g)
Lard 3 oz (90 g)

Method: Grease a shallow dish with lard and place herrings and pork in layers with onions. Season, add beer, vinegar, chopped dill and water. Sprinkle with crumbs and grated cheese and bake at 380°F for 45 minutes.

SWEETS

PUOLUKKALIEMI
Finnish apples and berries

Ingredients:

Short pastry 8 oz (240 g)

Filling:

Sliced apples 8 oz (240 g)

Cranberries or blue berries 4 oz (120 g)
Castor sugar 5 oz (150 g)
Pinch of cinnamon

Method: Place sliced apples and berries in a pie dish. Add sugar and cinnamon and cover with pastry. Brush with eggwash and bake at 380°F for 25 minutes. Dust top with icing sugar and serve with cream or ice cream.

SOLSKENSKAKA
Pineapple pudding with apricot sauce

Ingredients:

Margarine or butter 4 oz (120 g)
Castor sugar and brown sugar 4 oz (120 g)
2 eggs
Flour 5 oz (150 g)
8 pineapple rings
Butter 4 oz (120 g)
Rum 3 fl oz (90 mls)

Apricot sauce:

Apricot jam 4 oz (120 g)
Water 5 fl oz (150 mls)
Arrowroot ½ oz (15 g)
Cold water 5 fl oz (150 mls)

Method: Cream fat and sugar until fluffy and add beaten eggs gradually. Fold in flour lightly. Grease an oblong tin 2 inch deep with soft butter and place pineapple rings in the bottom. Sprinkle with rum and cinnamon and cover level with the cake mixture. Bake at 380°F for 40 minutes. Turn out on a dish.
Sauce: Melt apricot jam with water and thicken with arrowroot slurry. Pour sauce over the hot cake and serve hot or cold.

FINNISH RYE BREAD

Ingredients:

Baker's yeast 1 oz (30 g)
Water 1 pint (600 mls)
Salt ¾ oz (20 g)
Malt extract ¾ oz (20 g)

Lard ½ oz (15 g)
Caraway seeds ¼ oz (7 g)
Wheat flour 1 lb (480 g)
Rye flour 1 lb (480 g)

Method: Crumble yeast in water which has been
heated to 76°F. Dissolve salt and malt extract
in this liquid. Sift the two flours and blend to
liquid to form a tight dough. Knead well and add
lard and seeds. Roll into a ball and allow to ferment
for 10 minutes covered with an upside down basin.
Divide the dough into 8 oz (240 g) portions and
roll each piece into a ball. Flatten the ball and
roll into an oblong loaf. Place in a well greased
tin, brush with water and prove for 50 minutes.
Blend 1 oz (30 g) cornflour with ½ pint (300
mls) boiling water to obtain a glaze. Brush the
loaf with this mixture just before it is ready to
be baked at 420°F for 40 minutes.

Iceland

The coasts of Iceland have a legendary abundance of fish and the island itself has wonderful grazing land for sheep, so it comes as no surprise that the staple diet of these close relatives of the Vikings is fish and lamb or mutton. Despite its name, Iceland is one of the twenty-five hot-spots of the world, and the nation is quite literally sitting on a volcano. In 1973, a whole town, Eldfell, was engulfed by lava and a new mountain, 200 metres high, stands in the middle of this once busy port. But the volcanic activity has its uses; it provides natural heating for the houses as well as all the hot water. This same water also heats greenhouses in Reykjavik to supply the town with fresh vegetables and flowers.

The style of Icelandic food is very international in the Scandinavian manner in hotels and restaurants, but for those who are willing to experiment, there are specialised places where the traditional dishes are on the menu. Some of these specialities go back to the days of the Vikings and have their roots in antiquity, They are not to everyone's taste, but are uniquely Icelandic. That much I know. I was stationed in Iceland during the early part of the war when I served as a petty officer cook in the Royal Navy — and Icelandic fish was our daily fare.

One such speciality is *thorramatur*, a dish of pickled whale, shark and seal meat; another is *hakarl*, shark which has been buried in sand for a time. *Hardfiskur* is fish, usually haddock, dried until it is quite brittle, aided by being allowed to freeze during the drying process. It will keep for years, and instead of being cooked, it is hammered thoroughly until it is soft and crumbly. It is torn from the skin and served with butter.

Smoked lamb is a delicious change from the raw hams and smoked beef of Europe, and is a traditional Icelandic Christmas Eve dish. *Svid* is a singed sheep's head, made into a head cheese and preserved in whey, and *blodmor* is a unique food made from sheep's blood, salted, thinned with water then thickened with barley or rye flour and suet from the innards of the sheep. The mixture is then put into bags made of the intestines of the sheep and boiled for three hours before being preserved in sour whey.

The sour whey, a traditional Scandinavian way of preserving food, comes as a by-product from a soft cheese like a yoghurt, known as *skyr*. This used to be a staple food of the Scandinavians, but now is made only in Iceland. It is made from skim milk, pasteurised and cooled to blood heat. A fermenting agent is added to curdle the milk, after which the curds are separated from the whey. The curds are the *skyr*, and eaten with sugar and cream.

More usual specialities include ptarmigan, eaten at Christmas with a tasty sauce; wild bilberries, eaten with *skyr*, and the delicious small lobster known as *humar* caught in summer off south Iceland. It has a particularly delicate flavour when well prepared. Fish roes are a favourite dish in Iceland, especially in mid-winter when they are small in size with a firm texture. Cooked fresh with fish liver, they are one of the national dishes of Iceland. But the best dishes of Iceland are undoubtedly the fresh fish, which are so good that they require no sauce when perfectly poached, grilled or baked. A wedge of lemon, a pat of butter and a slice of brown farm bread make a feast fit for a Viking god.

Soup

RAEKJUSUPA
Shrimp soup

Hors d'Oeuvre (Humar)

HUMARHALAR I DILLSOSU
Norway prawns (scampi) in dill sauce

SALTSILD I KRYDDSOSU
Salt herrings in spice sauce

SILDARSALAT
Herring cocktail

Fish Dishes

OFNBOKUO SALTSILDARFLOK
Oven baked herring fillets with potatoes and
onions

GUFUSOOIN FISHFLOK MEO EPLUM OG
BANONUM
Plaice fillets with apples and bananas

FYLLTUR SKARKOLI
Fillet of plaice Icelandic style

Meat Dishes

SOOIO LAMBAKJOT MEO SPERGLI OG
RAEJUM
Boiled lamb with asparagus and shrimps

Sweets

RJOMAPONNUKOKUR
Pancake served cold with jam and whipped cream

SOUP

RAEKJUSUPA
Shrimp soup

Ingredients:

Fish stock:

Water 2½ pint (1,500 mls)
Tomato puree or powder 1 oz (30 g)
Sliced onions 3 oz (90 g)
Shrimps with shells (preferably uncooked)
    4 oz (120 g)
Fish heads (cod, haddock) or bones 8 oz (240 g)
Margarine 2 oz (60 g)
1 bouquet garni

Creaming:

2 egg yolks
Cornflour 1 oz (30 g)
Juice and rind of 1 lemon
Cream 5 fl oz (150 mls)

Garnishing:

Peeled cooked shrimps 4 oz (120 g)

Salt and pepper
Pinch of paprika

Method: Sweat sliced onions with margarine, add
fish and shrimps and cook for 8 minutes, add
water and tomato puree and boil for 20
minutes to produce a stock. Add bouquet garni
for last 5 minutes of cooking time. Strain stock.
Blend egg yolks, cornflour and cream in a bowl,
add ½ pint of the stock while stirring and pour
this mixture into the remainder of the stock.
Season and add lemon juice and grated rind at
the last minute with the shrimps.

HORS D'OEUVRE (HUMAR)

HUMARHALAR I DILLSOSU
Norway prawns (scampi) in dill sauce

The fresh scampi known as Dublin Bay prawns
in Britain, Langoustines in France and Nephtops
Norvegicus (Bot) or Norwegian prawns are all
the same but species vary in size and form.

Ingredients:

Prawns with shell (must be alive) 2 lb (960 g)
Margarine 4 oz (120 g)
Oil 1 fl oz (30 mls)
Chopped carrots 2 oz (60 g)
Chopped onions 2 oz (60 g)
Chopped leeks 2 oz (60 g)
Sprig of celery
1 bouquet garni
Flour 2 oz (60 g)
Margarine 2 oz (60 g)
Cream 5 fl oz (150 mls)
Chopped dill 1 tbs
Salt and pepper
Boiled rice 8 oz (240 g)

Method: Heat margarine and oil in a saucepan
and saute the vegetables without colouring for 5
minutes. Add the live prawns, cover with a lid
and cook for a further 5 minutes. Add 2 pints
of water, bouquet garni and boil for 10 minutes.
Remove prawns and shell the tails. Pound the
head to a paste and add to liquor. Boil for 30
minutes and strain. Thicken with a roux: cook
margarine and flour to a sandy texture and
gradually add fish liquor. Season and strain.
Reboil with cream and add chopped dill and
shelled prawns. Serve with plain boiled rice or
potatoes. A little lemon juice, sour cream or
yoghurt can be added to the sauce.

If frozen scampi are used, toss scampi in
margarine or oil for 5 minutes and drain. Add to
a white sauce which has been flavoured with
chopped dill.

SALTSILD I KRYDDSOSU
Salt herrings in spice sauce

If salt herrings are used they should be placed in
cold water and left to soak for 12 hours under a
running tap. If fresh herrings are available the
following recipe is more quickly prepared.

Ingredients:

Filleted herrings 8 by 4 oz (120 g) each

Marinade:

Wine or cider vinegar 1 pint (600 mls)
Water ½ pint (300 mls)
Sugar 8 oz (240 g)
Sliced onion 5 oz (150 g)
4 peppercorns
Mustard seeds 1 tsp
Few sprigs of dill
4 cloves
2 bay leaves
Salt 3 oz (90 g)

Method: Boil marinade ingredients for 5 minutes and cool. When cold place the herring fillets in an earthenware dish and add the cold marinade. Cover with a lid and store in the refrigerator for 48 hours. The vinegar is the preservative agent.

Arrange rings of onion and chopped dill on top and serve with bread and butter and hot boiled potatoes.

SILDARSALAT
Herring cocktail

Ingredients:

Marinaded herring fillets cut in 1 inch squares
   1 lb (480 g)
Tomato ketchup 4 fl oz (120 mls)
White wine 4 fl oz (120 mls)
Chopped onions 2 oz (60 g)
2 hard-boiled eggs
Sprig of dill
Salt and pepper
Fried bread croutons or sippets

Method: Blend tomato ketchup with white wine, add onions, chopped eggs, seasoning and dill and mix the herring pieces with this sauce. Serve with fried croutons or buttered toasts.

FISH DISHES

OFNBOKUO SALTSILDARFLOK
Oven-baked herring fillets with potatoes and
   onions (4 to 8 portions)

Ingredients:

8 filleted herrings with roes 2 lb (960 g)
Sliced potatoes 1 lb (480 g)
Sliced onions 8 oz (240 g)
Salt and pepper
Chopped dill
Lard or oil 3 oz (90 g)
Parsley butter 2 oz (60 g) – made with 1 tbs
   chopped parsley
Lemon juice 3 fl oz (60 mls)
Cream 5 fl oz (150 mls)
Breadcrumbs

Method: Clean, scale, gut and fillet herrings. Wash and dry. Season the fish, place on a buttered dish and cover with a layer of potatoes and dill. Fry sliced onions, without browning, for 6 minutes and add to the potatoes. Place alternate layers of fish, potatoes and onions until dish is full. Season and dot with parsley butter. Sprinkle breadcrumbs on top and bake for 20 minutes at 360°F. Pour cream over the dish and rebake for a further 5 minutes. Sprinkle with lemon juice and serve with bread and butter.

GUFUSOOIN FISHFLOK MEO EPLUM OG BANONUM
Plaice fillets with apples and bananas

Ingredients:

4 plaice fillets 6 oz (180 g) each
Seasoned flour 2 oz (60 g)
1 apple
1 banana
Butter 4 oz (120 g)
Oil 2 fl oz (60 mls)
Pinch of curry powder
Salt and pepper
Juice and rind of 1 lemon
Chopped onions 1 oz (30 g)
Tomato juice 3 fl oz (90 g)
Cabbage 2 lb (960 g)

Method: Sweat onions in butter and oil for 5 minutes without colouring. Add lemon and tomato juice, curry powder and seasoning. Blend sliced apples and bananas. Pass the fish fillets in seasoned flour and place in a shallow dish which has been well coated with butter. Cover fish with apple and banana mixture and season. Bake for 15 minutes at 380°F, basting occasionally. Shred cabbage and wash well. Boil for 10 minutes, add seasoning and serve with the fish.

FYLLTUR SKARKOLI
Fillet of plaice Icelandic style

Ingredients:

Thinly sliced potatoes 1 lb (480 g)
Thinly sliced onions 8 oz (240 g)
Chopped dill 1 tbs
Butter 2 oz (60 g)
Water ½ pint (300 mls)
Salt and pepper
4 plaice fillets 8 oz (240 g) each
Seasoned flour 2 oz (60 g)
Butter 3 oz (90 g)
Sliced mushrooms 4 oz (120 g)

Icelandic sauce:

Fish stock 1 pint (600 mls) — see shrimp soup
   recipe, p. 000
Cream 5 fl oz (150 mls)
2 egg yolks
Cornflour 1 oz (30 g)
Butter 1 oz (30 g)
Juice and rind of 1 lemon
Cooked chopped shrimps 2 oz (60 g)
Chopped dill 1 tbs

Method: Wash, peel and slice potatoes and onions. Place in a shallow dish which has been well greased with lard or butter. Add water, seasoning and chopped dill and bake for 20 minutes at 400°F. Remove from oven.

Clean, gut and fillet fish. Wash and dry and pass in seasoned flour. Dip in melted butter and place fish over cooked potatoes with sliced white mushrooms. Squeeze juice of lemon over the mushroom slices and bake for 15 minutes at 400°F, basting from time to time with melted butter.

Sauce: Boil fish stock and thicken with a slurry of cream, egg yolks and cornflour which have been blended together in a bowl. Add gradually to the boiling stock while stirring or whisking. Add shrimps and butter and season. Add chopped dill last. Pour this sauce over the fish and serve.

The alternative to this sauce is to prepare a real Hollandaise sauce (see Dutch chapter, p. 233).

MEAT DISHES

SOOIO LAMBAKJOT MEO SPERGLI OG RAEJUM
Boiled lamb with asparagus and shrimps

Ingredients:

Stewing lamb from shoulder or middle neck cut
   in ½ inch cubes 2 lb (960 g)
Sliced onions 5 oz (150 g)
Water 3 pints (1,800 mls)
Leeks 2 oz (60 g)
Sliced carrots 4 oz (120 g)
1 bouquet garni
Few sprigs dill
Salt and pepper

Roux:

Margarine 2 oz (60 g)
Flour 2 oz (60 g)

Garnish:

Fresh asparagus 1 lb (480 g)
Peeled cooked shrimps 8 oz (240 g)

Cream finish:

Cream 5 fl oz (150 mls)
2 egg yolks

Method: Place diced lean lamb in cold water and bring to the boil gently. Remove scum as it rises and when clear add vegetables and cook for 1 hour. Add bouquet garni and simmer for a further 10 minutes. Strain and reheat liquor. Cook a roux and add gradually to the boiling stock. Blend cream and yolks in a bowl, add ½ pint of the stock and stir well. Pour this mixture into the remainder of the stock, bring to the boil again and season. Add meat to sauce. Add the shrimps to the sauce also and serve asparagus separately with boiled potatoes. Sprinkle chopped dill over the meat and vegetables.

SWEETS

RJOMAPONNUKOKUR
Pancake served cold with jam and whipped cream

Ingredients:

1 egg
Flour 3 oz (90 g)
Milk 5 fl oz (150 mls)
Pinch of salt and sugar
Vanilla essence
Lard 2 oz (60 g) for cooking pancakes
Whipped cream 5 fl oz (150 mls)
Sugar 1 oz
Blackcurrant or black cherry jam

Method: Beat egg and add to milk with sugar and salt and vanilla essence. Add flour and beat to a smooth batter. Rest for 30 minutes. Heat pan with a little lard and cook pancakes. Cool and when cold spread with jam. Pipe a layer of cream, sprinkle with sugar and roll the pancake. Serve cold.

Instead of whipped cream a blob of ice cream can be used and the pancake rolled up in the same way.

Spain

The cooking of Spain is a blend of many ingredients artfully combined to blend them without disguising their own tastes. The food is usually plain in appearance and appetising because of its fresh look rather than the art of the chef — disguises and heavily spiced dishes have no appeal to the Spaniard.

Spanish gastronomy is the product of an originally Arabic culture, and the unusual mixtures of fish and several types of meat may be traced to these foundations. The same origins have given the Spaniard a tooth for sweet things, and syrup-soaked fried pastries and the use of sesame seeds, aniseed and honey shows the influence of the Middle East. Early journeys to the New World have also made Spain one of the first European countries to adopt chocolate, both as a flavouring and as a drink. It often replaces coffee as a breakfast drink, and chunks of chocolate are used to give a rich flavour to many stews, as in Mexican cookery.

Because of Spain's hot climate, fruits and the more exotic vegetables flourish, but there is little lush grass to pasture dairy herds, so that butter and cream play no part in Spanish cookery. Tomatoes, onions, garlic and peppers are used in many dishes and the valuable saffron is extensively used as an aromatic flavouring.

Olive oil is the constant ingredient of Spanish cooking. The best oil is obtained from fruit gathered in December, when it is fully ripe, and pressed cold after the skins and stones have been taken out. The second quality is expressed from the whole fruit, and lower grades are made from the skins, stones and residue by means of solvents and pressure.

Seafood is colourful and plentiful with a wide variety of delicious things from the Mediterranean and the Atlantic. Freshwater fish abound in the rivers which cross the Iberian Peninsula and are cooked in imaginative ways; fried before being put into a soup, or grilled with rough salt and a touch of ham fat.

Fiercely independent and individualistic, the Spaniards do not believe in collective action, and each region of the country clings to its own way of cooking. They even go so far as to give basic dishes local names; so the Iberian stew — based on what is available in the local market in the way of vegetables, with beef and chicken — is called *olla podrida* in central Spain, *cocido madrileno* in Madrid, *cocido andaluz* in Andulasia, and by a variety of names all over the country. Yet it is basically the same delicious, slow-simmered stew.

Many travellers have come back from a Spanish holiday, bitterly disappointed with Spanish fare, condemning it as greasy and over-spiced. It may be so in some hotels, but true Spanish food is never highly spiced and rarely greasy. In fact, Spanish food is the base upon which French cuisine has been built, and many centuries ago there were Spanish cooks at the court of Louis XIII of France. His wife, Anne of Austria, the Infanta of Spain, brought her cooks to his court and the kitchens were professionally organised by them. Their first introduction was the Spanish sauce, the basis of all classical sauces, followed by the mayonnaise, known then as *Mahonesa* from Mahon in the Balearic Isles. Mayonnaise was popularised by the chef of Cardinal Richelieu.

The reign of the French King Henri IV made Spanish food even more popular; he was the son of the Queen of Navarre, a province of Spain, and when he promised that every French family would be able to afford a fowl in the pot once a week, he was probably thinking of the Spanish *cocido*.

When Maria Theresa married Louis XIV of France, she brought a complete retinue of cooks and chefs, confectioners and bakers, among whom were the ancestors of the Conil family, who settled in Picardy in the seventeenth century.

Rich in history and culture, Spain was for a long time a poor country, and the cooking of Spain is essentially that of the people. Many recipes are adaptable in the amount of meat they use, and while a rich man might have a whole chicken plus beef, veal, *chorizo*, ham and blood sausage in his *cocido*, on the table of the poor a very similar dish will appear but with emphasis on the potatoes, carrots, chickpeas, cabbage and very little meat.

The typical diet of Spain still contains a high proportion of the cheaper filling foods such as potatoes, rice, dried salt fish, beans, peas and lentils.

When one thinks of Spain the temptation is to visualise the hot, red dry soil of Andulasia, with its flamenco and riots of colourful flowers on the slopes leading down to the sea. Yet there are regions of Spain where the flamenco is unknown. There is the lush green of Galicia, with its mists and rain on a rocky Atlantic shore; there is the dry, arid soil of Castille, blown by the summer wind; there are the scorched hills of the south and the snow-capped Pyrenees in the north-east; there are the rice swamps of Valencia and the Guadarrama mountains where an icy wind blasts the rocky peaks.

The basic ingredients may be similar, the olive oil, the garlic and the parsley may be universally Iberian, but the style of cooking varies with the area. Broadly speaking, the five zones of gastronomy in Spain are the north, the area for sauces; the centre, for roasts and game; the south for fried foods; the east for rice dishes; and the areas of the Bay of Biscay for seafood. In addition there is the land of the Basques, those true gourmets who do not know from where they come nor how their language originated, but who are the best cooks in the entire peninsula.

The Basque Country

Fish dominates the culinary style of this picturesque region situated between France and Spain. The *Sopa de Pescado a la Vasca* is a mixture of white fish and mussels with vegetables, and the *Ttorro* an interesting stew of prawns, mussels, five different fish with red peppers and tomatoes. *Bacalao a la Vizcaina* is a dish of dried salted cod and *angulas a la bilbaino* is a dish of young eels. There is a Basque version of *Paella* and other rice dishes, and the giant crab, crayfish and lobsters are prepared with various sauces. *Chipirones en su Tinta* are the small squid caught in the Bay of Biscay, cooked in their own ink. It may look like bits of rubber in engine oil, but it tastes divine; the ink thickens the sauce and after a while, even the murky depths of the blackness look appetising.

The Basques also have many dishes of meat with beans, the original precursors of the French *cassoulet*. The *chorizo* of the Basques is pencil-thin, with a crisp skin and dark tasty pork inside. A wonderful cheese is made from the milk of the shaggy Basque sheep called *lachas*. *Txakoli* is a crisp, tart dry white wine found nowhere else.

Asutria and Galicia

The people of this region are said to be Celtic in origin, and indeed their dances are traditionally accompanied by the music of bagpipes rather than guitars and castanets. The local way of cooking tripe, similar to the *tripes a la mode de Caen*, is also Celtic. The most wonderful dish of this region is a bean stew, the *fabada*, made with a locally-grown bean which is thick and white and never goes mealy. The stew includes pork, ham, bacon, blood sausage, sometimes pig's ears and trotters, and is simmered for many hours in an earthenware pot, very like the *cassoulet*.

Galicia is noted for its seafood and is the most important fishing region in the whole of Spain. The scallops, clams, tiny crabs and mussels are prepared simply, often by steaming or boiling. Parsley and garlic are used in many of the sauces which accompany the delicious seafood, and the unique wine called Rosal is dry, white and delicately sparkling — the perfect foil for the sea-fresh sweetness of the fish.

From Galicia also comes the *empanada*, a pie which can be of any size and filled with any kind of meat, fish or vegetables in any number of combinations. Turnip tops are a widely used vegetable in this verdant part of Spain.

Bread of the region is often made of cornmeal, and the almond tarts made in Galicia are a delicious sweet. The chestnuts of the area are as big as apples and are candied or eaten raw.

Madrid

The capital of Spain, Madrid is a cosmopolitan city which has taken the best dishes from all over the peninsula and improved them to very high standards. The Madrilenos' appetites are as legendary as the Basques', and there is a saying that they eat all day and part of the night. Modern nutritionists are beginning to note that the cult of slimness is starting to have an effect on the habits of the people of Madrid, but portions are still vast in restaurants and there are traditionally five meals in the day.

The *Cocido Madrileno* is a rich stew of beef and chicken with chickpeas and assorted vegetables. It is traditionally eaten in three courses, the first being the strong broth, followed by the vegetables served separately, and lastly the meats, which may include *chorizos*, ham, bacon or blood sausages.

Another excellent speciality from Madrid is the *sopa de ajo*, a hot garlic soup made from garlic and slices of bread sauted in olive oil, with water and beaten eggs stirred into it. Instead of soup, the hungry Madrileno may well choose the copious *entremeses* or hors d'oeuvres which would include onions, beans, peas, young artichoke hearts, olives, slices of *chorizo* and the smoked ham known as *jamon serrano*.

Meat courses are rich and flavourful in this heart of Spain, often with game like venison or wild boar, still hunted in the traditional way with a spear on horseback. For the poorer classes, the main course could be based on a stew of lentils, rich, filling and satisfying with a minimum of meat to give flavour, and often eaten with a few slices of raw onion. Dried codfish is another inexpensive meal typical of Madrid.

The Madrilenos, rich or poor, eat lightly at breakfast, with coffee or chocolate and a roll. The second meal is elevenses, possibly an omelette or some fried sausages. At about 2.30 in the afternoon, everything shuts for the main midday meal, an important affair of three or four courses finishing with a solid dessert — rice pudding and caramel custards are excellent. A lighter ending to a meal might be a piece of cheese or fruit in season. The institution of the siesta is beginning to die out, or at least getting shorter. Spanish dieticians are beginning to notice that the decline of the post-prandial nap is bringing about a decrease in diseases of the liver and gall bladder.

Coffee and pastries make an appearance at about six in the evening, and the last meal of the day is eaten between ten and midnight. It is usually a light meal, perhaps an omelette, invented by the Spanish but probably based on the Roman *ovamelitta*, a kind of pancake sweetened with honey. When it was first introduced to France at the court of Louis XIV is was known as *Tortilla a la Cartuja*, and could have been a creation of the Carthusian monks; the French developed it into the souffle omelette. The Spanish omelette is usually flat and it can be stuffed with all kinds of meat, vegetables or even fish. Potatoes and onions are the main ingredients of the omelette of Andalusia, and often onions, tomatoes, peppers and ham are used.

The surrounding area of Madrid, Castile, is the heart of Spain. But it is often a cold heart, and when the icy wind blows from the Guadarrama mountains, the food of Castile has to be substantial to cope with the climate. There is an abundance of game, with wild turkey, pheasants, partridge and quail as well as the more usual hare, rabbit and venison. Roasts are delicious in this area, especially the tiny sucking pigs of four kilos or less, roasted whole, in wood-burning ovens.

Vegetables are used in combinations, finely chopped and sauted, with some ham or eggs stirred in at the last to give some protein content to an essentially cheap dish. Tripes are cooked with tomatoes, *chorizos* and red peppers, all typical of this area.

Navarro and Aragon

These two provinces follow the Basque style of good cooking in the French manner rather than being typically Spanish. The people of Aragon like garlic, and it is a key ingredient in the delicious fricassee of lamb with minced onion, parsley and a hint of lemon juice. Chocolate is often used to make sauces rich and dark, notably in the *tongue a la aragonesa* with its cordon of carrots, potatoes and turnips, and in the sauce served with game in Navarro, based on tiny onions, deliciously glazed.

The trout of Navarro is excellent and is served most often marinated in a dry white wine with a variety of mountain herbs and onion. It is poached in the marinade, which is then thickened with egg yolks to make a sauce. Navarro also produces a wonderful ewe's milk cheese known as *Roncal*.

The Western Provinces

Leon, Zamora, Salamanca, Extremadura, Caceres and Badajoz are picturesque regions not very well known by tourists but of great individuality. From this region comes the *chanfaina*, a tasty dish of globe artichokes stuffed with a mixture of meat from the head, feet and lungs of an animal, often deer. Garlic soup *a la Salmantina* is made with giblets and *chorizo* sausages, and in Caceres game birds are prepared in rich, wine-dark sauces. The best wine of the region is Fruto Solesto.

Barcelona and Catalonia

All types of food in season with special emphasis on the fruits of the sea are the offerings of this northern Mediterranean area. Barcelona is an important port where Columbus landed on his return from America; now it is an international city with many five-star hotels and luxurious restaurants. Cooking *en papillote* is a local speciality, and there is a Barcelona version of a *paella*, every bit as good as the one from Valencia. One of the most exciting dishes I have ever tasted is the *Langoustines Costa Brava* at the Ritz; scampi in white wine with brandy and tomatoes, rather like lobster *a l'americaine*.

The Catalans have their own *cocido*, which includes meatballs, and the *zarzuela de mariscos* is a medley of seafoods in a light sauce, every bit as good as the *bouillabaisse*. *Rustido a la Catalan* is a wonderful, succulent joint of veal flavoured with garlic and dark rum.

The *Crema Catalana* is a light egg custard, and its close relative is the *leche frita*, a fried custard cream. *Pan de Santa Teresa* is a sweet bread dipped in eggs and fried.

Valencia and the Levante

This is the area of rice in all its forms, and the true home of the *paella*. The excellence of a good *paella* is in its combination of ingredients with due regard to taste, colour and texture, and in having each grain of rice separate without being too dry. Ingredients for the traditional *paella* include olive oil, chicken, lean pork, cured ham, eels, beans, snails, crayfish, clams, mussels, green peppers, garlic, onions and herbs, all flavoured with a good pinch of saffron to lend its perfumed brilliance to the finished dish.

Most dishes of this region are either based on rice or designed to complement the rice. An outstanding sweet speciality is *turron*, a nougat made of toasted almonds, honey, and egg whites, sometimes flavoured with coriander, nuts and cinnamon.

Andalusia

This is the region of strong sunlight, red earth and the *flamenco*. The summer heat has affected Andalusian cooking so that most dishes are light and easily digestible. The *gazpacho*, a liquid salad rather than a soup, comes from this area.

Fried foods in most countries tend to be heavy, but not so in Andalusia, and this southern province of Spain is also known as the land of the frying pan. Fried fish of a deliciously light texture and with no hint of greasiness is sold in the streets as a snack, or can be taken to the nearest cafe to enjoy with a glass or two of dry white wine or fine sherry. Another summer drink is sangria, a mixture of red wine, with lemon, borage, soda water and ice.

The best smoked ham comes from this province, from the mountains near the town of Huelva. The ham, *jamon serrano*, is laid out in the sun on the snow to prevent it decaying while the sun dries out the moisture and preserves it. It is most often eaten with a rich, scented melon like a cantaloup and is a favourite starter all over Spain.

The Andalusians also have an almost Arabic sweet tooth, and there are many syrup-soaked cakes, flavoured with nuts, sesame seeds and anis.

The wines of Spain are internationally renowned and come in a wide variety of identities. The best are Rioja and Navarra, high quality red wines suitable for aging, and Carinena, robust wines of a deep red. The dry Malaga, white Allela, Valdepenas and Huelva are white wines of distinction. The sherry of Spain is one of her most unique contributions to international gastronomy and is drunk extensively all over the world. It is also delicious in cooking.

The cooking of Spain is a riot of colours, flavours and textures — never to be taken too seriously, but to be savoured and above all — enjoyed.

BILL OF FARE

Soup

SOPA DE PESCADO A LA VISCA
Fish soup

SOPA DE AJO TERESA
Garlic soup

PUCHERO or OLLA PODRIDA
Spanish hot pot

GAZPACHO
Cold soup

GAZPACHUELO
Cold fish soup

ESCUDILLA DE PAGES JULIA
Haricot bean soup

Hors d'Oeuvre

PICADILLO
Oranges, red peppers, haddock, olives and onions
  with vinaigrette sauce

'FRICCO'
Tomato and cucumber salad with peppers and
  black olives

COSTA BRAVA
Large prawns (preferably fresh) cooked with
  tomatoes and sherry sauce

ANDALUSIA
Rice salad blended with mayonnaise and
  vegetables

'OVA SPAGNA'
Egg mayonnaise with anchovy fillets and
  olives

Fish Dishes

MERLUZA A LA GALLEGA
Baked hake with potatoes and onions

TRUCHA A LA NAVARRA
Stuffed trout wrapped in pancakes

ZARZUELA A LA CONIL
Spanish seafood mixture modified by Conil

ALMEJAS A LA MARINERA
Clams fishermen style

BESUGO ASADO
Baked sea bream or mullet

LANGOSTINA CATALANA
Crawfish with tomatoes and sherry

Meat Dishes

'OVA MELITTA SPAGNA'
Spanish omelette

PAELLA BARCELONA
Spanish national dish

PAELLA VALENCIANA
Chicken casserole with rice

GALLINA VIVA EL TORO
Chicken Spanish style

CALLOS MADRILENA
Tripe Spanish style

CONEJO A LA JUANA
Tame rabbit Spanish style

TERNERA A LA CONDESITA
Veal casserole in sherry

COCIDO CASTELLANO
Beef and gammon casserole Spanish style

COCHINILLO A LA CONIL
Pork escalope Basquaise style

BUTIFARRA CON JUDIAS
Sausages and baked beans

FAISAN A LA MODA DE ALCANTARA
Roast pheasant with liver and truffles

PERDIZ CHOCOLATE
Partridge in chocolate sauce

CARNERO ASADO A LA MANCHEGA
Leg of mutton with beans

FABADA ASTURIANA
Haricot beans and cabbage with pork and
  sausages

Vegetables

COL DE BRUSELAS
Sprouts fried in breadcrumbs

ESPINACA
Spinach with anchovies

PISTO A LA RIOJANA
Mixed vegetable casserole

Sweets and Desserts

CREMA LECHE FRITA CATALANA
Egg custard

PAN DE SANTA PAULA
Fried egg and bread fritters

ARROZ IMPERATRIZ EUGENIE
Cream rice with raspberry jelly and liqueur fruits

SOUP (SOPA)

SOPA DE PESCADO A LA VISCA
Fish soup (6 to 8 portions)

Ingredients:

Fish stock:

Fish bones and heads 1 lb (480 g)
Sliced onions 6 oz (180 g)
1 bouquet garni (bay leaf, celery, thyme)
Margarine or oil 2 fl oz (60 mls)
Water 3 pint (1,800 mls)
Good pinch of salt
Pinch of monosodium glutamate

Julienne of leeks (cut in strips 1½ inch long)
   2 oz (60 g)
Julienne of celery 2 oz (60 g)
Julienne of carrots 2 oz (60 g)
Margarine or oil 2 oz (60 g)
Clove of garlic
Salt and pepper
Tomatoes (skinned and seeded) 8 oz (240 g)
Dry sherry 5 fl oz (150 mls)
Haddock or hake fillets 6 oz (180 g) per person

Method: Place margarine in a saucepan and saute
sliced onions for 3 minutes. Add fish bones and
cover with lid. Let onions and bones sweat for 4
minutes and add water and bouquet garni. Boil
for 20 minutes without lid and strain. Season
with salt and monosodium glutamate.

   Grease a shallow dish with margarine and
sprinkle with julienne of vegetables. Cover with
fish fillets and season. Pour on sherry and stock
and arrange tomato pulp and chopped garlic on
each fish. Cover with a lid and bake at 380°F for
25 minutes. Serve with 1 oz (30 g) cooked rice
on each plate.

SOPA DE AJO TERESA
Garlic soup (6 to 8 portions)

Ingredients:

Duck or goose fat or oil 1 oz (30 g)
Garlic 1 oz (30 g)

1 bouquet garni
Water 3 pint (1,800 mls)
4 egg yolks
4 slices of French bread
Juice of 1 lemon
Chopped parsley, 1 tbs
2 chicken bouillon cubes or use chicken stock
   instead of water

Method: Place the egg yolks in a soup tureen with
1 oz (30 g) oil. Crush the garlic and boil with
water, chicken bouillon and bouquet garni for 10
minutes. Strain and pour into the soup tureen.
Whisk stock and egg yolks and add toasted
slices of French bread. Let the bread soak up the
soup for 4 minutes and sprinkle with chopped
parsley and lemon juice.

PUCHERO or OLLA PODRIDA
Spanish hot pot (12 portions)

Every country has its own hot pot. In my family,
such soup was prepared every day of the week.
The Spanish came to France with my ancestors
on my mother's and father's side who settled in
Picardy from the fourteenth century. (Conil,
Gorriez and Demagnez are all Spanish names.)
We owe the popularity of the hot pot to Henry IV
of Navarre who was connected to the Spanish
royal blood and later became King of France.

   The Spanish hot pot contains as many types of
meat as you can afford (bacon, beef, fowl and
many vegetables). The broth is drunk as soup
with bread soaked into the liquid and the
vegetables and meats are served as the main dish.

Ingredients:

Water 6 pints (3,600 mls)
Thick flank 1 lb (480 g)
1 fowl 4 lb (1,920 g)
Knuckle of bacon 1 lb (480 g)
1 carrot
1 turnip
1 small cabbage
Sprig of celery
4 leeks tied up in a bundle
1 onion studded with 3 cloves

1 bouquet garni
1 small peeled beetroot
Salt and pepper
4 slices of brown bread

Method: Clean and truss the fowl. Place in a
large stockpot with the meats and cover with
water. Bring gently to the boil, and, as the scum
rises, skim carefully until the broth is clear.
Simmer for 1½ hours. Add the carrot, turnip
and onion and boil for another 30 minutes.
Add the quartered cabbage, leeks, beetroot,
bouquet garni and celery. Add more water at
this stage, to keep the same level of liquid. Boil
for a further 30 minutes. Remove all the vegetables and arrange neatly on a dish to be served
as an accompaniment for the meat. Remove the
fowl and meats and use as much as is needed for
one meal. Either slices of each of the meats or
one only is required. Place the toasted bread
slices into a soup tureen and pour in the broth.
Season to taste.

This recipe which has been handed down in my
family, has given the best results. Note that the
beetroot will not only add a sweeter flavour but
also will give the broth a richer golden colour.
Beetroot only turns red with an acid or vinegar
and *yellow* in an alkaline solution.

GAZPACHO
A cold soup

Ingredients:

Garlic ½ clove (5 g)
Chopped onions 2 oz (60 g)
Chopped seedless green pepper 2 oz (60 g)
Skinned seedless tomatoes 2 oz (60 g)
Water 1½ pints (900 mls)
Oil 2 fl oz (60 mls)
Salt and pepper
Diced cucumber 3 oz (90 g)
Diced fried croutons 2 oz (60 g)
Vinegar 1 tbs

Method: Pound garlic, onions and peppers and add
tomatoes and cucumber. Mix in vinegar and seasoning and pass through a liquidiser to make a smooth

paste. Add 1½ pints of iced water and oil and
liquidise again to obtain a smooth well-emulsified
mixture. Serve croutons of fresh bread separately.

GAZPACHO MADRILENO

This is the same as above but flavoured with a
pinch of cumin and the diced cucumber served as
a garnish after the soup is made.

GAZPACHO ESTREMENO

Ingredients:

Garlic ½ clove (5 g)
3 egg yolks
Green pepper 2 oz (60 g)
Breadcrumbs 4 oz (120 g)
Water 5 fl oz (150 mls)
Oil 2 fl oz (60 mls)
Vinegar ½ fl oz (15 mls)
Salt and pepper

Method: Crush garlic with seedless green pepper
and salt. Add breadcrumbs (soaked in iced water
but squeezed dry). Add egg yolks to the mixture
and liquidise until smooth. Gradually add olive
oil and lastly mix in vinegar and complete
seasoning.

GAZPACHUELO
Cold fish soup

Ingredients:

Water 1½ pints (900 mls)
Filleted white fish 1 lb (480 g)
Potatoes 8 oz (240 g)
Lemon juice 1 fl oz (30 mls)
3 egg yolks and 3 egg whites
Olive oil 5 fl oz (150 mls)
Salt and pepper
1 clove of garlic

Method: Poach skinned fish until soft and then
remove bones. Strain stock and cook sliced
potatoes until tender. Prepare mayonnaise in a

bowl. Add yolks, a little lemon and salt and gradually mix in oil, whisking until thick. Add a finely chopped clove of garlic to this mixture and gradually add the stock of the soup to the mayonnaise to obtain a smooth mixture. Place fish and potatoes in a soup tureen and add egg mixture. Poach the whites of egg in a greased mould until set hard and cut in thin slices. Use as a garnish or decoration. In Malaga this soup is eaten lukewarm.

ESCUIDILLA DE PAGES JULIA
Haricot bean soup

This is the same as *Puchero* or *Olla Podrida*, but add 1 lb (480 g) cooked haricot beans to the soup.

HORS D'OEUVRE

PICADILLO
Oranges, red peppers, haddock, olives and
    onions with vinaigrette sauce

Ingredients:

Smoked haddock 1 lb (480 g)
Cooked diced potatoes 1 lb (480 g)
Red peppers 4 oz (120 g)
Orange segments 6 oz (180 g)
Onion rings 4 oz (120 g)
Black olives 3 oz (90 g)

Vinaigrette sauce:

Orange juice 2 fl oz (60 mls)
Lemon juice 2 fl oz (60 mls)
White vinegar 2 fl oz (60 mls)
Spanish olive oil 5 fl oz (150 mls)
Grated rind of half a lemon and orange
Salt and pepper
Clove of garlic finely chopped
Made mustard 1 tsp

Method: Poach the haddock in water for 10 minutes. Remove the bone and skin. Split the red pepper and grill to blister the skin for easier removal. Cut in strips. Grate orange and lemon

peel. Remove pith from two oranges and cut in segments. Arrange fish fillets and diced cooked potatoes in a shallow dish with strips of pepper and black olives. Surround with orange segments and top with rings of raw onion overlapping each other. Blend all ingredients of the sauce and pour over the salad. Serve remaining sauce in a sauceboat.

'FRICCO'
Tomato and cucumber salad with peppers and
    black olives

Ingredients:

Tomatoes 8 oz (240 g)
Peeled cucumber 8 oz (240 g)
White breadcrumbs 4 oz (120 g)
Chopped garlic 1 clove (10 g)
Salt and pepper
Black olives
Oil 3 tbs
Lemon juice or white vinegar 2 tbs
Chopped parsley 1 tbs
Chopped onions 1 tbs
2 chopped hard-boiled eggs

Method: Slice the tomatoes vertically from stem downwards. Slice cucumber. Sprinkle with salt to remove excess bitter juice and leave for 20 minutes. Rinse and drain. Alternate the tomato and cucumber slices in a shallow hors d'oeuvre dish. Place the crumbs in a bowl with lemon juice or vinegar, salt and pepper and oil. Add garlic and chopped onions. Pour this dressing over the salad and decorate with black olives and sprinkle with chopped parsley and hard-boiled eggs.

COSTA BRAVA
Large prawns (preferably fresh) cooked with
    tomatoes and sherry sauce

Ingredients:

Fresh Dublin Bay prawns 2 lb (960 g) or frozen
    scampi 1½ lb (720 g)
Chopped onions 2 oz (60 g)

Seasoned flour 2 oz (60 g) (used only with frozen
    scampi)
Oil 2 fl oz (60 mls)
Vinegar 3 tbs
Clove garlic
Water ½ pint (300 mls)
Bouquet garni
Dry sherry 5 fl oz (150 mls)
Skinned and seeded tomatoes 5 oz (150 g)
Pinch of dry thyme
Salt and pepper

Liaison:

Cream 5 fl oz (150 mls)
2 egg yolks
Cornflour ½ oz (15 g)

Method: Saute the chopped onions until
translucent in a large saucepan for 5 minutes. Add
the fresh prawns without shelling them. Place a lid
on the pan and toss for about 5 minutes. Add
water, vinegar and bouquet garni and boil for 10
minutes. Strain the water and remove prawns.
Shell and tail the prawns and keep the flesh in a
shallow dish while completing the sauce. Blend the
stock, sherry, tomato pulp, thyme and seasoning.
Boil for 10 minutes. Mix cream and egg yolks with
cornflour in a bowl and add ¾ pint of the stock
and stir. Pour the egg mixture back to remaining
stock and reheat until it thickens while stirring.
Add cooked prawns, check seasoning and serve hot
or cold.

Method for frozen scampi: Pass scampi in seasoned
flour and pan fry in oil for 5 minutes. Remove and
in same fat fry onion until translucent. Add
tomato pulp and sherry and boil for 5 minutes.
Thicken with cream and egg yolks as above. Blend
cooked scampi and season. A little fish stock can
be made with a few fish bones and same amount
per weight of water, boiled down for 20 minutes
with a bouquet garni and 1 oz (30 g) of onion.

ANDALUSIA
Rice salad blended with mayonnaise and vegetables

Ingredients:

Long grain rice 4 oz (120 g)

Water 1 pint (600 mls)
Tomato 8 oz (240 g)
Red and green peppers 4 oz (120 g)
Black olives 8
1 onion 4 oz (120 g) cut in thin rings

Spanish Mayonnaise: ½ pint (300 mls)
2 egg yolks
Made mustard 1 tsp
Olive oil ½ pint (300 mls)
Juice of 1 lemon
Salt and pepper

Method: Boil rice for 20 minutes. Pass under
the water tap to rinse away starch, drain and
dry. Make the mayonnaise as follows: place
mustard, salt and pepper in a bowl with egg
yolks. Warm the oil slightly at 80°F and add to
egg mixture in a thin trickle while stirring with
a whisk to obtain a perfect emulsion. Continue
pouring slowly until the mayonnaise is thick
and lastly add the lemon juice. Use only half of
the amount of mayonnaise made above and keep
the rest for the next recipe Ova Spagna. Blend rice
with mayonnaise, add diced red and green peppers
and stir. Decorate salad with tomato slices and
black olives. Surround the tomatoes with onion
rings.

'OVA SPAGNA'
Egg mayonnaise with anchovy fillets and olives

Ingredients:

4 hard-boiled eggs
8 anchovy fillets 4 oz (120 g)
8 stuffed olives
Mayonnaise ¼ pint (150 mls)
8 orange segments
4 lettuce leaves

Method: Cut eggs in halves. Place on lettuce leaves
and coat each half with mayonnaise. Decorate
with washed and drained anchovy fillets and sliced
stuffed olives. Surround with orange segments.

FISH DISHES

MERLUZA A LA GALLEGA
Baked hake with potatoes and onions

Ingredients:

Olive oil 3 fl oz (90 mls)
Potatoes 8 oz (240 g)
Onions 8 oz (240 g)
Filleted hake 2 lb (960 g)
Clove of garlic
Tomato pulp 8 oz (240 g)
Chopped red peppers 4 oz (120 g)
Salt and pepper
Water 5 fl oz (150 mls)
Dry sherry 5 fl oz (150 mls)
Chopped parsley 1 tbs
Powdered thyme 1 pinch

Method: Slice potatoes and onions and place in a saucepan with water, sherry, garlic and thyme. Boil for 12 minutes covered with a lid. Transfer into a shallow dish and place fish fillets on top. Season and cover with tomatoes and red peppers. Add a little oil and bake for 20 minutes at 400°F. Sprinkle with chopped parsley on serving.

TRUCHA A LA NAVARRA
Stuffed trout wrapped in pancakes

Ingredients:

4 trout fillets 2 lb (960 g)
Seasoned flour 2 oz (60 g)
4 large pancakes 8 inch diameter
4 large thin slices of ham
Chopped or sliced mushrooms 3 oz (90 g)
Chopped onions 2 oz (60 g)
Clove of garlic
1 hard-boiled egg
Mayonnaise ¼ pint (150 mls)
Chopped parsley 1 tbs
Salt and pepper
Pinch of ground thyme
Oil 4 fl oz (120 mls)

Method: Wash and dry fish and pass in seasoned flour. Place a slice of ham over each pancake and arrange 1 fillet of trout on the centre. Spread following mixture over each fish: pan fry chopped onions, garlic and mushrooms for 4 minutes in oil until soft. Remove from heat and blend with chopped hard-boiled egg, parsley and mayonnaise. Cream mixture to a paste, add seasonings. Roll the pancakes and place in a greased shallow dish. Brush with melted butter and bake for 20 minutes at 400°F.
For batter use: 1 egg, 3 oz (90 g) flour and 5 fl oz (150 mls) water blended together.

ZARZUELA A LA CONIL
A spanish seafood mixture modified by Conil

Ingredients:

Chopped onions 4 oz (120 g)
Clove of garlic
Oil 3 fl oz (90 mls)
Tomatoes skinned and seeded 8 oz (240 g)
Pinch of saffron
Dry sherry 5 fl oz (150 mls)
Pernod or absinthe liqueur 3 fl oz (90 mls)
Water 5 fl oz (150 mls)
White vinegar 2 tbs
Salt and pepper
Pinch of cayenne pepper
Chopped parsley 1 tbs
Pinch chopped tarragon
12 shelled raw mussels, cleaned and free from seaweed
4 x 6 oz (180 g) hake fillets
12 large scampi (frozen)
4 sippets of fried bread or garlic bread

Garlic bread mixture:

Butter 4 oz (120 g)
Chopped parsley 1 tbs
Pernod 1 tbs
1 or 2 cloves of chopped garlic
Small french loaf or 4 crisp rolls

Method: Saute chopped onions and crushed garlic in oil in a large pan until translucent. Add tomato pulp, saffron, sherry and water and boil for 5 minutes. Place fish into a shallow dish and arrange mussels and scampi around the sides. Cover with the tomato mixture and season. Add spices, vinegar and tarragon and bake for 20 minutes at 400°F. Serve in the same dish. Lastly pour the pernod over the fish and sprinkle with chopped parsley. Cream the garlic butter mixture and shape into a roll. Wrap in paper and freeze. Cut into pats and insert 1 in each bread roll and bake for 3 minutes. Serve warm.

ALMEJAS A LA MARINERA
Clams fishermen style

Ingredients:

Clams 2½ lb (1,200 g)
Chopped onions 2 oz (60 g)
Oil 2 fl oz (60 mls)
White vinegar 2 tbs
Clove of garlic
Breadcrumbs 2 oz (60 g)
Pinch of ground thyme
1 bay leaf
Dry sherry or Spanish white wine ½ pint (300 mls)
Salt and black pepper
Chopped parsley 1 tbs
Butter 3 oz (90 g)

Method: Soak clams in cold water for 2 hours. Drain and rinse. Saute onions in a large saucepan with oil for 5 minutes until translucent. Add clams, garlic and remaining ingredients. Cover with a lid and boil for 7 minutes until the clams open their shell. Remove clams to another dish and boil sauce for a further 5 minutes. Add butter and when melted add sauce to clams. Sprinkle with fresh chopped parsley.

BESUGO ASADO
Baked sea bream or mullet

Ingredients:

4 sea breams 2 lb (960 g)
Juice and rind of 2 lemons
4 slices of lemon cut in halves or quarters
Honey 4 oz (120 g)
Salt and pepper

Olive oil 4 fl oz (120 mls)
Breadcrumbs 4 oz (120 g)

Method: Clean fish and make small cuts or slits on top of the flesh. Insert halves of lemon into these slits and place in a dish. Melt honey and lemon juice and pour over the fish. Season with salt and pepper. Pour oil over the fish and bake for 20 minutes at 400°F. Sprinkle with fried breadcrumbs on serving the fish.

LANGOSTINA CATALANA
Crawfish with tomatoes and sherry

Ingredients:

4 medium crawfish 1½ lb each (720 g)
Oil 4 fl oz (120 mls)
Chopped onions 5 oz (150 g)
Chopped tomato pulp (skinned and deseeded
    tomatoes) 8 oz (240 g)
Tomato puree 2 oz (60 g)
Water ½ pint (300 mls)
Dry sherry ½ pint (300 mls)
Saffron 1 pinch
Salt and pepper
Chopped parsley 1 tbs

Butter paste:

Butter 2 oz (60 g)
Cornflour 1½ oz (45 g)

4 fried bread croutons (fried in oil)

Method: Cut live crawfish with shell in small pieces (split the head first, remove gravel from between the eyes and cut tail in 3 sections across). Heat a large pan and saute the pieces in oil for 10 minutes. Add chopped onions and cook for 5 more minutes without browning the onions. Add rest of ingredients. Cover with a lid and cook for 20 minutes. Thicken the sauce by adding the butter which has been creamed with the cornflour to make a paste. Boil for 5 minutes and sprinkle with chopped parsley. Serve with fried bread croutons. Crawfish or rock lobsters have no claws.

MEAT DISHES

'OVA MELITTA SPAGNA'
Spanish omelette

Ingredients:

8 eggs
Oil 3 fl oz (60 mls)

Garnish:

Chopped onions 1 oz (30 g)
Diced cooked potatoes 2 oz (60 g)
Diced raw green and red peppers 2 oz (60 g)
Clove of chopped garlic
Chopped ham 2 oz (60 g)
Tomato pulp 1 oz (30 g)

Methods: Pan fry onions in oil until translucent and add remaining garnish. Toss until brown and season. In another pan heat oil and add beaten eggs, scramble a little and add garnish. Stir to blend all ingredients and allow to set like a thick pancake. Toss on to the other side and then slide on to a plate. Brush with melted butter and sprinkle with chopped parsley.

It is best to make an individual omelette using 2 eggs and a quarter of the garnish mixture. The garnish must always be fried separately before adding to the eggs.

A Spanish omelette is a meal in itself and the items of the garnish can be as varied as the resources permit.

PAELLA BARCELONA
Spanish national dish

Paella is a flat cooking dish with hollowed cavities in which various ingredients are served as part of a composite dish. All types of Paella should always include rice. The dish originated with the Moors and, to the European gastronomists, the mixture of fish and meat in one dish is an absolute heresy. I do not wish to join the chorus of these sophisticated palates as I believe that a good Paella has a place in our international repertoire and such a dish can figure in any menu without fear of being outclassed by a less incongruous dish.

The original Paella was made with rice, eels and snails cooked in oil. The traditional Paella Valenciana contains snails, chicken and rice but the Barcelona version is more exotic with mussels, scampi, crawfish or lobsters and pork meat. Squid can also be included in both recipes.

This is the recipe produced by the chef for the late King Alphonse XIII. It was given to me thirty years ago by that chef.

Ingredients:

First pan:

Diced belly of pork 5 oz (150 g)
Diced veal 5 oz (150 g)
Diced raw chicken or turkey meat 5 oz (150 g)
Oil 2 fl oz (60 mls)
Long grain rice 10 oz (300 g)
Pinch of saffron
Salt and pepper
Water 3½ pint (2,100 mls)

Second pan:

Oil 3 fl oz (90 mls)
Diced red and green peppers 2 oz (60 g)
Peeled and seeded tomatoes 5 oz (150 g)
Peas 3 oz (90 g)
Artichoke hearts cut in small cubes 5 oz (150 g)
　(canned artichokes can be used)

Third pan:

Hake fillets cut in small squares 8 oz (240 g)
Frozen scampi 8 oz (240 g)
Seasoned flour 2 oz (60 g)
12 mussels or 12 snails stuffed with garlic butter

Fourth pan:

Oil 2 fl oz (60 mls)
Ox tongue cut in strips 2 oz (60 g)
Cooked ham cut in strips 2 oz (60 g)
Sliced mushrooms 2 oz (60 g)

Fifth pan:

Thin escalopes of calf's liver 6 oz (180 g)
Seasoned flour 2 oz (60 g)
Thin slices of beef fillets 8 oz (240 g)

Method: The final dishing out operation will involve the presentation of all these cooked items in 1 or 2 Paella dishes depending on the number of guests. Allow 2 dishes per 4 guests.

First pan: Pan fry all the diced meats and chicken until brown and add rice. Stir well into oil and season. Sprinkle with saffron and add water or stock. Cook gently for 45 minutes.

Second pan: Pan fry all the vegetables for 5 minutes and add to the first pan after draining off surplus oil.

Third pan: Pass the fish in seasoned flour and pan fry for 10 minutes. Add scampi and pan fry for a further 2 minutes only. Keep the fish in reserve at this stage.

Fourth pan: Saute strips of meat and mushrooms in oil for 30 minutes. Add to the main ingredients.

Fifth pan: Pass liver and fillets in seasoned flour and pan fry quickly for 5 minutes. Keep in reserve.

At this stage all ingredients are cooked and can now be dished out properly. Place the meats with some of the vegetables in 1 Paella and in another place the fish surrounded by stuffed snails or mussels in half of their shells with some of the vegetables and broth. Sprinkle with chopped parsley and serve. All items must be distinctly separated in the dish except the vegetables and rice which are mixed in the sauce or stock.

PAELLA VALENCIANA
Chicken casserole with rice

The officials of the National Rice Cooperative of Valencia have established a new ruling for this dish advising the use of less incongruous ingredients. This is the recipe which is likely to be more acceptable in Northern Europe.

Ingredients:

Water 3½ pint (2,100 mls)
Chicken giblets 8 oz (240 g)
Leeks 4 oz (120 g)
Carrots 4 oz (120 g)
1 onion studded with 3 cloves
1 bouquet garni

Pinch of saffron
Tomato puree 2 oz (60 g)
Celery sprig 4 oz (120 g)

For the preparation of a basic stock boil the above ingredients for 1 hour and strain.

Main ingredients:

1 chicken 3½ lb (1,680 g)
Seasoned flour 2 oz (60 g)
Oil 3 fl oz (90 mls)
Chopped garlic 1 clove
Long grain rice 5 oz (150 g)
Diced french beans 4 oz (120 g)
Peas 3 oz (90 g)
Skinned and seeded tomatoes 8 oz (240 g)
Salt and pepper
12 cooked mussels or clams
Stock 3 pint (1,800 mls)
12 prawns
Chopped parsley 1 tbs

Method: Cut chicken in 16 pieces on the bones. Pass in seasoned flour and pan fry in oil until golden for 5 minutes. Add chopped garlic and rice and stir well. Add rest of vegetables, except tomatoes, and stock and cook for 40 minutes. Add chopped tomatoes and seasoning and sprinkle with chopped parsley on serving the dish. When complete, the liquid should be level to the solid ingredients. Decorate with cooked mussels and prawns in their shells.

GALLINA VIVA EL TORO
Chicken Spanish style

Ingredients:

Skinned almonds 3 oz (90 g)
Oil 2 fl oz (60 g)
Pinch of saffron
1 chicken 3½ lb (1,680 g)
Seasoned flour 2 oz (60 g)
Salt and pepper
Tomato pulp 8 oz (240 g)
Pitted olives 3 oz (90 g)
Spanish sherry ½ pint (300 mls)

Sliced onions 2 oz (60 g)
Clove of garlic

Method: Pan fry the skinned almonds in oil until
brown. Remove oil and almonds and pound to a
paste. Brew the saffron for 5 minutes in hot sherry
and strain. Cut chicken in 8 pieces (4 pieces from
legs and 4 from breasts and wings). Pass in seasoned
flour and pan fry until golden brown for 15
minutes. Cover with a lid. Add almond paste, wine
and remaining ingredients and cook for 5 minutes.
Transfer to a shallow dish, season, cover with a lid
and bake for 30 minutes at 400°F.

CALLOS MADRILENA
Tripe Spanish style

Ingredients:

Calf's tripe 2½ lb (1,200 g)
Water 2 pint (1,200 mls)
Dry sherry ½ pint (300 mls)
Vinegar 4 fl oz (120 mls)
Skinned and deseeded tomatoes 1 lb (120 g)
Oil 4 fl oz (120 mls)
2 calf's trotters
1 bouquet garni
Clove of garlic
Sliced carrots 4 oz (120 g)
Sliced onions 4 oz (120 g)
Salt, pepper and paprika
4 *choriza* (spicy sausages)
Tomato puree 1 oz (30 g)
Diced ham 2 oz (60 g)
Chopped onions 2 oz (60 g)

Method: Cut the tripe in small strips and scrape
the trotters. Place in water with onions, carrots
and bouquet garni. Boil for 2 hours and remove
scum as it rises. Fry chopped onions in oil until
translucent and add chopped tomatoes, garlic,
diced ham, vinegar and tomato puree and ½ pint
(300 mls) stock from tripe. Boil for 10 minutes
and put in the tripe mixture with the *chorizo*
and simmer for a further 30 minutes. Serve with
a sprinkling of chopped parsley.

CONEJO A LA JUANA
Tame rabbit Spanish style

Cut rabbit in 10 pieces, pass in seasoned flour and
pan fry until golden brown. Add ingredients as
listed for Gallina Viva El Toro and cook for 1½
hours in a casserole dish.

TERNERA A LA CONDESITA
Veal casserole in Sherry

Ingredients:

4 veal escalopes 4 oz (120 g)
Sherry 5 fl oz (150 mls)
½ lemon
Oil 3 fl oz (90 mls)
1 beaten egg
Garlic ½ clove (5 g)
Seasoned flour 2 oz (60 g)
Gravy ½ pint (300 mls)

Method: Soak veal escalopes in dry sherry (or
medium) with a little oil and lemon juice. Chop the
garlic very finely and blend with beaten egg. Drain
and dry escalopes and pass in seasoned flour and
beaten egg. Pan fry in oil for 8 minutes until
cooked and serve with a tomato salad. Collect
sherry and add to gravy. Boil up and serve
separately.

COCIDO CASTELLANO
Beef and gammon casserole Spanish style

Ingredients:

Silverside or topside of beef cut in 1 inch cubes
    1 lb (480 g)
Water 6 pint (3,600 mls)
Lean green gammon cut in 1 inch cubes 8 oz
    (240 g)
Potatoes cut in 1 inch cubes 1 lb (480 g)
4 *chorizo* sausages
Leeks 5 oz (150 g)
Carrots 5 oz (150 g)
Turnips 5 oz (150 g)
Whole onion studded with 3 cloves 5 oz (150 g)
1 bouquet garni

Dumplings:

Flour 2 oz (60 g)
Breadcrumbs 5 oz (150 g)
Chopped parsley 1 tbs
1 egg
Pork sausagemeat
Salt and pepper
Flat noodles 5 oz (150 g)

Method: Place the meats in a large saucepan with water. Bring to the boil and remove the scum as it rises. When the broth is clear add bouquet garni and simmer for 1¼ hours. Add vegetables and simmer for another 45 minutes.
Dumplings: Blend all ingredients to a solid mass and divide into 12 dumplings. Place into the dish (Cocido) and cover with a lid. Simmer for 15 minutes and season. Serve with noodles which have been boiled separately in salted water for 15 minutes. Sprinkle with chopped parsley.

BUTIFARRA CON JUDIAS
Sausages and baked beans

This dish consists of baked sausages and beans with garlic and tomato pulp all cooked separately and assembled in a shallow dish to be reheated together for 10 minutes before serving.

FAISAN A LA MODA DE ALCANTARA
Roast pheasant with liver and truffles

Ingredients:

1 young pheasant 2½ lb (1,200 g)
Salt and pepper
Seasoned flour 2 oz (60 g)
Chicken liver 4 oz (120 g)
Truffles 1 oz (30 g)
Medium sherry ½ pint (300 mls)
Water ¼ pint (150 mls)
Oil 2 fl oz (60 mls)
Diced carrots 2 oz (60 g)
Diced onions 2 oz (60 g)
Diced streaky bacon 2 oz (60 g)
1 bouquet garni

Tomato puree 1 oz (30 g)
Chopped parsley 1 tbs

Slurry:

Cornflour ½ oz (15 g)
Water 5 fl oz (150 mls)

Method: Clean and truss pheasant and season. Clean chicken liver and remove gall. Pass in seasoned flour and pan fry quickly for 5 minutes in oil. Remove and chop finely. Add diced truffles or mushrooms and stuff the pheasant with this mixture. Saute the vegetables and bacon in remaining oil until brown and place in a casserole dish. Arrange pheasant on top and roast for 15 minutes at 400°F. Add sherry, water, bouquet garni, and cover with a lid and braise for 30 minutes at 380°F until the pheasant is cooked. Remove bouquet garni. Remove the pheasant and carve into portions. Place the pieces on a dish and transfer the contents of the casserole; vegetables, bacon and gravy, to a small saucepan. Boil for 5 minutes with tomato puree and thicken with a slurry of cornflour. Cook for 5 more minutes and season. Strain sauce over the pieces of pheasant and sprinkle with chopped parsley.

PERDIZ CHOCOLATE
Partridge in chocolate sauce

Ingredients:

4 partridges (use old partridges), split in two
Oil 2 fl oz (60 mls)
Water 1 pint (600 mls)
Chopped onions 2 oz (60 g)
Diced carrots 2 oz (60 g)
Medium sherry 5 fl oz (150 mls)
1 bouquet garni
3 cloves
Pinch of mace and nutmeg
1 chilli pepper or pinch of cayenne
Cocoa powder 5 g (small tsp) ⎫
Cornflour 5 g ⎪
Water 5 fl oz (150 mls) ⎬ blended to a paste
Oil 2 fl oz (60 mls) ⎪
Salt and pepper ⎭

Method: Roast the partridges at $380°$F for 15 minutes and place in a casserole of saucepan with water, sherry and vegetables. Simmer for 1 hour and season. Strain liquor and thicken with a slurry of oil, cocoa and cornflour blended together with 5 fl oz (150 mls) water. Add chocolate mixture to boiling stock and cook until it thickens while stirring to avoid lumps. Strain sauce and pour over the partridges. Young partridges need not be boiled, just roast for 15 minutes.

CARNERO ASADO A LA MANCHEGA
Leg of mutton with beans

Remove pelvic bone from leg and make a few slits in various parts of the leg near the handle and in the thick part. Insert peeled garlic cloves into each cavity and season. Roast for 1½ hours at $400°$F and serve with a dish of freshly boiled haricot beans or flageolets (green haricot beans, *not the pods*). (Baste leg with oil and butter during roasting and make a gravy with juices as usual).

FABADA ASTURIANA
Haricot beans and cabbage with pork and sausages

Ingredients:

Dry haricot beans 1 lb (480 g)
Water 4 pint (2,400 mls)
Diced streaky bacon 4 oz (120 g)
Diced red peppers 4 oz (120 g)
1 carrot cut in 4
½ cabbage cut in shreds
4 small *chorizos*
4 *chorizos*
1 onion studded with 4 cloves
Salt and pepper

Method: Soak the beans in distilled water, if the water is hard, for 24 hours. Cook in same water and remove scum as it rises. When the water is clear add carrot, cabbage, bacon, onions, seasoning and red peppers and cover with a lid. Bake at $300°$F until the beans are tender and season. Pan fry the pork chops and *chorizos* and add to the stew of

beans 15 minutes before the end of cooking time. Serve sprinkled with chopped parsley.

VEGETABLES

COL DE BRUSELAS
Sprouts fried in crumbs

Ingredients:

Fresh sprouts 1 lb (480 g)
Water 3 pint (1,800 mls)
2 beaten eggs
Seasoned flour flavoured with garlic salt
Crumbs 4 oz (120 g)
Salt
Oil for frying

Method: Blanch the sprouts for 4 minutes in salted water, drain and dry. Pass in seasoned flour, beaten eggs and crumbs and deep fry for 4 minutes until golden.

ESPINACA
Spinach with anchovies

Ingredients:

Spinach 2 lb (960 g)
Anchovy fillets 2 oz can (60 g)
Butter 2 oz (60 g)
Diced fried bread 3 oz (90 g)

Method: Boil cleaned spinach in salted water for 4 minutes, drain and dry. Squeeze out surplus water and gather into small 2 oz (60 g) dumplings. Reheat in butter with chopped anchovy and serve with croutons of fried bread.

PISTO A LA RIOJANA
Mixed vegetable casserole

Ingredients:

Peeled aubergines 5 oz (150 g)
Peeled courgettes 5 oz (150 g)
Chopped onions 2 oz (60 g)

Chopped garlic 1 clove
Chopped, skinned and seeded tomatoes 8 oz (240 g)
Oil 2 fl oz (60 mls)
Salt and pepper
Sugar 1 tsp
Vinegar 1 tbs
Red and green peppers cut in fine shreds 4 oz
  (120 g)
Water ½ pint (300 mls)
Chopped parsley

Method: Saute all the vegetables in oil, add water
and vinegar and simmer covered with a lid. Season
and serve with chopped parsley.

SWEETS AND DESSERTS

Spanish desserts are the same as in all hot countries
where fruits and nuts are in abundance. Ice creams
and sorbets with fruit salad are much preferred in
the summer but in the winter certain egg custard
sweets are also popular.

Cakes made with almonds are famed for their
quality and many chocolate and confectionery
goods are still trade secrets.

CREMA LECHE FRITA CATALANA
Egg custard

Ingredients:

Milk 1 pint (600 mls)
Pinch of cinnamon
Castor sugar 2 oz (60 g)
6 egg yolks and 2 egg whites
Cornflour 1 oz (30 g)
4 egg whites
Breadcrumbs 5 oz (150 g)
Flour 2 oz (60 g)
Oil
Orange blossom essence, few drops

Method: Bring milk to the boil. Beat egg yolks and
2 whites with sugar. Add cornflour, cinnamon,
orange essence and 3 fl oz (90 mls) of cold milk.
Pour the boiling milk into the egg mixture and
stir. Reheat until the mixture thickens while

whisking. Grease a tray with oil and pour in
mixture to cool. Use a tray with 2 inch sides. When
cold cut rounds or squares of the set custard and
pass each in flour, beaten egg whites and crumbs.
Pan fry in oil or a mixture of melted butter and
oil. Cook on both sides like fritters for 4 minutes.
Serve with jam or fruit compote.

PAN DE SANTA PAULA
Fried egg and bread fritters

Ingredients:

4 slices of bread
2 beaten eggs
Vanilla essence
Rum 1 tbs
Oil for frying
Butter 2 oz (60 g)
Granulated sugar 2 oz (60 g)

Method: Beat eggs and rum together and steep
slices of bread in this mixture until well soaked.
Heat oil and butter in a pan and fry the bread as
for fritters. Drain and sprinkle with granulated
sugar.

ARROZ IMPERATRIZ EUGENIE
Cream rice with raspberry jelly and liqueur fruits

This dish was created by the Chef of Napoleon III
in honour of the Spanish Empress Eugenie, his
wife.

Ingredients:

Milk 1 pint (600 mls)
Pudding rice 3 oz (90 g)
Castor sugar 3 oz (90 g)
Vanilla essence, few drops
4 egg yolks
Ground gelatine 1 oz (30 g)
Whipped cream ½ pint (300 mls)
Castor sugar 2 oz (60 g)
Orange liqueur 2 fl oz (60 mls)
Mixed glacé peels 1 oz (30 g)
Raspberry juice 5 fl oz (150 mls)
Ground gelatine ½ oz (15 g)

Castor sugar 3 oz (90 g)
Whipped cream for decoration ¼ pint (150 mls)
Fresh raspberries 8 oz (240 g)
Redcurrant jelly 3 oz (90 g)
Kirsch 3 fl oz (90 mls)
Glacé cherries 2 oz (60 g)
Angelica 1 oz (30 g)

Shortbread:

Ground almonds 2 oz (60 g)
Flour 3 oz (90 g)
Butter 5 oz (150 g)
Castor sugar 4 oz (120 g)
Lemon and almond essence, few drops
2 beaten eggs

Method: Cook the rice in 5 fl oz (150 mls) water
for 15 minutes, add milk and continue to cook
for 30 minutes until the rice is tender. Add sugar,
vanilla essence and 4 egg yolks. Mix ground
gelatine and castor sugar and dissolve in hot rice.
Cool mixture and when cold whisk for 5 minutes
to a cream, blend whipped cream and orange
liqueur and add mixed glacé peels. Line a decorative crown mould with raspberry jelly made as
follows: mix ground gelatine and castor sugar
together. Boil raspberry juice and dissolve the
gelatine in this mixture and cool. When cold line
the mould to coat the bottom and sides. This
operation is speed up by placing the mould on ice
cubes. When the jelly is set fill the mould with
rice mixture and chill. Turn the rice pudding out
on to a flat dish when set. Decorate the top with
rosettes of piped cream and floral arrangements of
glace cherries and angelica. Fill the cavity of the
mould with fresh raspberries. Boil the redcurrant
jam and add Kirsch and cool. Pour over the
raspberries and serve with Spanish shortbread made
as follows: cream butter and sugar until fluffy. Add
beaten eggs gradually and lastly the ground
almonds, essences and flour. Mix to a stiff
dough and rest in the refrigerator for 20 minutes.
Roll on floured pastry board to ¼ inch thick. Cut
rounds 3 inch diameter with a pastry cutter and
place on a greased tray. Make designs with a fork
and brush with egg white. Sprinkle with granulated
sugar and bake for 10 minutes at 400°F. Cool and
serve with Arroz Imperatriz.

Portugal

Portuguese cookery is very similar to Spanish, yet different in very significant ways. Spices and herbs are used with much more abandon, and chopped fresh coriander leaves make an appearance in a great number of dishes. Sauces are widely used, and sea foods are plentiful and delicious.

The area of the Minho has as its most characteristic dish a green kale soup, known as *Caldo Verde* and consumed in every home. Along the coast the speciality is salted cod, made into *Margarida da Praça*, or the *Bacalhau*, the national dish of Portugal. The fish is soaked for a day or so to remove the salt, and then poached until tender. It is then sauted with onions and flavoured with herbs, spices and vegetables to make any one of a dozen specialities. *Bacalhau Gomes de Sa* is made with potatoes, onions and eggs, while *Bacalhau a Braz* has the potatoes boiled with the fish, then everything is fried with onions, garlic and scrambled eggs. *Balinhos de Bacalhau* is like the French *Brandade de Morue*, where the fish is pounded into a paste and emulsified with oil and lemon juice, to the consistency of a soft cream. Half the amount is then blended with creamed potatoes, eggs and cooked chopped onions. The mixture is cooled and fried like fish cakes when needed.

The Minho region is rich in fresh vegetables and the rivers provide wonderful freshwater fish. Often the fish is coated in mayonnaise and browned in the oven so that the eggs in the mayonnaise cook as in a custard—a particularly Portuguese way of using mayonnaise. The two great sauces of professional cookery, *Madeira* and *Portugaise*, come from this region.

Sonhos is a type of pudding, rather like a steamed or baked sponge served with a cinnamon- and lemon-flavoured syrup. Oporto and the Douro region have wonderful dishes of tripe, often combined with tomatoes and baked with beans. Port wine with everything is the message in this part of the world, and the various types of Port are used to add flavour and strength to everything from white fish through roast chicken to fresh strawberries and melons.

Bread is used to thicken the unusual soup called *açorda,* made with fish and shrimps, and better than most bisques. The combinations of fish and meat are unusual and not always successful to the international gourmet, but hake with *chourico,* the smoked sausage, is interesting and good, and clams are served with pork, in another surprising taste sensation, very similar to the original Chowder so popular in the USA.

Bragança has a simple but succulent sardine pie, where fresh or canned sardines are placed on a bed of cooked onions and wrapped in pastry. *Bola de Carne* is another wrapped dish, this time a mixture of ham and chicken in yeast dough and looking like a large football. *Sopa Dourada* is a bread and egg custard pudding, and the French *pain perdu* makes yet another appearance, bread soaked in beaten eggs and fried in oil, sprinkled with sugar. There is a delicate almond cake called *Torta a Quinta do Passadouro* with a spongy centre like a bakewell tart.

In the centre of Portugal are the Beiras, Alta, Baixa and Litoral. The Beira soup with beans, potatoes and tomatoes is refreshing and the ox tongue with madeira sauce is rich and unctuous. *Frango a moda da Beira* is cooked chicken and ham topped with creamed cheese and browned in the oven. *Batalda* is a sweet potato cake made with eggs and orange salads are light and refreshing, especially my version of strawberries with sliced oranges flavoured with *creme de cacao*.

Lisbon is an international city and its restaurants offer the best on classical cooking with a uniquely individual Portuguese touch. The *Caldeira a Fragateira do Lisboa* is a local version of fish stew with tomatoes, garlic, onions and white port. French beans picked when young and made into a fritter is a local speciality, and broad beans with bacon, onions, smoked sausages and fresh coriander is another. Something similar is done with chickpeas.

My favourite dish is *Molho Escabeche,* mackerel covered with a mixture of fried onions with a *vinaigrette* sauce and a touch of garlic, served as an *hors d'oeuvre*. The succulent local clams meet their fate with a clove of garlic, coriander seed and basil in the *Ameijoas a Bulhao Pâté*. *Aroz de Tuna* is a rice dish with flaked tuna and onions and *Lulas a Pousada* is a dish of squid fried with a tomato sauce. The *Lagosta Suada* is very similar to the *Lobster Americaine,* whose creation is claimed by practically every chef of my generation. But this dish, with port wine or Madeira, with or without brandy, has been cooked in this part of Portugal for centuries, and we might do well to simply rename the dish *Lobster Portugues* and go on to more creative arguments.

The Arrabida region offers a choice of delicious fish and oysters in cream sauce. I am a purist and do not really approve of cooking these delicious molluscs, but the local oysters are shallow and coarse and the cream sauce does improve them. Five minutes' cooking is enough. *Sopa de Agrioes* is a potato and cress soup lightened with cream and egg yolks well worth trying.

The Alentejo has a bread porridge to which meat, fish and eggs may be added and is a tasty way of using leftover stale bread.

The Algarve is a lush province of figs, almonds and olives with dazzling white beaches and a treasure of seafood. There are rice and pomegranates, grapes, bananas, cumquats, sugary melons and courgettes. Tuna fish is plentiful and the fat mussels go into the soup called *Sopa de Conquilhas*. *Sopa a pescador* is a crayfish soup with rice. A wealth of seafood with onions, hot red pepper and paprika goes into the *cataplana,* a heavy metal casserole with a fitting lid in which food steams while the flavour intensifies. *Bolas de Figo* are dried figs stuffed with marzipan and coated in chocolate, a sweetmeat rather than dessert.

The Island of Madeira offers a wealth of tropical fruits and splendid fish—but the wine of Madeira is never used in cooking on the island. Ths is left to the French chefs, who use it to enhance baked ham, steak *au poivre*, scallops and consomme. My preference is to use dry Madeira with fish and lobster, and it could even be used in trifle and Christmas cake. The notion of using Madeira as an aperitif is French and to sip it with cheese is British. But the traditional way is to have it for mid-morning break with a slice of Madeira cake, like Queen Victoria.

The food of Portugal is tasty, unusual and in many cases excellent. But it is still essentially a peasant cuisine—and that is its chief charm.

BILL OF FARE

Soup

CALDO VERDE
Green cabbage soup

SOPA DE AGRIOES
Watercress soup

SOPA ALENTEJANA
Coriander leaf soup

CANJA
Chicken and rice soup

SOPA DE CAMARAO
Prawn soup

Hors d'Oeuvre

PAO DE ESPINAFRES
Bread roll filled with spinach and eggs

TORTILHA DE SARDINHAS
Pancakes stuffed with sardines

OVOS VERDES
Hard-boiled eggs in spicey herb sauce

TOMATES RECHEADOS
Stuffed tomatoes

ALGARVE OYSTERS
Poached oysters Portuguese style

AÇORDA DE MARISCO COM ALFACE
Portuguese seafood cocktail

ESCABECHE DE PEIXE
Fillets of bream in tomato sauce

OVOS COM ATUM
Surprise eggs

TOMATES MIRAMAR
Tomatoes stuffed with sardines and eggs

PAO TORRADO DE PEIXE
Anchovy fingers

BATATAS E SARDINHAS
Hot potato and sardine sandwiches

SALADA DE PEIXE
Tunny fish salad

BATATAS E OVOS
Tasty morsels

OVOS RIVIERA
Riviera eggs

MANTEIGA DE SARDINHAS
Sardine butter

BOLACHAS A MANTEIGA DE ATUM
Small biscuits with tunny fish butter

ESPINAFRES COM SARDINHAS
Sardine pyramids

Fish Dishes

DOURADO LOZIDA AL DAO
John Dory fish in port wine

CALDE VERDE PISCADORE PORTUGUESA
Stuffed cod baked with onions

Meat Dishes

COZIDO PORTUGUESA
Hot pot

ESTUFADO DE LINGUA DE VACA
Braised tongue Portuguese style

FRANGO COM ARROZ
Chicken a la Castelo Vide with tomatoes and
mushrooms

COELHO PORCALHOTA
Stewed rabbit with tomatoes

FEBRAS DE PORCO ASSADAS
Fillets of loin of pork Portuguese style with orange
sauce

COSTELETA DE PORCO GRELHADA
Pork chop with tomatoes and red peppers

CABRITO ASSADO
Goat stew with rice in Port wine

ISCAS A PORTUGUESA
Marinaded liver in wine sauce

ROLO DE PORCO
Meat roll in Port wine sauce

CARNEIRO ASSADO
Stuffed leg of mutton Portuguese style

FRANGO A PORTUGUESA
Chicken Portuguese style

MOLHO DE VINHO DA MADEIRA
Madeira sauce

MOLHO DE VINHO DO PORTO
Port wine sauce

Vegetables

FAVAS A MODA DO PESCADOR
Beans cooked with cod

TOMATES PORTUGUESES
Stuffed tomatoes

Sweets and Desserts

CASTANHAS
Chestnut cake

TORTA PORTUGUESA
Mixed fruit flan

PUDIM PORTUGUES
Walnut souffle pudding

TORTA DE AMENOAS
Almond flan

SOUP

CALDO VERDE
Green cabbage soup

Ingredients:

Sliced peeled potatoes 8 oz (240 g)
Sliced green cabbage 8 oz (240 g)
Water or bacon stock 3½ pint (2,100 mls)
Shredded spinach 6 oz (180 g)
Oil 2 fl oz (60 mls)
Chopped onions 2 oz (60 g)
Chopped garlic 1 clove
Smoked sausages or garlic sausage 4 oz (120 g)
Salt and pepper

Method: Heat oil in a saucepan and sweat
vegetables for 10 minutes without colouring. Add
water and boil for 20 minutes. Pass soup through
a liquidiser or sieve and season. Reheat and add
garlic sausages cut in thin slices. Season with black
pepper.

SOPA DE AGRIOES
Watercress soup

Ingredients:

Chicken stock or water 3½ pint (2,100 mls)
Sliced peeled potatoes 1 lb (480 g)
Sliced or chopped watercress 1 bunch
Chopped onions 2 oz (60 g)
Oil

Thickening:

Cream 5 fl oz (150 mls)
2 egg yolks
Cornflour 1 oz (30 g)

Salt and pepper
Pinch of grated nutmeg

Method: Heat oil in saucepan and sweat potatoes
and onions for 10 minutes without browning.
Add watercress and flood with water. Boil for 20
minutes and pass through a sieve or liquidiser.
Season. Place egg yolks, cream and cornflour
in a bowl, add ¼ pint of the puree and stir well.

Pour this mixture into the soup and reheat until
it thickens while stirring. Season and serve with
sippets of bread.

SOPA ALENTEJANA
Coriander leaf soup

Ingredients:

Water 3½ pint (2,100 mls)
Chopped onions 8 oz (240 g)
Oil 2 fl oz (60 mls)
1 small sprig of fresh coriander leaves with few
   seeds
Bread sippets 8 oz (240 g)
Salt and pepper
Clove of garlic

Method: Pound the coriander seeds and leaves
with onions and garlic to a paste. Add oil to
obtain an emulsion, whisking while pouring.
Boil water and add to oil mixture. Season and
place bread sippets in a soup tureen and pour
in soup. Let the bread soak for a while and
serve.

CANJA
Chicken and rice soup

Ingredients:

1 fowl 4 lb (1,920 g)
1 knuckle of bacon 1 lb (480 g)
Water 6 pint (3,600 mls)
1 onion studded with 4 cloves
Green peas 4 oz (120 g)
Rice 4 oz (120 g)
Fresh mint 1 sprig
1 bouquet garni
Tomato puree 1 tbs
Pinch of saffron
Salt and black pepper

Method: Clean fowl and knuckle and place in
water. Bring to the boil and remove scum as it
rises. When clear add bouquet garni and onion and

boil for 1½ hours. Remove fowl and use as the main meal. Reheat broth and cook rice, mint, peas, tomato puree and saffron for 30 minutes. Season and serve. A garnish of sliced chicken and knuckle can be served with the broth.

SOPA DE CAMARAO
Prawn soup

Ingredients:

Dublin Bay prawns 1 lb (480 g)
Onions 5 oz (150 g)
Sliced carrots 1 lb (480 g)
Garlic 1 clove (10 g)
Oil 3 fl oz (90 mls)
Chopped skinned tomatoes 5 oz (150 g)
Water 3½ pint (2,100 mls) or fish stock
Salt and pepper
Pinch of saffron
Rice 2 oz (60 g)
1 bouquet garni

Method: Saute prawns with chopped onions and carrots in oil. Add rice, tomatoes, garlic and bouquet garni and cook for another 10 minutes. Add water and saffron and boil for 20 minutes. Shell prawns. Discard shells and add meat to soup. Season. Remove bouquet garni before serving.

HORS D'OEUVRE

PAO DE ESPINAFRES
Bread roll filled with spinach and eggs

Ingredients:

Spinach 8 oz (240 g)
Butter 2 oz (60 g)
1 clove chopped garlic
4 small crisp bread rolls
2 hard-boiled eggs
Anchovy fillets 2 oz (60 g)

Method: Blanch spinach in salted water for 5 minutes. Drain and squeeze surplus moisture. Reheat in butter and chopped garlic. Chop up. Scoop out the crumbs of 4 crisp rolls by cutting two-thirds of each roll. Stuff with spinach mixture. Top with slices of hard-boiled egg and two fillets of anchovy. Bake in hot oven for 3 minutes.

TORTILHA DE SARDINHAS
Pancakes stuffed with sardines

Ingredients:

4 small pancakes
8 large sardines (canned)
Sliced onion rings 2 oz (60 g)
2 hard-boiled eggs, sliced
Seasoned flour 2 oz (60 g)
2 beaten eggs
Breadcrumbs 4 oz (120 g)
Salt and pepper
Vinegar
Oil for frying

Method: Make batter using the 135 mixture (1 egg, 3 oz flour and 5 fl oz water). Cook pancakes 6 inch diameter. Place 2 sardines, 2 onion rings and 2 slices hard-boiled egg on each pancake. Season and sprinkle a few drops of vinegar. Wrap and fold the pancake. Pass in seasoned flour, beaten eggs and crumbs. Deep fry until golden for 5 minutes at 380°F.

OVOS VERDES
Hard-boiled eggs in spicy herb sauce

Ingredients:

8 hard-boiled eggs
Chopped onions 2 oz (60 g)
Curry powder ½ oz (15 g)
Oil 2 fl oz (60 mls)
Chopped parsley 1 tbs
Salt and pepper
Mayonnaise ½ pint (300 mls)
4 lettuce leaves

Method: Boil eggs for 10 minutes. Shell and cut in half. Remove egg yolks and pass through a sieve. Sweat chopped onions in oil until translucent. Add curry powder and cook for 3 minutes. Cool. Blend egg yolks and remaining ingredients, using only half of the mayonnaise sauce for binding the mixture. Fill cavity of whites with mixture. Coat eggs with mayonnaise and serve on a bed of lettuce.

TOMATES RECHEADOS
Stuffed tomatoes

Ingredients:

4 large tomatoes 1 lb (480 g)—use ribbed variety
Chopped garlic 1 clove (10 g)
Grated cheese 4 oz (120 g)
1 beaten egg
Breadcrumbs 1 oz (30 g)
Salt and pepper
Chopped parsley 1 tbs
Butter 1 oz (30 g)
Oil 2 fl oz (60 mls)

Method: Cut tomatoes near the stem and scoop out seeds. Blend all remaining ingredients except oil to a paste and fill cavity of tomatoes. Place in a shallow tray. Sprinkle a little oil over the tomatoes and bake for 15 minutes at 400°F. Serve hot or cold.

ALGARVE OYSTERS
Poached oysters Portuguese style

Ingredients:

2 doz Portuguese oysters (shallow shell type)

Sauce:

Chopped onions or shallots 2 oz (60 g)
Oil 2 fl oz (60 mls)
1 clove of finely chopped garlic
Pinch of powdered thyme
Portuguese wine ½ pint (300 mls)
Chopped parsley 1 tbs
Breadcrumbs 1 oz (30 g)
Salt and pepper

Thickening:

Cream 5 fl oz (150 mls)
Cornflour ½ oz (15 g)
2 egg yolks

Garnish:

Grated cheese

Method: Sweat chopped onions in a saucepan with oil until translucent. Add chopped garlic, thyme and white wine. Boil for 10 minutes.

Open oysters and strain the liquor through a cloth. Collect it and add to the sauce. Poach oysters for 8 minutes, without too much ebulltion. Drain. Replace oysters in their wide, shallow shell. Boil sauce for 5 minutes and thicken with a slurry of cream, egg yolks, breadcrumbs and cornflour. Add chopped parsley to sauce. Pour some of the sauce over the oysters and serve remainder in a sauceboat. Serve with sippets of bread to mop up this delicious sauce. Sprinkle a little grated cheese on top of each oyster.

AÇORDA DE MARISCO COM ALFACE
Portuguese seafood cocktail

Ingredients:

Cooked peeled shrimps 2 oz (60 g)
Cooked scampi 2 oz (60 g)
Diced lobsters 2 oz (60 g)
Diced boiled white fish 5 oz (150 g)
Cooked mussels 4 oz (120 g)
Raw oysters—1 per person

Garnish:

1 shredded lettuce
Shredded green peppers 2 oz (60 g)
Shredded red peppers 2 oz (60 g)
Grated celeriac 2 oz (60 g)
Grated carrots 2 oz (60 g)

Sauce:

Mayonnaise ¼ pint (150 mls)
Tabasco 1 tsp
Tomato ketchup 2 fl oz (60 mls)
Apple puree 2 oz (60 g)
Juice and grated rind of 1 lemon

1 chopped hard-boiled egg
Chopped parsley 1 tbs

Method: Blend all the main ingredients in a bowl. Mix all the mayonnaise with ketchup, apple puree, lemon juice and rind and Tabasco. Season to taste. Blend half of the sauce into the ingredients. Reserve some for topping the cocktails.

Half fill glasses with shredded lettuce mixture, grated carrots, celeriac and peppers. Top it with seafood. Cover with a spoonful of sauce. Sprinkle with chopped hard-boiled eggs and chopped parsley.

ESCABECHE DE PEIXE
Fillets of bream in tomato sauce

Ingredients:

8 small fillets of bream 2 lb (960 g)
Seasoned flour 2 oz (60 g)
Oil 3 fl oz (90 mls)

Sauce:

Chopped onions 2 oz (60 g)
1 clove of garlic
1 bouquet garni
1 sprig of fresh mint
Chopped, skinned and seeded tomatoes 1 lb (480 g)
Sliced button mushrooms 6 oz (180 g)
White vinegar 3 fl oz (90 mls)
Sugar 1 oz (30 g)
Salt and pepper
Chopped parsley 1 tbs

Method: Pass cleaned fillets in seasoned flour and fry in oil for 5 minutes on each side. Transfer fillets into a shallow dish and prepare the sauce. Sweat chopped onions and garlic in same oil until translucent. Add rest of ingredients. Boil for 10 minutes. Cover fish with mixture and bake for 15 minutes at 400°F. Cool. Serve cold.

OVOS COM ATUM
Surprise eggs

Hard-boil some eggs, peel them, slice off 1 end to form a lid, shave a slice from other end so that eggs will stand up, carefully remove yolks. Mash the drained contents of a tin of Portuguese tunny fish and pass through a sieve; mix with oil from the tin and beat well. Fill the egg whites with this stuffing, stand them on a fireproof dish, place on their little lids and cover with cheese sauce—white sauce in which grated cheese, preferably Parmesan, has been stirred. Heat in moderate oven for a few minutes but do not allow to brown. Just before serving, sprinkle with egg yolk previously passed through a coarse sieve or a potato masher.

TOMATES MIRAMAR
Tomatoes stuffed with sardines and eggs

Use small tomatoes of equal size. Cut off a thin slice to serve as lid, scoop out and dust the cavity with salt and pepper. Fill and put on lids.
Fillings: Drain the contents of a tin of boneless Portuguese sardines; cut sardines into small dice. Stir diced fish and 2 chopped hard-boiled eggs into well seasoned mayonnaise. A tin of Portuguese tunny fish can be used instead of sardines for making the filling.

PAO TORRADO COM PEIXE
Anchovy fingers

Open 2 tins of Portuguese anchovies, drain, pass contents of 1 tin through a sieve and mix with an equal quantity of fresh butter. Spread this puree on fingers of bread or toast, put an anchovy in the middle and border all round with chopped hard-boiled egg and chopped parsley.

BATATAS E SARDINHAS
Hot potato and sardine sandwiches

Boil some large potatoes in their jackets, taking care not to overcook them; peel and cut into thick slices. Skin, bone and mash with a fork the contents of a tin of Portuguese sardines, season with pepper, mix with a little finely chopped parsley and a chopped hard-boiled egg. Use this mixture as a filling between 2 slices of potato.

When all the little sandwiches have been made, flour them, dip in beaten egg and fry. Serve very hot with a green vegetable, such as beans or peas, or with cauliflower.

SALADA DE PEIXE
Tunny fish salad

Have ready some cooked and cold haricot beans, diced potatoes, diced carrots, French beans or other vegetables as preferred. Drain the contents of a large tin of Portuguese tunny fish and cut the fish in neat pieces. Arrange the vegetables separately and alternately in layers in a salad bowl, interspersing them with layers of tunny fish. Pour over a well-mixed dressing of 3 parts oil to 1 part vinegar, mustard, salt, pepper and chopped parsley. Sprinkle top of salad with chopped hard-boiled egg.

BATATAS E OVOS
Tasty morsels

Have ready some rather thick slices of cold, boiled potatoes. Sprinkle chopped hard-boiled egg on centre of each slice and surround with Portuguese anchovy fillets.

OVOS RIVIERA
Riviera eggs

Choose well-shaped tomatoes of equal size and cut into slices of medium thickness. Sprinkle chopped, hard-boiled egg on centre of each slice, leaving a border of tomato showing. Top the chopped egg with sardine butter. Arrange on a dish and garnish with Portuguese anchovies, each rolled round a caper.

MANTEIGA DE SARDINHAS
Sardine butter

Open a tin of boneless sardines. Drain the sardines, break them up with a fork, pass through a sieve.

Mix with twice their bulk of fresh butter, season with salt and pepper. This sardine butter is excellent for preparing hors d'oeuvre.

BOLACHAS A MANTEIGA DE ATUM
Small biscuits with tunny fish butter

Mix well some Portuguese tunny fish in a mortar; add a good quantity of fresh butter, flavour this with some pepper, lemon juice and grated cheese (with sweetish flavour). Stir all until it becomes a very smooth paste.

Place a portion of the tunny fish butter into a large syringe and pipe small pieces of the mixture on the biscuits. Trim the top of them with stuffed olive with red sweet pepper.

ESPINAFRES COM SARDINHAS
Sardine pyramids

Cut slices of bread, remove crust, stamp out rounds with a cutter and fry in dripping or other fat. Pile up mounds of spinach puree on the fried bread and top with a peak of sardine cream (see recipe for sardine butter). Sprinkle with chopped hard-boiled egg. Serve alone, or with the sauce for which directions are given under the recipe for Fried Sardines.

FISH DISHES

Portuguese cookery is widely spread in some of their former colonies in Africa: Angola and Mozambique and in Brazil in South America where a new blend of gastronomy has been developed. Salted fish was, in fact, promoted by the Portuguese and passed on to their slaves and the African diet became accustomed to dried fish and onions with spices to this day.

DOURADO PORTUENSE NA FRIGIDEIRA
John Dory fish in Port wine

Ingredients:

4 large John Dory fish fillets 8 oz (240 g) each
Seasoned flour 2 oz (60 g)
Oil 4 fl oz (120 mls)

Garnish:

Sliced onions 2 oz (60 g)
Tomato pulp 2 oz (60 g)
Sliced red and green peppers 2 oz (60 g)
Garlic ½ clove (5 g)
Chopped parsley
Almonds
8 olives (stuffed)
4 anchovy fillets
Salt and pepper and pinch of cayenne
1 lemon
1 orange
Port wine (white)

Method: Pass the fish fillets in seasoned flour and
pan fry in oil until golden on both sides. Transfer
to a dish. Fry onions, red and green peppers and
tomatoes for 5 minutes and add garlic. When
cooked add port wine and boil up for 5 minutes.
Season with a pinch of cayenne and salt and pepper.
Place this mixture on top of the fish and decorate
with anchovy fillets and sliced stuffed olives.
Sprinkle with flaked toasted almonds and chopped
parsley and surround the dish with serrated slices
of lemon and orange. Serve with rice pilaff
coloured yellow with saffron or turmeric.

BACALHAU A JARDINEIRA
Stuffed cod baked with onions

Ingredients:

Cod fillet with skin on 1 lb (480 g)
Butter 4 oz (120 g)

Filling:

Mushrooms 3 oz (90 g)
Brown breadcrumbs
Chopped onions 3 oz (90 g)
Grated cheese

Hard-boiled eggs 3 oz (90 g) chopped
2 eggs
Chopped anchovies 2 oz (60 g)
Flour 2 oz (60 g)
Sweetcorn 2 oz (60 g)
Cooked spinach 3 oz (90 g)
Chopped parsley 1 oz (30 g)
1 sprig of fresh mint
Salt and pepper
Port wine (white)

Method: Lay a large fillet of cod on the table and
spread first with butter and then the following
stuffing on the white flesh: blend brown
breadcrumbs and grated cheese with chopped
mushrooms, onions, anchovies, hard-
boiled eggs and cooked sweetcorn. Add fresh eggs
and flour to obtain a soft spreadable mixture.
Season to taste. Blend chopped parsley, spinach
and fresh mint also as the filling must be greenish.
After spreading stuffing on fish place into a shallow
tray and cover with white port wine. Bake for 20
minutes at 360°F.

MEAT DISHES

COZIDO A PORTUGUESA
Hot pot

Ingredients:

Oil 2 fl oz (60 mls)
Chopped onions 2 oz (60 g)
Diced carrots 2 oz (60 g)
Sliced celery 2 oz (60 g)
Turnips 2 oz (60 g)
Crushed garlic 1 clove
Diced bacon 3 oz (90 g)
8 lamb chump chops 2½ lb (1,200 g)
1 bouquet garni
1 sprig of fresh mint
Green beans 4 oz (120 g)
Peas 4 oz (120 g)

Tomato puree 1 oz (30 g)
Madeira wine ½ pint (300 mls)
Water ½ pint (300 mls)
Salt and pepper
Cooked rice 8 oz (240 g)

Method: Heat oil in a saucepan and brown chops
and bacon for 5 minutes. Add vegetables and cook
for 5 more minutes. Add remaining ingredients
and simmer for 1½ hours on a slow heat. Season
to taste and remove bouquet garni. Serve with
cooked rice.

ESTUFADO DE LINGUA DE VACA
Braised tongue Portuguese style

Ingredients:

1 pickled ox tongue 1½ lb (720 g)
1 carrot 5 oz (150 g)
1 onion studded with cloves 5 oz (150 g)
1 bouquet garni
1 sprig of celery 3 oz (90 g)
Water 4 pint (2,400 mls)

Sauce:

Lard 2 oz (60 g)
Chopped onions 2 oz (60 g)
Sliced mushroom stalks 2 oz (60 g)
Diced bacon 2 oz (60 g)
Flour 1 oz (30 g)
Tomato puree 2 oz (60 g)
Madeira wine ½ pint (300 mls)
Stock from tongue ½ pint (300 mls)
Wine vinegar 3 tbs
Salt and pepper
Pinch of clove and mace

Method: Clean, wash and boil the ox tongue for
2 hours. Remove tough skin and throat fibres.
Cut in thin slices and coat with Madeira sauce
made as follows: fry onions, mushroom stalks,
carrots and bacon in lard until slightly brown. Add
flour, cook for 5 minutes and stir in tomato puree,
wine and vinegar and lastly water or stock. Boil
sauce for 20 minutes. Season and strain.

FRANGO COM ARROZ
Chicken a la Castelo Vide with tomatoes and
mushrooms

Ingredients:

1 fowl 4 lb (1,920 g)
1 onion studded with 3 cloves 4 oz (120 g)
1 large carrot 3 oz (90 g)
1 sprig of celery 3 oz (90 g)
1 bouquet garni
Water 5 pint (3,000 mls)

Garnish:

Chopped skinned and seeded tomatoes 8 oz (240 g)
Chopped onions 2 oz (60 g)
Sliced white mushrooms 5 oz (150 g)
Madeira wine ¼ pint (150 mls)
Oil 2 oz (60 g)
Rice 4 oz (120 g)
3 egg yolks
Cornflour 1 oz (30 g)
Salt and pepper
Grated nutmeg

Method: Boil the fowl in water for 1 hour and
remove scum as it rises. Add vegetables and
bouquet garni and simmer for 35 minutes. Remove
the chicken and cut in small pieces or slices.
Place in a shallow dish and cover with tomatoes
and raw mushrooms. Boil rice in 1 pint stock for
20 minutes and add to chicken. Fry chopped
onions in oil until translucent, add Madeira wine
and boil for 10 minutes. Cool. Place egg yolks and
cornflour into a bowl with half the Madeira liquor.
Stir well and add to rest of Madeira and onion
mixture. Reheat until liquid thickens like custard
and pour this sauce over the chicken and rice.
Season and bake in moderate oven for 15
minutes. The remaining vegetables and stock can
be made into a soup.

COELHO PORCALHOTA
Stewed rabbit with tomatoes

Ingredients:

1 young tame rabbit 3 lb (1,440 g)
Seasoned flour 2 oz (60 g)

Lard or oil 3 oz (90 g)
Small onions 8 oz (240 g)
Button mushrooms 8 oz (240 g)
Skinned and chopped tomatoes 8 oz (240 g)
1 bouquet garni
Madeira wine or white Port ¼ pint (150 mls)
Water ½ pint (300 mls)
Salt and black pepper
Ground clove and mace
1 clove of crushed garlic
1 small piece of fresh ginger finely chopped
Chopped parsley 1 tbs

Method: Cut rabbit in 8 pieces (2 legs, split the 2
back legs and the loin cut in 2). Include the liver
to be added at the last moment. Pass all the meat
in seasoned flour and pan fry in oil until golden
brown for 10 minutes. Transfer the rabbit to a
shallow dish. Saute onions and mushrooms in
same oil until brown for 5 minutes, add tomatoes,
wine, water and bouquet and boil for 5 minutes.
Pour over the rabbit pieces and cover with a lid.
Bake in oven for 1½ hours at 360°F. Season,
remove bouquet garni, sprinkle with chopped
parsley and serve with baked potatoes or rice.

FEBRAS DE PORCO ASSADAS
Fillets or loin of pork Portuguese style with orange
    sauce

Ingredients:

1 small loin of pork, cured in salt, 3 lb (1,440 g)
Lard 2 oz (60 g)
1 bouquet garni
1 large carrot 5 oz (150 g)
1 large onion 5 oz (150 g)

Sauce:

Lard 2 oz (60 g)
Flour 1½ oz (45 g)
Tomato puree 1 oz (30 g)
Fresh chopped mint 1 tbs
Juice of 1 lemon and orange
Vinegar 3 fl oz (90 mls)
Sugar 1 oz (30 g)
Water 1 pint (600 mls)
Salt and pepper

Garnish:

Segments of 2 oranges
White port 5 fl oz (150 mls)
Strips of orange cut thinly without white skin
    1 oz (30 g)

Thickening:

Water ¼ pint (150 mls)
Cornflour 1 oz (30 g)

Method: Remove rind from the pork, season and
lard and rub with lemon juice. Place on a trivet of
bones with carrot, onion and ¼ pint hot water.
Roast at 400°F for 1¼ hours, basting from time
to time. Remove gravy and place in a saucepan
with brown carrot and onion, add bouquet
garni, fresh mint and port and boil for 10 minutes
to produce a sauce. Burn the sugar to caramel in
a saucepan with vinegar and add this to the
sauce with the juice of 1 orange. Season and
thicken with a slurry of cornflour and water. Boil
for 5 minutes and strain. Boil orange strips for
10 minutes, refresh, drain and add to the sauce.
Carve the meat and place in a shallow dish.
Surround with segments of orange and pour half
the sauce over the meat. Serve remaining sauce
in a sauceboat.

COSTELETA DE PORCO GRELHADA
Pork chop with tomatoes and red peppers

Ingredients:

4 pork chops 8 oz (240 g) each
Red peppers 8 oz (240 g)
Oil 2 fl oz (60 mls)
Seasoned flour 2 oz (60 g)
Chopped onions 4 oz (120 g)
Tomato puree 2 oz (60 g)
White port wine ¼ pint (150 mls)
Water ¼ pint (150 mls)
Salt, pepper and grated nutmeg
Chopped parsley and fresh mint 1 tbs

Method: Remove bones and surplus fat from chops.
Bat or beat with rolling pin to thin down the
pieces of meat. Pass in seasoned flour and pan fry
until golden on both sides for 8 minutes. Transfer

to a shallow dish. Fry chopped onions and shredded red peppers in same oil for 5 minutes. Add tomato puree, wine, water and seasoning and boil for 8 minutes. Pour this over the pork and cover with a lid. Bake for 1 hour in a moderate oven at 360°F. Serve with a sprinkling of chopped herbs.

CABRITO ASSADO
Goat stew with rice in wine

Ingredients:

Kid's meat from leg, loin or shoulder cut in 1 inch
    cubes 3 lb (1,440 g)
Oil 2 fl oz (60 mls)
Chopped onions 8 oz (240 g)
Flour 2 oz (60 g)
Tomato puree 2 oz (60 g)
Red Portuguese wine ¾ pint (450 mls)
Water 1½ pint (900 mls)
1 bouquet garni
Soaked haricot beans 8 oz (240 g) (use red or
    black variety)
Sait and pepper
Pinch of fresh rosemary and summer savoury
Vinegar 3 tbs

Method: Pass kid's meat in seasoned flour and fry in pan with oil for 10 minutes. Add chopped onions and stir, cook for 5 more minutes. Sprinkle on flour and stir, add tomato puree, water, wine and remaining ingredients and cover with a lid. Bake in a moderate oven for 1½ hours. Serve in the same casserole.

ISCAS A PORTUGUESA
Marinaded liver in wine sauce

Ingredients:

Pig's liver 2 lb (960 g)
Red wine ½ pint (300 mls)
Water ½ pint (300 mls)
Wine vinegar 4 fl oz (120 mls)
1 bouquet garni
1 crushed clove of garlic
6 coriander seeds
Oil 2 fl oz (60 mls)
Seasoned flour 2 oz (60 g)
Chopped parsley 1 tbs

Method: Denerve and skin liver and cut in thin escalopes. Place in an earthenware casserole with wine, vinegar, water, garlic, seeds and bouquet garni. Soak for 1 hour and remove. Drain and dry. Pass in seasoned flour and pan fry in oil for 6 minutes. Place in a dish. Boil marinade for 15 minutes, strain and pour over the liver. Sprinkle with chopped parsley and serve with chips.

ROLO DE PORCO
Meat roll in Port wine sauce

Ingredients:

Minced beef 8 oz (240 g)
Minced pork 8 oz (240 g)
Breadcrumbs 3 oz (90 g)
Soya bean granules 1 oz (30 g)
1 egg
White Port wine 3 fl oz (90 mls)
Salt and pepper
Chopped onion 1 oz (30 g)
Chopped fresh parsley 1 tbs
Pinch of nutmeg, clove and ground mace
1 clove of garlic finely chopped
Brown breadcrumbs 3 oz (90 g)

Sauce:

Oil 2 fl oz (60 mls)
Chopped onions 2 oz (60 g)
Flour 1 oz (30 g)
Tomato puree 1 oz (30 g)
White port wine ¼ pint (150 mls)
Water ¼ pint (150 mls)
Salt and pepper

Method: Blend all the ingredients, except brown breadcrumbs, of the first mixture and pass through the mincer again. Grease an oblong aluminium container and fill with mixture. Bake in the oven at 360°F for 1½ hours. Cool and turn on to a dish. Sprinkle with brown breadcrumbs and reheat in the oven.
Sauce: Pan fry chopped onions in oil until

translucent, add flour and tomato puree and cook for 5 minutes. Add water and wine and boil for 15 minutes, season and strain. Serve with meat loaf and a dish of pasta or rice.

CARNEIRO ASSADO
Stuffed leg of mutton Portuguese style

Ingredients:

1 boned leg of lamb 3½ lb (1,680 g)
Sausage meat ¼ lb (120 g)
Soya protein 1 oz (30 g)
1 egg
White breadcrumbs 1 oz (30 g)
Chopped garlic 1 clove   } for stuffing
Chopped onion 2 oz (60 g)
Salt and pepper
2 large carrots 5 oz (150 g)
1 large onion 5 oz (150 g)
1 sprig of celery
1 bouquet garni
Brandy 5 fl oz (150 mls)
White Port wine ½ pint (300 mls)
Butter 2 oz (60 g)
Tomato puree 1 oz (30 g)
Button mushrooms 8 oz (240 g)
Pinch of nutmeg, mace, paprika and saffron
Chopped mint 1 tbs
Salt and pepper

Method: Blend the stuffing and place inside the meat to refill the bone cavity. Tie up with string and rub with butter and season all over. Place joint in a roasting tin and bake for 20 minutes at 400°F or until the outside is brown. Transfer the joint into a large casserole dish and add all remaining ingredients. Cover with a lid and bake gently at 360°F for 1¾ hours. Season and serve in the same dish. The carving is done in front of the guests. Serve with rice pilaff or baked beans.

FRANGƠ A PORTUGUESA
Chicken Portuguese style

Ingredients:

1 roasting chicken 4 lb (1,920 g)
Sliced onions 3 oz (90 g)
Portuguese tomato puree 3 oz (90 g)
Portuguese oil 3 fl oz (90 mls)
Skinned and seeded tomatoes 3 oz (90 g)
½ clove crushed garlic (5 g)
Chopped parsley 1 tsp (5 g)
White portuguese wine 5 fl oz (150 mls)
Chicken bouillon cube (10 g)
Water 5 fl oz (150 mls)
Salt and pepper
Seasoned flour 2 oz (60 g)
Pinch of oregano herbs

Method: Cut chicken in eight pieces and pass in seasoned flour. Fry in oil until golden and cover with a lid. Turn from time to time and allow 20 minutes for legs and 15 minutes for white meat. Drain the pieces and in same oil fry the onions until tender but not brown. Add fresh tomatoes and saute for 5 minutes. Add tomato puree, wine, water and garlic and boil up for 10 minutes. Crumble the bouillon cubes in this liquid and cook for 5 more minutes. Place chicken in a casserole dish, cover with the sauce, season to taste and bake in the oven for 20 minutes and serve with a sprinkling of chopped parsley and herbs.

MOLHO DE VINHO DA MADEIRA
Madeira sauce

Ingredients:

Tomato puree 2 oz (60 g)
2 beef bouillon cubes (20 g)

Stock:

Water 1 pint (600 mls)
Leeks 1 oz (30 g)
Carrots 1 oz (30 g)
Bacon trimmings 2 oz (60 g)
Diced stewing veal 4 oz (120 g)
Onions 2 oz (60 g)
Celery tops 1 oz (30 g)
1 bay leaf
Sprig of thyme
Portuguese oil 1 fl oz (30 mls)
Flour 1 oz (30 g)

Madeira wine 5 fl oz (150 mls)
Salt and pepper
Pinch of rosemary

Method: Saute all chopped vegetables, meat, bacon and herbs in oil until brown. Add tomato puree and cook for 5 minutes more. Flood mixture with water and boil until vegetables and meat are tender for 1 hour. Add bouillon cubes and boil for 5 more minutes. Prepare a roux by cooking the flour in oil till brown for 10 minutes over a low heat. Add this to mixture and boil for 15 minutes. Strain and season. Add Madeira wine to sauce.
Note: If a stock can be made from meat or veal bones the flavour and viscosity of the sauce will be more unctuous.

MOLHO DE VINHO DO PORTO
Port wine sauce

The classic tawny, red or white dessert wine from the region around Porto (Oporto) is used for this exquisite sauce: same procedure as above, substituting Port for Madeira.

Madeira sauce can be used for any kind of chicken or veal and also ham or bacon dishes. Port wine sauce is particularly flavoursome for chicken or game dishes, also duck.

VEGETABLES

Chickpeas, marrow peas, baked beans and lentils are frequently used in all the countries of the Spanish and Portuguese peninsula. The water to soak them is not hard like in Britain and the gentle cooking makes these dried vegetables soft and tender.

The classical peabean or Navy bean, cooked in bacon stock, then flavoured in rich tomato sauce is an example.

The Chilli con Carne of meat cooked with red or black beans or lentils with bacon seems to blend well with the entire pulse family of legumes which are particularly rich in essential protein and therefore can be eaten instead of meat as a complete food.

FAVAS A MODA DO PESCADOR
Beans cooked with cod

Ingredients:

Haricot beans ½ lb (240 g)
Onions 5 oz (150 g)
Carrots 5 oz (150 g)
1 bouquet garni
Vinegar 1 tbs
Salt and pepper
Tomato puree 2 oz (60 g)
Garlic 1 clove
White port 5 fl oz (150 mls)
Cod 5 oz (150 g) per portion
Seasoned flour 1 oz (30 g)
Chopped parsley 2 tbs
1 onion chopped 5 oz (150 g)
Oil

Method: Soak beans in distilled water (Britain) for 6 hours. Cook in the same water with 1 onion and 1 carrot till tender. Remove water and drain.

Saute chopped onions in oil till tender. Add tomato puree, garlic, vinegar, bouquet garni and a glass of white port wine. Boil for 5 minutes, season and mix with beans. Pass diced cod in seasoned flour and fry quickly in oil till golden brown. Place fish on top of beans. Remove bouquet garni, then cover with sauce and sprinkle with chopped parsley. Season to taste.

TOMATES PORTUGUESES
Stuffed tomatoes

Ingredients:

8 large tomatoes
Olive oil 3 fl oz (90 mls)
Butter 2 oz (60 g)
Chopped onions 2 oz (60 g)
Garlic 1 clove (10 g)
Chopped fresh cod 4 oz (120 g)
1 lemon
Crumbs 2 oz (60 g)
Salt and pepper
3 beaten eggs for scrambling
Grated cheese 2 oz (60 g)
Flaked almonds

Method: Split the large tomatoes two-thirds so as to have a large cavity to fill. Remove seeds.

Fry in a pan with butter and oil, chopped onions, garlic and chopped fresh cod. Season and add juice of lemon and crumbs.

Fill the tomatoes with this mixture half way up. Top with creamy scambled eggs. Sprinkle grated cheese and flaked almonds and bake in oven at 400°F for about 12 minutes. Decorate with uncooked tomato cap.

SWEETS AND DESSERTS

CASTANHAS
Chestnut cake

Ingredients:

Peeled chestnuts (baked or boiled) 1 lb (480 g)
3 oranges
Black grapes 8 oz (240 g)
Water 1 pint (600 mls)
Sugar 1 lb (480 g)
Orange liqueur 5 fl oz (150 mls)
Honey 2 oz (60 g)

Method: Split chestnuts and bake till tender. Remove hard and soft skin. Prepare a syrup: boil water, sugar and honey. Add grated orange rind and orange liqueur. Peel oranges and cut in segments without white skin. Split the large grapes and remove seeds. Place all ingredients in syrup and let them soak up overnight and serve cool.

TORTA PORTUGUESA
Mixed fruit flan

Ingredients:

Puff pastry 8 oz (240 g)

Filling:

2 oz (60 g) each of the following—total 1 lb (480 g)

Dates, figs, apples, almonds, walnuts, honey, butter, grated peel
Cinnamon for flavour

Method: Line a flan ring with puff pastry and place all the ingredients finely minced together. Cover with a layer of pastry. Glaze and prick top with prongs of a fork. Bake at 430°F for 30 minutes. Serve hot or cold with a Lemon Sabayon.

PUDIM PORTUGUESA
Walnut souffle pudding

Ingredients:

Walnuts 2 oz (60 g)
5 yolks
5 egg whites
Castor sugar 5 oz (150 g)
Cornflour 1 oz (30 g)
Sauce Sabayon ½ pint (300 mls)—flavoured with orange liqueur (see Italian chapter)

Method: Pound the walnuts to a paste. Beat yolks and sugar until foamy. Add cornflour and walnut paste. Fold the whites, beaten to a meringue, and place in a greased mould (souffle dish) two-thirds full. Bake for 45 minutes in a tray half filled with water at 380°F. Serve in the same mould with an Orange Sabayon.

TORTA DE AMENDOAS
Almond flan

Ingredients:

Sweet short pastry 8 oz (240 g)
Orange marmalade

Almond paste:

Butter 2 oz (60 g)
Castor sugar 2 oz (60 g)
2 eggs
Flour 1 oz (30 g)
Ground almonds 2 oz (60 g)
Orange liqueur 1 fl oz (30 mls)
Flaked almonds 1 oz (30 g)

Method: Line a flan ring with short pastry. Fill bottom with orange marmalade flavoured with Cointreau or other orange liqueur. Fill to the top with almond paste and sprinkle flaked almonds. Bake for 35 minutes at 380°F.

To make almond paste, cream butter and sugar. Add eggs and ground almonds. Add a little orange liqueur and then flour.

Technical Guide

OVEN TEMPERATURES

	Electric	Celsius	Gas
Very cool	225 F	110 C	¼
Very slow	250 F	120 C	½
Slow	275 F	140 C	1
Cool	300 F	150 C	2
Warm	325 F	160 C	3
Very moderate	350 F	180 C	4
Moderate	375 F	190 C	5
Moderately hot	400 F	200 C	6
Hot	425 F	220 C	7
Very hot	450 F	230 C	8
Very hot	475 F	240 C	9

This temperature guide is an informative guide, however as cookers do vary, it is always best to check with the cooker's instruction booklet.

CONVERSIONS*

From $°F$ to $°C$ the formula is: $(°F - 32) \times 5 \div 9 = °C$

e.g. $225°F - 32 = 193 \times 5 = 965 \div 9 = 107°C$.

From $°C$ to $°F$ the formula is: $°C \times 9 \div 5 = x + 32 = °F$

e.g. $107°C \times 9 = 963 \div 5 = 193 + 32 = 225°F$.

* Temperatures rounded off the the nearest whole figure.

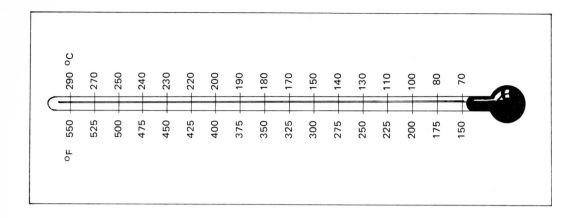

MEASURES

1 level teaspoon = 5 g
1 level tablespoon = 20 g
1 heaped tablespoon = 30 g

1 liquid pint = 600 mls
1 gallon = 8 pt
1 litre = 1,000 mls
1 teaspoon liquid = 5 mls
1 tablespoon liquid = 20 mls

1 tbs = 1 tablespoon
1 tsp = 1 teaspoon

1 pint = 20 fl oz (600 mls)
1 breakfast cup = 8 oz or ½ pint liquid
1 pinch = 1 g
40 drops essence = 5 mls (approx.)
2 drops essence per meal = 0.5 mls

The ratio of measurement in all the recipes has been based on a rounded figure, e.g. 1 oz exactly = 28.35 g but this has been rounded to 30 g so 1 heaped tablespoon = 1 oz (30 g).

USEFUL PERCENTAGES & QUANTITIES

Seasoning: Salt for liquid should be 1 per cent of total weight, e.g. salt needed for 1 pt (600 mls) = $^1/_5$ oz (6 g).

Salt for solid (hot or minced) meat should be 1½ per cent of total weight — for pastry and pie mixture this should be increased to 2 per cent.

Spicing: Black or white pepper ground for liquid should be 0.01 per cent of total weight, or 0.1 g per litre.

Black or white pepper ground for solid pate, meat or fish should be 0.2 per cent, e.g. pepper needed for 1 lb (480 g) = 0.96 g, or 2 g per 1,000 g.

Ginger, ground clove, mace, nutmeg, paprika and curry powder are the same as pepper for quantities. Chilli and cayenne pepper should be 0.001 per cent as they are very hot.

Sweetening: Twelve per cent or 2½ oz sugar is needed per pint of sweet sauce or custard (75 g to 600 mls).

Sugar required for cakes is 20.25 per cent of total weight of ingredients.

Flavouring: Fruit and spice flavouring in liquid form (vanilla, lemon and orange) should be 0.1 per cent or 1 ml (4 drops) or 6 drops per pint (600 mls) of sauce or mixture to be flavoured.

For almond and peppermint essences, use half the vanilla quantity.

For fruit cake use 1 drop of each flavour.

Thickening: Roux: Flour and fat required should be 5 per cent each of the total weight of the sauce or liquid to be thickened, e.g. flour and fat needed for 1 pt (600 mls) = 1 oz (30 g) flour and 1 oz (30 g) fat.

Cornflour, arrowroot, potato flour or tapioca flour should be 4 per cent of total weight, e.g. starch needed for 1 pt (600 mls) = $^4/_5$ oz (24 g).

Cohering:

6 yolks will cohere 1 pint of milk for custard sauce.
10-12 yolks will cohere 1 pint of wine for wine sabayon.
4 yolks will emulsify 1 pint of oil for mayonnaise.
4 whole eggs will set into a firm custard with 1 pint of milk.
4 yolks and 1 oz starch will thicken 1 pint of milk (confectioner's custard).

Fat: Use 2½ oz (75 g) butter or margarine to 1 oz (30 g) lard or oil for sauce making with same amount of flour.

Use 1 oz (30 g) butter or oil for sauce or gravy thickened with 1 oz (30 g) cornflour or pure starch.

Farinaceous products: To make rice pudding use 2 oz (60 g) to 2½ oz (75 g) rice per 1 pint (600 mls) milk. The same applies to semolina, tapioca and sago.

PORTIONS

Lean meat: Allow 4 oz (120 g) raw meat for 2 oz (60 g) cooked meat.
Lamb cutlets: Allow 2 per person.
Pork chops: Allow 1 X 8 oz (240 g) chop per person.
Beef steak: Allow 8 oz (240 g) raw meat per person.
Fish: Allow 6-8 oz (180-240 g) per portion when filleted. On the bone allow 2 oz (60 g) more or 10 oz (300 g).
Vegetables: Allow 8 oz (240 g) raw for 4-5 oz (120-150 g) cooked.
Pasta: Allow 3 oz (90 g) uncooked for 9 oz (270 g) cooked.
Sauce: Allow 1 pt (600 mls) for 6 portions.
Gravy: Allow 1 pt (600 mls) for 8 portions.
Soup: Allow ½ pt (300 mls) per portion.

COLOUR

The colour of food is important and many colouring agents are available in liquid and powder form. Natural colouring agents are:

Ground paprika for red

Turmeric for yellow
Juice of green vegetables like spinach for green

A complete range of artificial colouring in powder and liquid form is used in confectionery.

WINE IN COOKING

Plain wines can be used in sauces and stews to a maximum of 40 per cent of the total solid. On average, at least 25 per cent wine to the total weight of meat or fish should be used for good flavour.

If fortified wines are used, like port, madeira, sherry, marsala or vermouth, 10 per cent is enough, e.g. for 1 pt (600 mls) sauce use 2 fl oz (60 mls) fortified wine. The fortified wines are always added at the end when the sauce is made. Ordinary wines must be boiled with the aromatic agents (onions, mushrooms, herbs).

SPIRITS AND LIQUEURS

Five per cent of any spirit added at the end to sweets or sauces is sufficient to impart a good flavour. It is a mistake to flambe a spirit. This is done more for effect than flavour. In sweets the amount of liqueur can be increased to 8 per cent, e.g. in Crepes Grand Marnier allow 2 fl oz (60 mls) per portion of 2 pancakes.

USEFUL REFERENCES

1 egg yolk = 20 g	20 egg whites = 1 pint
30 yolks = 1 pint	1 whole egg (without weight of shell) = 50 g
1 egg white = 30 g	12 eggs = 1 pint

1 oz of baking powder will aerate 1 lb of plain flour.

1 egg will aerate 2 oz of flour so a cake with 1 lb flour requires 8 eggs, but by using baking powder and eggs together, fewer eggs are needed. Half a pound of flour needs ¼ oz baking powder and 2 eggs to do the same aeration as 4 eggs with ½ lb flour.

NUMERALS TO REMEMBER

135 = *1* egg, *3* oz flour and *5* fl oz water/milk for batter used in pancakes and Yorkshire puddings.

1258 = *1* egg, *2* oz icing sugar, *5* oz margarine and *8* oz flour for sweet short pastry.

119 = *1* lb flour, *1* lb butter/margarine and *9* oz water for puff pastry.

4444 = *4* oz margarine, *4* oz sugar, *4* oz eggs (2 eggs) and *4* oz flour for perfect cake.

55551 = *5* oz margarine, *5* oz sugar, *5* oz ground almonds, *5* oz egg and *1* oz flour for a perfect almond sponge.

12481 = *1* onion, *2* oz margarine, *4* oz fish bones, *8* fl oz water and *1* bouquet garni for fish stock.

1311 = *1* lb meat, skin and bones, *3* pt water, *1* lb mixed vegetables (leek, carrot and onion) and *1* bouquet garni for meat stock.

TEMPERATURE CHART FOR BOILING SUGAR

Stage	Temperature in °F	Temperature in °C	Cooking use
Boiling	212	100	water boils
Thread	212—225		jellies, jams, liqueurs and bonbons
Thick thread	230—235		transparent icing for glazing fruits
Blow feather	240—242		light meringue
Soft ball	240		marzipan, soft toffee
	245		fondant, fudge
Hard ball	250—280	121—136	marshmallow, Italian merginue, coconut ice, and candies
	278—280		nougat
Small crack	285—300		rock sugar, butterscotch and spun sugar
Crack	310		flowers, pulled sugar and dipping fruits
Hard crack	320		modelling
Caramel	330		caramel
Blackjack	over 340		

OBSERVATIONS ON COOKING SUGAR

1. 230-224 °F Syrup spins a 2 inch thread when dropped from a spoon.
2. 234-240 °F Syrup, when dropped in cold water, forms a soft ball which flattens on removal.
3. 244-248 °F Same as above, but the ball does not flatten on removal.
4. 250-265 °F Syrup forms a hard ball when dropped in cold water. It holds its shape and begins to become a little brittle.
5. 270-290 °F Syrup dropped in water is brittle and hard, breaking like glass.
6. 300-310 °F Syrup separates in very hard threads and is very brittle.
7. 320 °F Sugar liquifies.
8. 340 °F Sugar darkens.

SUGAR DENSITY CHART

Water		Sugar		Degree Beaume (French measure)	Purpose
				33½°	for crystallising
1 pint	(600 mls)	2 lb	(960 g)	32°	''
1½ pints	(900 mls)	''	''	30°	
1¼ pints	(750 mls)	''	''	28°	stock syrup
2 pints	(1,200 mls)	''	''	25°	
2½ pints	(1,500 mls)	''	''	22°	baba syrup
3 pints	(1,800 mls)	''	''	20°	for compote de fruits
4 pints	(2,400 mls)	''	''	17°	for water ices

Index

CLASSIFICATION OF INDEX

HORS D'OEUVRES

SOUP

EGG DISHES

PASTA DISHES

FISH DISHES

MEAT, POULTRY AND GAME DISHES

VEGETABLE, CEREAL AND SALAD DISHES

SAVOURIES

SAUCES

SWEETS

CAKES

Humarhalar i dillsosu (prawns) 385

Jansson's frest else (anchovy and potato) 353
Jatkan lohipotti (salmon) 379

Kartoffelsalat (sausage salad) 183
Kleftedhes (rissoles) 219
Kvass (beer) 319
Kyopoolou 288

Lax med pepparrotsgrade (salmon) 353
Lofoten caviar 365

Mantaqeiga de sardinhas (sardine butter) 417
Medaljonger av rakor (shrimp) 354
Melidzanes (aubergine) 205
Midia yemista (mussels) 203
Mushroom caviar 325
Moskowskaya kusnik (chicken) 325

Nadivane kornoutky z praske sunky (ham) 44
Norwegian prawn pâte 365
Norwegian quiche 365
'Ova Spagna' (egg) 399-400
Ovos com atum 416
Ovos Riviera 417
Ovos verdes 414

Pandzaria (beetroot) 204
Pao de espinafres (spinach and eggs) 414
Pao torrado de peixe (anchovy) 416
Pâté de campagne 117
Pâté Luxembourgeois 117
Pâté Maitre-Jean 145
Petit pâté en croute 146
Picadillo 398
Polish cheese 299
Potted ham and chicken 62
Prassa (leek) 217
Prawn mousse Elizabeth 61

Quiche aux fruits de mer 142

Rokt laxlada (smoked salmon) 354

Salada de peixe (tuna) 417
Salata psari me yaorti (fish) 205
Salingria (snails) 204
Saltsild i Kryddsosu (salted herrings) 385
Scampi Morecambe 62
Scampi Rosslare 62
Sedano Dolcelatte 251
Sildarsalat 386
Smoked herring salad 232
Smoked mackerel pâté 61
Smoked salmon tartlet 85
Smorgas platter 363

Smorrebrod 371
Spetsofagi (sausages) 204

Tarama kefteded (fish roe) 203
Taramosalata 219
Talattoure (cucumber) 219
Tiganites Kolokithakia (courgette) 204
Tivoli salad 353
Tomates Miramar 416
Tomates recheados 415
Tyropites (cream cheese) 203

Xydata kremmidia (onions) 220

Zucchine agrodolce (marrow) 251

SOUP

Anglia soup (ham and pea) 60
Anraith Aint Chlair 103
Anraith meidreach clarrat (vegetable) 103
Anraith oinniun gealach (onion with whiskey) 103
Anraith prath Tir edgain (potatoes and turnips) 103
Anraith Tiobraid arawn (vegetable) 104
Arter med flask (split pea with pork) 352

Batwinija (cold herb) 323
Blabaersuppe (blueberry) 363
Bohmisher pivo polevka (beer) 44
Borscht 321
Bucharest hot pot 282

Canja (chicken and rice) 413
Canton Schoyz cheese soup 167
Caldo verde (cabbage) 413
Ceska polevka (gammon with sour cream) 44
Chicory soup 231
Cock-a-leekie 84
Clear beet barszcz 298

Dutch chicory soep 229
Erwntensoep (pea and gammon) 231
Escudilla de pages Julia (haricot bean) 398

Faki xidhati (lentil) 218

Game soup with rose-hip 182
Gazpacho (cold) 397
Gazpachuelo (cold fish) 397
Gower oyster soup 95
Groenaerte suppe med gaase (goose and pea) 371
Gruner aal hamburger art (smoked eel) 182
Gsod suppe (bean and bacon) 167
Gulyas (beef paprika) 33

Hochepot a la Gantoise (hot pot) 116

Kalakeitto (fish chowder) 379
Kalfspoeletsoep (veal) 231
Kalsoppa med frikadeller (beef and cabbage) 352
Kasapski-djuvec (mutton and vegetable) 274
Kesakeitto (scampi) 378
Kurban chorba (mutton) 288

Lebernockerlsuppe (liver) 21
Louvana (yellow pea) 218
Luxembourg leek soup 116

Masova polevka po cesku (chicken and leek) 44
Mayeritsa (offal) 202
Millefanti (broth) 249
Minestrone 249
Moularde, la (mussel) 144

Nasselkal (nettle) 352

Olla podrida (hot pot) 396
Olmsuppe (beer) 363
Orja soup (pork) 33

Paloc soup (mutton) 33
Partan bree (crab) 84
Patsha (brain) 218
Puchero (hot pot) 396

Raekjusupa (shrimp) 385
Rassolnik (cucumber and kidney) 322
Rye zur 298

Sauerkraut 321
Scotch broth 84
Shchi (cabbage) 321
Solyanka (fish) 322
Song of Grieg (veal) 363
Sopa de agrioes (watercress) 413
Sopa de ajo Teresa (garlic) 396
Sopa alentejana (coriander) 413
Sopa de camardo (prawn) 414
Sopa de pescado a la visca 396
Soupe à l'oignon au madére 144
Soupa avgolemenó (egg and lemon) 218
Spanakosoupa (spinach) 202
Szeged (fish) 33

Tahinosoupa (peanut butter) 202
Tarator (cucumber and yoghurt) 288

Ujhazi (vegetable) 33
Uszka (dumplings) 296

Waterzooisoep (fish and vegetable) 233
Westphalian biersuppe 182
Windsor (calf's head) 60

Zalewajka (onion) 299
Zuppa pavese 249
Zuppa al pesto 250

EGG DISHES

Cheese à la shoppe 287

Egg ragoût 171

Gehaktnestjes (with minced beef) 229

Ova Spagna 399
Ova melitta Espagna 402
Ovos batatas 417
Ovos riviera 417
Ovos tunny 416
Ovos verdes 414

Poached eggs pannomia (with fish) 34

PASTA DISHES

Bilbao filling tortelini 255
Blinis (pancake) 326

Canneloni Romana 254

Farfallette Sophia Loren 258

Gnocchi Romana (semolina) 255

Iszka Polish dumplings 298

Noodle paste 253

Pizza 255
Polenta sole mio 256

Ravioli marinara (cod and prawns) 254
Ravioli tacchino delizioso (turkey, chestnuts and sprouts) 256
Rollatine impottite alla Fiorentina (pancakes with beef and spinach) 252
Russian pelmeni (ravioli) 334

Spatzle 189
Spaghetti Bolognese 257
Stuffed pancakes hortobagy (veal) 32

Tagliatelle verdi alla marinara (fish) 252

Vatrushka (doughnut filled with sour cream) 344

FISH DISHES

Aigran gealach trinsuir cill mantain (mixed seafood) 104
Almejas à la marinera (clam) 401
Anguilles au vert (eel) 117
Aoibneas an bradan shanagarry (salmon) 104
Arbroath smokie pie (haddock) 85

Bacahlhau a jardiniera (cod) 418
Bacaliaro kleftedhes (rissoles) 220
Bakalairos skordalia (fish and tomato) 207
Ballen from Lake Zug (trout) 167
Baluga in brine 327
Besugo asado (sea bream) 401

Carp à la rac 33
Carp umplut mamaia 282
Cockle pie 95
Codling Juliana 233
Codling Wilhelmina 233
Crab pie Lithuania 329
Crustaceans 149

Dourado portuense na frigideira (John Dory) 418
Dover sole Nelson 63
Dover sole Prince Philip 64

Estonian smoked sprat 327

Fevig mackerel 366
Filets de sole au fruit de la vigne, les 148
Fiskboller (haddock) 366
Fische mit apfel Kummelkraut 184
Fish fillet mornay au gratin 167
Fish solyanka (tomato and garlic) 328
Fogas Adriatic (perch) 274
Friesischer pfannfisch (potatoes, mustard and beer) 184
Fritto misto di mare 258
Fyllda pannkatkor (pancakes) 354
Fylltur skarkoli (plaice) 387

Gefilte fish 300
Gefusooin fishflok (plaice) 386

Haddock strachur 85
Halastle (stew) 34
Halibut Red Army 329
Heilbutt unter dem schneeberg (cream sauce) 184
Herring casserole 95
Herring in sour cream 180
Homard au pernod, le 150

Kaiserhummer mit huhn (chicken and lobster) 185
Kalamaria Kathista (squid) 221
Kapr na cerno (carp) 45
Kipper fish cake 95
Koft lutfisk (salted cod) 355

Koulibiac Moscoviana (poached salmon) 330

Lakspudding (salmon) 366
Langouste au gratin 147
Langostina catalana 401
Lobster 64
Lobster Ascot 65
Lobster Clarence 65

Mackerel in fennel 96
Marinovany kapr po cesku (carp) 45
Merluza a la gallega (hake) 400
Moules Ostendaise 118

Norwegian quiche 362

Ofnbokuo saltsildarflok (herring) 386

Patakukko (with onion) 379
Pesce persico in umido (casserole) 259
Pike in aspic 296
Plukfish (cod) 372
Pstruh po cesku (salmon trout) 44
Psari gratini 206
Psari marinato 205
Psari roullo (fish loaf) 206

Quenelles de saumon (salmon dumplings) 150

Rakpaprikas (scampi or crayfish) 274
Rollmops 185
Rospaette (plaice) 372

Salmon royal 64
Sardine a beccafico 258
Savoro (with garlic) 220
Scampi dorati 259
Scampi tallin 328
Scorcolea (walnut paste) 282
Shashlik of sturgeon Latvia (with bacon or ham) 328
Skoumbri yahni (mackerel) 206
Sole 63,148
Soupies yahni (cuttlefish) 207
Steamed sprat pudding 326
Sterlet Carpathian 34
Stuffed fish Russian style 327

Telnoye (fish loaf) 327
Trucha a la Navarra (trout) 400
Truite Luxembourg 118
Turban de Colin (hake) 148
Turbot boulonnaise 148
Torskrompastej (cod's roe) 355

Waterzoisoep (soup) 233

Zarzuela a la Conil 400

MEAT, POULTRY AND GAME DISHES

Aargau sausage fritters 169
Afelia of pork 222
Aphelia avgolemeno 210
Arfugi i flotesaus (ptarmigan) 367
Arni giouvetsi (lamb) 208
Arni stithos me kolokithakia (with courgettes) 207

Bacon and cauliflower 303
Bagun agus cabaiste (bacon and cabbage) 106
Ballekes (meat balls) 120
Beef Stroganoff 333
Beef Wellington 58
Bigos (pork and bacon) 303
Bitterballen (pork) 235
Boeuf braisé 121
Bollito misto verde (mixed boiled meats) 262
Boudin entre-ciel-et-terre (black pudding) 120
Brains Polish style 300
Braised ox heart Victoria 69
Brigand's roast 37
Burger Maritza (lamb) 303
Butifarra con Judias (sausages and beans) 405

Cabrito assado (goat) 421
Callos madrilena (tripe) 404
Canard à l'orange 153
Caneton aux cerises 123
Carbonnade Flamande (steak) 122
Carneiro assado (mutton) 422
Carnero asado a la manchega (mutton) 406
Casserole of beef with kvass 331
Casseruola si animelle al Marsala (sweetbread) 260
Cervello dorato al burro (calves' brains) 260
Cevapeici with ajvarsalata (hamburger) 276
Chanakhi (lamb stew) 332
Chicken Kiev 332
Chicken Polish style 302
Choesels au Madère 120
Cocido Castellano (beef and gammon) 404
Coelho porcalhota (rabbit) 419
Conejo la Juana (tame rabbit) 394
Costeleta de porco grelhada 420
Cozida de Portuguesa (hotpot) 418
Cumberland mutton pie 70
Culloden collops 86
Cyprus stuffing 217

Dillilammas (mutton with dill) 380
Dolmades yemista (stuffed vine leaves) 222
Duck Polish style 302

Einin Ballysadara (duckling) 102
Emince de veau Zurichoise 170
Escalope de veau Cyrano de Bergerac 142
Esterhazy achem (veal) 35

Estufado de lingua de vaca (tongue) 419

Faar i kaal (mutton and cabbage) 366
Fabada Asturiana (pork and sausages) 406
Faisan à la Brabançonne (pheasant) 122-3
Faisan a la moda de Alcantara (pheasant) 405
Farsumagru (veal) 262
Febras de porco assadas (pork) 420
Fegato di vitello alla Veneziana (calf's liver) 261
Fenalaar (mutton) 367
Forster goulash (venison) 21
Frango com arroz (chicken) 419
Frango Portuguesa 422
Fricadelles (meat balls) 120

Gallina viva el toro (chicken) 403
Gansebraten mit apfeln (goose) 187
Gehaktnestjes (minced beef) 234
Geschnetzeltes (veal) 171
Golubtsy (stuffed cabbage balls) 332
Goose liver casserole 35
Goulash 21
Grenadin of pork Chopin 301
Glukars smijetana sausaum (grouse) 336

Haggis 86
Ham pasties 58
Hare Polish style 303
Hirono avgolemeno (pork) 209
Hues mat ram (hare) 122

Iscas a Portuguesa (liver) 421

Kalalaatiko (pork) 381
Kalbsrolle (veal) 188
Karjalanpaisti (game) 380
Kasseler rippespeer (bacon) 186
Kazakh (minced beef) 344
Kebab Bulgarian style 290
Kebaches (veal and pork) 289
Keftedes tis skaras (lamb) 209
Keshy yena Utrecht (beef) 236
Kisslija kapuska (frankfurter) 335
Klosse (bacon dumplings) 188
Knedliki (bacon dumplings) 301
Kokt griljerad skinda (ham) 356
Konigsberger klosses (meat dumplings) 180
Krautfleisch (pork) 22
Kreatopitta kefalonais (lamb) 208
Krvoret morbrad med champignonsovs (pork) 372
Kydonato (lamb) 209

Lancashire hot pot 68
Leg of mutton chops 170
Leg of mutton Yugoslavian 275
Liver in sour cream 331
London city sirloin 70

Makaronia tou fournou (beef) 222
Makasalaatiko (liver) 380
Meat dumplings 169
Meat loaf Polish style 300
Meat pie Valais style (veal) 169
Mici (hamburger) 283
Mignonettes d'agneau (lamb) 151
Moscaraki roullo (veal) 209
Moussaka 210
Mutton Djuvec 273
Mutton Yugoslavian 275

Nadivana hovezi pecene s omackou (beef) 46

Oie de visé (goose) 121
Oiseaux sans tête et sans ésprit (veal or beef) 123
Oison aux poires et marrons (goose) 155
Osso buco alla Lombardia (veal) 263
'Ova Melitta Spagna' (Spanish omelet) 402

Paella Barcelona 402
Paella Valenciana 403
Paillard de veau 152
Paprika chicken 36
Paprika esirke (chicken) 35
Pâté de lapin (rabbit) 114
Pâté d'oie (gosling) 114
Perdriz chocolate (partridge) 405
Perdreau belle-fleur (partridge) 155
Petti di pollo cavour (chicken) 264
Pintadeau sans rival (guinea fowl) 154
Podarakia arnou avgolemono (sheep's trotters) 208
Poek kavarma (pork) 290
Pork and cabbage rissoles 301
Pork chop Amsterdam 236
Pork djuvec 276
Pork szekely 35
Poulet sauté au Médoc 153
Psito of lamb 221
Pushkin steak 333
Pyzy Warsaw (potato and meat) 301

Rabbit Polish style 302
Rebrucken mit rotweinsosse (venison) 186
Ris de veau Lucullus (sweatbread) 152
Rognons de veau Montparnasse (calves' kidneys) 151
Rolo de porco 421
Royal crown of English lamb 66
Royal Scotch grouse 87
Runderlappen (steak) 234
Russian hotpot Ljubushchkin (oxtail) 336
Russian pelmeni (ravioli) 334

Saddle of hare 36
Salsiccia alla Diavola (chipolatas) 259
Saltimbocca alla Romana (veal) 263
Sarma (minced beef) 276

Sauerbraten (braised beef) 188
Scalopina di tacchino alla Toscanini (turkey) 264
Scaltan naomh Padraig (chicken) 105
Seven leaders' tokany (casserole) 37
Shashlik Brezhnev (lamb and kidney) 333
Sjomansbiff (beef stew) 356
Sma Kottbullar (meat dumplings) 355
Solyanka Tolstoy (meat stew) 330
Sooio lambakjot meo spergli og raejum (lamb) 387
Souvlakia 208
Spiced beef Prince Charlie 87
Steak Balmoral 86
Steak, kidney and mushroom pudding 68
Steak and mushroom pie 67
Stegt svineham (pork) 373
Steig gaillimh 106
Steig gambun 105
Steig gealach 107
Stekte hjortekoteletters (venison) 367
Stobach gealach (Irish Stew) 106
Stomna (lamb) 286
Stuffed cabbage 32
Stuffed pepper 32
Stuffed pullet Godolfo (chicken) 36
Sarmi (stuffed vine leaves) 290
Surrey jugged hare 69
Suss-saure bratwurst 187
Svickova na Smetane (salted beef) 46
Sykoti Tiganito (liver) 210

Tatws a cig yn y popty (lamb) 96
Tava (lamb) 221
Teleci na kmine (veal) 46
Ternera a la condesita (veal) 404
Tessin spiessli (kebab) 169
Transylvanian Hungarian mixed grill 37
Trippa alla Emiliana 260
Tschakkum-bili (chicken) 335
Tsyplenok-tabaka (chicken) 335

Uitsmijter (ham) 235

Veal cutlets a la Magyarovar 36
Veal saddle 22
Veal Valkenburg 235
Veal Zrazy 331
Venison steak Tito 275
Vitello alla Marengo 261
Vitello tonnatto (veal with tuna) 264

Waterzoi de volaille (chicken) 124
Welsh lamb pie 96
Welsh mutton venison style 97
Wiener schnitzel 22
Wiener vierli 21

Zurcher leberspiessli (liver and bacon) 171

VEGETABLE, CEREAL AND SALAD DISHES

Aardappel broodjes (potato cakes) 237
Aran boxty (potato cakes) 107
Asparagus regency 71

Bamies (okra) 223
Banffshire potatoes 88
Bara lawr (laver bread) 97
Basel spinach frog 171
Beets in sour cream 304
Bohmen mit apfeln (haricot beans) 191
Bonor och svamp (green beans) 356
Bramborova kase (potatoes) 47

Can ceannann (cabbage and potato) 108
Caponata (egg plant) 265
Casserole beetroot 337
Cauliflower Polish style 304
Cauliflower au gratin Elizabeth II 67
Caws pobi (Welsh rarebit) 98
Champignons sous cloche 156
Choux de Bruxelles (sprouts) 125
Choux rouges Luxembourgeois (red cabbage) 125
Col de bruselas (sprouts) 406
Courgettes Mathilda 156
Cutlets doytoski 337
Cyprus stuffing (rice) 222

Devonshire stew 71
Dill cucumber 305

Endives braisées de Bruxelles 124
Endives meunière 124
Espinaca (spinach) 406

Fava a moda de pescadori (beans) 423
Fazole po cesku (beans) 47

Gefullter sellerie (celeriac) 190
Ghivecin calugaresc (mixed vegetables) 282
Gratin Parisien (potato) 156
Grune bohnen mit birnen (runner beans) 191

Halusky (cheese and potato) 48
Haricots enkhuizen (flageolet beans) 236

Jets de houblons (hop shoots) 125

Kale brose 88
Kartoffelklosse (potato) 190
Knedlik (dumplings) 48
Kohlrabi in sour cream 304
Kolokithakia plaki (courgettes) 211
Kopýtka (potato) 305
Kounoupidi me avga (cauliflower) 211
Kurbisbrei mit kase (pumpkin) 190

Lahanopitta (spinach) 223
Laver salad 97
Leek Northumbria 72
Leek porridge 97
Lesco (pepper and eggplant) 38
Lincoln croquette 71
Lofschotel (chicory) 237

Mamaliga gnocchi 283
Marrow Cambridgeshire 72
Mohren (carrots) 190
Mushroom with eger sauce 34
Mushroom Hungarian style 37

Onion cake 88
Onion East Anglia 72

Pantog (potato pancakes) 108
Pilafia (rice) 212
Piperies yemistes (green pepper) 211
Pisto a la Riojana 406
Polenta crisons (cornmeal) 172
Potato Hungarian style 38
Potato knishi 336
Potato oladyi 336
Potato Zapekanka 337
Punchnep (potato and turnip) 89

Rice pilaff Metternich 23
Risotto Boscaiolo 256
Rode Kool (red cabbage) 237
Roschti (potato) 171
Rotkohl mit apfeln (red cabbage) 191

Salade du père Conil 157
Salade Flamande 125
Salade de grand-mère Mathilda 157
Sauerkraut 191
Selinoriza tiganti (celeriac) 211
Souffle d'epinard (spinach) 157
Spinaci alla Piemontese 265
Stilton cucumber 72
Sukkebrunede kartofler (potatoes) 373
Sweet and sour spinach 337

Teisen hlonod (onion) 98
Tomates Portugueses 423

Vitkalsoppa 356

Wiener rotkraut (red cabbage) 20
Wyau ynys môn (leek and eggs) 98

Zucchini alla Vaticano 265

SAVOURIES

Angels on horseback (oysters and bacon) 73

Caws pobi (Welsh rarebit) 98
Cheese flan Bulgarian style 291
Cheese Fribourgeoise 168
Cheese pie Bulgarian style 291
Cheese à la shoppe (with egg) 291
Cheese balls St Gall 168
Cheese Vaudoise 168

Devils on horseback (prunes with liver and bacon) 73

Halusky (cheese and potato) 48

Knaves on horseback (mushrooms with chicken liver) 73
Knights on horseback (kidney with bacon) 73

Swiss fondue 168
Swiss pizza 168

Welsh rarebit 98

SAUCES

Dutch sauce 233

Fish sauce for quenelles 150

German sauce 189
Gravy 66

Kvass (fermented beer) 326

Molho de vinho Madeira 422-3
Molho de vinho Porto 423
Mustard sauce 364

Polish sour cream sauce 300
Prawn sauce 366

Skordalia (garlic) 212

SWEETS

Apfelkuchen (apple tart) 193
Appelkuch Luxembourg (custard apple tart) 126
Apple tart Hungarian 38
Aran agus ira putog (cream pudding) 108
Armenian rice ararat 339
Arroz Imperatriz Eugenie (cream rice) 407
Athol brose (whisky cream) 91
Austrian strudel 24

Baba 305
Baklava (nuts and syrup) 225
Beignets soufflés Flamande 128
Bertines Mandelbunn (almond meringue) 368
Beschuitkoek (bread fritter) 238
Briewecka (fruit bread loaf) 194
Brandy snaps 78
Brown bread and butter pudding 76
Buckwheat porridge 339

Cassata Italiana 266
Chausson Charleroi (almond cream) 127
Chausson Mathilda (apple and apricot) 127
Chelsea bun 77
Clafouti aux cerises (cherry flan) 160
Colchester pudding (tapioca) 75
Conil's shortbread 76
Cottage cheese pudding 343
Coulibiac (dough mixture) 343
Cream cheese pancakes 343
Cream ice 266
Crema leche frita Catalana (egg custard) 407
Crema mama mia (lemon cheese) 267
Cyprus tart (lemon curd) 223

Danish pastry 373
Drambuie cream 89
Drie in pan (fruit pancakes) 238
Dutch advocaat 239
Dutch meringue pie 239
Dutch peach Queen Wilhelmina 238

Egg ice bomb 266
Elizabeth silver jubilee pudding 74

Figs in ouzo 224
Filfar oranges 224
Finnish rye bread 381
Flamichou aux pommes (apples) 128
Flan Lorrain (almond) 126
Flapjacks 78
Flensjes Rembrandt (butterscotch) 238
Florentiner (fruit and nut toffee) 25
Fruchtspeise (apple and blackberry) 193

Gaufres Flamande (waffles) 126
Gaufrettes Suisses (waffles) 172
Gooseberry fool 76
Gozinakh (walnut) 342

Halvas simigdalenio (semolina) 212

Ice cream 266
Iyran (yoghurt) 225

Jahosovy (trifle) 50
Julglogg (wine cup) 359

CAKES